Africa and the West
A Documentary History from the Slave Trade to Independence

William H. Worger
Nancy L. Clark
Edward A. Alpers

Oryx Press
2001

© 2001 by The Oryx Press
4041 North Central at Indian School Road
Phoenix, Arizona 85012-3397
www.oryxpress.com

Library of Congress Cataloging-in-Publication Data

Africa and the West : a documentary history from the slave trade to independence / [compiled] by William H. Worger, Nancy L. Clark, and Edward A. Alpers.
    p. cm.
Includes bibliographical references and index.
  ISBN 1-57356-247-5 (alk. paper)
  1. Africa, Sub-Saharan—Relations—Europe—History—Sources. 2. Europe—Relations—Africa, Sub-Saharan—History—Sources. 3. Africa, Sub-Saharan—Relations—America—History—Sources. 4. America—Relations—Africa, Sub-Saharan—History—Sources. 5. Slave-trade—History—Sources. I. Worger, William H. II. Clark, Nancy L. III. Alpers, Edward A.
  DT353.5.E9 A34 2000
  967'.02—dc21
                              00-010718
                              CIP

Contents

List of Illustrations   vi

List of Maps   vi

Preface   vii

Part 1: Africa in the Era of the Slave Trade   1
Introduction   3
1. The beginnings of a regular European trade in slaves from Africa.   5
2. The Pope grants to the Portuguese a monopoly of trade with Africa.   13
3. The King of Spain regulates the importation of African slaves into the Americas.   16
4. British attempts to break the Portuguese and Spanish monopolies of slave trading.   17
5. A Jesuit justifies the trade in African slaves to a skeptical colleague.   19
6. The importation of slaves into the Cape of Good Hope.   20
7. An attempt to create an English monopoly of trade in West Africa.   21
8. Sources of slaves for the Royal African Company.   22
9. The log of the *Arthur*, a ship carrying slaves for the Royal African Company from West Africa to Barbados.   23
10. The Council of the Indies answers questions from the King of Spain concerning the introduction of slaves into Spanish America.   27
11. The voyage of the *Hannibal*, carrying slaves from West Africa to Barbados.   29
12. Willem Bosman describes the Dutch trade for slaves on the West African Coast.   35
13. In support of slavery and against monopoly.   37
14. Venture Smith describes his capture into slavery.   39
15. Olaudah Equiano becomes a slave.   42

16. Anders Sparrman describes the treatment of slaves in South Africa.   50
17. Alexander Falconbridge describes his experiences as a physician on slave ships.   54
18. The plan of the slave ship *Brookes*.   64
19. In support of the continued importation of slaves into South Africa.   65
20. Mungo Park describes taking slaves from the interior of Africa to the coast.   67
21. Britain and the United States enact legislation to abolish the trade in slaves.   77
22. Ali Eisami recounts how he was taken into slavery and then freed.   81
23. Samuel Crowther escapes slavery.   85
24. The Asante king questions British motives in ending the slave trade.   91
25. A slave revolt in South Africa.   93
26. A Muslim explains the morality and practices of slavery.   98
27. Tippu Tip, the "leopard."   103
28. Chisi Ndjurisiye Sichyajunga, slave.   105

Part 2: From Abolition to Conquest   109
Introduction   111
1. The subordination of labor in South Africa.   113
2. The trade question in West Africa.   115
3. The King of Asante disputes the text of a treaty.   118
4. The impact of the abolitionists on labor legislation.   122
5. The settlers' revolt.   123
6. A missionary talks with a king.   125
7. Dingane kills the first settlers.   129
8. Advance by treaty in West Africa.   130

Contents

9. The secretary of state for the colonies proposes a more interventionist policy to end the slave trade. 132
10. Treaties with "barbarians" are different from those with "civilized" people. 136
11. The persistence of "illegal" slaving. 139
12. Samuel Crowther on the role of African missionaries. 149
13. Christianity and cattle killing. 152
14. Boer slaving. 155
15. Legislating race and religion. 159
16. Expanding trade by taking territory, Lagos 1861. 161
17. French ambitions in West Africa. 163
18. Africanus B. Horton on an autonomous Africa. 167
19. Diamonds. 172
20. Cecil Rhodes dreams of empire. 175
21. The sack of Kumasi. 179
22. Cetshwayo describes Zulu society. 185
23. A university for Africa. 189
24. The scramble for Africa begins. 194
25. The Berlin conference. 196
26. Rhodes reaches north. 198
27. The imperialism of chartered companies. 200
28. Voices of imperialism. 201
29. Voices of resistance. 218

Part 3: Colonialism and Its Critics 229
Introduction 231
1. Making colonialism appear "traditional." 233
2. Africa for the African. 236
3. Evidence of colonial atrocities in the Belgian Congo. 239
4. Frederick Lugard instructs his officials on how to implement indirect rule. 241
5. The French practice direct rule to enforce submission. 246
6. A German school examination for African children. 249
7. The Natives Land Act, South Africa, 1913. 250
8. The ANC in South Africa. 253
9. W.E.B. Du Bois describes an Atlantic world bounded by racial exploitation. 255
10. An appeal for the equal treatment of Africans and people of African descent. 259
11. Harry Thuku explains why he formed a political movement for all East Africans. 260
12. Creating a national movement for all West Africans. 266
13. Organizing African workers. 268
14. Charlotte Maxeke describes the impact of colonialism on women and the family. 272
15. Education in the United States of America. 275
16. Colonial rule equals taxes and forced labor. 277
17. Colonial rule equals police harassment. 281
18. Colonial rule equals censorship. 285
19. The impact of World War II. 286
20. The dream of the warrior. 292
21. Freedom in our lifetime. 294
22. Women and men on strike. 296
23. Colonial officials take note of African discontent. 303
24. Hendrik Verwoerd explains apartheid. 304
25. Nelson Mandela's "No Easy Walk to Freedom." 309
26. Jomo Kenyatta in court. 316
27. Mau Mau's daughter. 319
28. The Freedom Charter. 323
29. Freedom! Freedom! Freedom! 325
30. Verwoerd reaffirms South Africa's commitment to white supremacy. 328
31. Patrice Lumumba writes his last letter to his wife. 331

Part 4: The Contradictions of Post-Colonial Independence 335
Introduction 337
1. Frantz Fanon discusses the limits of African independence. 340
2. Nkrumah on pan-Africanism as an answer to neo-colonialism. 344

3. Julius Nyerere argues for African democracy, self-reliance, and socialism. 347
4. The African National Congress (ANC) adopts a policy of violence. 355
5. "The Civilized Man's Burden." 357
6. Eduardo Mondlane rejects Portuguese apologetics. 359
7. Is neo-colonialism rationalized imperialism? 361
8. A man of the people. 365
9. Tearing things apart. 368
10. Black consciousness. 372
11. An emperor and his court. 375
12. Who will start another fire? 379
13. The fate of political dissisents. 379
14. The rebellion begins, South Africa, June 1976. 385

15. Torture under apartheid. 388
16. A task which shook my whole being. 391
17. Another coup in Ghana. 396
18. The crisis of the state in Africa. 398
19. The elements of democracy in Africa. 404
20. Negotiating democracy in South Africa. 407
21. Scrubbing the furious walls of Mikuyu prison. 409
22. An intimate genocide. 410
23. Nelson Mandela and a new Africa. 414

Index 419

List of Illustrations

The slave ship *Brookes* 65
Ali Eisami 82
Tippu Tip 104
Branding a female slave 141
Gang of slaves met at Mbame's on the way to Tete, 1861 158
David Livingstone 158
James Africanus B. Horton 169
The cost of African animals to Western zoos 173
Death mask of Cecil John Rhodes, 1902 178
Maxim automatic gun, 1887 203
F.D. Lugard 203
Baden-Powell's army column, 1895-1896 209
Submission of King Prempeh, January 20, 1896 210
Colonial atrocity, Mashonaland, 1896 220
Hendrik Witbooi 222
Delegation to Great Britain of leaders of the South African Native National Congress protesting the 1913 Natives Land Act 251
H.F. Verwoerd 305
Kwame Nkrumah 326
Patrice Lumumba in the hands of General Mobutu's men, 1960 333
Ellen Kuzwayo 392
Nelson Mandela voting in South Africa's first post-apartheid election, 1994 415

List of Maps

Portuguese maritime exploration, fifteenth and sixteenth centuries 7
Central Africa according to geographers of the sixteenth and seventeenth centuries 38
Mungo Park's travels, 1795-1806 69
Sketch of Natal, South Africa, 1850 126
David Livingstone's travels in Central and Southern Africa, 1840-1873 156
A hunter's map of Africa, 1875 174
The proportionate area covered by the Congo River and its affluents superimposed on a map of Europe 195
Territory owned by Cecil Rhodes's British South Africa Company in 1900 199
Gold Coast Colony, 1886 204
Africa in 1891 and 1914 206
Sketch map of the march to Kumasi, 1895-1896 212
Revenue divisions of the Congo Free State, 1906 240
Nigeria, 1912 243
Africa, 1960 327
South Africa's Homelands, 1986 393
Africa, 1999 416

Preface

Through primary documents, this book tells the story of the colonial encounter between Africa and the West from the beginning of the fifteenth century to the end of the twentieth. It begins with the first Portuguese settlements established along the northwest coast of Africa (especially on the Atlantic islands of the Azores, Madeira, Cape Verde, and the Canaries) and, from the latter part of the fifteenth century onward, with the consequent forcible removal of Africans who were taken across the Atlantic to colonize the Americas as servile laborers, not as free settlers. The book ends as we enter a new millennium, with all Africa finally regaining independence (South Africa in 1994 became the last state to return from European—or white settler—to African rule, almost half a century after Ghana won independence in 1957). Yet the continent remains politically fragile, bound economically to the West, and mired in poverty. The first-hand accounts and other primary documents in this book reveal the ways in which 400 years of slavery, little more than half a century of direct European rule for most Africans (including the bulk of South Africa's black population), and another half century of Cold War politics have left their imprint on post-colonial Africa.

The book focuses on the history of Africa south of the Sahara. Though there is a long history of direct contact between Europe and North Africa (and thereby into the Sahara and the Nile hinterland), with the beginning of the Atlantic slave trade a fundamentally new relationship developed between Africa and Europe. We have chosen to follow the developing contours of this relationship, particularly the ways in which Africans were incorporated into an Atlantic world that used their labor and their agricultural produce to build wealth in the West but poverty on the African continent.

The book is organized thematically. Attempting comprehensiveness across such a large continent with populations as diverse as those of Africa would be impossible (though we have focused on two countries in particular—Ghana and South Africa—because of the importance of each in the history of the encounter between Africa and the West, and because of the richness of sources that allows us to document that encounter).[1] Part 1 focuses on Africa and Europe during the era of the Atlantic slave trade, from the beginnings of an export trade by the Portuguese in the fifteenth century, to the growth and persistence of slavery within Africa into the twentieth century. Part 2 examines the ways in which the rhetoric of abolition, in the context of changing European needs for African labor and agricultural goods, was put into the service of imperialism, despite the eloquent pleas of Africans (many of them ex-slaves converted to Christianity) that they could initiate whatever changes they wanted free of outside intervention. Part 3 starts with the aims of colonialism, as expressed by some of its architects, and the concurrent criticisms made by colonial subjects (or victims as they increasingly saw themselves); it follows the growth and development of anti-colonial rhetoric through to the independence of Ghana in 1957, though noting the defiant support of racism by white South Africa, and the early violence resulting from the Cold War. Part 4 deals with the struggle (ultimately successful) of people in the Portuguese and white settler-ruled areas of Africa (Angola, Guinea-Bissau, Mozambique, Namibia, South Africa, and Zimbabwe) to achieve independence and of the difficulties and contradictions of life "after" colonialism for people in the rest of Africa. While "freedom," in Kwame Nkrumah's stirring words, came to Africa with the end of formal colonialism, political independence has not translated into the types of freedom that most people expected.

The 120 documents collected here were written by people who participated in the events described. They capture, in first-person narratives, in poetry, in letters, in formal political speeches, and in many other forms of writing, the hopes, aspirations, doubts, and, sometimes, hypocrisy, that mark all human endeavors. Editorially, we have aimed to present selections lengthy enough to enable the reader to capture a sense of what each author intended. We have avoided cutting texts to reflect certain lines of interpretation, and we have kept the explanatory text to the minimum (though clearly the selection of the documents itself reflects our collective and individual points of view). With the exception of minor changes in punctuation, the replacement of "f" by "s" in some of the older English documents, and the reduction of some excessive capitalization (by today's standards), we have maintained the spelling, grammatical forms, and some capitalization from the original documents. We have also retained without exception the original language—always powerful, moving, and sometimes rough—of the documents. The people whose words you read here were and are exceptionally eloquent.

We have endeavored in this collection to compile a text that will be of interest to a wide range of audiences, from middle school, high school, and college students and beyond to anyone interested in the history of the African continent. For some of us—and the authors are of a generation that came of age in the 1960s and the 1970s—decolonizing Africa was a place of hope and the names of people like Frantz Fanon, Kwame Nkrumah, and Julius Nyerere will be very familiar. For later generations there is likely to be greater familiarity with those who fought against continuing oppression in Africa, whether it be Nelson Mandela and his struggles to end apartheid in South Africa, or Jack Mapanje denouncing the shortcomings of Malawi's president-for-life Hastings Banda, or perhaps there will be little awareness of Africa except as a place of poverty and political unrest. Believing as historians that the present cannot be explained without understanding the past, we hope that readers of every generation will find these documents of value in understanding the history of Africa and gaining some insight into the problems and potential currently facing the continent.

This book has been a collaborative enterprise. The idea for the volume was first presented to the authors by Jake Goldberg, then of Oryx Press, who envisaged a single-volume source book for any student interested in the history of Africa from the slave trade to the lending policies of Western financial institutions at the end of the twentieth century. In tackling this daunting task, we shared responsibilities in the following manner. Nancy L. Clark, assisted by her extremely able research assistant Henry Trotter, took primary responsibility for identifying key issues of historical significance across the continent and for all time periods, and for making an initial selection of documents. Subsequently, working from this foundation and independently, the three authors divided up the sub-continent, primarily though not completely on a geographic basis, as they selected documents to be included in the final draft.

Nancy L. Clark took responsibility for post-1900 southern Africa and for economic issues affecting the entire sub-continent in the latter half of the twentieth century. William H. Worger dealt with West and Central Africa and with pre-1900 southern Africa. Edward A. Alpers took responsibility for East Africa. William Worger made the final selections, jointly with Nancy Clark, wrote the introductions to each of the four parts of the volume, and drafted the annotations for most of the documents (excepting those on East Africa, which Edward Alpers wrote).

Nancy Clark and William Worger would like to thank Henry Trotter for his research skills, his energy, and his enthusiasm. We are delighted that his experience working on this volume has caused him to change his career goal from being a scholar of African literature to one of African history. William Worger would also like to thank Gibril Cole and Karen Flint for assistance in locating relevant materials. Edward Alpers expresses his appreciation to UCLA for support from the Committee on Research of the Academic Senate and to Karen Flint and Kristin Haines for research assistance. We are all grateful to Sean Tape and Anne Thompson of Oryx Press for bringing this project so efficiently to completion.

References

1. On Ghana, see Part 1: documents 7, 11, 17, 24; Part 2: documents 2, 3, 8, 10, 11, 17, 18, 21, 28; Part 3: documents 12, 23, 29; and Part 4: documents 2, 17. On South Africa, see Part 1: documents 6, 16, 17, 19, 25; Part 2: documents 1, 4, 5, 6, 7, 13, 14, 15, 19, 20, 22, 26, 27, 28, 29; Part 3: 1, 7, 8, 13, 14, 21, 24, 25, 28, 30; and Part 4: documents 4, 10, 14, 15, 16, 23.

PART 1
Africa in the Era of the Slave Trade

Introduction

Although Europe had obtained goods from Africa since before the Christian era, these items (gold especially) had been acquired through African intermediaries. With the rise of Islam, access to African gold—the main source of that precious metal until the discovery of the Americas—became even more difficult and expensive for the Christian West. With the development of new methods of navigation in the fifteenth century, however, Europeans were able to gain direct access to the coast of sub-Saharan Africa and to interior trade networks without having to deal with Muslim intermediaries. Between the 1430s and the end of the century, the Portuguese moved steadily southward: along the northwestern coast of the continent in the 1430s and 1440s (including the Atlantic islands of the Azores, Madeira, and Canary), south of the Senegal and Gambia rivers to what became known as the Gold Coast (present-day Ghana) by the 1470s, to the mouth of the Congo River by the mid-1480s, and the southern tip of the continent at the end of the 1480s. In 1497, Vasco da Gama traveled around the Cape of Good Hope into the Indian Ocean, where he came in contact with the Swahili trading towns of the East African coast and reached southern India and the spice trade networks of the East. Though Portuguese voyaging aimed initially at getting direct access to West African gold producers, and locating in East Africa the legendary Christian monarch Prester John (viewed as a possible ally in the religious wars against Islam), an export trade in African slaves dominated practically all interaction between the West and Africa from the 1440s onward until the nineteenth century. During those four centuries, between 10 and 15 million Africans, two-thirds of them males, were forcibly taken from Africa and sent across the Atlantic to work in new colonies established primarily by the Spanish, the Portuguese, and the British in the Americas. The bulk of the slaves went to the Caribbean and to Portuguese South America (Brazil); the smallest number (approximately half a million) were landed in the U.S. South. These people were purchased from African agents and transported for re-sale in the Americas by merchants from every European country in a trade that did not cease completely until the end of the nineteenth century.

Europeans initially landed in Africa looking for a variety of goods, particularly gold, and turned to a trade in human beings almost as an afterthought (document 1). Trading in people and bringing them to Portugal for sale as slave workers provided an additional means by which the early voyagers could turn a profit on their voyages. The rise of plantation agriculture, however—first in sugar on Mediterranean islands, then on islands of the coast of Africa (especially São Tomé and Principe), and most significant of all in the Americas with such labor intensive crops as sugar, cotton, and tobacco—created a huge new demand for cheap labor. The economic benefits of plantation agriculture were so great that the Pope sanctioned the slave trade in an effort to maintain a Catholic monopoly in the face of attempts by competing traders to get access to such a highly profitable commerce (documents 2, 3, 4, 5, 7, 8, 10).

Whereas the first slaves had been captured in raids, or were war captives or criminals acquired through trade with local African leaders, over time the production of slaves became a major industry within Africa. Because of their susceptibility to local diseases, Europeans remained based along the West African coastline in a series of trading forts, dependent for their continued presence on the favor of local kings. In these forts, European merchants traded manufactured goods such as cloth and firearms for people on terms that were subject to constant negotiation (documents 11, 12). The slaves were brought from the interior, acquired often by raids especially for the purpose of taking people into bondage or through wars increasingly fought for the same purpose, and transported to the coast along the river networks that served as the hub of internal trade. Frequently such slaves changed owners several times in a series of transactions, and the trip to the coast could be very lengthy (documents 14, 14, 20). At the coast, the slaves were sold to European merchants who in constant attempts to secure as high profits as possible transported them across the Atlantic in the most appalling conditions (documents 15, 16, 17, 18). While the memoirs of those transported into slavery are riveting, so too are the "business-as-usual" accounts of those who managed the trade (document 11). The matter-of-fact business rationale of slavery is evident too in the justifications for the use of imported slave labor in the Cape of Good Hope, the only significant European colony in Africa prior to the nineteenth century, and one whose agricultural economy was built on slave labor imported from East Africa, Madagascar, and southeast Asia (documents 6, 19).

While millions of people were enslaved, they did not go peaceably. They fought against their captors, took flight when they had the chance, and rose up in revolt on occasion (document 25). Several hundred shipboard uprisings have been recorded by historians. Growing public revulsion at the practices of slave traders, especially as documented by writers like Olaudah Equiano (document 15); the frightening prospect of perhaps more successful slave revolts such as that of Toussaint l'Ouverture in Haiti; and the growing demand for free labor rather than servile as a result of the impact of the Industrial Revolution together reinforced demands for the end of the trade in slaves.

Britain and the United States passed legislation banning the export of people at the beginning of the nineteenth century, but slave trading continued (documents 21, 22, 23, and Part 2). Indeed, slave exports reached their highest peak ever in the 1820s and 1830s, when an average of almost 120,000 people a year were shipped across the Atlantic. Though Britain and the United States sent out ships to interdict the trade, and freed some people who were then landed in Sierra Leone and Liberia (established by British and U.S. antislavers respectively as havens for freed slaves), slavers moved their bases of operations, with a huge increase in slave raiding (much of it run by Muslim slavers) on the East Coast of Africa and its hinterland in the nineteenth century (documents 26, 27, 28).

The slave trade had an enormous impact on Africa. It resulted in a great increase in violence within the continent. Some of this violence was perpetrated by states (like Dahomey) that built their power and wealth on raiding other societies for a product that could be sold for export. Other states, like Asante, did not engage in slave-raiding for commercial purposes but did view the export trade as a useful way to rid itself of captives acquired in wars of conquest who otherwise might practice sedition (document 24). The removal from Africa of so many people during the most productive years of their lives (slave traders did not want the old, the ill, and the infirm), cannot but have had a huge impact on production within Africa. Moreover, instead of encouraging the production of local goods for trade within Africa, the slave trade led to a focus on the export of people in exchange for European manufactured goods (especially cloth, but also guns which were used to expand the mercenary trade, metal manufactures, and other items). The demographic impact was also likely to have been considerable with so many people removed from the continent. Some estimates have suggested that Africa's population by the end of the nineteenth century was perhaps 50 percent less than it would have been without the slave trade. Indeed, when Europeans finally explored the interior of the continent in the mid-nineteenth century, they remarked on the violence witnessed, the low levels of population in large areas, and the apparent (or at least to them) lack of an active internal economy other than that built around slavery; they did not consider how much of what they witnessed was a product of 400 years of trade with Europe.

~ ~ ~

1. The beginnings of a regular European trade in slaves from Africa.

From the 1430s until his death in 1460, Prince Henry of Portugal sent out a series of voyages to explore the West African coast. The Portuguese were seeking direct sea access to the gold of West Africa (otherwise obtainable only via Muslim traders who transported it across the Sahara), and hoped also to locate the legendary Christian monarch, Prester John, reputed to live on the East Coast of Africa and viewed as a potential ally for the Portuguese in their wars against the followers of Islam. The earliest and most complete record of these early Portuguese voyages was compiled by Gomes Azurara, royal librarian, chronicler, and keeper of the Portuguese archives. Using the testimony of participants as much as possible, Azurara, who completed his account in 1453, charted how the initial quest for gold and allies turned into a pattern of raiding for African slaves to work on farms and plantations in Portugal. The events described take place on the coast of present-day Mauritania.[1]

---

[1] Gomes Eannes De Azurara, *The Chronicle of the Discovery and Conquest of Guinea*, vol. 1, trans. Charles Beazley and Edgar Prestage (London: Hakluyt Society, 1896–97), pp. 39–50, 54–58, 60–68, 79–83.

How Antam Gonçalvez brought back the first Captives.

Now it was so that in this year 1441, when the affairs of this realm [Portugal] were somewhat more settled though not fully quieted, that the Infant [Prince Henry] armed a little ship, of the which he made captain one Antam Gonçalvez, his chamberlain, and a very young man; and the end of that voyage was none other, according to my Lord's commandment, but to ship a cargo of the skins and oil. . . .

But when he had accomplished his voyage, as far as concerned the chief part of his orders, Antam Gonçalvez, called to him Affonso Goterres, another groom of the chamber . . . and all the others that were in the ship, being one and twenty in all, and spoke to them in this wise: "Friends and brethren! We have already got our cargo, as you perceive, by the which the chief part of our ordinance is accomplished, and we may well turn back, if we wish not to toil beyond that which was principally commanded of us; but I would know from all whether seemeth to you well that we should attempt something further, that he who sent us here may have some example of our good wills; for I think it would be shameful if we went back into his presence just as we are. . . . O how fair a thing it would be if we, who have come to this land for a cargo of such petty merchandise, were to meet with the good luck to bring the first captives before the face of our Prince. . . . I would fain go myself this next night with nine men of you (those who are most ready for the business), and prove a part of this land along the river to see if I find any inhabitants; for I think we of right ought to meet with some, since 'tis certain there are people here, who traffic with camels and other animals that bear their freights. Now the traffic of these men must chiefly be to the seaboard; and since they have as yet no knowledge of us, their gathering cannot be too large for us to try their strength; and, if God grant us to encounter them, the very least part of our victory will be the capture of one of them, with the which the Infant will feel no small content, getting knowledge by that means of what kind are the other dwellers of this land. And as to our reward, you can estimate what it will be by the great expenses and toil he has undertaken in years past, only for this end." . . . they determined to do his bidding, and follow him as far as they could make their way. And as soon as it was night Antam Gonçalvez chose nine men who seemed to him most fitted for the undertaking, and made his voyage with them as he had before determined. And when they were about a league distant from the sea they came on a path which they kept, thinking some man or woman might come by there whom they could capture; but it happened otherwise; so Antam Gonçalvez asked the others to consent to go forward and follow out his purpose; for, as they had already come so far, it would not do to return to the ship in vain like that. And the others being content they departed thence, and, journeying through that inner land for the space of three leagues, they found the footmarks of men and youths, the number of whom, according to their estimate, would be from forty to fifty, and these led the opposite way from where our men were going. The heat was very intense, and so by reason of this and of the toil they had undergone in watching by night and travelling thus on foot, and also because of the want of water, of which there was none, Antam Gonçalvez perceived their weariness that it was already very great, as he could easily judge from his own sufferings: So he said, "My friends, there is nothing more to do here; our toil is great, while the profit to arise from following up this path meseemeth small, for these men are travelling to the place whence we have come, and our best course would be to turn back towards them, and perchance, on their return, some will separate themselves, or may be, we shall come up with them when they are laid down to rest, and then, if we attack them lustily, peradventure they will flee, and, if they flee, someone there will be less swift, whom we can lay hold of according to our intent; or may be our luck will be even better, and we shall find fourteen or fifteen of them, of whom we shall make a more profitable booty." Now this advice was not such

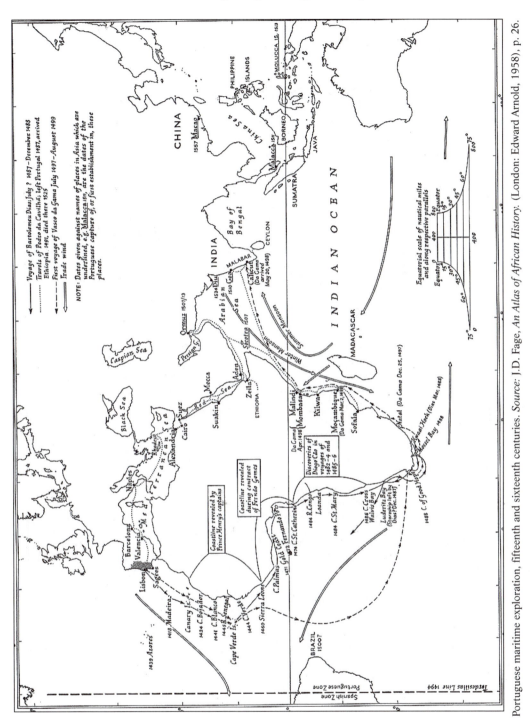

Portuguese maritime exploration, fifteenth and sixteenth centuries. *Source:* J.D. Fage, *An Atlas of African History.* (London: Edward Arnold, 1958), p. 26.

as to give rise to any wavering in the will of those men, for each desired that very thing. And, returning towards the sea, when they had gone a short part of the way, they saw a naked man following a camel, with two assegais [spears] in his hand, and as our men pursued him there was not one who felt aught of his great fatigue. But though he was only one, and saw the others that they were many; yet he had a mind to prove those arms of his right worthily and began to defend himself as best he could, shewing a bolder front than his strength warranted. But Affonso Goterres wounded him with a javelin, and this put the Moor in such fear that he threw down his arms like a beaten thing. And after they had captured him, to their no small delight, and had gone on further, they espied, on the top of a hill, the company whose tracks they were following, and their captive pertained to the number of these. And they failed not to reach them through any lack of will, but the sun was now low, and they wearied, so they determined to return to their ship, considering that such enterprise might bring greater injury than profit. And, as they were going on their way, they saw a black Mooress come along (who was slave of those on the hill), and though some of our men were in favour of letting her pass to avoid a fresh skirmish . . . Antam Gonçalvez bade them go at her; for if (he said) they scorned that encounter, it might make their foes pluck up courage against them. And now you see how the word of a captain prevaileth among men used to obey; for, following his will, they seized the Mooress. And those on the hill had a mind to come to the rescue, but when they perceived our people ready to receive them, they not only retreated to their former position, but departed elsewhere, turning their backs to their enemies. . . .

Now . . . Nuno Tristam, a youthful knight . . . brought with him an armed caravel, with the special command of his Lord, that he should pass beyond the Port of the Galley, as far as he could, and that he should bestir himself as well to capture some of the people of the country, as best he could. And he, pursuing his voyage, now arrived at the place where

Antam Gonçalvez was,. . . "You . . . my friend Antam Gonçalvez, are not ignorant of the will of the Infant our Lord, and you know that to execute this purpose of his he hath incurred many and great expenses, and yet up till now, for a space of fifteen years, he hath toiled in vain in this part of the world, never being able to arrive at any certainty as to the people of this land, under what law or lordship they do live. And although you are carrying off these two captives, and by their means the Infant may come to know something about this folk, yet that doth not prevent what is still better, namely, for us to carry off many more; for, besides the knowledge which the Lord Infant will gain by their means, profit will also accrue to him by their .service or ransom. Wherefore, it seemeth to me that we should do well to act after this manner. That is to say, in this night now following, you should choose ten of your men and I another ten of mine—from the best which each of us may have—and let us then go together and seek those whom you have found. And since you say that, judging from the fighting you had with them, they were not more than twenty men fit for battle, and the rest women and boys, we ought to capture them all very quickly. And even if we do not meet with the very same that you encountered, nevertheless we shall surely find others, by means of whom we can make as good a booty, or perhaps even better."

"I cannot well believe," replied Antam Gonçalvez, "that our expedition in search of those we found before, will have any sure result, for the place is all one great bare hill, in the which there is no house or hut where one could fancy they would lodge, and the more so since we saw them turn again like men that had come there from another part. And what seemeth to me worst of all is that those men will have forewarned all the others, and, peradventure, when we think to capture them we may ourselves become their booty.". . . .

Yet, although this counsel of Antam Gonçalvez was good . . . there were there two squires, in whom these reasons did not suffice to oppose their desire of doing brave deeds . . . And these two persuaded the Council to depart from the advice which Antam Gonçalvez had given . . . [and] as soon as it was night, they set out according to the order that Nuno Tristam gave at first. And so it chanced that in the night they came to where the natives lay scattered in two encampments, either the same that Antam Gonçalvez had found before or other like it. The distance between the encampments was but small, and our men divided themselves into three parties, in order that they might the better hit upon them. For they had not yet any certain knowledge of the place where they lay, but only a perception of them; as you see the like things are perceived much more readily by night than by day. And when our men had come nigh to them, they attacked them very lustily, shouting at the top of their voices, "Portugal" and "Santiago"; the fright of which so abashed the enemy, that it threw them all into disorder. And so, all in confusion, they began to fly without any order or carefulness. Except indeed that the men made some show of defending themselves with their assegais (for they knew not the use of any other weapon), especially one of them, who fought face to face with Nuno Tristam, defending himself till he received his death. And besides this one, whom Nuno Tristam slew by himself, the others killed three and took ten prisoners, what of men, women and boys. And it is not to be doubted that they would have slain and taken many more, if they had all fallen on together at the first onslaught. But among those who were taken there was one greater than the rest, who was called Adahu, and was said to be a noble; and he shewed in his countenance right well that he held the pre-eminence of nobility over the others. . . . Then those captains returned to the ships and bade that Arab [translator] whom Nuno Tristam had brought with him, to sit with those Moors but they were not able to understand him, because the language of these people was not Moorish, but Azaneguy of Sahara, for so they name that land [between present-day Morocco and Senegal]. But the noble, in that he was of better breeding than the other captives, so had he seen more things and better than they; and had

been to other lands where he had learned the Moorish tongue; forasmuch as he understood that Arab and answered to whatever matter was asked of him by the same. And the further to try the people of the land and to have of them more certain knowledge, they put that Arab on shore, and one of the Moorish women whom they had taken captive; who were to say to the others, that if they wished to come and speak to them about the ransom of some of those whom they had taken prisoners, or about traffick in merchandise, they might do so. And at the end of two days there came to that place about 150 Moors on foot and thirty-five on horses and camels, bringing the Moorish slave with them. And although outwardly they seemed to be a race both barbarous and bestial, yet was there not wanting in them something of astuteness, wherewith they sought to ensnare their enemies. For only three of them appeared on the shore, and the rest lay in ambush, to the end that our men, being unaware of their treachery, might land, when they who lay hid could seize them, which thing they might have done by sheer force of numbers, if our men had been a whit less cautious than they. But the Moors, perceiving that their wiles were discovered by us—because they saw that the men in the boat turned about on seeing that the slave did not appear—revealed their dissembling tricks and all came into sight on the shore, hurling stones and making gestures. And there they also displayed that Arab who had been sent to them, held as one whom they wished to keep in the subjection of a captive. And he called out to them that they should be on their guard against those people; for they would not have come there, except to take them at a disadvantage if they could. Thereupon our men turned back to the ships, where they made their partition of the captives, according to the lot of each, and the other Moors betook themselves to their encampments, taking the Arab with them. And Antam Gonçalvez, because he had now loaded his ship with cargo, as the Infant had commanded, returned to Portugal. . . .

How Antam Gonçalvez went to make the first ransom.

As you know that naturally every prisoner desireth to lie free, which desire is all the stronger in a man of higher reason or nobility whom fortune has condemned to live in subjection to another; so that noble [Adahu] of whom we have already spoken, seeing himself held in captivity, although he was very gently treated, greatly desired to be free, and often asked Antam Gonçalvez to take him back to his country, where he declared he would give for himself five or six Black Moors; and also he said that there were among the other captives two youths for whom a like ransom would be given.

And here you must note that these blacks were Moors like the others, though their slaves, in accordance with ancient custom, which I believe to have been because of the curse which, after the Deluge, Noah laid upon his son Cain, cursing him in this way—that his race should be subject to all the other races of the world.

And from his race these blacks are descended, as wrote the Archbishop Don Roderic of Toledo, and Josephus in his book on The Antiquities of the Jews. . . .

The will of Antam Gonçalvez to return to that land, for desire of the ransom and profit he would get, was not so great as his desire to serve the Infant his lord—and therefore he asked leave to go on this journey, saying, that (forasmuch as he perceived the great desire his Grace had to know part of that land) if that were not sufficient which he had ascertained from that Moor, that he should give him license to go and ransom him and the other captive youths with him.

For as the Moor told him, the least they would give for them would be ten Moors, and it was better to save ten souls than three—for though they were black, yet had they souls like the others, and all the more as these blacks were not of the lineage of the Moors but were Gentiles, and so the better to bring into the path of salvation.

Also he said that the blacks could give him news of land much further distant, and he promised that when he spoke about the traffic with the natives, he would find means to learn as much news as possible.

The Infant answered all this and said that he was obliged by his offer, and that he not only desired to have knowledge of that land, but also of the Indies, and of the land of Prester John, if he could.

Antam Gonçalvez made ready to go with his captives . . . and arriving at the boundaries of that land where the ransom had to be made, they resolved to put on shore that Moorish noble, that he might go and make ready his ransom at the place where he had agreed to meet Antam Gonçalvez again.

The Moor was very well clad in garments given him by the Infant, who considered that, for the excellence of his nobility that he had above the others, if he received benefits, he would be able to be of profit to his benefactors by encouraging his own people and bringing them to traffic. But as soon as he was free, he forgot very quickly all about his promises, on the security of which Antam Gonçalvez had trusted him, thinking that the nobility he displayed would be the chief hindrance of any breach of faith on his part; but his deceit thenceforth warned all our men not to trust one of that race except under the most certain security.

And now Antam Gonçalvez entering the Rio D'Ouro with his ship for a space of four leagues, dropped anchor, and waited for seven days without getting a message from any, or a glimpse of one single inhabitant of that land; but on the eighth day there arrived a Moor seated on a white camel, and another with him, who gave a message that they should await the others who would come and make the ransom, and that on the next day they would appear, as in fact they did.

And it was very clear that those youths [Gonçalvez's captives] were in great honour among them, for a good hundred Moors, male and female, were joined in their ransom, and Antam Gonçalvez received for his two captives, ten blacks, male and female, from various countries—one Martin Fernandez, the Infant's Alfaqueque [captive ransomer], managing the business between the parties.

And it was clear that the said Martin had great knowledge of the Moorish tongue, for he was understood among these people, where the other Arab, who was Moor by nation, could only find one person to understand him.

And besides the blacks that Antam Gonçalvez received in that ransom, he got also a little gold dust and a shield of ox-hide, and a number of ostrich eggs, so that one day there were served up at the Infant's table three dishes of the same, as fresh and as good as though they had been the eggs of any other domestic fowls. And we may well presume that there was no other Christian prince in this part of Christendom, who had dishes like these upon his table.

And according to the account of those Moors there were merchants in that part, who traded in that gold, which it seemed was found among them; but the Moorish noble never returned to fulfil his promise, neither did he remember the benefits he had received.

And by thus losing him, Antam Gonçalvez learnt to be cautious where before he was not. And returning to the Infant, his lord, he received his reward. . . .

The growth of the trade in slaves.

[A]t the beginning of the colonisation of the islands [Canary Islands and Cape Verde], people murmured as greatly as if he [Prince Henry] were spending some part of their property on it. . . . But when they saw the first Moorish captives brought home, and the second cargo . . . they confessed their mistake. . . . And so they were forced to turn their blame into public praise; for they said it was plain the Infant [Prince Henry] was another Alexander; and their covetousness now began to wax greater. And, as they saw the houses of others full to overflowing of male and female slaves, and their property increasing, they thought about the whole matter, and began to talk among themselves.

And because that after coming back from Tangier, the Infant usually remained always in the kingdom of Algarve, by reason of his town which he was then having built, and because the booty that his captains brought

back was discharged at Lagos, therefore the people of that place were the first to move the Infant to give them license to go to that land whence came those Moorish captives. . . .

And the first who interposed to beg for this license, was a squire [Lançarote] . . . [who was] Almoxarife [collector of taxes] for the King in that town of Lagos. . . . A man of great good sense, he understood well how the matter stood, and the profit that he would be able to gain by his expedition. . . . So Lançarote prepared six armed caravels to carry out his purpose and spoke to the Infant about a license; saying that he begged he would grant it him that he might do him service, as well as obtain honour and profit for himself. . . .

And the Infant was very glad of this and at once commanded his banners to be made, with the Cross of the Order of Jesus Christ, one of which each caravel was to hoist. . . .

And pursuing their voyage, they arrived at the Isle of Herons [in the Bay of Arguin], on the eve of Corpus Christi Day. . . . [T]hey took with them thirty men, to wit, six in each boat, and set out from the island where they were, about sunset. And rowing all that night, they arrived about daybreak at the island that they sought. . . .

[T]hey looked towards the settlement and saw that the Moors, with their women and children, were already coming as quickly as they could out of their dwellings, because they had caught sight of their enemies. But they, shouting out "St. James," "St. George," "Portugal," at once attacked them, killing and taking all they could.

Then might you see mothers forsaking their children, and husbands their wives, each striving to escape as best he could. Some drowned themselves in the water; others thought to escape by hiding under their huts; others stowed their children among the seaweed, where our men found them afterwards, hoping they would thus escape notice. And at last our Lord God, who giveth a reward for every good deed, willed that for the toil they had undergone in his service, they should that day obtain victory ever their enemies, as well as a guerdon and a payment for all their labour and expense; for they took captive of those Moors, what with men, women, and children, 165, besides those that perished and were killed. And when the battle was over, all praised God for the great mercy that he had shewn them, in that he had willed to give them such a victory, and with so little damage to themselves. And as soon as they had their captives put safely in their boats, and others securely tied on land (because the boats were small and they were not able to store so many in them at once), they sent a man to go as far as possible along the shore, to see if he could get sight of the caravels. He set out at once; and one full league from the place where the others were staying, he had sight of the caravels coming; for Lançarote, as he had promised, had started as soon as it was dawn. . . .

And when Lançarote, with those squires and brave men that were with him, had received the like news of the good success that God had granted to those few that went to the island; and saw that they had enterprised so great a deed; and that God had been pleased that they should bring it to such a pass; they were all very joyful, praising loudly the Lord God for that he had deigned to give such help to such a handful of his Christian people. . . .

Lançarote did not forget to learn from the Moorish prisoners what it was his duty to learn, about the place in which he was now staying and its opportunities; and he ascertained of them by his interpreter, that all about there were other inhabited islands, where they would be able to make large captures with little trouble. . . .

The caravels arrived at Lagos, whence they had set out, having excellent weather for their voyage, for fortune was not less gracious to them in the serenity of the weather than it had been to them before in the capture of their booty.

And from Lagos the news reached the Infant. . . . And next day Lançarote, as he who had taken the main charge of the expedition, said to the Infant: "My lord, your grace well knoweth that you have to receive the fifth of these Moors, and of all that we have gained in that land, whither you sent us for the service of God and of yourself. . . . The Infant said that he was well pleased, and on the next

day very early, Lançarote bade the masters of the caravels that they should put out the captives, and take them to that field, where they were to make the divisions. . . . But before they did anything else in that matter, they took as an offering the best of those Moors to the church of that place; and another little Moor, who afterwards became a friar of St. Francis, they sent to St. Vincent do Cabo, where he lived ever after as a Catholic Christian, without having understanding or perception of any law than that true and holy law in which all we Christians hope for our salvation. And the Moors of that capture were in number 235. . . .

O, Thou heavenly Father—who with Thy powerful hand, without alteration of Thy divine essence, governest all the infinite company of Thy Holy City, and controllest all the revolutions of higher worlds, divided into nine spheres, making the duration of ages long or short according as it pleaseth Thee— I [Azurara] pray Thee that my tears may not wrong my conscience; for it is not their religion but their humanity that maketh mine to weep in pity for their sufferings. And if the brute animals, with their bestial feelings, by a natural instinct understand the sufferings of their own kind, what wouldst Thou have my human nature to do on seeing before my eyes that miserable company, and remembering that they too are of the generation of the sons of Adam.

On the next day, which was the 8th of the month of August, very early in the morning, by reason of the heat, the seamen began to make ready their boats, and to take out those captives, and carry them on shore, as they were commanded. And these, placed all together in that field, were a marvellous sight; for amongst them were some white enough, fair to look upon, and well proportioned; others were less white like mulattoes; others again were as black as Ethiops, and so ugly, both in features and in body, as almost to appear (to those who saw them) the images of a lower hemisphere. But what heart could be so hard as not to be pierced with piteous feeling to see that company? For some kept their heads low and their faces bathed in tears, looking one upon another; others stood groaning very dolorously, looking up to the height of heaven, fixing their eyes upon it, crying out loudly, as if asking help of the Father of Nature; others struck their faces with the palms of their hands, throwing themselves at full length upon the ground; others made their lamentations in the manner of a dirge, after the custom of their country. And though we could not understand the words of their language, the sound of it right well accorded with the measure of their sadness. But to increase their sufferings still more, there now arrived those who had charge of the division of the captives, and who began to separate one from another, in order to make an equal partition of the fifths; and then was it needful to part fathers from sons, husbands from wives, brothers from brothers. No respect was shewn either to friends or relations, but each fell where his lot took him. . . .

And who could finish that partition without very great toil? for as often as they had placed them in one part the sons, seeing their fathers in another, rose with great energy and rushed over to them; the mothers clasped their other children in their arms, and threw themselves flat on the ground with them; receiving blows with little pity for their own flesh, if only they might not be torn from them.

And so troublously they finished the partition; for besides the toil they had with the captives, the field was quite full of people, both from the town and from the surrounding villages and districts, who for that day gave rest to their hands (in which lay their power to get their living) for the sole purpose of beholding this novelty. And with what they saw, while some were weeping and others separating the captives, they caused such a tumult as greatly to confuse those who directed the partition.

The Infant was there, mounted upon a powerful steed, and accompanied by his retinue, making distribution of his favours, as a man who sought to gain but small treasure from his share; for of the forty-six souls who fell to him as his fifth, he made a very speedy partition of these, for his chief riches lay in his purpose; for he reflected with great pleasure upon the salvation of those souls that before were lost.

And certainly his expectation was not in vain; for . . . as soon as they understood our language they turned Christians with very little ado; and I who put together this history into this volume, saw in the town of Lagos boys and girls (the children and grandchildren of those first captives, born in this land) as good and true Christians as if they had directly descended, from the beginning of the dispensation of Christ, from those who were first baptised.

2. The Pope grants to the Portuguese a monopoly of trade with Africa.

Prince Henry argued that navigation of the African coast was part of a holy war and sought the support of the Catholic Church both for his missionary enterprise and to ward off other European powers. During the 1440s, Pope Eugenius IV had remained neutral with regard to the competing claims of Portugal and Spain, but in a papal bull issued in 1452, Pope Nicholas V gave King Alfonso of Portugal "power to conquer and enslave pagans." In another issued in 1455, Nicholas extended the king of Portugal's authority to include "exclusive control over the newly discovered territory." Note that "Guinea" in the papal bulls, and in the correspondence of the Portuguese, referred generally to all of West Africa south of the Saharan desert. [2]

---

[2] Frances Davenport, *European Treaties Bearing on the History of the United States and its Dependencies to 1648*, vol. 1 (Washington, DC: Carnegie Institute, 1917), pp. 20–24. Davenport has the original Latin text as well as this translation into English.

Papal Bull, January 8, 1455.

The Roman pontiff, successor of the key-bearer of the heavenly kingdom and vicar of Jesus Christ, contemplating with a father's mind all the several climes of the world and the characteristics of all the nations dwelling in them and seeking and desiring the salvation of all, wholesomely ordains and disposes upon careful deliberation those things which he sees will be agreeable to the Divine Majesty and by which he may bring the sheep entrusted to him by God into the single divine fold, and may acquire for them the reward of eternal felicity, and obtain pardon for their souls. This we believe will more certainly come to pass, through the aid of the Lord, if we bestow suitable favors and special graces on those Catholic kings and princes, who, like athletes and intrepid champions of the Christian faith, as we know by the evidence of facts, not only restrain the savage excesses of the Saracens and of other infidels, enemies of the Christian name, but also for the defense and increase of the faith vanquish them and their kingdoms and habitations, though situated in the remotest parts unknown to us, and subject them to their own temporal dominion, sparing no labor and expense, in order that those kings and princes, relieved of all obstacles, may be the more animated to the prosecution of so salutary and laudable a work.

We have lately heard, not without great joy and gratification, how our beloved son, the noble personage Henry, infante of Portugal, uncle of our most dear son in Christ, the illustrious Alfonso, king of the kingdoms of Portugal and Algarve, treading in the footsteps of John, of famous memory, king of the said kingdoms, his father, and greatly inflamed with zeal for the salvation of souls and with fervor of faith, as a Catholic and true soldier of Christ, the Creator of all things, and a most active and courageous defender and intrepid champion of the faith in Him, has aspired from his early youth with his utmost might to cause the most glorious name of the said Creator to be published, extolled, and revered throughout the whole world, even in the most remote and undiscovered places,

and also to bring into the bosom of his faith the perfidious enemies of him and of the life-giving Cross by which we have been redeemed, namely the Saracens and all other infidels whatsoever, [and how] after the city of Ceuta, situated in Africa [on the northwestern tip nearest Spain], had been subdued by the said King John to his dominion, and after many wars had been waged, sometimes in person, by the said infante, although in the name of the said King John, against the enemies and infidels aforesaid, not without the greatest labors and expense, and with dangers and loss of life and property, and the slaughter of very many of their natural subjects, the said infante being neither enfeebled nor terrified by so many and great labors, dangers, and losses, but growing daily more and more zealous in prosecuting this his so laudable and pious purpose, has peopled with orthodox Christians certain solitary islands [Azores, Madeira, Canary Islands] in the ocean sea, and has caused churches and other pious places to be there founded and built, in which divine service is celebrated. Also by the laudable endeavor and industry of the said infante, very many inhabitants or dwellers in divers islands situated in the said sea, coming to the knowledge of the true God, have received holy baptism, to the praise and glory of God, the salvation of the souls of many, the propagation also of the orthodox faith, and the increase of divine worship.

Moreover, since, some time ago, it had come to the knowledge of the said infante that never, or at least not within the memory of men, had it been customary to sail on this ocean sea toward the southern and eastern shores, and that it was so unknown to us Westerners that we had no certain knowledge of the peoples of those parts, believing that he would best perform his duty to God in this matter, if by his effort and industry that sea might become navigable as far as to the Indians who are said to worship the name of Christ, and that thus he might be able to enter into relation with them, and to incite them to aid the Christians against the Saracens and other such enemies of the faith, and might also be able forthwith to subdue certain gentile or pagan peoples, living between, who are entirely free from infection by the sect of the most impious Mahomet [Mohammed], and to preach and cause to be preached to them the unknown but most sacred name of Christ, strengthened, however, always by the royal authority, he has not ceased for twenty-five years past to send almost yearly an army of the peoples of the said kingdoms, with the greatest labor, danger, and expense, in very swift ships called caravels, to explore the sea and coast lands toward the south and the Antarctic pole. And so it came to pass that when a number of ships of this kind had explored and taken possession of very many harbors, islands, and seas, they at length came to the province of Guinea, and having taken possession of some islands and harbors and the sea adjacent to that province, sailing farther they came to the mouth of a certain great river commonly supposed to be the Nile, and war was waged for some years against the peoples of those parts in the name of the said King Alfonso and of the infante, and in it very many islands in that neighborhood were subdued and peacefully possessed, as they are still possessed together with the adjacent sea. Thence also many Guineamen and other negroes, taken by force, and some by barter of unprohibited articles, or by other lawful contract of purchase, have been sent to the said kingdoms. A large number of these have been converted to the Catholic faith, and it is hoped, by the help of divine mercy, that if such progress be continued with them, either those peoples will be converted to the faith or at least the souls of many of them will be gained for Christ.

But since, as we are informed, although the king and infante aforesaid (who with so many and so great dangers, labors, and expenses, and also with loss of so many natives of their said kingdoms, very many of whom have perished in those expeditions, depending only upon the aid of those natives, have caused those provinces to be explored and have acquired and possessed such harbors, islands, and seas, as aforesaid, as the true lords of them), fearing lest strangers induced by covetousness should sail to those parts, and desiring to usurp to themselves the perfection, fruit, and praise of this work, or at least to hinder it, should therefore, either for the sake of gain or through malice, carry or transmit iron, arms, wood used for construction, and other things and goods prohibited to be carried to infidels, or should teach those infidels the art of navigation, whereby they would become more powerful and obstinate enemies to the king and infante, and the prosecution of this enterprise would either be hindered, or would perhaps entirely fail, not without great offense to God and great reproach to all Christianity, to prevent this and to conserve their right and possession, [the said king and infante] under certain most severe penalties then expressed, have prohibited and in general have ordained that none, unless with their sailors and ships and on payment of a certain tribute and with an express license previously obtained from the said king or infante, should presume to sail to the said provinces or to trade in their ports or to fish in the sea, [although the king and infante have taken this action, yet] in time it might happen that persons of other kingdoms or nations, led by envy, malice, or covetousness, might presume, contrary to the prohibition aforesaid, without license and payment of such tribute, to go to the said provinces, and in the provinces, harbors, islands, and sea, so acquired, to sail, trade, and fish; and thereupon between King Alfonso and the infante, who would by no means suffer themselves to be so trifled with in these things, and the presumptuous persons aforesaid, very many hatreds, rancors, dissensions, wars, and scandals, to the highest offense of God and danger of souls, probably might and would ensue. We weighing all and singular the premises with due meditation, and noting that since we had formerly by other letters of ours granted among other things free and ample faculty to the aforesaid King Alfonso—to invade, search out, capture, vanquish, and subdue all Saracens and pagans whatsoever, and other enemies of Christ wheresoever placed, and the kingdoms, dukedoms, principalities, dominions, possessions, and all movable and immovable goods whatsoever held and possessed by them and to reduce their persons to perpetual slavery, and to apply and appropriate to himself and his successors the kingdoms, dukedoms, counties, principalities, dominions, possessions, and goods, and to convert them to his and their use and profit— by having secured the said faculty, the said King Alfonso, or, by his authority, the aforesaid infante, justly and lawfully has acquired and possessed, and doth possess, these islands, lands, harbors, and seas, and they do of right belong and pertain to the said King Alfonso and his successors . . . We do by the tenor of these presents decree . . . to the aforesaid king and to his successors and to the infante . . . that the right of conquest which in the course of these letters we declare to be extended from the capes of Bojador and of Não [on the northwest African coast just south of the Canary Islands], as far as through all Guinea, and beyond toward that southern shore, has belonged and pertained, and forever of right belongs and pertains, to the said King Alfonso, his successors, and the infante, and not to any others.

3. The King of Spain regulates the importation of African slaves into the Americas.

The regular shipment of slaves from Africa to European possessions in the Americas began in the early 1500s (although the greatest growth was not to take place until the spread of plantation agriculture, especially sugar, after the 1640s). The colonial labor needs arose from a combination of the exhaustion of indigenous stores of precious metals by European looting, together with the decimation of the local populations by diseases introduced from Europe. To make their colonies pay, the Spanish needed workers to produce goods, and people able to resist the diseases that caused such high death rates among Native Americans and European settlers. The first slaves imported on a regular basis were Africans from Portugal who had first been converted to Christianity. As the demand for slave labor increased, the requirement of conversion was allowed to lapse, as did the practice of importing only Africans who had first been brought to Europe. At the same time, the Spanish crown anticipated earning considerable revenues from monopolizing and licensing slave imports into the Americas (which the Pope had proclaimed a Spanish possession). The first significant license granted by the crown was that given in 1518 by King Charles to Lorenzo de Gomenot, governor of Bresa, for the right to ship 4,000 Africans to Hispaniola, Cuba, Jamaica, and Puerto Rico.[3]

The King. Our officials who reside in the city of Seville in our House of Trade of the Indies; Know ye that I have given permission, and by the present [instrument] do give it, to Lorenzo de Gorrevod, [Gomenot], governor of Bresa, member of my Council, whereby he, or the person or persons who may have his authority therefor, may proceed to take to the Indies, the islands and the mainland of the ocean sea already discovered or to be discovered, four thousand negro slaves both male and female, provided they be Christians, in whatever proportions he may choose. Until these are all taken and transported no other slaves, male or female, may be transported, except those whom I have given per-

---

[3] Elizabeth Donnan, ed., *Documents Illustrative of the History of the Slave Trade to America*, vol. 1 (Washington, DC: Carnegie Institute, 1930), pp. 41–42. Reprinted with the agreement of the Carnegie Institute.

mission [to take] up to the present date. Therefore, I order you to allow and consent to the governor of Bresa aforesaid or the person or persons aforesaid who may have his said authority to transport and take the four thousand slaves male and female, without molesting him in any way; and, if the said governor of Bresa or the persons aforesaid who may have his authority, should make any arrangements with traders or other persons to ship the said slaves, male or female, direct from the isles of Guinea and other regions from which they are wont to bring the said negroes to these realms and to Portugal, or from any other region they please, even though they do not bring them to register in that house, they may do so provided that you take sufficient security that they bring you

proof of how many they have taken to each island and that the said negroes male and female, have become Christians on reaching each island, and how they have paid the customs duties there, in order that those taken be known and be not in excess of the aforesaid number. Notwithstanding any prohibition and order that may exist to the contrary, I require you and order you in regard to this not to collect any duty in that house [of trade] on the said slaves but rather you are to allow them to be taken freely and this my cedula shall be written down in the books of that house [of trade].

Done in Saragossa, the eighteenth day of August of the year 1518.

I THE KING

4. British attempts to break the Portuguese and Spanish monopolies of slave trading.

The papal bulls excluded all Europeans other than those approved by the Portuguese and Spanish crowns from the export trade in slaves from Africa and the import trade into the Americas. Such formal prohibition did not prevent buccaneers attracted by the profits of the trade from attempting to participate, and in the 1560s Sir John Hawkins, an English sailor and trader, made three expeditions to West Africa in quest of slaves that he planned to sell to Spanish settlers in the Caribbean. As these excerpts from his accounts of his second and third voyages demonstrate, success in these endeavors was very difficult especially because of the actions taken by African rulers to use the European intruders for their own purposes.[4]

Hawkins' second voyage, 1564.

The 27th [December, 1564] the captain was advertised by the Portugals of a town of the Negros called Bymba, being in the way as they returned [from the interior], where there was not only great quantity of gold, but also that there were not above forty men, and an hundred women and children in the town, so that if he would give the adventure upon the same, he might get a hundred slaves: with the which tidings he being glad . . . deter-

mined to stay before the town three or four hours to see what he could do: and thereupon prepared his men in armour and weapon together, to the number of forty men well appointed, having to their guides certain Portugals, in a boat, who brought some of them to their death: we landing boat after boat, and diverse of our men scattering themselves, contrary to the captain's will, by one or two in a company, for the hope that they had to find gold in their houses, ransacking the same, in the meantime the Negros came

---

[4] Richard Hakluyt, *The Principal Navigations, Voyages, Traffiques & Discoveries of the English Nation Made by Sea or Over-land to the Remote and Farthest Distant Quarters of the Earth at Any Time Within the Compasse of these 1600 Yeeres*, vol. 10 (London: G. Gishop, R. Newberie, and Barker, 1598–1600), pp. 21–23, 65–67.

upon them, and hurt many being thus scattered, whereas if five or six had been together, they had been able, as their companions did, to give the overthrow to 40 of them, and being driven down to take their boats, were followed so hardly by a route of Negros, who by that took courage to pursue them to their boats, that not only some of them, but others standing on shore, not looking for any such matter by means that the Negros did flee at the first, and our company remained in the town, were suddenly so set upon that some with great hurt recovered their boats; othersome not able to recover the same, took the water, and perished by means of the ooze. While this was doing, the captain who with a dozen men, went through the town, returned finding 200 Negros at the watersside, [the English] shooting at them in the boats, and cutting them in pieces which were drowned in the water, at whose coming, they all ran away: so he entered his boats, and before he could put off from the shore, they returned again, and shot very fiercely and hurt diverse of them. Thus we returned back somewhat discomforted, although the captain in a singular wise manner carried himself, with countenance cheerful outwardly, as though he did little weigh the death of his men, not yet the great hurt of the rest, although his heart inwardly was broken in pieces for it; done to this end, that the Portugals being with him, should not presume to resist against him, nor take occasion to put him to further displeasure or hindrance for the death of our men: having gotten by our going ten Negros, and lost seven of our best men. . . . and we had 27 of our men hurt.

Hawkins' third voyage, 1567–1568.

The ships departed from Plymouth, the second day of October, Anno 1567 . . . and arrived at Cape Verde, the eighteenth of November; where we landed 150 men, hoping to obtain some Negros, where we got but few, and those with great hurt and damage to our men, which chiefly proceeded of their envenomed arrows; and although in the beginning they seemed to be but small hurts, yet there hardly escaped any that had blood drawn of them, but died in strange sort, with their mouths shut some ten days before they died, and after their wounds were whole; where I myself had one of the greatest wounds, yet thanks be to God, escaped. From thence we past the time upon the coast of Guinea, searching with all diligence the rivers from Rio Grande, unto Sierra Leone, till the twelfth of January, in which time we had gotten together a hundred and fifty Negros . . . thus having nothing wherewith to seek the coast of the West Indies, I was with the rest of our company in consultation to go to the coast of the Mina [Elmina], hoping there to have obtained some gold for our wares, and thereby to have defrayed our charge. But even in that present instant, there came to us a Negro, sent from a king, oppressed by other Kings his neighbours, desiring our aide, with promise that as many Negros as by these wars might be obtained as well of his part as of ours, should be at our pleasure; whereupon we concluded to give aid, and sent 120 of our men, which the 15 of January, assaulted a town of the Negros of our allies adversaries, which had in it 8000 inhabitants, being very strongly impaled and fenced after their manner, but it was not so well defended, that our men prevailed not, but lost six men and forty hurt: so that our men sent forthwith to me for more help: whereupon considering that the good success of this enterprise might highly further the commodity of our voyage, I went myself, and with the help of the king of our side, assaulted the town, both by land and sea, and very hardly with fire (their houses being covered with dry palm leaves) obtained the town, put the inhabitants to flight, where we took 250 persons, men, women, & children, and by our friend the king of our side, there were taken 600 prisoners, whereof we hoped to have had our choice; but the Negro (in which nation is seldom or never found the truth) meant nothing less: for that night he removed his camp and prisoners, so that we were fain to content us with those few which we had gotten ourselves.

Now we had obtained between four and five hundred Negros, wherewith we thought it somewhat reasonable to seek the coast of the West Indies, and there, for our Negros, and other [of] our merchandize, we hoped to obtain, whereof to countervail our charges with some gains, whereunto we proceeded with all diligence . . . and departed the coast of Guinea the third of February [1568]....

5. A Jesuit justifies the trade in African slaves to a skeptical colleague.

Not all Europeans engaged in the early slave trade accepted without question the legal and moral basis of the commerce in persons. In 1610, a Catholic priest in Brazil, Father Sandoval, inquired of a colleague in Angola, Luis Brandaon, rector of the College of the Society of Jesus at St. Paul de Loando [Luanda], Angola, as to the ways in which Africans were enslaved and how they were treated before being exported. Angola was the main source of slaves for Portuguese possessions in the Americas. It was also, for practically the entire period of the Atlantic slave trade, the largest supplier by far of slaves shipped to the Americas, accounting for almost half of all slave exports from Africa in the 1700s and the 1800s.[5]

Brother Luis Brandaon to Father Sandoval, March 12, 1610.

Your Reverence writes me that you would like to know whether the negroes who are sent to your parts have been legally captured. To this I reply that I think your Reverence should have no scruples on this point, because this is a matter which has been questioned by the Board of Conscience in Lisbon, and all its members are learned and conscientious men. Nor did the bishops who were in São Thomé, Cape Verde, and here in Loando—all learned and virtuous men—find fault with it. We have been here ourselves for forty years and there have been [among us] very learned Fathers; in the Province of Brazil as well, where there have always been Fathers of our order eminent in letters, never did they consider this trade as illicit. Therefore we and the fathers of Brazil buy these slaves for our service without any scruple. Furthermore, I declare that if any one could be excused from having scruples it is the inhabitants of those regions, for since the traders who bring those negroes bring them in good faith, those inhabitants can very well buy from such traders without any scruple, and the latter on their part can sell them, for it is a generally accepted opinion that the owner who owns anything in good faith can sell it and that it can be bought. Padre Sánchez thus expresses this point in his Book of Marriage, thus solving this doubt of your Reverence. Therefore, we here are the ones who could have greater scruple, for we buy these negroes from other negroes and from people who perhaps have stolen them; but the traders who take them away from here do not know of this fact, and so buy those negroes with a clear conscience and sell them out there with a clear conscience. Besides I found it true indeed that no negro will ever say he has been captured legally. Therefore your Reverence should not ask them whether they have been legally captured or not, because they will always say that they were stolen and captured illegally, in the hope that they will be given their liberty. I declare, moreover, that in the fairs where these negroes are bought there are always a few who have been captured illegally because they were stolen or because the rulers of the land order them to be sold for offenses so slight that they do not deserve captivity, but these are few in

---

[5] Elizabeth Donnan, ed., *Documents Illustrative of the History of the Slave Trade to America*, vol. 1 (Washington, DC: Carnegie Institute, 1930), pp. 123–24. Reprinted with the agreement of the Carnegie Institute.

number and to seek among ten or twelve thousand who leave this port every year for a few who have been illegally captured is an impossibility, however careful investigation may be made. And to lose so many souls as sail from here—out of whom many are saved—because some, impossible to recognize, have been captured illegally does not seem to be doing much service to God, for these are few and those who find salvation are many and legally captured.

6. The importation of slaves into the Cape of Good Hope.

In 1652, the Dutch East Indies Company, established to break the monopoly of the Portuguese and Spanish on trade to Africa and Asia, founded a settlement on the southern coast of Africa from which to resupply ships sailing between Holland and trading ports along the West and East African coasts and in South and Southeast Asia. Initially, the directors of the company hoped to use local people to provide the labor needs of the settlement. The refusal, however, of local Khoisan to work on the terms offered by the company led the first governor, Jan van Riebeeck, to send an expedition to the East Coast of Africa in search of foodstuffs and slaves. From the 1650s until the first half of the nineteenth century, settlers at the Cape of Good Hope relied on slaves imported from Madagascar, Mauritius, the East Coast of Africa, and parts of South and Southeast Asia for their domestic and agricultural labor needs. While all European forts and settlements along the West and East African coasts used some slave labor, the Dutch settlement at the Cape produced the largest and most continuous use of slave labor by Europeans within Africa. [6]

Instructions for the Officers of the *Roode Vos* on the voyage to Mauritius and Madagascar, May 8, 1654.

As you are well aware from our resolution of the 27th April, why the galiot [galley] is to proceed to the above named islands [the settlement had been "reduced to great straits," had "nothing left of beans, cadjang, arrack, etc.," and had "resolved to send for supplies to Madagascar"], we merely now order you to proceed with the first fair wind straight to Mauritius and deliver our letter to the Commander there, and obtain the information required for trading at Madagascar, in order to secure rice, arrack, etc., hastening as much as possible to reach that island with the men which he may give you, that you may trade for the following provisions for the [Cape]

station: 25 or 30 tons rice, among them one or two padi. Arrack as much as you can stow away in casks or pots. . . . Besides 30 or 40 slaves, more or less as you may be able to conveniently take on board—among them 10 or 12 slave girls from 12 to 15 or 16 years of age—the men slaves, however, to range in age between 16 to 20 and 23 years.

Should you meet with amber, musk, silver, ivory, skins or anything profitable for the Company you may bring us some as a trial. Also some sandal or other wood to see whether some profits may not likewise be secured for India. Above all, provide yourselves with rice, as we are much in want of it, and the men will long for it with their empty stomachs—for this especially the voyage is to be made with the hope that Providence will make it successful. Amen.

---

[6] H. C. V. Leibbrandt, *Précis of the Archives of the Cape of Good Hope, Letters Despatched from the Cape, 1652–1662*, vol. 1 (Cape Town, South Africa: W. A. Richards and Sons, 1900), pp. 300–02.

7. An attempt to create an English monopoly of trade in West Africa.

With British buccaneering attempts to break the Portuguese and Spanish monopolies meeting only with limited success or with failure, the English crown sought to create trading monopolies of its own in an attempt to carve out a large share of trade on the West African Coast. In 1618, James I chartered the Company of Adventurers of London Trading into Parts of Africa, but all its trading voyages ended in disaster with the ships lost at sea or the traders attacked on shore. Charles I in 1631 gave another group of English traders an exclusive right to regulate commerce in West Africa for 31 years, though again none of the expeditions were particularly successful. With the growth of English sugar plantations in the Caribbean from the mid-1600s onward, however, the demand for slave labor grew enormously. To meet this demand, the English sought to establish a new monopoly company for West Africa, matching the East India Company that controlled English trade in South Asia and along the East African Coast. The new enterprise, the Royal African Company, first chartered as the "Company of Royal Adventurers Trading to Africa" at the time of the restoration of the monarchy in 1660, and then reorganized in 1672, aimed to create an English monopoly that would challenge those of its European competitors (particularly the French and the Dutch who by the mid-1600s had largely pushed the Portuguese out of much of West Africa). The company traded primarily in gold and slaves, and based its African enterprises at Cape Coast Castle on the Gold Coast (present-day Ghana). According to the terms of its 1672 charter, the company had the right not only to an exclusive monopoly of West African trade, but also to raise armies, declare wars, and enslave "Negroes."[7]

The Charter of the Royal African Company, 1672.

We [Charles the Second by the Grace of God King of England Scotland France and Ireland, Defender of the Faith, etc.] do hereby, for us, our heirs and Successors, grant unto the said Royal African Company of England and their Successors, that it shall and may be lawful to and for the said Company and their Successors, and none others, from time to time to set to Sea such and so many ships, pinnaces, and barks as shall be thought fitting . . . And shall hereafter have, use and enjoy all mines of Gold and Silver . . . which are or shall be found in any of the places above mentioned, And the whole, entire and only Trade, liberty, use and privilege of Trade and Traffic into and from the said parts of Africa above mentioned (that is to say) . . . all . . . places now or at any time heretofore called or known by the name or names of South Barbary, Guinny, Buiny or Angola . . . or any other Region or Countries or places within the bounds and limits aforesaid, and into and from all and singular Ports, Havens, Rivers, Creeks, Islands and places in the parts of Africa to them or any of them belonging, or being under the obedience of any King, State, or Potentate, of any Region, Dominion or Country in South Barbary, Guinny, Buiny or Angola, or limits aforesaid, for the buying, selling, bartering, and exchanging of, for, or with any Gold, Silver, Negroes, Slaves, goods, wares and merchandizes whatsoever

---

[7] Elizabeth Donnan, ed., *Documents Illustrative of the History of the Slave Trade to America*, vol. 1 (Washington, DC: Carnegie Institute, 1930), pp. 177–92. Reprinted with the agreement of the Carnegie Institute.

to be rented or found at or within any of the Cities, Towns, places, Rivers situate or being in the Countries, islands, Places, Ports and Coasts aforementioned. . . .

[W]e do hereby. . . prohibit and forbid, all the subjects of us . . . to visit, frequent, trade or adventure to traffic into or from the said Regions . . . and places aforesaid or any of them or to import any Red Wood, Elephant's Teeth, Negro Slaves, Hydes, Wax, Gums, grains or any other of the Commodities of the said Countries . . . unless it be with license and consent of the said Company. . . .

We do hereby . . . grant and give full power and authority unto the said Royal African Company of England and their successors for the time being, that they, by themselves, their factors, deputies and assigns, shall and may, from time to time, and at all times hereafter, enter into any Ship, Vessel, house, shop, Cellar or work-house and attack, arrest, take and seize all manner of ships, vessels, Negroes, Slaves, goods, Wares and Mer–chandizes whatsoever which shall be brought from or carried to the places before mentioned, or any of them, contrary to our Will and pleasure. . . .

And we do . . . give and grant unto the Said Royal African Company of England . . . full power to make and declare war with any of the heathen nations that are or shall be natives of any countries within the said terri-tories within the said parts of Africa . . . [W]e do . . . give to them [the governors of the company] full power and authority to raise armies, train and muster such military forces as to them shall seem requisite and neces-sary and to execute and use within the said plantations the Laws called the Marshall Laws, for the defence of the said plantations against any foreign or domestic insurrection or Rebellion. . . .

We have thought fit to erect and establish . . . a Court of Judicature to be held at such place or places, for our forts, plantations or factories upon the said coasts . . . which Court shall consist of one person learned in the Civil Laws, and two merchants, . . . [who] shall have cognizance and power to hear and de-termine all case of forfeiture and seizures of any ship or ships, goods and merchandizes trading and coming upon any of the said coasts . . . and also all causes of mercantile or maritime bargains buying selling and bar-tering of wares whatsoever . . . and all cases of trespasses, injuries and wrongs done or committed upon the high sea or in any of the regions, territories, countries or places afore-said concerning any person or persons re-siding coming or being in the parts of Africa within the bounds and limits aforesaid. . . .

In Witness etc., Witness the king at West-minster the seven and twentieth day of Sep-tember [1672]. BY THE KING

8. Sources of slaves for the Royal African Company.

The Royal African Company held a legal monopoly of English trade on the West African Coast until 1698. One of its main trading forts was on an island in the mouth of the Gambia River, and from this base, company traders annu-ally acquired thousands of African slaves. In the following extract, the local agent of the company, Thomas Thurloe, reports to his London superiors on trading conditions on the West African coast.[8]

Thomas Thurloe to the Royal African Company, Gamboa, 15th March 1678.

The next most considerable place for Trade is within this River of Gamboa for Slaves, Teeth, Wax and Hydes and may yield yearly between 5 and 6000 Slaves, 14 or 15 tuns of Teeth and wax and about 10,000 Hydes, the prices differ according to the persons the Goods are bought of, the dearest rates are those we give to the Portugueze which are

---

[8] Elizabeth Donnan, ed., *Documents Illustrative of the History of the Slave Trade to America*, vol. 1 (Washington, DC: Carnegie Institute, 1930), pp. 234–35. Reprinted with the agreement of the Carnegie Institute.

30 Bars for a Slave 18 Barrs per Cent for Teeth 16 for wax and 3 Hydes per b'l. To the natives wee give not so much but agree with them as wee can. But wee buy farr more of the Portugueze than of the Natives. If the Portugueze be kept poore then they will certainly bring their goods to the Islands but if they begin to grow rich then they will stand upon high terms and carry their goods to any Interloper's Strange Ship that comes in unless wee comply with them in every particular therefore this method ought to be used, to lend the best of them soe much and no more as with the proffitt of the goods wee lend them they may pay us againe and just maintaine their families soe that they wilbe allwayes in a necessity of borrowing and consequently only trade for us and not dare to sell what they gett to any strange Ship for fear wee should deny the lending of them. Once a Year (*vizt.*) about the ende of February a Vessell should be sent up the River to buy Slaves and Teeth of Merchants who come to such a particular place about 200 leagues up on purpose to meet with us and the Portugueze where those Comodityes are purchased at a cheaper rate than here below; and there is itt where wee buy the Country clothes which are very necessary to buy provisions here for wee spend 10 or 1200 every Year.

A third place to Trade in is betweene Cape Verde and this Rivers mouth which yields a good quantity of Negroes and Hydes but dearer then here for being an open place the French and Spaniards use it continually which hath raised the price of their Comodities, wee have not used that place because the Dutch had a Factor there; but since their Island hath been taken per the French, I sent thither to see what might be done and In a month or five weeks time bought 26 Negroes and 1400 Hydes, and if Goree were settled per the English, for the Dutch are taken and the French have left it, soe that tis free for the first commer, without wee might have a Considerable trade upon that Coast for it yields at best 500 Negroes and 50,000 hydes Yearly.

As for the sending out of Ships hither, it would be convenient to order it soe that none may be here In the raine time for that may prove the overthrow of a Voyage. 4 every Year would be enough (*Vizt.*) 2 for Negroes one to goe from hence at Christmas and the other at the latter end of May, and may both be dispatched from hence, for all the time betweene June and Christmas will be to buy ones Cargoe and from Christmas to June the other . . . this day I have sent another Ship to that Coast to buy Slaves and Hydes.

9. The log of the *Arthur*, a ship carrying slaves for the Royal African Company from West Africa to Barbados.

The Arthur *was part of the "triangular" trade, sailing from England to West Africa to purchase slaves, paying primarily with cloth manufactured in Europe and imported from India, beads, cowrie shells (the main form of currency used in Africa), and pieces of brass. The slaves were then shipped to the Caribbean and sold for sugar, which was then transported by the same vessels back to England. The log of the* Arthur *reprinted here details particularly the daily occurrence of death among the captives.*[9]

Journal of the *Arthur*, December 5, 1677 to May 25, 1678.

Dec. 5th 1677. A Journall of a voyage att New Callabarr in the shipp the *Arthur* Capt'n Rob't Doegood Commander: one the accompt of the Royall Affrican Company of England, of all actions and transactions from Gravesend to New Callabar and from thence to the Island of Barbados our portt of Discharge.

---

[9] Elizabeth Donnan, ed., *Documents Illustrative of the History of the Slave Trade to America*, vol. 1 (Washington, DC: Carnegie Institute, 1930), pp. 226–34. Reprinted with the agreement of the Carnegie Institute.

Feb. 1678. Wed. 5 Wee Brake ground at Gravesend by five of the Clock in the mourninge and came to Anchor againe 7th day att twelve the wind att s.e. . . .

Munday 11 February 1678. This day aboutt nine in the morninge Came one Board the Kinge of New Calabarr with some others of his gen'tes and after a Long discourse Came to Agreem'tt for Currentt for negro man 36 Copper Barrs: for one negro woman 30 and for one monello eight yames.

Tuesday 12th Feb'y 1678. This morninge Came one Board of us some Cannowse [canoes] Belonninge to Bandy with negroes but nott any wee did like: from which persons wee had Intelligence of Capt'n Wilkinse your Hon'rs Ship and that he had been gone from thence aboutt two moones and whilst he lay there was enforced to putt his negroes all on shore By reason of fire which appeared to be in his forecastell insoemuch that hee was very Likely to have Lost his ship By fire had nott the inhabitants [on] shore been kinde to him and helped him in the quenching of the fire and did honnorably deliver him againe all his negroes.

Wednesday 13 February 1678. The 12th day wee Bought 3 men 3 women as your

hon'rs will finde one my Books of Acc'tt and this day we Bo[ought] 14 men and

18 women very good and young negroes with some provisions for them. . . .

Sunday 17th Feby. 1678. Bo't 10 men 5 women 1 Boy and 3 girles all very likely negroes nott one of them exceedinge 30 years nor one under 14 yeares

Monday 18th Feby 1678. This day wee Bo't 4 men and 4 women havinge noe encouridgrn't to By more by Reason of shore Remissniss in Bringinge us provisions Doubtinge wee should have more Negroes then wee were Likely to have provisions and soe they to take advantage that did forbarre to Bye sendinge away again severall negroes and keepinge only such as we had minde to.

Wednesday 20th Feb. 1678. This day we had Cannows from Callabar and wee Bought 6 men 6 women and one Boye but had very Littell provisions for them.

Thursday 21st Feby 1678. This day we had severall Cannows on Board of us with Negroes Butt very few provitions wee Bo't 9 men and 11 women which were very stoute negroes indeed Butt nott many yames more then what before this day was promised to Bee Brought: the goods in our hands we kept till such Tyme as they had Brought enough for those negroes we had Bo't of them.

Friday Feby 22 1678. This day we sentt our Boat att Donus to see whatt might be done there, wee findinge negroes to be Brought one Board of us fast enough but were nott free to deale in many fearing lest wee should take in negroes and have noe provitions for them and the Boate returned againe with 1000 yames which they had purchased from severall of those on shore findinge yames very scarce this day, wee Bo't 7 men and 4 Women with some provitions as your hon'r may finde one the Booke of acc'tt. . . .

Sattday 2 March 1678. This day wee Brought 2 men and 2 women havinge nott many Cannows one Board of us did Forbare to Buy too many expectinge to have as wee did Resolve our Choice of negroes: wee have made Choice of negroes to the Best of our skill and judgm'tt and as likely negroes as a man should see yett wee finde that some of them doe decay and grow Leane and some are sick they want for no thinge havinge dealy as much provition as they cann make use of neither doe the[y] want for any Comfortt not sufferinge any man one Board to strike them.

Acctt of what Negroes Dyd every day.

Sunday 3 March 1678. This day wee Bought 5 men and 5 women and some provisions: aboutt 2 in the morning died one of our seamen after 5 days sickness and about 4 in the afternoon died one negro man: have 5 others sick.

Monday 4 March 1678. This day wee Bought 3 men and 4 women and 7 Girles very Likely Captives wee had some provisions and some oyle for them as will appere pr accontt.

Tuesday 5. This day wee Bought 5 men and 5 women wee forgett nott your hon'rs Interests mindeinge if possible to gett most men: if they are any way promisinge Butt as yett wee finde the women generally Better then the men.

Wednesday 6. This day wee Bought 3 men: 1 women with some provitions as pr accompt will appeare very good negroes nott forgetfinge your hon'rs orders that none exceed the age of fourteen neither under the age of twelve yeeres as heatherto had Been minded and accordingly Bo't.

Fryday 8. This day wee Bought 2 men and 1 woman haveinge nott many Cannows one Board to take greater Choice therfore did forbare to purchase expecting more for to Chuse for your hon'rs Better advantage Resolvinge as was befor minded to Buye not any Butt such as might If Life might bee permitted Answer your hon'rs expectation and advantage:

The 7 day aboutt four in the afternoon died one woman. This day as will appeare y're accompt wee did nott purchase any Negroes Butt some provitions for negroes: wee have many sick Captives Butt take the greatest Care wee can to preserve [them].

Sattday 9, March 1678 This day wee Bought 8 men and 6 women very Likely Negroes with some provitions—wee had died this day one man and severall others that are sick nottwithstandinge our Care with the Docktors phisick there is nothinge wantinge to them.. . .

Tuesday 12, March 1678 This day wee purchased 1 man 4 women and 1 Boy with some provitions as will appeare pr Accontt and att 10 in the forenoon died one man which to our knolidge had nott been sick 12 houres.

Wednsday 13, March 1678. This day haveinge many Cannows on Board wee Bought 9 men and 8 women with some provitions many others wee might have Bott more but wee had noe Reason findinge many bad negroes, and the sickniss of ours one Board did soe much troble us takeing them in very Likely and stout negroes to fall sick in soe

short Tyme that wee Littell in Curagm'tt. this day died 1 man and 1 Boy.

Thursday 14, March 1678. This day wee Bought 1 man and 1 woman with some provitions wee are nott free to Buy to many all one Tyme our Complem'tt Beinge all most up Butt are very Likely to Loose more here haveinge many very sick.

Fryday 15. This day wee haveinge many Cannewes on bord and very Likely negroes wee Bought 11 men, 4 women, 2 Boyes and 1 Girle wee had not purchase soe many Butt findeinge them very Likely negroes and haveinge then many sick: . . . died this day one man.

Sattday 16. This day wee Bought 3 men and 1 woman with some provitions wee hope to depart this place in few dayes our Complement beinge up: nether intend to purchase one negroe more except more dye to make our full number when wee shall come clare ofe: wee have many sick and doubt will not long live. the reason of ouer Byinge is bye the Loss of Negroes here.. . .

Monday 18. haveing soe many very sick expecting in few dayes the Loss of some negroes and haveinge very likely Negroes By the side wee Bought 4 men and some provitions: this day died 1 woman.. . .

Wedsday 20. died this day one man and one woman.

Thursday 21 . . . died one man haveing many more very sick . . . .

Wednsday 27. . . . this day died one man. died of our negroes befor such tyme as wee could gett over the Barr 12 men 6 woman and 1 Boy: have sevarall others sick.

Thursday 28. . . . in the afternoone I causd a muster of the negroes haveinge all that were well downe btween deck and soe told them up, on and on, giveinge all tobaco as they came up: and found to bee one Board a life 175 men: 135 women: 9 Boyes: and 10 Girles and nott one Negro more in the Shipp; myselfe sarchinge both betwen decks: and likewise the hold: and am very Certaine there was not one Negroe more Bought for I paied the goods my selfe for every Negroe was purchasd this voyage, this day died one man: and 2 women.

Fryday 29. . . . this day died one woman.

Sattday 30. . . . this day wee had died two men—haveinge att Least 30 more very sick.

Sunday 31. . . . in the morninge died one of our seamen and in the afternoon that day died our docktor w'ch wee did accon'tt a great Lost haveinge 6 white men very sick and many negroes sick: had not been sick passinge three dayes and wee had Been att sea of from the Barr when he died, 5 dayes this day died one woman and one Girle.

Aprill, 1678.

Munday 1. . . . this day died one man and one woman.

Tuesday 2. . . . this day died two men—wee haveinge many more sick takeinge the greatest Care wee Could for there preservation.

Munday 8. . . . our negroes fallinge sick very many to our greate Troble Resolved to goe at Cape Lopuse [Cape Lopez] to take some Refreshinge for them there aboutt 4 in the afternoon wee had a fresh gale: this day died one man.

Tuesday 9. . . . died this day and last night [two women].

Wedsday 10. there was att Cape Lopus when wee Came in a Dutchman, Belonginge to the mine [Elmina], which had traded upon the Coast 5 months for Teeth, the next day after wee Came in he went away from Cape Lopus this day wee sentt our Boat one shore for water: this day died [one woman].

Thursday 11. This morninge our men went ashore woodinge and some for water, wee had one Board Load of wood this day and 4 Tunn of Water: this day died one man.

Fryday 12. This day wee had 2 Boates Load of wood on Board and some water. wee finde our Negroes to a mend and to be very well Refreshed wee Concludee itt to be By Reson of the Change of the water: this day died one woman.

Sattday 13. Wee are now Cleeninge our ship: in the hold throwinge away the Rotton yames wch are a great many more than wee thought. wee doubt wee shall not have good in the ship 30,000 yames and shall be forced to take in provition here. this day died one woman. . . .

Munday 15. This day aboutt 2 of the Clock in the morninge wee sett seale from Cape Lopus. . . . wee finde that the negroes are greatly refreshed By the stoping a Littell tyme. this day died one man.

Tuesday 16. . . . this day died one man.

Fryday 19. . . . this day and Last night died 2 negro men.

Sunday 21. . . . this day died one Negroe man: some more wee have sick and though wee have noe Docktor yett wee doe the Best wee Cann for them giveinge them Brandy and Mallagetta: there is nothinge wantinge to them. this day died one man.

Munday 22. This day the winde nott Blowinge soe Fresh I did Muster the Negroes Causeing all to goe Downe Between decks that were weell and soe counted them up giveinge as they Came up one after one, Beinge all out of sheckells, Tobacco: and found to be alife 155 men 119 women 9 Boyes 9 Girles and noe more, this afternoone died one woman . . .

May.

Wedsday 1. our negroes are now for the most part in health.

Tuesday 14. . . . this day died one man—wee finde our negroes provitions to fall shortt By Reason of the many yames w'ch are Rotten.

Wedsday 15. . . . I tooke acco'tt of the Negroes Causeinge all that were well to goe downe Between decks: and soe Countinge the sick alought in the fore Castell and upon deck first: then Causeing the woman to Come up first one after one: and after the men: and I found to bee alife then 144 men: 110, women: 9 Boyes and 9 Girles and noe more, this eveninge about seaven of the Clock died one woman.

Thursday 16. this morninge and Last night died two men: one Boye: god Continue the gale otherwise wee doubt itt will be hard for us all intendinge to give our Negroes white mens provitions if theres should fall shortt w'ch wee doubt as yett wee have nott abated the negroes any thinge of there victialls but have as much as att first.

Sattday 18. . . . this afternoone died one man.

Tuesday 21. . . . aboutt 4 of the Clock in the afternoone wee had sight of the Island of Barbadoss, suppossinge too Late to gett in that night wee stood away.

Wednsday 22. The morninge Beinge hasie and darke wee Could not see the Island for two houres after wee stood towards itt wee made seale and seald N. W. and By 12 Of the Clock that day wee Anchord in Caleele Bay in Barbadoss: aboutt two houres after wee Came to Anchor; the Commander ordered his Boat to be mand who goes one shore and gives your hon'rs agentts accompt of the ships arrivall: my selfe Contininge on Board: expecting there Worshipps, on Board that night.

Thursday 23. This day wee expected your hon'rs Agentts on Board but did not Come. I went into the hold to see what was Left of the Negroes provition and found about 240 yames a few dryed plantaines w'ch was Left of that wee tooke in att Cape Lopus: 18 stock Fish: 3 parts of a hdd. of Beanes: a very small matter of Mallagetta [pepper] and about 10 l. of Tobaco: this is that w'ch was Left of there provitions: w'ch was not enough to give them Sattisfacktion three dayes: wherefor your honrs Agentts did order partatoes one Board whiles the Remaind there.

Fryday 24. This day I wentt one shore to your hon'rs Agentts and gave there W'rships the Charter p'tt and alsoe an accompt of what Negroes wee Bought what died one the Coast: what in the passage and how many wee Brought into Barbadoss alife: alsoe there worshipps had the sight of the Invoyces with the Declaration and proclamation: there worships intendinge the next day to Bee one Board and Lotte the negroes: w'ch after I had sattisfied there worshipps what they desired I went one Board againe. died one woman.

Sattday 25. This day your hon'r Agentts were one Board and Lotted the Negroes: which beinge done I showed there Worships my Booke of Accompt and whatt provitions was Left alsoe the Accompt of Teeth purchased and what goods Remayned of the Cargoe shipt one Board by your hon'rs Beinge now in the ship the *Arthur* eight hole Cest of Copper Barrs: and 34 Barrs in a Broken Chest, 26 Iron Barrs 16 Tapseels [type of cloth from India] 10 pentadoss [type of cloth from Southeast Asia] 16 dozen of Knives—this day died one negro man w'ch your hon'rs agentts had the sight of.

Sunday 26. Tuesday Followinge is intended the day for sale of Negroes: I am ordered to Tarry one Board w'ch accodingly doe. this day died one man.

Tuesday 28. This day were many of your hon'rs Negroes sold: the next day Beinge Keept: there were none sold untill Thursday. Wednsday Beinge the 29 May.

Thursday 30. this day the negroes were very thinn upon haveinge nott many Left.

31. The next day Rainy weather were not many Buyers one Board: if itt had Been Fare Weather suppose had sold all the Negroes—there were 23 Left unsold [the *Arthur* contained 265 living slaves when the sale began]: and the next day Beinge Satterday Mr. man Came on Board By your hon'rs Agentts order and Caused them to be Caryed away. I suppose the[y] were sold: after the negroes were all outt I Left the shipp and went one shore and the 7th of June Came outt of Barbadoss in the shipp the *Edward and Ann* Captn Nathaniell Green Commander: in Company with eleven seale more Bound for England.

Your Hon'rs Sav't

Geo. Kingston

10. The Council of the Indies answers questions from the King of Spain concerning the introduction of slaves into Spanish America.

In 1685, the king of Spain, Charles II, asked the Council of the Indies to explain the need for slavery in the Americas, and to answer whether the religious aims of the Catholic Church were being undermined by contracting with

"Dutch heretics" to obtain large supplies of slaves. In their reply, the members of the Council argued that the use of "heretics" did not undermine the religious aims of the Spanish colonists. Moreover, they stressed that without the use of slave labor Spain could not afford to retain its American colonies.[10]

Question:

By decree of July 5, 1685, his Majesty was pleased to order the Council of the Indies to inform him at once concerning the advantage of the negroes in America and what damage would follow in case they could not be had; whether there had been held any meetings by theologians and jurists to decide whether it was considered lawful to buy them as slaves and form asientos [concessions or contracts] for them; whether there were any authors who had written about this particular matter and who they were. . . .

The Council answered as follows:

[The committee of the Council] unanimously declared that they had no doubt with regard to this matter [the religious question] . . . the intercourse was lawful when there was no danger of perversion; and this could not be feared even remotely, for, although the administration of the contract was entrusted to Dutch persons, this present manager had to reside in these realms [Spanish], the business dealings were to be handled by Catholics, and if any Dutch trader had to assist tradesmen in their dealings, they were to obtain the advantages of such an one who had never had any business experiences in the Indies. Although many heretics of different sects have gone to the Indies, not one of them has ever tried to introduce his creed there. In case any such should go there, measures had been taken and orders had been given to the officials of the Inquisition, to punish them through their tribunal if they trespassed the permission granted them. The Faith was so firmly rooted in the Indies, and especially at ports where transports with negro slaves had to put in, that it could safely be said that it

could not be more assured in the ports of Castile. There were no Indians at these ports nor even at a great distance from them, among whom they might, on account of their ready compliance, introduce their erroneous beliefs; and they cannot go into the interior of the country, because of the prohibitions in the laws of the Indies. As many cautions as possible were taken with regard to the two warships allowed to be manned by Flemish and Dutch crews in order to prevent these men from going ashore and from having any intercourse whatsoever with the Catholics. . . . [Moreover, the intercourse was lawful] since it was certain that the Indies could not be maintained without negroes, because the lack of Indians has made it necessary that they be supplemented by making use of these people both for the labor of the estates, and for service in the families, as it is impossible to obtain Spaniards or creoles who are willing to do this kind of work; also the Dutch own the factories whence the negroes are brought. The public reason for maintaining those realms makes the trading lawful, because the Catholic could purchase from the infidel what was distinctly for necessary use, and not only the purchase is lawful, but also the delivery of the goods by the same hand, especially when, notwithstanding the many efforts made, no Spaniard could be found who was willing to take the asiento, inasmuch as the Consulado, which alone could handle the trade and which had done so before, refused it. Wherever the public weal is concerned, intercourse and trading are not only permitted but also the alliance with and use of armed auxiliaries, even of heretics, in defense of those domains proper, in case assistance cannot be obtained in any other way, as has been done in many instances in the past. . . .

---

[10] Elizabeth Donnan, ed., *Documents Illustrative of the History of the Slave Trade to America*, vol. 1 (Washington, DC: Carnegie Institute, 1930), pp. 346–51. Reprinted with the agreement of the Carnegie Institute.

From the absolute need of these slaves, the fatal consequences which would result from not having them were easily deduced, for if they are the ones who cultivate the haciendas, and there is no one else who could do it, because of a lack of Indians, and where Indians were to be found they would not be forced to render personal services, it would follow that if a prohibition were issued to discontinue bringing them, the food needed for the support of the whole kingdom would cease to be produced; the landed properties, the main wealth of which consists chiefly of negro slaves, would be lost, and America would face absolute ruin. This was experienced when the kingdom of Portugal separated itself from the Spanish crown [1640], for since [then] the asientos had lapsed and the bringing of negroes from Cape Verde and the factories owned by the Portuguese in Africa had ceased, and although certain permits were issued, they were not half enough to provide America where great poverty was suffered in consequence. It was then, in order to repair the loss, because the public weal demanded the support of those dominions, that the asiento was made with Domingo Grillo, slaves were provided, and immediately the benefit of their introduction was felt. Everything else connected with this question and deemed useful was considered.

11. The voyage of the *Hannibal*, carrying slaves from West Africa to Barbados.

This account of a slave voyage differs from that of the Arthur *in that the author, Thomas Phillips, provides information on the negotiations over slave prices that took place between African and European trader. He also describes in some detail the conditions to which slaves were subjected on the Atlantic crossing and recounts the ways in which they struggled to escape their recent captivity. Phillips had purchased the* Hannibal, *a vessel of 450 tons and 36 guns, in 1693 with funds supplied by one of the London members of the Royal African Company, Sir Jeffrey Jeffreys, who was interested particularly in trade to Virginia. Other members of the Company also invested as part-owners with Phillips and Jeffreys. The* Hannibal, *together with five other ships, departed the English coast in October 1693 for a slaving voyage to West Africa. The vessels arrived at Cape Coast Castle near the end of February 1694, and then sailed along the coast until reaching Whydah (in present-day Benin) in late May.*[11]

Our factory [at Whydah] lies about three miles from the sea-side, where we were carry'd in hamocks, which the factor Mr. Joseph Peirson, sent to attend our landing, with several arm'd blacks that belong'd to him for our guard; we were soon truss'd in a bag, toss'd upon negroes heads, and convey'd to our factory. . . .

Our factory built by Capt. Wiburne, Sir John Wiburne's brother, stands low near the marshes, which renders it a very unhealthy place to live in; the white men the African company send there, seldom returning to tell their tale: 'tis compass'd round with a mud-wall, about six foot high, and on the southside is the gate; within is a large yard, a mud thatch'd house, where the factor lives, with

---

[11] Thomas Phillips, "A Journal of a Voyage made in the *Hannibal* of London…," published originally in Awnsham and John Churchill, *Collection of Voyages and Travels,* 6 vols. (London: H. Lintot, 1744–1746); here excerpted from Elizabeth Donnan, ed., *Documents Illustrative of the History of the Slave Trade to America*, vol. 1 (Washington, DC: Carnegie Institute, 1930), pp. 399–410. Reprinted with the agreement of the Carnegie Institute.

the white men; also a store-house, a trunk for slaves, and a place where they bury their dead white men, call'd, very improperly, the hog-yard; there is also a good forge, and some other small houses. . . . And here I must observe that the rainy season begins about the middle of May, and ends the beginning of August, in which space it was my misfortune to be there, which created sicknesses among my negroes aboard, it being noted for the most malignant season by the blacks themselves, who while the rain lasts will hardly be prevail'd upon to stir out of their huts. . . .

The factory prov'd beneficial to us in another kind; for after we had procured a parcel of slaves, and sent them down to the sea-side to be carry'd off, it sometimes proved bad weather, and so great a sea, that the canoes could not come ashore to fetch them, so that they returned to the factory, where they were secured and provided for till good weather presented, and then were near to embrace the opportunity, we sometimes shipping off a hundred of both sexes at a time.

The factor, Mr. Peirson, was a brisk man, and had good interest with the king, and credit with the subjects, who knowing their tempers, which is very dastard, had good skill in treating them both civil and rough, as occasion requir'd; most of his slaves belonging to the factory, being gold coast negroes, who are very bold, brave, and sensible, ten of which would beat the best forty men the king of Whidaw [Whydah] had in his kingdom; besides their true love, respect and fidelity to their master, for whose interest or person they will most freely expose their own lives. . . .

As soon as the king understood of our landing, he sent two of his cappasheirs, or noblemen, to compliment us at our factory, where we design'd to continue, that night, and pay our devoirs to his majesty next day, which we signify'd to them, and they, by a foot-express, to their monarch; whereupon he sent two more of his grandees to invite us there that night, saying he waited for us, and that all former captains used to attend him the first night: whereupon being unwilling to infringe the custom, or give his majesty any offence, we took our hamocks, and Mr.

Peirson, myself, Capt. Clay, our surgeons, pursers, and about 12 men, arm'd for our guard, were carry'd to the king's town, which contains about 50 houses. . . .

We returned him thanks by his interpreter, and assur'd him how great affection our masters, the royal African company of England, bore to him, for his civility and fair and just dealings with their captains; and that notwithstanding there were many other Places, more plenty of negro slaves that begg'd their custom, yet they had rejected all the advantageous offers made them out of their good will to him, and therefore had sent us to trade with him, to supply his country with necessaries, and that we hop'd he would endeavour to continue their favour by his kind usage and fair dealing with us in our trade, that we may have our slaves with all expedition, which was the making of our voyage; that he would oblige his cappasheirs to do us justice, and not impose upon us in their prices; all which we should faithfully relate to our masters, the royal African company, when we came to England. He answer'd that the African company was a very good brave man; that he lov'd him; that we should be fairly dealt with, and not impos'd upon; But he did not prove as good as his word; nor indeed (tho' his cappasheirs shew him so much respect) dare he do any thing but what they please . . . so after having examin'd us about our cargoe, what sort of goods we had, and what quantity of slaves we wanted, etc., we took our leaves and return'd to the factory, having promised to come in the morning to make our palavera, or agreement, with him about prices, how much of each of our goods for a slave.

According to promise we attended his majesty with samples of our goods, and made our agreement about the prices, tho' not without much difficulty; he and his cappasheirs exacted very high, but at length we concluded as per the latter end; then we had warehouses, a kitchen, and lodgings assign'd us, but none of our rooms had doors till we made them, and put on locks and keys; next day we paid our customs to the king and cappasheirs, as will appear hereafter; then the bell was order'd to go about to give notice to all people to bring their slaves to the trunk to sell us: this bell is a hollow piece of iron in shape of a sugar loaf, the cavity of which could contain about 50 lb. of cowries: This a man carry'd about and beat with a stick, which made a small dead sound. . . .

Capt. Clay and I had agreed to go to the trunk to buy the slaves by turns, each his day, that we might have no distraction or disagreement in our trade, as often happens when there are here more ships than one, and the commanders can't set their horses together, and go hand in hand in their traffick, whereby they have a check upon the blacks, whereas their disagreements create animosities, underminings, and out-bidding each other, whereby they enhance the prices to their general loss and detriment, the blacks well knowing how to make the best use of such opportunities, and as we found make it their business, and endeavour to create and foment misunderstandings and jealousies between commanders, it turning to their great account in the disposal of their slaves.

When we were at the trunk, the king's slaves, if he had any, were the first offer'd to sale, which the cappasheirs would be very urgent with us to buy, and would in a manner force us to it ere they would shew us any other, saying they were the Reys Cosa [slaves of the king], and we must not refuse them, tho' as I observ'd they were generally the worst slaves in the trunk, and we paid more for them than any others, which we could not remedy, it being one of his majesty's prerogatives: then the cappasheirs each brought out his slaves according to his degree and quality, the greatest first, etc. and our surgeon examin'd them well in all kinds, to see that they were sound wind and limb, making them jump, stretch out their arms swiftly, looking in their mouths to judge of their age; for the cappasheirs are so cunning, that they shave them all close before we see them, so that let them be never so old we can see no grey hairs in their heads or beards; and then having liquor'd them well and sleek with palm oil, 'tis no easy matter to know an old one from a middle-age one, but by the teeths decay; but our greatest care of all is to buy none that are pox'd, lest they should infect the rest aboard. . . .

When we had selected from the rest such as we liked, we agreed in what goods to pay for them, the prices being already stated before the king, how much of each sort of merchandize we were to give for a man, woman, and child, which gave us much ease, and saved abundance of disputes and wranglings, and gave the owner a note, signifying our agreement of the sorts of goods; upon delivery of which the next day he receiv'd them; then we mark'd the slaves we had bought in the breast, or shoulder, with a hot iron, having, the letter of the ship's name on it, the place being before anointed with a little palm oil, which caus'd but little pain, the mark being usually well in four or five days, appearing very plain and white after.

When we had purchas'd to the number of 50 or 60 we would send them aboard, there being a cappasheir, intitled the captain of the slaves, whose care it was to secure them to the water-side, and see them all off; and if in carrying to the marine any were lost, he was bound to make them good, to us, the captain of the trunk being oblig'd to do the like, if any ran away while under his care, for after we buy them we give him charge of them till the captain of the slaves comes to carry them away: These are two officers appointed by the king for this purpose, to each of which every ship pays the value of a slave in what goods they like best for their trouble, when they have done trading; and indeed they discharged their duty to us very faithfully, we not having lost one slave thro' their neglect in 1300 we bought here.

There is likewise a captain of the sand, who is appointed to take care of the merchandize we have come ashore to trade with, that the negroes do not plunder them, we being often forced to leave goods a whole night on the sea shore, for want of porters to bring them up; but notwithstanding his care and authority, we often came by the loss, and could have no redress.

When our slaves were come to the sea-side, our canoes were ready to carry them off to the longboat, if the sea permitted, and she convey'd them aboard ship, where the men were all put in irons, two and two shackled together, to prevent their mutiny, or swimming ashore.

The negroes are so wilful and loth to leave their own country, that they have often leap'd out of the canoes, boat and ship, into the sea, and kept under water till they were drowned, to avoid being taken up and saved by our boats, which pursued them; they having a more dreadful apprehension of Barbadoes than we can have of hell, tho' in reality they live much better there than in their own country; but home is home, etc: we have likewise seen divers of them eaten by the sharks, of which a prodigious number kept about the ships in this place, and I have been told will follow her hence to Barbadoes, for the dead negroes that are thrown over-board in the passage. I am certain in our voyage there we did not want the sight of some every day, but that they were the same I can't affirm.

We had about 12 negroes did wilfully drown themselves, and others starv'd themselves to death; for 'tis their belief that when they die they return home to their own country and friends again.

I have been inform'd that some commanders have cut off the legs and arms of the most wilful, to terrify the rest, for they believe if they lose a member, they cannot return home again: I was advis'd by some of my officers to do the same, but I could not be perswaded to entertain the least thought of it, much less put in practice such barbarity and cruelty to poor creatures, who, excepting their want of Christianity and true religion (their misfortune more than fault) are as much the works of God's hands, and no doubt as dear to him as ourselves; nor can I imagine why they should be despis'd for their colour, being what they cannot help, and the effect of the climate it has pleas'd God to appoint them. I can't think there is any intrinsick value in one colour more than another, nor that white is better than black, only we think so because we are so, and are prone to judge favourably in our own case, as well as the blacks, who in

odium of the colour, say, the devil is white, and so paint him. . . .

The present king often, when ships are in a great strait for slaves, and cannot be supply'd otherwise, will sell 3 or 400 of his wives to compleat their number, but we always pay dearer for his slaves than those bought of the cappasheirs, his measure for booges [type of cowry shell] being much larger than theirs, and he was allow'd accordingly in all other goods we had.

For every slave the cappasheirs sold us publickly, they were oblig'd to pay part of the goods they receiv'd for it to the king, as toll or custom, especially the booges, of which he would take a small dishfull out of each measure; to avoid this they would privately send for us to their houses in the night, and dispose of two or three slaves at a time, and we as privately would send them the goods agreed upon for them; but this they did not much practise for fear of offending the king, should he come to know it, who enjoyns them to carry all their slaves to be sold publickly at the trunk with his own; sometimes after he had sold one of his wives or subjects, he would relent, and desire us to exchange for another, which we freely did often, and he took very kindly. . . .

After we are come to an agreement for the prices of our slaves, ere the bell goes round to order all people to bring their slaves to the trunk to be sold, we are oblig'd to pay our customs to the king and cappasheirs for leave to trade, protection and justice; which for every ship are as follow, *viz*.

To the king six slaves value in cowries, or what other goods we can perswade him to take, but cowries are most esteem'd and desir'd; all which are measur'd in his presence, and he would wrangle with us stoutly about heaping up the measure.

To the cappasheirs in all two slaves value, as above.

The usual charges here which we pay at our departure when we have finish'd our trade, in any goods that remain, are One slave value to the captain of the trunk for his care of our slaves while there; one slave value to the captain of the sand for his care of our goods; one ditto to the captain of the slaves who conducts them safe to the sea-side; one ditto to captain Tom the interpreter, for his trouble; one ditto for filling water; half a slave, or as much cowries as the cavity of the bell can contain, to the bell-man.

Besides all which our factory charges, victualling the negroes after bought till they get aboard, and hire of porters to bring up the goods from the sea-side, which is seven miles at least, and the stoutest fellow would not bring above two bars of iron at a time, and make but one trip in a day, took up great quantities of our cowries, we paying these last charges in nothing else but these shells.

The best goods to purchase slaves here are cowries, the smaller the more esteem'd; for they pay them all by tale, the smallest being as valuable as the biggest, but take them from us by measure or weight, of which about 100 pounds for a good man-slave.

The next in demand are brass neptunes or basons, very large, thin, and flat; for after they have bought them they cut them in pieces to make anilias or bracelets, and collars for their arms legs and necks.

The other preferable goods are blue paper sletias, cambricks or lawns, caddy chints, broad ditto [all types of cloth], coral, large, smooth, and of a deep red, rangoes [beads] large and red, iron bars, powder, and brandy.

With the above goods a ship cannot want slaves here, and may purchase them for about three pounds fifteen shillings a head, but near half the cargo value must be cowries or booges, and brass basons, to set off the other goods that we buy cheaper, as coral, rangoes, iron, etc. else they will not take them; for if a cappasheir sells five slaves, he will have two of them paid for in cowries, and one in brass, which are dear slaves; for a slave in cowries costs us above four pounds in England; whereas a slave in coral, rangoes, or iron, does not cost fifty shillings; but without the cowries and brass they will take none of the last goods, and but small quantities at best, especially if they can discover that you have good store of cowries and brass aboard, then no other goods will serve their turn, till they have got as much as you have; and after, for

the rest of the goods they will be indifferent, and make you come to their own terms, or else lie a long time for your slaves, so that those you have on board are dying while you are buying others ashore; therefore every man that comes here, ought to be very cautious in making his report to the king at first, of what sorts and quantities of goods he has, and be sure to say his cargo consists mostly in iron, coral, rangoes, chints, etc. so that he may dispose of those goods as soon as he can, and at last his cowries and brass will bring him slaves as fast as he can buy them; but this is to be understood of a single ship: or more, if the captains agree, which seldom happens; for where there are divers ships, and of separate interests, about buying the same commodity they commonly undermine, betray, and out-bid one the other; and the Guiney commanders words and promises are the least to be depended upon of any I know use the sea; for they would deceive their fathers in their trade if they could. . . .

The only money they have here are these cowries or shells we carry them, being brought from the East-Indies, and were charg'd to us at four pounds per cent. of which we gave 100 lb. for a slave; as soon as the negroes have them, they bore holes in the backs of them, and string them on rushes, 40 shells on each, which they call a foggy; and five of such foggys being tied together, is call'd a galina, being 200 shells, which is their way of accounting their shell-money. . . .

The canoes we buy on the gold coast, and strengthen them with knees and weatherboards fore and aft, to keep the sea out, they plunging very deep when they go against a sea . . . those that are most fit for the use at Whidaw, are five hand or seven hand canoes; of which each ship that buys many slaves ought to carry two, for they are very incident to be staved by the great sea when they overset, and here is none for supply, and without them there is no landing or coming off for goods or men: The canoe-men we bring from Cape Corce being seven in number, of which one is boatswain, and is commonly one of the most skillful canoe-men in Guiney . . . .

their pay is certain and stated, half of which we pay them in gold at Cape Corce [Cape Coast Castle], and the rest in goods when we have done with them at Whidaw; 'tis also customary to give them a canoe to carry them back, and cut up the other for fire-wood, unless an opportunity offers to sell it, which is very rare. They lost us six or seven barrels of cowries, above 100 bars of iron, and other goods, by the over-setting of the canoes in landing them, which we could never recover, or have the least satisfaction for, but were forced to give them good words, lest they should, in revenge, play us more such tricks; we kept two men ashore here constantly to fill water, which lay and eat at the factory, which fill'd our small hogsheads in the night, and roll'd them over the sand to the sea-side, ready to raft off in the morning, before the sea breeze came in, which is the only time, we having no other way to get it off but by rafting, and in halling off to the longboat the great sea would often break our raft, and stave our cask, whereby we lost a great many. . . .

When our slaves are aboard we shackle the men two and two, while we lie in port, and in sight of their own country, for 'tis then they attempt to make their escape, and mutiny; to prevent which we always keep sentinels upon the hatchways, and have a chest full of small arms, ready loaden and prim'd, constantly lying at hand upon the quarter-deck, together with some granada shells; and two of our quarter-deck guns, pointing on the deck thence, and two more out of the steerage, the door of which is always kept shut, and well barr'd; they are fed twice a day, at 10 in the morning, and 4 in the evening, which is the time they are aptest to mutiny, being all upon deck; therefore all that time, what of our men are not employ'd in distributing their victuals to them, and settling them, stand to their arms; and some with lighted matches at the great guns that yaun upon them, loaden with partridge, till they have done and gone down to their kennels between decks: Their chief diet is call'd dabbadabb, being Indian corn ground as small as oat-meal, in iron mills, which we carry for that purpose; and after mix'd with

water, and boil'd well in a large copper furnace, till 'tis as thick as a pudding, about a peckful of which in vessels, call'd crews, is allow'd to 10 men, with a little salt, malagetta [pepper], and palm oil, to relish; they are divided into messes of ten each, for the easier and better order in serving them: Three days a week they have horse-beans boil'd for their dinner and supper, great quantities of which the African company do send aboard us for that purpose; these beans the negroes extremely love and desire, beating their breast, eating them, and crying Pram! Pram! which is Very good! they are indeed the best diet for them, having a binding quality, and consequently good to prevent the flux, which is the inveterate distemper that most affects them, and ruins our voyages by their mortality: The men are all fed upon the main deck and forecastle, that we may have them all under command of our arms from the quarter-deck, in case of any disturbance; the women eat upon the quarter-deck with us, and the boys and girls upon the poop; after they are once divided into messes, and appointed their places, they will readily run there in good order of themselves afterwards; when they have eaten their victuals clean up, (which we force them to for to thrive the better) they are order'd down between decks, and every one as he passes has a pint of water to drink after his meat, which is serv'd them by the cooper out of a large tub, fill'd before-hand ready for them. . . .

When we come to sea we let them all out of irons, they never attempting then to rebel, considering that should they kill or master us, they could not tell how to manage the ship, or must trust us, who would carry them where we pleas'd; therefore the only danger is while we are in sight of their own country, which they are loth to part with; but once out of sight out of mind: I never heard that they mutiny'd in any ships of consequence, that had a good number of men, and the least care; but in small tools where they had but few men, and those negligent or drunk, then they surpriz'd and butcher'd them, cut the cables, and let the vessel drive ashore, and every one shift for himself. However, we have some 30 or 40 gold coast negroes, which we buy, and are procur'd us there by our factors, to make guardians and overseers of the Whidaw negroes, and sleep among them to keep them from quarrelling; and in order, as well as to give us notice, if they can discover any caballing or plotting among them, which trust they will discharge with great diligence: they also take care to make the negroes scrape the decks where they lodge every morning very clean, to eschew any distempers that may engender from filth and nastiness; when we constitute a guardian, we give him a cat of nine tails as a badge of his office, which he is not a little proud of, and will exercise with great authority. We often at sea in the evenings would let the slaves come up into the sun to air themselves, and make them jump and dance for an hour or two to our bagpipes, harp, and fiddle, by which exercise to preserve them in health; but notwithstanding all our endeavour, 'twas my hard fortune to have great sickness and mortality among them.

Having bought my compliment of 700 slaves, *viz.* 480 men and 220 women, and finish'd all my business at Whidaw, I took my leave of the old king, and his cappasheirs, and parted, with many affectionate expres-

sions on both sides, being forced to promise him that I would return again the next year, with several things he desired me to bring him from England; and having sign'd bills of lading to Mr. Peirson, for the negroes aboard, I set sail the 27th of July in the morning, accompany'd with the *East-India Merchant*, who had bought 650 slaves, for the island of St. Thomas, with the wind at W.S.W. . . .

We supply'd ourselves with some Indian corn, figolas, or kidneybeans, plantins, yams, potatoes, cocoa-nuts, limes, oranges, etc., for the use and refreshment of our negroes. . . .

Having completed all my business ashore in fourteen days that I lay here, yesterday in the afternoon I came off with a resolution to go to sea. Accordingly about six in the evening we got up our anchors, and set sail for Barbadoes, being forc'd to leave the *East-India Merchant* behind, who could not get ready to sail in nine or ten days; which time I could not afford to stay, in respect to the mortality of my negroes, of which two or three died every day, also the small quantity of provisions I had to serve for my passage to Barbadoes . . . I deliver'd alive at Barbadoes to the company's factors 372, which being sold, came out at about nineteen pounds per head. . . .

12. Willem Bosman describes the Dutch trade for slaves on the West African Coast.

During the seventeenth century, Dutch traders expanded aggressively into the international seaborne trade, driving the Portuguese from many of their bases in West and East Africa, the Indian subcontinent, and Southeast Asia. They conquered much of Brazil from the Portuguese in 1630 (though were driven out in 1654) and established their own sugar plantations in the Caribbean. In search of slaves for their own plantations, and making considerable profits as suppliers of slaves to other European settlers, the Dutch had their main base at Elmina (in present-day Ghana), which they seized from the Portuguese in 1637. Willem Bosman, the author of the extract below, had first traveled to West Africa as a 16-year-old in the late 1680s. Later he returned as head of the Dutch trading fort at Elmina and published one of the earliest and most thorough accounts of slave trading on the African coast.[12]

---

[12] Willem Bosman, *A New and Accurate Description of the Coast of Guinea, Divided into the Gold, the Slave, and the Ivory Coasts* (London: J. Knapton, 1705; first published in a Dutch edition in 1704), pp. 363–65.

The first business of one of our factors [agents] when he comes to Fida [Whydah], is to satisfy the customs of the king and the great men, which amount to about 100 pounds in guinea value, as the goods must yield there. After which we have free licence to trade, which is published throughout the whole land by the crier.

But yet before we can deal with any person, we are obliged to buy the king's whole stock of slaves at a set price; which is commonly one third or one fourth higher than ordinary: After which we obtain free leave to deal with all his subjects of what rank soever. But if there happen to be no stock of slaves, the factor must then resolve to run the risk of trusting the inhabitants with goods to the value of one or two hundred slaves; which commodities they send into the inland country, in order to buy with them slaves at all markets, and that sometimes two hundred miles deep in the country: For you ought to be informed that markets of men are kept here in the same manner as those of beasts with us.

Not a few in our country fondly imagine that parents here sell their children, men their wives, and one brother the other: But those who think so deceive themselves; for this never happens on any other account but that of necessity, or some great crime: But most of the slaves that are offered to us are prisoners of war, which are sold by the victors as their booty.

When these slaves come to Fida, they are put in prison all together, and when we treat concerning buying them, they are all brought out together in a large plain; where, by our surgeons, whose province it is, they are thoroughly examined, even to the smallest member, and that naked too both men and women, without the least distinction or modesty. Those which are approved as good are set on one side; and the lame or faulty are set by as invalids, which are here called *mackrons*. These are such as are above five and thirty years old, or are maimed in the arms, legs, hands or feet, have lost a tooth, are grey-haired, or have films over their eyes; as well as all those which are affected with any venereal distemper, or with several other diseases.

The invalids and the maimed being thrown out, as I have told you, the remainder are numbered, and it is entered who delivered them. In the mean while a burning iron, with the arms or name of the companies, lies in the fire; with which ours are marked on the breast.

This is done that we may distinguish them from the slaves of the English, French or others; (which are also marked with their mark) and to prevent the Negroes exchanging them for worse; at which they have a good hand.

I doubt not but that this trade seems very barbarous to you, but since it is followed by mere necessity it must go on; but we yet take all possible care that they are not burned too hard, especially the women, who are more tender than the men.

We are seldom long detained in the buying of these slaves, because their price is established, the women being one fourth or fifth part cheaper than the men. The disputes which we generally have with the owners of these slaves are, that we will not give them such goods as they ask for them, especially the *boesies* [cowry shells] (as I have told you, the money of this country); of which they are very fond, though we generally make a division on this head in order to make one sort of goods help off another, because those slaves which are paid for in *boesies* cost the company one half more than those bought with other goods. . . .

When we have agreed with the owners of the slaves, they are returned to their prison; where from that time forwards they are kept at our charge, cost us two pence a day a slave; which serves to subsist them, like our criminals, on bread and water: So that to save charges we send them on board our ships with the very first opportunity; before which their masters strip them of all they have on their backs; so that they come aboard stark naked as well women as men. In which condition they are obliged to continue, if the master of the ship is not so charitable (which he commonly is) as to bestow something on them to cover their nakedness.

You would really wonder to see how these slaves live on board; for though their number sometimes amounts to six or seven hundred, yet by the careful management of our masters of ships, they are so regulated that it seems incredible: And in this particular our nation exceeds all other Europeans; for as the French, Portuguese and English slave-ships, are always foul and stinking; on the contrary ours are for the most part clean and neat.

The slaves are fed three times a day with indifferent good victuals, and much better than they eat in their own country. Their lodging-place is divided into two parts; one of which is appointed for the men the other for the women; each sex being kept apart. Here they lie as close together as is possible for them to be crowded.

We are sometimes sufficiently plagued with a parcel of slaves, which come from a far inland country, who very innocently persuade one another, that we buy them only to fatten and afterwards eat them as a delicacy.

When we are so unhappy as to be pestered with many of this sort, they resolve and agree together (and bring over the rest to their party) to run away from the ship, kill the Europeans, and set the vessel ashore; by which means they design to free themselves from being our food.

I have twice met with this misfortune; and the first time proved very unlucky to me, I not in the least suspecting it; but the uproar was timely squashed by the master of the ship and myself, by causing the abettor to be shot through the head, after which all was quiet.

But the second time it fell heavier on another ship, and that chiefly by the carelessness of the master, who having fished up the anchor of a departed English ship, had it laid in the hold where the male slaves were lodged; who, unknown to any of the ship crew, possessed themselves of a hammer; with which, in a short time, they broke all their fetters in pieces upon the anchor: after this they came above deck and fell upon our men; some of whom they grievously wounded, and would certainly have mastered the ship, if a French and English ship had not very fortunately happened to lie by us; who perceiving by our firing a distressed gun, that something was in disorder of board, immediately came to our assistance with shallops [a type of sloop] and men, and drove the slaves under deck: Notwithstanding which before all was appeased about twenty of them were killed.

The Portuguese have been more unlucky in this particular than we; for in four years time they have lost four ships in this manner.

13. In support of slavery and against monopoly.

Not all merchants believed that profits could be won only through the establishment of national monopolies like that of the Royal African Company. Joshua Gee, a London merchant, argued that only the final demise of the company would encourage competition and result in much greater numbers of slaves being exported from Africa to British plantations in the Caribbean. At the time of Gee's writing, the company was already well into decline. Within two decades it disappeared altogether and was replaced in 1752 by the Company of Merchants Trading to Africa, membership in which was open to all English traders.[13]

---

[13] Joshua Gee, *The Trade and Navigation of Great-Britain Considered* (London: S. Buckley, 1729), pp. 25–26.

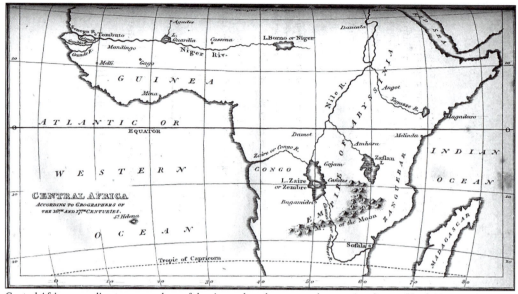

Central Africa according to geographers of the sixteenth and seventeenth centuries. *Source:* Hugh Murray, *Historical Account of Discoveries and Travels in Africa, by the Late John Leyden, M.D. . . .,* vol. 2 (Edinburgh: Archibald Constable and Company, 1817, after p. 370.

Trade between England and Africa.

Our trade with Africa is very profitable to the Nation in general; it has this Advantage that it carries no Money out, and not only supplies our Plantations with Servants, but brings in a great Deal of Bullion for those that are sold to the Spanish West Indies, beside Gold Dust, and other Commodities, as Red-wood, Teeth, Guinea Grain, &c. some of which are re-exported. The supplying our Plantations with Negroes is of that extraordinary Advantage to us, that the Planting Sugar and Tobacco, and carrying on Trade there could not be supported without them; which Plantations, as I have elsewhere observed, are the great Causes of the Increase of the Riches of the Kingdom. There has been great Struggles by the African Company to engross that Trade to themselves; by which Means they would not only prevent the large Profits that are brought into the Nation by the Trade private Adventurers drive thither, but would also be one great Means of ruining our Plantations; for, as I have already observed, our Plantations are supported by the Labour of Slaves, and our Profit either more or less, according to the Numbers there employed; and as the Trade is now drove on by private Adventures, they push it with all imaginable Vigour, and the Planters have not only very great Numbers of Slaves brought in, but they are also afforded them at moderate Prices. But if this Trade should fall into the Hands of the Company, the Management, I am afraid, would be as it has been in some other Companies, carried on to the enriching particular Persons, who too often trade away the Company's Estates; whereas private Traders put themselves into all Methods of Frugality, Industry and good Management; which indeed evidently appears by the Trade the Company drove and what private Adventurers have done. For the Company at best, by what I apprehend, never traded for above Five or Six Thousand Negroes yearly, whereas private Adventureres have traded for Thirty Thousand or upwards; And if ever our Trade should come to be put under a Company, I shall take it for granted, that our Improvements in the Plantations, which is carried on by the Labour of Negroes, would soon decline.

14. Venture Smith describes his capture into slavery.

Broteer, or Venture Smith as he was later named, was born the son of a West African prince. Captured in the 1730s by enemies of his father when only six years old, Broteer was transported to the coast and sold into slavery. He was transported to the United States where eventually he was able to purchase his freedom at the age of 36. Later he also purchased the freedom of his wife, two sons, and a daughter and became a man of some property even buying three slaves of his own. When he died in Connecticut in 1805, he left a hundred-acre farm and three houses to his heirs. He published his autobiography in 1798, and like that of his near contemporary Olaudah Equiano (see document 15), Broteer's text became an important weapon in the hands of those calling at the end of the eighteenth century for the abolition of the slave trade.[14]

I was born at Dukandara, in Guinea, about the year 1729. My father's name was Saungm Furro, Prince of the Tribe of Dukandara. My father had three wives. Polygamy was not uncommon in that country, especially among the rich, as every man was allowed to keep as many wives as he could maintain. By his first wife he had three children. The eldest of them was myself, named by my father, Broteer. The other two were named Cundazo and Soozaduka. My father had two children by his second wife, and one by his third. I descended from a very large, tall and stout race of beings, much larger than the generality of people in other parts of the globe, being commonly considerable above six feet in height, and every way well proportioned.

The first thing worthy of notice which I remember was, a contention between my father and mother, on account of my father marrying his third wife without the consent of his first and eldest, which was contrary to the custom generally observed among my countrymen. In consequence of this rupture, my mother left her husband and country, and travelled away with her three children to the eastward. I was then five years old. She took not the least sustenance along with her, to support either herself or children. I was able to travel along by her side; the other two of her offspring she carried one on her back, and the other being a sucking child, in her arms. When we became hungry, our mother used to set us down on the ground, and gather some of the fruits which grew spontaneously in that climate. These served us for food on the way. At night we all lay down together in the most secure place we could find, and reposed ourselves until morning. Though there were many noxious animals there; yet so kind was our Almighty protector, that none of them were ever permitted to hurt or molest us. Thus we went on our journey until the second day after our departure from Dukandara, when we came to the entrance of a great desert. During our travel in that we were often affrighted with the doleful howlings and yellings of wolves, lions, and other animals. After five days travel we came to the end of this desert, and immediately entered into a beautiful and extensive interval country. Here my mother was pleased to stop and seek a refuge for me. She left me at the house of a very rich farmer. I was then, as I should judge, not less than one hundred and forty miles from my native place, separated from all my relations and acquaintance. At this place my mother took her farewell of me, and set out for my own country. My new guardian, as I shall call the man with whom I was left, put me into the business of tending sheep, immediately after I was left with him. The flock

---

[14] Venture Smith, *A Narrative of the Life and Adventures of Venture, a Native of Africa, but Resident above Sixty Years in the United States of America* (New London, CT: C. Holt, 1798), pp. 5–13.

which I kept with the assistance of a boy, consisted of about forty. We drove them every morning between two and three miles to pasture, into the wide and delightful plains. When night drew on, we drove them home and secured them in the cote. In this round I continued during my stay here. One incident which befell me when I was driving my flock from pasture, was so dreadful to me in that age, and is to this time so fresh in my memory, that I cannot help noticing it in this place. Two large dogs sallied out of a certain house and set upon me. One of them took me by the arm, and the other by the thigh, and before their master could come and relieve me, they lacerated my flesh to such a degree, that the scars are very visible to the present day. My master was immediately sent for. He came and carried me home, as I was unable to go myself on account of my wounds. Nothing remarkable happened afterwards until my father sent for me to return home. . . . My father sent a man and horse after me. After settling with my guardian for keeping me, he took me away and went for home. It was then about one year since my mother brought me here. Nothing remarkable occurred to us on our journey until we arrived safe home.

I found then that the difference between my parents had been made up previous to their sending for me. On my return, I was received both by my father and mother with great joy and affection, and was once more restored to my paternal dwelling in peace and happiness. I was then about six years old.

Not more than six weeks had passed after my return, before a message was brought by an inhabitant of the place where I lived the preceding year to my father, that that place had been invaded by a numerous army, from a nation not far distant, furnished with musical instruments, and all kinds of arms then in use; that they were instigated by some white nation who equipped and sent them to subdue and possess the country; that his nation had made no preparation for war, having been for a long time in profound peace; that they could not defend themselves against such a formidable train of invaders, and must therefore necessarily evacuate their lands to the fierce enemy, and fly to the protection of some chief; and that if he would permit them they would come under his rule and protection when they had to retreat from their own possessions. He was a kind and merciful prince, and therefore consented to these proposals.

He had scarcely returned to his nation with the message, before the whole of his people were obliged to retreat from their country, and come to my father's dominions.

He gave them every privilege and all the protection his government could afford. But they had not been there longer than four days before news came to them that the invaders had laid waste their country, and were coming speedily to destroy them in my father's territories. This affrighted them, and therefore they immediately pushed off to the southward, into the unknown countries there, and were never more heard of.

Two days after their retreat, the report turned out to be but too true. A detachment from the enemy came to my father and informed him, that the whole army was encamped not far out of his dominions, and would invade the territory and deprive his people of their liberties and rights, if he did not comply with the following terms. These were to pay them a large sum of money, three hundred fat cattle, and a great number of goats, sheep, asses, etc.

My father told the messenger he would comply rather than that his subjects should be deprived of their rights and privileges, which he was not then in circumstances to defend from so sudden an invasion. Upon turning out those articles, the enemy pledged their faith and honor that they would not attack him. On these he relied and therefore thought it unnecessary to be on his guard against the enemy. But their pledges of faith and honor proved no better than those of other unprincipled hostile nations; for a few days after a certain relation of the king came and informed him, that the enemy who sent terms of accommodation to him and received tribute to their satisfaction, yet meditated an attack upon his subjects by surprise and that probably they would commence their attack in less than one day, and concluded with advising him, as he was not prepared for war, to order a speedy retreat of his family and subjects. He complied with this advice.

The same night which was fixed upon to retreat, my father and his family set off about the break of day. The king and his two younger wives went in one company, and my mother and her children in another. We left our dwellings in succession, and my father's company went on first. We directed our course for a large shrub plain, some distance off, where we intended to conceal ourselves from the approaching enemy, until we could refresh ourselves a little. But we presently found that our retreat was not secure. For having struck up a little fire for the purpose of cooking victuals, the enemy who happened to be encamped a little distance off, had sent out a scouting party who discovered us by the smoke of the fire, just as we were extinguishing it, and about to eat. As soon as we had finished eating, my father discovered the party, and immediately began to discharge arrows at them. This was what I first saw, and it alarmed both me and the women, who being unable to make any resistance, immediately betook ourselves to the tall thick reeds not far off, and left the old king to fight alone. For some time I beheld him from the reeds defending himself with great courage and firmness, till at last he was obliged to surrender himself into their hands.

They then came to us in the reeds, and the very first salute I had from them was a violent blow on the back part of the head with the fore part of a gun, and at the same time a grasp round the neck. I then had a rope put about my neck, as had all the women in the thicket with me, and were immediately led to my father, who was likewise pinioned and haltered for leading. In this condition we were all led to the camp. The women and myself being pretty submissive, had tolerable treatment from the enemy, while my father was closely interrogated respecting his money which they knew he must have. But as he gave them no account of it, he was instantly cut and pounded on his body with great inhumanity, that he might be induced by the torture he suffered to make the discovery. All this availed not in the least to make him give up his money, but he despised all the tortures which they inflicted, until the continued exercise and increase of torment, obliged him to sink and expire. He thus died without informing his enemies where his money lay. I saw him while he was thus tortured to death. The shocking scene is to this day fresh in my mind, and I have often been overcome while thinking on it. He was a man of remarkable stature. I should judge as much as six feet and six or seven inches high, two feet across his shoulders, and every way well proportioned. He was a man of remarkable strength and resolution, affable, kind and gentle, ruling with equity and moderation.

The army of the enemy was large, I should suppose consisting of about six thousand men. Their leader was called Baukurre. After destroying the old prince, they decamped and immediately marched towards the sea, lying to the west, taking with them myself and the women prisoners. In the march a scouting party was detached from the main army. To the leader of this party I was made waiter, having to carry his gun, etc. As we were a scouting we came across a herd of fat cattle, consisting of about thirty in number. These we set upon, and immediately wrested from their keepers, and afterwards converted them into food for the army. The enemy had remarkable success in destroying the country wherever they went. For as far as they had penetrated, they laid the habitations waste and captured the people. The distance they had now brought me was about four hundred miles. All the march I had very hard tasks imposed on me, which I must perform on pain of punishment. I was obliged to carry on my head a large flat stone used for grinding our corn, weighing as I should suppose, as much as twenty-five pounds; besides victuals, mat and cooking utensils. Though I was pretty large and stout at my age, yet these burdens were very grievous to me, being only six years and a half old.

We were then come to a place called Malagasco. When we entered the place we could not see the least appearance of either houses or inhabitants, but upon stricter search found, that instead of houses above ground they had dens in the sides of hillocks, contiguous to ponds and streams of water. In these we perceived they had all hid themselves, as I suppose they usually did on such occasions. In order to compel them to surrender, the enemy contrived to smoke them out with faggots. These they put to the entrance of the eaves and set them on fire. While they were engaged in this business, to their great surprise some of them were desperately wounded with arrows which fell from above on them. This mystery they soon found out. They perceived that the enemy discharged these arrows through holes on the top of the dens directly into the air. Their weight brought them back, point downwards on their enemies heads, whilst they were smoking the inhabitants out. The points of their arrows were poisoned, but their enemy had an antidote for it, which they instantly applied to the wounded part. The smoke at last obliged the people to give themselves up. They came out of their caves, first spatting the palms of their hands together, and immediately after extended their arms, crossed at their wrists, ready to be bound and pinioned. I should judge that the dens above mentioned were extended about eight feet horizontally into the earth, six feet in height and as many wide. They were arched over head and lined with earth, which was of the clay kind, and made the surface of their walls firm and smooth.

The invaders then pinioned the prisoners of all ages and sexes indiscriminately, took their flocks and all their effects, and moved on their way towards the sea. On the march the prisoners were treated with clemency, on account of their being submissive and humble. Having come to the next tribe, the enemy laid siege and immediately took men, women, children, flocks, and all their valuable effects. They then went on to the next district which was contiguous to the sea, called in Africa, Anamaboo. The enemies provisions were then almost spent, as well as their strength. The inhabitants knowing what conduct they had pursued, and what were their present intentions, improved the favorable opportunity, attacked them, and took enemy, prisoners, flocks and all their effects. I was then taken a second time. All of us were then put into the castle, and kept for market. On a certain time I and other prisoners were put on board a canoe, under our master, and rowed away to a vessel belonging to Rhode Island, commanded by Captain Collingwood, and the mate Thomas Mumford. While we were going to the vessel, our master told us all to appear to the best possible advantage for sale. I was bought on board by one Robertson Mumford, steward of said vessel, for four gallons of rum, and a piece of calico, and called VENTURE, on account of his having purchased me with his own private venture. Thus I came by my name. All the slaves that were bought for that vessel's cargo, were two hundred and sixty.

15. Olaudah Equiano becomes a slave.

Olaudah Equiano, also known by his slave name, Gustavus Vassa, was born in the mid-1740s. An Igbo-speaker from the eastern part of present-day Nigeria, Equiano, along with his sister, was captured by local slave raiders in the mid-1750s and eventually sold to slavers bound for the British Caribbean. Near the end of his life (he died in 1797), he became a well-known opponent of the slave trade and a strong supporter of the repatriation of freed slaves to the British colony of Sierra Leone. His autobiography, published in 1789, won considerable support for the abolitionist cause with its graphic depiction of the horrors of slavery. It was an enormous publishing success, going into over nine editions in England alone within five years of its first publication, circulating in multiple editions in the United States, and being translated into Dutch, German, and Russian in the 1790s. So powerful was the impact of Equiano's two-volume account of his life on public opinion that contemporary advocates of the slave trade sought to question (without apparent factual basis and without success) its veracity by claiming that the author had been born in the Caribbean and had never set foot in Africa until he returned later in life as an advocate of slave repatriation.[15]

My father, besides many slaves, had a numerous family, of which seven lived to grow up, including myself and a sister, who was the only daughter. As I was the youngest of the sons, I became, of course, the greatest favorite with my mother, and was always with her; and she used to take particular pains to form my mind. I was trained up from my earliest years in the art of war: my daily exercise was shooting and throwing javelins; and my mother adorned me with emblems, after the manner of our greatest warriors. In this way I grew up till I was turned the age of eleven, when an end was put to my happiness in the following manner. Generally when the grown people in the neighborhood were gone far in the fields to labor, the children assembled together in some of the neighboring premises to play; and commonly some of us used to get up a tree to look out for any assailant, or kidnapper, that might come upon us, for they sometimes took those opportunities of our parents' absence, to attack and carry off as many as they could seize. One day as I was watching at the top of a tree in our yard, I saw one of those people come into the yard of our next neighbor but one to kidnap, there being many stout young people in it. Immediately on this I gave the alarm of the rogue, and he was surrounded by the stoutest of them, who entangled him with cords, so that he could not escape till some of the grown people came and secured him. But, alas! ere long it was my fate to be thus attacked, and to be carried off, when none of the grown people were nigh. One day, when all our people were gone out to their works as usual, and only I and my dear sister were left to mind the house, two men and a woman got over our walls, and in a moment seized us both, and, without giving us time to cry out, or make resistance, they stopped our mouths, and ran off with us into the nearest wood. Here they tied our hands, and continued to carry us as far as they could, till night came on, when we reached a small house, where the robbers halted for refreshment, and spent the night. We were then unbound, but were unable to take any food; and, being quite overpowered by fatigue and grief, our only relief was some sleep, which allayed our misfortune for a short time. The next morning we left the house, and continued travelling all the day. For a long time we had kept the woods, but at last we came into a road which I believed I knew. I had now some hopes of being delivered; for we had advanced but a little way before I discovered some people at a distance, on which I began to cry out for their assistance; but my cries had no other effect than to make them tie me faster and stop my mouth, and then they put me into a large sack. They also stopped my sister's mouth, and tied her hands; and in this manner we proceeded till we were out of sight of these people. When we went to rest the following night, they offered us some victuals, but we refused it; and the only comfort we had was in being in one another's arms all that night, and bathing each other with our tears. But alas! we were soon deprived of even the small comfort of weeping together. The next day proved a day of greater sorrow than I had yet experienced; for my sister and I were then separated, while we lay clasped in each other's arms. It was in vain that we besought them not to part us; she was torn from me, and immediately carried away, while I was left in a state of distraction not to be described. I cried and grieved continually; and for several days did not eat any thing but what they forced into my mouth. At length, after

[15] Olaudah Equiano, *The Interesting Narrative of the Life of Olaudah Equiano, or Gustavus Vassa, the African, Written by Himself*, vol. 1 (London: self-published, 1789), pp. 30–52.

many days travelling, during which I had often changed masters, I got into the hands of a chieftain, in a very pleasant country. This man had two wives and some children, and they all used me extremely well, and did all they could to comfort me; particularly the first wife, who was something like my mother. Although I was a great many days' journey from my father's house, yet these people spoke exactly the same language with us. This first master of mine, as I may call him, was a smith, and my principal employment was working his bellows, which were the same kind as I had seen in my vicinity. They were in some respects not unlike the stoves here in gentlemen's kitchens, and were covered over with leather; and in the middle of that leather a stick was fixed, and a person stood up, and worked it in the same manner as is done to pump water out of a cask with a hand pump. I believe it was gold he worked, for it was of a lovely bright yellow color, and was worn by the women on their wrists and ankles. I was there I suppose about a month, and they at last used to trust me some little distance from the house. This liberty I used in embracing every opportunity to inquire the way to my own home; and I also sometimes, for the same purpose, went with the maidens, in the cool of the evenings, to bring pitchers of water from the springs for the use of the house. I had also remarked where the sun rose in the morning, and set in the evening, as I had travelled along; and I had observed that my father's house was towards the rising of the sun. I therefore determined to seize the first opportunity of making my escape, and to shape my course for that quarter; for I was quite oppressed and weighed down by grief after my mother and friends; and my love of liberty, ever great, was strengthened by the mortifying circumstance of not daring to eat with the free-born children, although I was mostly their companion. While I was projecting my escape one day, an unlucky event happened, which quite disconcerted my plan, and put an end to my hopes. I used to be sometimes employed in assisting an elderly slave to cook and take care of the poultry; and one morning, while I was feeding some chickens, I happened to toss a small pebble at one of them, which hit it on the middle, and directly killed it. The old slave, having soon after missed the chicken, inquired after it; and on my relating the accident (for I told her the truth, for my mother would never suffer me to tell a lie), she flew into a violent passion, and threatened that I should suffer for it; and, my master being out, she immediately went and told her mistress what I had done. This alarmed me very much, and I expected an instant flogging, which to me was uncommonly dreadful, for I had seldom been beaten at home. I therefore resolved to fly; and accordingly I ran into a thicket that was hard by, and hid myself in the bushes. Soon afterwards my mistress and the slave returned, and, not seeing me, they searched all the house, but not finding me, and I not making answer when they called to me, they thought I had run away, and the whole neighborhood was raised in the pursuit of me. In that part of the country, as in ours, the houses and villages were skirted with woods, or shrubberies, and the bushes were so thick that a man could readily conceal himself in them, so as to elude the strictest search. The neighbors continued the whole day looking for me, and several times many of them came within a few yards of the place where I lay hid. I expected every moment, when I heard a rustling among the trees, to be found out, and punished by my master; but they never discovered me, though they were often so near that I even heard their conjectures as they were looking about for me, and I now learned from them that any attempts to return home would be hopeless. Most of them supposed I had fled towards home; but the distance was so great, and the way so intricate, that they thought I could never reach it, and that I should be lost in the woods. When I heard this I was seized with a violent panic, and abandoned myself to despair. Night, too, began to approach, and aggravated all my fears. I had before entertained hopes of getting home, and had determined when it should be dark to make the attempt; but I was now convinced it was fruitless, and began to consider that, if possibly I could escape all other animals, I could not those of the human kind; and that, not knowing the way, I must perish in the woods. Thus was I like the hunted deer—

'Every leaf and every whisp'ring breath,
Convey'd a foe, and every foe a death,'

I heard frequent rustlings among the leaves, and being pretty sure they were snakes, I expected every instant to be stung by them. This increased my anguish and the horror of my situation became now quite insupportable. I at length quitted the thicket, very faint and hungry, for I had not eaten or drank any thing all the day, and crept to my master's kitchen, from whence I set out at first, which was an open shed, and laid myself down in the ashes with an anxious wish for death, to relieve me from all my pains. I was scarcely awake in the morning, when the old woman slave, who was the first up, came to light the fire, and saw me in the fire place. She was very much surprised to see me, and could scarcely believe her own eyes. She now promised to intercede for me, and went for her master, who soon after came, and, having slightly reprimanded me, ordered me to be taken care of, and not ill treated.

Soon after this, my master's only daughter, and child by his first wife, sickened and died, which affected him so much that for some time he was almost frantic, and really would have killed himself, had he not been watched and prevented. However, in short time afterwards he recovered, and I was again sold. I was now carried to the left of the sun's rising, through many dreary wastes and dismal woods, amidst the hideous roarings of wild beasts. The people I was sold to used to carry me very often, when I was tired, either on their shoulders or on their backs. I saw many convenient well built sheds along the road, at proper distances, to accommodate the merchants and travellers, who lay in those buildings along with their wives, who often accompany them; and they always go well armed.

From the time I left my own nation, I always found somebody that understood me till I came to the sea coast. The languages of different nations did not totally differ, nor where they so copious as those of the Europeans, particularly the English. They were therefore, easily learned; and, while I was journeying thus through Africa, I acquired two or three different tongues. In this manner I had been travelling for a considerable time, when, one evening, to my great surprise, whom should I see brought to the house where I was but my dear sister! As soon as she saw me, she gave a loud shriek, and ran into my arms. I was quite overpowered: neither of us could speak; but, for a considerable time, clung to each other in mutual embraces, unable to do any thing but weep. Our meeting affected all who saw us; and, indeed, I must acknowledge, in honor of those sable destroyers of human rights, that I never met with any ill treatment, or saw any offered to their slaves, except tying them, when necessary, to keep them from running away. When these people knew we were brother and sister, they indulged us to be together; and the man, to whom I supposed we belonged, lay with us, he in the middle, while she and I held one another by the hands across his breast all night; and thus for a while we forgot our misfortunes, in the joy of being together; but even this small comfort was soon to have an end; for scarcely had the fatal morning appeared when she was again torn from me forever! I was now more miserable, if possible, than before. The small relief which her presence gave me from pain, was gone, and the wretchedness of my situation was redoubled by my anxiety after her fate, and my apprehensions lest her sufferings should be greater than mine, when I could not be with her to alleviate them. Yes, thou dear partner of all my childish sports! thou sharer of my joys and sorrows! happy should I have ever esteemed myself to encounter every misery for you and to procure your freedom by the sacrifice of my own. Though you were early forced from my arms, your image has been always rivetted in my heart, from which neither time nor fortune have been able to remove it; so that, while the thoughts of your sufferings have damped my prosperity, they have mingled with adversity and increased its bitterness. To that Heaven which protects the weak from the strong, I commit the care of your innocence and virtues, if they have not already received their full reward, and if your youth and delicacy have not long since fallen victims to the violence of the African trader, the pestilential stench of a Guinea ship, the seasoning in the European colonies, or the lash and lust of a brutal and unrelenting overseer.

I did not long remain after my sister. I was again sold, and carried through a number of places, till after travelling a considerable time, I came to a town called Tinmah, in the most beautiful country I had yet seen in Africa. It was extremely rich, and there were many rivulets which flowed through it, and supplied a large pond in the centre of the town, where the people washed. Here I first saw and tasted cocoa nuts, which I thought superior to any nuts I had ever tasted before; and the trees which were loaded, were also interspersed among the houses, which had commodious shades adjoining, and were in the same manner as ours, the insides being neatly plastered and whitewashed. Here I also saw and tasted for the first time, sugar-cane. Their money consisted of little white shells, the size of the finger nail. I was sold here for one hundred and seventy-two of them, by a merchant who lived and brought me there. I had been about two or three days at his house, when a wealthy widow, a neighbor of his, came there one evening, and brought with her an only son, a young gentleman about my own age and size. Here they saw me; and, having taken a fancy to me, I was bought of the merchant, and went home with them. Her house and premises were situated close to one of those rivulets I have mentioned, and were the finest I ever saw in Africa: they were very extensive, and she had a number of slaves to attend her. The next day I was washed and perfumed, and when meal time came, I was led into the presence of my mistress, and ate and drank before her with her son. This filled me with astonishment; I could scarce help expressing my surprise that the young gentleman should suffer me, who was bound, to eat with him who was free; and not only so,

but that he would not at any time either eat or drink till I had taken first, because I was the eldest, which was agreeable to our custom. Indeed, every thing here, and all their treatment of me, made me forget that I was a slave. The language of these people resembled ours so nearly, that we understood each other perfectly. They had also the very same customs as we. There were likewise slaves daily to attend us, while my young master and I, with other boys, sported with our darts and bows and arrows, as I had been used to do at home. In this resemblance to my former happy state, I passed about two months; and I now began to think I was to be adopted into the family, and was beginning to be reconciled to my situation, and to forget by degrees my misfortunes, when all at once the delusion vanished; for, without the least previous knowledge, one morning early, while my dear master and companion was still asleep, I was awakened out of my reverie to fresh sorrow, and hurried away even amongst the uncircumcised.

Thus, at the very moment I dreamed of the greatest happiness, I found myself most miserable; and it seemed as if fortune wished to give me this taste of joy only to tender the reverse more poignant. The change I now experienced, was as painful as it was sudden and unexpected. It was a change indeed, from a state of bliss to a scene which is inexpressible by me, it discovered to me an element I had never before beheld, and till then had no idea of, and wherein such instances of hardship and cruelty continually occurred, as I can never reflect on but with horror.

All the nations and people I had hitherto passed through, resembled our own in their manners, customs, and language: but I came at length to a country, the inhabitants of which differed from us in all those particulars. I was very much struck with this difference, especially when I came among a people who did not circumcise, and ate without washing their hands. They cooked also in iron pots, and had European cutlasses and cross bows, which were unknown to us, and fought with their fists among themselves. Their women were not so modest as ours, for they ate, and drank, and slept with their men. But above all, I was amazed to see no sacrifices or offerings among them. In some of those places the people ornamented themselves with scars, and likewise filed their teeth very sharp. They wanted sometimes to ornament me in the same manner, but I would not suffer them; hoping that I might some time be among a people who did not thus disfigure themselves, as I thought they did. At last I came to the banks of a large river which was covered with canoes, in which the people appeared to live with their household utensils, and provisions of all kinds. I was beyond measure astonished at this, as I had never before seen any water larger than a pond or a rivulet: and my surprise was mingled with no small fear when I was put into one of these canoes, and we began to paddle and move along the river. We continued going on thus till night, and when we came to land, and made fires on the banks, each family by themselves; some dragged their canoes on shore, others stayed and cooked in theirs, and laid in them all night. Those on the land had mats, of which they made tents, some in the shape of little houses; in these we slept; and after the morning meal, we embarked again and proceeded as before. I was often very much astonished to see some of the women, as well as the men, jump into the water, dive to the bottom, come up again, and swim about. Thus I continued to travel, sometimes by land, sometimes by water, through different countries and various nations, till, at the end of six or seven months after I had been kidnapped, I arrived at the sea coast. . . .

The first object which saluted my eyes when I arrived on the coast, was the sea, and a slave ship, which was then riding at anchor, and waiting for its cargo. These filled me with astonishment, which was soon converted into terror, when I was carried on board. I was immediately handled, and tossed up to see if I were sound, by some of the crew; and I was now persuaded that I had gotten into a world of bad spirits, and that they were going to kill me. Their complexions, too, differing so much from ours, their long hair, and the language they spoke (which was very different

from any I had ever heard), united to confirm me in this belief. Indeed, such were the horrors of my views and fears at the moment, that, if ten thousand worlds had been my own, I would have freely parted with them all to have exchanged my condition with that of the meanest slave in my own country. When I looked round the ship too, and saw a large furnace of copper boiling, and a multitude of black people of every description chained together, every one of their countenances expressing dejection and sorrow, I no longer doubted of my fate; and, quite overpowered with horror and anguish, I fell motionless on the deck and fainted. When I recovered a little, I found some black people about me, who I believed were some of those who had brought me on board, and had been receiving their pay they talked to me in order to cheer me, but all in vain. I asked them if we were not to be eaten by those white men with horrible looks, red faces, and long hair. They told me I was not: and one of the crew brought me a small portion of spirituous liquor in a wine glass, but, being afraid of him, I would not take it out of his hand. One of the blacks, therefore, took it from him and gave it to me, and I took a little down my palate, which, instead of reviving me, as they thought it would, threw me into the greatest consternation at the strange feeling it produced, having never tasted any such liquor before. Soon after this, the blacks who brought me on board went off, and left me abandoned to despair.

I now saw myself deprived of all chance of returning to my native country, or even the least glimpse of hope of gaining the shore, which I now considered as friendly; and I even wished for my former slavery in preference to my present situation, which was filled with horrors of every kind, still heightened by my ignorance of what I was to undergo. I was not long suffered to indulge my grief; I was soon put down under the decks, and there I received such a salutation in my nostrils as I had never experienced in my life: so that, with the loathsomeness of the stench, and crying together, I became so sick and low that I was not able to eat, nor had I the least desire to taste any thing. I now wished for the last friend, death, to relieve me; but soon, to my grief, two of the white men offered me eatables; and, on my refusing to eat, one of them held me fast by the hands, and laid me across, I think the windlass, and tied my feet, while the other flogged me severely. I had never experienced any thing of this kind before, and although not being used to the water, I naturally feared that element the first time I saw it, yet, nevertheless, could I have got over the nettings, I would have jumped over the side, but I could not; and besides, the crew used to watch us very closely who were not chained down to the decks, lest we should leap into the water; and I have seen some of these poor African prisoners most severely cut, for attempting to do so, and hourly whipped for not eating. This indeed was often the case with myself. In a little time after, amongst the poor chained men, I found some of my own nation, which in a small degree gave ease to my mind. I inquired of these what was to be done with us? they gave me to understand, we were to be carried to these white people's country to work for them. I then was a little revived, and thought, if it were no worse than working, my situation was not so desperate; but still I feared I should be put to death, the white people looked and acted, as I thought, in so savage a manner; for I had never seen among any people such instances of brutal cruelty; and this not only shown towards us blacks, but also to some of the whites themselves. One white man in particular I saw, when we were permitted to be on deck, flogged so unmercifully with a large rope near the foremast, that he died in consequence of it; and they tossed him over the side as they would have done a brute. This made me fear these people the more; and I expected nothing less than to be treated in the same manner. I could not help expressing my fears and apprehensions to some of my countrymen; I asked them if these people had no country, but lived in this hollow place? (the ship) they told me they did not, but came from a distant one. "Then," said I, "how comes it in all our country we never heard of them?" They told me because they lived so very far off. I then asked where were their women? had they

any like themselves? I was told they had. "And why," said I, "do we not see them?" They answered, because they were left behind. I asked how the vessel could go? they told me they could not tell but that there was cloth put upon the masts by the help of the ropes I saw, and then the vessel went on and the white men had some spell or magic they put in the water when they liked, in order to stop the vessel. I was exceedingly amazed at this account, and really thought they were spirits. I therefore wished much to be from amongst them, for I expected they would sacrifice me; but my wishes were vain—for we were so quartered that it was impossible for any of us to make our escape.

While we stayed on the coast I was mostly on deck; and one day, to my great astonishment, I saw one of these vessels coming in with the sails up. As soon as the whites saw it, they gave a great shout, at which we were amazed; and the more so, as the vessel appeared larger by approaching nearer. At last, she came to an anchor in my sight, and when the anchor was let go, I and my countrymen who saw it, were lost in astonishment to observe the vessel stop and were now convinced it was done by magic. Soon after this the other ship got her boats out, and they came on board of us, and the people of both ships seemed very glad to see each other. Several of the strangers also shook hands with us black people, and made motions with their hands, signifying I suppose, we were to go to their country, but we did not understand them.

At last, when the ship we were in, had got in all her cargo, they made ready with many fearful noises, and we were all put under deck, so that we could not see how they managed the vessel. But this disappointment was the least of my sorrow. The stench of the hold while we were on the coast was so intolerably loathsome, that it was dangerous to remain there for any time, and some of us had been permitted to stay on the deck for the fresh air; but now that the whole ship's cargo were confined together, it became absolutely pestilential. The closeness of the place, and the heat of the climate, added to the number in the ship, which was so crowded that each had scarcely room to turn himself, almost suffocated us. This produced copious perspirations, so that the air soon became unfit for respiration, from a variety of loathsome smells, and brought on a sickness among the slaves, of which many died—thus falling victims to the improvident avarice, as I may call it, of their purchasers. This wretched situation was again aggravated by the galling of the chains, now became insupportable; and the filth of the necessary tubs, into which the children often fell, and were almost suffocated. The shrieks of the women, and the groans of the dying, rendered the whole a scene of horror almost inconceivable. Happily perhaps, for myself, I was soon reduced so low here that it was thought necessary to keep me almost always on deck; and from my extreme youth I was not put in fetters. In this situation I expected every hour to share the fate of my companions, some of whom were almost daily brought upon deck at the point of death, which I began to hope would soon put an end to my miseries. Often did I think many of the inhabitants of the deep much more happy than myself. I envied them the freedom they enjoyed, and as often wished I could change my condition for theirs. Every circumstance I met with, served only to render my state more painful, and heightened my apprehensions, and my opinion of the cruelty of the whites.

One day they had taken a number of fishes; and when they had killed and satisfied themselves with as many as they thought fit, to our astonishment who were on deck, rather than give any of them to us to eat, as we expected, they tossed the remaining fish into the sea again, although we begged and prayed for some as well as we could, but in vain; and some of my countrymen, being pressed by hunger, took an opportunity, when they thought no one saw them, of trying to get a little privately; but they were discovered, and the attempt procured them some very severe floggings. One day, when we had a smooth sea and moderate wind, two of my wearied countrymen who were chained together (I was near them at the time), preferring death to such a life of misery, somehow made through the nettings and jumped into

the sea: immediately, another quite dejected fellow, who, on account of his illness, was suffered to be out of irons, also followed their example; and I believe many more would very soon have done the same, if they had not been prevented by the ship's crew, who were instantly alarmed. Those of us that were the most active, were in a moment put down under the deck, and there was such a noise and confusion amongst the people of the ship as I never heard before, to stop her, and get the boat out to go after the slaves. However, two of the wretches were drowned, but they got the other, and afterwards flogged him unmercifully, for thus attempting to prefer death to slavery. In this manner we continued to undergo more hardships than I can now relate, hardships which are inseparable from this accursed trade. Many a time we were near suffocation from the want of fresh air, which we were often without for whole days together. This, and the stench of the necessary tubs, carried off many.

During our passage, I first saw flying fishes, which surprised me very much; they used frequently to fly across the ship, and many of them fell on the deck. I also now first saw the use of the quadrant; I had often with astonishment seen the mariners make observations with it, and I could not think what it meant. They at last took notice of my surprise; and one of them, willing to increase it, as well as to gratify my curiosity, made me one day look through it. The clouds appeared to me to be land, which disappeared as they passed along. This heightened my wonder; and I was now more persuaded than ever, that I was in another world, and that every thing about me was magic. At last, we came in sight of the island of Barbadoes, at which the whites on board gave a great shout, and made many signs of joy to us. We did not know what to think of this; but as the vessel drew nearer, we plainly saw the harbor, and other ships of different kinds and sizes, and we soon anchored amongst them, off Bridgetown. Many merchants and planters now came on board, though it was in the evening. They put us in separate parcels, and examined us attentively. They also made us jump, and pointed to the land, signifying we were to go there. We thought by this, we should be eaten by these ugly men, as they appeared to us; and, when soon after we were all put down under the deck again, there was much dread and trembling among us, and nothing but bitter cries to be heard all the night from these apprehensions, insomuch, that at last the white people got some old slaves from the land to pacify us. They told us we were not to be eaten, but to work, and were soon to go on land, where we should see many of our country people. This report eased us much. And sure enough, soon after we were landed, there came to us Africans of all languages.

We were conducted immediately to the merchant's yard, where we were all pent up together, like so many sheep in a fold, without regard to sex or age. As every object was new to me, every thing I saw filled me with surprise. What struck me first, was, that the houses were built with bricks and stories, and in every other respect different from those I had seen in Africa; but I was still more astonished on seeing people on horseback. I did not know what this could mean; and, indeed, I thought these people were full of nothing but magical arts. While I was in this astonishment, one of my fellow-prisoners spoke to a countryman of his, about the horses, who said they were the same kind they had in their country. I understood them, though they were from a distant part of Africa; and I thought it odd I had not seen any horses there; but afterwards, when I came to converse with different Africans, I found they had many horses amongst them, and much larger than those I then saw.

We were not many days in the merchant's custody, before we were sold after their usual manner, which is this. On a signal given (as the beat of a drum), the buyers rush at once into the yard where the slaves are confined, and make choice of that parcel they like best. The noise and clamor with which this is attended, and the eagerness visible in the countenances of the buyers, serve not a little to increase the apprehension of terrified Africans, who may well be supposed to consider them as the ministers of that destruction to which they think themselves devoted. In this manner, without scruple, are relations and friends separated, most of them never to see each other again. I remember, in the vessel in which I was brought over, in the men's apartment, there were several brothers, who, in the sale, were sold in different lots; and it was very moving on this occasion, to see and hear their cries at parting. O, ye nominal Christians! might not an African ask you— Learned you this from your God, who says unto you, Do unto all men as you would men should do unto you? Is it not enough that we are torn from our country and friends, to toil for your luxury and lust of gain? Must every tender feeling be likewise sacrificed to your avarice? Are the dearest friends and relations, now rendered more dear by their separation from their kindred, still to be parted from each other, and thus prevented from cheering the gloom of slavery, with the small comfort of being together, and mingling their sufferings and sorrows? Why are parents to lose their children, brothers their sisters, or husbands their wives? Surely, this is a new refinement in cruelty, which, while it has no advantage to atone for it, thus aggravates distress, and adds fresh horrors even to the wretchedness of slavery.

16. Anders Sparrman describes the treatment of slaves in South Africa.

Anders Sparrman (1748–1820) was a Swedish physician and naturalist who had trained as a student of Carl Linneaus. He first traveled overseas as a ship's surgeon on a voyage to China in 1765. In 1772, he visited the Cape at the direction of the Swedish East India Company with instructions to investigate the natural life of the country. Later that same year, he joined Captain James

Cook's expedition to the South Pacific and Antarctica, returning to the Cape in 1775 after 28 months' voyaging. Before returning to Sweden in 1776, Sparrman made a lengthy expedition into the interior of the Cape. His three-volume Swedish (two-volume English) account of these travels focused on the flora and fauna of the Cape, but it also provided detailed commentary on all the people that he encountered. Sparrman, who later gave testimony in England about the cruelties of the slave trade, was highly critical of the Dutch. In this excerpt, he uses a story told to him in April 1776 about the sufferings of a Dutch woman whose husband had been killed by a slave as an opportunity to discuss the harsh ways in which slaves were treated at the Cape.[16]

In the evening we came to *Nana-rivier* [two days ride east of Cape Town]. At this time there lived here a widow, whose husband had several years before met with the dreadful catastrophe of being beheaded by his own slaves. His son, then about 13 or 14 years of age, was obliged to be eye-witness to his father's fate, and was even threatened with being made to partake of it, but luckily found an opportunity of giving them the slip; and after eluding their most vigilant search, hid himself up close from the forenoon till it was dark at night; when at last he ventured forth, with a view to seek a safer asylum at a neighbouring farm, and to accuse his father's murderers. These villains had resolved likewise to murder the mother, who was expected that day home from the Cape; but fortunately for her, though very much to her dissatisfaction, she was delayed by some accident on the road till the next day. By means of her son, who had made his escape, she received advice of what had happened. As the whole premises on the farm consisted merely of two houses, situated on a plain quite open on all sides, excepting that it was covered with a few straggling bushes, which grew along the little river or brook that ran close by the spot, the lad's contrivance to hide himself, though in fact extremely painful as well as singular, was the only one that could at this time possibly save him. It consisted in this, viz. that he sat, or rather sank himself up to his nose in the river; taking care at the same time to hide his face behind the boughs that hung over the water. The murderers not being able to find him any where, he having as it were entirely vanished out of their sight, immediately began to conclude, that, in order to avoid the stroke of the bloody axe, he had rather chose to put an end to his life himself, by jumping into the river: notwithstanding this, however, they attempted to make themselves certain whether he was drowned or not. The means they took in order to effect this, was to sound the brook all over with the branches of a tree; but they luckily forgot just the particular place where the boy was sitting, probably as the river was in that part shallower, and had a brisker current.

I should doubtless have brought the tears into the eyes of our hosts, and at the same time made them a bad return for their civilities, had I, by questioning them closely concerning the particulars of this story, endeavoured so unseasonably to satisfy my curiosity. For this reason, I have contented myself with taking it down, just as I have related it above, from the accounts given me by Mr. Immelman and others; and consequently was not able to learn with any certainty, whether the deceased had by any unusual act of severity provoked his slaves to commit this crime, by way of revenging themselves; or else whether these latter had acted thus, from a persuasion that the same crimes and predatory practices by which violence had been offered to their persons, and they had been deprived of their liberties, might likewise lawfully be had recourse to, for the recovery of

---

[16] Anders Sparrman, *A Voyage to the Cape of Good Hope, Towards the Antarctic Polar Circle and Round the World: But Chiefly into the Country of the Hottentots and Caffres, from the Year 1772 to 1776*, vol. 2 (London: G. G. J. and J. Robinson, 1785), pp. 337–44.

this precious right bestowed on them by nature, and might consequently be very pardonable when exercised on their tyrants.

Yet, whatever might be the real reason of the committing this dreadful crime, I am convinced, that it has its origin in the very essence and nature of the commerce in slaves, in whatever manner and in whatever country it may be practised; a motive which I found had as much influence among the Christians in many places, as among the Turks on the coast of Barbary, to induce the unhappy slaves, and still more their tyrannical masters, to behave very strangely; nay, sometimes to be guilty of the most horrid cruelties. I have known some colonists, not only in the heat of their passion, but even deliberately and in cool blood, undertake themselves the low office (fit only for the executioner) of not only flaying, for a trifling neglect, both the backs and limbs of their slaves by a peculiar slow lingering method, but likewise, exceeding the very tigers in point of cruelty, throw pepper and salt over the wounds. But what appeared to me more strange and horrible, was to hear a colonist, not only describe with great seeming satisfaction the whole process of this diabolical invention, but even pride himself on the practice of it; and rack his brains, in order to find sophisms in defence of it, as well as of the slave trade; in which occupation the important post he enjoyed in the colony, and his own interest, had engaged him. He was, however, an European by birth; of a free and civilized nation; and, indeed, gave evident proofs of possessing a kind and tender heart; so that, perhaps, it would be difficult to shew any where a greater contradiction in the disposition of man, though in a world composed almost entirely of contradictions.

Many a time, especially in the mornings and evenings, have I seen in various places unhappy slaves, who with the most dismal cries and lamentations, were suffering the immoderately severe punishments inflicted on them by their masters; during which, they are used, as I was informed, to beg not so much for mercy, as for a draught of water; but as long as their blood was still inflamed with the pain and torture, it was said that great care

must be taken to avoid allowing them the refreshment of any kind of drink; as experience had shewn, that in that case, they would die in the space of a few hours, and sometimes the very instant after they had drank it. The same thing is said to happen to those who are impaled alive, after having been broken upon the wheel, or even without having previously suffered this punishment. The spike in this case is thrust up along the backbone and the vertebrae of the neck, between the skin and the cuticle, in such a manner, that the delinquent is brought into a sitting posture. In this horrid situation, however, they are said to be capable of supporting life for several days, as long as there comes no rain; as in that case, the humidity will occasion their sores to mortify, and consequently put an end to their sufferings in a few hours.

I am glad that, during my residence in the town, no opportunity presented itself to me of seeing any one undergo this punishment; which, though it is only destined for incendiaries, or for such as are guilty of sedition or murder, aggravated with peculiar circumstances of cruelty and barbarity, appears not less shocking and revolting to human nature, than the very crimes themselves, and actually irritates more than it is generally thought to do, the other slaves in the town; whom I have seen compelled to be present even at such public punishments as do not affect the life of the culprit, in order that they might take warning from it. But the slave who is punished for sedition, is always, in the eyes of his fellow-slaves a martyr, that suffers for the common cause, and for having maintained the dearest rights bestowed upon them by nature, which is their liberty. Spikes, wheels, red-hot pincers, and all the rest of the horrid apparatus employed by their executioners, will never have with the sufferers the effect of convincing them of the contrary doctrine; on the contrary, they become still more obstinate in supposing themselves tyrannized over, and in thinking that such of their fellow-slaves as have had the courage to take away the lives of their own tyrants, and prefer death and tortures to the basely groveling and crawling any longer upon the earth in an opprobrious state of bondage, are examples worthy of imitation, and that at least they deserve to be venerated, pitied, and even revenged. . . .

I have before observed, that the Bugunese slaves [brought to the Cape from Dutch possessions in the Celebes islands of Southeast Asia] are particularly strict and scrupulous with respect to the administration of justice. Those slaves are a sort of Mohamedans, and nearly of the same complexion as the people of Java, though they are taken upon other islands in the East-Indies. They are not moreover of a humour to put up with harsh expressions or abusive language, still less when they are not deserving of it, and not at all from a woman; looking upon it as the greatest shame, to suffer themselves to be disciplined by the weaker sex. Many a master and mistress of a family, who have happened to forget themselves with respect to this point, have, when a proper opportunity has offered, been made to pay for this mistake of theirs with their lives. These same slaves, on the other hand, when they know that they are in the wrong, are said to thank their master for each stroke he bestows upon them; at the same time commending his rigour and justice, nay even kissing his feet; a circumstance of which I myself have been an eye-witness. In fine, they are reported to be capable of bearing the most cruel torments with wonderful fortitude, as though they were entirely devoid of feeling. There have been instances of their not having uttered the least cry or complaint when impaled alive, or broken upon the wheel. But should a Bugunese slave at any time happen to betray the least want of resolution in this point, his countrymen are said to feel themselves hurt by it, considering it as a reproach to the whole nation. The female slaves belonging to these people, are reported to be extremely constant in love, as likewise to exact the strictest fidelity from their lovers. In short, the bold and intrepid character of this nation, is the cause that people at the Cape are not fond of buying them; and that the importation of them is prohibited, though in fact it is sometimes practised. The slaves from other parts, such

as from Mosambique, Madagascar, Malabar, etc. are in general not so dangerous to their unreasonable and tyrannical masters. On account of this great tameness shewn by them, they are more generally made to bow beneath the yoke; and the mistress of a family may venture to give as free a scope to all her whims and fancies as her husband himself, with respect to these slaves. There is a law, indeed, existing in the colonies, which prohibits masters from killing their slaves, or from flogging or otherwise chastising them with too great severity; but how is a slave to go to law with his master, who is, as it were, his sovereign, and who, by the same laws, has a right (or at least may by dint of bribes purchase that right) to have him flogged at the public whipping-post, not absolutely to death, indeed, yet not far from it; and this merely on the strength of the master's own testimony, and without any farther inquisition into the merits of the case? The master has, besides, so far his slave's life in his hands, that by rating and abusing him day after day, as likewise by proper family discipline, as it is called, such as heavy iron chains, hard work, and little meat, he may, without controul, by little and little, though soon enough for his purpose, worry the poor fellow out of his life. In consequence of this, the unhappy slaves, who are frequently embued with finer feelings and nobler sentiments of humanity, though for the most part actuated by stronger passions than their white masters, often give themselves up totally to despondency, and commit various acts of desperation and violence. Divers circumstances and considerations may, perhaps, concur to induce a wretch in this situation to exempt his tyrant from the dagger, which he plunges in his own bosom; content with being thus able to put an end to his misery, and at the same time to disappoint his greedy master of the profits arising from the sweat of his brow. A female slave, who had been just bought at a high price, and rather prematurely treated with severity by her mistress, who lived in the Roode-zand district, hanged herself the same night out of revenge and despair, just at the entrance of her new mistress's bedchamber. A young man and woman, who were slaves at the Cape, and were passionately fond of each other, solicited their master, in conformity to the established custom, for his consent to their being united in wedlock, though all in vain, as from some whim or caprice he was induced absolutely to forbid it. The consequence was, that the lover was seized with a singular fit of despair, and having first stabbed the heart of the object of his dearest wishes, immediately afterwards put an end to his own life. But how many hundred instances, not less dreadful than these, might be produced for this purpose! These, however, may suffice to create all that abhorrence for the slave trade, which so unnatural a species of commerce deserves; we will, therefore, at present dismiss this disagreeable subject.

17. Alexander Falconbridge describes his experiences as a physician on slave ships.

Criticism of the treatment of slaves and of the Atlantic slave trade grew throughout the latter half of the eighteenth century, reaching a peak in the late 1780s. In response to the criticism, the English parliament held a series of official inquiries into slavery and the export of slaves from Africa. One of the most riveting accounts of the slave trade was written by Alexander Falconbridge, a physician who had served as ship's surgeon on four slaving voyages. On the basis of his shipboard experiences he became a strong supporter of abolition, testifying against the trade before official British commissions, working closely with leading abolitionists such as Thomas Clarkson, and volunteering to travel to Sierra Leone, established in 1787 as a colony for freed slaves, to rebuild settlements burnt down by slavers.[17]

The Manner in Which the Slaves are Procured.

After permission has been obtained for *breaking trade*, as it is termed, the captains go ashore, from time to time, to examine the negroes that are exposed to sale, and to make their purchases. The unhappy wretches thus disposed of, are bought by the black traders at fairs, which are held for that purpose, at a distance of upwards of two hundred miles from the sea coast; and these fairs are said to be supplied from an interior part of the country. Many negroes, upon being questioned relative to the places of their nativity have asserted that they have travelled during the revolution of several moons (their usual method of calculating time) before they have reached the places where they are purchased by the black traders. At these fairs, which are held at uncertain periods, but generally every six weeks, several thousands are frequently exposed to sale, who had been collected from all parts of the country for a very considerable distance round. While I was upon the coast, during one of the voyages I made, the black traders brought down, in different canoes, from twelve to fifteen hundred negroes, which had been purchased at one fair. They consisted chiefly of men and boys, the women seldom exceeding a third of the whole number. From forty to two hundred negroes are generally purchased at a time by the black traders, according to the opulence of the buyer; and consist of those of all ages, from a month, to sixty years and upwards. Scarce any age or situation is deemed an exception, the price being proportionable. Women sometimes form a part of them, who happen to be so far advanced in their pregnancy, as to be delivered during their jour-

[17] Alexander Falconbridge, *An Account of the Slave Trade on the Coast of Africa* (London: J. Phillips, 1788), pp. 12–36.

ney from the fairs to the coast; and I have frequently seen instances of deliveries on board ship. The slaves purchased at these fairs are only for the supply of the markets at Bonny, and Old and New Calabar.

There is great reason to believe, that most of the negroes shipped off the coast of Africa, are *kidnapped*. But the extreme care taken by the black traders to prevent the Europeans from gaining any intelligence of their modes of proceeding; the great distance inland from whence the negroes are brought; and our ignorance of their language (with which, very frequently, the black traders themselves are equally unacquainted), prevent our obtaining such information on this head as we could wish. I have, however, by means of occasional inquiries, made through interpreters, procured some intelligence relative to the point, and such, as I think, puts the matter beyond a doubt.

From these I shall select the following striking instances. While I was in employ on board one of the slave ships, a negroe informed me, that being one evening invited to drink with some of the black traders, upon his going away, they attempted to seize him. As he was very active, he evaded their design, and got out of their hands. He was however prevented from effecting his escape by a large dog, which laid hold of him, and compelled him to submit. These creatures are kept by many of the traders for that purpose; and being trained to the inhuman sport, they appear to be much pleased with it.

I was likewise told by a negroe woman, that as she was on her return home, one evening, from some neighbours, to whom she had been making a visit by invitation, she was kidnapped; and, notwithstanding she was big with child, sold for a slave. This transaction happened a considerable way up the country, and she had passed through the hands of several purchasers before she reached the ship. A man and his son, according to their own information, were seized by professed kidnappers, while they were planting yams, and sold for slaves. This likewise happened in the interior parts of the country, and after

passing through several hands, they were purchased for the ship to which I belonged.

It frequently happens, that those who kidnap others, are themselves, in their turns, seized and sold. A negroe in the West-Indies informed me, that after having been employed in kidnapping others, he had experienced this reverse. And he assured me, that it was a common incident among his countrymen.

Continual enmity is thus fostered among the negroes of Africa, and all social intercourse between them destroyed; and which most assuredly would not be the case, had they not these opportunities for finding a ready sale for each other.

During my stay on the coast of Africa, I was an eye-witness of the following transaction. A black trader invited a negroe, who resided a little way up the country, to come and see him. After the entertainment was over, the trader proposed to his guest, to treat him with a sight of one of the ships lying in the river. The unsuspicious countryman readily consented, and accompanied the trader in the canoe to the side of the ship, which he viewed with pleasure and astonishment. While he was thus employed, some black traders on board, who appeared to be in the secret, leaped into the canoe, seized the unfortunate man, and dragging him into the ship, immediately sold him.

Previous to my being in this employ, I entertained a belief, as many others have done, that the kings and principal men *breed* negroes for sale, as we do cattle. During the different times I was in the country, I took no little pains to satisfy myself in this particular; but notwithstanding I made many inquiries, I was not able to obtain the least intelligence of this being the case, which it is more than probable I should have done, had such a practice prevailed. All the information I could procure, confirms me in the belief, that to *kidnapping*, and to crimes (and many of these fabricated as a pretext) the slave trade owes its chief support.

The following instance tends to prove, that the last mentioned artifice is often made use of. Several black traders, one of whom was a person of consequence, and exercised an authority somewhat similar to that of our magistrates, being in want of some particular kind of merchandize, and not having a slave to barter for it, they accused a fisherman, at the river Ambris, with extortion in the sale of his fish; and as they were interested in the decision, they immediately adjudged the poor fellow guilty, and condemned him to be sold. He was accordingly purchased by the ship to which I belonged, and brought on board.

As an additional proof that kidnapping is not only the general, but almost the sole mode, by which slaves are procured, the black traders, in purchasing them, choose those which are the roughest and most hardy; alleging, that the smooth negroes have been *gentlemen*. By this observation we may conclude they mean that nothing but fraud or force could have reduced these smooth-skinned gentlemen to a state of slavery.

It may not be here unworthy of remark, in order to prove that the wars among the Africans do not furnish the numbers they are supposed to do, that I never saw any negroes with recent wounds; which must have been the consequence, at least with some of them, had they been taken in battle. And it being the particular province of the surgeon to examine the slaves when they are purchased, such a circumstance could not have escaped my observation. As a further corroboration, it may be remarked, that on the Gold and Windward Coasts, where fairs are not held, the number of slaves procured at a time are usually very small.

The preparations made at Bonny by the black traders, upon setting out for the fairs which are held up the country, are very considerable. From twenty to thirty canoes, capable of containing thirty or forty negroes each, are assembled for this purpose; and such goods put on them as they expect will be wanted for the purchase of the number of slaves they intend to buy. When their loading is completed, they commence their voyage, with colours flying and musick playing; and in about ten or eleven days, they generally return to Bonny with full cargoes. As soon as the canoes arrive at the trader's landing-place, the purchased negroes are cleaned, and oiled with palm oil; and on the following day they are exposed for sale to the captains.

The black traders do not always purchase their slaves at the same rate. The speed with which the information of the arrival of the ships upon the coast is conveyed to the fairs, considering it is in the interest of the traders to keep them ignorant, is really surprising. In a very short time after the ships arrive upon the coast, especially if several make their appearance together, those who dispose of the negroes at the fairs are frequently known to increase the price of them.

These fairs are not the only means, though they are the chief, by which the black traders on the coast are supplied with negroes. Small parties of them, from five to ten, are frequently brought to the houses of the traders, by those who make a practice of kidnapping; and who are constantly employed in procuring a supply, while purchasers are to be found.

When the negroes, whom the black traders have to dispose of, are shewn to the European purchasers, they first examine them relative to their age. They then minutely inspect their persons, and inquire into the state of their health; if they are afflicted with any infirmity, or are deformed, or have bad eyes or teeth; if they are lame, or weak in the joints, or distorted in the back, or of a slender make, or are narrow in the chest; in short, if they have been, or are afflicted in any manner, so as to render them incapable of much labour; if any of the foregoing defects are discovered in them, they are rejected. But if approved of, they are generally taken on board the ship the same evening. The purchaser has liberty to return on the following morning, but not afterwards, such as upon re-examination are found exceptionable.

The traders frequently beat those negroes which are objected to by the captains, and use them with great severity. It matters not whether they are refused on account of age, illness, deformity, or for any other reason. At New Calabar, in particular, the traders have frequently been known to put them to death. Instances have happened at that place, that the traders, when any of their negroes have

56

been objected to, have dropped their canoes under the stern of the vessel, and instantly beheaded them, in sight of the captain.

Upon the Windward Coast, another mode of procuring slaves is pursued; that is, by what they term *boating*; a mode that is very pernicious and destructive to the crews of the ships. The sailors, who are employed upon this trade, go in boats up the rivers, seeking for negroes, among the villages situated on the banks of them. But this method is very slow, and not always effectual. For, after being absent from the ship during a fortnight or three weeks, they sometimes return with only from eight to twelve negroes. Numbers of these are procured in consequence of alleged crimes, which, as before observed, whenever any ships are upon the coast, are more productive than at any other period. Kidnapping, however, prevails here.

I have good reason to believe, that of one hundred and twenty negroes, which were purchased for the ship to which I then belonged, then lying at the river Ambris, by far the greater part, if not the whole, were kidnapped. This, with various other instances, confirms me in the belief that kidnapping is the fund which supplies the thousands of negroes annually sold off these extensive Windward, and other Coasts, where boating prevails.

The Treatment of the Slaves.

As soon as the wretched Africans, purchased at the fairs, fall into the hands of the black traders, they experience an earnest of those dreadful sufferings which they are doomed in future to undergo. And there is not the least room to doubt, but that even before they can reach the fairs, great numbers perish from cruel usage, want of food, travelling through inhospitable deserts, etc. They are brought from the places where they are purchased to Bonny, etc., in canoes; at the bottom of which they lie, having their hands tied with a kind of willow twigs, and a strict watch is kept over them. Their usage in other respects, during the time of the passage, which generally lasts several days, is equally cruel. Their allowance of food is so scanty, that it is barely sufficient

to support nature. They are, besides, much exposed to the violent rains which frequently fall here, being covered only with mats that afford but a slight defence; and as there is usually water at the bottom of the canoes, from their leaking, they are scarcely ever dry.

Nor do these unhappy beings, after they become the property of the Europeans (from whom, as a more civilized people, more humanity might naturally be expected) find their situation in the least amended. Their treatment is no less rigorous. The men negroes, on being brought aboard the ship, are immediately fastened together, two and two, by hand-cuffs on their wrists, and by irons rivetted on their legs. They are then sent down between the decks, and placed in an apartment partitioned off for that purpose. The women likewise are placed in a separate apartment between decks, but without being ironed. And an adjoining room, on the same deck, is besides appointed for the boys. Thus are they all placed in different apartments.

But at the same time, they are frequently stowed so close, as to admit of no other posture than lying on their sides. Neither will the height between decks, unless directly under the grating, permit them the indulgence of an erect posture; especially where there are platforms, which is generally the case. These platforms are a kind of shelf, about eight or nine feet in breadth, extending from the side of the ship towards the centre. They are placed nearly midway between the decks, at the distance of two or three feet from each deck. Under these the negroes are stowed in the same manner as they are on the deck underneath.

In each of the apartments are placed three or four large buckets, of a conical form, being near two feet in diameter at the bottom, and only one foot at the top, and in depth about twenty-eight inches; to which, when necessary, the negroes have recourse. It often happens, that those who are placed at a distance from the buckets, in endeavouring to get to them, tumble over their companions, in consequence of their being shackled. These accidents, although unavoidable, are productive of continual quarrels, in which some of them are always bruised. In this distressed situation, unable to proceed, and prevented from getting to the tubs, they desist from the attempt; and, as the necessities of nature are not to be repelled, ease themselves as they lie. This becomes a fresh source of broils and disturbances, and tends to render the conditions of the poor captive wretches still more uncomfortable. The nuisance arising from these circumstances, is not infrequently increased by the tubs being much too small for the purpose intended, and their being usually emptied but once every day. The rule for doing this, however, varies in different ships, according to the attention paid to the health and convenience of the slaves by the captain.

About eight o'clock in the morning the negroes are generally brought upon deck. Their irons being examined, a long chain, which is locked to a ring-bolt, fixed in the deck, is run through the rings of the shackles of the men, and then locked to another ring-bolt, fixed also in the deck. By this means fifty or sixty, or sometimes more, are fastened to one chain, in order to prevent them from rising, or endeavouring to escape. If the weather proves favourable, they are permitted to remain in that situation till four or five in the afternoon, when they are disengaged from the chain, and sent down.

The diet of the negroes, while on board, consists chiefly of horse-beans, boiled to the consistence of a pulp; of boiled yams and rice, and sometimes of a small quantity of beef or pork. The latter are frequently taken from the provisions laid in for the sailors. They sometimes make use of a sauce, composed of palm-oil, mixed with flour, water, and pepper, which the sailors call *slabber-sauce*. Yams are the favourite food of the Eboe, or Bight negroes, and rice or corn, of those from the Gold and Windward Coasts; each preferring the produce of their native soil.

In their own country, the negroes in general live on animal life and fish, with roots, yams, and Indian corn. The horse-beans and rice, with which they are fed aboard ship, are chiefly taken from Europe. The latter, indeed,

is sometimes purchased on the coast, being far superior to any other.

The Gold Coast negroes scarcely ever refuse any food that is offered them, and they generally eat larger quantities of whatever is placed before them, than any other species of negroes, whom they likewise excel in strength of body and mind. Most of the slaves have such an aversion to the horse-beans, that unless they are narrowly watched, when fed upon deck, they will throw them overboard, or in each other's faces when they quarrel.

They are commonly fed twice a day, about eight o'clock in the morning and four in the afternoon. In most ships they are only fed with their *own food* once a day. Their food is served up to them in tubs, about the size of a small water bucket. They are placed around these tubs in companies of ten to each tub, out of which they feed themselves with wooden spoons. These they soon lose, and when they are not allowed others, they feed themselves with their hands. In favourable weather they are fed upon the deck, but in bad weather their food is given them below. Numberless quarrels take place among them during their meals; more especially when they are put upon short allowance, which frequently happens, if the passage from the coast of Guinea to the West-India islands proves of unusual length. In that case, the weak are obliged to be content with a very scanty portion. Their allowance of water is about half a pint at every meal. It is handed round in a bucket, and given to each negroe in a pannekin; a small utensil with a strait handle, somewhat similar to a sauce-boat. However, when the ships approach the islands with a favourable breeze, they are no longer restricted.

Upon the negroes refusing to take sustenance, I have seen coals of fire, glowing hot, put on a shovel, and placed so near their lips, as to scorch and burn them. And this has been accompanied with threats, of forcing them to swallow the coals, if they any longer persisted in refusing to eat. These means have generally had the desired effect. I have also been credibly informed, that a certain captain in the slave trade, poured melted lead on such of the negroes as obstinately refused their food.

Exercise being deemed necessary for the preservation of their health, they are sometimes obliged to dance, when the weather will permit their coming on deck. If they go about it reluctantly, or do not move with agility, they are flogged; a person standing by them all the time with a cat-o'-nine-tails in his hand for that purpose. Their musick, which upon these occasions, consists of a drum, sometimes with only one head; and when that is worn out, they do not scruple to make use of the bottom of one of the tubs before described. The poor wretches are frequently compelled to sing also; but when they do, their songs are generally melancholy lamentations of their exile from their native country.

The women are furnished with beads for the purpose of affording them some diversion. But this end is generally defeated by the squabbles which are occasioned, in consequence of their stealing them from each other.

On board some ships, the common sailors are allowed to have intercourse with such of the black women whose consent they can procure. And some of them have been known to take the inconstancy of their paramours so much to heart, as to leap overboard and drown themselves. The officers are permitted to indulge their passions among them at pleasure, and sometimes are guilty of such brutal excesses, as disgrace human nature.

The hardships and inconveniences suffered by the negroes during the passage, are scarcely to be enumerated or conceived. They are far more violently affected by the sea-sickness than the Europeans. It frequently terminates in death, especially among the women. But the exclusion of the fresh air is among the most intolerable. For the purpose of admitting this needful refreshment, most of the ships in the slave-trade are provided, between the decks, with five or six air-port on each side of the ship, of about five inches in length, and four in breadth; in addition to which, some few ships, but not one in twenty, have what they denominate wind-sails. But whenever the sea is rough, and the rain heavy, it becomes necessary to shut these, and every conveyance by which the air is admitted. The fresh air being thus excluded, the negroes rooms very soon grow intolerably hot. The confined air, rendered noxious by the effluvia exhaled from their bodies, and by being repeatedly breathed, soon produces fevers and fluxes, which generally carries off great numbers of them.

During the voyages I made, I was frequently witness to the fatal effects of this exclusion of the fresh air. I will give one instance, as it serves to convey some idea, though a very faint one, of the sufferings of those unhappy beings whom we wantonly drag from their native country, and doom to perpetual labour and captivity. Some wet and blowing weather having occasioned some port-holes to be shut, and the grating to be covered, fluxes and fevers among the negroes ensued. While they were in this situation, my profession requiring it, I frequently went down among them, till at length their apartments became so extremely hot, as to be only sufferable for a very short time. But the excessive heat was not the only thing that rendered their situation intolerable. The deck, that is, the floor of their rooms, was so covered with the blood and mucus which had proceeded from them in consequence of the flux, that it resembled a slaughter-house. It is not in the power of the human imagination to picture to itself a situation more dreadful or disgusting. Numbers of the slaves having fainted, they were carried upon deck, where several of them died, and the rest were, with great difficulty, restored. It had nearly proved fatal to me also. The climate was too warm to admit the wearing of any clothing but a shirt, and that I had pulled off before I went down; notwithstanding which, by only continuing among them for about a quarter of an hour, I was so overcome with the heat, stench and foul air, that I had nearly fainted; and it was not without assistance, that I could get upon deck. The consequence was, that I soon fell sick of the same disorder, from which I did not recover for several months.

A circumstance of this kind, sometimes repeatedly happens in the course of a voyage; and often to a greater degree than what has just been described; particularly when the slaves are much crowded, which was not the case at that time, the ship having more than a hundred short of the number she was to have taken in.

This devastation, great as it was, some few years ago was greatly exceeded on board a Liverpool ship. I shall particularize the circumstances of it, as a more glaring instance of an insatiable thirst for gain, or of less attention to the lives and happiness of even of that despised and oppressed race of mortals, the sable inhabitants of Africa, perhaps was never exceeded; though indeed several similar instances have been known.

This ship, though a much smaller ship than that in which the event I have just mentioned happened, took on board at Bonny, at least six hundred negroes; but according to the information of the black traders, from whom I received the intelligence immediately after the ship sailed, they amounted to near *seven hundred*. By purchasing so great a number, the slaves were so crowded, that they were even obliged to lie one upon another. This occasioned such a mortality among them, that, without meeting with unusual bad weather, or having a longer voyage than common, nearly one half of them died before the ship arrived in the West-Indies.

That the publick may be able to form some idea of the almost incredible small space into which so large a number of negroes were crammed, the following particulars of this ship are given. According to Liverpool custom she measured 235 tons. Her width across the beam, 25 feet. Length between the decks, 92 feet, which was divided into four rooms, thus:

Store room, in which there were not any negroes placed		15 feet
Negroes rooms	mens room	about 45 feet
	womens ditto	about 10 feet
	boys ditto	about 22 feet
Total room for negroes		77 feet

Exclusive of the platform before described, from 8 to 9 feet in breadth, and equal in length to that of the room.

It may be worthy of remark, that the ships in this trade, are usually fitted out to receive only one third women negroes, or perhaps a smaller number, which the dimensions of the room allotted for them, above given, plainly shew, but in a greater disproportion.

One would naturally suppose, that an attention to their own interest, would prompt the owners of the Guinea ships not to suffer the captains to take on board a greater number of negroes than the ship would allow room sufficient for them to lie with ease to themselves, or, at least, without rubbing against each other. However that may be, a more striking instance than the above, of avarice, completely and deservedly disappointed, was surely never displayed; for there is little room to doubt, but that in consequence of the expected premium usually allowed to the captains, of 6 per cent sterling on the produce of the negroes, this vessel was so thronged as to occasion such a heavy loss.

The place allotted for the sick negroes is under the half deck, where they lie on the bare planks. By this means, those who are emaciated, frequently have their skin, and even their flesh, entirely rubbed off, by the motion of the ship, from the prominent parts of the shoulders, elbows, and hips, so as to render the bones in those parts quite bare. And some of them, by constantly lying in the blood and mucus, that had flowed from those afflicted with the flux, and which, as before observed, is generally so violent as to prevent their being kept clean, have their flesh much sooner rubbed off, than those who have only to contend with the mere friction of the ship. The excruciating pain which the poor sufferers feel from being obliged to continue in such a dreadful situation, frequently for several weeks, in case they happen to live so long, is not to be conceived or described. Few, indeed, are ever able to withstand the fatal effects of it. The utmost skill of the surgeon is here ineffectual. If plaisters be applied, they are very soon displaced by the friction of the ship; and when bandages are used, the negroes very soon take them off, and appropriate them to other purposes.

The surgeon, upon going between decks, in the morning, to examine the situation of the slaves, frequently finds several dead; and among the men, sometimes a dead and living negroe fastened by their irons together. When this is the case, they are brought upon the deck, and being laid on the grating, the living negroe is disengaged, and the dead one thrown overboard.

It may not be improper here to remark, that the surgeons employed in the Guinea trade, are generally driven to engage in so disagreeable an employ by the confined state of their finances. An exertion of the greatest skill and attention could afford the diseased negroes little relief, so long as the causes of their diseases, namely the breathing of a putrid atmosphere, and wallowing in their own excrements, remain. When once the fever and dysentery get to any height at sea, a cure is scarcely ever effected.

Almost the only means by which the surgeon can render himself useful to the slaves, is, by seeing that their food is properly cooked, and distributed among them. It is true, when they arrive near the markets for which they are destined, care is taken to polish them for sale, by an application of the lunar caustic to such as are afflicted with the yaws. This, however, affords but a temporary relief, as the disease most assuredly breaks out, whenever the patient is put upon a vegetable diet.

It has been asserted, in favour of the captains in this trade, that the sick slaves are usually fed from their tables. The great number generally ill at a time, proves the falsity of such an assertion. Were even a captain *disposed* to do this, how could he feed half the slaves in the ship from his own table? for it is well known, *that more than half* are often sick at a time. Two or three perhaps may be fed.

The loss of slaves, through mortality, arising from the causes just mentioned, are frequently very considerable. In the voyage lately referred to (not the Liverpool ship beforementioned) one hundred and five, out of three hundred and eighty, died in the passage. A proportion seemingly very great, but by no means uncommon. One half, sometimes two

thirds, and even beyond that, have been known to perish. Before we left Bonny River, no less than fifteen died of fevers and dysenteries, occasioned by their confinement. On the Windward Coast, where slaves are procured more slowly, very few die, in proportion to the numbers which die at Bonny, and at Old and New Calabar, where they are obtained much faster; the latter being of a more delicate make and habit.

The havock made among the seamen engaged in this destructive commerce, will be noticed in another part; and will be found to make no inconsiderable addition to the unnecessary waste of life just represented.

As very few of the negroes can so far brook the loss of their liberty, and the hardships they endure, so as to bear them with any degree of patience, they are ever upon the watch to take advantage of the least negligence in their oppressors. Insurrections are frequently the consequence; which are seldom suppressed without much bloodshed. Sometimes these are successful, and the whole ship's company is cut off, They are likewise always ready to seize every opportunity for committing some act of desperation to free themselves from their miserable state; and notwithstanding the restraints under which they are laid, they often succeed.

While a ship, to which I belonged, lay in Bonny River, one evening, a short time before our departure, a lot of negroes, consisting of about ten, was brought on board; when one of them, in a favourable moment, forced his way through the net-work on the larboard side of the vessel, jumped overboard, and was supposed to have been devoured by the sharks.

During the time we were there, fifteen negroes belonging to the vessel from Liverpool, found means to throw themselves into the river; very few were saved; and the residue fell a sacrifice to the sharks. A similar instance took place in a French ship while we lay there.

Circumstances of this kind are very frequent. On the coast of Angola, at the River Ambris, the following incident happened. During the time of our residing on shore, we erected a tent to shelter ourselves from the weather. After having been there several weeks, and being unable to purchase the number of slaves we wanted, through the opposition of another English slave vessel, we determined to leave the place. The night before our departure, the tent was struck; which was no sooner perceived by some of the negroe women on board, than it was considered a prelude to our sailing; and about eighteen of them, when they were sent between decks, threw themselves into the sea through one of the gun ports; the ship carrying guns between decks. They were all of them, however, excepting one, soon picked up; and that which was missing, was, not long after, taken about a mile from the shore.

I once knew a negroe woman, too sensible of her woes, who pined for a considerable time, and was taken ill of a fever and dysentery; when declaring it to be her determination to die, she refused all food and medical aid, and, in about a fortnight after, expired. On being thrown overboard, her body was instantly torn to pieces by the sharks.

The following circumstance also came within my knowledge. A young female negroe, falling into a desponding way, it was judged necessary, in order to attempt her recovery, to send her on shore, to the hut of one of the black traders. Elevated with the prospect of regaining her liberty by this unexpected step, she soon recovered her usual cheerfulness; but hearing, by accident, that it was intended to take her on the ship again, the poor young creature hung herself.

It frequently happens that the negroes, on being purchased by the Europeans, become raving mad; and many of them die in that state; particularly the women. While I was one day ashore at Bonny, I saw a middle aged stout woman, who had been brought down from a fair the preceding day, chained to the post of a black trader's door, in a state of furious insanity. On board a ship in Bonny River, I saw a young negroe woman chained to the deck, who had lost her senses, soon after she was purchased and taken on board. In a former voyage, on board a ship to which I belonged, we were obliged to confine a female negroe, of about twenty-three years of age, on her becoming a lunatic. She was afterwards sold during one of her lucid intervals.

One morning, upon examining the place allotted for the sick negroes, I perceived that one of them, who was so emaciated as scarcely to be able to walk, was missing, and was convinced that he must have gone overboard in the night, probably to put a more expeditious period to his sufferings. And, to conclude on this subject, I could not help being sensibly affected, on a former voyage, at observing with what apparent eagerness a black woman seized some dirt from off an African yam, and put it into her mouth; seeming to rejoice at the opportunity of possessing some of her native earth.

From these instances I think it may be clearly deduced, that the unhappy Africans are not bereft of finer feelings, but have a strong attachment to their native country, together with a just sense of the value of liberty. And the situation of the miserable beings above described, more forcibly urge the necessity of abolishing a trade which is the source of such evils, than the most eloquent harangue, or persuasive arguments could do.

Sale of the slaves.

When the ships arrive in the West-Indies (the chief mart for this inhuman merchandize), the slaves are disposed of, as I have before observed, by different methods. Sometimes the mode of disposal, is that of selling them by what is termed a *scramble*; and a day is soon fixed for that purpose. But previous thereto, the sick, or refuse slaves, of which there are frequently many, are usually conveyed on shore, and sold at a tavern by vendue, or public auction. These, in general, are purchased by the Jews and surgeons, but chiefly the former, upon speculation, at so low a price as five or six dollars a head. I was informed by a mulatto woman, that she purchased a sick slave at Grenada, upon speculation, for the small sum of one dollar, as the poor wretch was apparently dying of the flux. It seldom happens that any, who are carried ashore in the emaciated state to which they are generally reduced by that disorder, long survive their landing. I once saw fifteen conveyed on shore, and sold in the foregoing manner, the whole of them died before I left the island, which was within a short time after. Sometimes the captains march their slaves through the town at which they intend to dispose of them; and then place them in rows where they are examined and purchased.

The mode of selling them by scramble having fallen under my observation the oftenest, I shall be more particular in describing it. Being some years ago, at one of the islands in the West-Indies, I was witness to a sale by scramble, where about 250 negroes were sold. Upon this occasion all the negroes scrambled for bear an equal price; which is agreed upon between the captains and the purchasers before the sale begins.

On a day appointed, the negroes were landed, and placed together in a large yard, belonging to the merchants to whom the ship was consigned. As soon as the hour agreed on arrived, the doors of the yard were suddenly thrown open, and in rushed a considerable number of purchasers, with all the ferocity of brutes. Some instantly seized such of the negroes as they could conveniently lay hold of with their hands. Others, being prepared with several handkerchiefs tied together, encircled with these as many as they were able. While others, by means of a rope, effected the same purpose. It is scarcely possible to describe the confusion of which this mode of selling is productive. It likewise causes much animosity among the purchasers, who, not infrequently upon these occasions, fall out and quarrel with each other. The poor astonished negroes were so much terrified by these proceedings, that several of them, through fear, climbed over the walls of the court yard, and ran wild about the town; but were soon hunted down and retaken.

While on a former voyage from Africa to Kingston in Jamaica, I saw a sale there by scramble, on board a scow. The negroes were collected together upon the main and quarter decks, and the ship was darkened by sails suspended over them, in order to prevent the purchasers from being able to see, so as to pick or chuse. The signal being given, the buyers rushed in, as usual, to seize their prey; when the negroes appeared to be extremely terrified, and near thirty of them jumped into the sea. But they were all soon retaken, chiefly by boats from other ships.

On board a ship, lying at Port Maria, in Jamaica, I saw another scramble; in which, as usual, the poor negroes were greatly terrified. The women, in particular, cling to each other in agonies scarcely to be conceived, shrieking through excess of terror, at the savage manner in which their brutal purchasers rushed upon them, and seized them. Though humanity, one would imagine, would dictate the captains to apprize the poor negroes of that mode by which they were to be sold, and by that means to guard them, in some degree, against the surprize and terror which must attend it, I never knew that any notice of the scramble was given to them. Nor have I any reason to think that it is done; or that this mode of sale is less frequent at this time, than formerly.

Various are the deceptions made use of in the disposal of the sick slaves; and many of these, such as must excite in every humane mind, the liveliest sensations of horror. I have been well informed, that a Liverpool captain boasted of his having cheated some Jews by the following stratagem. A lot of slaves, afflicted with the flux, being about to be landed for sale, he directed the surgeon to stop the anus of each of them with oakum. Thus prepared, they were landed, and taken to the accustomed place of sale; where, being unable to stand but for a very short time, they are usually permitted to sit. The Jews, when they examine them, oblige them to stand up, in order to see if there be any discharge, and when they do not perceive this appearance, they consider it as a symptom of recovery. In the present instance, such an appearance being prevented, the bargain was struck, and they were accordingly sold. But it was not long before a discovery ensued. The excruciating pain which the prevention of a discharge of such an acrimonious nature occasioned, not being able to be borne by the poor wretches, the temporary obstruction was removed, and the deluded purchasers were speedily convinced of the imposition.

So grievously are the negroes sometimes afflicted with this troublesome and painful disorder, that I have seen large numbers of them, after being landed, obliged by the virulence of the complaint, to stop almost every minute, as they passed on.

18. The plan of the slave ship *Brookes*.

The Brookes *was one of 18 Liverpool slave ships officially examined and measured in 1788 during parliamentary discussions about possible regulation of slave vessels. Using these measurements, Thomas Clarkson, a prominent abolitionist, had a sketch of the* Brookes *drawn to show what the ship would look like when fully loaded with slaves. The sketch, though slightly incorrect in failing to show the spaces by which slaves could be fed and dead bodies removed, proved a highly effective piece of propaganda. When Clarkson visited France in 1789 to gain support for the abolitionist cause, Louis XVI's chief minister refused to show the sketch to the king on the grounds that it would distress him too much, while future revolutionaries such as Condorcet, Mirabeau, and Lafayette were all much impressed. Mirabeau had a model of the* Brookes *made in wood, the better to depict the barbarity of the slaves' conditions, and Lafayette became a supporter of the anti-slavery cause. Nearly 4,000 copies of the diagram were distributed by abolitionists in Philadelphia.[18]*

Captain Perry, the official who measured the 18 Liverpool slave ships in 1788, described the dimensions of the *Brookes* as follows.

Length of the lower deck, gratings and bulkheads included, at A A, 100 feet, breadth of beam on lower deck inside, B B, 25 feet 4 inches, depth of Hold, O O O, from ceiling to ceiling, 10 feet, height between decks, from deck to deck, 5 feet 8 inches, length of the men's room, C C, on the lower deck, 46 feet, breadth of the men's room, C C, on the lower deck, 25 feet 4 inches, length of the platforms, D D, in the men's room, 46 feet, breadth of the platforms in the men's room on each side, 6 feet, length of the boys' room, E E, 13 feet 9 inches, breadth of the boys' room, 25 feet, breadth of platforms, F F, in boys' room, 6 feet, length of women's room, G G, 28 feet 6 inches, breadth of women's room, 23 feet 6 inches, length of platforms, H H, in women's room, 28 feet 6 inches, breadth of platforms in women's room, 6 feet, length of gun-room, I I, on the lower deck, 10 feet 6 inches, breadth of the gun-room on the lower deck, 12 feet, length of the quarter-deck, K K, 33 feet 6 inches, breadth of the quarter-deck, 19 feet, 6 inches, length of the cabin, L L, 14 feet, height of the cabin, 6 feet 2 inches, length of the half-deck, M M, 16 feet 6 inches, height of the half-deck, 6 feet 2 inches, length of the platforms, N N, on the half-deck, 16 feet 6 inches, breadth of the platforms on the half-deck, 6 feet, upper deck, PP. . . .

Let it now be supposed that the above are the real dimensions of the ship *Brookes*, and further, that every man slave is to be allowed six feet by one foot four inches for room, every woman five feet ten by one foot four, it will follow that the annexed plan of a slave vessel will be precisely the representation of the ship *Brookes*, and of the exact number of persons neither more nor less, that could be stowed in the different rooms of it upon these

[18] Elizabeth Donnan, ed., *Documents Illustrative of the History of the Slave Trade to America*, vol. 2 (Washington, DC: Carnegie Institute, 1930), p. 592, and facing 592. Reprinted with the agreement of the Carnegie Institute.

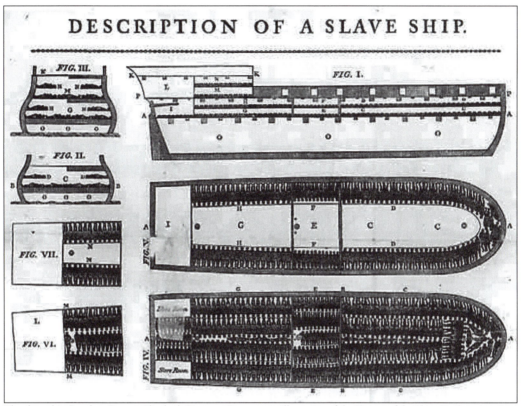

DESCRIPTION OF A SLAVE SHIP.

The slave ship *Brookes. Source:* Elizabeth Donnan, *Documents Illustrative of the History of the Slave Trade to America,* vol. 2 (Washington: Carnegie Institute, 1930), facing p. 592.

data. These, if counted [deducting the women stowed at Z in figs. VI and VII since by an act of Parliament that space was re-allocated to seamen], will be found to amount to *four hundred and fifty-one.* Now, if it be considered that the ship *Brookes* is of three hundred and twenty tons, and that she is allowed to carry by act of Parliament *four hundred and fifty-four persons,* it is evident that if three more could be wedged among the number represented in the plan, this plan would contain precisely the number which the act directs.

19. In support of the continued importation of slaves into South Africa.

Despite the growing calls for abolition in the late eighteenth century, pro-slavers continued to speak with a dominant voice, especially by pointing out the economic basis of slavery. In 1795, when the British, concerned that the French might gain control of the sea route to India, conquered the Dutch East Indies Company's settlement at the Cape of Good Hope, they instructed the first governor, Lord Macartney, to examine the feasibility of ending the importation of slaves. For advice on this question, Macartney turned to W. S. van Ryneveld who, despite being a member of the Company's governing body at the time of conquest, was considered an expert on matters of local administration. Van Ryneveld argued that ending the importation of slaves would result in the eco-

nomic collapse of the Cape. The British took van Ryneveld's advice. Between 1795 and 1808, they imported another 3,500 slaves into South Africa and, even after the passage of legislation prohibiting the trade, brought another 2,100 "prize negroes" into the colony between 1808 and 1816. The latter were captives "released" from slaving vessels interdicted by British frigates and forced to enter 14-year "apprenticeships" with European employers at the Cape.[19]

Question: What material injury or inconvenience would result to the Colony, if the importation of slaves were to be prohibited?

Answer: An immediate interdiction to the importation of slaves, would, of course, effectuate that the culture, especially the two principal branches thereof . . . corn and wine, first would begin to languish, and afterwards entirely to decay.

We know very well, that here, both within and without the Colony, no sufficient number of white people can be obtained to perform in culture the labour of the slaves; and, on the other hand, experience shows us every day that the procreation of slaves, in proportion to number, is very trifling, and even not worth mentioning; and that, moreover, a very considerable number of slaves is lost by continual disorders, especially by bile and putrid fevers, to which they are very subject.

The political state of this Colony, I think, is actually of that nature that, however injurious slavery of itself may be to the morals and industry of the inhabitants, still the keeping of slaves has now become, as it is styled, a necessary evil; and, at least, a sudden interdiction to the importation of slaves would occasion a general injury, as long as such a number of hands as is requisite for the culture cannot be obtained from another part, at a rate that may be thought proportionate to the produce arising from the lands . . . It is very true that at present there may be found some white or free persons apt for that purpose; yet apart from the number of these persons not being sufficient in any degree to supply the number of slaves wanted, the high hire and expensive maintenance of such free labourers would still render the employing of them impracticable. . . .

Question: If there were no slaves at the Cape, would not the white peasants become more industrious and useful to the State? Does not the facility of procuring slaves, and the general custom of making use of them, render the white inhabitants more haughty, more lazy and more brutal? . . .

Answer: There are (to return properly to my subject) two principle causes that prevent the white people here from doing rural labour, viz.:

1st. The great extent of the country, without sufficient population, so that the country is really in want of hands for carrying on the tillage;

2nd. The introduction of slavery.

I perfectly acknowledge . . . that if there were no slaves at the Cape the peasants would then be more industrious and useful to the State, and that the facility of procuring slaves renders the inhabitants of this country lazy, haughty and brutal.

Every kind of vice and a perfect corruption of morals is owing to that. But how to help it? If slavery had been interdicted at the first settling of this Colony, then the inhabitants would doubtless have become more industrious and useful to each other; they would be obliged to associate in a narrower compass of land, and the Colony would never have so exceedingly extended beyond its ability and beyond the exigence of its population.

Yet, the business is done. Slavery exists and is now even indispensable. It is absolutely necessary because there are no other hands to till this extensive country, and therefore it will be the work, not of years, but as it were

---

[19] Replies of W. S. Ryneveld to Governor Macartney's questionnaire, November 29, 1797, reprinted in Andre Du Toit and Hermann Giliomee, eds., *Afrikaner Political Thought*, vol. 1 (Berkeley: University of California Press, 1983), pp. 46–49. Reprinted with the permission of the University of California Press.

of centuries to remove by attentive and proper regulation this evil established with the first settling of the Colony. Should the slaves be now declared free, that would immediately render both the country and these poor creatures themselves miserable; not only all tillage would then be at an end, but also the number of freemen, instead of their being (as now) useful members of, would then really become a charge to, society. And should the importation of slaves be interdicted, on a sudden, without any means being provided towards supplying other hands for the tillage, then the Colony would thereby be caused to languish (the procreation of slaves being so inconsiderable in comparison with their mortality) and especially the culture of grain would thereby be reduced to decay.

In order to improve gradually the industry of this Colony, it will be absolutely necessary, on the one hand, to obviate the further enlarging of this settlement. As long as one may infringe upon the countries of the Kaffirs, Bushmen, etc., to take their lands and to live upon the breeding of cattle, then so long no person will be anxious about the state of his children, so long no sufficient number of hands will be to be obtained in the country itself to carry on the tillage, so long the inhabitants will never enter into the service of each other, and, finally, so long the importation of slaves also will be necessary for the sake of the culture of grain. While on the other hand a person will never scruple to settle himself throughout the whole country of Africa among all the nations, and, by so doing, at length to become like those wild nations.

The Government, intending to frame from this Colony a regular Society, where diligence and industry are to compose the foundation of the prosperity of the people, ought therefore, and in the first place, to take care that no person do in future settle beyond the boundaries of this Colony, and that by that regulation the young people be, of course, obliged to endeavour to earn their subsistence in the bosom of the Colony itself; from doing which, sufficient motives will then always and in proportion to the increase of population arise, to be industrious and so to promote both their own welfare and the prosperity of the community in general. . . .

20. Mungo Park describes taking slaves from the interior of Africa to the coast.

Like his South African contemporary van Ryneveld, Mungo Park (1771–1806), the first European to explore the hinterland of the Gambia River, considered slavery a necessary evil. Park, who had trained as a surgeon at Edinburgh University and was a protégé of Sir Joseph Banks (famed naturalist and president of the Royal Society), embarked on his travels at the direction of the African Association, an organization founded in 1788 by, as Park put matters, "noblemen and gentlemen, associated for the purpose of prosecuting discoveries in the interior of Africa." One of their main aims was to gain information about the legendary trading cities of the interior, especially Timbuktu, still renowned as it had been three hundred years earlier in the publications of Ibn Battuta and Leo Africanus as the chief entrepôt for the transfer of African gold across the Sahara. Park began his expedition into the interior with "a passionate desire to examine into the productions of a country so little known, and [aiming] to become experimentally acquainted with the modes of life and character of the natives." Though exhaustion and illness prevented him from reaching Timbuktu on his first trip, he explored more of the interior of West Africa than any other European up to that point. He returned again in 1806 but was killed when, firing on Africans who he believed to be unfriendly, he and a companion were attacked in turn. In the following extract from his published journal, Park provides an eyewitness description of the collection of slaves in the interior, their transfer to the coast, and the Atlantic crossing.[20]

Park arrives at Kamalia, northeast of the headwaters of the Gambia River, on September 16, 1796.

On my arrival at Kamalia, I was conducted to the house of a Bushreen [Muslim] named Karfa Taura . . . He was collecting a coffle [caravan] of slaves, with a view to sell them to the Europeans on the Gambia, as soon as the rains should be over. I found him sitting in his baloon [visitor's room], surrounded by several Slatees [African merchants], who proposed to join the coffle. He was reading to them from an Arabic book; and inquired, with a smile, if I understood it. Being answered in the negative, he desired one of the Slatees to fetch the curious little book, which had been brought from the west country. On opening this small volume, I was surprised and delighted, to find it our *Book of Common Prayer*; and Karfa expressed great joy to hear that I could read it: for some of the Slatees, who had seen the Europeans upon the coast, observing the colour of my skin (which was now become very yellow from sickness), my long beard, ragged clothes, and extreme poverty; were unwilling to admit that I was a white man, and told Karfa that they suggested I was some Arab in disguise. . . . [I]n the beginning of December, a Sera-Woolli Slatee, with five slaves, arrived from Sego: this man too, spread a number of malicious reports concerning me; but Karfa paid no attention to them, and continued to show me the same kindness as formerly. As I was one day conversing, with the slaves which this Slatee had brought, one of them begged me to give him some victuals. I told him I was a stranger, and had none to give. He replied, "I gave *you* victuals when you was hungry. Have you forgot the man who brought you milk at

Karrankalla? But (added he with a sigh) *the irons were not then upon my legs!*" I immediately recollected him, and begged some ground nuts from Karfa to give him, as a return for his former kindness. He told me that he had been taken away by the Bambarrans the day after the battle of Joka, and sent to Sego, where he had been purchased by his present master, who was carrying him down to Kajaaga. Three more of these slaves were from Kaarta, and one from Wassela, all of them prisoners of war. They stopped four days at Kamalia, and were then taken to Bala, where they remained until the river Kokoro was fordable, and the grass burnt.

In the beginning of December, Karfa proposed to complete his purchase of slaves; and for this purpose collected all the debts which were owing to him in his own country, and on the 19th, being accompanied by three Slatees, he departed for Kancaba, a large town on the banks of the Niger; and a great slave market. Most of the slaves who are sold at Kancaba come from Bambarra; for Mansong, to avoid the expence and danger of keeping all his prisoners at Sego, commonly sends them in small parties, to be sold at the different trading towns; and as Kancaba is much resorted to by merchants, it is always supplied with slaves, which are sent thither up the Niger in canoes. . . .

The slaves in Africa, I suppose, are nearly in the proportion of three to one to the freemen. They claim no reward for their services except food and clothing, and are treated with kindness or severity, according to the good or bad disposition of their masters. Custom, however, has established certain rules with regard to the treatment of slaves, which it is thought dishonourable to violate. Thus, the

[20] Mungo Park, *Travels in the Interior Districts of Africa: Performed under the Direction of the African Association, in the Years 1795, 1796, and 1797* (London: G. and W. Nicol, 1799), pp. 253, 256–57, 287–90, 318–21, 323–25, 327–28, 330, 331–34, 338–40, 346–50, 353–54, 356–57, 360–62.

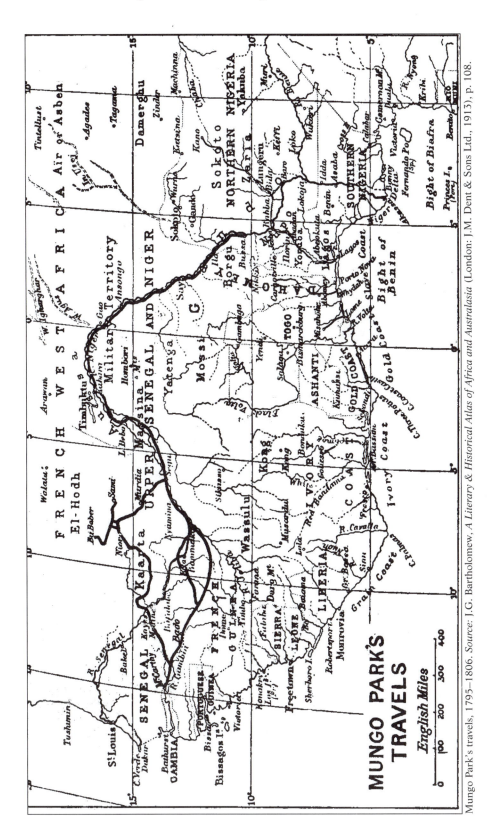

MUNGO PARK'S TRAVELS

English Miles

0   100   200   300   400

Mungo Park's travels, 1795–1806. *Source:* J.G. Bartholomew, *A Literary & Historical Atlas of Africa and Australasia* (London: J.M. Dent & Sons Ltd., 1913), p. 108.

domestic slaves, or such as are born in a man's own house, are treated with more lenity than those which are purchased with money. The authority of the master over the domestic slave . . . extends only to reasonable correction; for the master cannot sell his domestic, without having first brought him to a public trial, before the chief men of the place. But these restrictions on the power of the master extend not to the case of prisoners taken in war, nor to that of slaves purchased with money. All these unfortunate beings are considered as strangers and foreigners, who have no right to the protection of the law, and may be treated with severity, or sold to a stranger, according to the pleasure of their owners. There are, indeed, regular markets, where slaves of this description are bought and sold, and the value of a slave, in the eye of an African purchaser, increases in proportion to his distance from his native kingdom: for when slaves are only a few days' journey from the place of their nativity, they frequently effect their escape, but when one or more kingdoms intervene, escape being more difficult, they are more readily reconciled to their situation. On this account, the unhappy slave is frequently transferred from one dealer to another, until he has lost all hopes of returning to his native kingdom. The slaves which are purchased by the Europeans on the Coast, are chiefly of this description; a few of them are collected in the petty wars, hereafter to be described, which take place near the Coast; but by far the greater number are brought down in large caravans from the inland countries, of which many are unknown, even by name, to the Europeans. The slaves which are thus brought from the interior may be divided into two distinct classes; *first*, such as were slaves from their birth, having been born of enslaved mothers; *secondly*, such as were born free, but who afterwards, by whatever means, became slaves. Those of the first description are by far the most numerous; for prisoners taken in war (at least such as are taken in open and declared war, when one kingdom avows hostilities against another), are generally of this description. . . . it must be observed that men

of free condition have many advantages over the slaves, even in war time. They are in general better armed, and well mounted, and can either fight or escape with some hope of success; but the slaves who have only their spears and bows, and of whom great numbers are loaded with baggage, become an easy prey. Thus, when Mansong, King of Bambarra, made war upon Kaarta . . . he took in one day nine hundred prisoners, of which number not more than seventy were free men. This account I received from Daman Jumma, who had thirty slaves at Kemmoo, all of whom were made slaves by Mansong. Again, when a free man is taken prisoner, his friends will sometimes ransom him, by giving two slaves in exchange; but when a slave is taken, he has no hopes of such redemption. To these disadvantages, it is to be added, that the Slatees, who purchase slaves in the interior countries, and carry them down to the Coast for sale, constantly prefer such as have been in that condition of life from their infancy, well knowing that these have been accustomed to hunger and fatigue, and are better able to sustain the hardships of a long and painful journey, than free men; and on their reaching the Coast, if no opportunity offers of selling them to advantage, they can easily be made to maintain themselves by their labour; neither are they so apt to attempt making their escape, as those who have once tasted the blessings of freedom.

Slaves of the second description [those born free], generally become such by one of the following causes, 1. *Captivity.* 2. *Famine.* 3. *Insolvency.* 4. *Crimes.* A free man may, by the established customs of Africa, become a slave by being taken in war. War is, of all others, the most productive source, and was probably the origin of slavery. . . .

On the 24th of January [1797] Karfa returned to Kamalia with a number of people, and thirteen prime slaves which he had purchased. . . .

The slaves which Karfa had brought with him were all of them prisoners of war; they had been taken by the Bambarran army in the kingdoms of Wassela and Kaarta, and carried to Sego, where some of them had remained three years in irons. From Sego they were sent, in company with a number of other captives, up the Niger, in two large canoes, and offered for sale at Yamina, Bammakoo, and Kancaba; at which places the greater number of the captives were bartered for gold dust, and the remainder sent forward to Kankaree.

Eleven of them confessed to me that they had been slaves from their infancy; but the other two refused to give any account of their former condition. They were all very inquisitive; but they viewed me at first with looks of horror, and repeatedly asked if my countrymen were cannibals. They were very desirous to know what became of the slaves after they had crossed the salt water. I told them, that they were employed in cultivating the land; but they would not believe me; and one of them putting his hand upon the ground, said with great simplicity, "have you really got such ground as this, to set your feet upon?" A deeply rooted idea, that the whites purchase Negroes for the purpose of devouring them, or of selling them to others that they may be devoured hereafter, naturally makes the slaves contemplate a journey towards the Coast with great terror; insomuch, that the Slatees are forced to keep them constantly in irons, and watch them very closely, to prevent their escape. They are commonly secured by putting the right leg of one, and the left of another, into the same pair of fetters. By supporting the fetters with a string, they can walk, though very slowly. Every four slaves are likewise fastened together by the necks, with a strong rope of twisted thongs; and in the night, an additional pair of fetters is put on their hands, and sometimes a light iron chain passed round their necks.

Such of them as evince marks of discontent, are secured in a different manner. A thick billet of wood is cut, about three feet long, and a smooth notch being made upon one side of it, the ankle of the slave is bolted to the smooth part by means of a strong iron staple, one prong of which passes on each side of the ankle. All these fetters and bolts are made from native iron; in the present case they were put on by the blacksmith, as soon

as the slaves arrived from Kancaba, and were not taken off until the morning on which the coffle departed for Gambia.

In other respects, the treatment of the slaves during their stay at Kamalia, was far from being harsh or cruel. They were led out in their fetters, every morning, to the shade of the tamarind tree, where they were encouraged to play at games of hazard, and sing diverting songs, to keep up their spirits; for though some of them sustained the hardships of their situation with amazing fortitude, the greater part were very much dejected, and would sit all day in a sort of sullen melancholy, with their eyes fixed upon the ground. In the evening their irons were examined, and their hand fetters put on; after which they were conducted into two large huts, where they were guarded during the night by Karfa's domestic slaves. But notwithstanding all this, about a week after their arrival, one of the slaves had the address to procure a small knife, with which he opened the rings of his fetters, cut the rope, and made his escape; more of them would probably have got off had they assisted each other: but the slave no sooner found himself at liberty, than he refused to stop, and assist in breaking the chain which was fastened round the necks of his companions.

As all the Slatees and slaves belonging to the coffle were now assembled, either at Kamalia, or at some of the neighbouring villages, it might have been expected that we should have set out immediately for Gambia; but though the day of our departure was frequently fixed, it was always found expedient to change it. Some of the people had not prepared their dry provisions; others had gone to visit their relations, or collect some trifling debts, and last of all, it was necessary to consult whether the day would be a lucky one. On account of one of these, or other such causes, our departure was put off, day after day, until the month of February was far advanced, after which, all the Slatees agreed to remain in their present quarters, until the *fast moon was over*. . . .

April 19th. The long-wished-for day of our departure was at length arrived, and the

Slatees having taken the irons from their slaves, assembled with them at the door of Karfa's house, where the bundles were all tied up, and every one had his load assigned him. The coffle, on its departure from Kamalia, consisted of twenty-seven slaves for sale, the property of Karfa and four other Slatees; but we were afterwards joined by five at Maraboo and three at Bala; making in all thirty-five slaves. The free men were fourteen in number, but most of them had one or two wives, and some domestic slaves, and the school-master, who was now upon his return for Woradoo, the place of his nativity, took with him eight of his scholars; so that the number of free people and domestic slaves amounted to thirty-eight, and the whole amount of the coffle was seventy-three. Among the free men were six Jillakeas (singing men), whose musical talents were frequently exerted, either to divert our fatigue, or obtain us a welcome from strangers. When we departed from Kamalia, we were followed for about half a mile, by most of the inhabitants of the town, some of them crying, and others shaking hands with their relations, who were now about to leave them; and when we had gained a piece of rising ground from which we had a view of Kamalia, all the people belonging to the coffle were ordered to sit down in one place, with their faces towards the west, and the townspeople were desired to sit down in another place, with their faces towards Kamalia. In this situation, the schoolmaster with two of the principal Slatees, having taken their places between the two parties, pronounced a long and solemn prayer; after which they walked three times round the coffle, making an impression in the ground with the ends of their spears, and muttering something by way of charm. When this ceremony was ended, all the people belonging to the coffle sprang up, and without taking a formal farewell of their friends, set forwards. As many of the slaves had remained for years in irons, the sudden exertion of walking quick, with heavy loads upon their heads, occasioned spasmodic contractions of their legs; and we had not proceeded above a mile, before it was found necessary to take two of them from the rope, and allow them to walk more slowly until we reached Maraboo, a walled village where some people were waiting to join the coffle. Here we stopt about two hours, to allow the strangers time to pack up their provisions, and then continued our route. . . .

As this was the first town [Kinytakooro] beyond the limits of Manding, greater etiquette than usual was observed. Every person was ordered to keep in his proper station, and we marched towards the town, in a sort of procession, nearly as follows. In front, five or six singing men, all of them belonging to the coffle; these were followed by the other free people; then came the slaves fastened in the usual way by a rope round their necks, four of them to a rope, and a man with a spear between each four; after them came the domestic slaves, and in the rear the women of free condition, wives of the Slatees, etc. In this manner we proceeded, until we came within a hundred yards of the gate; when the singing men began a loud song, well calculated to flatter the vanity of the inhabitants, by extolling their known hospitality to strangers, and their particular friendship for the Mandingoes. When we entered the town we proceeded to the Bentang, where the people gathered round us to hear our *dentegi* (history). This was related publicly by two of the singing men: they enumerated every little circumstance which had happened to the coffle, beginning with the events of the present day, and relating everything in a backward series, until they reached Kamalia. When this history was ended, the master of the town gave them a small present, and all the people of the coffle, both free and enslaved, were invited by some person or other, and accommodated with lodging and provisions for the night. . . .

As soon as we had crossed the river [Wonda] Karfa gave orders, that all the people of the coffle should in future keep close together, and travel in their proper station; the guides and young men were accordingly placed in the van, the women and slaves in the centre, and the free men in the rear. In this order we travelled with uncommon expedition. . . .

April 24th. Before daybreak the Bushreens said their morning prayers, and most of the free people drank a little *moening* (a sort of gruel), part of which was likewise given to such of the slaves as appeared least able to sustain the fatigues of the day. One of Karfa's female slaves was very sulky, and when some gruel was offered to her, she refused to drink it. As soon as day dawned we set out, and travelled the whole morning over a wild and rocky country, by which my feet were much bruised; and I was sadly apprehensive that I should not be able to keep up with the coffle during the day; but I was, in a great measure, relieved from this anxiety, when I observed that others were more exhausted than myself. In particular, the woman slave, who had refused victuals in the morning, began now to lag behind, and complain dreadfully of pains in her legs. Her load was taken from her, and given to another slave, and she was ordered to keep in the front of the coffle. About eleven o'clock, as we were resting by a small rivulet, some of the people discovered a hive of bees in a hollow tree, and they were proceeding to obtain the honey, when the largest swarm I ever beheld, flew out, and attacking the people of the coffle, made us fly in all directions. I took the alarm first, and I believe was the only person who escaped with impunity. When our enemies thought fit to desist from pursuing us, and every person was employed in picking out the stings he had received, it was discovered that the poor woman abovementioned, whose name was Nealee, was not come up; and as many of the slaves in their retreat had left their bundles behind them, it became necessary for some persons to return, and bring them. In order to do this with safety, fire was set to the grass, a considerable way to the eastward of the hive, and the wind driving the fire furiously along, the party pushed through the smoke, and recovered the bundles. They likewise brought with them poor Nealee, whom they found lying by the rivulet. She was very much exhausted, and had crept to the stream, in hopes to defend herself from the bees by throwing water over her body; but this proved ineffectual; for she was stung in the most dreadful manner.

When the Slatees had picked out the stings as far as they could, she was washed with water, and then rubbed with bruised leaves; but the wretched woman obstinately refused to proceed any farther; declaring, that she would rather die than walk another step. As entreaties and threats were used in vain, the whip was at length applied; and after bearing patiently a few strokes, she started up, and walked with tolerable expedition for four or five hours longer, when she made an attempt to run away from the coffle, but was so very weak, that she fell down in the grass. Though she was unable to rise, the whip was a second time applied, but without effect; upon which Karfa desired two of the Slatees to place her upon the ass which carried our dry provisions; but she could not sit erect; and the ass being very refractory, it was found impossible to carry her forward in that manner. The Slatees however were unwilling to abandon her, the day's journey being nearly ended: they therefore made a sort of litter of bamboo canes, upon which she was placed, and tied on it with slips of bark: this litter was carried upon the heads of two slaves, one walking before the other, and they were followed by two others, who relieved them occasionally. In this manner the woman was carried forward until it was dark, when we reached a stream of water, at the foot of a high hill called Gankaran-Kooro; and here we stopt for the night, and set about preparing our supper. As we had only eat one handful of meal since the preceding night, and travelled all day in a hot sun, many of the slaves, who had loads upon their heads, were very much fatigued; and some of them *snapt their fingers*, which among the Negroes is a sure sign of desperation. The Slatees immediately put them all in irons; and such of them as had evinced signs of great despondency, were kept apart from the rest, and had their hands tied. In the morning they were found greatly recovered.

April 25th. At daybreak poor Nealee was awakened; but her limbs were now become so stiff and painful, that she could neither walk nor stand; she was therefore lifted, like a corpse, upon the back of the ass; and the Slatees endeavoured to secure her in that situation, by fastening her hands together under the ass's neck, and her feet under the belly, with long slips of bark; but the ass was so very unruly, that no sort of treatment could induce him to proceed with his load; and as Nealee made no exertion to prevent herself from falling, she was quickly thrown off, and had one of her legs much bruised. Every attempt to carry her forward being thus found ineffectual, the general cry of the coffle was, *kang-tegi, kang-tegi,* "cut her throat, cut her throat"; an operation I did not wish to see performed, and therefore marched onwards with the foremost of the coffle. I had not walked above a mile, when one of Karfa's domestic slaves came up to me, with poor Nealee's garment upon the end of his bow, and exclaimed *Nealee affilita* (Nealee is lost). I asked him whether the Slatees had given him the garment, as a reward for cutting her throat; he replied, that Karfa and the schoolmaster would not consent to that measure, but had left her on the road; where undoubtedly she soon perished, and was probably devoured by wild beasts.

The sad fate of this wretched woman, notwithstanding the outcry beforementioned, made a strong impression on the minds of the whole coffle, and the schoolmaster fasted the whole of the ensuing day, in consequence of it. We proceeded in deep silence, and soon afterward crossed the river Furkoomah, which was about as large as the river Wonda. We now travelled with great expedition, every one being apprehensive he might otherwise meet with the fate of poor Nealee. It was however with great difficulty that I could keep up, although I threw away my spear, and every thing that could in the least obstruct me. About noon we saw a large herd of elephants, but they suffered us to pass unmolested, and in the evening we halted near a thicket of bamboo, but found no water; so that we were forced to proceed four miles farther, to a small stream, where we stopt for the night. We had marched this day, as I judged, about twenty-six miles . . . .

In the afternoon [April 28] we passed several villages, at none of which could we procure a lodging; and in the twilight we received information, that two hundred Jallonkas had assembled near a town called Melo, with a view to plunder the coffle. This induced us to alter our course, and we travelled with great secrecy until midnight, when we approached a town called Koba. Before we entered the town, the names of all the people belonging to the coffle were called over, and a freeman and three slaves were found to be missing. Every person immediately concluded that the slaves had murdered the freeman, and made their escape. It was therefore agreed, that six people should go back as far as the last village, and endeavour to find his body, or collect some information concerning the slaves. In the meantime the coffle was ordered to lie concealed in a cotton field near a large nitta tree, and nobody to speak, except in a whisper. It was towards morning before the six men returned, having heard nothing of the man or the slaves. As none of us had tasted victuals for the last twenty-four hours, it was agreed that we should go into Koba, and endeavour to procure some provisions. We accordingly entered the town before it was quite day, and Karfa purchased from the chief man, for three strings of beads, a considerable quantity of ground nuts, which we roasted and ate for breakfast; we were afterwards provided with huts, and rested here for the day.

About eleven o'clock, to our great joy and surprise, the freeman and slaves, who had departed from the coffle the preceding night, entered the town. One of the slaves, it seems, had hurt his foot, and the night being very dark, they soon lost sight of the coffle. The free man, as soon as he found himself alone with the slaves, was aware of his own danger, and insisted on putting them in irons. The slaves were at first rather unwilling to submit, but when he threatened to stab them one by one with his spear, they made no further resistance, and he remained with them among the bushes until morning, when he let them out of irons, and came to the town in hopes of hearing which route the coffle had taken. The information that we received concerning the Jallonkas, who intended to rob the coffle, was this day confirmed, and we were forced to remain here until the afternoon of the 30th; when Karfa hired a number of people to protect us, and we proceeded to a village called Tinkingtang. Departing from this village on the day following, we crossed a high ridge of mountains to the west of the Black river, and travelled over a rough stony country until sunset, when we arrived at Lingicotta, a small village in the district of Woradoo. Here we shook out the last handful of meal from our dry provision bags, this being the second day (since we crossed the Black river), that we had travelled from morning until night, without tasting one morsel of food . . . .

May 13th. In the morning, as we were preparing to depart, a coffle of slaves belonging to some Serawoolli traders, crossed the river, and agreed to proceed with us to Baniserile, the capital of Dentila; a very long day's journey from this place. We accordingly set out together, and travelled with great expedition, through the woods, until noon, when one of the Serawoolli slaves dropt a load from his head, for which he was smartly whipped. The load was replaced; but he had not proceeded above a mile before he let it fall a second time, for which he received the same punishment. After this he travelled in great pain until about two o'clock, when we stopt to breathe a little, by a pool of water, the day being remarkably hot. The poor slave was now so completely exhausted, that his master was obliged to release him from the rope, for he lay motionless on the ground. A Serawoolli therefore undertook to remain with him, and endeavour to bring him to the town during the cool of the night: in the meanwhile we continued our route, and after a very hard day's travel, arrived at Baniserile late in the evening . . . .

About eight o'clock the same evening, the Serawoolli, who had been left in the woods to take care of the fatigued slave, returned and told us that he was dead; the general opinion, however, was, that he himself had killed him, or left him to perish on the road; for the Serawoollis are said to be infinitely more cruel in their treatment of slaves than the Mandingoes. We remained at Baniserile two days, in order to purchase native iron, Shea-butter, and some other articles for sale on the Gambia; and here, the Slatee who had invited me to his house, and who possessed three slaves, part of the coffle, having obtained information that the price on the coast was very low, determined to separate from us, and remain, with his slaves, where he was, until an opportunity should offer of disposing of them to advantage . . . [May 16 traveled from Baniserile to Kirwani]

Departing from Kirwani, on the morning of the 20th, we entered the Tenda Wilderness of two days' journey. The woods were very thick, and the country shelved towards the south-west. About ten o'clock we met a coffle of twenty-six people, and seven loaded asses, returning from Gambia. Most of the men were armed with muskets, and had broad belts of scarlet cloth over their shoulders, and European hats upon their heads. They informed us that there was very little demand for slaves on the Coast, as no vessel had arrived for some months past. On hearing this, the Serawoollies who had travelled with us from Falemé river, separated themselves and their slaves from the coffle. They had not, they said, the means of maintaining their slaves in Gambia until a vessel should arrive; and were unwilling to sell them to disadvantage: they therefore departed to the northward for Kajaaga. We continued our route through the Wilderness, and travelled all day through a rugged country, covered with extensive thickets of bamboo . . . .

[May 30th] . . . Here [the town of Jallacotta] one of the slaves belonging to the coffle, who had travelled with great difficulty for the last three days, was found unable to proceed any farther; his master (a singing man) proposed therefore to exchange him for a young slave girl, belonging to one of the townspeople. The poor girl was ignorant of her fate, until the bundles were all tied up in the morning, and the coffle ready to depart; when, coming with some other young women to see the coffle set out, her master took her by the hand and delivered her to the singing man. Never was a face of serenity more suddenly changed into one of the deepest distress; the terror she manifested on having the load put upon her head, and the rope fastened around her neck, and the sorrow with which she bade adieu to her companions, were truly affecting . . . .

Being now [June 2, 1797] arrived within a short distance of Pisania, from whence my journey originally commenced, and learning that my friend Karfa was not likely to meet with an immediate opportunity of selling his slaves on the Gambia, it occurred to me to suggest to him, that he would find it for his interest to leave them at Jindey, until a market should offer. Karfa agreed with me in this opinion, and hired, from the chief man of the town, huts for their accommodation, and a piece of land on which to employ them, in raising corn, and other provisions for their maintenance. With regard to himself, he declared that he would not quit me until my departure from Africa. We set out accordingly, Karfa, myself, and one of the Foulahs belonging to the coffle, early on the morning of the 9th; but although I was now approaching the end of my tedious and toilsome journey, and expected, in another day, to meet with countrymen and friends, I could not part, for the last time, with my unfortunate fellow-travellers, doomed, as I knew most of them to be, to a life of captivity and slavery in a foreign land, without great emotion. During a wearisome peregrination of more than five hundred British miles, exposed to the burning rays of a tropical sun, these poor slaves, amidst their own infinitely greater sufferings, would commiserate mine; and frequently, of their own accord, bring water to quench my thirst, and at night collect branches and leaves to prepare me a bed in the Wilderness. We parted with reciprocal expressions of regret and benediction. My good wishes and prayers were all I could bestow upon them, and it afforded me some consolation to be told that they were sensible I had no more to give . . . .

[O]n the 15th [June], the ship *Charles-Town*, an American vessel, commanded by Mr. Charles Harris, entered the river. She came for slaves, intending to touch at Goree to fill up, and to proceed from thence to South Carolina. As the European merchants on the Gambia had at this time a great many slaves on hand, they agreed with the captain to purchase the whole of his cargo, consisting chiefly of rum and tobacco, and deliver him slaves to the amount, in the course of two days. This afforded me such an opportunity of returning (through a circuitous route) to my native country, as I thought was not to be neglected. I therefore immediately engaged my passage in this vessel for America. . . . I embarked at Kaye on the 17th day of June.

Our passage down the river was tedious and fatiguing, and the weather was so hot, moist, and unhealthy, that before our arrival at Goree, four of the seamen, the surgeon, and three of the slaves, had died of fevers. At Goree we were detained, for want of provisions, until the beginning of October.

The number of slaves received on board this vessel, both on the Gambia, and at Goree, was one hundred and thirty, of whom about twenty-five had been, I suppose, of free condition in Africa, as most of those, being Bushreens, could write a little Arabic. Nine of them had become captives in the religious war between Abdulkader and Damel, mentioned in the latter part of the preceding chapter. Two of the others had seen me as I passed through Bondou, and many of them had heard of me in the interior countries. My conversation with them, in their native language, gave them great comfort; and as the surgeon was dead, I consented to act in a medical capacity in his room for the remainder of the voyage. They had in truth need of every consolation in my power to bestow; not that I observed any wanton acts of cruelty practised either by the master, or the seamen, towards them; but the mode of confining and securing Negroes in the American slave ships, owing chiefly to the weakness of their crews, being abundantly more rigid and severe than in British vessels employed in the same traffic, made these poor creatures to suffer greatly, and a general sickness prevailed amongst them. Besides the three who died on the Gambia, and six or eight while we remained at Goree, eleven perished at sea, and many of the survivors were reduced to a very weak and emaciated condition.

In the midst of these distresses, the vessel, after having been three weeks at sea, became so extremely leaky, as to require constant exertion at the pumps. It was found necessary, therefore, to take some of the ablest of the Negro men out of irons, and employ them at this labour, in which they were often worked beyond their strength. This produced a complication of miseries not easily to be described. We were, however, relieved much sooner than I expected, for the leak continuing to gain upon us, notwithstanding our utmost exertions to clear the vessel, the seamen insisted on bearing away for the West Indies, as affording the only chance of saving our lives. Accordingly, after some objections on the part of the master, we directed our course for Antigua, and fortunately made that island in about thirty-five days after our departure from Goree. Yet even at this juncture we narrowly escaped destruction, for on approaching the north-west side of the island, we struck on Diamond Rock, and got into St John's harbour with great difficulty. The vessel was afterwards condemned as unfit for sea, and the slaves, as I have heard, were ordered to be sold for the benefit of the owners . . . .

21. Britain and the United States enact legislation to abolish the trade in slaves.

In 1807, the governments of Britain and the United States enacted legislation to restrict the trade in slaves from Africa. By terms of its legislative act, Great Britain aimed to end the export trade from Africa, making it illegal for anyone, no matter the nationality of the offender, to engage in the "Purchase, Sale, Barter, or Transfer of Slaves, or of Persons intended to be sold, transferred, used, or dealt with as Slaves, practised and carried on, in, at, to or from any Part of the Coast or Countries of Africa." The United States focused on the import trade to North America rather than the export trade from Africa, prohibiting the importation of any "negro, mulatto, or person of colour, with intent to hold, sell, or dispose of such . . . as a slave, or to be held to service or labour."[21]

Great Britain, An Act for the abolition of the slave trade, June 10 and 24, 1806, May 1, 1807.

Whereas the Two Houses of Parliament did, by their Resolutions of the Tenth and Twenty-fourth Days of June One thousand eight hundred and six, severally resolve, upon certain Grounds therein mentioned, that they would, with all practicable Expedition, take effectual Measures for the Abolition of the African Slave Trade, in such Manner, and at such Period as might be deemed adviseable: And Whereas it is fit upon all and each of the Grounds mentioned in the said Resolutions, that the same should be forthwith abolished and prohibited, and declared to be unlawful; be it therefore enacted by the King's most Excellent Majesty, by and with the Advice and Consent of the Lords Spiritual and Temporal, and Commons, in this present Parliament assembled, and by the Authority of the same, That from and after the First Day of May One thousand eight hundred and seven, the African Slave Trade, and all manner of dealing and trading in the Purchase, Sale, Barter, or Transfer of Slaves, or of Persons intended to be sold, transferred, used, or dealt with as

---

[21] Elizabeth Donnan, ed., *Documents Illustrative of the History of the Slave Trade to America* (Washington, DC: Carnegie Institute, 1930), vol. 2, pp. 659–669; vol. 4, pp. 666–671. Reprinted with the agreement of the Carnegie Institute.

Slaves, practised and carried on, in, at, to or from any Part of the Coast or Countries of Africa, shall be, and the same is hereby utterly abolished, prohibited, and declared to be unlawful; and also that all and all manner of dealing, either by way of Purchase, Sale, Barter, or Transfer, or by means of any other Contract or Agreement whatever, relating to any Slaves, or to any Persons intended to be used or dealt with as Slaves, for the Purpose of such Slaves or Persons being removed and transported either immediately or by Transhipment at Sea or otherwise, directly or indirectly from Africa, or from any Island, Country, Territory, or Place whatever, in the West Indies, or in any other Part of America, not being in the Dominion, Possession, or Occupation of His Majesty, to any other Island, Country, Territory or Place whatever, is hereby in like Manner utterly abolished, prohibited, and declared to be unlawful; and if any of His Majesty's Subjects, or any Person or Persons resident within this United Kingdom, or any of the Islands, Colonies, Dominions, or Territories thereto belonging, or in His Majesty's Occupation or Possession, shall from and after the Day aforesaid, by him or themselves, or by his or their Factors or Agents or otherwise howsoever, deal or trade in, purchase, sell, barter, or transfer, or contract or agree for the dealing or trading in, purchasing, selling, bartering, or transferring of any Slave or Slaves, or any Person or Persons intended to be sold, transferred, used, or dealt with as a Slave or Slaves contrary to the Prohibitions of this Act, he or they so offending shall forfeit and pay for every such Offence the Sum of One hundred Pounds of lawful Money of Great Britain for each and every Slave so purchased, sold, bartered, or transferred, or contracted or agreed for as aforesaid, the One Moiety thereof to the Use of His Majesty, His Heirs and Successors, and the other Moiety to the Use of any Person who shall inform, sue, and prosecute for the same. . . .

And be it further enacted, That from and after the said First Day of May One thousand eight hundred and seven, it shall be unlawful for any of His Majesty's Subjects, or any Person or Persons resident in this United Kingdom, or in any of the Colonies, Territories or Dominions thereunto belonging, or in His Majesty's Possession or Occupation, to carry away or remove, or knowingly and wilfully to procure, aid, or assist in the carrying away or removing, as Slaves, or for the Purpose of being sold, transferred, used, or dealt with as Slaves, any of the Subjects or Inhabitants of Africa, or of any Island, Country, Territory, or Place in the West Indies, or any other Part of America, whatsoever, not being in the Dominion, Possession, or Occupation of His Majesty, either immediately or by Transhipment at Sea or otherwise, directly or indirectly from Africa, or from any such Island, Country, Territory, or Place as aforesaid, to any other Island, Country, Territory, or Place whatever. . . .

And Whereas it may happen, That during the present or future Wars, Ships or Vessels may be seized or detained as Prize, on board whereof Slaves or Natives of Africa, carried and detained as Slaves, being the Property of His Majesty's Enemies, or otherwise liable to Condemnation as Prize of War, may be taken or found, and it is necessary to direct in what Manner such Slaves or Natives of Africa shall be hereafter treated and disposed of: And Whereas it is also necessary to direct and provide for the Treatment and Disposal of any Slaves or Natives of Africa carried, removed, treated or dealt with as Slaves, who shall be unlawfully carried away or removed contrary to the Prohibitions aforesaid, or any of them, and shall be afterwards found on board any Ship or Vessel liable to Seizure under this Act, or any other Act of Parliament made for restraining or prohibiting the African Slave Trade, or shall be elsewhere lawfully seized as forfeited under this or any other such Act of Parliament as aforesaid; and it is expedient to encourage the Captors, Seizors and Prosecutors thereof; Be it therefore further enacted, That all Slaves and all Natives of Africa, treated, dealt with, carried, kept or detained as Slaves, which shall at any Time from and after the said First Day of May next be seized or taken as Prize of War, or liable to Forfeiture, under this or any other Act of Parliament made for restraining or prohibiting the African Slave Trade, shall and may, for the Purposes only of Seizure, Prosecution, and Condemnation as Prize or as Forfeitures, be considered, treated, taken, and adjudged as Slaves and Property, in the same Manner as Negro Slaves have been heretofore considered, treated, taken, and adjudged, when seized as Prize of War, or as forfeited for any Offence against the Laws of Trade and Navigation respectively; but the same shall be condemned as Prize of War, or as forfeited to the sole Use of His Majesty, His Heirs and Successors, for the Purpose only of divesting and barring all other Property, Right, Title, or Interest whatever, which before existed, or might afterwards be set up or claimed in or to such Slaves or Natives of Africa so seized, prosecuted and condemned; and the same nevertheless shall in no case be liable to be sold, disposed of, treated or dealt with as Slaves, by or on the Part of His Majesty, His Heirs or Successors, or by or on the Part of any Person or Persons claiming or to claim from, by or under His Majesty, His Heirs and Successors, or under or by force of any such Sentence of Condemnation: Provided always, that it shall be lawful for His Majesty, His Heirs and Successors, and such Officers, Civil or Military, as shall, by any general or special Order of the King in Council, be from Time to Time appointed and empowered to receive, protect, and provide for such Natives of Africa as shall be so condemned, either to enter and enlist the same, or any of them, into His Majesty's Land or Sea Service as Soldiers, Seamen or Marines, or to bind the same, or any of them, whether of full Age or not, as Apprentices, for any Term not exceeding Fourteen Years, to such Person or Persons, in such Place or Places, and upon such Terms and Conditions, and subject to such Regulations, as to His Majesty shall seem meet, and as shall by any general or special Order of His Majesty in Council be in that Behalf directed and appointed; and any Indenture of Apprenticeship duly made and executed, by any Person or Persons to be for that Purpose appointed by any such Order in Council, for

any Term not exceeding Fourteen Years, shall be of the same Force and Effect as if the Party thereby bound as an Apprentice had himself or herself, when of full Age upon good Consideration, duly executed the same; and every such Native of Africa who shall be so enlisted or entered as aforesaid into any of His Majesty's Land or Sea Forces as a Soldier, Seaman, or Marine, shall be considered, treated, and dealt with in all Respects as if he had voluntarily so enlisted or entered himself.

United States of America, Act to prohibit the importation of slaves into the United States, March 2, 1807.

An Act to prohibit the importation of Slaves into any place within the jurisdiction of the United States, from and after the first day of January, in the year of our Lord one thousand eight hundred and eight.

Be it enacted by the Senate and House of Representatives of the United States of America in Congress assembled, That from and after the first day of January, one thousand eight hundred and eight, it shall not be lawful to import or bring into the United States or the territories thereof from any foreign kingdom, place, or country, any negro, mulatto, or person of colour, with intent to hold, sell, or dispose of such negro, mulatto, or person of colour, as a slave, or to be held to service or labour.

Sec. 2. *And be it further enacted,* That no citizen or citizens of the United States, or any other person, shall, from and after the first day of January, in the year of our Lord one thousand eight hundred and eight, for himself, or themselves, or any other person whatsoever, either as master, factor, or owner, build, fit, equip, load or otherwise prepare any ship or vessel, in any port or place within the jurisdiction of the United States, nor shall cause any ship or vessel to sail from any port or place within the same, for the purpose of procuring any negro, mulatto, or person of colour, from any foreign kingdom, place, or country, to be transported to any port or place whatsoever, within the jurisdiction of the United States, to be held, sold, or disposed of as slaves, or to be held to service or labour; and if any ship or vessel shall be so fitted out for the purpose aforesaid, or shall be caused to sail so as aforesaid, every such ship or vessel, her tackle, apparel, and furniture, shall be forfeited to the United States, and shall be liable to be seized, prosecuted, and condemned in any of the circuit courts or district courts, for the district where the said ship or vessel may be found or seized.

Sec. 3. *And be it further enacted*, That all and every person so building, fitting out, equipping, loading, or otherwise preparing or sending away, any ship or vessel, knowing or intending that the same shall be employed in such trade or business, from and after the first day of January, one thousand eight hundred and eight, contrary to the true intent and meaning of this act, or any ways aiding or abetting therein, shall severally forfeit and pay twenty thousand dollars, one moiety thereof to the use of the United States, and the other moiety to the use of any person or persons who shall sue for and prosecute the same to effect.

Sec. 4. *And be it further enacted*, If any citizen or citizens of the United States or any person resident within the jurisdiction of the same, shall, from and after the first day of January, one thousand eight hundred and eight, take on board, receive or transport from any of the coasts or kingdoms of Africa, or from any other foreign kingdom, place, or country, any negro, mulatto, or person of colour, in any ship or vessel, for the purpose of selling them in any port or place within the jurisdiction of the United States as slaves, or to be held to service or labour or shall be in any ways aiding or abetting therein, such citizen or citizens, or person, shall severally forfeit and pay five thousand dollars, one moiety thereof to the use of any person or persons who shall sue for and prosecute the same to effect; and every such ship or vessel in which such negro, mulatto, or person of colour, shall have been taken on board, received, or transported as aforesaid, her tackle, apparel, and furniture, and the goods and effects which shall be found on board the same, shall be forfeited to the United States,

and shall be liable to be seized, prosecuted, and condemned in any of the circuit courts or district courts in the district where the said ship or vessel may he found or seized. And neither the importer, nor any person or persons claiming from or under him, shall hold any right or title whatsoever to any negro, mulatto, or person of colour, nor to the service or labour thereof, who may be imported or brought within the United States, or territories thereof, in violation of this law, but the same shall remain subject to any regulations not contravening the provisions of this act, which the legislatures of the several states or territories at any time hereafter may make, for disposing of any such negro, mulatto, or person of colour.

Sec. 5. *And be it further enacted*, That if any person or persons whatsoever, shall, from and after the first day of January, one thousand eight hundred and eight, purchase or sell any negro, mulatto, or person of colour, for a slave, or to be held to service or labour, who shall have been imported, or brought from any foreign kingdom, place, or country, or from the dominions of any foreign state, immediately adjoining to the United States, into any port or place within the jurisdiction of the United States, after the last day of December, one thousand eight hundred and seven, knowingly at the time of such purchase or sale, such negro, mulatto, or person of colour, was brought within the jurisdiction of the United States as aforesaid, such purchaser and seller shall severally forfeit and pay for every negro, mulatto, or person of colour, so purchased or sold as aforesaid, eight hundred dollars; one moiety thereof to the United States, and the other moiety to the use of any person or persons who shall sue for and prosecute to the same effect: *Provided*, that the aforesaid forfeiture shall not extend to the seller or purchaser of any negro, mulatto, or person of colour, who may be sold or disposed of in virtue of any regulation which may hereafter be made by any of the legislatures of the several states in that respect, in pursuance of this act, and the constitution of the United States . . . .

22. Ali Eisami recounts how he was taken into slavery and then freed.

Though Britain outlawed the trade in slaves and sent armed vessels to patrol the West African coast and intercept slaving ships, the export trade across the Atlantic continued, especially so long as slavery remained legal throughout the Americas. Between 1801 and 1867, more than three million West Africans were transported as slaves across the Atlantic. Some of these slaves were victims of a series of religious wars that erupted in West Africa during the first decades of the nineteenth century when Islamic reformers engaged in jihads (holy wars) against societies that they considered had become corrupt. Ali Eisami was born in the late 1780s in the Gazir province of Bornu, an Islamic state in the northeast of present-day Nigeria. The relatively privileged son of a Muslim scholar-teacher, Ali Eisami found his life transformed after 1808 when Fulbe reformers attacked Bornu. Ali was taken into slavery in 1818 and, after a series of transactions, ended up being sold to European slave merchants. By chance— the British had only two ships patrolling the entire West African coast in 1818— the vessel on which Ali Eisami was being transported to the Americas was interdicted, and Ali was released in Sierra Leone, at that time the only significant British territorial holding in West Africa. Ali Eisami dictated the story of his life to S. W. Koelle, a German linguist employed by the Church Missionary Society.[22]

In the town of Magriari Tapsoua, there was a man, named Mamade Atshi, son of Kodo, and he was my father. He was already a priest when he went and sought to marry my mother: so when their great people had consulted together, and come to a mutual understanding, my father prepared himself, sought a house, and the time for the wedding was fixed, which having arrived, my mother was married, and brought into my father's house. After they had been living in their house one year, my elder sister, Sarah, was born, next my elder brother Mamade, and after him myself; next to me, my younger sister Pesam, and then my younger sister Kadei were born; on their being born, our mother did not bear any more. As to myself, I was put to school when I was seven years of age. Then my younger sister Kadei and mine elder brother Mamade died, so that only three of us remained, of whom two were females and I alone a male. When I had been reading at school till I was nine years of age,

they took me from school, and put me into the house of circumcision; and after passing through the rite of circumcision, I returned to school, and having remained there two years longer, I left off reading the Koran. When I left off reading the Koran, I was eleven years old.

Two years later, there was an eclipse of the sun, on a Saturday, in the cold season. One year after this, when, in the weeding time, in the rainy season, about two o'clock in the afternoon, we looked to the West, the Kaman-locusts were coming from the West, forming a straight line (across the sky), as if one of God's thunder-storms were coming, so that day was turned into night. When the time of the locusts was past, the famine Ngeseneski took place, but did not last long, only three months. After it, the pestilence came, and made much havock in Bornu, completely destroying all the great people. Next, the wars of the Phula [Fulbe] came up. In the rainy season the Phula put to flight the

---

[22] Sigismund William Koelle, *African Native Literature, or Proverbs, Tales, Fables, & Historical Fragments in the Kanuri or Bornu Language* (London: Church Missionary House, 1854), pp. 248–56.

Ali Eisami. *Source:* S.W. Koelle, *Grammar of the Bornu or Kanuri Language* (London: Church Missionary House, 1854), frontispiece.

Deia King with his family, and, as they were coming to our town, my Father said to me, "My son, times will be hard for you: this year thou hast been nineteen years of age, and though I said that, when thou art twenty, I will seek a girl for thee, and let thee marry, yet now the Phula have unsettled the land, and we do not know what to do: but what God has ordained for us, that shall we experience." When the guinea-corn which we were weeding had become ripe, and the harvest was past, the Phula roused both us and the Deiaese, so we went, and remained near the Capital, till the Phula arose and came to the Capital, on a Sunday, about two o'clock in the afternoon. When they were coming, the Commander went out to encounter them; but, after they had met and been engaged in a battle till four o'clock, the Commander's power was at an end. The King arose, passed out through the Eastgate, and started for Kurnoa. Then the Commander left the Phula, and followed the King; on seeing which, all the Phula came and entered the Capital. Af-

ter they had entered, the tidings reached us about seven o'clock in the evening. When the tidings came, none knew where to lay their head. On the following morning, a great priest of the Phula said to us, "Let every one go and remain in his house, the war is over: let all the poor go, and each cultivate land!" Then my father called his younger brother, and we arose and went to our town; but when we came, there was nothing at all to eat. So my father called my mother at night, when all the people were gone, and said to her, "This our town is ruined; if we remain, the Phula will make an end of us: arise, and load our things upon our children!" Now there was a town, Magerari by name, which is subject to the Shoas; and the Phula never meddle with any place that is subject to the Shoas. So we arose, and went to that town; but when we had lived there one year, the King went, turned the Phula out of the Capital, and went in himself and abode there.

About one year after this event, when my father had died, as it were to-day, at two o'clock in the afternoon, and we had not yet buried him, intending to do so next day, then we slept, and on the following morning, my mother called me, and my elder and my younger sister, and said to us, "Live well together, ye three; behold, your father lies here a corpse, and I am following your father." Now there was just a priest with us who said to my mother, "Why dost thou say such things to thy children?" but my mother replied to the priest, "I say these things to my children in truth." Then she called me, and I rose up, went, and sat down before her. When I had sat down, she said to me, "Stretch out thy legs, that I may lay my head upon thy thighs." So I stretched out my legs, and she took her head, and laid it upon my thighs; but when the priest who was staying with us saw that my mother was laying her head upon my thighs, he arose, came, sat down by me, stretched out his legs, and took my mother's head from my thighs, and laid it upon his own. Then that moment our Lord sought my mother.

After this there came tears from mine eyes, and when the priest saw it, he said to me, "Let me not see tears in thine eyes! will thy father and thy mother arise again, and sit down, that thou mayest see them, if thou weepest?" I attended to what the priest said, and did not weep any more. With the corpse of our father before us, and with the corpse of our mother before us, we did not know what to do, till the people of the town went and dug graves for both of them, side by side, in one place, and came back again, when we took the corpses, carried and buried them, and then returned.

After waiting two months at home, I took my younger sister, and gave her to a friend of my father's in marriage, my elder sister being already provided with a husband. On one occasion I got up after night had set in, without saying any thing to my little mother, took my father's spear, his charms, and one book which he had, set out on a journey, and walked in the night, so that it was not yet day when I reached the town of Shagou, where there was a friend of my father's, a Shoa; and, when I came to the dwelling place of this friend of my father's, they were just in the place for prayer. When I came to him, and he saw me, he knew me, and I knew him. I having saluted him, he asked me, "Where is thy father?" I replied to him, saying, "My father is no more, and my mother is no more, so I left both my elder and my younger sister, and came to thee"; whereupon he said to me, "Come, my son, we will stay together; thy father did do good to me, and now since he is no more, and thou didst like me and come to me, I also like thee: I will do to thee what I do to my own son."

After I had been there about three years, I called a companion, saying, "Come and accompany me!" for I had a friend in a town of the name of Gubr. The youth arose, and we started together, but as we were going towards the town of Gubr, seven Phula waylaid us, seized us, tied our hands upon our backs, fettered us, put us in the way, and then we went till it became day. When it was day, both they and we became hungry in a hostile place, the land being the land of Ngesm. In this place we sat down, and ate the fruit of a certain tree called Ganga, till it became dark, when they took us again, and carried us to

the town of Ngololo to market. On that day Hausas bought us, took us into a house, and put iron fetters on our feet; then, after five days, we arose, and were twenty-two days, ere we arrived in the Hausa land. When we arrived, we went to a town called Sangaya, where there are a great many dates. In this town we remained during the months of Asham, Soual, and Kide; but when only three days of (the month of) Atsbi were passed, they roused me up, and in a week we came to the Katsina Capital, where they slew the Easter-lamb, and after five days they rose again, and we started for Yauri. After marching a fortnight, we arrived at the Yauri Capital. Here the Hausas sold us, and took their goods, whilst Bargas bought us. The Bargas roused us up, and when we came to their town, the man who had bought me, did not leave me alone at all: I had iron fetters round my feet, both by night and by day. After I had stayed with him seven days, he took me, and brought me to the town of Sai, where a Yoruban bought me.

The Yoruban who bought me was a son of the Katunga King; he liked me, and called me to sit down before him, and, on seeing my tattoo-marks, he said to me, "Wast thou the son of a King in your country?" To this I replied, "My father, as for me, I will not tell lies, because times are evil, and our Lord has given me into slavery: my father was a scholar." Then he said, "As for this youth and his father, his father must have been a fine man; I will not treat him ill"; and so he kept me in his house. In this place I remained a long time, so that I understood their language. After I had been there four years, a war arose: now, all the slaves who went to the war, became free [these were likely among the soldiers who captured Samuel Crowther—see the next extract]; so when the slaves heard these good news, they all ran there, and the Yorubans saw it. The friend of the man who had bought me, said to him, "If thou dost not sell this slave of thine, he will run away, and go [to] the war, so that thy cowries will be lost, for this fellow has sound eyes." Then the man took hold of me, and bound me, and his three sons took me to the town of Atshashe, where white men had landed; then they took off the fetters from my feet, and carried me before them to the white people, who bought me, and put an iron round my neck. After having bought all the people, they took us, brought us to the seashore, brought a very small canoe, and transferred us one by one to the large vessel.

The people of the great vessel were wicked: when we had been shipped, they took away all the small pieces of cloth which were on our bodies, and threw them into the water, then they took chains, and fettered two together. We in the vessel, great and small, were seven hundred, whom the white men had bought. We were all fettered round our feet, and all the stoutest died of thirst, for there was no water. Every morning they had to take many, and throw them into the water: so we entreated God by day and by night, and, after three months, when it pleased God to send breezes, we arose in the morning, and the doors were opened. When we had all come on deck, one slave was standing by us, and we beheld the sky in the midst of the water.

When I looked at the horizon, mine eye saw something far away, like trees. On seeing this, I called the slave, and said to him, "I see a forest yonder, far away"; whereupon he said to me, "Show it to me with thy finger!" When I had shown it to him, and he had seen the place at which my finger pointed, he ran to one of the white men who liked me, and would give me his shirts to mend, and then gave me food, he being a benefactor; now, when the slave told it him, the white man who was holding a roasted fowl in his hand, came to me, together with the slave. This slave who understood their language, and also the Hausa, came and asked me, saying, "Show me with thy finger what thou seest, that the white man also may see it!" I showed it, and when the white man brought his eye, and laid it upon my finger, he also saw what I pointed at. He left the roasted fowl which he held in his hand and wanted to eat, before me, and ran to their Captain. Then I took the fowl, and put it into my bag.

All of them ran, and loaded the big big guns with powder and their very large iron. We, not knowing what it was, called the Hausa who understood it, and said to him, "Why do the white men prepare their guns?" and he said to us, "What thou sawest were not trees, but a vessel of war is coming towards us." We did not believe it, and said, "We have never seen any one make war in the midst of water"; but, after waiting a little, it came, and when it was near us, our own white men fired a gun at them; but it still went on. When the white men with us had fired a gun nine times, the white man of war was vexed and fired one gun at our vessel, the ball of which bit the middle mast with those very large sails, cut it off, and threw it into the water. Then the white men with us ran to the bottom of the vessel, and hid themselves. The war-chief, a short man, of the name of Captain Hick, brought his vessel side by side with ours, whereupon all the war-men came into our vessel, sword in band, took all our own white men, and carried them to their vessel. Then they called all of us, and when we formed a line, and stood up in one place, they counted us, and said, "Sit down!" So we sat down, and they took off all the fetters from our feet, and threw them into the water, and they gave us clothes that we might cover our nakedness, they opened the water-casks, that we might drink water to the full, and we also ate food, till we had enough. In the evening they brought drums, and gave them to us, so that we played till it was morning. We said, "Now our Lord has taken us out of our slavery," and thanked him. Then came a white man, stood before me, and, after looking at me, slapped both my cheeks, took me to the place where they cooked food, and said to me, "Thou hast to cook, that thy people may eat." So I cooked food, and distributed the water with mine own hand, till they brought us and landed us in this town [Freetown, Sierra Leone], where we were a week in the King's house, and then they came and distributed us among the different towns.

We went and settled in the forests, at Bathurst. We met a white man in this town whose name was Mr. Decker, and who had a wife, and was a reverend priest. On the following morning we all went, and stood up in his house, and having seen all of us, he came, took hold of my hand, and drew me into his house, and I did not fear him; but I heard inside the house that my people without were talking, and saying, "The white man has taken Ali, and put him into the house, in order to slaughter him." So I looked at the white people, and they looked at me. When the white man arose and went to the top of the house, I prepared myself, and thought, "If this white man takes a knife, and I see it in his hand, I will hold it"; but the white man was gone up to fetch shirts, and trowsers, and caps down. On coming down, he said to me, "Stand up!" So when I stood up, he put me into a shirt, put trowsers over my legs, gave me a jacket, and put a cap upon my head. Then he opened the door, and when we came out, all our people were glad. He called a man who understood the white man's language, and said to him, "Say that this one is the chief of all his people"; then the man told me so.

When they carried us to the forest the day before, my wife followed after me; and on the day after our arrival the white man married us, and gave me my wife, so we went and remained in the house of our people.

The white man was a benefactor, and he liked me. But, after a few days, his wife became ill, so we took her, and carried her to the town of Hog-brook; and then the illness exceeded her strength, and our Lord sought her. After this he arose in our town, and we took his things, and carried them to Freetown, where he said to us, "Go, and remain quiet; I go to our own country, not knowing whether I shall come back again, or not." Then he shook hands with us, bid us farewell, and went to their own country.

Until now our Lord has preserved me, but "God knows what is to come," say the Bornuese. I also heard the great men say, "What is to come even a bird with a long neck cannot see, but our Lord only." This is an account of what I experienced from my childhood till to-day, and what I have been telling thee is now finished.

23. Samuel Crowther escapes slavery.

Samuel Crowther was born around 1806 in the southwestern part of present-day Nigeria. His father was a weaver, his mother a descendant of one of the Yoruba kings of Old Oyo and a renowned priestess in her own right. Crowther's life intersected with that of Ali Eisami in a number of ways. (See document 22.) It was Yoruba people who at one point acquired Ali Eisami as a slave, before selling him to European merchants. On the other hand, Crowther's hometown was sacked by a Muslim army made up of freed slaves from Old Oyo, the same town where Eisami had spent time as a slave. Crowther was captured by these Islamic reformers in 1821–22 and sold to merchants in Lagos who placed him on a slave ship bound for Brazil. The slave ship was intercepted by a British man of war, and Crowther and his fellow captives put ashore at Freetown, Sierra Leone. Crowther converted to Christianity, became an active member of the Church Missionary Society, and was consecrated in 1864 as the first Anglican bishop of West Africa.[23]

---

[23] *Journals of the Rev. James Frederick Schön and Mr. Samuel Crowther, who with the Sanction of Her Majesty's Government Accompanied the Expedition up the Niger, in 1841, in Behalf of the Church Missionary Society. With Appendices, and Map.* (London: Hatchard and Son, 1842), pp. 371–85.

Letter of Mr. Samuel Crowther to the Rev. William Jowett, in 1837, then Secretary of the Church Missionary Society, detailing the circumstances connected with his being sold as a slave.

Fourah Bay, Feb. 22, 1837

Rev. and Dear Sir,

As I think it will be interesting to you to know something of the conduct of Providence in my being brought to this Colony, where I have the happiness to enjoy the privilege of the Gospel, I give you a short account of it; hoping I may be excused if I should prove rather tedious in some particulars.

I suppose some time about the commencement of the year 1821, I was in my native country, enjoying the comforts of father and mother, and the affectionate love of brothers and sisters. From this period I must date the unhappy—but which I am now taught, in other respects, to call blessed day, which I shall never forget in my life. I call it *unhappy* day, because it was the day in which I was violently turned out of my father's house, and separated from relations; and in which I was made to experience what is called to be in slavery:—with regard to its being called *blessed*, it being the day which Providence had marked out for me to set out on my journey from the land of heathenism, superstition, and vice, to a place where His Gospel is preached.

For some years, war had been carried on in my Eyò [Oyo] country, which was always attended with much devastation and bloodshed; the women, such men as had surrendered or were caught, with the children, were taken captives. The enemies who carried on these wars were principally the Eyò Mahomedans, with whom my country abounds—with the Foulahs [Fulbe], and such foreign slaves as had escaped from their owners, joined together, making a formidable force of about 20,000, who annoyed the whole country. They had no other employment but selling slaves to the Spaniards and Portuguese on the coast.

The morning in which my town, Ochógu [Osugun], shared the same fate which many others had experienced, was fair and delightful; and most of the inhabitants were engaged in their respective occupations. We were preparing breakfast without any apprehension; when, about 9 o'clock A.M., a rumour was spread in the town, that the enemies had approached with intentions of hostility. It was not long after when they had almost surrounded the town, to prevent any escape of the inhabitants; the town being rudely fortified with a wooden fence, about four miles in circumference, containing about 12,000 inhabitants, which would produce 3,000 fighting men. The inhabitants not being duly prepared, some not being at home—those who were, having about six gates to defend, as well as many weak places about the fence to guard against, and, to say in a few words, the men being surprised, and therefore confounded–the enemies entered the town after about three or four hours' resistance. Here a most sorrowful scene imaginable was to be witnessed!—women, some with three, four, or six children clinging to their arms, with the infants on their backs, and such baggage as they could carry on their heads, running as fast as they could through prickly shrubs, which, hooking their . . . loads, drew them down from the heads of the bearers. While they found it impossible to go along with their loads, they endeavoured only to save themselves and their children: even this was impracticable with those who had many children to care for. While they were endeavouring to disentangle themselves from the ropy shrubs, they were overtaken and caught by the enemies with a noose of rope thrown over the neck of every individual, to be led in the manner of goats tied together, under the drove of one man. In many cases a family was violently divided between three or four enemies, who each led his away, to see one another no more. Your humble servant was thus caught—with his mother, two sisters (one an infant about ten months old), and a cousin—while endeavouring to escape in the manner above described. My load consisted in nothing else than my bow, and five arrows in the quiver; the bow I had lost in the shrub, while I was extricating myself, before I could think of making any use of it against my enemies. The last view I had of my father was when he came from the fight, to give us the signal to flee: he entered into our house, which was burnt some time back for some offence given by my father's adopted son. Hence I never saw him more—Here I must take thy leave, unhappy, comfortless father!—I learned, some time afterward, that he was killed in another battle.

Our conquerors were Eyọ̀ Mahomedans, who led us away through the town. On our way, we met a man sadly wounded on the head, struggling between life and death. Before we got half way through the town, some Foulahs, among the enemies themselves, hostilely separated my cousin from our number . . . The town on fire . . . We were led by my grandfather's house, already desolate; and in a few minutes after we left the town to the mercy of the flame, never to enter or see it any more. . . . We were now out of Ochó-gu, going into a town called Iseh'i [Iseyin], the rendezvous of the enemies, about twenty miles from our town. On the way, we saw our grandmother at a distance, with about three or four of my other cousins taken with her, for a few minutes. . . . Several other captives were held in the same manner as we were: grandmothers, mothers, children, and cousins, were all led captives. O sorrowful prospect!—The aged women were to be greatly pitied, not being able to walk so fast as their children and grandchildren: they were often threatened with being put to death upon the spot, to get rid of them, if they would not go as fast as others; and they were often as wicked in their practice as in their words. O pitiful sight! Whose heart would not bleed to have seen this? Yes, such is the state of barbarity in the heathen land. Evening came on; and coming to a spring of water, we drank a great quantity; which served us for breakfast, with a little parched corn and dried meat previously prepared by our victors for themselves.

During our march to Iseh'i, we passed several towns and villages which had been reduced to ashes. It was almost midnight before we reached the town, where we passed our doleful first night in bondage. . . .

On the next morning our cords being taken off our necks, we were brought to the Chief of our captors—for there were many other Chiefs—as trophies at his feet. In a little while, a separation took place, when my sister and I fell to the share of the Chief, and my mother and the infant to the victors. We dared not vent our grief by loud cries, but by very heavy sobs. My mother, with the infant, was led away, comforted with the promise that she should see us again, when we should leave Iseh'i for Dah'dah [Dada], the town of the Chief. In a few hours after, it was soon agreed upon that I should be bartered for a horse in Ishe'i, that very day. Thus was I separated from my mother and sister for the first time in my life; and the latter not to be seen more in this world. Thus, in the space of twenty-four hours, being deprived of liberty and all other comforts, I was made the property of three different persons. About the space of two months, when the chief was to leave Iseh'i for his own town, the horse, which was then only taken on trial, not being approved of, I was restored to the chief, who took me to Dah'dah; where I had the happiness to meet my mother and infant sister again with joy, which could be described by nothing else but tears of love and affection; and on the part of my infant sister, with leaps of joy in every manner possible. Here I lived for about three months, going for grass for horses with my fellow captives. I now and then visited my mother and sister in our captor's house, without any fears or thoughts of being separated any more. My mother told me that she had heard of my sister; but I never saw her more.

At last, an unhappy evening arrived, when I was sent with a man to get some money at a neighbouring house. I went; but with some fears, for which I could not account; and, to my great astonishment, in a few minutes I was added to the number of many other captives, enfettered, to be led to the market-town early the next morning. My sleep went from me; I spent almost the whole night in thinking of my doleful situation, with tears and sobs, especially as my mother was in the same town, whom I had not visited for a day or two. There was another boy in the same situation with me: his mother was in Dah'dah. Being sleepless, I heard the first cock-crow. Scarcely the signal was given, when the traders arose, and loaded the men slaves with baggage. With one hand chained to the neck, we left the town. My little companion in affliction cried and begged much to be permitted to see his mother, but was soon silenced by punishment. Seeing this, I dared not speak, although I thought we passed by the very house my mother was in. Thus was I separated from my mother and sister, my then only comforts, to meet no more in this world of misery. After a few days' travel, we came to the market-town, I-jah'i [Ijaye]. Here I saw many who had escaped in our town to this place; or those who were in search of their relations, to set at liberty as many as they had the means of redeeming. Here we were under very close inspection, as there were many persons in search of their relations; and through that, many had escaped from their owners. In a few days I was sold to a Mahomedan woman, with whom I travelled to many towns in our way to the Popo country, on the coast, much resorted to by the Portuguese, to buy slaves. When we left I-jah'i, after many halts, we came to a town called Tó-ko [Itoko]. From I=jah'i to Tó-ko all spoke the Ebwah [Egba] dialect, but my mistress Eyò, my own dialect. Here I was a perfect stranger, having left my own Eyò country far behind. I lived in Tó-ko about three months; walked about with my owner's son with some degree of freedom, it being a place where my feet had never trod: and could I possibly have made my way out through many a ruinous town and village we had passed, I should have soon become a prey to some others, who would have gladly taken the advantage of me. . . .

Now and then my mistress would speak with me and her son, that we should by-and-bye go to the Popo country, where we should buy tobacco, and other fine things, to sell at our return. Now, thought I, this was the signal of my being sold to the Portuguese; who,

they often told me during our journey, were to be seen in that country. Being very thoughtful of this, my appetite forsook me, and in a few weeks I got the dysentery, which greatly preyed on me. I determined with myself that I would not go to the Popo country; but would make an end of myself, one way or another. In several nights I attempted strangling myself with my band; but had not courage enough to close the noose tight, so as to effect my purpose. May the Lord forgive me this sin! I determined, next, that I would leap out of the canoe into the river, when we should cross it in our way to that country. Thus was I thinking, when my owner, perceiving the great alteration that took place in me, sold me to some persons. Thus the Lord, while I knew Him not, led me not into temptation and delivered me from evil. After my price had been counted before my own eyes, I was delivered up to my new owners, with great grief and dejection of spirit, not knowing where I was now to be led. After the first cock-crowing, which was the usual time to set out with slaves, to prevent their being much acquainted with the way, for fear an escape should be made, we set out for Jabbo [Ijebu], the third dialect from mine.

After having arrived at Ik-ke-ku Yé-re [Ikereku-iwre], another town, we halted. In this place I renewed my attempt of strangling, several times at night; but could not effect my purpose. It was very singular, that no thought of making use of a knife ever entered my mind. However, it was not long before I was bartered, for tobacco, rum, and other articles. I remained here, in fetters, alone, for some time, before my owner could get as many slaves as he wanted. He feigned to treat us more civilly, by allowing us to sip a few drops of White Man's liquor, rum; which was so estimable an article, that none but chiefs could pay for a jar or glass vessel of four or five gallons: so much dreaded it was, that no one should take breath before he swallowed every sip, for fear of having the string of his throat cut by the spirit of the liquor. This made it so much more valuable.

I had to remain alone, again, in another town in Jabbo, the name of which I do not now remember, for about two months. From hence I was brought, after a few days' walk, to a slave-market, called I'-ko-sy [Ikosi], on the coast, on the bank of a large river, which very probably was the Lagos on which we were afterwards captured. The sight of the river terrified me exceedingly, for I had never seen any thing like it in my life. The people on the opposite bank are called E'-ko. Before sun-set, being bartered again for tobacco, I became another owner's. Nothing now terrified me more than the river, and the thought of going into another world. Crying was nothing now, to vent out my sorrow: my whole body became stiff. I was now bade to enter the river, to ford it to the canoe. Being fearful at my entering this extensive water, and being so cautious in every step I took, as if the next would bring me to the bottom, my motion was very awkward indeed. Night coming on, and the men having very little time to spare, soon carried me into the canoe, and placed me among the corn-bags, and supplied me with an Ab'-alah [steamed pudding] for my dinner. Almost in the same position I was placed I remained, with my Ab'-alah in my hand, quite confused in my thoughts, waiting only every moment our arrival at the new world; which we did not reach till about 4 o'clock in the morning. Here I got once more into another dialect, the fourth from mine; if I may not call it altogether another language, on account of now and then, in some words, there being a faint shadow of my own. Here I must remark that, during the whole night's voyage in the canoe, not a single thought of leaping into the river had entered my mind; but, on the contrary, the fear of the river occupied my thoughts.

Having now entered E'-ko [Lagos], I was permitted to go any way I pleased; there being no way of escape, on account of the river. In this place I met my two nephews, belonging to different masters. One part of the town was occupied by the Portuguese and Spaniards, who had come to buy slaves. Although I was in E'-ko more than three months, I never once saw a White Man; until one evening, when they took a walk, in company of about six, and came to the street of the

house in which I was living. Even then I had not the boldness to appear distinctly to look at them, being always suspicious that they had come for me: and my suspicion was not a fanciful one; for, in a few days after, I was made the eighth in number of the slaves of the Portuguese. Being a veteran in slavery, if I may be allowed the expression, and having no more hope of ever going to my country again, I patiently took whatever came; although it was not without a great fear and trembling that I received, for the first time, the touch of a White Man, who examined me whether I was sound or not. Men and boys were at first chained together, with a chain of about six fathoms in length, thrust through an iron fetter on the neck of every individual, and fastened at both ends with padlocks. In this situation the boys suffered the most: the men sometimes, getting angry, would draw the chain so violently, as seldom went without bruises on their poor little necks; especially the time to sleep, when they drew the chain so close to ease themselves of its weight, in order to be able to lie more conveniently, that we were almost suffocated, or bruised to death, in a room with one door, which was fastened as soon as we entered in, with no other passage for communicating the air, than the openings under the eaves-drop. Very often at night, when two or three individuals quarrelled or fought, the whole drove suffered punishment, without any distinction. At last, we boys had the happiness to be separated from the men, when their number was increased, and no more chain to spare: we were corded together, by ourselves. Thus we were going in and out, bathing together, and so on.—The female sex fared not much better.—Thus we were for nearly the space of four months.

About this time, intelligence was given that the English were cruising the coast. This was another subject of sorrow with us—that there must be war also on the sea as well as on land—a thing never heard of before, or imagined practicable. This delayed our embarkation. In the meanwhile, the other slaves which were collected in Popo, and were intended to be conveyed into the vessel the nearest way from that place, were brought into E'-ko, among us. Among this number was Joseph Bartholomew, my Brother in the service of the Church Missionary Society.

After a few weeks' delay, we were embarked, at night, in canoes, from E'-ko to the beach; and on the following morning were put on board the vessel, which immediately sailed away. The crew being busy embarking us, 187 in number, had no time to give us either breakfast or supper; and we, being unaccustomed to the motion of the vessel, employed the whole of this day in sea-sickness, which rendered the greater part of us less fit to take any food whatever. On the very same evening, we were surprised by two English men-of-war; and on the next morning found ourselves in the hands of new conquerors, whom we at first very much dreaded, they being armed with long swords. In the morning, being called up from the hold, we were astonished to find ourselves among two very large men-of-war and several other brigs. The men-of-war were, His Majesty's ships *Myrmidon*, Captain H. J. Leeke, and *Iphigenia*, Captain Sir Robert Mends, who captured us on the 7th of April 1822, on the river Lagos.

Our owner was bound with his sailors; except the cook, who was preparing our breakfast. Hunger rendered us bold; and not being threatened at first attempts to get some fruits from the stern, we in a short time took the liberty of ranging about the vessel, in search of plunder of every kind. Now we began to entertain a good opinion of our conquerors. Very soon after breakfast, we were divided into several of the vessels around us. This was now cause of new fears, not knowing where our misery would end. Being now, as it were, one family, we began to take leave of those who were first transshipped, not knowing what would become of them and ourselves. About this time, six of us, friends in affliction, among whom was my Brother Joseph Bartholomew, kept very close together, that we might be carried away at the same time. It was not long before we six were conveyed into the *Myrmidon*, in which we discovered not any trace of those who were

transshipped before us. We soon came to a conclusion of what had become of them, when we saw parts of a hog hanging, the skin of which was white–a thing we never saw before; for a hog was always roasted on fire, to clear it of the hair, in my country—and a number of cannonshots were arranged along the deck. The former we supposed to be the flesh, and the latter the heads of the individuals who had been killed for meat. But we were soon undeceived, by a close examination of the flesh with cloven foot, which resembled that of a hog; and, by a cautious approach to the shot, that they were iron.

In a few days we were quite at home in the man-of-war: being only six in number, we were selected by the sailors, for their boys; and were soon furnished with clothes. Our Portuguese owner and his son were brought over into the same vessel, bound in fetters; and, thinking that I should no more get into his hand, I had the boldness to strike him on the head, while he was shaving by his son–an act, however, very wicked and unkind in its nature. His vessel was towed along by the man-of-war, with the remainder of the slaves therein. But after a few weeks, the slaves being transshipped from her, and being stripped of her rigging, the schooner was left alone on the ocean. . . .

One of the brigs, which contained a part of the slaves, was wrecked on a sand-bank: happily, another vessel was near, and all the lives were saved. It was not long before another brig sunk, during a tempest, with all the slaves and sailors, with the exception of about five of the latter, who were found in a boat after four or five days, reduced almost to mere skeletons, and were so feeble, that they could not stand on their feet. One hundred and two of our number were lost on this occasion.

After nearly two months and a half cruising on the coast, we were landed at Sierra Leone, on the 17th of June, 1822. The same day we were sent to Bathurst, formerly Leopold, under the care of Mr. Davey. Here we had the pleasure of meeting many of our country people, but none were known before. They assured us of our liberty and freedom;

and we very soon believed them. But a few days after our arrival at Bathurst, we had the mortification of being sent for at Freetown, to testify against our Portuguese owner. It being hinted to us that we should be delivered up to him again, notwithstanding all the persuasion of Mr. Davey that we should return, we entirely refused to go ourselves, unless we were carried. I could not but think of my ill-conduct to our owner in the man-of-war. But as time was passing away, and our consent could not be got, we were compelled to go by being whipped; and it was not a small joy to us to return to Bathurst again, in the evening, to our friends.

From this period I have been under the care of the Church Missionary Society; and in about six months after my arrival in Sierra Leone, I was able to read the New Testament with some degree of freedom. . . . The Lord was pleased to open my heart to hearken to those things which are spoken by His servants; and being convinced that I was a sinner, and desired to obtain pardon through Jesus Christ, I was baptized on the 11th of

December, 1825 [and took the name Samuel Crowther after that of a benefactor of the Church Missionary Society]. . . . May I ever have a fresh desire to be engaged in the service of Christ, for it is *perfect freedom*. . . .

Thus the day of my captivity was to me a blessed day, when considered in this respect; though certainly it must be unhappy also, in my being deprived on it of my father, mother, sisters, and all other relations. I must also remark, that I could not as yet find a dozen Ochó-gu people among the inhabitants of Sierra Leone. I was married to a Christian woman on the 21st of September 1829. She was captured by His Majesty's Ship *Bann*, Capt. Charles Phillips, on the 31st of October 1822. Since, the Lord has blessed us with three children—a son, and two daughters.

That the time may come when the Heathen shall be fully given to Christ for His inheritance, and the uttermost part of the earth for His possession, is the earnest prayer of

Your humble, thankful, and obedient Servant

Samuel Crowther

24. The Asante king questions British motives in ending the slave trade.

Not all Africans welcomed British attempts to end the trade in slaves. The Asante king, Osei Bonsu, for one expressed doubt that those who were opposed to the trade were influenced by humanitarian reasons. For his part, he argued that he had never enslaved people except through war (and then not wars fought for the purpose of getting slaves but for other reasons entirely), and that it was necessary for him to sell war captives lest they rise against him. Osei Bonsu expressed these points in a discussion in 1820 with Joseph Dupuis, sent by the British to be their counsel in the Asante capital city of Kumasi. Dupuis had been instructed by his superiors "to nurture the seeds of an accidental friendship as an essential preliminary step to the advancement of certain hopeful expectations connected with the manufacturing and commercial interests of Great Britain." Osei Bonsu wondered what he would trade with if he could not trade slaves for European manufactured goods.[24]

---

[24] Joseph Dupuis, *Journal of a Residence in Ashantee, Comprising Notes and Researches Relative to the Gold Coast, and the Interior of Western Africa; Chiefly Collected from Arabic MSS. And Information Communicated by the Moslems of Guinea: To Which Is Prefixed an Account of the Origin of the Causes of the Present War* (London: Henry Colburn, 1824), pp. 162–64.

"Now," said the king, after a pause, "I have another palaver, and you must help me to talk it. A long time ago the great king liked plenty of trade, more than now; then many ships came, and they bought ivory, gold, and slaves; but now he will not let the ships come as before, and the people buy gold and ivory only. This is what I have in my head, so now tell me truly, like a friend, why does the king, do so?" "His majesty's question," I replied, "was connected with a great palaver, which my instructions did not authorise me to discuss. I had nothing to say regarding the slave trade." "I know that too," retorted the king, "because, if my master liked that trade, you would have told me so before. I only want to hear what you think as a friend: this is not like the other palavers." I was confessedly at a loss for an argument that might pass as a satisfactory reason, and the sequel proved that my doubts were not groundless. The king did not deem it plausible, that this obnoxious traffic should have been abolished from motives of humanity alone; neither would he admit that it lessened the number either of domestic or foreign wars.

Taking up one of my observations, he remarked, "the white men who go to council with your master, and pray to the great God for him, do not understand my country, or they would not say the slave trade was bad. But if they think it bad now, why did they think it good before. Is not your law an old law, the same as the Crammo [Muslim] law? Do you not both serve the same God, only you have different fashions and customs? Crammos are strong people in fetische, and they say the law is good, because the great God made the book; so they buy slaves, and teach them good things, which they knew not before. This makes every body love the Crammos, and they go every where up and down, and the people give them food when they want it. Then these men come all the way from the great water [Niger], and from Manding, and Dagomba, and Killinga; they stop and trade for slaves, and then go home. If the great king would like to restore this trade, it would be good for the white men and for me too, because Ashantee is a coun-

try for war, and the people are strong; so if you talk that palaver for me properly, in the white country, if you go there, I will give you plenty of gold, and I will make you richer than all the white men."

I urged the impossibility of the king's request, promising, however, to record his sentiments faithfully. "Well then," said the king, "you must put down in my master's book all I shall say, and then he will look to it, now he is my friend. And when he sees what is true, he will surely restore that trade. I cannot make war to catch slaves in the bush, like a thief. My ancestors never did so. But if I fight a king, and kill him when he is insolent, then certainly I must have his gold, and his slaves, and the people are mine too. Do not the white kings act like this? Because I hear the old men say, that before I conquered Fantee and killed the Braffoes and the kings, that white men came in great ships, and fought and killed many people; and then they took the gold and slaves to the white country: and sometimes they fought together. That is all the same as these black countries. The great God and the fetische made war for strong men every where, because then they can pay plenty of gold and proper sacrifice. When I fought Gaman, I did not make war for slaves, but because Dinkera (the king) sent me an arrogant message and killed my people, and refused to pay me gold as his father did. Then my fetische made me strong like my ancestors, and I killed Dinkera, and took his gold, and brought more than 20,000 slaves to Coomassy. Some of these people being bad men, I washed my stool in their blood for the fetische. But then some were good people, and these I sold or gave to my captains: many, moreover, died, because this country does not grow too much corn like Sarem, and what can I do? Unless I kill or sell them, they will grow strong and kill my people. Now you must tell my master that these slaves can work for him, and if he wants 10,000 he can have them. And if he wants fine handsome girls and women to give his captains, I can send him great numbers."

25. A slave revolt in South Africa.

In 1825, a 26-year-old slave named Galant, angered by constant floggings he received from his "master," Willem van der Merwe, and inspired by reports of the development of abolitionist sentiment in Britain, gathered together fellow slaves equally unhappy with their situation. Galant killed van der Merwe and two other farmers and took control of his master's farm but within days was captured along with those slaves who had joined him in revolt and was put on trial for treason. Though this uprising was only the second insurrection to occur in 200 years of slavery at the Cape, and limited to one farm, slaveholders perceived Galant's revolt as a powerful threat to their way of life. The uprising took place during a period when the institution of slavery was coming under strong attack in Britain and in the Cape, with missionaries in particular denouncing the ways in which Dutch slaveholders treated their servants. Moreover, less than two decades earlier in the Cape, in October 1808, more than 300 slaves, determined to overthrow slavery, had marched on Cape Town, and memories of that insurrection (which ended with the capture of the slaves and the execution of five of their leaders) remained strong in the minds of slaves and slaveholders alike. These connections were made clear in Galant's testimony, and in the prosecutor's (D. Denyssen) demand for the death penalty for the prisoners.

The trial of Galant and twelve other defendants concluded with two found not guilty and the remainder guilty. Galant, along with two co-conspirators, was ordered to be hanged until dead, and his head, along with that of his chief ally, to be displayed publicly on iron spikes "until consumed by time and the birds of the air." The others convicted were sentenced to various forms of torture (scourging, branding, and flogging) and to lengthy terms of imprisonment.[25]

Testimony of Galant.

Question: With what intention did you assemble?

Answer: We meant to murder all the masters that did not treat their people well, to lay waste the country if we were strong enough, and then to escape to Caffreland; and if the Commando should be too strong, to remain at the places of the murdered people.

Question: As you say in the beginning of your statement that you had spoken with Abel [one of the accused] and the other people, had you any other conversation with them than about the ill usage?

Answer: Abel said he had heard his Master reading the newspaper about making the slaves free, and that he had heard his master say he would rather shoot all his slaves than make them free . . . .

Question: Do you persist in this statement, and have you anything to add to or take from it?

Answer: I have something more to state, namely my master told me himself that he would shoot me. My master once when I came from the work also said to me that there was a newspaper come from another country which stated that a black cat had been hatched under a white hen. The next day my

---

[25] A full transcript of the court case is printed in G. M. Theal, ed., *Records of the Cape Colony*, vol. 20 (London, 1905), pp. 188–341. The excerpts here are from pp. 208–11, 312–16, 318–20, 322–23, 328–30.

master asked me what I understood by that expression? to which I answered that I did not know. My master repeated the question, and I said again, that I did not understand it; my Master then asked Achilles and Antony [both accused] if they also had an intention of going to their own Country, to which they answered yes, but said that they could not find the way there, but that they would go if the Governor would send them, although they were afraid their parents were dead and that they should not be known by their nation. My master was thereupon silent, but my mistress said to my wife, a Hottentot named Betje, that a Newspaper was come from the Cape which she dare not break open, but that a time would be prescribed when it might be opened. When the Newspaper was opened my mistress said that it stood therein that there was another great nation that was unknown; that there were orders come to make the Slaves free, and that if it was not done the other nation would then come to fight against the Farmers. My mistress afterwards further told me that it was also said in the Newspapers that the Slaves must be free, but if the Farmers would not allow it then it would not take place, to which I did not say anything. Another Newspaper came afterwards, when my wife Betje told me that her mistress had said if we would go to the King for the money and bring it to her on the table, that then we might be free. I desired her to keep it quiet, which she did. Some time after, another Newspaper came, when my wife told me that her Mistress had said that the first Englishman who came to make the slaves free should be shot, as well as the slaves; upon which I again advised her to be silent, for that if our master should hear of it he would punish us, and that she must not tell it to anybody else; but I desired her to ask the Mistress why the slaves were to be free, as she spoke so often about it. She told me afterwards that she had asked her, and that her Mistress had said it was because there came too many white children among the black Negroes, and therefore that they must be free. I then desired her again not to tell it to anyone, and not to talk so much about it. An-

other Newspaper then came, when she informed me that her Mistress had said that the Farmers were too hardly off, and that they were obliged to put up with too much from the Blacks. My wife came to me one day to the land weeping, and on my asking her the reason she said that while she was in the kitchen she had asked for a piece of bread, and that her Master was so angry that he said he would shoot her and all the people in a lump, and leave us to be devoured by the crows and vultures. I again told her to be quiet, for that I could not well believe her although she was my wife, as she could not read or write no more than myself. Once that Barend van der Merwe [a neighbor of Willem van der Merwe] was at my Master's place on his return from Worcester where he had been to fetch the slave Goliath who had made a complaint, I was in the stable preparing forage for the horses. It was dark, so that nobody could see me in the stable. My master called Barend van der Merwe out and came with him into the stable without seeing me, when I heard my master ask him whether he had had his slave flogged, to which he answered no, for that the black people had more to say with the Magistrate of late than the Christians; further saying but he shall nevertheless not remain without a flogging, for when I come home he shall have one. I also heard Barend van der Merwe say to my Master on that occasion I wish that the Secretaries or Commissioners had died rather than that they should have come here, for that since that time they had been obliged to pay so much for the *Opgaaf* [tax receipt] and also for the Slaves. My master gave for answer I wish that the first Commissioner who put his foot on the wharf from on board had broken his neck, for that it was from that time one was obliged to pay so much for the Slaves, which they were not worth. My Master likewise said to Baren van der Merwe that he must keep himself armed in order to shoot the first Commissioner or Englishman who should come to the Country to make the Slaves free, together with the Slaves all in one heap. B. van der Merwe thereupon rode home, some time after which I again heard my master speaking to Barend Lubbe who was at my Master's place, when he asked Lubbe how it was in the upper Country, to which Lubbe answered he did not know, that he not having any slaves had not once inquired about it, and that what the gentlemen did was well done; my master replied that although he had not any Slaves he must nevertheless stand up for his Country, further saying that he would shoot the first Commissioner, Englishman, or magistrate who should come to his place to make the Slaves free, but first the Slaves. Lubbe then asked van der Merwe whether he was not afraid if he fought against the Magistrates that the Slaves would attack him from behind, to which my master answered for that reason the Slaves must be first shot. Subsequently I heard my master speaking for the third time with Hans Lubbe and Jan Bothma, whom having asked how it was in their part of the Country, they answered bad, for the black heathens have more privileges than us, and if the Christians go to the Landdrost to complain of their slaves, the Landdrost will not even look at us, but turns his backside to us, on which my master said the best advice I can give you is that you remain armed and keep your powder and ball together. Lubbe replied the first Gentleman that comes to me I will shoot with all the Slaves in a heap. Again for the fourth time I heard my Master talking with Schalk Lubbe, likewise at my master's place, whom he asked how it was here in the upper Country and if he had heard anything of the Newspaper and about the Slaves, he answered no, on which my master said lately we heard every day of new laws. I have asked for nothing, but I keep myself armed to shoot the first magistrate who comes to my place and the Blacks likewise.

For the fifth time I heard my Master conversing at his place with Johannes Jansen and Jan Verlee [both of whom were killed along with van der Merwe]; the former had made an ox sambok [rawhide whip] which he brought into the house, on which my master desired me to drive in a pig that had got out, which I accordingly did. Standing before the door of the pigsty in order to fasten it, I heard my master say to Jansen, you must promise me something the same as Verlee has done, namely to shoot the magistrate when he comes. Jansen answered that he would do so, for that he would stand up for his mother Country; on that my Master said that he should give orders to all the Slaves, and that if they did not obey them he would supple the sambok on them the next day, for, said my Master, if you punish a slave you must do it that he cannot be known before a magistrate. My Master ordered us to smear the treading floor and that the floor must be well laid the next morning when he got up, on that we made the plan to murder all the farmers; we did not smear the floor because it was evening and was dark; we also told my master this, but he notwithstanding would have that the floor should be smeared against the next morning. My master did not say anything more about it that evening, and we then immediately formed the plan, as I have already stated.

Speech of Fiscal D. Denyssen as public prosecutor at the trial of the Bokkeveld insurgents, March 18, 1825.

. . . I shall begin with the head of the gang, namely the slave Galant. When we hear his statement, one will be easily led to suppose that he had been obliged to sigh under a continued chain of successive ill usage, that his child who could scarcely walk, had died in consequence of the repeated floggings he had received from his master, and this for no other reason than because he was displeased with his own wife; that he himself had been hoisted up by the arms and in this manner flogged by his master, that he had been incessantly maltreated by his Master in the same way, and that he scarcely received sufficient clothes or victuals.

How unfortunate it is for the impartial investigation of the truth that the man, whom all these accusations regard, now lies low and cannot refute them, and that his widow, who is likewise implicated in the charges, although she still lives, cannot possibly appear here without suffering too much under the consequences of the wound so cruelly inflicted on her.

In the meantime if it be considered worth the trouble to stop the mouth of the prisoner Galant of his foul charges, I believe there exist proofs enough which can be adduced with success.

We have already seen in the investigation of these charges, for as far as we could ascertain the truth, that the foulest slander constitutes their principal feature. . . . [I]t was not the ill treatment which Galant alleges to have suffered that brought him to the step, as he calls it, of fighting himself free; no, it was his disappointed hopes of freedom that induced him to it. I take his own words. When in his confrontation with the Witness Betje she says that Galant told her before the commencement of the present year he should wait til new year, and that if he were not made free then he would begin to murder, what else did Galant do than to acknowledge the truth of what Betje said, and to name the persons from whom he had heard last year that at the commencement of the new one a general freedom of the slaves should take place.

See there your Worships the ringleader's own confession, see there the pivot upon which the whole machine guided by his hand turned.

Such like false reports appear to have prevailed for some time, it is impossible to say how long they have been in circulation, but they have been communicated not only to the slaves but to the owners of slaves. No wonder then if some credulous and misled masters, imagining that their right of property to their slaves, which next to their lives they considered as most sacred, would be disputed, now and then expressed themselves in language characteristic of the bitterness of their internal feelings; and that the slaves, in whose presence such subjects were imprudently talked of, or who listened at such discourses or found an opportunity of getting a knowledge of them from the children of their masters, should on their part become exasperated against their owners from the opposition to their freedom which they supposed they met with at their hands.

No wonder if in this manner an enmity hitherto unknown arose and was cherished in the minds of slaves against their masters, and that the ruinous distrust of their masters, which so evidently appears in the statements of Galant, gained ground and produced those extremities to which they naturally must lead. It is in this point of view that I consider the statement of Galant with regard to the backwardness of the Masters to communicate to their slaves the news contained in the papers which they received from time to time, or the written orders which they received from the Landdrost respecting their slaves, and also with respect to his fishing out and listening to the discourses which he says were held between his master and others, and again those discourses themselves, which he states to have consisted in threats against his slaves and all others who should undertake to proclaim their freedom.

For why should we doubt of the truth of what Galant says, in this regard, that such discourses have been actually held by weak and credulous slave owners, who supposing that they were at once to be deprived of all their slaves, were driven by such an idea to the very borders of rage and despair.

It is not my task in the present prosecution to endeavour to trace out the authors of such evil and pernicious reports, this belongs to an investigation hereafter to be made by me. It is sufficient in the present instance if such reports did prevail, and if they were the leading cause, as Galant states them to have been, of his undertaking. . . .

If we compare the examples of murders committed on slaves by their masters with the number of those committed on and by others, we shall soon see that the slave here is almost as safe under the protection of his Master as the child under that of the father; and especially those slaves who are born in the house, of which description both Abel and Galant are, with respect to whom the natural feeling of affection combines with self interest to make them find true friends and protectors in their masters. . . .

Proceeding now to the grounds of my claim relative to the criminality and punishableness of the several points of accusation, I remark that the most heinous species of high treason consists in taking up arms against the state, and that all those are justly considered as guilty of this crime who combine to oppose the existing order of public affairs with violence and arms. . . .

In a country where slavery exists, a rising of the slaves to fight themselves free is nothing else than a state of war, and therefore to such a rising the name of war has been given more than once in the Roman history, and justly, for hence states can be, and we know have been, totally overthrown. . . .

One of the prisoners themselves, I believe Galant, called his act here in Court making *war*. According to the laws it is sufficient that the plan of such a rising and the junction of the partakers therein, is prepared, to consider the crime of sedition, properly called *Perduellis* (High treason) as consummated. . . .

And now, your Worships, as it has fallen to my lot to claim the punishment of death against so many culprits who now stand before you, it only remains for me to see whether I am at liberty to recommend any mitigation to the Court. There exists a right of mitigation that the law gives to the Judge, namely when legal reasons can be adduced why the Judge is allowed to mitigate the ordinary punishment. But among these reasons I certainly do not find that of having been led away by Galant; for all of them have attained that age, and possess that portion of understanding and judgment, which could prevent them having been so seduced.

The eagerness to shake off the yoke of slavery, which had never before led to such excesses here, cannot be considered in any other light than as a desire to withdraw themselves from the laws of the land and from obedience to Government; a desire for blood, war and confusion leading to the most disastrous anarchy, the desire of freedom thus directed is a reason for the aggravation of the punishment. But perhaps it will be said, when so many are to suffer, humanity requires that the example to deter should extend to all, but the punishment to only few. Of this we find instances in history where great crimes have been committed by many persons. But this belongs to the rights reserved to the Sovereign. As Judges I am humbly of opinion that this court cannot go farther than the right with which judicial authority is vested with regard to crimes and punishments. The reasons which might induce His Excellency the Governor to spare any of those who may appear to have been led away are not within the pale of that authority, and they cannot constitute a subject of discussion at the present moment.

I therefore claim and conclude that the first ten prisoners, Galant, Abel, Isaac Rooy, Isaac Thys, Hendrik, Klaas, Achilles, Antony, Valentyn, and Vlak, and the 12th prisoner Pamela [the charges against prisoners 11 and 13 had been dismissed] shall be declared by your Worships guilty of the crimes with which they are charged in the act of accusation; and the last mentioned prisoner Pamela in particular of not rendering any the least assistance to her Master and Mistress, but on the contrary deserting them, when she slept under the same roof and could have afforded help by warning them of the approaching evil and assisting them in their danger . . . and [recommend] therefore that they shall be condemned by sentence of your Worships to be brought to the usual place of execution here, and being there all with the exception of the 10th prisoner Vlak, delivered over to the executioner, the first eight prisoners, Galant, Abel, Isaac Rooy, Isaac Thys, Hendrik, Klaas, Achilles, and Antony, to be hanged by the necks till they are dead; the 12th prisoner Pamela to be strangled, and the 9th prisoner Valentyn to be tied to a stake and severely scourged with rods on the bare back, then branded, and thereupon confined to labour on the public works here for such term as this Worshipful Court shall deem requisite, that the bodies of the first six prisoners shall be afterwards taken down from the gallows and their heads separated therefrom with an axe at the public place of execution, and then thrown into sacks in order to be conveyed to Bokkeveld and there exposed to public view on separate poles to be erected on the most conspicuous places near the road, with a board over each, on which shall be painted in legible letters *The punishment of Rebels*; thus to remain till consumed by time and the birds of the air; and the 10th prisoner Vlak, after having witnessed the execution, to be severely flogged in the town prison by the black constables. . . .

26. A Muslim explains the morality and practices of slavery.

Even as the Atlantic slave trade continued in the nineteenth century, though at a lower level than the previous century, the use of slaves within Africa expanded. Many of those used as slaves were war captives and criminals who once would have been exported to the Americas but now were used for labor within Africa. There was a growing need for such labor, especially with the expansion of agricultural production to meet new European demands. As the export of slaves from the West Coast of Africa to the Americas declined in the face of increasing British pressure and larger naval squadrons, that from Central Africa to the East Coast and beyond grew. Arab spice plantations on the islands of Zanzibar and Pemba needed huge numbers of workers to meet the market demands of Europe. The French established plantations in the Indian Ocean to replace those that they had lost to slave revolts and British raids in the Caribbean. And Muslim communities in Egypt, the Sudan, and the Arabian peninsula continued to import slaves. Between 1801 and 1896, more than a million and a half Africans were exported to communities ringing the Indian Ocean (Arabia, Iran, India, Zanzibar, Pemba), as well as below the coast of southern Africa to Brazil. Many of these slaves lived in Muslim societies, and the leaders of these communities found it necessary to explain to European colonial officials why they considered slavery necessary and not the evil depicted by abolitionists.

This particular piece was recorded during the 1890s. A German linguist, Carl Velten, asked Swahili-speaking Africans living near the town of Bagamoyo in German East Africa (present-day Tanzania) to write down accounts of their traditions and customs. This they did in Arabic script which Velten translated into German. Velten's main informant was Bwana Mtoro Mwinyi Bakari, a Muslim who traveled to Germany with Velten and taught Arabic in Berlin. While in Europe Bwana Mtoro married a German woman but because of opposition from German settlers was unable to live with her when he returned to Tanzania with his bride. Bwana Mtoro and his wife both returned to Germany where they were able to spend the rest of their lives living openly as man and wife. [26]

Of Slavery: The Origin of Slaves.

The origin is that a man is struck by some disaster such as war between one country and another. Those who are taken prisoner in war are not killed, but roped and taken to the town and told to remain as slaves. They do so, and they marry among themselves, and their offspring are slaves too. Or slavery may arise from a debt of blood money. If somebody

---

[26] J. W. T. Allen, ed., *The Customs of the Swahili People: The Desturi za Waswahili of Mtoro bin Mwinyi Bakari and Other Swahili Persons* (Berkeley: University of California Press, 1981), pp. 169–77. Reprinted with the permission of the University of California Press.

has killed another and his family is poor and he has no money, he is liable for blood money; but if he cannot pay, he is taken and sold, or he goes as a slave to the creditor. If he has killed a freeman, the blood money is a large sum, and if he has a brother or an uncle, he also may accompany him into slavery. Or if a sorcerer has killed somebody, and is known to be a sorcerer, he is killed, or he may go as a slave to the place where the killing took place. Or if an adulterer has lain with another's wife, he has to pay compensation. If he cannot, he becomes a slave. Compensation for adultery used to be paid inland and on the coast, even among the Swahili. Or in time of famine people would sell themselves to each other. Or a person may pledge a child or a brother-in-law, and when he has not the money to redeem him, he becomes a slave. A man cannot pledge or sell his wife, even in a severe famine. If he cannot support her he will divorce her.

To return to consideration of the inland country: prisoners of war, pawns, and persons taken in adultery whose families cannot redeem them become slaves. Arab and other slave traders go inland and buy them and bring them to the coast and sell them to others. This is the origin of slavery. The purchaser of those brought to the coast must keep a close watch on them or they will run away, and some on arrival coast claim to be freemen.

In the time of Sayyid Barghash there was a famine, and the Zaramo sold and pawned each other. When the Zanzibar Arabs heard that slaves were easily obtained on the coast, they came to buy Zaramo slaves; but when they went to sleep at night, the Zaramo ran away and by morning was back at home. Once he was there it was hard to recover him. Those who were shipped to Zanzibar stayed for a month and then claimed not to be slaves but freemen and the courts were full of complaints. When Sayyid Barghash found out that the Arabs were going to the coast to buy Zaramo, he rebuked them, saying, "Anybody who goes to the coast to buy Zaramo is throwing his money into the sea, and in addition I shall give him six months in fetters."

The reason for this was that they were not being bought; when people were going out of the town into the country, and they saw Zaramo and children, they would seize them, gagging them so that they could not cry out, and bring them into the town to sell to the traders.

Many of the Arabs traveled inland to make war on the pagan tribes and to enslave those whom they made prisoner. Or a pagan would go to an Arab and offer his services. The Arab would agree, and if he had any family, they would come too. Then he made them slaves. That is why some of the inland or Maniema slaves give a lot of trouble on the coast, saying, "This Arab did not buy me. I took service with him, and now he wants to make a slave of me."

Types of Slaves.

Mzalia is one whose mother came from inland. On arrival she was married to another slave and had a child. He is called mzalia. There are two sorts of mzalia, first-generation mzalia, second-generation mzalia, et cetera, until the seventh generation. The meaning of the seventh generation is that his mother was born in the town and his father likewise. Such a person's status is that of a freeman, he is simply said to be of slave origin.

Then there are raw slaves. Raw means that he has just arrived on the coast and does not know the language or customs, nor how to wash clothes nor how to cook. He is called a raw slave, and if he is sold his price is smaller than that of a trained slave.

The mzalia was not often sold in the past, unless he had bad manners and was rude to freemen. A freeman would marry a mzalia, for they became part of the family. Children born to a mzalia by a freeman are not slaves.

The Work of Raw Slaves.

On purchase they were given new clothes and bought a hoe and sent to the fields. There there were an overseer and a headman. When the master came to the field, he called the overseer and the headman and said to them,

"I have brought you a recruit." They said, "Good, we see him."

In the morning the overseer and the headman showed him where to dig, and his plot was marked out for him. He was given a task, that is, a section in which he must dig cassava and plant vegetables and beans. The master did not have to give him the yield of this plot unless he wished to do so. If he grew rice or sorghum, he gave him a little rice as *pepeta* [seed rice given as a gift]or sorghum as *msima* [a spike of sorghum given as a tip] out of kindness.

Some slaves have three days and some two. They work in the fields from early morning until eleven o'clock, when they return to the houses. They go out again in the afternoon until five, when they knock off.

If a slave is unwell, he does not go to work. He tells the master that such a slave is unwell. If the illness is serious, the master treats him until he recovers. If he dies, he provides the winding sheet and tells the others to bury him.

Songs of Slaves after Work.

They sing:

Overseer, your work is done,

Give us something to straighten our backs.

or:

If you go to Malindi, kanzu [a long shirt] and vest,

If you get any money, let it roll,

Or Msengesi [a Zanzibarian Arab reputed to be a pederast] will ruin you.

or:

Sir, I am not well, send me to the field

To dig wild jasmine and pomegranate.

This is not smallpox but chicken pox.

or:

The silver dollar [Maria Therasa dollar coin] never tells a lie.

Though you put it in the mud

Your heart rejoices and you have no bitterness.

The Work of Mzalia.

The work of the mzalia is to serve in the house, to wash vessels and plates or clothes or to be taught to cook, to plait mats, to sweep the house, to go to the well to draw water, to go to the shop to buy rice or meat; when food is ready, to dish it up for the master, to hold the basin for him to wash his hands, sometimes to wash his feet, and to oil him; but only if his wife approves. If the wife wants to go into the country or to a mourning or a wedding, she accompanies her, and if she has an umbrella, she carries it for her.

A male mzalia travels with his master to tend him if he is unwell, to wash his clothes when they are dirty, to shop for him, and to do any other service that he wants. He may be sent into the yard to learn to sew a kanzu or to embroider clothes or caps, or to be taught carpentry, to make carved doors, or to build stone or timber houses. When he knows these things he retains his own profits, and if he is a good mzalia he remembers his master and gives part to him.

How Slave and Master Should Behave.

A slave should obey his master; if he is told to do something, he should do it. If he is called, he should come at once to hear his orders. He should not answer his master back. If he sees his master carrying something, he should take it from him. If he goes into his master's room, he should take off his cap. When he is with his master, he should not go in front, and if they go where there are stools, he should not take one. Every morning and evening he should wait on his master to do anything required. When a slave greets his master, he does not offer his hand, even when they are traveling, nor does he ever enter his master's room without speaking. A slave must eat any food that the gentry are eating; but he does not eat with them. A mzalia eats with his master.

Of Slaves in the Past.

In the past slaves were given no consideration by freemen on the coast. A slave was known by his dress, for never in his life did he wear a cap, whether a jumbe [a person with some royal authority, a chief] lived or died. He never wore sandals nor a kanzu long enough to cover his legs. Nor did a gentleman address him by name; he said, "You." He did not protect himself from the rain with an umbrella; although they did cover themselves in the rain with umbrellas made of doum palm. Nor did he ever in the house wear clogs. At parties they sat separately, not with the gentry, as the town crier said:

The news horn,

Its sound means that all is well.

The horn of the jumbe and of the forty,

Of the officers and the locally born slaves,

Of gentlemen and their sons,

Of the mzalia and of slaves.

After this introduction the required announcement was made. Female slaves accompanying free women do not wear a veil or a headcloth.

Nor does a slave sit on a cane chair nor have one in his house. If he does so, people say, "This slave thinks himself as good as us. He has cane chairs in his house."

Slaves began to give themselves airs some fifteen years ago. There was a jumbe who had many slaves. One day he went to the shop and bought kangas [cloth wrap] and *kayas* [headcloth]for his slave girls to wear. They were astonished, and the other jumbes heard that jumbe Kisoka had given kayas to his slaves. They went to ask him about it, and he said, "I want to please myself and my slaves, as anyone may do if he likes." All the jumbes were angry, and they wanted to oppose him; but others said, "That will not do; he has a lot of supporters, he is well born, and he has many relations in the town," but the jumbes hated him.

A year later there was in the quarter of Gongoni a jumbe called Gungurugwa, who said, "I am going to give my slaves kayas and umbrellas." The young citizens made no objection, and he put his domestic slaves into kayas, and they went around the town carrying umbrellas. The other jumbes were angry and said, "These jumbes are breaking the traditions and doing things that our ancestors never did. There will be trouble in the town. There will be a revolution if slaves are treated differently every month. Next time a jumbe dies, half the place will uncover in respect, and half will keep their caps on." There was a lot of disagreement, and to this day they do not uncover on the death of a jumbe. Very few do so because they do not think it necessary. And the slaves no longer do the work that they used to do. They do as they like, and if they do not like it they do not do it. If one is disobedient, his master cannot correct him. He takes him to court and says, "This slave is disobedient and will not work in the house." The government punishes him. That is the difference between slaves now and in the past.

Marriage of Slaves.

In the past, if a slave wanted a wife, he asked his master's permission to marry her. The master asked if they were agreed, and he said that they were. Then he told the slave to give him a dollar for his turban. A raw slave paid a dollar for the turban, which he gave to his master, and the bride-price was five dollars. After paying for the turban in accordance with old custom, they did not go to the teacher for the marriage, but the master said, "I marry you to your fellow slave so-and-so," and he went at once into his wife's house.

Now they go to the teacher to be married in accordance with custom. There are no wedding feast, no celebration, no invitations, and no sewing mattresses and pillows.These customs are not followed.

A freed slave does not inform his master of his proposal to a fellow slave. He finds the woman that he wants, and when they have agreed, he goes to his master to tell him that he wishes to get married, because to do so is respectful. The master says, "Very well, it is for you to decide."

On the day of the wedding the master comes to preside over the feast, for he is the father. If the freed slave can afford it, he has a celebration like a freeman with dancing and many invitations. The bride-price is ten to twenty dollars, and a turban of five dollars is given to the bride's father or brother or, if she has neither, to her owner. A freed slave, or, as the Swahili say, a slave of God, marries another slave of God. A freed domestic slave can marry a free woman, but a raw slave cannot.

Children both of whose parents are slaves are slaves. If a freeman marries a slave woman, their child is a slave; but if a free woman marries a slave man, their child is not a slave, because free birth is matrilineal.

Of Suria.

A suria is when a man buys a slave girl and introduces her into his house, and she learns cooking and all domestic customs. When she is of age, her master says to her, "You are my suria, and you may not go outside. If you want anything, tell others to buy it for you." When her fellows realize that the master has spoken so, they give her respect. She is bought a bed and a mat and pillows and is given her own room like a wife. If the master is married, he spends three nights with his wife and one with his suria. If he is not married, the suria is his wife. Some people prefer a suria to a wife, because they say that a suria is a piece of luggage, meaning that if you travel you take your suria with you; but a wife, first you have to persuade her, and then you have to consult her parents before you take her on a journey. That is why they prefer a suria. Others prefer a wife, because when they have a child, he can say, "My father is so-and-so and my grandfather so-and-so, and my mother is so-and-so and her father so-and-so," because he has good blood on both sides. That is the reason for preferring a wife. But the son of a suria is a freeman and may not be sold nor called a slave, although he has no rank through his mother.

Of Runaway Slaves.

If a slave runs away, if you bought him in the town, you go to the vendor and say, "My slave has run away, please bring him to me if you see him." Or you go to the river or the sea-shore and say to the ferrymen, "My slave has run away; his description is like this—he is wearing such clothes, his tribe is Ganda or Sukuma, he is a raw slave, short and dark. If you find him trying to cross, stop him, catch him, and bring him to me. I live at Bagamoyo near so-and-so, and my name is. . . ." Then he goes back to the town.

If the slave comes to the river and the ferrymen see him, they ask him what he wants, and he does not know what to say, so they catch him and take him to the man's house in the town, and he must pay a recovery fee of one dollar. In the old days the slave would be locked up in the house in a room by himself for two or three days. Then he was promised on oath that if he ran away again he should die.

Of Charms to Recover Slaves.

If a man ran away, a coil rope was bought and Ya sini [part of the Qur'an]was recited over seven knots in it by the teacher. It was given to the owner of the runaway to take home. There he stood in the doorway and called his slave by name seven times. Then the rope was hung over the door, and if he was lucky the slave came back or was caught and brought back by others.

Of Giving a Slave as Security.

Any debtor can send his slave as security, whether the slave likes it or not, if security is required of the master. Such a slave is allowed one day to go and visit his master and to return on the next day. A married slave can be used as security and his wife too, and they have to do the same work as they did for their master. If they are idle, he can send them back and demand his money.

Of Borrowing by Slaves.

A slave cannot incur a debt without his master's authority. If a merchant advances money to a slave, he knows that if the slave takes the money and goes inland or dies or runs away and does not return to the coast, his money has fallen into the sea. He cannot go to the master to claim it. If it is a written agreement and he wants to borrow, he may do so by himself if he is in need of money; because if he loses it, he alone, and not his master, is liable.

Of Manumission.

If a man has many slaves, he may see one under his authority and call him, saying, "Mabruk" or "Majuma, you shall have a deed of manumission and be no longer a slave." Or if he has but one slave who has been with him for many years, he may manumit him. If he has a little field, he gives it to him and makes him his brother or his son. Such deeds are usually written when a man is growing old and wants to do a good action, whether he has children or not. He says, "I wish to make slave so-and-so a slave of God, and when I die, let her be as your sister. Do not cast her off." Then a deed is written and given to her, and she is free. One with such a deed cannot be sold or used as security.

The Deed of Manumission.

If a man wants to give his slave a deed of manumission, he writes, "I, A, son of B, hereby declare that I set so-and-so free before God, a free person. None may dispute this while I am alive or after my death. Any person altering what I have written in this deed is answerable to God for altering it. I have made him free. Any person making him a slave contrary to this deed must answer to God."

Such was the bond; but nowadays they go to the court, and the deed is drawn there and stamped with the seal of the central government.

27. Tippu Tip, the "leopard."

The most renowned slave trader in mid-nineteenth century Africa was Tippu Tip who, with a base in Zanzibar, roamed far into central Africa in search of ivory and slaves. Tippu Tip established his own state in the interior of Africa, building roads, laying out plantations, collecting taxes, and attempting to impose a monopoly on the sale of ivory. Reaching the height of his power in the 1870s, he lost out to European competitors in the 1880s and retired to the East African coast still a rich man in the 1890s. Here he describes how he became a trader in ivory and slaves.[27]

1. When I was twelve, I started to go on local trips. I traded in gum-copal, together with my brother Muhammad bin Masud el Wardi and my uncle Bushir bin Habib, and Abdallah bin Habib el Wardijan. I only took small loads, as I was merely a youth. My brother and my uncles carried rather more. This trade we carried on for a year.

2. When I was eighteen, my father, Muhammed bin Juma, went on a journey; he and his kinsmen decided to go to Ugangi. He brought me the news, saying, "I have decided to go on a trip to Ugangi, come, let us go!" I went with him and we arrived at Ugangi. After the Ugangi trip I came to Zanzibar. Then my father decided to go to Unyamwezi country, to Tabora. In Tabora he was comparable to a Chief. He had married from childhood the daughter of Chief Fundi Kira, one Karunde, and Karunde's mother was Fundi Kira's first and chief wife. And the chief wife at that time in Unyamwezi held power comparable with the Chief, so that my father was greatly respected. Whatever he wanted in and around Tabora he got, and when he went down to the coast he took his

[27] W. H. Whitely, *Maisha ya Hamed bin Muhammad el Murjebi: Yanni Tippu Tip, kwa Maneno yake Mwenyewe* (Kampala: East African Literature Bureau, 1966) pp. 9, 11, 13, 15.

Tippu Tip. *Source:* Henry M. Stanley, *In Darkest Africa, or the Quest, Rescue, and Retreat of Emin Governor of Equatoria,* vol. 2 (New York: Charles Scribner's Sons, 1890), p. 68.

wife Karunde. He was given much ivory from the wealth of Chief Fundi Kira. He was also given other goods, was my father, and at this time he was as though Chief in the Nyamwezi manner, having much property and many followers, perhaps even as much as the Chiefs of Uganda and Karagwe.

3. At the time when I went to Tabora, I was stricken with smallpox en route, and when I reached Unyanyambe, Tabora, we stayed two months. My father decided to go on to Ujiji but when we arrived the price of ivory was rather high. Our fellow Arabs with whom we were travelling decided to go on to Urua, while my father preferred to return to Tabora, giving his property to a fellow from the Mrima coast at Mbwamaji, by name Mwinyi Bakari bin Mustafa. He said, "You go with him, travel together." At this time wealth at Urua was simply reckoned in beads and bangles, they didn't want cloth. And I replied, "I can't go on to Urua, with our property in the possession of a man from the Mrima coast and I following along with him. Better that I return with you." My father answered. "I wouldn't have given the stuff to the man had you not been a youth who was unversed in the practice of the area. That's why I gave it to him. But if you are able yourself to take the goods, so much the better." I

replied, "Yes, try; if I fail then give it to someone else next trip." He left the goods with me and left to return to Tabora.

4. As for us, we crossed Lake Tanganyika, and at that time there were no proper boats, only dug-outs. There were about twenty of us who made the trip. We arrived at Urua at Mrongo Tambwe's place. We found that trade was moderate, neither good nor bad. We bought ivory; large tusks were expensive while the small were extremely cheap. Everyone was buying the large tusks, so I decided to go for the small, and collected a large number. At that time the price of the large tusks was high; people wanted the large ones because on the coast they fetched a higher price, the Babu "Ulaya" than did the Babu "Kutch." When we had finished trading we returned. . . . . .

11. When I arrived in Zanzibar I was lucky. It was the small tusks which were fetching a good price and at the time a frasila (35 lbs.) fetched between 50-55 dollars (if this were the Maria Theresa dollar, value 3-4) and the tax was 9 dollars per frasila. So I sold the ivory and took back to my father the goods he had ordered. I did not go back again to Tabora but carried on my own business with my brother, Mohammed bin Masud el Wardi.

When my father and I had made our trip, he had gone to Ngao and Nyasa. Returning thence he went to Benadir. As for me, I had been to Mahenge to the Mafiti. I borrowed goods in Zanzibar about 1000 dollars' worth and went to Uhehe to Mtengera's.

There I had had to take a major decision, borrowed between 4000-7000 dollars and went on to Urori. There I found trade bad and so went on to Fipa, Nyamwanga, Ruemba and Urungu where I got a great quantity of ivory. Returning from this trip to Ruemba I saw my brother in Zanzibar for the first time in twelve years. Formerly, when I had arrived in Zanzibar, he had been in Ngao or Benadir; when he had been in Zanzibar I had been up-country; now when I returned from Ruemba he had just come from Benadir and that was when we met.

For my part, I had made tremendous profits, but he had resolved to have a change from sea-trips and so we decided to go up-country together. . . . .

13. I took 700 porters and left Zanzibar with the goods and went to Mbwamaji. We loaded (made into loads) the goods and when everything was ready the crowd of porters appeared and took off their loads. We started the journey and reached Mbezi, where we stayed seven days. Then we went off again and reached Mkamba. By this time the porters had eaten the maize and were carrying their loads on an empty stomach, so when we arrived at Mkamba we bought plenty of rice to give them adequate rations. For between there and Lufiyi (Rufiji) there was no likelihood of getting food and the porters were many. Each man was given food for six days because there was plenty available.

14. On the day we decided to leave, the porters were scattered throughout the many villages where they had set down their loads; a hundred men in one, sixty in another; they had dispersed.

In the morning we sounded the departure drum. There was no response. We sent out men to go and hurry them up but they encountered no one. All had deserted. When they brought me this news, I went myself to look in the villages where they had set down their loads. I saw no one. I lost my temper and brought the news to my brother and told him to bring me my guns, travelling clothes and a bed-roll and servants. Then I went back through the districts of Mbezi and Ndengereko. Within a few hours I had a force of eighty guns. I slept on the road and on the second day arrived in the porters' villages, but they had not yet arrived. I seized their elders and kinsmen, about 200 of them, and bound them up. Thereupon they beat their drums and met together, the whole lot of them. When they saw that we were ready they came back. I went on ahead to Ndengereko and then to Mbezi, seizing a large number of people. I went into every part of Zaramu country and in the space of five days had seized 800 men. They called me Kingugwa--the "leopard"—because the leopard attacks indiscriminately, here and there. I yoked the whole lot of them together and went back with them to Mkamba.

28. Chisi Ndjurisiye Sichyajunga, slave.

Whatever the justifications given by slaveholders and supporters of the slave trade, the lives of those subjected to this coercive institution remained hard throughout the nineteenth century. Indeed, slavery was not denied a legal status until late in the nineteenth or early in the twentieth century for much of Africa. It remained legal in Nigeria until 1901; in French West Africa until 1903; in Kenya until 1907; in Angola until 1910; in Tanganyika until 1922; in Sierra Leone, supposed home of freed slaves, until 1928; and in Ethiopia, always proud of not having been conquered by Europeans in the nineteenth century, until 1937. Chisi Ndjurisiye Sichyajunga, born around 1870 in Central Africa, was one such person who experienced slavery well into the colonial era in Africa.[28]

Childhood.

My home was in the Biza country, for we are Chawa. I do not know my family, for enemies carried me off when I was still a child. The name of my father was Sichyajunga, and the name of my mother was Ntundu.

I can just remember the death of my mother. I was a very little child and sat be-

---

[28] Marcia Wright, *Strategies of Slaves and Women: Life-stories from East/Central Africa* (New York: Lilian Barber Press, 1993), pp. 81–85. Reprinted with the permission of Marcia Wright and the Lilian Barber Press.

side her before the door of our hut. My mother fed the baby with gruel while I held its hands. Suddenly a lion sprang upon us, seized my mother and tore her with its teeth, and scratched my leg with its claws. People drove off the lion and rescued my mother, but she died of her wounds. Near our home there were many lions. The lion which killed my mother had also killed two of my mother's sisters, my aunts.

After my mother's death we were alone with my father, who looked after us. My grandmother cared for the baby.

My older sister, Nsigwa, lived with her husband in another village. She sent a messenger to my father who said, "Your daughter wishes you to know that she is with child." When my father heard this he called my brother and told him to go and see how my sister was. Then I began to cry and said, "Father, let me go, too." But my father replied, "No, you cannot walk so far. You must stay here. Your brother shall go alone." I screamed, "I will go with him." At last my father said, "Go, if you must."

My brother and I set out. Part of the way he carried me, part of the way I walked. When we came to the village where my sister lived we found it was as the messenger had said. My brother did not spend the night there, but set out for home the same day, and I stayed with my sister.

Stolen from Home.

Our land lies near the borders of the Bemba country, and the Bemba are our enemies. They are always making war on our land. That very night, as dawn was breaking while I lay asleep with my sister in her hut, the Bemba attacked the village.

There had been a beer drink the day before, so that everyone was drunk. The enemy killed all the men; not one escaped. Then they cut off their heads, put them in baskets, and carried them off to their own land to show to their chief.

Two of the enemy burst into our hut, seized my sister and me, and set out with us for luBemba. We spent the night on the way,

and during the night my sister gave birth to twins, both girls.

The next morning my sister could not walk. The man who had taken her said to his companion, "What shall I do now?" His companion replied, "You dare not kill her, for the chief has forbidden the killing of women. If you are going to leave her behind, leave her alive." But the man said, "No, I will not leave her behind, for I have no other wife at home. I will look after her, and when she is better she will be my wife. Let the girl stay behind with me, too, so that she can look after her sister, and later I will give her back to you." The other agreed to this and went on alone, leaving me with my sister. We camped in that place for one more night.

The next day at dawn the man said to my sister, "Come along. We shall travel slowly and I will care for you." My sister set out, carrying one of the children, while the man carried the other. We traveled very slowly and spent ten nights on the way. At last we reached luBemba with both children safe and well.

In luBemba the chief said to my captor, "This is the first person you have taken in a raid, so she belongs to me, for it is the custom that the first person taken belongs to the chief." So it came to pass that my sister stayed in the hut of the man who had stolen her and became his wife, but that I was given to the chief.

Slavery.

I stayed in luBemba for three years until I was ten or eleven years old. I must have been seven or eight years of age when I was stolen by the enemy. Then four coast people, an Arab and three black men, came to luBemba. After the chief had spoken with them in secret he brought them to the hut where I was and said, "Chisi, these men are my relations. You are to go home with them and stay with them. You shall return with me after a time when I go to visit them." Then he gave me meat and fish saying, "Eat this while you are with my relations."

I wept bitterly, but it was of no avail. The coast people took me to their hut, and there I met four boys and two girls. The coast people put food before me. I would not eat, but screamed and cried. At sunset we started our journey and traveled by night, for the moon was shining. We went toward wiNamwanga and were a long time on the way.

In wiNamwanga the Arab became so ill that he could not travel, and we stayed there for two and a half years.

When the Arab was somewhat better we set out once more and reached the village of Chief Zambi in uSafwa. We stayed there for three days. There the coast people said to one of the girls who was about my age, "You are to stay here with our relations until we come back and fetch you." But we found ivory in the hut and exclaimed, "Where did that come from? That was not here before! You have sold your sister for ivory!"

We left Zambi and traveled toward Intente. When we got there it was raining heavily and we were numb with cold. The coast people sat down and ate some honey. They said to my companion and me, "Go on, we shall catch up with you." The boys stayed with the men.

Escape.

As we walked on, the other girl, who was bigger than I, said, "Child, let us run away and hide in the tall grass, for these coast people will kill us. One of us has already been left behind in Zambi. She has been sold for the ivory they are carrying. They will sell us, too. Come along, let us hide in the grass and later we will make our way home." I answered, "It is all very well for you, my friend, for you are big and can run faster than I. You will go ahead and leave me behind, for I am small and very cold. But she said, "No, I promise not to leave you. Come on, let us be off."

She put down the Arab's cooking pot which she carried and we plunged into the high grass and fled. My companion ran quickly and I soon fell behind, so I turned aside and went down to the stream and hid in a cave in the bank. I heard my companion call, "Hurry up, child, come to me." But I did not want to follow her, and stayed in the cave.

The coast people came along the road and found the cooking pot. They followed our tracks through the grass, but they lost mine where I had turned aside to the stream. They followed the other girl, and I have never heard whether they caught her or not.

The water began to rise in the cave where I was hidden, for much rain had fallen that day. I crawled out and looked around. Nearby were fields of the Safwa of Itende. I went toward the fields and came on some boys who had been weeding and taken shelter, from the rain. I stood still and thought, The Safwa will find me in their fields and will call out, "Thief, you are stealing our maize!" So I went on toward a hut with smoke rising from it. I was shivering with cold and thought, "I will go to that hut and there I shall die."

Marriage.

I went up to the hut, which belonged to Ndeye. He was not there but his sister was in the hut. She looked up and said in Safwa "Where do you come from?" But I did not understand Safwa and the woman could not speak Biza. I tried to explain with signs another girl and I had run away from the coast people, but I did not know where she was. Then the woman signaled come to the fire, and I drew near and warmed myself.

Ndeye's wife came in and found me there and asked, "Where does this girl come from?" Ndeye's sister answered, "Just think, she was traveling with the coast people and she had run away from them with another girl. Where the other is I know not. This one came into the hut suddenly."

The wife of Ndeye went to the chief and said, "A girl has come to my hut. She says she was traveling with the coast people and ran away from them." When the chief heard this he said, "Do not let her leave the hut. Keep her hidden there until Ndeye comes back."

When Ndeye came back and heard the whole story, he said, "It is well; my ancestors have sent this girl to my hut." So I stayed in the hut of Ndeye.

After a year the chief sent for Ndeye and said to him, "Bring the girl to me. I want to see her." Ndeye led me before the chief, who said, "Look after the girl as though she were your own child. Let men woo her, and he who wants her must work for her." But Ndeye replied, "Not so, O Chief, if I keep this girl she shall be my wife." So I stayed in the hut of Ndeye and grew up there. After four years, when I was fully grown, I became the wife of Ndeye and bore him a son, Mbindijeriye.

Part 2
From Abolition to Conquest

Introduction

During the course of the nineteenth century, Europeans gradually developed a new relationship with the African continent, replacing the buying and selling of people with the appropriation of their lands and their human rights. The movement from an export trade in slaves to European conquest was not a quick and straightforward process, nor was it one foreordained by the nature of the relationship that existed between the West and Africa at the beginning of the nineteenth century. But it was a process that in fundamental ways grew out of 400 years of the Atlantic slave trade.

At the end of the eighteenth and the beginning of the nineteenth century, it was becoming evident to some European business leaders that the slave trade was on the decline and that new export products needed to be identified if they were to retain their commercial bases in Africa. People sent to explore the interior, such as Mungo Park, were instructed to seek certain types of knowledge (commercial above all) and were funded by business leaders who wanted to find out about and tap into the trading networks of the interior. The prospects did not look particularly good. Park favored continuing with the slave trade since he thought the other exports alone could not support an expanded European commercial presence in Africa (Part 1, document 20). In South Africa, the continuance of slavery was also deemed by many as being absolutely necessary for the economic survival of the Cape Colony (document 19, part 1), and if not slavery then certainly other forms of servile labor (document 1). Because of such testimony, by the early 1800s European powers like Britain and France were questioning the continued presence of their nationals in Africa (document 2). The only group really supporting the continuance of a European presence in Africa were missionaries, most of them members of the newly emergent middle class who argued to their peers at home and to potential converts in Africa about the importance of a missionary presence for Christianizing and "civilizing" the otherwise "barbarous" and "warlike" people of the continent (document 6). They clearly had a considerable impact on labor legislation in South Africa, but in part because of their complaints about settler treatment of the indigenous people, the area of white settlement expanded considerably as white farmers moved into the interior beyond the purview of British officials (documents 4, 5, 7).

From the 1810s onward though, European interest in Africa did grow, especially because of a growing demand in rapidly industrializing societies for the raw materials that could further fuel their growth—palm, ground nut, and peanut oils used increasingly for lubricants; indigo for dyes; and ivory for billiard balls and piano keys for the new middle classes in Europe and the United States. With the growing demand for these products there was also a rise in demand for labor to produce them. The result was a considerable expansion not only of these export goods, but also of the use of slave labor by African producers on newly established plantations and for collecting and transporting items such as

ivory, and a further shift (already evident during the slave trade) from food production. Europeans sought to acquire direct access to these goods by entering
into treaty arrangements with African kings, though the terms of these treaties
were often disputed when the resulting written form was explained to those
Africans who had signed them and who considered that their oral transactions
had been misrepresented (document 3). But then, Europeans often believed that
since Africans were "barbarians," they did not have to be treated as one would
treat a "civilized" person (documents 8, 9, 10).

Still, treaties were necessary because until the latter half of the nineteenth
century, fear of tropical diseases such as malaria kept Europeans from traveling into the interior of Africa. Often they relied on missionaries, sometimes
freed African slaves, to proselytize for a combination of Christianity and "civilization" (or export commerce) in the interior (documents 9, 12). New medical and technological developments at mid-century, however, made the reliance
on missionary initiative less important. Quinine proved a very effective pro-
phylactic against malaria, and European death rates in the West African interior and on the coast dropped to levels that were only two to three times those
experienced in Europe rather than a hundred times or more higher. Steam-
powered iron ships could be sailed upriver against the current, thereby enabling European merchants direct access to the riverine networks of the interior,
and the gunboats extended the reach of their cannons. Perhaps most significant of all was the immense development of European firepower from the
mid-nineteenth century onward, especially of rifled barrels and repeating
mechanisms, which for the first time gave Europeans a huge military advantage over their opponents. This advantage was cemented by the development
of early machine guns, especially the maxim gun.

Still, at mid-century there was yet no real momentum for conquest. In
South Africa, the Dutch-speaking settlers had established their own independent republics situated between African states, but these states were essentially semi-subsistence economies utilizing disguised forms of slave labor and
not likely to expand much (documents 14, 15). In West Africa, the British and
the French were interested in expanding their spheres of influence, especially
up the rivers—such as the Senegal, Gambia, and Niger—through which large
numbers of slaves were still illegally exported (documents 16, 17). But missionary-educated Africans, some who had never left Africa, others who had
returned from the Americas—like Samuel Crowther, Africanus Horton, and
Edward Blyden—could still reasonably envisage a future Africa learning from
Europe and other parts of the world but remaining politically autonomous
(documents 12, 18, 23).

The vision of an autonomous Africa changed in the 1870s. The discovery of
a vast store of diamonds in South Africa excited European expectations of finding new wealth in the continent. Images of Africa as poverty stricken and wracked
by never-ending warfare changed into visions of fortune. Yet, as the South
African diamond industry demonstrated, fortune could be ephemeral, and only
the securing of large supplies of cheap labor within Africa would make it possible for Europeans to exploit fully the potential wealth of their anticipated empires (documents 19, 20). Using an imperial rhetoric that denounced Africans

for being savage and announcing a European commitment to ridding Africa of slavery, empire boosters—most of them business speculators—scrambled in the 1870s and 1880s to seize as large a share of Africa as they could (documents 20, 21, 22). They organized themselves into companies chartered by their respective national states with a goal of obtaining a supposed monopoly of trade in the territories that they sought to acquire (documents 24).

The resulting competition was often self-defeating. As a result, the European powers (with participation by the United States), under the aegis of Otto von Bismarck, organized a conference in 1884–1885 to allocate territory in Africa. Significantly, the prime areas of concern were the riverine hinterlands that had been so important during the slave trade, especially those of the Niger and the Congo (document 25). The "scramble," already a decade in motion, was now much more carefully organized by the treaty signed in Berlin, with no African presence whatsoever at the negotiating table (despite endless rhetoric in the treaty about Europe's commitment to ending slavery in Africa). Significantly, the agreement banned any trade in arms to Africa (meaning in practice to Africans since it was accepted that weapons were necessary for Europeans to "pacify" the continent).

The process of conquest was frequently duplicitous and often bloody. In their private writings, and often in their public ones, the imperialists were not loath to admit that prospects of fortune drove them on and that trickery was often necessary to achieve their goals. And when trickery did not work, outright slaughter by means of the maxim gun was always a sure means of success (documents 27, 28). It was not just a racial conquest either, for when the control of South African gold was at issue, the British were quite ready to embark on their largest and most costly colonial campaign ever as they fought to destroy the Boer republics at the end of the nineteenth century and the beginning of the twentieth.

Conquest was a lengthy process. Africans did not give in easily in any part of the continent. Nor did initial defeats mean the end of resistance. Indeed, the process of conquest extended often over several decades and produced events and leaders who would long be celebrated for their resistance to European rule (document 29).

~~~

1. The subordination of labor in South Africa.

One of the results of the 1807 British legislation prohibiting the export trade in slaves was a growing shortage of labor within the one European settlement that depended extensively on the use of imported workers: the Cape of Good Hope. From the 1650s through to the beginning of the nineteenth century, European farmers at the Cape depended entirely on slaves imported from the East Coast of Africa, Madagascar, and Southeast Asia to meet their labor needs. To meet continued demands for workers, while also adhering to the British government's policy of ameliorating the conditions of forced labor, in 1809 the Cape colonial administration of the Earl of Caledon introduced legislation requiring that lo-

cal Khoisan peoples (known pejoratively as "Hottentots") be regulated "in re-gard to their places of abode and occupations." All male Khoisan were required to carry a "pass" stating whether they were entitled to live in a certain area of the colony, and whether they were employed by a European "master" and had fulfilled the conditions of their employment. Nonfulfillment of the conditions or lack of evidence of employment was regarded as the equivalent of vagrancy and thus punishable by the state. The terms of the 1809 legislation were ex-tended in 1812 to apply as well to children and young adults (euphemistically deemed "apprentices").[1]

Proclamation No. 14, By His Excel-lency Du Pre, Earl of Caledon, November 1, 1809.

WHEREAS it appears that the provisions made from time to time, for securing the ful-filling of Contracts of Hire between the In-habitants of this Colony and Hottentots, are not sufficient for the intended purpose; and, whereas for the benefit of this Colony at large, it is necessary, that not only the Individuals of the Hottentot Nation, in the same manner as the other Inhabitants, should be subject to proper regularity in regard to their places of abode and occupations, but also that they should find an encouragement for preferring entering the service of the Inhabitants to lead-ing an indolent life, by which they are ren-dered useless both for themselves and the community at large.

I therefore have thought proper to estab-lish and ordain, and by these Presents do es-tablish and ordain:

1. That all and every Hottentot in the dif-ferent Districts of this Colony, in the same manner as all Inhabitants, shall have a fixed Place of Abode in some one of the Districts, and that an entry of the same shall be made in the Office of the Fiscal, or the respective Landdrosts, and that they shall not be allowed to change their place of abode from one Dis-trict to another, without a Certificate from the Fiscal, or Landdrost of the District from which they remove; which Certificate they shall be bound to exhibit to the Fiscal, or Landdrost of the District where they intend to settle, for the purpose of being entered in their Office; while every Hottentot neglect-ing this order, shall be considered as a Vaga-bond, and be treated accordingly.

2. That every Inhabitant who engages a Hottentot in his service for the space of a month, or any longer period, shall be bound with the same to make his appearance before the Fiscal, or Landdrost, or the Field-Cornet of his Dis-trict, and there enter into, and sign *in triplo,* a proper written Contract, containing:

(a) The name of the Person who takes into service;

(b) The name of the Person who enters into service;

(c) The terms of the Contract;

(d) The amount of the Wages;

(e) The time of payment; and

(f) Such further Conditions as the Persons contracting shall agree upon. . . .

13. That the Hottentots engaged in the manner prescribed in the 2nd article, shall be bound diligently and honestly to serve their masters during the period of their contract, and to behave with proper submission; on pen-alty, that in case any founded complaints against their non-complying with their con-tract be lodged against them, to the fiscal or respective Landdrosts, they shall, by order of the same, be subjected to domestic correction; or, if their misconduct deserves a severer pun-ishment, they shall, upon a summary investi-gation of the case, by a committee of the court of justice or *heemraden,* be punished with con-fiscation of the wages due to them, or part of the same, or a temporary confinement, or a more severe domestic punishment. . . .

---

1. W. Wilberforce Bird, *State of the Cape of Good Hope in 1822* (London: John Murray, 1828), pp. 244–48.

15. That no Hottentot shall be taken into service without being provided with a certificate, either of his master, or the fiscal, landdrost, or field-cornet, under whose district he did serve, containing a declaration, that he has duly served out his time, or in case he has not served out his time, that he left the service of his former master with proper consent, or upon due authority. . . . any one taking into his service a Hottentot not provided with such certificate or discharge, shall forfeit one hundred rds [rix dollars, the local currency]; one-third for the informer, one-third for the public treasury, and one-third for the magistrate who carries on the prosecution.

16. Lastly, the Hottentots going about the country, either on the service of their masters, or on other lawful business, must be provided with a pass, either of their commanding officer, if in the military service, or the master under whom they serve, or the magistrate in the district, on penalty of being considered and treated as vagabonds. . . .

2. The trade question in West Africa.

The British legislation abolishing the export of slaves made illegal 90 percent of the trade engaged in by the Company of Merchants trading to Africa, the loose association of merchants that had succeeded the Royal African Company. This issue raised the question as to whether Britain should continue to maintain the 11 forts spread along 350 miles of the West African Coast that were used as bases by British slavers. On the surface, abandonment seemed to make economic sense. And the number of people based in the forts was miniscule, no more than about 35 Europeans "with a handful of men, half soldiers, half slaves." But proponents of abolition argued that by maintaining bases on the West African Coast, and fostering new forms of trade, Britain could promote "civilization." In this approach, the abolitionists were joined by members of the Company of Merchants, who, rapidly casting off their pro-slavery views of the past, took up the cause of anti-slavery in arguing for an expansion of the British presence in West Africa. The first selection below is from a letter by Zachary Macaulay, governor of Sierra Leone from 1793 to 1799 (administered by the St. George's Bay or Sierra Leone Company founded in 1791), to the British Secretary of State for War and the Colonies. The second is from a letter sent by the Company of Merchants to the British Treasury Lords. [2]

Zachary Macaulay to Lord Castlereagh, May 8, 1807.

The British Settlements in Africa form at present a very loose and disjointed whole, subjected to great diversity of management and pursuing ends which differ widely from each other. Goree is a Military Government immediately under the directions of His Majesty, Sierra Leone is at present governed by the Sierra Leone Company by the authority of a Charter of Justice obtained from the King.

Bance Island, a fortified settlement in the same river, is the property of Messrs. John and Alexander Anderson of London, who hold it by virtue of an Act of Parliament, and who have hitherto used it as a slave factory. The forts on the Gold Coast, seven or eight in number, are in the hands of the African Company, who receive annually from Parliament the sums required for their maintenance; and who continue a Company for the sole purpose of managing these forts, which were originally constructed and hitherto been

2. G. E. Metcalfe, ed., *Great Britain and Ghana: Documents of Ghana History, 1807–1957* (Legon: University of Ghana:, 1964), pp. 4–6, 22–25.

supported for the protection and encouragement of the slave trade.

With a view both to the British interests in Africa, and to the improvement of Africa itself it appears to deserve consideration whether these Establishments, as well as any other which may hereafter be formed in Africa, should not be taken under the immediate government of His Majesty, otherwise it is not likely that any uniform plan of policy can be pursued with respect to that country, nor any liberal and concurrent efforts made to amend the condition of its inhabitants. It was also in that case naturally become a question, whether the different settlements on the coast of Africa should be independent of each other, and subject only to the direct controul of which, the others might be placed. Supposing the latter, which seems the better plan, should be adopted, I should entertain no doubt, for reasons not now necessary to be specified, that Sierra Leone is the best situation for such a Presidency.

But whether the plan of uniting all our African Establishments under the Government of His Majesty is adopted or not, it appears to me that some steps might be taken, at the present moment, which would be attended with advantage both to Africa and Great Britain. . . .

It appears to be in the first place desirable that for the course of the next year or two vessels of war should be stationed at different parts of the African coast . . . with a view both of giving effect to the provisions of the Act for Abolishing the Slave Trade, and for other purposes of considerable moment. The Commanders of His Majesty's ships are almost universally regarded with respect and deference by the native chiefs on the coast of Africa. Being recognised as the representatives and accredited agents of His Majesty they naturally possess a very considerable influence among those chiefs.

If such Naval Commanders therefore as may visit the Coast of Africa, were directed to convey to the chiefs to whom they may have an opportunity of communicating favourable views of the principles which have guided the British Government in abolishing the slave trade, and to point out to them the various means within their reach of improving the condition of their country, their representations, I have little doubt, would produce a considerable and very beneficial effect. . . .

In particular it seems important to point out to them the advantage which they would derive from cultivating generally the *white* instead of the *red* rice, because in that case a vent might be easily obtained for their surplus produce of that article, either in Great Britain or the West Indies, the former species being a marketable article, while the other, though equally useful as food, would not find a sale out of Africa.

The other articles of exportable produce, the cultivation of which seems to me the best adapted to the present state of Africa are indigo, cotton and coffee, and these might be recommended to the attention of the chiefs. . . .

I have already expressed an opinion that the Settlement of Sierra Leone is better calculated than any other for the presidency of the African Coast. Its local advantages are great when compared either with Goree, or Cape Coast Castle, and without taking into account that Goree may be given up to France at a peace. The existence also of a colonial establishment at this place, together with a considerable extent of territory, will afford facilities for promoting the great object of African civilization which are enjoyed in no other place on the Coast, particularly as the circumstances, which hitherto have chiefly impeded this object will be removed by the abolition of the Slave Trade, and the transfer of the Colony from the Company to the Government. The example afforded by the Colony of a mild but firm and well-ordered Government, of rational liberty, and of secure and productive industry, would be of almost incalculable importance while the influence which its growing strength and respectability and its growing commercial importance must give it over the neighbouring chiefs, might be exerted in composing their differences, and inducing them to pursue plans of peaceful industry. . . .

The forts of the Gold Coast, if properly employed, might be made very important engines of promoting the mutual benefit of Great Britain and Africa. In addition to those which we already possess, it might be advisable to obtain possession of two or three Dutch forts situated on the same coast, which I apprehend would be a work of little difficulty. If this were effected, we should possess almost the entire controul of that line of Coast which extends from Cape Three Points to the Rio Volta. It is important here to remark, that at this moment the laws of this district of Africa are administered in a great degree by the Governors of these forts, who ordinarily proceed in administering them on the principles not of British but of African legislation. That is to say, the guilt of African criminals is tried, not by the received rules of evidence, but by the application of some ordeal which is regarded according to [the] effect which it produces, as decisive of guilt or innocence. Persons thus found guilty being liable to be sold as slaves, and the Governors of the forts being generally slave traders, it might be presumed that some degree of oppression has arisen from this source. It is obvious, however, that the power which has been thus employed, and that without being resisted, may be converted into an instrument of great good to Africa; and that the Governors who may now be appointed, being instructed to substitute equitable principles of law and benevolent maxims of policy, in place of those which have grown up under the former system, may by that change alone operate a very considerable amelioration in the civil condition of the inhabitants of a part of the coast which extends from three to four hundred miles in length. . . .

The African Committee of the Company of Merchants to the Lords of the Treasury, April 9, 1812.

Settlements on the coast of Africa have hitherto been deemed valuable on two grounds; first, as conferring an exclusive right of trade upon the Power possessing them; and, secondly, as the only medium through which it can be safely and advantageously carried on. The trade with the Gold Coast principally consists in a traffic of native merchants who travel from the interior, and frequently from very great distances, to exchange their goods for articles of foreign production. As these merchants cannot wait for the ships to arrive, nor the ships for them, it results that resident traders are necessary for their mutual accomodation; and that country will trade to the most advantage which has the greatest number of them established at convenient stations on the coast. For the sake of security, both to their persons and property, these traders must necessarily reside in forts, or under the immediate protection of them. . . .

By the abolition of the slave trade, the commerce of Africa was rendered so insignificant that it may have appeared scarcely worth the maintenance of the settlements on the coast. But it must be recollected that those settlements which are supported at so trifling an expense, were originally formed with no view to the slave trade, which was then neither in existence nor in contemplation and that one of the chief arguments urged for the abolition of that trade was that on the adoption of that measure, a new, more desirable, and more extensive commerce would, in process of time, be established in Africa. We will not pretend to determine the precise extent to which these bright anticipations are likely to be realized; but that considerable progress has already been made will appear from the [fact] . . . that in the three years which have elapsed since the abolition, the average export to that country has been £830,325, and that the imports have rapidly increased until they amounted in the year 1810 to above half a million sterling, exclusive of gold, which has been imported in far greater quantities than during the slave trade. . . .

Before any material improvement can be expected to take place in any district of Africa, the slave trade must be completely annihilated, or at least driven from that part of the coast; for so long as any people carrying on that trade are in possession of a single fort in the same neighbourhood, their influence will be superior to ours, and we shall be considered as opposed to the interests of the natives and be regarded with feelings of enmity. It is, besides, unquestionable that the British trade will not be able to exist where the slave trade is carried on. Those engaged in the latter will monopolize the whole. Ships can always carry more goods than are required to purchase their complement of negroes, and with little additional expense and without loss of time, the surplus goods may be converted into gold, ivory, &c; whereas the British merchant must fit out his vessel expressly for the purpose of purchasing those articles. . . .

So long as the vessels of other countries are allowed to frequent the coast, the forts will be unable to prevent the trade in slaves. Until, therefore, we can interdict such intercourse by foreign vessels, good policy would forbid our imposing the impracticable duty of at-tempting it by force, upon those whose prospects of success in the great work of introducing cultivation and civilization so essentially depend on their preserving the friendship, confidence and respect of the natives.

We are aware of but one mode by which the slave trade can be entirely abolished in this part of Africa, and that, we feel it our duty to recommend. It is the occupation by this nation of the whole of the Gold Coast . . . stationing good and respectable garrisons in the most commanding situation, [and,] at the rest, establishments sufficient to mark our possession. The sole right of external trade or internal being thereby vested in this country, two or three small ships of war, with some troops or an extra number of marines on board, should be kept constantly cruizing on the coast, to prevent the approach of all vessels not British. . . .

3. The King of Asante disputes the text of a treaty.

The British government accepted the views of the pro-expansionists and in 1821 took formal possession of the West African forts of the Company of Merchants. But staying meant finding new trade items to replace slaves. It also necessitated the establishment of treaty relationships with African rulers to ensure that British traders got a monopoly of the new trades. Treaty-making was a complex process, especially because of the limited understanding each party had of one another's language, and because of the eagerness of merchant representatives to claim to have received more than African rulers believed that they had given. The complexities are evident in the accounts left by participants to the first treaty that the British made with an African ruler, that with the king (or Asantehene) of Asante, Osei Bonsu, in 1817. The first three accounts come from Thomas Bowdich's description of his mission, on behalf of the Company of Merchants, to the Asante capital, Kumasi, in 1817. In the second of these extracts the Asante king complains of the British failure to force coastal Africans living near Cape Castle, his subjects by conquest since 1807, to make adequate tribute payments. The third extract is Bowdich's version (which implied that the king of Dwaben was co-equal with rather than a vassal of the Asantehene) of the 1817 treaty. In the fourth and fifth extracts, from Joseph Dupuis's account of his mission to Kumasi in 1821 and William Hutton's account of the same expedition, the objections of the Asantehene are detailed. Continuing disagreement between the British and the king of Asante over control of the West African Coast, especially the right of the Asante king to receive tribute from the coastal people, led to the British sending a punitive expedition under the command of the British governor, Sir Charles

Macarthy, into the interior in 1824. Macarthy's forces were defeated and the governor decapitated. His head was taken by victorious Asante to their capital of Kumasi where it remained in the royal palace for more than half a century.[3]

(A). Letter of instruction from the African Committee of the Company of Merchants to Thomas Bowdich.

[W]e wish you to obtain permission from the King [of Asante] to send an Embassy to his capital; if granted, you will select three gentlemen (one of them from the medical department) for that service. . . . In particular, it will be necessary for them to observe, and report upon, the nature of the country; its soil and products; the names, and distances, and the latitude and longitude of the principal places; and its most remarkable natural objects: the appearance, distinguishing characters, and manners of the natives; their religion, laws, customs, and forms of government, as far as they can be ascertained; and by whom each place is governed. When at Ashantee, they should endeavour to obtain the fullest information of the countries beyond, in each direction; particularly whether any high mountains, lakes, or large rivers are known; and the width, depth, course, and direction of the latter; and whether the water, as well of the lakes as the rivers, is salt or fresh. And how far, and under what circumstances, white men may travel with safety, especially in a northerly direction. They should collect the most accurate information possible of the extent, population, and resources of the Ashantee dominions, and should report fully their opinion of the inhabitants, and of the progress they may have made in the arts of civilized life. They should be directed also, to procure and bring away (with the consent of the chiefs) any specimens of vegetable and mineral productions they may be able: and to ascertain where

and how the natives collect the gold, and the extent to which the trade in that article, and in ivory, might be carried on. It would, we conceive, be a most important advantage if the King of Ashantee, and some of his chiefs, could be prevailed upon to send one or more of their children to the Cape, to be educated at the expense of the Committee (to be attended by their own servants, if required), under the guarantee of the Governor and Council for their personal safety, and that they should be sent back when required.

Another great object would be, to prevail upon the King to form, and keep open, a path not less than six feet wide, from his capital, as far as his territories extend towards Cape Coast, you engaging on the part of the Committee to continue it from that point to Cape Coast, which we presume may be done at a very small expense, by means of monthly allowances to the chiefs of such villages as be in that line; upon condition that they shall not allow the path to be overgrown with underwood, or otherwise obstructed. . . .

Besides the escort of which we have spoken, we think it necessary, or at least extremely important, that the Embassy should be accompanied by natives of character and consequence, conversant with the Ashantee language, in whom you have perfect confidence, selected, one from each of the towns of Cape Coast, Accra, and Appollonia, to whom you may make reasonable allowances for their time and trouble.

We have said that you should obtain the permission of the King of Ashantee to send the Embassy: we have doubts of the expediency of requiring hostages; but, we presume you will concur with us in thinking, it will be

3. (A) (B) (C), T. Edward Bowdich, *Mission from Cape Coast Castle to Ashantee, with a Descriptive Account of that Kingdom* (London: Griffith and Farran, new edition, 1873; first edition, 1819), pp. 3–7, 76–81, 143–45; (D), Joseph Dupuis, *Journal of a Residence in Ashantee, Comprising Notes and Researches Relative to the Gold Coast, and the Interior of Western Africa; Chiefly Collected from Arabic MSS. And Information Communicated by the Moslems of Guinea: To Which Is Prefixed an Account of the Origin of the Causes of the Present War* (London: Henry Colburn, 1824), p. 135; (E), William Hutton, *A Voyage to Africa: Including a Narrative of an Embassy to One of the Interior Kingdoms, in the Year 1820; with Remarks on the Course and Termination of the Niger, and Other Principal Rivers in that Country* (London: Longman, Hurst, Rees, Orme, and Brown, 1821), pp. 447–51.

necessary, before it leaves Cape Coast, that a man of consequence should be specially sent down by the King, to serve as a guide and protector; and who, on his journey to Cape Coast, may arrange with the messenger whom you may send to the King, respecting the places at which the Embassy may stop to refresh, and give directions to open the paths that may be overgrown.

The gentlemen whom you may select, will of course be well advised by you not to interfere with any customs of the natives, however absurd; or in any way to give them offence. And they cannot too strongly impress upon the minds of the King and people of Ashantee, that the only objects his Britannic Majesty has in view, are, to extend the trade with that country; to prevent all interruption to their free communication with the waterside; and to instruct their children in reading, writing, &c., from which, as may be easily pointed out, the greatest advantages must arise to the Ashantees . . . [Y]ou gentlemen will perceive, that in selecting the Embassy, it is important, that one of the persons composing it should be able to determine the latitude and longitude of places, and that both shall be seasoned to the climate of ability, physical and mental; of cool tempers and moderate habits; and possessed of fortitude and perseverance; and that in the selection of their escort also, regard be had to the qualifications of the parties in those respects. Among them there should be a bricklayer, carpenter, blacksmith, gunsmith, and cooper, with proper tools; if these persons can be spared for the purpose.

(B). Sai Tootoo Quamina, King of Ashantee and its Dependencies, to John Hope Smith, Esquire, Governor-in-Chief of the British Settlements on the Gold Coast of Africa.

The King sends his compliments to the Governor; he thanks the King of England and him very much for the presents sent to him, he thinks them very handsome. The King's sisters and all his friends have seen them, and think them very handsome, and thank him. The King thanks his God and his fetish that he made the Governor send the white men's faces for him to see, like he does now; he likes the English very much, and the Governor all the same as his brother.

The King of England has made war against all the other white people a long time, and killed all the people all about, and taken all the towns, French, Dutch, and Danish, all the towns all about. The King of Ashantee has made war against all the people of the water side, and all the black men all about, and taken all their towns.

When the King of England takes a French town, he says, "Come, all this is mine, bring all your books, and give me all your pay"; and if they don't do it, does the Governor think the King of England likes it? So the King [of Asante] has beat the Fantees now two times, and taken all their towns, and they send and say to him, "You are a great King, we want to serve you"; but he says, "Hah! you want to serve me, then bring all your books, what you get from the forts"; and then they send him four ackies [of tribute]; this vexes him too much . . . his captains swear that the Fantees are rogues and want to cheat him. When the white men see the Fantees do this, and the English officers bring him this four ackies, it makes him get up very angry, but he has no palaver with white men.

All Fantee is his, all the black man's country is his; he hears that white men bring all the things that come here; he wonders they do not fight with the Fantees, for he knows they cheat them. Now he sees white men, and he thanks God and his fetish for it. . .

This King, Sai, is young on the stool, but he keeps always in his head what old men say, for it is good, and his great men and linguists tell it him every morning. The King of England makes three great men, and sends one to Cape Coast, one to Annamaboe, and one to Accra; Cape Coast is the same as England. The King gets two ounces from Accra every moon, and the English wish to give him only four ackies for the big fort at Cape Coast, and the same for Annamaboe; do white men think this proper? . . .

The King knows the King of England is his good friend, for he has sent him handsome dashes; he knows his officers are his good friends, for they come to see him. The

King wishes the Governor to send to Elmina to see what is paid him there, and to write the King of England how much, as, the English say their nation passes the Dutch; he will see by the books given him by both forts. If the King of England does not like that, he may send him himself what he pleases, and then Sai can take it.

He thanks the King and Governor for sending four White men to see him. The old King wished to see some of them, but the Fantees stop it. He is but a young man and sees them, and so again he thanks God and his fetish.

Dictated in the presence of, T. EDWARD BOWDICH. WILLIAM HUTCHISON HENRY TEDLIE

(C). Treaty made and entered into by Thomas Edward Bowdich, Esquire, in the name of the Governor and Council at Cape Coast Castle, on the Gold Coast of Africa, and on behalf of the British Government, with Sai Tootoo Quamina, King of Ashantee and its Dependencies, and Boitinnee Quama, King of Dwabin and its Dependencies. *

1st. There shall be perpetual peace and harmony between the British subjects in this country and the subjects of the Kings of Ashantee *and Dwabin.*

2nd. The same shall exist between the subjects of the Kings of Ashantee *and Dwabin*, and all nations of Africa residing under the protection of the Company's Forts and Settlements on the Gold Coast, and, it is hereby agreed, that there are no palavers now existing, and that neither party has any claim upon the other.

3rd. The King of Ashantee guarantees *the security of* the people of Cape Coast from the hostilities threatened by the people of Elmina.

4th. In order to avert the horrors of war, it is agreed that in any case of aggression on the part of the natives under British protection, the Kings shall complain thereof to the Governor-in-Chief to obtain redress, and that they will in no instance resort to hostilities, *even against the other towns of the Fantee territory*, without

endeavoring as much as possible to effect an amicable arrangement, *affording the Governor the opportunity of propitiating it, as far as he may with discretion.*

5th. The King of Ashantee agrees to permit a British officer to reside constantly at his capital, for the purpose of instituting and preserving a regular communication with the Governor-in-Chief at Cape Coast Castle.

6th. The Kings of Ashantee *and Dwabin* pledges himself/*themselves* to countenance, promote and encourage the trade of his/*their* subjects with Cape Coast Castle and its dependencies to the extent of his/*their* power.

7th. The Governors of the respective Forts shall at all times afford every protection in their power to the persons and property of the people of Ashantee *and Dwabin* who may resort to the water-side.

8th. The Governor-in-Chief reserves to himself the right of punishing any subject of Ashantee *or Dwabin* guilty of secondary offences, but in case of any crime of magnitude, he will send the offender to the Kings, to be dealt with according to the laws of his country.

9th. The Kings agree(s) to commit *their* children to the care of the Governor-in-Chief, for education, at Cape Coast Castle, in full confidence of the good intentions of the British Government and of the benefits to be derived therefrom.

10th. The Kings promise(s) to direct diligent inquiries to be made respecting the officers attached to the Mission of Major John Peddie and Captain Thomas Campbell, and to influence and oblige the neighbouring kingdoms and their tributaries, to befriend them as the subjects of the British Government.

Signed and sealed at Coomassie, this seventh day of September, in the year of our Lord, one thousand eight hundred and seventeen.

The mark of Sai Tootoo Quamina X (L.S.)

The mark of Boitinnee Quama X (L.S.)

Thomas Edward Bowdich

In the presence of William Hutchison

Henry Tedlie

---

*Italicized words under section C are those that appear in Bowdich's version of the treaty but not in that of the Asantehene.

(D). Dupuis's comment on Bowdich's version of the treaty.

The Treaty, as published in Mr. Bowdich's work, compared with what was actually written, and deposited with the king, is a garbled statement. I cannot say less. In the original document, which is now in my keeping, the pompous name of Boitene Quama, king of Dwabin, is nowhere to be found. It would seem that this association of the two sovereigns was calculated to awaken a more lively interest, and thus only can I account for an attempt to deceive government and the public, by means, I believe, unprecedented in the annals of British diplomacy. The article, No. 9, showing the king's disposition to send his own children to Cape Coast for education is falsely inserted, and every other article is disfigured or misrepresented more or less.

(E). Declaration of Messrs. Hutton, Salmon, Collins, and Graves, relative to the Message sent up to the King of Ashantee, by Mr. Smith.

We, the undersigned officers and gentlemen, who accompanied the embassy, under charge of Consul Dupuis, being present at an audience . . . were witnesses to the truth of the following statement, resulting from a discussion which ensued between the king of Ashantee and the consul, on the subject of certain claims established by the former on the governor of Cape Coast Castle, and also on the town of Cape Coast, amounting, separately, to 1600 ounces of gold, and collectively to double the said sum.

The new treaty being read over and interpreted to the king, he expressed much dissatisfaction and declared it to be his determined resolution not to relinquish the demand he had made on the town of Cape Coast; alleging, at the same time, that he was actually negotiating with the governor of the Castle, who had become responsible to him for the payment of a certain sum of money. . . .

In reply to an observation, which was made by the consul at an early part of the debate, that the king of Ashantee had, in virtue of the treaty of 1817, consigned over to the protection of the British government the natives residing under the British forts, he, the king, produced the original treaties, preliminary and definitive, and caused them to be read over and explained to him, which, when done, he declared he had been deceived by the author of those documents, who did not truly explain to him their contents, for he never could or would resign the command he possessed over a conquered people, who were his slaves, and consequently should be obedient to him their master. He moreover declared, that he had consigned these people over to the English, resident on the coast, giving and granting them authority to make use of their services as they pleased; but he never transferred to them the power to interfere with his government, in any shape; nor would he permit it, as they were, "*bona fide*," his subjects only, as his dominions embraced the whole line of coast from Appollonia on the west to Danish Accra on the east (both inclusive).

4. The impact of the abolitionists on labor legislation.

Missionaries at the Cape of Good Hope criticized how settler farmers, most of them of Dutch origin, treated their black employees, slaves and Khoisan alike. Joined in their criticism by allies among British merchants (whom local farmers accused of hoping to benefit from the growth of larger markets for their goods among a better paid working class), the missionaries succeeded in pressuring the British government to rescind harsh labor regulations introduced earlier (especially the legislation of 1809 and 1812).[4]

4. G. W. Eybers, ed., *Select Constitutional Documents Illustrating South African History, 1795–1910* (New York: George Routledge and Sons, 1918), pp. 26–28.

Ordinance No. 20, For Improving the Condition of Hottentots and other free Persons of colour at the Cape of Good Hope, and for Consolidating and Amending the Laws affecting those Persons, July 17, 1828.

WHEREAS certain Laws relating to and affecting the Hottentots and other free persons of colour, lawfully residing in this Colony, require to be consolidated, amended, or repealed, and certain obnoxious usages and customs, which are injurious to those persons, require to be declared illegal and discontinued: Be it therefore enacted, by His Honour the Lieutenant-Governor in Council, That from and after the passing of this Ordinance, the Proclamations of the 16th day of July 1787, 9th day of May 1803, 1st day of November 1809, 23rd day of April 1812, 9th day of July 1819, and 23rd day of May 1823, shall be, and the same are hereby repealed. . . .

II. And whereas by usage and custom of this Colony, Hottentots and other free persons of colour have been subjected to certain restraints as to their residence, mode of life, and employment, and to certain compulsory services to which others of His Majesty's Subjects are not liable: Be it therefore enacted, that from and after the passing of this Ordinance, no Hottentot or other free Person of colour, lawfully residing in this Colony, shall be subject to any compulsory service to which other of His Majesty's Subjects therein are not liable, nor to any hindrance, molestation, fine, imprisonment or punishment of any kind whatsoever, under the pretence that such Person has been guilty of vagrancy or any other offence, unless after trial in due course of Law; any custom or usage to the contrary in any wise notwithstanding.

III. And whereas doubts have arisen as to the competency of Hottentots and other free Persons of colour to purchase or possess Land in this Colony: Be it therefore enacted, [all transfers of land made to or by such Hottentot or other free person of colour are legal; and it is lawful for such persons born in the Colony or granted deeds of burghership to possess land].

IV. And whereas it is expedient to protect ignorant and unwary Hottentots and other free Persons of colour as aforesaid from the effects of improvident Contracts for Service: Be it therefore enacted, [that it shall not be legal for any person to hire by written agreement any Hottentot or free person of colour for a longer period than one calendar month at a time, except as hereinafter provided]. . . .

5. The settlers' revolt.

Slave-owning farmers on the eastern frontier of the Cape of Good Hope reacted angrily to the legislation of 1828, considering it an unacceptable intrusion by the colonial government into employer-employee relations. They were particularly opposed to any official measures that prevented them from using physical means to punish their workers and to the enforcement of policies that resulted in the trial of farmers accused of ill-treating slaves and free black workers such as Khoisan. They were also unhappy with the refusal of the colonial administration to expand the eastern frontiers of the colony and thereby make more land available to farmers. From 1833 onward, organized parties of Dutch farmers, almost all of them from the eastern districts of the Cape, began moving into the interior of South Africa in an attempt to get beyond the reach of British authority and to find new areas to farm. During the rest of the decade, approximately 15,000 men, women, and children (about half of whom were Khoisan "servants") joined this "Great Trek" into the interior. One of the leaders of this movement was Piet Retief who, after an unsuccessful business career, little of which involved farming, declared bankruptcy in June 1836, eight months before he joined the trek. Despite this checkered past, he became the main spokesman for Dutch settler aspirations at the Cape.[5]

Manifesto of the EMIGRANT FARMERS, *Grahamstown Journal,* February 2, 1837.

A document has been handed to us, with a request to give it publicity, purporting to be the causes of the emigration of the colonial farmers, of which the following is a literal translation:

Numerous reports having been circulated throughout the colony, evidently with the intention of exciting in the minds of our countrymen of prejudice against those who have resolved to emigrate from a colony where they have experienced, for so many years past, a series of the most vexatious and severe losses; and, as we desire to stand high in the estimation of our brethren, and are anxious that they and the world at large should believe us incapable of severing that sacred tie which binds a Christian to his native soil, without the most sufficient reasons, we are induced to record the following summary of our motives for taking so important a step, and also our intentions respecting our proceedings towards the native tribes which we may meet with beyond the boundary:

1. We despair of saving the colony from those evils which threaten it by the turbulent and dishonest conduct of vagrants, who are allowed to infest the country in every part; nor do we see any prospect of peace or happiness for our children in any country thus distracted by internal commotions.

2. We complain of the severe losses which we have been forced to sustain by the emancipation of our slaves, and the vexatious laws which have been enacted respecting them.

3. We complain of the continual system of plunder which we have ever endured from the Caffres [Africans] and other coloured classes, and particularly by the last invasion of the colony, which has desolated the frontier districts and ruined most of the inhabitants.

4. We complain of the unjustifiable odium which has been cast upon us by interested and dishonest persons, under the cloak of religion, whose testimony is believed in England, to the exclusion of all evidence in our favour; and we can foresee, as the result of this prejudice, nothing but the total ruin of the country.

5. We are resolved, wherever we go, that we will uphold the just principles of liberty; but, whilst we will take care that no one shall be held in a state of slavery, it is our determination to maintain such regulations as may suppress crime, and preserve proper relations between master and servant.

6. We solemnly declare that we quit this colony with a desire to lead a more quiet life than we have heretofore done. We will not molest any people, nor deprive them of the smallest property; but, if attacked, we shall consider ourselves fully justified in defending our persons and effects, to the utmost of our ability, against every enemy.

7. We make known, that when we shall have framed a code of laws for our future guidance, copies shall be forwarded to the colony for general information; but we take this opportunity of stating, that it is our firm resolve to make provision for the summary punishment of any traitors who may be found amongst us.

8. We propose, in the course of our journey, and on arriving at the country in which we shall permanently reside, to make known to the native tribes our intentions, and our desire to live in peace and friendly intercourse with them.

9. We quit this colony under the full assurance that the English Government has nothing more to require of us, and will allow

---

5. G. W. Eybers, ed., *Select Constitutional Documents Illustrating South African History, 1795–1910* (New York: George Routledge and Sons, 1918), pp. 143–45.

us to govern ourselves without its interference in future.

10. We are now quitting the fruitful land of our birth, in which we have suffered enormous losses and continual vexation, and are entering a wild and dangerous territory; but we go with a firm reliance on an all-seeing, just, and merciful Being, whom it will be our endeavour to fear and humbly to obey.

By authority of the farmers who have quitted the Colony,

(Signed) P. RETIEF.

6. A missionary talks with a king.

Missionaries—British, French, and American—went into the interior of South Africa from the 1810s onward, aiming to introduce Christianity and "civilization" to Africans. George Champion was the first missionary to travel to the Zulu kingdom, established by Shaka in the late 1810s and 1820s, and ruled from 1828 onward by Dingane (or Dingaan, both spellings were current in the nineteenth century), Shaka's half-brother and his assassin as well. Accounts of the Zulu written by British traders who had visited Shaka in the 1820s stressed what they perceived as the brutality of his regime and that of his successor. Champion, however, found a king who was very inquisitive about the beliefs and practices of his European visitor.[6]

January 17, 1836, Sunday.

The king sent for us early; of course our present must go with us as an introduction. Providence had highly favoured us, in that we had been able to secure the services of the only white man in the country who can speak Dingaan's language well, and with whom the chief is well acquainted. Of course we were informed of all the minutiae of introduction and formality, on which often so much depends. Dingaan was sitting just outside of his cattle-kraal, in a large old-fashioned arm-chair just brought him by Mr. N [Norden]. He wore a cloak of red plush with two rows of buttons extending from head to foot in front. A strip of the same was tied round his forehead. This is the place where he sits every morning for the purpose of attending to business. Some fifty or eighty men were sitting in a semicircle on either side of him on the ground. During some minutes after we had approached near him all was silence. At length the chief sent his compliments to us, and wished to converse. He examined minutely the articles brought:

the razor, the umbrella, the pictures, and the lock of a tin trunk given him. A few beads also, a knife, a tea-canister, and some handkerchiefs were among them. He appeared much pleased, and said he should like to see our wagon. This he inspected narrowly. He found a piece of green baize which he fancied, and we gave it him. We mentioned to him that it was the Sabbath, and that we rested from all secular business. He seemed satisfied, and excused us till to-morrow. In the afternoon he sent a goat for slaughter, and through his means probably the people were kept away from our wagon, so that our day of rest has not been so much interrupted as we feared. A shower of rain also gave us a season of quiet. . . . We had brought with us a small turning-lathe, supposing that it would give the chief a better idea of some things than any explanation of ours. Some rosewood upon the wagon attracted his attention yesterday, and an enquiry brought the lathe on the carpet. He must have it with us in his palace to-day, and see its operation in the turning of a snuff-box. He sent for us early, to what may be called his hall of audi-

---

6. Journal of George Champion, printed in John Bird, ed., *The Annals of Natal, 1495 to 1845* (Pietermaritzburg: P. Davis and Sons, 1888), pp. 203–08.

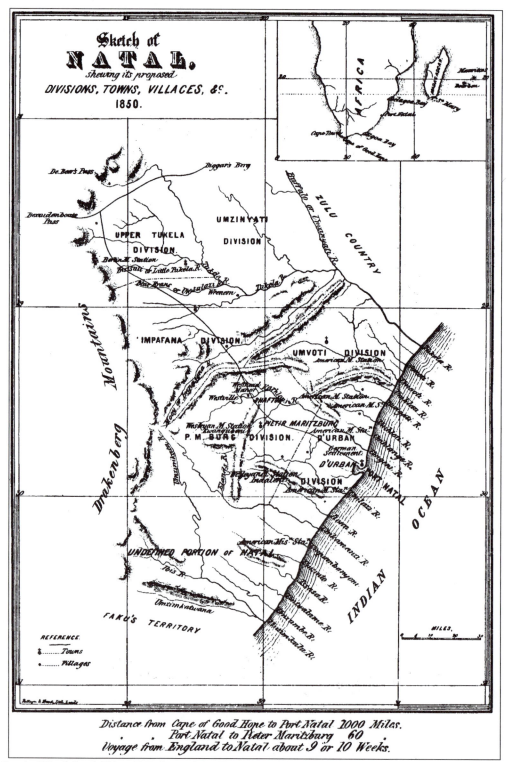

Sketch of Natal, South Africa, 1850. *Source:* James Erasmus Methley, *The New Colony of Port Natal: With Information for Emigrants, Accompanied with an Explanatory Map, by the Government Official Surveyor* (London: Houlston and Stoneman, 1850), facing p. 40.

ence. This is an apartment some-what in the shape of a triangle, with curved sides, surrounded by a fence of whittled sticks woven very ingeniously together, and seven or eight feet high. It has three or four gates, each one being surmounted by the sticks passing over the gateway, parallel to each other, in the shape of a semicircle; and continued down its side to the ground. The king's house stands in the centre, well constructed and very large, perhaps twenty feet high—but, after all, only a Kafir hut. The king's great chair or throne stands in this room. Beside it there is nothing but a mound of clay, on which the king often stands to survey his town and land, no doubt with some of the pride of the Babylonian monarch. The king took us to different parts of his abode. It consists of apartments resembling the first, but usually containing three houses. He led us from one place to another till we were absolutely tired, and thought that if left to ourselves we should find it difficult to escape out of the labyrinth. In one apartment sixty or seventy of his girls were dancing and singing; and that not without some harmony and precision. And it must be added that we saw in his palace some three hundred girls, of whom a few, apparently, were in the position of servants, but the others evidently filled a different sphere. Completely beyond all description, their hips and necks loaded with beads of various sorts, and with no clothing on most, except a short coat around the loins, they present "in toto," as they drag their load over the ground, and in this warm weather, an appearance which excites in a stranger both ridicule and disgust.

We crept into one of the houses at the king's request. The dark earthen floor bore a fine polish, and was as smooth as marble. It is smeared every morning, I am informed, with fat. The fireplace in the centre was constructed with much neat taste, and the roof was so wattled on the inside as to appear like some well-braided basket.

Returning to the lathe, we found it surrounded by a whole host of the royal family, greatly admiring every part and parcel of the instrument. At length the box was finished, greatly to the satisfaction of the owner. But

he must try his hand; and, to his credit it must be said, he succeeded very well for a beginner. He has an inquisitive mind, and often starts questions which show him to be superior to the generality of his people. Every part of the lathe underwent the strictest scrutiny, and nothing was left unexplained. But he is very proud and excessively fond of flattery. His subjects approach him in a bending posture or on the ground. No man comes into his palace without an express permit. His smith, however, was admitted to-day to view the curious machine. This man is of great service in fastening the rings and bangles upon his captains, and appears to be on very familiar terms with his chief. His language to the king is nothing but submissive adulation, as that of all his subjects, "Yes, father: O father! mighty chief," being appended to every sentence. He received a present of a file or two from Mr. Grout, whereat his eyes almost started out of his head for joy. . . .

20th. This morning early, the king sent for us. He was sitting in the presence of his people. The doctor's skill was for some time the topic. He asked him if he could heal all diseases; if he went by any spirit in his art, and whether he could cure a man who was affected by paralysis in an arm or leg. When told that the man could be cured, he told us his own complaint, but said he would wait and see if the paralytic were cured. He wished to see some money; asked us what we thought of his dress yesterday; informed us now and then that the people were praising him; and as we were leaving him, asked if we could perform feats of leaping, such as some white men had once done. He asked us if we could get a bead-maker to live with him. When God's name happened to be mentioned, he asked us how we knew of Him, and then childishly turned to something else.

Took a walk round the town. It would occupy half an hour's constant walking. On the upper side we found the smith's shop. His work is wholly in brass. A very hot fire is made from the dried leaves of the sloe. Here the small brass wire is melted down into plates, which again are fluted by sharp hammers on rude anvils of stone, and bent so as to form the broad covering for the forearm, given by Dingaan to none but the greatest of his captains. The principal work now going forward here is the making of shields. These are made of large ox-hides, oval in shape, and are given, the black to the boys, the red to the men. In fact, Gungunhlovu seems to be little else than a camp of soldiers. The chief is always talking of some warlike expedition, and inspiring them with a desire for plunder and blood. They live, as it were, at the king's table, and not on the fruits of their own labour. . . .

21st. Again at the king's this morning. He improves in his skill at the lathe, and his fondness for it led him to ask it of us. This we had to refuse. The girls were at work. Some of them were receiving their calabashes of morning's milk, some engaged in fastening the brass about another's neck, The person to be operated upon was lying down with her neck across a block, while the rings were made to meet by pounding with a hammer. Ever after, the victim finds it difficult to bend her neck any way.

The king sat in a chair, very like an European one, but carved with an assagai [spear] out of a single block of wood. He wished us to write an order for some *brass dancing-rods*. The subject of our visit was mentioned, and he said that this afternoon he would see about it.

22nd. The king had appointed yesterday for our conference; but a true African shower prevented. The thunder was very loud, with lightning exceedingly vivid, and hailstones as large as bullets, and in such profusion as to whiten the ground, pelted our cloth habitation roundly.

Early this morning the king's messenger came for us. He was sitting in his usual morning seat, with his "amabutu," or young soldiers, in a half-moon in front of him, at thirty or forty yard's distance. He invited us near him, and also the three captains left in the place of two indunas in their absence. Our business came at once on the carpet, without form or ceremony. Some short account of God's word was given, and our object briefly stated. A Testament was shown as a part of God's word. He wished to know how many

leaves it contained, and was surprised to hear us tell without counting them. He asked to hear some of it read. He then enquired about the Creation. A short account of the Saviour was given. They all seemed interested. One asked if God was not displeased with their treatment of His Son, and what He did to the people. We were asked if men knew anything about God before Christ came. One query was, if God was so powerful, why not pray to Him to take away all disease and misery?

Dingaan wished to know our relation to the Government of our country, and then said, "Here, now, are my three councillors, in place of the two great men; they must decide for you; I am favourable." The result was—for the councillors echoed but the voice of their chief—that they fear evils from the introduction of white men into their country, and wish the line of the whites to be beyond the Umtugela [river]; that they can hardly believe we can teach the people what we profess, to read and write; but that they wish the experiment to be tried in their country when we return with our wives. For this purpose we may begin in the district of Hlomenhline, containing several thousands. "And then," said the king, "if you succeed, I will bring the school right into the heart of my dominions, I will learn myself, and set an example to my people!"

We were mutually pleased. In present circumstances we can ask no more. Such is the gross darkness that reigns here, even in the mind of Dingaan, that the work must be gradual. In speaking of God to any of these people they have usually stared about the heavens in wonder, or listened to our words as an unmeaning story; and, perhaps, have interrupted us by asking for something that caught their eye. Soon we called upon the king for the last time. He was eating, and it was given us in very strict charge not to cough, or hem, or spit in his presence. He was in his hut. We were obliged absolutely to crawl in on our hands and knees. The chief was reclining on a mat, his head on a wooden bolster. Strung around the hut, behind his wives, were their bead dresses. The hut was not high within, but very wide, and supported by nine posts. In the centre the dogs were sleeping. We now saw the monarch reclining at his ease in our presence. Very little ceremony was required. He appeared to be our friend more than at any time previous. While in the house, we heard the loud song of his subjects previous to partaking of the king's meat. Several oxen are slaughtered daily by the chief. After a loud song, they all shout "God save the King," or its equivalent—and enter on the work of mastication.

Dingaan was as inquisitive as usual. He took much notice of a letter written for him to Mr. N. He asked us how we learned to read. He said it ran in his head that he should learn, and should ere long have one of us to teach him. Our interpreter received quite a rebuke for being a white man and not able to read and write. He then wished the names of all his girls, who were sitting around the sides

of the house, and of the dogs which were sleeping in the centre, to be written, and to be read by one who had been absent during the writing. He asked when we should return, and gave us beads, as specimens of those which he wished us to bring. We must then make for him some candle-wicks, that he might supply his lantern and candlestick during our absence; and then he went out, leaving as the sport of his childish girls, till the heat and confinement of the house obliged us also to leave it. We found him outside, near some tallow, which probably his royal skill would soon manufacture into some sort of candles. Here he gave orders for five cattle, in addition to the two we had already received, to be brought to us for most on our journey, and charging the doctor not to forget his medicine, he wished us a good journey, saying that he regarded us as his friends, and wished soon to see us.

7. Dingane kills the first settlers.

Though initially welcoming to his first European visitors, and always interested in discussing religion with missionaries, Dingane became concerned with the arrival of large numbers of Dutch settlers into his territory. He feared that they would undermine his authority, take his people's land, and perhaps even threaten his own life. In February 1838, he decided on a pre-emptive strike against the party of trekkers led by Piet Retief. This eyewitness account of the killing of the trekkers is by Francis Owen, a U.S. missionary who lived at Dingane's capital and who enjoyed the king's protection. Less than a year after Dingane's act, other trekkers, working in alliance with the Zulu monarch's half-brother, Mpande, defeated the Zulu at the battle of Blood River. Dingane fled north as a refugee, and within a few months was killed by Swazi enemies. Mpande succeeded him as king of the Zulu.[7]

February 6, 1838. A dreadful day in the annals of the mission. I shudder to give an account of it. This morning, as I was sitting in the shade of my wagon, reading the Testament, the usual messenger came, with hurry and anxiety depicted in his looks. I was sure that he was about to pronounce something serious. And what was his commission?

While it showed consideration and kindness in the Zulu monarch towards me, it disclosed a horrid instance of perfidy–too horrid to describe–towards the unhappy men who for a few days had been his guests, and are now no more. He sent to tell me not to be frightened, as he was going to kill the Boers. This news came like a thunderstroke to myself and

---

7. Journal of Francis Owen, printed in John Bird, ed., *The Annals of Natal, 1495 to 1845* (Pietermaritzburg: P. Davis and Sons, 1888), pp. 346–48, 351–52.

to every successive member of my family as they heard it. The reason assigned for this treacherous act was that they were going to kill him; that they had come here, and that he had now learnt all their plans. The messenger was anxious for my answer; but what could I say? I was fearful on the one hand of seeming to justify the treachery, and on the other of exposing myself and my family to probable danger if I appeared to take their part. Moreover, I could not but feel that it was my duty to apprise the Boers of the intended massacre; while certain death would have ensued, I apprehended, if I had been detected in giving them this information. However, I was released from this dilemma by beholding an awful spectacle. My attention was directed to the blood-stained hill nearly opposite my hut, and on the other side of my wagon, which hides it from view, where all the executions at this fearful spot take place, and which was destined now to add sixty more bleeding carcasses to the number of those who have already cried to heaven for vengeance. "There!" said some one, "they are killing the Boers now!" About nine or ten Zulus to each Boer were dragging their helpless, unarmed victims to the fatal spot— where those eyes which awaked this morning to see the cheerful light of day for the last time, are now closed in death. I laid myself down on the ground. Mrs. and Miss Owen were not more thunderstruck than myself. We comforted one another. Presently, the deed

of blood being accomplished, the whole multitude returned to the town to meet their sovereign; and, as they drew near to him, set up a shout which reached the [missionary] station, and continued for some time. Meanwhile, I myself had been kept from all fear for our personal safety; for I considered the message of Dingaan to me as an indication that he had no ill designs against the missionary. . . .

February 7. I did not give an adequate description of the dreadful carnage yesterday. I omitted to state that many of the Boers had children with them, some under eleven years of age, as I am informed–and these were all butchered. They also had their Hottentot servants, and these were likewise slaughtered, besides their interpreter and his servant. The number slain must have been nearer a hundred than sixty. . . . Dingaan afterwards sent for Mr. Venables and his interpreter. . . . He said that he should never send us away, or drive us out; but if the teachers at any time wished to go and see their own people, and would come and say "Hlala guhle" (farewell, or rest quietly), he would not stop them. . . .

February 9 . . . The king sent for my interpreter . . . and gave him a very plausible account of the late unhappy affairs. He said if he had not despatched the Boers, they would have fired at him and his people when they left; and that, when their guns were examined, they were all found to be loaded with ball.

8. Advance by treaty in West Africa.

Given the high financial and human costs of military action in West Africa, as evidenced by the fate of Governor Charles MacCarthy, the British officially pulled back somewhat and tried to advance their anti-slavery and commercial interests in West Africa by forming alliances with African leaders and negotiating treaties with potential enemies. The British hoped to build up a network of alliances that would extend their reach into the interior. They developed alliances with the Fante people of the coast and, assisted by militias formed by Danish and African merchants, inflicted a heavy defeat on the Asante in 1827. The British government returned control of the coast to a group of merchants who appointed George Maclean as their governor. Maclean negotiated a new peace treaty with the Asante in 1831 by the terms of which the latter agreed to give up their claims to the coastal areas.

The British also sought to extend their commercial interests in the Niger Delta and thereby gain access to the enormous trading hinterland of the Niger River (especially the trade in palm oil). Representatives of the British government entered into a series of treaty agreements in the 1830s and 1840s with the African merchant-kings who controlled the Niger Delta. They made annual payments (or "presents," or perhaps, in African eyes, "tribute") to get local rulers to desist from the export trade in slaves. Through treaties, they tried to establish the ways in which their merchants would be dealt with if disputes arose between European and African. In seeking to establish such extra-territorial jurisdiction, the British negotiated with one of the most important of the Niger Delta leaders, King Pepple of Bonny (a state that had grown throughout the eighteenth century as a center of the slave trade).[8]

(A). Peace treaty with Asante, April 27, 1831.

We, the undersigned . . . Namely, the Governor of the Cape Coast Castle and British settlements, on the part of His Majesty the king of England; the princess "Akianvah" and chief "Quagua," on the part of the king of Ashantee; "Aggery," king of Cape Coast; "Adookoo," king of Fantee; "Amonoo," king of Annamaboe; "Chibboo," king of Denkera; "Ossoo Okoo," king of Tufel; "Aminnie," king of Wassaw; "Chibboo," king of Assin; the chiefs of Adjumacon and Essacoomah, and the other chiefs in alliance with the king of Great Britain, whose names are hereunto appended—do consent to and hereby ratify the following treaty of peace and of free commerce between ourselves and such other chiefs as may hereafter adhere to it:

1. The king of Ashantee having deposited in Cape Coast Castle, in the presence of the above-mentioned parties, the sum of 600 ounces of gold, and having delivered into the hands of the Governor two young men of the royal family of Ashantee named "Ossor Ansah" and "Ossoo Inquantamissah," as security that he will keep peace with the said parties in all time coming, peace is hereby declared betwixt the said king of Ashantee and all and each of the parties aforesaid, to continue in all time coming. The above securities shall remain in Cape Coast Castle for the space of six years from this date.

2. In order to prevent all quarrels in future which might lead to the infraction of this treaty of peace, we the parties aforesaid, have agreed to the following rules and regulations for the better protection of the lawful commerce:

The paths shall be perfectly open and free to all persons engaged in lawful traffic, and persons molesting them in any way whatever, or forcing them to purchase at any particular market, or influencing them by any unfair means whatever, shall be declared guilty of infringing this treaty, and be liable to the severest punishment.

Panyarring [seizing as a pledge or security], denouncing and swearing on or by any person or thing whatever, are strictly forbidden, and all persons infringing this rule shall be rigorously punished; and no master or chief shall be answerable for the crimes of his servants, unless done by his orders or consent, or When under his control.

As the king of Ashantee has renounced all right or title to any tribute or homage from the kings of Dinkera, Assin, and others formerly his subjects, so, on the other hand, these parties are strictly prohibited from insulting, by improper speaking or in any other

---

8. (A), George Metcalfe, *Great Britain and Ghana: Documents of Ghana History, 1807–1957* (Legon: University of Ghana, 1964), pp. 133–34; (B), C. W. Newbury, ed., *British Policy Towards Africa: Select Documents, 1786–1874* (Oxford: Clarendon Press, 1965), pp. 375–76.

way, their former master, such conduct being calculated to produce quarrels and wars.

All "palavers" are to be decided in the manner mentioned in the terms and conditions of peace already agreed to by the parties to this treaty.

Signed in the great hall of Cape Coast Castle, this 27th day of April, 1831, by the parties to this treaty, and sealed with the great seal of the Colony, in their presence.

[Signed] George Maclean, Governor

(B). King Pepple's House, Grand Bonny, January 25, 1836.

Article I.

It is hereby agreed, between the undersigned H. B. Majesty's Subjects and the King of Bonny, that no English Subject shall from this time be detained on shore or maltreated in any way whatever by the King or natives of Bonny under any pretence; by so doing, they will bring themselves under the displeasure of the King of England, and be declared enemies of Great Britain, and that the Men of War, on any complaint will immediately come up the Bonny to protect the English Vessels.

2.

In case of any misunderstanding between the Captains of the English Vessels and the King or Gentlemen of Bonny, that all and every English Captain will go on shore, free of molestation and will, with the King and Gentlemen of Bonny, peaceably settle all disputes between the parties.

3.

English Captains having any complaint against any of the natives of Bonny, will come on shore, and lay his or their complaint before the King, and they hereby promise to give the complainant redress, by punishing the offender, and if any English seaman shall ill treat a Bonny man he shall be punished by the Captain of the Vessel to which he may belong.

4.

That for the future, all books made between the Traders and English Captains, shall bear the signature of such responsible officer, belonging to the Ship with the date and name; by his not doing so, the case shall be decided by the Captains of the Merchant Ships, lying in the River, who will see, that the Trader's or Native's loss be made good.

5.

That after the Captain or Supercargo has paid the regular Custom, the trade shall be opened, and upon no account, shall the trade of any Vessel be stopped; excepting the Captain or Supercargo act in opposition, to any of the annexed agreements, and refuses to pay the fine, imposed by the other Captains, for the infringing of these rules.

6.

That every vessel's property shall be properly protected, and that no King, Gentleman, or Native of Bonny, shall roll away the casks of any Vessel from the Cask house on any pretence whatever.

7.

That the King will be responsible for all monies, Oil, or goods, that may be owing to the English Captains, so that the Vessel may not be detained before sailing; and that the Captains of the English Ships, will see all just debts incurred by any vessel, are paid by her to Bonny men with Bars, or Oil, before leaving the River.

9. The secretary of state for the colonies proposes a more interventionist policy to end the slave trade.

By the end of the 1830s, it was becoming evident to British officials that their existing anti-slave trade policies were not working. A surreptitious trade in slaves was still active in the British forts along the coast. African leaders such as King Pepple insisted on higher cash payments to desist from the slave trade than the

British government was ready to pay. Moreover, Pepple and his peers refused to countenance any interference with their practices of domestic slavery. In these circumstances, Lord John Russell sent an official expedition up the Niger River in 1841 to meet with African leaders and to persuade them to cease the slave trade. The Niger commissioners traveled on three steamships, a new mode of transportation that for the first time allowed the British to sail against the outward flowing river currents and extend their sea power into the interior of Africa.[9]

Lord John Russell's instructions to Her Majesty's Niger Commissioners, January 30, 1841.

10. On your arrival at each native settlement, you will ascertain the proper mode for opening a communication with the Chief; and in all your intercourse with him, you will take care that you are treated by him with proper respect; and you will not neglect, also, to treat him with the respect which is due to the rank which belongs to him.

11. You will tell the Chief that you are sent by the Queen of Great Britain and Ireland to express Her Majesty's wish to establish friendly relations with him; and to settle and agree with him for the extinction of the Foreign Traffic in Slaves in his dominions; and for the substitution instead thereof of a full and free intercourse and barter of all articles of innocent trade between the subjects of Her Majesty and those of such Chief, for his profit and advantage, and for the mutual use, comfort, and benefit of the subjects of both countries. You will ask him what articles he and his subjects are in want of, and you will express generally the readiness of this country to supply them; you will ask him what articles of trade he and his subjects wish to dispose of; and you will express generally the readiness of this country to purchase them. You will inquire what further articles of native growth, or produce, or manufacture his country can supply as articles of useful export with Great Britain; and you will encourage him to the cultivation or production thereof, by expressing generally the readiness of this country to take off his hands, on fair and reasonable terms of barter, all such ar-

ticles of useful trade for this country as he can supply, in return for all such articles of use, and comfort, and advantage to himself as he requires.

12. You will show to him the advantages of putting down the Foreign Slave Trade, and of building upon the abolition a lawful and innocent trade. You will say to him, that his subjects will thereby be induced to cultivate the soil, to value their habitations, to increase their produce, and to behave well, in order to keep the advantage which that produce will give to them; that they will thus become better subjects, and better men, and that his possessions will thus become more full of what is valuable. You will impress upon him, that he himself will no longer need to make, or to keep up, quarrels with his neighbours, or to undertake distant and dangerous wars, or to seek out causes of punishment to his own subjects, for the sake of producing from the odious Trade in Slaves an income for himself. You will explain to him, that the people of his country will, out of the produce of labour in cultivating, gathering, and preparing articles for trade, bring to him more revenues, and be consequently more valuable to him.

13. You will tell him, that Her Majesty, desirous to make that innocent commerce which is a benefit to all nations, a peculiar benefit to himself, proposes that, upon his abolishing the Slave Trade, not only he and his subjects shall have this free and advantageous commerce; but that he himself shall have, for his own share, and without any payment on his part, a sum not exceeding one-twentieth part value of every article of British merchandize brought by British ships

---

9. *Papers Relative to the Expedition to the River Niger* (London: William Clowes and Sons, 1843), pp. 6–10.

and sold in his dominions; such proportion to be taken by himself without any reference to the amount of articles for which the remaining nineteen-twentieths shall be bartered with him or with his subjects; and you will make agreements with him on this subject conformable, as far as possible, with the draft agreement. You will, where possible, stipulate in return for a free right of barter for his subjects, and the abolition of any monopoly in his own favour, should such exist.

14. While explaining to the Chief the profit to be derived from the cultivation of the soil, you will not fail on all proper occasions, as far as you may deem it expedient and compatible with the main objects of your mission, to draw his attention to the superior advantages of free over slave labour: to impress upon him the impolicy as well as the injustice of slavery: and to acquaint him with the abhorrence in which it is held by Her Majesty and the people of England. You may remind him of the large tracts of waste land in his possession; state how unprofitable they are to him at present; and inform him that if he could procure such land to be cultivated by his subjects on a system of free labour, he would be justly entitled to receive a considerable share of the increased profits: far more than enough to counterbalance all the profits which could possibly arise from the continuance of the Slave Trade. You may further remind him that every man naturally works harder for himself than for another, and is more economical and more careful of his own property; consequently, that the produce of his country would be much greater by free labour than by any other system, and that he would derive a double advantage, first, from his share of the produce as a landlord, and afterwards from the duties he would get as Chief on the sale of the remainder. You may further intimate to him, that a compliance with the wish of Her Majesty's Government and her people, in this respect, would certainly increase Her Majesty's interest in his welfare, and enable Her Majesty and her people to render much greater assistance and encouragement in improving the condition of himself and his people, than could be af-

forded them during the continuance of a system of slave labour. But you must always bear in mind that the main object of your commission is the extinction of the Foreign Slave Trade, and all other points must for the present be considered subordinate.

15. You will, at the proper time, exhibit the presents with which you are furnished from Her Majesty, as proofs of the desire of friendship which the Queen entertains towards the Chief, and as samples of the articles, with which, among others, this country will be glad to supply himself and his subjects in as great a quantity as they shall want and wish, on fair and reasonable terms of barter. You should not distribute these presents to any of the Chiefs, except in those cases where you are satisfied that the interests of the commission in which you are employed imperatively require it; and further, you will also bear in mind the necessity of giving no more than is absolutely requisite; and especially with a view to avoid all possibility of in future impeding ordinary traffic with British or other merchants. In case any of the Chiefs or Head-men of the country should be willing to make presents, you are authorized to exercise your discretion in receiving or rejecting the same; all presents received being for the use of Her Majesty.

16. You will finally propose to him an Agreement upon the basis of the draft with which you are herewith furnished.

17. If, after earnestly discussing this matter with the Chief, you shall find that your arguments have not so far prevailed with him, as to induce him to enter into this Agreement for the Extinction of the Foreign Slave Trade in his dominions; and if he shall resolutely resist your suggestions and the wishes of Her Majesty to that effect; you will entreat and urge him to reconsider this matter, you will ask him to assemble his elders or head-men, and consult with them, before he finally rejects the proposals made by you.

18. You will, if permitted to be present at such conference, declare that the Queen your Sovereign, however powerful, is anxious only to promote peace and prosperity among them; that she offers them, through you, ev-

ery advantage that they can want and that she can give, towards increasing, in a harmless and sure way, the wealth and power of the country; that you come but to ask them to give up the custom of exporting human beings as slaves, and in return to offer them a more profitable substitute in innocent trade; that if they wish moreover any help towards the production of any article, or introduction of any commodity or art for the benefit of their country, your Sovereign is disposed to assist them, and her subjects will be willing to supply at a moderate rate what they desire; and that you will express to Her Majesty their wishes, and forward their views to that effect.

19. While you describe the power and wealth of your country, you will, in all your interviews with the African Chiefs, and with other African natives, on the subject of the suppression of the Slave Trade, abstain carefully from any threat or intimation, that hostilities upon their territory will be the result of their refusal to treat. You will state that the Queen and people of England profess the Christian Religion; that by this religion they are commanded to assist in promoting good will, peace, and brotherly love, among all nations and men; and that in endeavouring to commence a further intercourse with the African nations Her Majesty's Government are actuated and guided by these principles. You will make allowance for the motives of fear, of distrust, of jealousy, of suspicion, by which native Africans, unaccustomed to treat with Europeans in this formal way, may, at first, naturally view the overtures made to them; you will make allowance also for misunderstanding, either of language, of manner, or of conduct, or of your object in seeking intercourse with them; you will also allow for any hardness of feeling you may witness in them on the subject of Slave Trade, a hardness naturally engendered by the exercise of that traffic, and, perhaps, in some cases, increased by intercourse with the lowest and basest of Europeans. You will endeavour to convince them by courtesy, by kindness, by patience and forbearance, of your most persevering desire to be on good terms with them; and you will be most careful to exhibit no signs of needless mistrust. You will on all occasions keep a strict watch, so that no mischief may, from open force or secret wile of the natives, ensure to the lives, liberties, and properties of yourselves, and of others committed to your care; and with this view you will be careful to be provided with adequate means of defence as far as possible; but you will on no account have recourse to arms, excepting for the purpose of defence; and you will bear in mind, that the language and conduct prescribed to you in this paragraph is that which you are to observe on all occasions in the course of your commission.

20. If, after all your attempts to attain the immediate object of your commission, you shall fail in it, you will conclude by telling the Chief and his head-men, that Her Majesty is bound to use all her naval means in conformity with the treaties already entered into with other Great Powers to endeavour entirely to put a stop to the exportation of Slaves from the dominions of every African Chief; and that the Chief and his subjects will, when perhaps too late, see cause to regret their conduct.

21. In those cases in which, all your arguments and representations failing, you will have been obliged to leave the Chief and his country, without accomplishing the immediate objects of your mission, you will be careful still even at parting to leave that Chief and his country in a friendly manner, in order to give room for future overtures, and for a reconsideration of the kindly meant efforts of Her Majesty; and you will, if time and circumstances allow it, take an opportunity of visiting again those Chiefs, who in your first visit declined your overtures; and strengthened by the weight which your success elsewhere may have given to your negotiations, you will again urge the Chiefs to conclude an agreement, on the before-mentioned basis of the abolition of the Slave Trade. . . .

25 . . . It is considered desirable by Her Majesty's Government to have power to erect one or more small forts on the Niger, from whence, and by means of which, to watch over the due execution of the Agreements, to

assist in the abolition of the Slave Trade, and to protect and further the innocent trade of Her Majesty's subjects.

Bearing these views in mind, you will, in your course up that river, select some one or more appropriate spots for the erection of forts for the above-mentioned purposes; and you will make with the Chief of the country a conditional bargain for the land, stating the purpose for which it is intended; you will pay down a small portion of the price, as security for the purchase and permission; and you will send or bring home, for the consideration and ultimate decision of Her Majesty's Government, reports and drawings explanatory of the spot and its capabilities.

The spots should be chosen with reference both to defence and salubrity; to soil and to climate, not only of the spots themselves, but also of the immediate neighbourhood on both sides of the river; because the miasma from one side of a river will frequently, if carried by winds, produce diseases on the other side. They should be places where vessels may securely anchor and ride in safety. They should be in situations to which natives are likely to resort for trade; and if possible, in situations where natives have been accustomed to resort for the purpose. Means of a ready communication with the interior are also desirable for the positions; so that persons wishing to visit the interior from thence, for purposes of commerce or otherwise, may there find facilities for those objects. They should be in a neighbourhood where supplies for vessels may be got; and in a country where the inhabitants are well disposed towards friendly communication with British subjects; and they will be preferably situated not far from some considerable mass of habitations. The establishment of a position near to the confluence of the rivers Niger and Tchadda, would, with its other advantages, have the additional and important one, that it would assist the British trade with both rivers. . . .

33. If at any place, in an independent State within the range of your commission, it shall appear to you to be desirable, that a resident agent on the part of Her Majesty, shall be immediately appointed, and enter on his duties, you are empowered to leave at such a place provisionally, as British resident agent, any one of the gentlemen of your commission, or of the officers or others of the expedition, whom you may think competent and fitted to the duties of that situation. You may assure to such gentleman an allowance proportioned to the circumstances of his situation, for one year only.

10. Treaties with "barbarians" are different from those with "civilized" people.

Treaties that dealt ostensibly with anti-slavery policies had implications for African sovereignty. If an African leader agreed to bring an end to slavery and was unable to do so, did that mean that the British had the legal right (however they defined such right) to intervene? The template drawn up by the British for treaties with African chiefs began with expressions of "peace and friendship," moved on to measures to reduce the trade in slaves, and ended with a requirement that the "person and property of the agent [of the British monarch be treated as though] sacred." In practice, as the treaty with the King of Kataba shows, anti-slavery treaties with African leaders resulted in the transfer of considerable powers from indigenous leaders to the British monarch. James Stephen, under-secretary of state for colonies, noted in a minute regarding the treaty that such fundamental changes could take place because diplomatic agreements made with Africans were not really "treaties" but rather "arrangements" that could be amended as the secretary of state for foreign affairs saw fit. That was how one dealt with "barbarous" as distinct from "civilized" people.[10]

Draft agreement with African chiefs, July 1840.

Object:

There shall be peace and friendship between the people of England and the people of _____ and the slave trade shall be put down for ever in _____, and the people of England and the people of_____ shall trade together innocently, justly, kindly and usefully. And A and B do make the following agreement for these purposes:

Terms:

1. No white Christian persons shall be made slaves in the country in any case; and if any white Christians are now slaves in the _____country, or shall be brought into it as slaves, they shall instantly be set free by the Chief of _____, and he shall assist them to return to their own country.

2. No persons of any colour, or wherever born, shall be taken out of the_____country as slaves; and no person in the_____country shall be in any way concerned in seizing, keeping, carrying, or sending away any persons for the purpose of their being taken out of the _____ country as slaves. And the Chief of _____ shall punish severely all those who break this law.

3. The officers of the Queen of England may seize every vessel or boat of _____ found anywhere carrying on the trade in slaves, and may also seize every vessel or boat of other nations found carrying on the trade in slaves in the waters belonging to the Chief of _____, and the vessels and boats so seized shall be taken into an England possession to be tried by English law; and, when condemned, shall be sold, and the produce of the sale shall be divided equally between the Queen of England and the Chief of _____, and the slaves who were found on board shall be made free.

4. English people may come freely into the _____ country, and may stay in it or pass through it; and they shall be treated as friends while in it, and shall receive every supply they need there; they may freely practice the Christian religion there, and shall not be harmed nor troubled on that account; and they may leave the country when they please.

5. English people may always trade freely with the people of _____ in every article which they may wish to buy or sell; and neither the English people nor the people of _____ shall ever be forced to buy or to sell any article, nor shall they be prevented from buying or selling any article; and the customs and dues taken by the Chief of _____ on English goods shall in no case be more altogether than 1/__th part of the price of the goods sold.

6. The paths shall be kept open through the _____ country to other countries, so that English traders may carry goods of all kinds through the _____ country to sell them elsewhere; and the traders of other countries may bring their goods through the _____ country to trade with the English people.

7. English people may buy and sell or hire lands and houses in the country, and their houses shall not be entered without their consent, nor shall their goods be seized, nor their persons touched; and if English people are wronged or ill treated by the people of _____, and Chief of _____ shall punish those who wrong or ill treat the English people.

8. But the English people must not break the laws of the _____ country; and when they are accused of breaking the laws, the chiefs shall send a true account of the matter to the nearest place where there is an English force; and the commander of such English force shall send for the English person, who shall be tried according to English law, and shall be punished if found guilty.

---

10. C. W. Newbury, ed., *British Policy Towards Africa: Select Documents, 1786–1874* (Oxford: Clarendon Press, 1965), pp. 150–53, 224–26.

9. If the _____ people should take away the property of an English person, or should not pay their just debts to an English person, the Chief of _____ shall do all he can to make the _____ people restore the property and pay the debt; and if English persons should take away the property of the _____ people, or should not pay their just debts to the _____ people, the Chief of _____ shall make known the fact to the Commander of the English force, nearest to the _____ country, or to the resident agent, if there is one; and the English Commander, or the agent, whichever it may be, shall do all he can to make the English persons restore the property and pay the debt.

10. The Queen of England may appoint an agent to visit _____ or to reside there, in order to watch over the interests of the English people, and to see that this agreement is fulfilled; and such agent shall always receive honour and protection in the _____ country, and the _____ Chiefs shall pay attention to what the agent says; and the person and property of the agent shall be sacred.

11. The Chief of _____ shall, within 48 hours of the date of this agreement, make a law for carrying the whole of it into effect; and shall proclaim that law, and the Chief of _____ shall put that law in force from that time for ever. . . .

Additional terms for special cases:

Article 1. Moreover, the Queen of England, for _____ years to come, will have ready every year, at _____, the following articles, viz: _____ and an English officer shall inquire in each year whether the Chief of _____ and his people have faithfully kept the foregoing agreement, and if, after enquiry, he shall be satisfied that they have kept the agreement, he shall then deliver the articles to the chief, or to the chief's agent for him; but when the English officer is not satisfied, he shall not deliver the articles.

Article 2. The practice of making human sacrifice, on account of religious or political ceremonies or customs, shall cease for ever in _____.

Article 3. The Chief of _____ sells and makes over to the English people of the Queen of England, the land from _____ to _____ and everything in it, entirely and for ever, for the sum of _____, of which _____ is now paid to him. And the English people shall have possession of the said land, and of whatever may be upon it, when they shall have paid to the Chief of _____ the remainder of the price above stated; and when the land shall be delivered over to the English people, they may do with it as they please.

Article 4. The Queen of England will assist in protecting the Chief and people of _____ against any attack which other chiefs and people may make on them on account of anything they may do for the purpose of giving up the slave trade according to the present agreement.

The treaty with Kataba (upper Guinea coast), April 23, 1841.

. . . The Officer of England may seize every vessel or boat of Cartabar [Kataba] found anywhere carrying on the trade in Slaves, in the waters of Cartabar and the vessel and boats so seized shall be taken to an English possession to be tried by English law, and if condemned, shall with appurtenances and cargo be sold, the produce of the sale being equally divided between the Queen of England and the King of Cartabar.

Two Additional Articles:

1. The King of Cartabar seeing that he is unable of himself to prevent the incursion of neighbouring ill-disposed Chiefs delighting only in war and who have heretofore annually ravaged his Country, carrying off his people as Slaves; the cattle and produce; now and for ever places the Country of Cartabar under the sole protection of the Sovereign of England and he begs that Her Majesty Victoria the 1st, Queen of England, may become in his own royal person and for Her Heirs and successors, the protecting Sovereign of the Cartabar Country; And the King of Cartabar freely cedes forever, to the Queen of England Her Heirs and successors one square mile of land in such part of his country as shall be pointed out by the Lieutenant Governor of the British Settlements of the Gambia or other officer authorized to do so.

2. The King of Cartabar agrees that he will not enter any alliances, negotiations or communication of any political nature whatever, with any power in the world without the knowledge and consent of the Queen of England; and the King of Cartabar declares the whole of the annexed Treaty, and these two additional articles to be binding equally to himself as to His Heirs and successors forever. . . .

James Stephen's minute on the implications of the Kataba Treaty, September 6, 1841.

. . . When the Niger Expedition was resolved on, it was also resolved to make war on the Slave Trade by Treaties with the Chiefs of the Interior. A model of such a Treaty was prepared, and was sent to each of the Governors. Capt. Huntley, the Governor of the Gambia, accordingly made a Treaty with a Chief called the King of Cartabar. . . .

I have called this Agreement with the King of Cartabar a *Treaty*, but it should be observed that in devolving all these arrangements on this Office, Lord Palmerston [the prime minister] expressly stipulated against the use of any such Diplomatic language. He desired that the compacts to be made with the African Chiefs should be described as "*Arrangements* or *Agreements*," or by some other word which should exclude them from the class of Diplomatic Conventions. The distinction is not verbal or trivial. It means to reserve to the Secretary of State for Foreign Affairs his own exclusive power of negociating Treaties, and it is also meant to mark the distinction between Agreements with barbarous Chiefs and the international Compacts of Civilized States.

11. The persistence of "illegal" slaving.

Despite the 1807 British and U.S. legislation limiting the trade in slaves, and the activities of British anti-slavery squadrons along the West Coast of Africa, tens of thousands of Africans continued to be exported annually across the Atlantic. Though the export trade had been made illegal, Britain did not end slavery within its own colonial possessions until 1833, the United States not until 1865, and Brazil not until 1888. Moreover, travelers to Africa reported an increased use of slaves within indigenous communities, a result of using the labor of some of those previously exported for the production of other goods for export to meet the changing demands of European merchants. The growth in slavery within Africa during a period when Europeans were traveling into the interior for the first time, led to strong condemnations of slavery as a distinctly African phenomenon. Long-term European residents of Africa, however, such as Brodie Cruickshank, pointed out that slavery in Africa took a number of forms, including "pawning," and was not the same as the chattel slavery of the Americas.

A striking pattern that did arise from the anti-slave measures taken by the British and other European powers in the nineteenth century was a geographical shift in the slave export trade, with a decline along the West Coast of Africa, a continued large-scale export from the Portuguese-dominated coast of West Central Africa, and a huge growth on the East Coast. The expansion in the east (where exports had been negligible before c. 1800) resulted from a combination of a rising demand for slaves on newly established French plantations in the Indian Ocean (this despite French emancipation in 1848); the development of spice plantations worked by slave labor on the Arab-ruled islands of

Zanzibar, Pemba, and parts of the East African Coast; increasing exports to the Persian Gulf and India; and the activities of Brazilian, Spanish, and U.S. slavers seeking new sources of slaves for Brazil and Cuba to replace those under pressure on the West Coast.

The following extracts chart the move of the export trade from west to east and show the potential for African-European conflict arising from disputes about the terms of trade, the persistence and growth of slavery within Africa, and the issue of escapees. As on the West Coast, European slave traders had to obtain slaves and negotiate prices with local merchants, often Arabs based in Zanzibar. Likewise, they often had to make tribute payments to local rulers as, for example, the Portuguese did on an annual basis to the Zulu. Each of the authors spent different amounts of time in Africa and had quite different experiences. Brodie Cruickshank lived on the Gold Coast between 1834 and 1854, was a member of the first legislative council of the Gold Coast when the colony gained independence from the administration of Sierra Leone in 1850, and briefly served as acting governor of the colony. Paul du Chaillu's account is based on four trips he made to Africa in the 1850s, primarily to investigate the flora and fauna. (He "shot, stuffed, and brought home over 2,000 birds . . . and . . . killed upwards of 1,000 quadrupeds.") Barnard was a British naval lieutenant who spent three years on an anti-slavery patrol on the coast of Mozambique.[11]

(A). Brodie Cruickshank on indigenous slavery in West Africa, 1853.

The condition of the slaves in the countries under our protection is by no means one of unmitigated hardship. In ordinary cases, the slave is considered as a member of his master's family, and often succeeds to his property, in default of a natural heir. He eats with him from the same dish, and has an equal share in all his simple enjoyments. He intermarries with his children, and is allowed to acquire property of his own, over which, unless under very extraordinary circumstances, his master exercises no control. He sometimes even acquires wealth and consideration far superior to his master, who may occasionally be seen swelling his importance, by following in his train. They address each other as "my father" and "my son," and differ in little in their mutual relations from the respect and obedience implied in these endearing epithets.

We see in the whole of their domestic economy a complete transcript of the patriarchal age; the same participation in the cares, and sorrows, and enjoyments of life; the same community of feeling and of interest; and the same external equality, conjoined with a devoted obedience, so marked and decided, as to assume the form of a natural instinct. This quality in the mind of dependents has a tendency to destroy the idea of personal accountability. The will of the master is in most instances more than a counterpoise for the volition of the slave, who yields obedience to his commands with an instinctive submission, without the intervention of any external compulsion, and often under circumstances where the natural inclination of the slave is opposed to the particular conduct required of him. Slavery of body and mind is thus thor-

11. (A), Brodie Cruickshank, *Eighteen Years on the Gold Coast of Africa, Including an Account of the Native Tribes, and their Intercourse with Europeans*, vol. 2 (London: Hurst and Blackett, 1853), pp. 236–50; (B), Paul B. du Chaillu, *Explorations and Adventures in Equatorial Africa* (London: John Murray, 1861), pp. 141–47; (C), Frederick Lamport Barnard, R. N., *A Three Years' Cruize in the Mozambique Channel* (London: R. Bentley, 1848), pp. 137–38, 153–54, 206–07, 217, 223–25, 258–59.

Branding a female slave. *Source:* Theophile Conneau, *Captain Canot [Conneau]; or Twenty Years of an African Slaver.* . . (New York: D. Appleton and Company, 1854), facing p. 102.

oughly engrained in the constitution of the African. We have known cases of murder having been committed at the command of a master, and against the remonstrances of the slave, who however does not refuse compliance; and we have seen how completely the will of the master has been considered the test of the slave's conscience, by the perfect unconcern of the latter respecting the deed, and the absence of any idea of his accountability for it.

Scarcely would the slave of an Ashantee chief obey the mandate of his king, without the special concurrence of his immediate master; and the slave of a slave will refuse obedience to his master's master, unless the order be conveyed to him through his own master. This perfect identification of the mind of the slave with that of his master has no doubt given rise to the master's accountability for the acts of his slave, and to the laws which affect them. He has to pay his debts, and to make compensation and restitution for every injury committed by him, either wilfully or accidentally. This responsibility may be a cause of the kind and considerate treatment so often observable, the master's interest being so closely involved in the conduct of his slave, as to render him anxious to attach him to his person, and to engage his affectionate obedience. It will also account for the isolated cases of harshness and cruelty which occasionally come under our observation, the vindictive slave having it in his power to cause his master much annoyance and expense, for which the latter can only retaliate by corporal suffering. Where this discordant spirit exists, the master, after repeated ineffectual attempts to reclaim an incorrigible slave, gets rid of the annoyance by selling him.

There does not appear any limit to the extent of punishment which a master is permitted to inflict upon his slave. He is considered so entirely his property, that he may with impunity put him to death; although from applications for freedom, on the ground of severe personal injury, such as the loss of an eye or a tooth, there is reason to believe that, during some period of their history, the slave was protected by a more humane code of laws.

We have heard a slave argue for his emancipation on the score of the accidental loss of an eye, in his master's service, from the recoil of a branch of a tree, and appeal to a traditionary law which entitles him to this compensation.

Like the Hebrews, the Fantees make a distinction between the slaves, their countrymen, and those who have been taken in war, or purchased from another tribe. The latter, until they become amalgamated by a long period of servitude, and by intermarriage, do not receive the same considerate treatment. They are considered an inferior race, with the ordinary class of whom it is thought derogatory for the daughters of the land to intermarry. The burden of the labour of the country falls upon them. Immense numbers of these slaves are being annually imported into the country, through Ashantee, from the countries near the range of the Kong Mountains. Many of them, on their first arrival, manifest an extraordinary degree of stolidity and brutishness, and exhibit a very low type of intellect and breeding. They pass under the general name of "Donko," a word signifying a slave in the language of the interior, and which, from the great stupidity of these creatures, has come to be a word of reproach, tantamount to "fool." They are naturally a very obstinate, perverse, and self-willed race, upon whom it is difficult to make any impression by kindness. It is very difficult also to coerce them to labour; and yet, notwithstanding their many bad qualities, the Fantees eagerly purchase them from the Ashantees. They vary in price from £6 to £8, girls and boys being sold at a considerable reduction. They have scars on the face and person, distinctive of their native tribes; some with semicircular lines covering the whole face, some with a few scarred lines on each cheek, some with a single raised mark upon the forehead, and others seamed and scarred over the whole of the upper part of their persons. Among this servant race, we find also a good many mongrel Moors, little superior to the others.

If they arrive in the country at an early age, they are by no means slow in acquiring knowledge, and become very useful to their masters, and sometimes obtain a consideration equal to the native of the country, intermarrying with the Fantees, and becoming members of their families. But if the Donko be grown up before his arrival upon the coast, he generally remains a dull, stolid beast of burden all the days of his life. It is only by comparing the native Fantee with these, that we are sensible of the very great advancement of the former, who appears a very civilized being in comparison with this foreign race. And yet these are not altogether devoid of some of the better qualities of our nature. They evince much sympathy and compassion for each other, and readily assist one another in their difficulties. A common fate appears to unite them by the ties of a patriotic attachment, and they delight to sing, in the place of their captivity, the songs of their native land. Their treatment by their masters depends much upon their own conduct, for interest, as well as natural inclination, make the Fantee a kind master. The great stubbornness of the Donko, however, often brings down upon him a severe chastisement, to which he submits with a sullen insensibility. Some thousands of these are added to the population of the country under our protection every year. Various considerations have induced the local government to tolerate this internal slave trade, which it would be difficult to suppress. The objects of it are either taken in war by the Ashantees, received as tribute from subjugated states, or purchased by them. If they were not bought by the Fantees, many of them would be sacrificed at the Ashantee customs, or kept in a worse bondage in that country. By being brought into the countries under our protection, their lives are spared; they receive a more humane treatment; they are shielded from oppression, and are placed within the influence of a higher degree of civilization. Their condition, in every respect, is improved by the change, and the second generation becomes an effective addition to a by no means superabundant population.

It will be seen, then, that while the diffusion of wealth and the progress of knowledge are creating a spirit of industry, and exciting a desire for greater freedom among the native Fantees, a fresh tide of slavery is pouring into the country from another direction. It may be questioned how far this state of matters is to be approved. But when we reflect, that the Ashantee wars are not undertaken expressly to supply this demand; that the transfer of the slaves from the Ashantee to the Fantee country is not adding to the ranks of slavery generally; that it greatly ameliorates the condition of the slaves in question, and brings them and their descendants within the scope of many civilizing influences, to which they would otherwise have remained strangers; that, moreover, an increase to the population is desirable to bring out the resources of a rich and fertile country, we are warranted in concluding that the cause of general civilization and of humanity is advanced by this movement. It is not unreasonable to hope that, after centuries of progress, the tide of emigration may again recede into the interior, carrying with it the seeds of civilization and Christian knowledge.

Besides the native-born Fantee slaves, and those purchased from the interior, there remains to be noticed another species of slavery existing, under the name of "pawns," to which we have already adverted. It has been seen that individuals form, in the present state of commerce, no small portion of the currency of the country. To obtain a loan or pay a debt, a master does not hesitate to place one or more of his family, or slaves, in temporary bondage to another. The terms of this contract are, that the pawn shall serve his new master until such time as the person pawning him shall make good the sum lent, with 50 per cent interest; the services of the pawn, even if they should extend over a great number of years, counting for nothing in the liquidation of the debt. If a woman has been pawned, her new master has the right to make her his concubine, and her children continue to serve him also.

The cruel operation of this system will be best illustrated by an example. We will suppose A. to pawn his daughter B. to his friend C. for the sum of two ounces. He finds it impossible to redeem her, perhaps, under a period of many years, during which time we will suppose her to have borne seven children to her master. A. now is anxious to redeem his daughter, but he cannot do so without paying C. the original amount with interest, and four ackies and a half (22s. 6d.) for each child, which raises the original debt of two ounces (£8) to four ounces fifteen ackies and a half, or £9 17s. 6d. The money paid on account of the children is regarded as an equivalent for their maintenance.

If A. has had to borrow the money to effect this redemption, which frequently happens, it will be seen that the original sum of two ounces would go on accumulating at a rate which must eventually leave this family in a state of hopeless bondage. The death of the pawn does not cancel the debt. A. must substitute another pawn in her place, or pay the amount; but in this case B. generally, though not invariably, foregoes the interest. Neither is the master of a pawn, like the master of a slave, responsible for his pawn's debts. These recoil upon the head of the person pawning her.

A father cannot pawn his child without the concurrence of the mother's relations, unless she also be his slave. Neither can a mother pawn her child without the father's consent; but if he cannot advance the sum required, then she can do so. We have always regarded this system of pawning as much worse than actual slavery, and we have seen but too many of its victims irrecoverably reduced to perpetual bondage. The English authorities have greatly mitigated its hardships, by refusing to consider the loan in any other light than that of a common debt.

After the account which has been given, the reader will now be able to have a clear comprehension of the nature and condition of slavery upon the Gold Coast. It would appear that it is greatly influenced by the state of social progress, and that its exactions become more rigid in proportion to the advancement of a people. The closer the points of resemblance between the master and the slave, the easier will be the yoke; and where the improvement of both go on simultaneously, all distinctions gradually become effaced. We see the gradual operation of this process among the Fantee masters and their native-born slaves, while the diffusion of greater wealth among the former, and of increased knowledge, renders the condition of the "donkos," an inferior class, more truly that of a degrading servitude, and widens the distance between them and their masters. . . .

Another difficulty which our Gold Coast government has to contend against, is the disposal of runaway slaves from Ashantee. It was stipulated in our treaties with the king, that his fugitive subjects should be redelivered to him in the same way that Fantees, flying into his dominions, were to be restored to the governor. This arrangement was necessary to prevent malefactors escaping punishment. But in many cases, the runaway Ashantee seeks a refuge from the fate which is likely to overtake him at the murderous customs which are often taking place at Coomassie, and a natural repugnance is, of course, felt about surrendering him.

Our position and power, however, do not enable us to follow the course most consistent with our feelings. If we were to refuse to deliver these runaways, the King of Ashantee would retaliate by seizing all the Fantees in his country, where a large number may at all times be found prosecuting their trade. He has also the means of cutting off all intercourse with his country, a measure which he invariably adopts upon occasions of misunderstanding with the governor. If redress were refused, war would be the consequence, a calamity in the present hopeful state of progress which would go far to undo the good which has been already effected, and which of all things is most anxiously to be avoided. Under these circumstances, the governor is obliged to mediate as he best can, and refuses to deliver up the runaway, except upon condition of sufficient security being given that his life will be spared.

Although this restriction must be galling to the king, yet he is induced to submit to it, rather than incur the risk of a doubtful war, into which he and his chiefs would not hesitate to plunge if such a vital question as the non-surrender of runaway slaves were involved in the issue. The security given for their safety is simply "the king's great oath," taken on his behalf by his messengers. There is no instance known of this oath given under such circumstances being violated. We remember a case, which will show the fearful regard which the king has for oaths.

Upon application being made for some runaways, the messengers were required to take the usual oath before they were surrendered. The refugees, however, were not satisfied with this oath alone, and positively refused to return to Ashantee, unless the king's messengers would give additional security for their safety, by "kissing the white man's book." They did not hesitate to agree to this, as they were perfectly satisfied that the king's oath would not be violated, and that, therefore, there could be no danger in kissing the book. But when they returned to Coomassie, and the king found that they had bound him, not only by his own, but also by the white man's oath, he became alarmed, lest any accidental injury might happen to the persons thus protected, which might bring him under the penalty of its violation; and to get rid of the liability, he sent the refugees back to the Fantee country, preferring to lose them to the risk of incurring an unknown danger.

It will be thus seen, that both to avoid insurrection among the Fantees, and the horrors of a war with Ashantee, the British authorities are compelled to adopt a policy with regard to this slave question, which appears never to have been openly avowed, and which is never brought under the notice of the Colonial Office without exciting a feeling of uneasiness, and calling forth a renewed declaration that slavery cannot be recognized within our settlements upon the Gold Coast, thus throwing back upon the governor the responsibility of its recognition.

(B). Paul du Chaillu on the coast of West Central Africa, 1861.

The next day I made a visit to the barracoons, or slave-pens. Cape Lopez [on the coast of West Central Africa, north of the outlet of the Congo river and in the same longitude as the island of Sao Tōmé where the Portuguese had first established slave plantations in the fifteenth century], a great slave-dépôt—once one of the largest on the whole coast—and I had, of course, much curiosity to see how the traffic is carried on.

My way led through several of the villages which are scattered about the extensive plain. Every head of a family makes a separate little settlement, and the huts of his wives and slaves which surround his own make quite a little village. Each of these groups is hidden from view by surrounding clumps of bushes, and near each are the fields cultivated by the slaves. The object of building separately in this way is to prevent the destruction which used frequently to fall upon their larger towns at the hands of British cruisers, who have done their best several times to break up this nest of slave-dealing. A town could be shelled and burned down; these scattered plantations afford no mark. Cape Lopez boasts of two slave-factories. I now visited the one kept by the Portuguese. It was, from the outside, an immense enclosure, protected by a fence of palisades twelve feet high, and sharp-pointed at the top. Passing through the gate, which

was standing open, I found myself in the midst of a large collection of shanties surrounded by shade-trees, under which were lying about, in various positions, people enough to form a considerable African town.

An old Portuguese, who seemed to be sick, met and welcomed me, and conducted me to the white men's house, a two-story frame building, which stood immediately fronting the gate. This was poorly finished, but contained beds, a table, chairs, &c.

Unfortunately I do not speak either Spanish or Portuguese, and my conductor understood neither French nor English. We had, therefore, to make use of a native interpreter, who made slow work of our talk. The Portuguese complained that it was now very hard to land a cargo in the Brazils, as the Government was against them, and that each year the trade grew duller. To put myself on a right footing with him, I told him I had not come to trade, but to collect objects in natural history, and to see the country and hunt.

I was now led around. The large house I have mentioned was surrounded by a separate strong fence, and in the spacious yard which was thus cut off were the male slaves, fastened six together by a little stout chain which passed through a collar secured about the neck of each. This mode of fastening experience has proved to be the most secure. It is rare that six men are unanimous in any move for their own good, and it is found that no attempt to liberate themselves, when thus fastened, succeeds. They reposed under sheds or shelters built about the yard, and here there were buckets of water from which they could drink when they felt inclined.

Beyond this yard was another for the women and children, who were not manacled, but allowed to rove at pleasure through their yard, which was protected by a fence. The men were almost naked. The women wore invariably a cloth about their middle.

Behind the great houses was the hospital for sick slaves. It was not ill-arranged, the rooms being large and well-ventilated, and the beds—structures of bamboo covered with a mat—were ranged about the walls.

Outside of all the minor yards, under some trees, were the huge cauldrons in which the beans and rice, which serve as slave-food, were cooked. Each yard had several Portuguese overseers, who kept watch and order, and superintended the cleaning out of the yards, which is performed daily by the slaves themselves. From time to time, too, these overseers take the slaves down to the seashore and make them bathe.

I remarked that many of the slaves were quite merry, and seemed perfectly content with their fate. Others were sad, and seemed filled with dread of their future; for, to lend an added horror to the position of these poor creatures, they firmly believe that we whites buy them to *eat* them. They cannot conceive of any other use to be made of them; and wherever the slave-trade is known in the interior, it is believed that white men beyond sea are great cannibals, who have to import blacks for the market. Thus a chief in the interior country, having a great respect for me, of whom he had heard often, when I made him my first visit, immediately ordered a slave to be killed for my dinner, and it was only with great difficulty I was able to convince him that I did not, in my own country, live on human flesh.

The slaves here seemed of many different tribes, and but few even understood each other. The slave-trade has become so great a traffic here (here I speak of the country and foreign trade alike) that it extends from this coast quite to the centre of the continent; and I have met slaves on the coast who had been bought much farther in the interior than I ever succeeded in reaching. The Shekiani, Bakalai, and many other tribes far inland sell their fellows into slavery on various pretexts (chiefly witchcraft), and thus help to furnish the Sangatanga slave-barracoons. The large rivers which, joining, form the Nazareth, provide an easy access to the coast, and give Cape Lopez great advantages for obtaining a regular supply of slaves; and the creeks which abound hereabouts afford the vessels good chances to conceal themselves from the watchful cruisers. . . .

The next morning I paid a visit to the other slave-factory. It was a neater place, but arranged much like the first. While I was standing there, two young women and a lad of fourteen were brought in for sale, and bought by the Portuguese in my presence. The boy brought a twenty-gallon cask of rum, a few fathoms of cloth, and a quantity of beads. The women sold at a higher rate. Each was valued at the following articles, which were immediately paid over: one gun, one neptune (a flat disk of copper), two looking-glasses, two files, two plates, two bolts, a keg of powder, a few beads, and a small lot of tobacco. Rum bears a high price in this country.

At two o'clock this afternoon a flag was hoisted at the king's palace on the hill, which signifies that a slaver is in the offing. It proved to be a schooner of about 170 tons' burden. She ran in and hove to a few miles from shore. Immediately I saw issue from one of the factories gangs of slaves, who were rapidly driven down to a point on the shore nearest the vessel. I stood and watched the embarkation. The men were still chained in gangs of six, but had been washed, and had on clean cloths. The canoes were immense boats, managed by twenty-six paddles, and besides each about sixty slaves. Into these the poor creatures were now hurried, and a more piteous sight I never saw. They seemed terrified almost out of their sense; even those whom I had seen in the factory to be contented and happy were now gazing about with such mortal terror in their looks as one neither sees nor feels very often in life. They had been content to lie in the factory, where they were well treated and had enough to eat. But now they were being taken away they knew not whither, and the frightful stories of the white man's cannibalism seemed fresh in their minds.

But there was no time allowed for sorrow or lamentation. Gang after gang was driven into the canoes until they were full, and then they set out for the vessel, which was dancing about in the sea in the offing.

And now a new point of dread seized the poor wretches, as I could see, watching them from the shore. They had never been on rough water before, and the motion of the canoe, as it skimmed over the waves and rolled now one way now another, gave them fears of drowning, at which the paddlers broke into a laugh, and forced them to lie down in the bottom of the canoe.

I said the vessel was of 170 tons. Six hundred slaves were taken off to her, and stowed in her narrow hold. The whole embarkation did not last two hours, and then, hoisting her white sails away she sailed for the South American coast. She hoisted no colours while near the shore, but was evidently recognized by the people on shore. She seemed an American-built schooner. The vessels are, in fact, Brazilian, Portuguese, Spanish, sometimes Sardinian, but oftenest of all American. Even whalers, I have been told, have come to the coast, got their slave cargo, and departed unmolested, and setting it down in Cuba or Brazil, returned to their whaling business no one the wiser. The slave-dealers and their overseers on the coast are generally Spanish and Portuguese. One of the head-men at the factories here told me that he had been taken twice on board slave-vessels, of course losing his cargo each time. Once he had been taken into Brest by a French vessel, but by the French laws he was acquitted, as the French do not take Portuguese vessels. He told me that he thought he should make his fortune in a very short time now, and then he meant to return to Portugal.

The slave trade is really decreasing. The hardest blow has been struck at it by the Brazilians. They have for some years been alarmed at the great superiority in numbers of the Africans in Brazil to its white population, and the government and people have united to discourage the trade, and put obstacles in the way of its successful prosecution. If now the trade to Cuba could also be stopped, this would do more to put an end to the whole business than the blockading by all the navies of the world.

It is impossible for any limited number of vessels to effectually guard 4,000 miles of coast. Eight or ten years ago, when I was on the coast of Africa, the British kept some 26 vessels of light draught on the coast, several of which were steamers, while the rest were good sailors. The French also had 26 vessels there, and the Americans their complement. But, with all this force to hinder, the slave-trade was never more prosperous. The demand in Brazil and Cuba was good, and barracoons were established all along the coast. Many vessels were taken, but many more escaped. The profits are so great that the slave-dealers could afford to send really immense fleets, and count with almost mathematical certainty on making a great profit from those which escaped the cruisers. The barracoons were shifted from place to place to escape the vigilance of the men-of-war; and no sooner was one of these dépôts broken up than another was established in some neighbouring creek or bay. So great was the demand that fearful atrocities were sometimes practised on innocent negroes by shrewd captains, who begrudged even the small price they had to pay for slaves. Thus it is related of one that he invited a number of friendly natives on board of his vessel, then shut them under hatches, and sailed away with them to Cuba to sell them.

A pregnant sign of the decay of the business is that those engaged in it begin to cheat each other. I was told by Portuguese on the coast that within two or three years the conduct of Cuban houses had been very bad. They had received cargo after cargo, and when pressed for pay had denied and refused. Similar complaints are made of other houses; and it is said that now a captain holds on to his cargo till he sees the doubloons, and takes the gold in one hand while he sends the slaves over the side with the other. While the trade was brisk they had no occasion to quarrel. As the profits become more precarious, each will try to cut the other's throat.

Now there are not many barracoons north of the equator, and the chief trade centres about the mouth of the Congo. The lawful trade has taken the place of the slave traffic to the northward; and if the French will only abolish their system of "apprenticeship," lawful trade might soon make its way to the south.

(C). Lieutenant Barnard describes the slave trade on the coast of Mozambique, 1848.

In the evening I learnt that about a week before our arrival, a large barque had embarked from 700 to 800 slaves at Ouilinda, the river to the southward of Quillimane, and I have since found out, that this was the same *Julia* which Trou, the captain of the Gentil, had detained in May last, and that the slaves actually went from the town of Quillimane in launches. Three or four days after our last visit, 300 slaves had been burnt alive in a baracoon [slave barracks] some distance to the northward, where they had been sent ready for embarkation, one of them slipping his iron collar during the night, and setting fire to the building.

Upwards of 2,000 slaves were ready in the neighbourhood of the town for embarkation, purchased with merchandize, brought out by American vessels, and slave-vessels were expected from Rio daily, so that my arrival at Quillimane put those who had so much at stake in a great ferment, and I witnessed long and angry discussions amongst them as they came in and out of Azvedo's house. A brig, said to be under Sardinian colours, had attempted to land her captain at Luabo, where they say there is a flagstaff, but he with three of his boat's crew was drowned in crossing the bar, one man only reaching the shore, and no more has been heard of her.

The black schooner belonging to Senhor Isidore, which had embarked 400 slaves at Macuze, put back after having lost one-half of her human cargo, and relanded the wretched remnant half dead. . . .

I must now add another page to the dreadful horrors of slavery. The bark *Julia*, which I have twice mentioned before, after sailing with 700 slaves, was eight days afterwards wrecked on the Bassas da India Rocks, when every soul perished except the Captain and three of the crew, who escaped to the Macuze in a small gig. The current had drifted them close to the breakers before they knew their danger, and they had barely time to get out of her before she opened and went down.

Thus, in the short space of six months, I have detailed the untimely end of 1,200 Negroes, by fire, disease, and wreck; and the suffering they must have endured whilst driven from the interior must have thinned considerably the original number; for frequently have I seen them, soon after their arrival at Quillimane, mere skeletons, with death depicted in their countenances.

I saw the schooner on the beach: she was not coppered, and about ninety tons burden; and on board this were 400 human beings crammed for a passage across the Atlantic. . . .

When [Lieutenant William] Alexander [one of Bardard's fellow officers] first got on board in the cutter, he found that her crew had deserted her, leaving the steward and supercargo sick in the bunks on deck, with 420 slaves, the greater part under hatches, fastened down with spike nails, and left by the merciless wretches to be drowned or smothered. Never was there a more dreadful attempt at cool, deliberate, and wholesale murder; and yet there is no means of punishing the perpetrators; no judge nor magistrate residing at Mozambique, and the judge at Quillimane being a coloured man, formerly, a gentleman's servant, and one of the greatest slave-dealers in the place. Never was an officer placed in a more awkward position, the cutters being all but stoved, and there appearing every chance of the brig's being knocked to pieces as the tide went down. Alexander thought the best plan was to allow them to swim on shore, and the greater part of them reached it in safety. On the two following days, the boats were employed in completing the destruction of the brig by fire, and brought on board the two sick Portuguese and seven negroes who had remained on board. A few bodies were found on the beach and buried. . . .

The slaves that are brought from the interior are poor half-starved looking creatures, attached to each other by ropes round the neck; and famine is spreading its ravages throughout this ill-fated country. The province is in such a state of decay, that it cannot continue long under its present government, and a more powerful one would scarcely risk the expense and loss of life attendant upon the many changes that must take place before it could be bettered. . . .

As the principal object of all my visits to the town was to gain information respecting the movements of the slave-dealers and their agents, I was obliged to be constantly on the *qui vive*, and found myself both suspected and watched since the affair of the brig. However, I managed to get the following, bit by bit, from various quarters.

Paulo Roderigue, the captain of the *Defensivo*, and the shipper of 1,800 slaves at Inhamban and Delagoa Bay, was again expected at the former place, in two or three months, for 800 blacks, which were in readiness. He was to have two American brigs under their own colours, one of which was to be delivered over to the slave-dealers, whilst the other was to take both American crews on board, touch at Quillimane with money to pay the authorities, who have been in the habit of conniving at the slave trade, and return to Rio; so you may easily conceive what little chance there is of putting down this detestable traffic, whilst the star-spangled banner, that boasted flag of liberty, waves over and protects the miscreants, to put down whom England has expended so many hundreds of lives of her bravest, and so many millions of treasure. Look at the results.

There are now at Quillimane and its neighourhood 2,700 poor wretches for embarkation. Their owners are at Rio, 800 belonging to Manuel Pinto de Fonseca; 200 to Tavares, or Tavash; 2,000 to Bernadino de Sa'. Only one slave agent remained at Quillimane, named Martinbas, and he intended to leave for Rio in the American.

Of the 420 slaves allowed to swim on shore from the brig off Mariangombe, 110 were retaken, and the rest were supposed to have escaped into the interior. She had on board five officers, four of whom had died of fever since her destruction. Eight of her crew were taken and sent to Mozambique in the Don Juan de Castro, and the captain and steward remained at Quillimane, most probably soon to be victims of the approaching sickly season. . . .

I made diligent inquiries about the slave trade carried on at Angonha, and am led to believe that it has only of late become a place for the exportation of slaves for the Brazils, and that the *Lucy Penniman*, *Kentucky*, and two others which escaped, are the only vessels which have attempted to take in cargoes there. The Majojos have, however, for many years carried on a brisk trade in human flesh, by means of Arab dows, with Zanzibar, Johanna, and the Red Sea; but of late, the *Sappho*, *Mutine*, and *Helena*, have taken and destroyed several of these vessels, and put a temporary check on it. But there are so many rivers and inlets on this coast which a man-of-war cannot approach, that we might as well try to alter the currents in the Mozambique channel as stop the slave trade with sailing vessels.

12. Samuel Crowther on the role of African missionaries.

European missionaries had little success converting Africans to Christianity during the first half of the nineteenth century. David Livingstone, the most famous of the British proselytizers, persuaded only one African chief to convert and that individual soon repudiated his decision. But Africans freed from slave ships and released in Sierra Leone offered a potential source of indigenous missionaries. Many of the freed slaves worked for members of the Church Missionary Society (CMS) and converted to the Christian faith of their British employers and rulers. Unlike the European missionaries, the African converts knew the local languages. They had also often been captured into slavery from parts of Africa beyond the coastal reach of the British and could therefore lead the anti-slavery advance into the interior.

Samuel Crowther was the most prominent of these African missionaries in the nineteenth century. Born among the Igbo people of present-day Nigeria and given the name Ajayi by his parents, he had taken the name Samuel Crowther in 1825 when he was baptized in his late teens as a Christian and a member of the CMS. He trained first as a schoolteacher for the CMS, then after further education in England, was ordained a minister and in 1843 went to Abeokuta (southern Nigeria) as a missionary. During the 1840s and 1850s, Crowther accompanied several British expeditions organized by the African Inland Commercial Company exploring the course of the Niger. These expeditions aimed to investigate the commercial potential of the interior and to establish inland missions along the Niger.

Unlike the earlier expeditions to the interior of travelers like Mungo Park, which had relied on foot and dugout canoe and usually resulted in the death of all (as occurred on Park's final trip in 1805) or most of the European participants due to local diseases (malaria in particular), the mid-century ventures benefited from several key developments in European science. Steamships were first introduced on the Niger in the early 1830s and allowed British traders to bypass the African-controlled trading towns of the delta and sail inland. These ships were armed with cannons, allowing the British for the first time to extend their superior firepower into the interior. Most important of all, the adoption of quinine as a malaria preventative in the 1840s dramatically reduced European mortality rates which until then had averaged between 50 and 80 percent. The 1854 expedition up the Niger was the first to demonstrate the effectiveness of these new developments. The Pleiad, a 220-ton propeller steamer crewed by 12 Europeans and 54 Africans, and armed with four cannons, spent 112 days sailing up the Niger and Benue rivers and returned with not a single fatality from disease. Crowther's journal of this expedition focused, however, not on technological triumph but on the potential of opening Africa to the endeavors of indigenous Christian missionaries.[12]

On the need for African missionaries.

I believe the time is fully come when Christianity must be introduced on the banks of the Niger: the people are willing to receive any who may be sent among them. The English are still looked upon as their friends, with whom they themselves desire to have connexion as with the first nation in the world. Could the work have been begun since 1841, how imperfect soever it might it have been, yet it would have kept up the thread of connexion with England and the countries on the banks of the Niger. God has provided instruments to begin the work, in the liberated Africans in the Colony of Sierra Leone, who are the natives of the banks of this river.

If this time is allowed to pass away, the generation of the liberated teachers who are immediately connected with the present generation of the natives of the interior will pass away with it also; many intelligent men who took deep interest in the introduction of trade and Christianity by the Niger, who had been known to the people, have died since; so have many of the chiefs and people in the country, who were no less interested to be brought in connexion with England by seeing their liberated countrymen return. Had not Simon Jonas been with us, who was well known to Obi and his sons, we should have had some difficulty in gaining the confidence of the people at Aboh at our ascent.

It would be of very great advantage if the colony born young men were introduced by

12. Samuel Crowther, *Journal of an Expedition up the Niger and Tshadda Rivers, Undertaken by MacGregor Laird, Esq., in Connection with the British Government, in 1854* (London: Church Missionary House, 1854), pp. xvi–xviii, 21–22, 80–81.

their parents or countrymen to their father-land; it has many advantages which have not been sufficiently noticed. It cannot be expected that children born in the Colony should become acquainted with the countries and characters of the people so soon as their parents and countrymen. Though the parents are illiterate, yet if they are sincere followers of the Lord Jesus Christ, their service will be of much worth in introducing Christianity to their own people. They are brought back to their country as a renewed people, looked upon by their countrymen as superior to themselves, as long as they continue consistent in their Christian walk and conversation, and do not disgrace themselves by following heathenish practices. The language of the people of Abbeokuta will be that of the natives on the banks of the. Niger: "Let those who come from the white man's country teach us and condemn our heathenish practices, we shall listen to them." It takes great effect when returning liberated Christians sit down with their heathen countrymen and speak with contempt of their own former superstitious practices, of whom, perhaps, many now alive would bear testimony as to their former devotedness in their superstitious worship; all which he now can tell them he has found to be foolishness, and the result of ignorance; when he with all earnestness, invites them, as Moses did Hobab, Come with us, for the Lord has promised good to Israel; and all this in his own language, with refined Christian feelings and sympathy, not to be expressed in words, but evidenced by an exemplary Christian life. The services of such persons will prove most useful in the introduction of the Gospel of Jesus Christ among the heathens. Let such persons be employed as readers or Christian visitors, and thus they will gradually introduce their children into the country, who in the course of time will be able to carry on the work more effectually; as pioneers, we must not look for instruments of the keenest edge, anything that will open the path for the future improvement will answer as well at the onset.

Talking about Christianity.

July 23 [1854]: Sunday. Had service on board at half-past ten, and preached from St. John i. 29 [The next day John seeth Jesus coming unto him and saith, Behold the Lamb of God, which taketh away the sin of the world]. The boat was just ready for me after the service, to go on shore and speak a few words with the chief on religious subjects, and also to ask his permission to address the people of the town, when his canoe appeared from the creek, with numerous attendants, so I postponed my going till his return; but he remained so long on board, that there was no prospect of his soon going away. When Captain Taylor had done with him, I took the opportunity to speak with him at length on the subject of the Christian religion, Simon Jonas interpreting for me. The quickness with which he caught my explanation of the all-sufficient sacrifice of Jesus Christ, the Son of God, for the sin of the world, was gratifying. I endeavoured to illustrate it to him in this simple way. "What would you think of any persons, who, in broad daylight like this, should light their lamps to assist the brilliant rays of the sun to enable them to see better?" He said, "It would be useless; they would be fools to do so." I replied, "Just so"; that the sacrifice of Jesus Christ, the Son of God, was sufficient to take away our sins, just as one sun is sufficient to give light to the whole world; that the worship of country fashions, and numerous sacrifices, which shone like lamps, only on account of the darkness and ignorance of their superstition, though repeated again and again, yet cannot take away our sins; but that the sacrifice of Jesus Christ, once offered, alone can take away the sin of the world. He frequently repeated the names, "Oparra Tshuku! Oparra Tshuku!" Son of God! Son of God! As I did not wish to tire him out, I left my discourse fresh in his mind. The attention of his attendants, with the exception of a few, was too much engaged in begging and receiving presents, to listen to all I was talking about. I gave Tshukuma a Yoruba primer, in which I wrote his name; and left some with Simon Jonas, to teach the children, or any who should feel disposed to learn, the Alphabet and words of two letters. Tshukuma and his attendants were perfectly at home in the steamer, and it was not till a gentle hint was given them, that the gentlemen wanted to take their dinner, that he ordered his people to make ready for their departure.

Advice for European travelers.

What is generally related of the natives of Africa as to their hostility to Europeans is not strictly correct. The truth is, they take alarm, and consequently get ready for the defence of their country, which is divided by wars, marauding and robbery into many independent states, and every district must watch against surprize by its neighbours. It is but natural for such a people, shut out from communication with the civilized world, when they see for the first time such a huge and self-moving body as a steamer, to take alarm, not knowing the object of those who inhabit it, for to their ideas it is a town of itself. There

is one thing which enterprising European explorers overlook, I mean the continual fear and insecurity the Natives are in, from the constant treachery of their enemies. This causes them to go about always armed with their bows and arrows, and at the least alarm they are ready to discharge their deadly weapons. Though travellers fear nothing themselves, yet, they should endeavour to take due precautions to allay the fears of those whom they intend to visit, by previous communication, which will soon be circulated in the neighbourhood, and then all will be right. A prudent man will not consider an hour or two wasted to effect this purpose, rather than risk the painful result of misunderstandings which may never be remedied. As far as I know, there is no place in Africa uncontaminated with European slave dealers, which Europeans have visited with the intention of doing good, where such an event has not been hailed as the most auspicious in the annals of the country. Every chief considers himself highly honoured to have white men for his friends.

13. Christianity and cattle killing.

Though the missionaries won fewer converts than they hoped, their religious teaching, especially the apocalyptic aspects of Christianity, could have a profound impact on African societies under stress because of the expansion of European settlement. This was the case on the eastern frontier of settler expansion in South Africa where, from the 1770s onward, European and African competed for and fought over such essential resources as land and water. By the 1850s, conditions for the Xhosa people had become particularly dire. They had lost considerable amounts of land to European settlers backed by the military power of the British colonial state. The British administration seemed determined to end Xhosa political autonomy. Moreover, African cattle herds were being greatly reduced by an epidemic of lung-sickness during the middle of the decade. In this context of suffering, missionary teachings about redemption and resurrection had particular appeal. But Xhosa wanted to liberate themselves through a combination of Christianity and indigenous religious beliefs rather than accept missionary teachings as a form of submission to European intellectual authority.

In 1856, a Xhosa man, Mhlakaza, who had years earlier converted to Christianity and taken the name William Goliath, began spreading word of a vision seen by two young girls in which foreign visitors called on Xhosa to kill their cattle and consume all their corn. Mhlakaza was the first Xhosa confirmed as an Anglican (in April 1850) and worked for a number of years as the servant of an Anglican minister, joining with his employer on missionary trips along the eastern frontier. However, the minister dismissed Mhlakaza because his work as a servant was not satisfactory. Back among the Xhosa, Mhlakaza spread the message of his niece, Nongqawuse, that if the cattle were killed and the corn eaten, then all whites would be driven into the sea and the suffering of Xhosa would end. Many Xhosa followed Mhlakaza's precepts, with disastrous results. With most of their cattle slaughtered and their crops gone, tens of thousands of Xhosa starved to death (including Mhlakaza). Many of the survivors became refugees in the Cape Colony, seeking laboring work to stay alive. Most of the land of the Xhosa ended up in the possession of the British. Nongqawuse was captured, interrogated, and placed briefly in a paupers' lodge. Later released, she returned to the eastern Cape where she remained in obscurity until her death in the second or third decade of the twentieth century.[13]

Deposition made by NONQUASE, a Kafir Prophetess, in an Examination before the Chief Commissioner of British Kaffraria.

Examination, before the Chief Commissioner, of NONQUASE, a Kafir Prophetess, who was a niece of, and resided with, UMHLAKAZA [Mhlakaza]. She is a girl apparently between 15 and 16 years, intelligent, and gave her evidence freely. She was given over to Major Gawler, by MONY, Chief of the Amabomvanas.

My name is Nonquase. Umhlakaza was my uncle, and a counsellor of Xito, a petty chief. My father's name was Umhlanhla, of Kreli's tribe. He died when I was very young. I lived with Umhlakaza. He lived at Xaha on the Kei, near the sea. Umhlakaza is dead. He died about six moons ago of starvation. Umhlakaza's son, and elder brother, and my brother lived at the same kraal. After Umhlakaza's death we went and lived with the Amabomvana, across the Bashee, near Mony's kraal. We originally intended crossing the Umtato, but remained at this kraal near Mony.

Umhlakaza had many cattle before the talk about the new people. This talking commenced about seven sowing seasons back (two and a half years). It commenced after my having reported to Umhlakaza that I had seen about ten strange Kafirs in the gardens, and I told him I was afraid to go there. The people I saw were Kafirs—young men. I was afraid of them, because I did not know them. Umhlakaza told me not to be afraid of them, as they would do me no harm. He told me to speak to them, and ask them what they were doing there. I did so. They replied, "We are people who have come to order you to kill your cattle—to consume your corn—and not to cultivate any more." Umhlakaza asked them through me, "What are we to eat when we kill our cattle, &c?" They answered, "We will find you something to eat." The people then said that was enough for that day—they would return some other day. We asked them who sent them, they answered, "We have come of our own accord, as we wish every thing in the country to be made new." They said they had come from *a place of refuge* (engaba). I asked them where this place of refuge was. They said, "You would not know if we even told you." I always pressed them to tell me where the place of refuge was, but they gave me the same answer. The next day Umhlakaza killed one head of cattle. He then called a meeting of the people and told them that strangers had come to tell them to kill their cattle—to destroy their corn, and that great plenty would be provided for them here-

13. "Deposition made by NONQUASE, a Kafir Prophetess, in an Examination before the Chief Commissioner of British Kaffraria," (Cape Town, 1858), Cape of Good Hope Parliamentary Paper, G38, 1858. For the examination of Nonkosi, the other prophetess, see G5, 1858.

after. The people dispersed, and from that day they commenced killing their cattle, &c.; and Umhlakaza continued killing his cattle, one a day. The people killed more cattle than they could use. The dogs and wild beasts ate the carcases. About four days after we saw the strange Kafirs, three men came. We first heard of their arrival by an old woman, who told Umhlakaza that the people from the place of refuge had arrived. Umhlakaza took me with him to speak to them. I asked them for the news. They answered, "We do not know what news you expect; our only news is to tell you to kill your cattle—to consume your corn—and plenty will be provided for you." They left us the same day. In five days after two men came. I recognised them as two of the men who had come before. They said, "Our great chief has sent us to tell you, Umhlakaza, that all the people must kill their cattle, &c., as he wished to change the country; and that you must communicate this to Kreli and all the Kafir chiefs." Umhlakaza told me to ask them who their great chief was. They said they would not name him, for if they did, we would not know him, having never seen him or heard of him. They soon after left us. Umhlakaza then went to Xoti (Kreli's uncle), who is chief of the Galekas in the lower country between the Bashee and the Kei, and told him the news. Xito instructed Umhlakaza to spread the news, which he did. After Umhlakaza returned from visiting Xito's and other kraals, the three men came again. I heard Umhlakaza tell these men what he had told Xito, and that he had spread the news over the country. They answered him that he had done right. These men then said, "You must all be quick in killing your cattle, as in seven days the people will rise." I asked him what people? They replied, "The same people as ourselves—and they will rise at different kraals; that they would have cattle, corn guns, and assegais [spears]; and that they would drive the English out of the country, and make them run into the sea."

Within seven days Umhlakaza killed all his cattle, and the killing of cattle throughout the country became general. Kreli, Xito, Ungubo (Kreli's cousin), and Lindixowa, frequently visited Umhlakaza, and had private meetings with him. These meetings were quite confidential and secret. There was no one present. I was not there.

The following chiefs also visited Umhlakaza: Pama, Dondashe, Zono, Umgwebi, and Sigidi, Galekas. Also Dina (Pato's son), Qabimbola, Sandili, Macomo, Pato, Qasana, and Xoxo, Gaika and T'Slambie chiefs, and many others whose names I did not know. They came attended by counsellors, and many people. Kreli's counsellors supplied cattle to feed the chiefs and people at these meetings. The chiefs always slept several nights at Umhlakaza's kraal. They used to have secret meetings with Umhlakaza, at which I was not allowed to be present, and so I do not know what passed between them and Umhlakaza.

Shortly after the expiration of seven days, I saw the men who stated they had come from the place of refuge. They came with Kreli. I told them that Umhlakaza had killed all his cattle, but they made no reply.

Some time after this a petty chief, Lindixowa, came direct from Kreli, and told Umhlakaza that, though he (Umhlakaza) had killed his cattle, he was to remain where he was. Umhlakaza remained ten days after this, and then moved down towards the sea, for the purpose of living on roots and shell fish.

When we were starving, I often heard Umhlakaza regret his having killed his cattle and destroyed his corn. That he never thought he would be so reduced or come to such misery. I have often heard him blame Kreli as the sole cause of the cattle-killing, which was done for the purpose of leading the Kafirs to war, and driving the English out of the country. I heard Xito and Pama say, that the killing of cattle was to force the Kafirs to war with the English.

NOTE: Upon being asked whether she had heard any others than Umhlakaza, Xito, and Pama speak of war, she replied as follows:

"The three men stated they came from the place of refuge, and they intended fighting with the English and driving them out of the country. They spoke of the whole country where the English lived. They said that their great chief had informed them that his intention was to drive the English out of the country. I also recollect when Kreli paid his first visit to Umhlakaza, after the killing commenced, he, Kreli, told me, in Xito's presence, to tell the strange people that the English were in his way, and that these people must assist him to fight against the English and drive them out of the country. I delivered Kreli's message to these men; they answered 'Yes, we will assist Kreli to fight against the English and drive them out of the country.'

I went to Kreli, who was sitting near at hand, and gave him their answer. Kreli replied, "I am glad"; and called out in a voice sufficiently loud to be heard by the three men, "I thank you my friends. I have been at a loss to know what to do with the English, as they have been stronger than the Kafirs; you have come to strengthen us."

Xito was present upon this occasion; also a great many counsellors. I heard Kreli on several other occasions express his thanks in the same manner whenever he asked these people to assist them; and he also told them to be sure and keep their promise.

Did you hear of the Umpongo Prophetess? Yes. Her name is Nonkosi. I heard Umhlakaza say she spoke the same as I did. I also heard Umhlakaza tell his sons that Umhala had sent to him for news.

I have never seen Nonkosi. When Major Gawler came to the Bashee, Mony ordered me to be sent to him.

JOHN MACLEAN, Chief Commissioner
Truly Interpreted,
W. B. Chalmers, Clerk & Interpreter

14. Boer slaving.

Apart from wanting land, European settlers also wanted labor. And they wanted to get this labor as cheaply as possible, because the farming in which they were engaged was often little beyond subsistence level. After the British ended slavery at the Cape in 1828, the Dutch-speaking settlers had trekked into the interior of southern Africa from the 1830s onward, aiming to secure their labor needs from the African communities among which they lived. David Livingstone, whose journals chronicled the cruelties of Portuguese and Arab slaving, also denounced the ways in which Dutch settlers, or Boers, engaged in a new form of slavery. He also remarked on the way in which these Boers deemed themselves a "chosen people" of God, entitled by biblical teachings as well as by physical force to rule over Africans.[14]

ANOTHER adverse influence with which the mission had to contend was the vicinity of the Boers of the Cashan Mountains, otherwise "Magaliesberg." These are not to be confounded with the Cape colonists, who sometimes pass by the name. The word Boer simply means "farmer," and is not synonymous with our word boor. Indeed, to the Boers generally the latter term would be quite inappropriate, for they are a sober, industrious, and most hospitable body of peasantry.

Those, however, who have fled from English law on various pretexts, and have been joined by English deserters and every other variety of bad character in their distant localities, are unfortunately of a very different stamp. The great objection many of the Boers had, and still have, to English law, is that it makes no distinction between black men and white. They felt aggrieved by their supposed losses in the emancipation of their Hottentot slaves, and determined to erect themselves into a re-

14. David Livingstone, *Missionary Travels and Researches in South Africa: Including a Sketch of Sixteen Years' Residence in the Interior of Africa* (New York: Harper & Brothers, 1858), pp. 35–39.

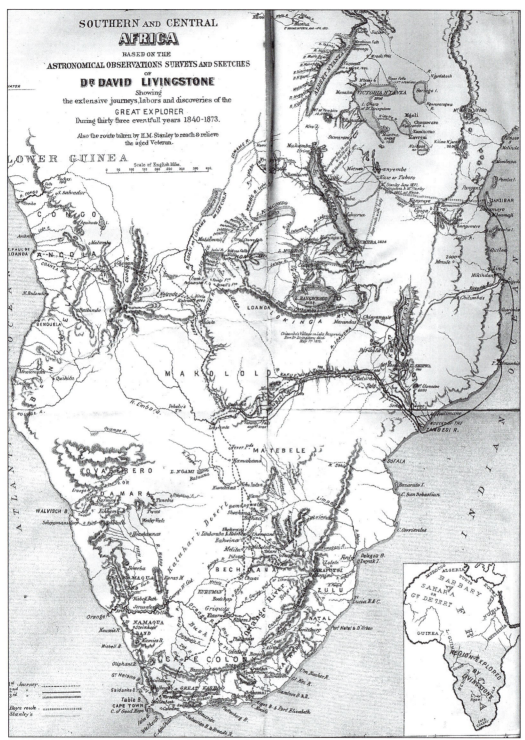

David Livingstone's travels in Central and Southern Africa, 1840–1873. *Source:* J.E. Chambliss, *The Life and Labors of David Livingstone . . .* (Philadelphia: Hubbard Brothers, 1876), facing p. 804.

public, in which they might pursue, without molestation, the "proper treatment of the blacks." It is almost needless to add that the "proper treatment" has always contained in it the essential element of slavery, namely, compulsory unpaid labor.

One section of this body, under the late Mr. Hendrick Potgeiter, penetrated the interior as far as the Cashan Mountains, whence a Zulu or Caffre chief, named Mosilikátze, had been expelled by the well-known Caffre Dingaan; and a glad welcome was given them by the Bechuana tribes, who had just escaped the hard sway of that cruel chieftain. They came with the prestige of white men and deliverers; but the Bechuanas soon found, as they expressed it, "that Mosilikátze was cruel to his enemies, and kind to those he conquered; but that the Boers destroyed their enemies, and made slaves of their friends." The tribes who still retain the semblance of independence are forced to perform all the labor of the fields, such as manuring the land, weeding, reaping, building, making dams and canals, and at the same time to support themselves. I have myself been an eyewitness of Boers coming to a village, and, according to their usual custom, demanding twenty or thirty women to weed their gardens, and have seen these women proceed to the scene of unrequited toil, carrying their own food on their heads, their children on their backs, and instruments of labor on their shoulders. Nor have the Boers any wish to conceal the meanness of thus employing unpaid labor; on the contrary, every one of them, from Mr. Potgeiter and Mr. Gert Krieger, the commandants, downward, lauded his own humanity and justice in making such an equitable regulation. "We make the people work for us, in consideration of allowing them to live in our country."

I can appeal to the Commandant Krieger if the foregoing is not a fair and impartial statement of the views of himself and his people. I am sensible of no mental bias toward or against these Boers; and during the several journeys I made to the poor enslaved tribes, I never avoided the whites, but tried to cure and did administer remedies to their sick, without money and without price. It is due to them to state that I was invariably treated with respect; but it is most unfortunate that they should have been left by their own Church for so many years to deteriorate and become as degraded as the blacks, whom the stupid prejudice against color leads them to detest.

This new species of slavery which they have adopted serves to supply the lack of field-labor only. The demand for domestic servants must be met by forays on tribes which have good supplies of cattle. The Portuguese can quote instances in which blacks become so degraded by the love of strong drink as actually to sell themselves; but never in any one case, within the memory of man, has a Bechuana chief sold any of his people, or a Bechuana man his child. Hence the necessity for a foray to seize children. And those individual Boers who would not engage in it for the sake of slaves can seldom resist the two-fold plea of a well-told story of an intended uprising of the devoted tribe, and the prospect of handsome pay in the division of the captured cattle besides.

It is difficult for a person in a civilized country to conceive that any body of men possessing the common attributes of humanity (and these Boers are by no means destitute of the better feelings of our nature) should with one accord set out, after loading their own wives and children with caresses, and proceed to shoot down in cold blood men and women, of a different color, it is true, but possessed of domestic feelings and affections equal to their own. I saw and conversed with children in the houses of Boers who had, by their own and their masters' account, been captured, and in several instances I traced the parents of these unfortunates, though the plan approved by the long-headed among the burghers is to take children so young that they soon forget their parents and their native language also. It was long before I could give credit to the tales of bloodshed told by native witnesses, and had I received no other testimony but theirs I should probably have continued skeptical to this day as to the truth of the accounts; but when I found the Boers themselves, some bewailing and denouncing, others glorying

Gang of slaves met at Mbame's on the way to Tete, 1861. *Source:* David and Charles Livingstone, *Narrative of an Expedition to the Zambesi and Its Tributaries; and of the Discovery of Lakes Shirwa and Nyassa, 1858-1864* (New York: Harper & Brothers, 1866), p. 376.

in the bloody scenes in which they had been themselves the actors, I was compelled to admit the validity of the testimony, and try to account for the cruel anomaly. They are all traditionally religious, tracing their descent from some of the best men (Huguenots and Dutch) the world ever saw. Hence they claim to themselves the title of "Christians," and all the colored race are "black property" or "creatures." They being the chosen people of God, the heathen are given to them for an inheritance, and they are the rod of divine vengeance on the heathen, as were the Jews of old. Living in the midst of a native population much larger than themselves, and at fountains removed many miles from each other, they feel somewhat in the same insecure position as do the Americans in the Southern States. The first question put by them to strangers is respecting peace; and when they receive reports from disaffected or envious natives against any tribe, the case assumes all the appearance and proportions of a regular insurrection. Severe measures then appear to the most mildly disposed among them as imperatively called for, and, however bloody the massacre that follows, no

qualms of conscience ensue: it is a dire necessity for the sake of peace. Indeed, the late Mr. Hendrick Potgeiter most devoutly believed himself to be the great peacemaker of the country.

David Livingstone. *Source:* J.E. Chambliss, *The Life and Labors of David Livingstone . . .* (Philadelphia: Hubbard Brothers, 1876), frontispiece.

But how is it that the natives, being so vastly superior in numbers to the Boers, do not rise and annihilate them? The people among whom they live are Bechuanas, not Caffres [Livingstone is here referring to Xhosa], though no one would ever learn that distinction from a Boer; and history does not contain one single instance in which the Bechuanas, even those of them who possess fire-arms, have attacked either the Boers or the English. If there is such an instance, I am certain it is not generally known, either beyond or in the Cape Colony. They have defended themselves when attacked, as in the case of Sechele [Livingstone's sole convert], but have never engaged in offensive war with Europeans. We have a very different tale to tell of the Caffres, and the difference has always been so evident to these border Boers that, ever since those "magnificent savages" obtained possession of fire-arms, not one Boer has ever attempted to settle in Caffreland, or even face them as an enemy in the field. The Boers have generally manifested a marked antipathy to any thing but "long-shot" warfare, and, sidling away in their emigrations toward the more effeminate Bechuanas, have left their quarrels with the Caffres to be settled by the English, and their wars to be paid for by English gold.

The Bakwains at Kolobeng had the spectacle of various tribes enslaved before their eyes—the Bakatla, the Batlókua, Bahúkeng, the Bamosétla, and two other tribes of Bakwains were all groaning under the oppression of unrequited labor. This would not have been felt as so great an evil but that the young men of those tribes, anxious to obtain cattle, the only means of rising to respectability and importance among their own people, were in the habit of sallying forth, like our Irish and Highland reapers, to procure work in the Cape Colony. After laboring there three or four years, in building stone dikes and dams for the Dutch farmers , they were well content if at the end of that time they could return with as many cows. On presenting one to their chief, they ranked as respectable men in the tribe ever afterward. These volunteers were highly esteemed among the Dutch, under the name of Mantátees. They were paid at the rate of one shilling a day and a large loaf of bread between six of them. Numbers of them, who had formerly seen me about twelve hundred miles inland from the Cape, recognized me with the loud laughter of joy when I was passing them at their work in the Roggefelt and Bokkefelt, within a few days of Cape Town. I conversed with them and with elders of the Dutch Church, for whom they were working, and found that the system was thoroughly satisfactory to both parties. I do not believe that there is one Boer, in the Cashan or Magaliesberg country, who would deny that a law was made, in consequence of this labor passing to the colony, to deprive these laborers of their hardly-earned cattle, for the very cogent reason that, "if they want to work, let them work for us their masters," though boasting that in their case it would not be paid for. I can never cease to be most unfeignedly thankful that I was not born in a land of slaves. No one can understand the effect of the unutterable meanness of the slave-system on the minds of those who, but for the strange obliquity which prevents them from feeling the degradation of not being gentlemen enough to pay for services rendered, would be equal in virtue to ourselves. Fraud becomes as natural to them as "paying one's way" is to the rest of mankind.

15. Legislating race and religion.

The Dutch settlers in the interior of southern Africa established two independent political communities, the Orange Free State (OFS) and the Transvaal Republic (also known as the South African Republic—SAR). Though the British did not recognize the independence of these states, they did not interfere with the political autonomy of these communities between the middle of the 1850s and the end of the 1870s. The OFS and the SAR were constituted as independent republics, with the right to vote given to all white males, but not to women nor to Africans of any gender. Though influenced in part by the constitution of the United States, the framers of the South African constitutions made explicit the connection that they considered essential between church and state, and limited official recognition to one church only, Dutch Reformed. [15]

General regulations of the South African Republic, February 1858.

1. This State shall bear the name of the South African Republic.

2. The form of government of this State shall be that of a Republic.

3. It desires to be acknowledged and respected by the civilised world as an independent and free people.

4. The people seek no extension of territory, and desire it only according to principles of justice, when the interests of the Republic render it advisable.

5. The people desire to possess and retain their territory unimpaired inclusive of their rights and claims to the territory towards the East and South-East of this Republic, so far as those rights and claims extend, and so in like manner towards the West and South-West. And the Government of the South African Republic shall be obliged as soon as possible to take steps for fixing and publishing by Proclamation the limits and boundaries.

6. Its territory is open to every stranger who submits to the laws of this Republic. All persons who happen to be within the territory of this Republic have equal claim to protection of person and property.

7. The lands or farms situated within this territory which have not yet been given out are declared to be the property of the State, but are none the less obtainable as heretofore by the Public. No farm inspected for that purpose shall be larger than 3000 morgen [a measure of land, approximately 6,000 acres]. And no one shall be entitled to apply for or to obtain lands until he has reached the age of sixteen.

8. The people demand as much social freedom as possible, and expect to obtain it by retaining their religious faith, by fulfilling their obligations, by submitting to law, order and justice, and by upholding these. The people permit the spread of the Gospel among the heathen subject to definite safeguards against fault and deception.

9. The people desire to permit no equality between coloured people and the white inhabitants, either in Church or State.

10. The people desire to put up with no trading in slaves nor with slavery in this Republic.

11. The people reserve to themselves alone the protection and defence of the independence and inviolability of Church and State, according to the laws.

12. The people delegate the function of legislation to a Volksraad, the highest authority in the country, consisting of representatives or plenipotentiaries of the people, elected by burghers possessing the franchise, but it is provided that a period of three months be given to the people to enable them to convey to the Volksraad their views on any proposed law, should they so desire, except in the case of laws which can brook no delay.

13. The people delegate the proposal and the administration of the laws to an Executive Council, which shall also recommend all public officials for appointment by the Volksraad. . . .

20. The people desire to retain the fundamental teachings of their Dutch Reformed Religion as laid down in the years 1618 and 1619 by the Synod of Dordrecht, and the Dutch Reformed Church shall be the State Church.

---

15. G. W. Eybers, ed., *Select Constitutional Documents Illustrating South African History, 1795–1910* (New York: George Routledge and Sons, 1918), pp. 363–67.

21. They prefer to allow no Roman Catholic Churches amongst them, nor any other Protestant Churches than those in which the same tenets of Christian belief are taught, as contained in the Heidelberg Catechism.

22. They shall appoint no other representatives to the Volksraad than those who are members of the Dutch Reformed Congregations. . . .

24. The people desire the development, prosperity and welfare of Church and State,

and with this view to provide for the wants of the Dutch Reformed Ministers and Teachers. . . .

32. The members of the Volksraad shall be chosen by a majority of the votes of the people. Every burgher, who has reached the age of 21 years or more, shall possess the franchise, provided he be a member of the Dutch Reformed Church. . . .

16. Expanding trade by taking territory, Lagos 1861.

Though African traders on the Niger Delta and the British had negotiated a commercial treaty in 1836, with the king of Bonny getting thereafter an annual payment to encourage him to reduce the trade in slaves, British officials became dissatisfied with the way the agreement worked in practice. They decided, as the following memorandum by Lord John Russell shows, that the formal acquisition of territory, preferably by treaty, would help attain two goals: encourage British trade up the Niger river by establishing a local administration that would assist British merchants in their dealings with Africans, and enable a more interventionist policy with regard to the suppression of slavery. The focus of British official activities was the trading city of Lagos, named after the town in Portugal from which the first regular trade in African slaves had begun in the fifteenth century.[16]

(A). Lord John Russell to the Duke of Newcastle, recommending the annexation of Lagos, February 7, 1861.

But there is another measure which would in my opinion be attended with the most beneficial results, both as regards the suppression of the Slave Trade, and the encouragement of lawful Commerce in the Bight of Benin, namely that the Town and Island of Lagos should be taken possession of by the British Government.

Since the establishment at Lagos of its present Chief, King Docemo, that Island has virtually been under British protection, the King's authority being only maintained by the continued presence in the Lagos Lagoon of one of Her Majesty's Gun Boats. If that pro-

tection were withdrawn, the place would, in all probability, shortly fall into the hands of its former Chief King Kosoko, under whose rule it would speedily become again the head quarters of Slave Dealers, as it was until Kosoko was expelled by a British force. King Docemo is moreover unable to govern the people under him, and to keep order among the traders assembled at Lagos without the constant support and interference of Her Majesty's Consul, who is in reality the Chief Authority in the place. Her Majesty's Government are thus in fact burdened with the responsibility of governing and defending Lagos, whilst they do not enjoy any of the advantages of Sovereignty.

If instead of this anomalous quasi Protectorate, Lagos were placed under British

16. C. W. Newbury, ed., *British Policy Towards Africa: Select Documents, 1786–1874* (Oxford: Clarendon Press, 1965), pp. 426–28, 429–30. Reprinted with the permission of Colin Newbury.

authority, the state of uncertainty and periodical alarm that prevails there would be put an end to, and the feeling of security which could not fail to spring up, would have a most beneficial influence in extending the valuable trade already carried on from Lagos and its neighbourhood, the existence of which is due to the expulsion of the Slave Dealers from Lagos by a British force in 1845 [*sic*], and their exclusion ever since, by the measures taken to prevent the return of Kosoko.

To shew Your Grace the extent and value of this Trade, and how rapidly it has sprung up, I have the honor to enclose for your information the accompanying Extracts from Reports which have been received from Her Majesty's late Consuls at Lagos. It will be seen from these Papers that the value of the Palm Oil & Cotton exported from the Bight of Benin in the Year 1857 amounted to the sum of £1,062,700 and the value of these exports since that date would have been made more considerable if it had not been for the Slave hunting Expeditions of the King of Dahomey.

I do not doubt that Your Grace will concur with me that it would be impossible for Her Majesty's Government to allow Lagos again to fall into the hands of the Slave Dealers, nor could they view with indifference the establishment there by French Agents of a Depôt for Negroes to be exported as Labourers to the French Colonies, a measure which might still be carried into effect if the French should fail in procuring a supply of labor for their Colonies from other than African sources.

But the defence of Lagos would be far more easy if the place was actually under British Government, and there would then be no difficulty in preventing the interference of foreign nations with Lawful Trade by Schemes of black Emigration.

Moreover, the occupation of so important a point as Lagos, could not fail to produce a great moral effect upon the minds of the Inhabitants of the surrounding Country, and would go far to secure the tranquillity of the neighbouring District. From this District we have, within the last few years, derived a supply of Cotton which tho' hitherto small, is rapidly increasing, and which, according to the information received by Her Majesty's Government, is capable of an almost unlimited extension.

For these reasons I do not hesitate to recommend to Your Grace's favorable consideration, that Lagos should be taken possession of and occupied. It might afterwards be considered whether it should be constituted a British Colony.

It would, it is believed, not be difficult to obtain from the present Chief the cession of his Rights, in return for which it would probably be necessary to assign him an allowance out of the Revenues of the Port, and there is no cause to doubt that the inhabitants would gladly become British Subjects.

The expense of maintaining such a Colony would not be considerable, and would, in my opinion, be amply repaid by the advantages which I have pointed out.

If your Grace should agree in these views, I would propose to trust Her Majesty's Consul at Lagos to enter into a negotiation with King Docemo for the cession of his rights.

(B). Lagos treaty of cession, August 6, 1861.

Treaty between Norman B. Bedingfeld, Commander of Her Majesty's Ship "Prometheus," and Senior Officer of the Bights Division, and William McCoskry, Esq., Her Britannic Majesty's Acting Consul, on the part of Her Majesty the Queen of Great Britain; and Docemo, King of Lagos, on the part of himself and Chiefs.

Article 1. In order that the Queen of England may be the better enabled to assist, defend, and protect the inhabitants of Lagos, and put an end to the slave trade in this and the neighbouring countries, and to prevent the destructive wars so frequently undertaken by Dahomey and others for the capture of slaves, I, Docemo, do, with the consent and advice of my Council, give, transfer, and by these presents grant and confirm unto the Queen of Great Britain, her heirs and successors for ever, the port and Island of Lagos, with all rights, profits, territories, and appurtenances whatsoever thereunto belonging, and as well the profits and revenue as the direct, full, and absolute dominion and sovereignty of the said port, island, and premises, with all the royalties thereof, freely, fully, entirely, and absolutely. I do also covenant and grant that the quiet and peaceable possession thereof shall, with all possible speed, be freely and effectually delivered to the Queen of Great Britain, or such person as Her Majesty shall thereunto appoint, for her use in the performance of this grant; the inhabitants of the said island and territories, as the Queen's subjects, and under her sovereignty, Crown, jurisdiction, and Government, being still suffered to live there.

Article 2. Docemo will be allowed the use of the title of King in its usual African signification, and will be permitted to decide disputes between natives of Lagos with their consent, subject to appeal to British laws.

Article 3. In the transfer of lands, the stamp of Docemo affixed to the document will be proofs that there are no other native claims upon it, and for this purpose he will be permitted to use it as hitherto.

In consideration of the cession as before-mentioned of the port and island and territories of Lagos, the representatives of the Queen of Great Britain do promise, subject to the approval of Her Majesty, that Docemo shall receive an annual pension from the Queen of Great Britain, equal to the net revenue hitherto annually received by him; such pension to be paid at such periods and in such mode as may hereafter be determined.

Additional Article to the Lagos Treaty of Concession, 18 February 1862. King Docemo having understood the foregoing Treaty, perfectly agrees to all the conditions thereof; and with regard to the 3d Article consents to receive as a pension, to be continued during his lifetime, the sum of 1,200 (twelve hundred) bags of cowries per annum, as equal to his net revenue; and I, the undersigned representative of Her Majesty, agree on the part of Her Majesty to guarantee to the said King Docemo an annual pension of (1,200) twelve hundred bags of cowries for his lifetime, unless he, Docemo, should break any of the Articles of the above Treaty, in which case his pension will be forfeited. The pension shall commence from the 1st of July of the present year, 1862, from which day he, the King, resigns all claim upon all former farmers of the revenue.

17. French ambitions in West Africa.

During the first half of the nineteenth century, while the British were spreading their trading efforts along much of the West African Coast and seeking entry to the interior via two riverine systems—that of the Gambia river, north of Sierra Leone, and that of the Niger—the French largely concentrated their presence at the mouth of the Senegal river. (They also developed trading posts along the Ivory Coast and in Dahomey.) From their coastal base, the French had traded for slaves in the seventeenth and eighteenth centuries, and, after the return of their territories at the conclusion of the Napoleonic wars (the British had seized France's colonial bases), for new products.

At first, the French focused on the indigenous gum trade (used for glazing textiles) and then, with the growing demand for lubricants in Europe, switched to groundnuts from the 1840s onward. The French acquired gum and groundnuts through trade with African merchants and producers. Increasingly, however, as the potential for huge profit in the oil trade became clear, the French hoped to re-negotiate the terms of trade by getting direct access to the areas of production. This goal meant looking to the interior, and especially to the hinterland of the Niger river with its great resources of palm oil, monopolized at mid-century by British traders moving into the interior up the Niger. The great "architect" of French ambitions at mid-century was Louis Faidherbe, governor of Senegal 1854–1861 and 1863–1865. In developing his expansionist ambitions, Faidherbe had the support of the French military (the outline for a new colonial army had been drawn up by an official Commission of French officers in 1850) and the clergy (the Holy Ghost Fathers quoted below were applying in 1858 for an official subsidy for their operations).[17]

(A). Louis Faidherbe drafts a policy for the French in West Africa, May 1864.

The situation of our establishments on the West Coast of Africa deserves the attention of the Government. For nearly five centuries our ships have been frequenting this coast, and it may be said that France was the first of all European nations to carry her flag and her civilising ideas into this part of the world. After enjoying an almost exclusive position and possessing numerous establishments over a long period, in consequence of disastrous set-backs on the seas she witnessed her possessions passing successively into the hands of the Dutch, the Portuguese, and the British, and the influence of those three naval powers gradually replacing that which she formerly exercised without dispute. . . . However, our forces soon recovered their advantage, Saint-Louis was recaptured, and by a Treaty signed on 3 September 1783 we received exclusive possession of the Senegal river and its dependencies, Gorée, and the *comptoir* of Albreda, situated a short distance from the mouth of the Gambia. England was confirmed in possession of the latter river and retained the right to trade for gum between the River St. John and Portendick. . . .

As for that portion of the coast between the left bank of the Gambia and the Sierra Leone river, it was not attributed exclusively to any nation; the French continued to share with the English and all other peoples the right to frequent these waters and to form new establishments at any point not occupied.

The Treaty of Paris (30 March 1814) confirmed these provisions, and restored to us *unreservedly* all the establishments which we possessed on the West Coast of Africa at 1 January 1792. . . . To these establishments have been added, in consequence of treaties with native chiefs, those of Grand Bassam (19 February 1842), Assinie, Dabou and Gabon (18 March 1842). . . . By a convention of 7 March 1857 we exchanged our *comptoir* of Albreda against the British right to trade for gum at Portendick. . . .

However, our commerce, which these establishments were intended to protect and attract to themselves, has not unreservedly entered upon the paths thus opened to it. At the same time as it was profiting from the support of our posts and the prestige of our arms in order to extend its operations in Senegal, it successively abandoned our *comptoirs* down the coast to try to find in the free rivers suitable conditions for trading without supervision or protection. The Department of the Marine and Colonies was soon obliged to recognise that, at the same time as business was expanding in the territories dependent on Saint-Louis, in the Senegal river, on the coast at Dakar, and in the rivers Sine, Saloum and Casamance, the factories on the Gold Coast and at Gabon were almost completely abandoned, while a considerable growth was taking place in transactions at points on the coast not submitted to our authority and open to foreign competition, especially in the Gambia, where the trade is almost exclusively French.

The position may be summarised thus. French trade with the West Coast of Africa may be estimated at an annual value of 40 million francs, namely 24,000,000 francs of imports into France and 15,600,000 francs of exports. Of this sum Senegal (Saint-Louis and Gorée) accounts for a value of 19 millions (8 millions of imports into France, 11

17. John Hargreaves, ed., *France and West Africa: An Anthology of Historical Documents* (London: Macmillan, 1969), pp. 99–101, 102–04, 144–47. All translations are by Hargreaves. Reprinted with permission of Macmillan Publishers Ltd.

millions of exports); Gabon accounts for 500,000 francs only. At Grand Bassam and Assinie trade is almost nil. Thus the trade which we carry out in competition with other European powers, either on parts of the coast which are open to all comers or in actual foreign establishments, accounts for *more than half* of the general movement of French shipping to the West Coast of Africa. The creation of our *comptoirs* has had almost no discernible influence on this state of things, and although our trade has found for the most part a régime concerned to give it exclusive protection, it has successively abandoned these points, where for twenty years, at an annual cost of 470,000 francs to the government, and of regrettable casualties caused by fever in the ranks of the administrative and naval personnel, we have maintained our occupation without serious results for our shipping or our influence. The moment seems come to draw clear conclusions from this situation. Two principal facts emerge from our experience. The first is the *stable* character of our interests in the Senegal district [*cercle*], the second the essentially *inconstant* nature of our relations on other parts of the coast. Our commerce, which seems to have found at Saint-Louis, under effective and progressive supervision, a centre from which to spread out, inland by the river and southwards through our coastal establishments, is leaving Gabon and our posts on the Gold Coast and resolutely facing in other districts—often with marked success—the hazards of a trade exposed to arbitrary acts of the natives and to the difficulties of competition.

It appears that we would be responding to these present tendencies of our traders, in the first place by consolidating the territorial base so well established around Saint-Louis, and then by guaranteeing them on the rest of the coast, instead of a limited and costly armed protection about which they seem to care very little, active general supervision in their relations with the natives, and favourable treatment from European nations. To achieve this double purpose it would be appropriate to enter into an arrangement with England, the only power which today competes seriously with us in these waters. . . . In exchange for the Gambia, the English might be offered Gabon, Assinie . . . Grand Bassam and Dabou, together with the rights conferred on us by the Protectorate of Porto Novo, which is considerably impeding British designs upon Dahomey . . . [If this compensation were judged insufficient, one might go so far as to grant access for their flag to our colony of Saint-Louis.] We would further stipulate for equality of customs, shipping and port duties in all places thus exchanged.

After such a transaction, our Senegalese colony would form a compact and homogeneous territory, bounded by its natural frontiers; all the sources from which the trade of these coasts is drawn would be completely in our hands. Those who are resisting our plans for colonisation and development would receive no more supplies with which to do so, and caravans from the interior would henceforth follow the routes we saw fit to indicate. The great projects which might be conceived for extending our influence towards Timbuktu and the upper Niger would henceforth have a large and solid base. . . .

This negotiation would in my view be the starting point for a system on which I believe the commercial future of the West Coast of Africa depends, and which might be the culmination of European policies in these waters; I mean the neutralisation of the coast, and the admission of all countries and nations to trade in its rich products, under the guarantee of an agreement concluded among the great powers, and under the protection of all the navies of Europe. [The final paragraph was deleted from the official version.]

(B). Plans for a new type of colonial army.

[I]t is highly desirable that the Senegalese infantry should be composed of European and native troops in equal parts. Black soldiers have always given excellent service in the colony. Among others, those who belong to the Bambara race are, it may be said, as good as white soldiers, and they have the advantage over them of being immune to all the hardships of the climate. One can thus well appreciate the value which the support of such a force might have for Senegal in a host of circumstances, especially for the garrisons up-river. This is indisputably one of the most urgent needs of the locality. The remaining companies, already much reduced in strength following successive liberations of their personnel, will soon be run down completely, when the remainder have received their discharge. The Commission attaches the greatest urgency to consideration of methods of reconstructing this force.

There are two ways in which this reconstruction might be effected. Firstly, one might consider subjecting the population of Senegal to the metropolitan law of recruitment. But we must recognise that populations unaccustomed to military service would accept such obligations only with extreme repugnance. Moreover they could hardly provide an intake of more than 25 or 30 men a year, which is clearly insufficient for present needs. The alternative method of recruitment, the most hopeful and indeed the only effective one, would be that formerly employed, which consists of going up-country to enrol captives, to whom the sum needed to purchase their freedom is given as enrolment bounty. The Commission is aware that the terms of the emancipation decree [1848] now seem to put legal obstacles in the way of such an operation. It is also aware of the moral and humanitarian reasons which led to the inclusion in this act of a prohibition of long-term contracts of service—and which indeed had already caused them to be forbidden by the previous regime. These contracts, handed over to private interests as they formerly were in the Colony, had indeed degenerated into a veritable slave trade, and could no longer be tolerated. But if they are strictly confined to the needs of military recruitment and entrusted exclusively to the hands of the administration, they cannot give rise to any abuse. What after all is their effect?—that the government restores to freedom a certain number of captives who would otherwise be doomed to almost certain death, on the sole condition that they serve the government for several years. One might add that when these men return to their homelands at the end of their military service they should become excellent agents for the diffusion into the interior of Africa of the first notions of civilisation and commerce. In view of the major political interest, supported by this humanitarian interest, in not merely maintaining but increasing the strength of the black companies in Senegal, the Commission feels quite justified in asking that all steps be taken to reconcile the requirements of existing legislation with the obvious needs of our position in Senegal.

It further recommends that these troops should be completely assimilated to troops sent from Europe in regard to pay and rations, though care should be taken that they are organised in separate units. . . .

(C). The Holy Ghost Fathers explain the role of missionary education for Africans.

These are the objectives which the Missionaries of the Holy Ghost and the Sacred Heart of Mary have set themselves, and these are the needs of their establishment. Our general aim is the religious—and thus, the social—regeneration of the Negroes of Africa; the means to this will be our holy religion, and next to religious knowledge, work. Literary and scientific work for those who have the capacity to engage in it; manual work supplemented by a certain cultivation of the intelligence for those whose vocation is more humble. Our particular aim is to provide the French possessions with intelligent and loyal servants.

Consequently there is a dual objective. On the one hand, to produce well-educated and responsible young men, able to render real and valuable services in the colony and in the trading-posts as employees of the administration, the engineering department, the military and naval establishments; on the other to make honest and competent workmen, who would assist and if necessary even supervise those whom the colonial government already has at its disposal. Hence we have a primary and secondary school, and a trades school.

In the former we study the child, who usually comes to us young, at the age of five or six. If his intellectual qualities permit his education will be continuous; he will pass in succession from the primary school to the secondary school, where so far as our resources allow he will receive the same education as in a French college. If a pupil's undeveloped intelligence does not allow him to undertake such a heavy curriculum, we content ourselves with giving him some knowledge of the elementary principles of the French language, arithmetic and writing, and we make a workman of him.

At present we are educating seventy children at Dakar, and among them we have printers, book-binders, blacksmiths, joiners, wood-turners, cooks, shoemakers, weavers and tailors.

There is no need to dwell further on the real advantages for the French government of such an establishment on the African coast. Our colonies and trading-posts need honest, intelligent and loyal workmen, and especially foremen who can supervise the Negroes; they will be found among the children brought up in our work-shops, formed by a rule of discipline and accustomed to obey.

The better-off families from Saint-Louis, Gorée and elsewhere give their children an education beyond what the Brothers can offer in the Colony. Our secondary school will accept them. Our boarding fees, more in line with their present resources than those in France, will allow a large number of families to send their children; the climate of Dakar, being that in which they were born, will not prove unhealthy for these children, as that of France so often does; finally these young men, knowing only Africa, will not wish to leave it, but to serve in their own fatherland the French government, which will have become their own father. It is quite otherwise with those educated in France, who return home only with regret, and live only for the moment of leaving again.

Moreover, now Dakar is French it is destined to become the centre of all the maritime and commercial operations of Africa, and this will allow all points on the coast to send representatives there. We already have children from Gabon, Principe Island, Grand Bassam, Rio Pongos, Rio Nunez, Casamance, Bathurst, Gambia, the kingdoms of Sine and Baol, Gorée, Saint-Louis and Galam.

The Sisters of Immaculate Conception have a similar establishment within ten minutes of our own and their programme for the education and instruction of children is the same as ours, in due proportion. . . .

18. Africanus B. Horton on an autonomous Africa.

James Africanus Horton, a near contemporary of Samuel Crowther, was born in 1835, the son of an Igbo man who had been freed from a slave ship by a British naval squadron and who had settled in Sierra Leone. Identified by Church Missionary Society (CMS) missionaries as a talented scholar, Africanus Horton was recommended by his teachers to the British army as a likely candidate for medical training. He trained in Scotland and in 1859 graduated with an M.D. and a dissertation on "The Medical Topography of West Africa." Horton spent his career in the British army, serving in medical stations along the West African Coast and accompanying British expeditions against the Asante in 1864 and 1873–1874. He retired in 1880 with the rank of surgeon-major and died prematurely in 1882.

Horton was a strong admirer of the British, especially with regard to their systems of education and rule, and he thought that Africa benefited from their presence. But he also believed that Africans could change their societies themselves without outside intervention, and he was an opponent of the expansion of formal empire. He criticized in particular the rise of pseudo-scientific racism in Europe and the United States, arguing that Africans were in no way inferior to other peoples. He also stressed that Africans had themselves developed organized systems of governance, in his view full of shortcomings yet quite unlike the images of barbarity popularized in most of the accounts of European travelers. A strong critic of the Asante, he favored the creation of a federation of the Fante peoples of the Gold Coast, independent of the Asantehene (king), though under the influence of the British. The extracts below are from a book Horton published in 1868, a critical time in his view for West Africa. In 1865, a parliamentary committee had recommended that Britain withdraw any official presence it had on the West Coast other than in Sierra Leone, and the Asante had begun their campaign to re-conquer the Fante. Horton wanted the British to stay, but only to allow Africans to develop new forms of self-government, not to conquer.[18]

On racism.

It must appear astounding to those who have carefully and thoughtfully read the history of England in connexion with the subject of the African race, when its greatest statesman, so long ago as 1838, stated in Parliament the endeavours his Government had been making to induce the various continental and transatlantic ones to put down slavery, that the abolition of that institution in the Southern States of America should have produced so much bile amongst a small section in England; who, although they have had undeniable proofs of the fallacy of their arguments, and inconsistency of their statements with existing facts, have formed themselves into an association (*sic* Anthropological Society) to rake up old malice and encourage their agents abroad to search out the worst possible characteristics of the African, so to furnish material for venting their animus against him. "Its object," as has been stated, "is to prove him unimprovable, therefore unimproved since the beginning and, consequently, fitted only to remain a hewer of wood and drawer of water for the members of that select society." It would have been sufficient to treat this with the contempt it deserves, were it not that leading statesmen of the present day have shown themselves easily carried away by the malicious views of these

negrophobists, to the great prejudice of that race.

It is without doubt an uphill work for those who have always combated that vile crusade of prejudice, especially when considering themselves at the point of putting a crowning stroke to the superstructure which had taken them years to erect, to find the foundation undermined by rats of a somewhat formidable size, and therefore requiring a renewed and a more unassailable structure. One of the anthropological myths is to prove that, up to the age of puberty, the negro can combat successfully, and even show a precocity superior to that of the more enlightened race of a temperate climate, but that after this period, which corresponds to the closing of the sutures, he is doomed—a limit is set upon his further progress. But to prove more convincingly that this malign statement is fallacious, let those who are interested in the subject refer to the Principals of the Church Missionary College, Islington; King's College, London; and Fourah Bay College, Sierra Leone; where full-blooded Africans, who have had the complete development of their sutures, have been under tuition, and they will then be able to form an opinion from unbiassed testimony. I do not for a moment attempt here to prove that, as a whole, a race whose past generations have been in utter darkness, the mental faculty of whose ances-

18. James Africanus B. Horton, *West African Countries and Peoples, British and Native, with the Requirements Necessary for Establishing that Self Government Recommended by the Committee of the House of Commons, 1865, and a Vindication of the African Race* (London: W. J. Johnson, 1868), pp. v–vii, 31–34, 39, 113–16, 246–49.

tors has never received any culture for nearly a thousand years, could attempt to compete successfully in their present state with one whose ancestors have successively been under mental training and moulding for centuries. To think so would be to expect an ordinary-bred horse to have equal chances in a grand race with a thorough-bred one. But I say that the African race, as exemplified by the results of enterprizes in Western Africa, if put in comparison with any race on the face of the globe, whether Caucasian, Mongolian, Teutonic, Celtic, or any other just emerging from a state of barbarism, as they are, will never be found a whit behind. But to draw deductions by comparing their present

James Africanus B. Horton. *Source:* James Africanus B. Horton, *West African Countries and Peoples British and Native with the Requirements for Establishing that Self Government Recommended by the Committee of the House of Commons, 1865, and a Vindication of the African Race* (London: W.J. Johnson, 1868), frontispiece.

state with the civilization of the nineteenth century is not only absurd, but most unphilosophical.

Even Captain [Richard] Burton, the *noli me tangere* of the African race, the greatest authority in the present school of English anthropologists (their vice-president), who, from his writings, has led everyone to believe that he has a fiendish hatred against the negro, whilst animadverting in all his works on Western Africa, in the most unmistakably malicious language, on the impossibility of improving that race he so hates, forgot himself in one place, and exclaimed, as to their intellectual superiority, "There are about 100 Europeans in the land; amongst these there are many excellent fellows, *but it is an unpleasant confession to make*, the others appear to be inferior to the Africans, native as well as mulatto. The possibility of such a thing had never yet reached my brain. At last, in colloquy with an old friend upon the Coast, the idea started up, and, after due discussion, we adopted it. I speak of *morale*. In intellect *the black race is palpably superior, and it is fast advancing in the path of civilization.*" The first and last italics are ours. . . .

Dr [Robert] Knox regards everything to be subservient to race; and his arguments are brought forward to show that the negro race, in spite of all the exertions of Exeter Hall, or as his commentators most sneeringly call them, the "broad-brimmed philanthropy and dismal science school," will still continue as they were. To him, as he says, "Race is everything—literature, science, art—in a word, civilization depends on it. . . . With me race or hereditary descent is everything, it stamps the man."

Of late years a society has been formed in England in imitation of the Anthropological Society of Paris, which might be made of great use to science had it not been for the profound prejudice exhibited against the negro race in their discussions and in their writings. They again revive the old and vexed question of race, which the able researches of Blumenbach, Prichard, Pallas, Hunter, Lacepède, Quatrefages, Geoffroy St Hilaire, and many others, had years ago (as it was thought) settled. They placed the structure of the anthropoid apes before them, and then commenced the discussion of a series of ideal structures of the negro which only exist in their imagination, and thus endeavour to link the negroes with the brute creation. Some of their statements are so barefacedly false, so utterly the subversion of scientific truth, that they serve to exhibit the writers as perfectly ignorant of the subjects of which they treat. . . .

Carl Vogt, who, perhaps, has never seen a negro in his life, and who is perfectly ignorant as to the capabilities of the negro race, must needs deceive his pupils in Geneva on subjects that he knows nothing about. He tells them that as the young orangs and chimpanzees are goodnatured, so is the young negro; but that after puberty and the necessary transformation has taken place, as the former becomes an obstinate savage beast, incapable of any improvement, so the intellect of the negro becomes stationary, and he is incapable of any further progress; that, in fact, the supposed sudden metamorphoses (which rests only in his ideas) in puberty, said to have taken place in the negro at this period, is not only intimately connected with physical development, but is a repetition of the phenomena occurring in the anthropoid apes. . . .

Now, is this not a base prostitution of scientific truth? I have seen more than a hundred thousand negroes, but have not been able to find these characteristic differences which Carl Vogt, who has never seen one, or Prunner Bey, who saw Egyptian negro slaves, essay to describe. Indeed, as amongst every other tribe, white or black, there are to be found some with short necks, and others whose necks are peculiarly long; but where are to be found negroes with pendulous bellies as the anthropoid apes? Not in Africa surely, for from Senegal to the Cameroons the negroes I have met with are peculiar for the perfect flatness of their bellies. But Carl Vogt descends from the absurd to the ridiculous; when, writing on the peculiarities of the human foot as characters differentiating man and ape, he went on to state that "the foot of the gorilla is more anthropoid than that of any other ape, and the foot of the negro more apelike than that of the white man. The bones of the tarsus in the gorilla exactly resemble

those in the negro." We must only dismiss these absurdities by referring him to M. Aeby's measurements, which led him to the conclusion that individual races are not distinguishable from each other when the proportion of their limbs and these parts are examined; that the difference between the forearm of the European and the negro amounts to less than one per cent, and even he thinks that this slight difference which he has obtained may, by further and more extended measurement, be greatly reduced. Thus, therefore, there is no material difference in the proportion of the limbs between the European and negro.

On self-government.

Our government will . . . exercise sole authority over the countries from the Sweet River, near Elmina, to the River Volta. This should be divided into two separate independent self-governments—viz., the *Kingdom of Fantee*, extending from the Sweet River, to the borders of Winnebah; and the *Republic of Accra*, extending from Winnebah to the River Volta; the former to comprise the kingdoms of Denkera, Abrah, or Abacrampah, Assin, Western Akim, and Goomoor; the latter Eastern Akim, Winnebah, Accra, Aquapim, Adangme, and Crobboe.

The next point to be considered is the political union of the various kings in the kingdom of Fantee under one political head. A man should be chosen, either by universal suffrage, or appointed by the [British] Governor, and sanctioned and received by all the kings and chiefs, and crowned as King of Fantee. He should be a man of great sagacity, good common sense, not easily influenced by party spirit, of a kind and generous disposition, a man of good education, and who has done good service to the Coast Government. He should be crowned before all the kings and caboceers within the kingdom of Fantee; the kings should regard him as their chief; his authority should be recognized and supported by the Governor of the Coast, who should refer to him matters of domestic importance relative to the other native kings, advise him as to the course he should pursue, and see that his decisions be immediately carried out.

He should be assisted by a number of councillors, who, for the time, should swear allegiance to the British Government, until such time as the country is considered fit for delivery over to self-government. They should consist not only of men of education and good, sound common sense, residing in the Coast towns, but also of responsible chiefs, as representatives of the various kings within the kingdom.

One most important consideration is the yearly vote of a round sum out of the revenue as stipend to the king elect whilst under this probationary course, such as would allow him to keep up a certain amount of State dignity, and would enable him to carry out his authority over the kings and chiefs. Each State should be made to contribute towards the support of the temporary Government; a native volunteer corps should be attached to the Government, officered by natives of intelligence, who should be thoroughly drilled by paid officers and sergeants, supplied from West Indian regiments stationed on the Coast. The English language should be made the diplomatic language with foreign nations; but Fantee should be made the medium of internal communication and therefore ought at once to be reduced to writing.

The territory of the kingdom of Ashantee is larger than that of the Protected Territory of the Gold Coast, but we find the reigning king possesses absolute power over the different tribes composing it. True enough, the edifice was constructed on the blood of several nationalities, which gives it greater strength; but the kingdom of Fantee must be erected on a peaceable footing, supported, for a time at least, by a civilized Government, with a prince at the head who is versed in native diplomacy . . . a prince who would be able, like the potentate of Ashantee, to concentrate a large force at a very short notice, at any given point, when menaced by their powerful neighbours. . . .

The aim, therefore, should be to form a strong, compact native Government, which would command the obedience of all the na-

tive kings and chiefs, and which would immediately undertake the quelling of all disturbances in the interior, and command the native force if attacked. . . .

Let them, therefore, have a ruler in whom they have confidence, and generals experienced in bush fighting; let them be united, offensive and defensive, to one another, under one head, whose authority is paramount; let good, large, open roads be made connecting the kingdoms with one another . . . let the strength of every kingdom be known by the head centre . . . and I guarantee that a compact, powerful, and independent Government will be formed, which would defy Ashantee and give confidence to the whole country. . . .

Advice to the rising generation in West Africa.

Let the younger portion of the population, who are so susceptible and ready to take offence and retort at the least occasion, remember that all Europeans who enter their country, by the higher degree of intellectual and moral cultivation which they, as a race, have received, are entitled to a certain degree of respect as the harbingers of civilization, imitating the good and virtuous, while shunning those whose actions are a disgrace to civilization. . . . [L]et them be uniformly courteous, cultivate their minds, and strive zealously for substantial worth. Let them seek independence without bravado, manliness without subserviency; and let them put their shoulders to the work. . . .

They should make it their ruling principle to concentrate their mental powers, their powers of observation, reasoning, and memory. . . .

Let them consider that their own interest is intimately bound up in the interest of their country's rise; and that by developing the principle of public interest they will bring the Government to take an interest in themselves, and thus their interest and that of the Government will not clash, but become identical. . . .

Let the rising generation, therefore, study to exert themselves to obtain the combined attractive influence of knowledge and wisdom, wealth and honesty, great place and charity, fame and happiness, book-learning and virtue, so that they may be made to bring their happy influences to bear on the regeneration of their country. . . .

19. Diamonds.

In 1869, the year after Africanus Horton published his major work on West Africa, reports of a huge diamond find in the interior of southern Africa reached Europe. Within a few years, thousands of people, African and European, had traveled to the diamond fields. The new industry was hugely profitable for the few, such as Cecil Rhodes who succeeded in monopolizing control of the diamond mines, and enormously demanding for the Africans who labored in the mines. Gwayi Tyamzashe, a Xhosa convert to Christianity and a minister in the United Free Church of Scotland, came to the new city of Kimberley to engage in missionary work. Here he describes the urban culture developed at the diamond fields, noting especially the huge range of people coming from every part of southern and central Africa to work in the mining industry. Tyamzashe's son, Henry Daniel, became one of the chief aides to Clements Kadalie in organizing the Industrial and Commercial Workers' Union in South Africa during the 1920s.[19] (See Part 3, document 13.)

We have often heard of the industrious city—the Metropolis of Great Britain; the crowding of its streets, and the noise of the machinery and workmen. But I question if the noise there has ever been anything approaching what I have heard at the New Rush [Kimberley]. The hurry and din of the wheels, pulleys, wires, and buckets, in conveying the diamondiferous ground out of the gigantic mine; the noise of waggons, carts, carriages, sieves, sorting tables, and all the like, combined with the barbarous yells of the native labourers, and accompanied with a hurrah for every trifling thing that seems to be out of place, these things are as familiar to us at Kimberley as the touch bells are to you at Lovedale.

On my first arrival at the New Rush I observed that nearly every evening was devoted to private and public amusements, insomuch that there seemed to be no room left for the great work for which we had come. The evenings resounded with the noise of the concert, the circus, and all sorts of dances from one end of the camp to the other. The life then of both coloured and whites was so rough that I thought this place was only good for those who were resolved to sell their souls for silver, gold, and precious stones, or for those who were determined to barter their lives for the pleasures of a time. Diamond stealing was also regularly carried on a large scale by persons of colour as well as whites. Even in the present days of order, peace, and good government, I fear that diamond stealing is still practised systematically and ingeniously. It is very effectively done by companies consisting of several natives and a European diamond buyer who is at the head of the Company. Like the old Spartans, these natives are taught to steal so that they cannot be found out, and are well compensated for it.

During the short period of about two years there has been a wonderful change with regard to the moral condition of the Diamond Fields. The invincible power of the Gospel has made itself felt in the hearts of many, so that now there are two opposite forces acting

19. Gwayi Tyamzashe, article published in the bilingual missionary journal, *Kaffir Express/Isigidimi* (August 1874), reprinted in Francis Wilson and Dominique Perrot, eds., *Outlook on a Century: South Africa 1870–1970* (Lovedale, South Arica: Lovedale Press, 1972), pp. 19–21. Reprinted with the permission of the Lovedale Press.

APPENDIX.

ANIMALS.

Believing that zoological gardens might wish in the future to make collections of animals in Central Africa, I made the following estimate, which was approved by those who had an extended acquaintance with the business:

No.	Animals.	Kinds.	Age.	Price.			
1..	Elephant	2	10 years ...	$200	× 8	=	$1,600
2..	Giraffe.	1	3 years	100	× 4	=	400
3..	Hippopotami	1	2 years . ..	100	× 4	=	400
4..	Ostrich	8	2 years . ..	25	× 12	=	300
5..	Lions	1	2 months ..	10	× 8	=	80
6..	Leopards	1	2 months ..	10	× 4	=	40
7..	Panther	1	2 months ..	10	× 4	=	40
8..	Wild Cat.	1	2 months ..	10	× 4	=	40
9..	Linx	1	2 months ..	10	× 4	=	40
0..	Monkeys.	8	1 month ...	5	×100	=	500
1..	Wild Ass.	1	2 months ..	100	× 4	=	400
12..	Wild Cat.	....	2 years ...	5	× 4	=	20
13..	Hyena	2	2 months ..	10	× 8	=	80
14..	Fox.	8		5	× 12	=	60
15..	Abyssinian Cat.	1		20	× 4	=	80
16..	Dromedary	2	5 years	100	× 8	=	800
17..	Antelopes	20		20	× 80	=	1,600
18..	Camel	......		20	× 4	=	80
19..	Rhinoceros.	1		100	× 4	=	400
20..	Zebra	1		100	× 4	=	400
21..	Crocodiles.	1		10	× 8	=	80
				Ani'ls, 290			$6,770

Cost of animals	$6,770
Chains, 200 × $3	600
Cages, 150 × $10	1,500
Cases	1,000
To get the animals ready	3,000
For care	1,000
Hunting expedition	500
Hunters, 10 × $100	1,000
Men, 30 × $50	1,500
Gunpowder, etc	2,000
Boats to Alexandria, 12 × $200	2,400
	$21,270
Cost of transportation to New York, including cases	10,000
Total	$31,270

The cost of African animals to Western zoos. *Source:* Alvan S. Southworth, *Four Thousand Miles of African Travel: A Personal Record of a Journey Up the Nile . . .* (New York: Baker, Pratt & Co., Publishers, 1875), p. 381.

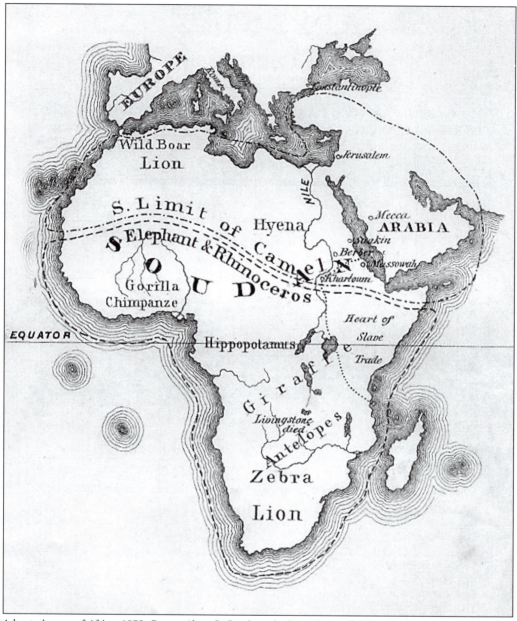

A hunter's map of Africa, 1875. *Source:* Alvan S. Southworth, *Four Thousand Miles of African Travel: A Personal Record of a Journey Up the Nile . . .* (New York: Baker, Pratt & Co., Publishers, 1875), facing p. 1.

against each other, whereas before only one—namely, the evil influence—seemed to be the one ruling power in this camp.

Instead of the bustle and confusion of 1872, we have now that quietude and security of life and property which is characteristic of proper legislation and good government. About two years ago human life was, so to speak, reckoned as of less value than silver, gold, and precious stones. At that time you would hear nothing but cursing, swearing, screaming, and shouts of hurrah for new comers from the interior, for fighters, for a well dressed lady, for a diamond being found, and so forth. It is vain to expect order and smoothness here. The very purpose for which the people have rushed and crowded together in this camp—to get rich rapidly—speaks of itself that there can be neither order nor smoothness in such a rush as this. Add to this the severity of the climate and the unruly character of the diggers. All who have ever visited the fields will have complained of excessive heat, extreme cold, and choking dust occasioned by the every day storms of wind raising the gigantic heaps of sorted gravel, sometimes rendering the sun invisible, and breathing also difficult. You would be surprised to find at the Colesberg Kopje a person whom you knew to have been a respectable gentleman, dressed like a common labourer, with only a pair of trousers, a big flannel shirt purposely unbuttoned, and a big heavy belt round his waist. Every one who succeeds in making a fortune, whether he be white or coloured, will first have to be contented to live day after day like the Kaffir Bakwetas or white boys. When they are all at work you can hardly distinguish the whites from the coloured, for they all resemble the diamondiferous soil they are working.

A lady or a well dressed gentleman dare not come near the mine during the hours of labour, for the native labourers will make shouts of hurrah for them all round the Kopje. Day after day you hear shouts of hurrah for a diamond being found, for a rope or wire breaking, for a bucket falling and injuring some one, for a portion of a claim breaking down and burying some person or persons underneath it.

This is the reason why many persons wanting patience and perseverance have been thoroughly disappointed when they came here. To bear on for a year or so at this picnic life requires no ordinary degree of patience on the part of the digger. The summation of the above statements with regard to life at the Diamond Fields may be comprehended under the two English words, *rough and hard.* . . .

In a mission point of view, it is not easy to deal with such a mixture of tribes as we have at the Diamond Fields. There are Bushmen, Korannas, Hottentots, Griquas, Batlaping, Damaras, Barolong, Barutse, Bakhatla, Bakwena, Bamangwatu, Bapeli, Magalaka, Batsuetla, Baganana, Basutu, Magwaba, Mazulu, Maswazi, Matswetswa, Matonga, Matebele, Mabaca, Mampondo, Mamfengu, Batembu, Maxosa, etc. Many of these can hardly understand each other, and in many cases they have to converse through the medium of either Dutch, Sisutu, or Kaffir. Those coming from far up in the interior, such as the Bakwena, Bamangwatu, Mapeli, Matebele, etc., come with the sole purpose of securing guns. Some of them therefore resolve to stay no longer here than is necessary to get some six or seven pounds for the gun. Hence you will see hundreds of them leaving the Fields, and as many arriving from the north almost every day. . . .

20. Cecil Rhodes dreams of empire.

The most famous of the diamond magnates was Cecil Rhodes. Born in 1853, the son of an English clergyman, Rhodes made a fortune in diamonds while still in his twenties, monopolized control of the industry with his company, De Beers Consolidated Mines (which controls world diamonds to the present day), became prime minister of the Cape Colony, and established his own private colony, Rhodesia. Interested both in business and in politics, and an enthusiastic supporter of the British Empire, he attempted to perpetuate his beliefs by leaving practically his entire estate to fund scholarships for university study. These Rhodes scholarships would enable "young Colonists" (including some Americans), males only (though with no restriction as to race), to study at Oxford University (which Rhodes himself had attended, paying his own way from diamond profits) to acquire an understanding of "the advantage to the Colonies as well as to the United Kingdom of the retention of the unity of the Empire." While a student at Oxford, Rhodes had sketched out his long-term

aims in a "confession of faith," reproduced below with Rhodes's original spell-
ing and punctuation. The scholarships, the qualifications for which Rhodes
detailed in his will (B), were meant to create the society of Empire-boosters
envisaged in the confession.[20]

(A). Rhodes' confession of faith, June 2, 1877.

It often strikes a man to inquire what is the chief good in life; to one the thought comes that it is a happy marriage, to another great wealth, and as each seizes on his idea, for that he more or less works for the rest of his existence. To myself thinking over the same question the wish came to render myself useful to my country. I then asked myself how could I and after reviewing the various methods I have felt that at the present day we are actually limiting our children and perhaps bringing into the world half the human beings we might owing to the lack of country for them to inhabit that if we had retained America there would at this moment be millions more of English living. I contend that we are the finest race in the world and that the more of the world we inhabit the better it is for the human race. Just fancy those parts that are at present inhabited by the most despicable specimens of human beings what an alteration there would be if they were brought under Anglo-Saxon influence, look again at the extra employment a new country added to our dominions gives. I contend that every acre added to our territory means in the future birth to some more of the English race who otherwise would not be brought into existence. Added to this the absorption of the greater portion of the world under our rule simply means the end of all wars, at this moment had we not lost America I believe we could have stopped the Russian-Turkish war by merely refusing money and supplies. Having these ideas what scheme could we think of to forward this object. I look into history and I read the story of the Jesuits I see what they were able to do in a bad cause and I might say under bad leaders.

In the present day I become a member in the Masonic order I see the wealth and power they possess the influence they hold and I think over their ceremonies and I wonder that a large body of men can devote themselves to what at times appear the most ridiculous and absurd rites without an object and without an end.

The idea gleaming and dancing before ones eyes like a will-of-the-wisp at last frames itself into a plan. Why should we not form a secret society with but one object the furtherance of the British Empire and the bringing of the whole uncivilised world under British rule for the recovery of the United States for the making the Anglo-Saxon race but one Empire. What a dream, but yet it is probable, it is possible. I once heard it argued by a fellow in my own college, I am sorry to own it by an Englishman, that it was a good thing for us that we have lost the United States. There are some subjects on which there can be no arguments, and to an Englishman this is one of them, but even from an American's point of view just picture what they have lost, look at their government, are not the frauds that yearly come before the public view a disgrace to any country and especially their's which is the finest in the world. Would they have occurred had they remained under English rule great as they have become how infinitely greater they would have been with the softening and elevating influences of English rule, think of those countless 000's of Englishmen that during the last 100 years would have crossed the Atlantic and settled and populated the United States. Would they have not made without any prejudice a finer country of it than the low class Irish and German emigrants? All this we have lost and that country loses owing to whom? Owing to two

---

20. (A), John Flint, *Cecil Rhodes* (London: Hutchinson, 1976), pp. 248–52. Reprinted with permission of John Flint. (B), Lewis Michell, *The Life of the Rt. Hon. Cecil John Rhodes, 1853–1902*, vol. 2 (London: Edward Arnold, 1910), pp. 326–27.

or three ignorant pig-headed statesmen of the last century, at their door lies the blame. Do you perhaps ever feel mad? do you ever feel murderous? I think I do with those men. I bring facts to prove my assertion. Does an English father when his sons wish to emigrate ever think of suggesting emigration to a country under another flag, never—it would seem a disgrace to suggest such a thing I think that we all think that poverty is better under our own flag than wealth under a foreign one.

Put your mind into another train of thought. Fancy Australia discovered and colonised under the French flag, what would it mean merely several millions of English unborn that at present exist we learn from the past and to form our future. We learn from having lost to cling to what we possess. We know the size of the world we know the total extent. Africa is still lying ready for us it is our duty to take it. It is our duty to seize every opportunity of acquiring more territory and we should keep this one idea steadily before our eyes that more territory simply means more of the Anglo-Saxon race more of the best the most human, most honourable race the world possesses.

To forward such a scheme what a splendid help a secret society would be a society not openly acknowledged but who would work in secret for such an object.

I contend that there are at the present moment numbers of the ablest men in the world who would devote their whole lives to it. I often think what a loss to the English nation in some respects the abolition of the Rotten Borough System has been. What thought strikes a man entering the house of commons, the assembly that rules the whole world? I think it is the mediocrity of the men but what is the cause. It is simply an—assembly of wealth of men whose lives have been spent in the accumulation of money and whose time has been too much engaged to be able to spare any for the study of past history. And yet in the hands of such men rest our destinies. Do men like the great Pitt, and Burke and Sheridan not now exist. I contend they do. There are men now living with I know no other term the μέγα χόχέγις of Aristotle but there are not ways for enabling them to serve their Country. They live and die unused unemployed. What has been the main cause of the success of the Romish Church? The fact that every enthusiast, call it if you like every madman finds employment in it. Let us form the same kind of society a Church for the extension of the British Empire. A society which should have its members in every part of the British Empire working with one object and one idea we should have its members placed at our universities and our schools and should watch the English youth passing through their hands just one perhaps in every thousand would have the mind and feelings for such an object, he should be tried in every way, he should be tested whether he is endurant, possessed of eloquence, disregardful of the petty details of life, and if found to be such, then elected and bound by oath to serve for the rest of his life in his Country. He should then be supported if without means by the Society and sent to that part of the Empire where it was felt he was needed.

Take another case, let us fancy a man who finds himself his own master with ample means on attaining his majority whether he puts the question directly to himself or not, still like the old story of virtue and vice in the Memorabilia a fight goes on in him as to what he should do. Take if he plunges into dissipation there is nothing too reckless he does not attempt but after a time his life palls on him, he mentally says this is not good enough, he changes his life, he reforms, he travels, he thinks now I have found the chief good in life, the novelty wears off, and he tires, to change again, he goes into the far interior after the wild game he thinks at last I've found that in life of which I cannot tire, again he is disappointed. He returns he thinks is there nothing I can do in life? Here I am with means, with a good house, with everything that is to be envied and yet I am not happy I am tired of life he possesses within him a portion of the μέγα χόχέγις of Aristotle but he knows it not, to such a man the Society should go, should test, and should finally show him the greatness of the scheme and list him as a member.

Take one more case of the younger son with high thoughts, high aspirations, endowed by nature with all the faculties to make a great man, and with the sole wish in life to serve his Country but he lacks two things the means and the opportunity, ever troubled by a sort of inward deity urging him on to high and noble deeds, he is compelled to pass his time in some occupation which furnishes him with mere existence, he lives unhappily and dies miserably. Such men as these the Society should search out and use for the furtherance of their object.

(In every Colonial legislature the Society should attempt to have its members prepared at all times to vote or speak and advocate the closer union of England and the colonies, to crush all disloyalty and every movement for the severance of our Empire. The Society should inspire and even own portions of the press for the press rules the mind of the people. The Society should always be searching for members who might by their position in the world by their energies or character forward the object but the ballot and test for admittance should be severe). [The section in parentheses did not appear in the first draft but was added later when Rhodes was back in Kimberley, and then deleted when he wrote his will.]

Once make it common and it fails. Take a man of great wealth who is bereft of his children perhaps having his mind soured by some bitter disappointment who shuts himself up separate from his neighbours and makes up his mind to a miserable existence. To such men as these the society should go gradually disclose the greatness of their scheme and entreat him to throw in his life and property with them for this object. I think that there are thousands now existing who would eagerly grasp at the opportunity. Such are the heads of my scheme.

For fear that death might cut me off before the time for attempting its development I leave all my worldly goods in trust to S. G. Shippard and the Secretary for the Colonies at the time of my death to try to form such a Society with such an object.

(B). Codicil to the last will and testament of Cecil Rhodes, October 11, 1901.

23. My desire being that the students who shall be elected to the Scholarships shall not be merely bookworms I direct that in the election of a student to a Scholarship regard shall be had to (i) his literary and scholastic attainments (ii) his fondness of and success in manly outdoor sports such as cricket football and the like (iii) his qualities of manhood truth courage devotion to duty sympathy for the protection of the weak kindliness unselfishness and fellowship and (iv) his exhibition during school days of moral force of character and of instincts to lead and to take an interest in his schoolmates for those latter attributes will be likely in afterlife to guide him to esteem the performance of public duties as his highest aim. As mere suggestions for the guidance of those who will have the choice of students for the Scholarships I record that (i) my ideal qualified student

Death mask of Cecil John Rhodes, 1902. *Source:* Lewis Mitchell, *The Life of Rt. Hon. Cecil John Rhodes, 1853-1902*, vol. 2 (London: Edward Arnold, 1910), frontispiece.

would combine these four qualifications in the proportions of 3/10ths for the first 2/10ths for the second 3/10ths for the third and 2/10ths for the fourth qualification so that according to my ideas if the maximum number of marks for any Scholarship were 200 they would be apportioned as follows: 60 to each of the first and third qualifications and 40 to each of the second and fourth qualifications (ii) the marks for the several qualifications would be awarded independently as follows (that is to say) the marks for the first qualification by examination for the second and third qualifications respectively by ballot by the fellow-students of the candidates and for the fourth qualification by the head master of the candidates school and (iii) the results of the awards (that is to say the marks obtained by each candidate for each qualification) would be sent as soon as possible for consideration to the Trustees or to some person or persons appointed to receive the same and the person or persons so appointed would ascertain by averaging the marks in blocks of 20 marks each of all candidates the best ideal qualified students.

24. No student shall be qualified or disqualified for election to a Scholarship on account of his race or religious opinions.

21. The sack of Kumasi.

In the mid-1860s, the British had considered abandoning their possessions in West Africa, with the exception of Sierra Leone, on the grounds that administrative costs were too high, the dangers of getting entangled in wars with African communities too great, and trading profits not sufficient to make staying worthwhile. But by the 1870s, perhaps anticipating economic returns like those newly developed in the southern African diamond fields, they had decided to stay. Staying meant dealing with the two issues that had bedeviled relations between the British and the Asante kingdom since the conclusion of the 1831 peace treaty: the authority of the Asantehene over African coastal peoples, and whether or not the British had to return to the Asantehene people (believed by the British to be mostly slaves) fleeing the king's authority. For the Asante, the ending of the slave trade had begun a long decline in their economic and political fortunes. In the late 1860s, the new Asantehene, Kofi Karikari (reigned 1867–1874), went on the offensive. He argued that the treaty terms of 1831 did not give the British authority beyond the reach of their guns at Cape Coast Castle, and he fought a series of successful military campaigns against the coastal Fante people. He also argued that the Dutch, who formerly had been his allies and tributaries, had no right to transfer their territory, including especially the coastal fort of Elmina, when the British "bought out" the Dutch in 1872.

Having to decide between withdrawal from the Gold Coast, continuous frontier wars, or further intervention, the British in 1873 decided to crush the Asante militarily. In the selections below, the Asantehene asserts his rights to the coast, the British colonial secretary instructs Sir Garnet Wolseley, the officer in charge of British forces (and the model for Gilbert and Sullivan's famous music hall figure, "the very model of the modern major-general"), as to his duties, and Henry Brackenbury, secretary to Sir Garnet, describes the sacking of Kumasi. Brackenbury's account, with its emphasis on Asante barbarity and bloodletting, became a very influential text in the development of an impe-rialistic literature at the end of the nineteenth century. By terms of the Treaty of Fomena (February 13, 1874), the defeated Kofi Karikari accepted the terms demanded by the British and gave up Asante claims to the coast (though re-taining autonomy for the much reduced territory of the Asante). In May 1874, the British consolidated their possessions on the Gold Coast into a single colony, bringing an end to the Fante Confederation that, supported by people such as Africanus Horton, had attempted to bring about a self-governing state between 1867 and 1874. Later in 1874 the British banned the "selling, buying, or dealing in slaves," and emancipated all slaves in their Gold Coast territories, the first time that any colonial power had made slavery illegal in Africa since the emancipation of slaves in South Africa in 1833–1834.[21]

(A). Letter from King Kofi Karikari to Governor R. W. Harley with regard to Asante claims to the coastal commu-nities of Elmina, Denkyera, Akim, and Assin, March 20, 1873.

Sir . . . His Majesty states that, he being the grandson of Ossai Tutu, he owns the Elminas to be his relatives, and consequently the fort at Elmina and its dependencies being his, he could not understand the Administrator-in-Chief's sending Attah, *alias* Mr. H. Plange, to tell him of his having taken possession of them for Quake Fram, and notifying him also that in four months, he, the Administrator, would come to Ashantee to take power away from him.

He states that he has been made angry by this, and it was this which led to his sending great captains and forces to bring him Quake Fram, of Denkerah, who dares to take his Elmina fort, &c., and also the Assins and Akims, who are his slaves, and who have united with the Denkerahs to take power from him.

His Majesty further states that your Honour's restoring him these tribes . . . back to their former position as his subjects, and also restoring the Elmina fort and people back in the same manner as they were before, will be the only thing or way to appease him, for he has no quarrel with white men; but should

your Honour come in to interfere as he hears you are, that you have not to blame him, be-cause he will then start himself. . . .

(B). Instructions from the Earl of Kimberley to Sir Garnet Wolseley, September 10, 1873.

Sir,

Her Majesty's Government wish to leave you a large discretion as to the terms which you may think it advisable to require from the king of Ashantee, but may I point out to you that the Treaty which was concluded with Ashantee in 1831 . . . seems to afford a rea-sonable basis for any fresh Convention.

It would certainly be desirable to include in such a Convention an explicit renewal by the king of Ashantee of the renunciation, con-tained in the Treaty of 1831, of all claim to tribute or homage from the native kings who are in alliance with Her Majesty; and further, a renunciation of all pretension on his part to supremacy over Elmina or over any of the tribes formerly connected with the Dutch, and to any tribute or homage from such tribes, as well as to any payment or acknowledgement in any shape by the British Government in respect of Elmina or any other of the British forts or possessions on the coast.

The king should also, for his own interest no less than with a view to the general ben-

---

21. (A) and (B), G. E. Metcalfe, ed., *Great Britain and Ghana: Documents of Ghana History, 1807–1957* (Legon: University of Ghana, 1964), pp. 349, 351–52; (C), Henry Brackenbury, *The Ashanti War: A Narrative Prepared from the Official Documents by Permission of Major-General Garnet Wolseley C.B. K.C.M.G.*, vol. 2 (Edinburgh: William Blackwood and Sons, 1874), pp. 223–44.

efit of the country, engage to keep the paths open through his dominions, to promote lawful commerce to and through the Ashantee country, and to protect all peaceful traders passing through his dominions to the coast; and it might be expedient that a stipulation should be made that a resident British Consul or Agent should be received at the Ashantee capital, if Her Majesty should think fit at any time to appoint one.

You will, of course, be careful to avoid as far as possible anything which may endanger the lives of the European missionaries and their families who have so long been held in captivity at Coomassie [Kumasi], without any fault of their own, so far as Her Majesty's Government are aware, and you will use every effort to secure their safe release. You will also endeavour to procure the surrender of all the prisoners taken by the Ashantees from the tribes in alliance with Her Majesty.

It is a usual practice with the native tribes to demand hostages for the faithful performance of Treaties of Peace. This was done in 1831, when two hostages of high rank were delivered over to the British Government by the king of Ashantee. If you should find it advisable to make a similar demand on the present occasion, you will bear in mind that the hostages should be men of high rank and position in Ashantee.

It would be reasonable to exact from the king the payment of such an indemnity as may be within his means, which are said to be considerable, for the expenses of the war and the injuries inflicted on Her Majesty's allies.

Lastly, the opportunity should not be lost for putting an end, if possible, to the human sacrifices and the slave hunting which, with other barbarities, prevail in the Ashantee kingdom.

(C). Brackenbury describes the sack of Kumasi, February 1874.

This entry into Coomassie is in its circumstances unrivalled in the annals of war. The town was full of armed men. The first wide open place reached immediately after crossing the swamp had houses on the right and left, in all of which armed men were seen, who ran away on the approach of our skirmishers, but returned again to watch the passage of the long column, disappearing into the bush if any attempt was made to disperse them. In the great main street hundreds of armed men were collected to observe the entry, yet not a single shot was fired. So strong, indeed, seemed their confidence in the white man, that they deliberately walked through the market-place, past the front of our troops, carrying their arms and ammunition away into the bush; and officers of rank were seen chasing and tripping men carrying kegs of powder on their heads, and rifles and ammunition-boxes in their hands. The main street commands both the town and the palace, and the Brigadier on arrival had placed the artillery so that it could sweep the streets ascending to the market-place, and thrown out picquets. A party was at once sent down to the king's palace. . . . The palace was reached, but the king was nowhere to be found: he, the queen-mother, Prince Mensah, and all other personages of distinction, had disappeared.

Thus Coomassie was taken, and the goal of our enterprise was reached; the king had done his best, both by negotiations and the sterner policy of battle, to prevent our reaching his capital; but his efforts had failed. His policy of deceit and fraud had recoiled, broken to pieces upon the straightforward truthful dealing of our commander; and his troops had been scattered to the winds by the brave soldiers who had so well seconded the forethought, skill, and courage with which they had been directed by their general.

The king had in person been with his army; not in the fore-front of the battle; not seeking, like a brave man, to aid his troops by example, or staking his own life while others were staking theirs for him, but carried in his litter in rear, where no bullets came. But his presence showed the great effort that was made. "In Ashanti," said Prince Ansah, long before we went out, "the king never joins his army except on occasions when the full strength of the Ashanti power is to be put forth, and in pursuance of some solemn vow." And now, defeated, he takes refuge in flight, and, in his cowardly fear to come in, leaves his city and his people to be destroyed. . . .

Of course the main question now occupying the Major-General's mind was to conclude a peace with the king, and if possible to obtain from him a treaty. His palace was left unmolested, only a guard being placed upon it. . . . The following letter was addressed by Sir Garnet to the king:

"Coomassie, February 4, 1874
KING, You have deceived me, but I have kept my promise to you.

I am in Coomassie, and my only wish is to make a lasting peace with you. I have shown you the power of England, and now I will be merciful.

As you do not wish to give up your mother and Prince Mensa, send me some other hostages of rank, and I will make peace with you tomorrow on the terms originally agreed upon.

If either your majesty, or your royal mother, or Prince Mensa, will come to see me tomorrow early, I will treat you with all the honour due to your royal dignity, and allow you to return in safety. You can trust my word, I am, &c.,

(Signed) G. J. WOLSELEY

Major-General and Administrator, Gold Coast

To His Majesty Koffee Kalkalli, King of Ashanti, Coomassie"

The writer [Brackenbury] was commissioned to deliver this letter to the messengers, and at the same time to explain to them what were Sir Garnet's views; and it was impressed upon them that his Excellency had still only one wish—to make a lasting peace with the king; that he had no desire to break up his Majesty's kingdom, or to injure his position in the eyes of his people; that he had shown him how utterly impossible it was for him to resist the power of England, and had proved by coming to Coomasie that the white man always keeps his word. He now wished to make friends with the king, and urged upon him to come in person and treat with him. In order that he might do so, his palace was left untouched, and a guard was to be placed

upon it in order to preserve unharmed everything that his Majesty had left. If the king himself would not come to see the Major-General, his Excellency would treat with his royal mother, or with Prince Mensa, the heir to the crown, but with no lesser personage. His Excellency promised that the king or either of these royal personages should be considered free, and treated with all respect due to their rank and dignity; and he would accept lesser chiefs as hostages for the payment of the indemnity which it was his duty to demand. If the king would thus come and treat, Coomassie should be left untouched, and the troops should leave it as they found it. At the same time, Owoosoo Koko [a representative of the Asantehene] was warned that every precaution had been taken against treachery; and that if in the night, or during our stay at Coomassie, one single shot was fired against our troops, Coomassie should be destroyed, and every living person in it unhesitatingly put to death. . . .

[T]he Major-General and his staff lay down crowded together . . . to seek such rest as might be found. But there was little rest that night for any one in Coomassie. In the first place, the excitement of the day rendered us but little inclined for sleep; in the next place, we were sleeping or trying to sleep near the southern end of the town, and were sickened and nauseated by the loathsome smell of human bodies that pervaded this quarter, and which the fires in front of our place of shelter altogether failed to keep away. But even more sleep repelling was the fact, that at an early hour of the night, fires—evidently the work of incendiaries—sprang up all over the town, and through the night the troops were engaged in putting them out. . . .

[The next day] the Major-General visited the palace. . . . Descending the hill past the great fetish tree, which had blown down and shivered to pieces on the very day that Sir Garnet's summons to the king had left . . . past some other huge trees, whose gnarled roots spread across the road, passing on the left some large chiefs' houses, and on the right the house of the king's mother, we reached the high wooden paling which bounds the enclosure of the palace, and entered by a gate nearly opposite to a large enclosure on the opposite side of the road, where the bodies of dead kings and princes are buried for a year before being removed to the royal mausoleum at Bantama; and by the side of which enclosure is the mound on which human sacrifices are made on the occasions of great customs.

Entering by the gate in the paling, we found ourselves in the enclosure of the palace—a very large irregular pile of building, partly formed of thick walls of masonry, enclosing rooms two stories high, and partly of great open courts similar to those already described at Fommanah, only on a far larger scale, with the same raised rooms open to the court, and the same high pitched roofs. There are several entrances to the palace but we passed in, not by the porch on the south side, but by a large door on the west side of the palace, leading by a long passage, past some small courts to the right and left, which were apparently full of Ashantis, to the large court where the king holds receptions. . . .

The great court would have held 200 men. The supporting pillars of the roofs of all the recesses were highly ornamented with scroll-work in glazed red clay, and the floor of the recess at the southern end, in which the king sits, to receive embassies . . . had the floor ornamented with various devices in white paint. At the foot of the steps leading up to this recess was a little wicker semi-circular fence, enclosing a tortoise, and some rubbish of different sorts, which we were told was great fetish. In another court was a splendid bird, apparently quite tame— a bird of many gorgeous colours, and most beautifully crested; this, too, was fetish. We also saw some of the king's cats, of which he has many, and with which the missionaries had told us he was very fond of playing. In one place we found a quantity of enormous umbrellas of various materials, amongst them the State umbrella sent home to her Majesty, and in the same court numerous litters covered with silks and velvets or the skins of animals, in which the king was wont to be carried. In rooms up-stairs were stored heaps of boxes, which appeared to contain articles of value, and silks, and many other treasures

in profusion; all showed the signs of a hasty flight; and yet it was wonderful these things had not been carried away in the night.

Other things we saw of a different nature, which brought vividly before us the horrors of which this place had been a witness. There was the great death drum surrounded with human skulls and thigh-bones—the great drum on which three peculiar beats are given whenever a human victim is slaughtered as an offering to fetish. There were stools—the concave wooden stools common in the country—covered with clotted blood standing out from them in huge thick lumps, the blood of hundreds of human victims, in which they had been bathed as an offering to the memories of the king's ancestors, to whom they had belonged. Loathsome they were to see, as the flies rose in dense clouds from them at our approach.

We entered the king's bedchamber, closed by a heavy door, on which were many stamped placques of gold and silver; and we saw his Majesty's gorgeous four-post bed covered with silk, and on a stand beside it a large brass bowl filled with a compound of foul-smelling materials—the preparation of the fetish priests. But Sir Garnet Wolseley would not remain long enough in the palace where every association was horrible to the thought. Only, he had remained long enough to see that it would be well to protect it with a European guard, and that the guard must be a large one.

A hundred of the Rifle Brigade had already been ordered down, and the writer was left to see that the sentries were so posted as to prevent all ingress to, and egress from, the palace. Captain Carey accompanied the writer round the entire enclosure of the palace, and we endeavoured to post sentries, so that it should be impossible to enter it or leave it without being observed. The task was a most difficult one. On the north side there were but two entrances into the palace; on the west side but one; the eastern side also we easily protected by two sentries; but on the southern side, the palace itself in many places merged into one irregularly built cluster of houses, which we learnt belonged to the king's wives. Some idea of the size of the building and of its irregularity, may be gained from the fact that we posted 13 sentries in such positions that they were only just able to protect all the inlets to the building. After having apparently been all round the building once, we again marched round to see whether a sentry could not be economised; and though in one place we were enabled to remove one, we found that the whole of a long gallery, evidently the women's quarters, had been omitted, and we had to place another at the entrance of this. The guard of 100 men was placed in the great central court, and 1000 men might easily have been quartered in the main building.

In the mean time the Major-General had again received messages professing to come from the king, to the effect that his Majesty would come in in the course of the morning, and then that he would come later in the day. More messengers were sent, who professed that they would go to the king, urging him to come in, and saying that his palace was still at his disposal. But the king came not; the persons who professed to be his messengers, notably Owoosoo Koko and Boossumra Intakura, were found collecting arms and ammunition and endeavouring to pass them out of the town, and were arrested. The policy of fraud and of deception which the king had hitherto displayed was again being attempted, and it was now scarcely to be hoped that the king would be wise enough to take the one last step in his power to save his capital by coming in, or sending his mother or his nephew to make peace. . . .

A succession of tornadoes had seemingly set in; there seemed no apparent probability of their ceasing for some time; and the natives assured us that this was the prelude to the rainy season, evidently about to begin earlier than usual. The afternoon had passed, and the king had not fulfilled the promise said to have been made by him that he would come in; and there was now no probability of his doing so. His actual present position could not be ascertained; and even if we had found out where he was, it would have been impossible to capture him, as every village is surrounded with bush, and nothing would be easier than to escape. To chase the king from one place to another was abso-

lutely out of the question; it would but have been to add failure to what had hitherto been unbroken success; and whatever was to be done must now be accomplished without taking into consideration the possibility even of a meeting with his Majesty or his relations. In reply to all the invitations to act like a sensible man and make peace, the king, or those representing him, had only sent deceiving messages; and now the problem was, should the Major-General remain another day at Coomassie, and take advantage of it to march to Bantama, the royal mausoleum, or should he at once destroy Coomassie, and retire? . . .

It was out of the question to undertake any operation that might involve another battle; because any increment to our list of sick and wounded would have placed it beyond his [Wolseley's] power to remove them back to Agemmamu, as there would neither have been hammocks nor bearers sufficient for the purpose. A report was therefore circulated in the course of the afternoon, that the king having played the Governor false, and not having come in to make a treaty of peace, the army would advance in pursuit of him; and it was given out that all Ashantis found in the town after six o'clock the next morning would be shot. . . .

As night set in, the rain again came down with merciless force, and peals of thunder shook the very earth. As soon as possible after dark, the prize agents proceeded to the palace to collect what they could of value; and the writer was allowed to accompany them. That night is one to be remembered with interest. The prize agents, and one or two other European officers, assisted by Andooa, chief of Elmina, and Vroom, Captain Buller's interpreter, worked with most ardent energy in despoiling King Koffee of his property. Candles were scarce at Coomassie; and only four were available for the search, of which economy forbade that more than two should be alight at a time. By the light of these two candles the search began. The first room visited was one which during the day had been seen to be full of boxes, some of which, at all events, contained articles of much value. Here were found those gold masks, whose object it is so difficult to divine, made of pure gold hammered into shape. One of these, weighing more than forty-one ounces, represented a ram's head, and the others the faces of savage men, about half the size of life. Box after box was opened and its contents hastily examined, the more valuable ones being kept, and the others left. Necklaces and bracelets of gold, Aggery beads, and coral ornaments of various descriptions, were heaped together in boxes and calabashes. Silver-plate was carried off, and doubtless much left behind. Swords, gorgeous ammunition-belts, caps mounted in solid gold, knives set in gold and silver, bags of gold-dust and nuggets; carved stools mounted in silver, calabashes worked in silver and in gold, silks embroidered and woven, were all passed in review. The sword presented by her Majesty to the king was found and carried off; and thousands of things were left behind that would be worth fabulous sums in cabinets at home. . . .

Engineer labourers under Lieutenant Hare had set the town on fire. Commencing by applying their torches at the north edge of the town, they had worked down to the south. The town burnt furiously, all these three days of rain failing in any way to impede the progress of the devouring element. The thick thatched roofs of the houses, dry as tinder except just on the outside, blazed as though they had been ready prepared for the bonfire, and the flames ran down the framework which supported the mud walls. In the larger houses, more substantially built, only the roofs caught fire but the destruction was prac-tically complete. Slowly huge dense columns of smoke curled up to the sky, and the lighted fragments of thatch drifting far and wide upon the wind showed to the King of Ashanti, and to all his subjects who had fled from the capital, that the white man never failed to keep his word.

At nine o'clock the firing party had reached the point where the rear-guard was stationed, and Major Home arrived with his Sappers from the palace, reporting that his work there was completed, that two of his eight mines had already exploded, and that the fuses of the remainder were lit. No sounds of explosion had been heard, the mines being so arranged that the thick masonry of the palace walls would be shaken throughout by their discharge, and would totter with the shock and fall.

Anxiety was exhibited by some of those remaining with the rear-guard at the great delay in the firing of the mines at the palace, and the distance which in consequence existed between the main body and the 42d, which was to follow; but no such anxiety was shown by Colonel M'Leod. The same quiet demeanour was shown here as under the enemy's hottest fire; and he remained behind the rear company, till the party of Sappers and the last Engineer labourer had passed to the front.

At nine o'clock he rose and waved his hand; it was the signal for the rear company to march, and Coomassie was left a heap of smoking ruins.

22. Cetshwayo describes Zulu society.

During the 1870s and early 1880s, the British government engaged in a series of wars to cement imperial control over southern Africa. This was a considerable change from previous policies, which had kept colonial frontiers as restricted as possible. The change was occasioned by the huge economic growth set off by the discovery of diamonds and the resulting demand for cheap African labor. In 1879, the British went to war with the Zulu. Their forces under the command of Sir Garnet Wolseley, the British denounced the Zulu as barbarians, ruled by tyrants, and with no understanding of regularized forms of law and government. Though the Zulu defeated a British army at Isandlwana (the worst defeat of the British in a colonial war), their forces were soon crushed by the superior firepower of their opponents. Their king, Cetshwayo, was deposed and sent into exile.

In the early 1880s, the British established an official commission to provide advice as to the most effective manner in which the newly conquered African peoples of southern Africa could be governed. One of the most important witnesses to appear before the commission was Cetshwayo who, despite the evident biases of his questioners, argued that Zulu society was not a barbaric autocracy but a society that operated along certain recognized rules and practices, and in which common people and women were treated not as slaves (as commonly argued by European missionaries) but as having certain rights to their persons and to property.[22]

Sir J. D. Barry, judge, and president of the Native Laws and Customs Commission, questions the king, July 7, 1881.

137. Did Mpanda ever acknowledge that he owed any fealty to the Boers?—No; at one time when Dingaan was killed by his subjects, Mpanda came over to the Boers and was protected by them, because it was intended to kill him too. Shortly afterwards he was taken back to Zululand and lived there as king, and of course the Zulus thought that everything was settled between them and the Boers, but in a few days the Boers came and said they were going to fight Mpanda. There was a breach between the Zulus and the Boors [Boers], and then the English came to Natal.

138. Did Mpanda ever do anything to show that he acknowledged the Boer authority over him?—No.

139. Did Mpanda ever acknowledge the English authority over him?—No, the Zulus never acknowledged the authority of the English at any time, but they were like relations of the English. They always sent to the English, and told them anything that happened in Zululand, and wanted their help. . . . The Zulus said they would not have anything more to do with the Boers, because the Boers could not look after them. At the time when the Boers intended to invade Zululand, the English came to Natal and attacked the Boers,

and the Boers could do nothing against the Zulus after that; but in my reign they did, and in the latter days of Mpanda.

140. After Mpanda's death, before you succeeded, did you in an way acknowledge the authority of Shepstone over you?—The king says, when his father died, he sent messenger with a large ox to Shepstone, to report it to him, and to say that he wished Shepstone to see about the country being settled under him, because the Zulu nation was a relation of the English.

141. Did not Shepstone influence your father in making his will in your favour?—No, Shepstone had no influence in any way. The Zulu nation and Mpanda himself told Shepstone that Cetywayo [Cetshwayo] was the heir, and was to be king after his death.

142. Before you were crowned by Shepstone, did you do anything to show that Shepstone had any authority over you, or did you consider up to that time that he had any authority over you?—No; the king says he did nothing to acknowledge the authority of Shepstone, but he used to talk to Shepstone in a friendly way, and he acknowledged the Queen.

143. You did acknowledge the Queen before you were crowned by Shepstone as the Queen's servant?—The king says he acknowledged the authority of the Queen in this way, that he would have nothing to do with

22. *Report and Proceedings with Appendices of the Government Commission on Native Laws and Customs* vol. 2, pt. 1 (Cape Town: W. A. Richards and Sons, Government Printers, 1883), pp. 523–30, Cape of Good Hope Parliamentary Paper, G4 1883.

the Boers or any other nation, and he acknowledged Shepstone as her officer.

144. As king of the Zulus, was all power invested in you, as king, over your subjects?—In conjunction with the chiefs of the land.

145. How did the chiefs derive their power from you as king?—The king calls together the chiefs of the land when he wants to elect a new chief, and asks their advice as to whether it is fit to make such a man a large chief, and if they say "yes" the chief is made.

146. If you had consulted the chiefs, and found they did not agree with you, could you appoint a chief by virtue of your kingship?—In some cases, if the chiefs don't approve of it, the king requires their reasons, and when they have stated them he often gives it up. In other cases he tries the man to see whether he can perform the duties required of him or not.

147. In fact, you have the power to act independently of the chiefs in making an appointment, although you always consult them?—No; the king has not the power of electing an officer as chief without the approval of the other chiefs. They are the most important men. But the smaller chiefs he can elect at his discretion. . . .

150. Are there any hereditary claims to the appointment of induna [civil or military officials]?—It is not hereditary with the small chiefs, but with the important men of the land. The son of the chief wife is heir to the property of this important man.

151. Has the heir to this property of a chief the right to claim to be a chief?—No; if a man was known to be fit to hold the post he would be appointed.

152. What are the duties of the indunas?—They look after the land, and decide different cases.

153. Cases of murder?—Every criminal case.

154. Do you allot a particular province to each induna?—The king allots different parts of the country to different chiefs.

155. And each induna in his own province tries all the cases which arise in that province?—He is called "induna" when he is at the military kraal [settlement], but when he

goes to his residence he is called headman, and he has to look after the cases which arise in that part of the country.

156. How is he assisted at the trials?—He calls together all the chief men of that district, and they discuss the case.

157. After they have discussed it, does he retire and form his own opinion upon all the evidence and discussion, and come to a conclusion alone, or does he give his judgment sitting with the other men altogether?—No; the headman does not hear the evidence and then go home and consider it, but he sits there and listens to the assembly talking about the case. Then they ask his opinion, and he says, "I think so and so." If they don't agree with him, they give their reasons.

158. And he gives the final verdict?—Yes; the headman.

159. Does the headman award the punishment upon his own decision, or does he consult the others upon it first?—The headman and the assembly award the punishment.

160. But suppose they differ, who finally decides?—Then the case is taken to the king's kraal.

161. Has the king absolute power to decide?—The chief men of the land talk about the case first, and bring it up to him.

162. And he finally decides?—Sometimes they decide before they come to him, and they come and tell him which way they decide, and he approves or disapproves as the case may be, and as he thinks it right or wrong.

163. Suppose there is a difference among them, who finally decides?—The king has the power to decide in this way, that when he has decided the chief men of the country have nothing to say against it, because they will not say that the king has decided against their wish.

164. Is all law and right of property supposed to come from the king in consultation with his chiefs?—The right of property comes from the king, but he does not exercise that power. The country has remained like it is now since the king's father and grandfather reigned. . . .

168. If you want to make a new law, to be applicable to all Zululand, how do you set about it?—The king has a discussion with

the chiefs about it, and they give out the law, but he cannot make a law without their consent. He consults the chiefs and gives his reasons, and if they conclude to agree to it, it is the law, but he cannot make a law against the wishes of his chiefs. . . .

171. In England our laws are written, and so there is no misunderstanding them, but suppose there is a dispute in Zululand, as to what the law really is, who is supposed to be the best authority upon the law as given out by the chiefs?—The king cannot say, because it never happened that there was any doubt about the law of the country. . . .

173. Have the people, independently of these chiefs and you as king, any sort of voice in the making of any laws? Are they heard directly or indirectly?—No. . . .

175. Is every man bound to serve in Zululand as a soldier?—The old men of the country are called the white part of the nation, that is to say they are not soldiers; the young men are the soldiers.

176. Have all these old men been soldiers before?—Yes. Some of these are retired and old, and unable to serve any more, but the younger ones who have the [head]rings on can go to the king and serve as they please, and return home as they like. The young men are not forced to be soldiers.

177. Is there any young man there who is not a soldier?—No, everyone wishes to be a soldier. If anyone stops at home, the others laugh at him, and say he is a "Ungogo" = Button quail. . . .

180. What are the duties of the petty chiefs?—They principally superintend work for their superior chiefs, and for the king. The larger chiefs send them out to look after men who are doing work for the king. . . .

183. The people are never consulted about either big or little matters? The only consultation is between you and your big chiefs in big matters, and between you and your small chiefs in smaller matters?—Yes, he has a voice in that; he can go to a chief and say it should be done in this or in that way. . . .

196. Is there not one particular divine power, who is supposed to be above all spirits and to be the father of the whole human race?—Yes.

197. What is he called?—Nkulunkulu. . . .

199. What does "Zulu" mean?—The name of the nations' ancestor; the first man of the Zulu nation.

200. Where is he supposed to be?—At the military kraal in Zululand. "Zulu" also means "heaven." Zulu was one of the king's ancestors, the king of Zululand.

201. Are the Zulus all supposed to come from heaven or to go there?—Yes, every man came from heaven because he was made by God, the white as well as the Zulus.

202. Why are the old chiefs called "white men"?—Because they generally live at the military kraal, and go home when they wish; and because they have a white shield instead of a black one.

203. You told us that you make these laws. Are you bound to govern in accordance with the laws which you and your ancestors have made?. . . —Yes.

204. What is your law as to land? To whom does it belong, and how is it apportioned?—The whole country belongs to the king, and different portions of it are inhabited by headmen, and smaller portions by common people.

205. Who allots the land?—The king. . . .

218. The Zulus generally have a great wife, a right-hand and a left-hand wife?—Yes.

219. But the great wife is not necessarily the first wife that he marries?—No. . . .

223. When a man has a number of wives, does he keep them all in one kraal?—No; in different kraals. . . .

230. Every woman, married or unmarried, belongs to some one, to her husband, her father, or her father's heir?—Yes.

231. Can any woman require property for herself?—No; only the king's wife.

232. If a married woman obtains anything it becomes the property of her husband?—Yes.

233. And if an unmarried woman obtains anything it is the property of her father or her father's heir?—If a father wishes his daughter to have anything she can have it, and if a son wants it he can ask his sister for it, but she can keep it if she likes.

234. Has any woman the right of property independent of the will of her father or

her husband?—Yes; they can have property independent of the father or husband. . . .

291. How many missionaries were there in your country?—The king is not quite sure, but he thinks about fourteen. . . .

293. Did you like to have them there?—Yes, they did good, they were able to help the people by giving them medicine; they were kind people; they were not troublesome. . . .

295. Altogether you think it was good to have them?—There was a German missionary whom the king did not like, but as a whole he liked the missionaries very much because they were no trouble.

296. What trouble did this man give?—He quarrelled with the people, and was too fast with thrashing. . . .

23. A university for Africa.

Edward Blyden was born in the Danish Caribbean in 1832, the descendant of African slaves. As a teenager, he accompanied an American Presbyterian to the United States to pursue higher education, but because of the racial discrimination he experienced, he moved in 1851 to Liberia where he remained for most of the rest of his life. In 1861, he became a professor at the newly established Liberia College, and in 1881, he was appointed its president. Later he became Liberia's ambassador to London, was nominated as a candidate for the presidency of Liberia, and then worked for the British colonial service in Lagos and Sierra Leone, dealing primarily with the education of Muslim Africans. He died in Freetown in 1912. West African leaders in the first half of the twentieth century viewed him as a pioneer of pan-Africanism, someone who saw a basic unity between peoples of African descent on both sides of the Atlantic. In his inaugural address to Liberia College, he argued for a program of study for Africans that built on what he saw as the strengths of Western education, but that also incorporated study of Africa and of the Muslim world, and avoided those European works produced during the era of the slave trade and imperialism.[23]

Edward Blyden's inaugural address as president of Liberia College, January 5, 1881.

A college in West Africa, for the education of African youth by African instructors, under a Christian government conducted by Negroes, is something so unique in the history of Christian civilization, that wherever, in the civilized world, the existence of such an institution is heard of, there will be curiosity as to its character, its work, and its prospects. A college suited, in all respects, to the exigencies of this nation and to the needs of the race cannot come into existence all at once. It must be the result of years of experience, of trial, of experiment.

Every thinking man will allow that all we have been doing in this country so far, whether in church, in state, or in school—our forms of religion, our politics, our literature, such as it is, is only temporary and transitional. When we advance further into Africa, and become one with the great tribes on the continent, these things will take the form which the genius of the race shall prescribe.

The civilization of that vast population, untouched by foreign influence not yet affected by European habits, is not to be organized according to foreign patterns, but will organize itself according to the nature of the people and the country. Nothing that we are doing now can be absolute or permanent,

23. Edward W. Blyden, *Christianity, Islam and the Negro Race* (London: W. B. Whittingham & Co, 1887), pp. 71–93.

because nothing is normal or regular. Everything is provisional or tentative.

The College is only a machine, an instrument to assist in carrying forward our regular work, devised not only for intellectual ends, but for social purposes, for religious duty, for patriotic aims, for racial development; and when as an instrument, as a means, it fails, for any reason whatever, to fulfil its legitimate functions, it is the duty of the country, as well as the interest of the country, to see that it is stimulated into healthful activity; or, if this is impossible, to see that it is set aside as a pernicious obstruction. We cannot afford to waste time in dealing with insoluble problems under impossible conditions. . . .

We have in our curriculum, adopted some years ago, a course of study corresponding, to some extent, to that pursued in European and American colleges. To this we shall adhere as nearly as possible; but experience has already suggested, and will, no doubt, from time to time suggest, such modifications as were required by our peculiar circumstances.

The object of all education is to secure growth and efficiency, to make a man all that his natural gifts will allow him to become; to produce self-respect, a proper appreciation of our own powers and of the powers of other people; to beget a fitness for one's sphere of life and action, and ability to discharge the duties it imposes. Now, if we take these qualities as the true outcome of a correct education, then every one who is acquainted with the facts must admit that, as a rule, in the entire civilized world, the Negro, notwithstanding his two hundred years' residence with Christian and civilized races, has nowhere received anything like a correct education. We find him everywhere, in the United States, in the West Indies, in South America, largely unable to cope with the responsibilities which devolve upon him. Not only is he not sought after for any position of influence in the political movements of those countries, but he is even denied admission to ecclesiastical appointments of importance. . . .

To a certain extent, perhaps to a very important extent, Negroes trained on the soil of Africa have the advantage of those trained in foreign countries; but in all, as a rule, the intellectual and moral results, thus far, have been far from satisfactory. There are many men of book-learning, but few, very few, of any capability, even few who have that amount, or that sort, of culture, which produces self-respect, confidence in one's self, and efficiency in work. Now, why is this? The evil, it is considered, lies in the system and methods of European training to which Negroes are, everywhere in Christian lands, subjected, and which everywhere affects them unfavourably. Of a different race, different susceptibility, different bent of character from that of the European, they have been trained under influences in many respects adapted only to the Caucasian race. Nearly all the books they read, the very instruments of their culture, have been such as to force them from the groove which is natural to them, where they would be strong and effective, without furnishing them with any avenue through which they may move naturally and free from obstruction. Christian and so-called civilized Negroes live, for the most part, in foreign countries, where they are only passive spectators of the deeds of a foreign race; and where, with other impressions which they receive from without, an element of doubt as to their own capacity and their own destiny is fastened upon them, and inheres in their intellectual and social constitution. They deprecate their own individuality, and would escape from it if they could. And in countries like this, where they are free from the hampering surroundings of an alien race, they still read and study the books of foreigners, and form their idea of everything that man may do, or ought to do, according to the standard held up in those teachings, Hence, without the physical or mental aptitude for the enterprises which they are taught to admire and revere, they attempt to copy and imitate them, and share the fate of all copyists and imitators. Bound to move on a lower level, they acquire and retain a practical inferiority, transcribing, very often, the faults rather than the virtues of their models. . . .

In all English-speaking countries the mind of the intelligent Negro child revolts against the descriptions given in elementary books—geographies, travels, histories—of the Negro;

but, though he experiences an instinctive revulsion from these caricatures and misrepresentations, he is obliged to continue, as he grows in years, to study such pernicious teachings. After leaving school he finds the same things in newspapers, in reviews, in novels, in *quasi* scientific works; and after a while . . . they begin to seem to him the proper things to say and to feel about his race, and he accepts what, at first, his fresh and unbiased feelings naturally and indignantly repelled. Such is the effect of repetition. . . .

Those who have lived in civilized communities, where there are different races, know the disparaging views which are entertained of the blacks by their neighbours—and often, alas! by themselves. The standard of all physical and intellectual excellencies in the present civilization being the white complexion, whatever deviates from that favoured colour is proportionally depreciated, until the black, which is the opposite, becomes not only the most unpopular but the most unprofitable colour. Black men, and especially black women, in such communities, experience the greatest imaginable inconvenience. They never feel at home. In the depth of their being they always feel themselves strangers in the land of their exile, and the only escape from this feeling is to escape from themselves. And this feeling of self-depreciation is not diminished as I have intimated above, by the books they read. Women, especially, are fond of reading novels and light literature; and it is in these writings that flippant and eulogistic reference is constantly made to the superior physical and mental characteristics of the Caucasian race, which, by contrast, suggest the inferiority of other races, especially of that race which is furthest removed from it in appearance.

It is painful in America to see the efforts which are made by Negroes to secure outward conformity to the appearance of the dominant race.

This is by no means surprising; but what is surprising is that, under the circumstances, any Negro has retained a particle of self-respect. Now in Africa, where the colour of the majority is black, the fashion in personal matters is naturally suggested by the personal characteristics of the race, and we are free from the necessity of submitting to the use of "incongruous feathers awkwardly stuck on." Still, we are held in bondage by our indiscriminate and injudicious use of a foreign literature; and we strive to advance by the methods of a foreign race. In this effort we struggle with the odds against us. We fight at the disadvantage which David would have experienced in Saul's armour. The African must advance by methods of his own. He must possess a power distinct from that of the European. It has been proved that he knows how to take advantage of European culture, and that he can be benefited by it. This proof was perhaps necessary, but it is not sufficient. We must show that we are able to go alone, to carve out our own way. We must not be satisfied that, in this nation, European influence shapes our polity, makes our laws, rules in our tribunals, and impregnates our social atmosphere. We must not suppose that the Anglo-Saxon methods are final, that there is nothing for us to find for our own guidance, and that we have nothing to teach the world. There is inspiration for us also. We must study our brethren in the interior, who know better than we do the laws of growth for the race. We see among them the rudiments of that which, with fair play and opportunity, will develop into important and effective agencies for our work. We look too much to foreigners, and are dazzled almost to blindness by their exploits—so as to fancy that they have exhausted the possibilities of humanity. . . .

I propose now to sketch the outlines of a programme for the education of the students in Liberia College, and, I may venture to add, of the Negro youth everywhere in Africa who hope to take a leading part in the work of the race and of the country. I will premise that, generally, in the teaching our youth, far more is made of the importance of imparting information than of training the mind. Their minds are too much taken possession of by mere information drawn from European sources. . . .

We shall devote attention principally, both for mental discipline and information, to the earlier epochs of the world's history. It is decided that there are five or six leading epochs in the history of civilization. I am following Mr. Frederic Harrison's classification. First, there was the great permanent, stationary system of human society, held together by a religious belief, or by social custom growing out of that belief. This has been called the Theocratic state of society. The type of that phase of civilization was the old Eastern empires. The second great type was the Greek Age of intellectual activity and civic freedom. Next came the Roman type of civilization, an age of empire, of conquest, of consolidation of nations, of law and government. The fourth great system was the phase of civilization which prevailed from the fall of the Roman Empire until comparatively modern times, and was called the Medieval Age, when the Church and Feudalism existed side by side. The fifth phase of history was that which began with the breaking-up of the power of the Church on the one side, and of feudalism on the other, the foundation of modern history, or the Modern Age. That system has continued down to the present; but, if sub-divided, it would form the sixth type, which is the Age since the French Revolution, the Age of social and popular development, of modern science and industry.

We shall permit in our curriculum the unrestricted study of the first four epochs, but especially the second, third and fourth, from which the present civilization of Western Europe is mainly derived. There has been no period of history more full of suggestive energy, both physical and intellectual, than those epochs. Modern Europe boasts of its period of intellectual activity, but none can equal, for life and freshness, the Greek and Roman prime. No modern writers will ever influence the destiny of the race to the same extent that the Greeks and Romans have done.

We can afford to exclude, then, as subjects of study, at least in the earlier college years, the events of the fifth and sixth epochs, and the works which, in large numbers, have been written during those epochs. I know that during these periods some of the greatest works of human genius have been composed. I know that Shakespeare and Milton, Gibbon and Macaulay, Hallam and Lecky, Froude, Stubbs and Green, belong to these periods. It is not in my power, even if I had the will, to disparage the works of these masters; but what I wish to say is, that these are not the works on which the mind of the youthful African should be trained. It was during the sixth period that the transatlantic slave trade arose, and those theories—theological, social, and political—were invented for the degradation and proscription of the Negro. This epoch continues to this day, and has an abundant literature and a prolific authorship. It has produced that whole tribe of declamatory Negrophobists, whose views, in spite of their emptiness and impertinence, are having their effect upon the ephemeral literature of the day, a literature which is shaping the life of the Negro in Christian lands. His whole theory of life, quite contrary to what his nature intends, is being influenced, consciously and unconsciously, by the general conceptions of his race entertained by the manufacturers of this literature, a great portion of which, made for to-day, will not survive the next generation. . . .

The instruments of culture which we shall employ in the College will be chiefly the Classics and Mathematics. By Classics I mean the Greek and Latin languages and their literature. In those languages there is not, as far as I know, a sentence, a word, or a syllable disparaging to the Negro. He may get nourishment from them without taking in any race-poison. They will perform no sinister work upon his consciousness, and give no unholy bias to his inclinations. . . .

Passing over, then, for a certain time, the current literature of Western Europe, which is, after all, derived and secondary, we will resort to the fountain head, and in the study of the great masters, in the languages in which they wrote, we shall get the required mental discipline without unfavourably affecting our sense of race individuality or our own self respect. There is nothing that we need to know for the work of building up this country, in its moral, political and religious character, which we may not learn from the ancients. There is nothing in the domain of literature, philosophy, or religion for which we need be dependent upon the moderns. Law and philosophy we may get from the Romans and the Greeks, religion from the Hebrews. . . .

But we shall also study Mathematics. These, as instruments of culture, are everywhere applicable. A course of Algebra, Geometry, and Higher Mathematics must accompany, step by step, classical studies. Neither of these means of discipline can be omitted without loss. The qualities which make a man succeed in mastering the Classics and Mathematics are also those which qualify him for the practical work of life.

It will be our aim to introduce into our curriculum also the Arabic, and some of the principal native languages, by means of which we may have intelligent intercourse with the millions accessible to us in the interior, and learn more of our own country. We have young men who are experts in the geography and customs of foreign countries; who can tell all about the proceedings of foreign statesmen in countries thousands of miles away; can talk glibly of London, Berlin, Paris, and Washington; know all about Gladstone, Bismarck, Gambetta, and Hayes; but who knows anything about Musahdu, Medina, Kankan, or Sego, only a few hundred miles from us? Who can tell anything of the policy or doings of Fanfi-doreh, Ibrahima Sissi, or Fahqueh-queh, or Simoro of Boporu, only a few steps from us? These are hardly known. Now as Negroes, allied in blood and race to these people, this is disgraceful; and as a nation, if we intend to grow and prosper in this country, it is impolitic, it is short-sighted, it is unpatriotic; but it has required time for us to grow up to these ideas, to understand our position in this country. In order to accelerate our future progress, and to give to the advance we make the element of permanence, it will be our aim in the College to produce men of ability. Ability or capability is the power to use with effect the instruments in our hands. The bad workman complains of his tools; but, even when he is satisfied with the excellence of his tools, he cannot produce the results which an able workman will produce, even with indifferent tools.

I trust that arrangements will be made by which girls of our country may be admitted to share in the advantages of this College. I cannot see why our sisters should not receive exactly the same general culture as we do. I think that the progress of the country will be more rapid and permanent when the girls receive the same general training as the boys; and our women, besides being able to appreciate the intellectual labours of their husbands and brothers, will be able also to share in the pleasures of intellectual pursuits. We need not fear that they will be less graceful, less natural, or less womanly; but we may be sure that they will make wiser mothers, more appreciative wives, and more affectionate sisters. . . .

In the religious work of the College, the Bible will be our textbook, the Bible without note or comment, especially as we propose to study the original language in which the New Testament was written; and we may find opportunity, in connection with the Arabic, to study the Old Testament. The teachings of Christianity are of universal application. "Other foundation can no man lay than that which is laid." The great truths of the Sermon on the Mount are as universally accepted as Euclid's axioms. The meaning of the Good Samaritan is as certain as that of the forty-seventh proposition, and a great deal plainer. . . .

All our traditions and experiences are connected with a foreign race. We have no poetry or philosophy but that of our taskmasters. The songs that live in our ears and are often on our lips are the songs which we heard sung by those who shouted while we groaned and lamented. They sang of their history, which was the history of our degradation. They recited their triumphs, which contained the records of our humiliation. To our great misfortune, we learned their prejudices and their passions, and thought we had their aspirations and their power. Now, if we are to make an independent nation—a strong nation—we must listen to the songs of our unsophisticated brethren as they sing of their history, as they tell of their traditions, of the wonderful and mysterious events of their tribal or national life, of the achievements of what we call their superstitions; we must lend a ready ear to the ditties of the Kroomen who pull our boats, of the Pessah and Golah men, who till our farms; we must read the compositions, rude as we may think them, of the Mandingoes and the Veys. We shall in this way get back the strength of the race, like the giant of the ancients, who always gained strength, for his conflict with Hercules, whenever he touched his Mother Earth.

And this is why we want the College away from the seaboard—with its constant intercourse with foreign manners and low foreign ideas—that we may have free and uninterrupted intercourse with the intelligent among the tribes of the interior; that the students, even from the books to which they will be allowed access, may conveniently flee to the forests and fields of Manding and the Niger, and mingle with our brethren and gather fresh inspiration and fresh and living ideas. . . .

The time is past when we can be content with putting forth elaborate arguments to prove our equality with foreign races. Those who doubt our capacity are more likely to be convinced of their error by the exhibition, on our part, of those qualities of energy and enterprise which will enable us to occupy the extensive field before us for our own advantage and the advantage of humanity—for the purposes of civilization, of science, of good government, and of progress generally—than by any mere abstract argument about the equality of races. The suspicions disparaging to us will be dissipated only by the exhibition of the indisputable realities of a lofty manhood as they may be illustrated in successful efforts to build up a nation, to wrest from Nature her secrets, to lead the van of progress in this country, and to regenerate a continent.

24. The scramble for Africa begins.

At the same time that Africanus Horton was developing his ideas for an independent confederation of Fante peoples, Edward Blyden was elaborating his plans for a new university curriculum, and Cetshwayo was testifying as to the regularized system of governance operating in Zulu society, European speculators and adventurers were pursuing plans to access the reputed wealth of the interior of the continent. Expectations of interior wealth had grown enormously with the growth of the diamond industry and accelerated even more with news of potentially vast gold finds, also in southern Africa, in 1886. From the 1870s onward, European merchants competed against one another to get privileged access to African territory, primarily by negotiating treaties with indigenous rulers. In the Niger basin, for example, British representatives of the National African Company Limited (founded 1882), and its successor, the Royal Niger Company (established by royal charter in 1886), concluded 343 separate treaties between 1884 and 1892. Representatives of the two companies used various templates in this treaty-making process; those printed below are the first template (used in 25 treaties) and the tenth (used in 22 cases).[24]

Form No. 1.

After the _____ year's experience, we, the undersigned _____, fully recognize the benefit accorded to our country and people by our intercourse with the National African Company (Limited), and, in recognition of this, we now cede the whole of our territory to the National African Company (Limited), and their administrators, for ever. In consid-

---

24. Edward Hertslet, *The Map of Africa by Treaty*, vol. 1 (London: Her Majesty's Stationery Office, 1894), pp. 457–58, 476–77.

eration of this, the National African Company (Limited) will not interfere with any of the native laws and also not encroach on any private property unless the value is agreed upon by the owner and said Company.

The National African Company (Limited) will reserve to themselves the right of excluding foreign settlers.

Any palaver [negotiation] that may exist with any other tribe at any time, or in the event of any dispute arising between the _____ and territory, shall at once be referred to the National African Company (Limited) or their representative at the time.

We, the _____ and district, do hereby agree to afford assistance at any time for the protection of the said Company's property and people.

As per mutual consent of the _____ of the foregoing Agreement, the National African Company (Limited) agreed to pay _____

Pro the National African Company (Limited),

David McIntosh

Form No. 10.

Treaty made on the _____ day of _____, 18__, between _____ on the one hand, and the Royal Niger Company (Chartered and Limited), for themselves and their assigns, for ever, hereinafter called "The Company," on the other hand.

1. We, the undersigned Kings and Chiefs of _____, with the view of bettering the condition of our country and people, do this day cede to the Company, including as above their assigns, for ever, the whole of our territory, but the Company shall pay private landowners a reasonable amount for any portion of land that the Company may require from time to time.

2. We hereby give to the Company and their assigns, for ever, full jurisdiction of every kind, and we pledge ourselves not to enter into any war with other tribes without the sanction of the Company.

3. We give to the Company and their assigns, for ever, the sole right to mine in any portion of our territory.

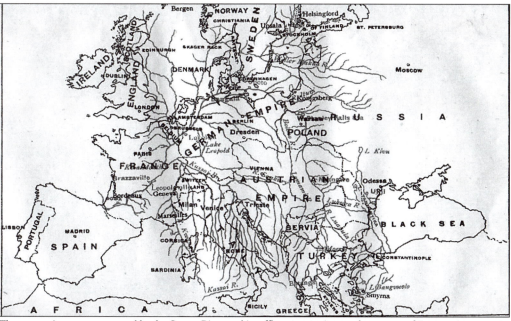

The proportionate area covered by the Congo River and its affluents superimposed on a map of Europe. *Source:* E.D. Morel, *Red Rubber: The Story of the Rubber Slave Trade which flourished on the Congo for Twenty Years, 1890-1910*, new and revised edition (Manchester: The National Labour Press, 1920), facing p. 1.

4 . We bind ourselves not to have any intercourse as representing our tribe or state, on tribal or state affairs, with any person or persons other than the Company, who are hereby recognized as the authorized Government of our territories: but this provision shall in no way authorize any monopoly of trade, direct or indirect, by the Company or others, nor any restriction of private or commercial intercourse with any person or persons of any nation whatsoever, subject, however, to administrative dispositions in the interest of commerce and order.

5. In consideration of the foregoing, the Company bind themselves not to interfere with any of the native laws or customs of the country, consistently with the maintenance of order and good government, and the progress of civilization.

6. The Company bind themselves to protect, as far as practicable, the said King and Chiefs from any attacks of any neighbouring aggressive tribes.

7. In consideration of the above, the Company have this day paid the King and Chiefs of _____ goods to the value of _____, receipt of which is hereby acknowledged.

This Treaty having been interpreted to us, the above-mentioned King and Chiefs of _____, we hereby approve and accept it for ourselves and for our people, and in testimony of this, having no knowledge of writing, do affix our marks below.

We, the undersigned witnesses, do hereby solemnly declare that the King and Chiefs whose names are placed opposite their respective marks have, in our presence, affixed their marks of their own free will and consent, and that _____ on behalf of the Company, has, in our presence, affixed his signature.

I, _____, for and on behalf of the Company, do hereby approve and accept the above Treaty, and hereby affix my hand.

Declaration by Interpreter. I, _____, native of _____, do hereby solemnly declare that I am well acquainted with the _____ language, and that on the _____ day of _____, 18_, I truly and faithfully explained the above Treaty to all the native signatories, and that they understood its meaning.

Witnesses to the above _____ mark or signature: Done in triplicate at _____, this _____ day of _____, 18_.

25. The Berlin conference.

Treaty making like that engaged in by the National African Company and competitors from Britain, France, Germany, Belgium, and Portugal, set off a rush for territory. Between November 1884 and February 1885, an international conference, called together by Chancellor Otto von Bismarck of Germany, met in Berlin to regulate this competitive rush. The main concern of the countries represented (every European state as well as the United States) was not the partition of Africa but rather ensuring that their nationals not be excluded from any of the main trading areas of the continent, particularly the river basins of the Niger and the Congo. At the same time, they found it expedient in the interests of public opinion – strongly influenced by David Livingstone's anti-slavery writings and by the accounts of Henry Morton Stanley of traveling "Through Darkest Africa" in search of the lost missionary–to link commercial aims with a statement that greater intervention in Africa would lead to the suppression of the internal slave trade so graphically described by Livingstone and Stanley. The signatories to the treaty also agreed to ban the importation of firearms into Africa except when used by their own agents for self-protection or to suppress the slave trade. In practice, this meant that Europeans claimed (though were seldom able to achieve) a monopoly of guns.[25]

General Act of the Conference of Berlin, relative to the Development of Trade and Civilization in Africa; the free Navigation of the Rivers Congo, Niger etc.; the suppression of the Slave Trade by Sea and Land; the occupation of Territory on the African coasts, etc. Signed at Berlin, February 26, 1885.

Chapter I. Declaration relative to freedom of trade in the basin of the Congo, its mouths and circumjacent regions. . . .

Art. I. The trade of all nations shall enjoy complete freedom. . . .

Art. V. No power which exercises or shall exercise sovereign rights in the above-mentioned regions shall be allowed to grant therein a monopoly or favour of any kind in matters of trade. . . .

Art. VI. All the Powers exercising sovereign rights or influence in the aforesaid territories bind themselves to watch over the preservation of the native tribes, and to care for the improvement of the conditions of their moral and material well-being, and to help in suppressing slavery, and especially the slave trade.

They shall, without distinction of creed or nation, protect and favour all religions, scientific, or charitable institutions, and undertakings created and organized for the above ends, or which aim at instructing the natives and bringing home to them the blessings of civilization.

Christian missionaries, scientists, and explorers, with their followers, property, and collections, shall likewise be the objects of especial protection.

Freedom of conscience and religious toleration are expressly guaranteed to the natives, no less than to subjects and to foreigners. . . .

Chapter II. Declaration relative to the slave trade.

Art. IX. Seeing that trading in slaves is forbidden in conformity with the principles of international law as recognized by the Signatory Powers, and seeing also that the operations, which, by sea or land, furnish slaves to trade, ought likewise to be regarded as forbidden, the Powers which do or shall exercise sovereign rights or influence in the territories forming the Conventional basin of the Congo declare that these territories may not serve as a market or means of transit for the trade in slaves, of whatever race they may be. Each of the Powers binds itself to employ all the means at its disposal for putting an end to this trade and for punishing those who engage in it. . . .

Chapter VI. Declaration relative to the essential conditions to be observed in order that the new occupations on the coasts of the African continent may be held to be effective.

Art. XXXIV. Any Power which henceforth takes possession of a tract of land on the coasts of the African Continent outside of its present possessions, or which, being hitherto without such possessions, shall acquire them, as well as the Power which assumes a Protectorate there, shall accompany the respective act with a notification thereof, addressed to the other Signatory Powers of the present Act, in order to enable them, if need be, to make good any claims of their own.

Art. XXXV. The signatory Powers of the present Act recognize the obligation to insure the establishment of authority in regions occupied by them on the coasts of the African Continent sufficient to protect existing rights, and, as the case may be, freedom of trade and of transit under the conditions agreed upon.

---

25. Edward Hertslet, *The Map of Africa by Treaty*, vol. 1 (London: Her Majesty's Stationery Office, 1894), pp. 20–45.

26. Rhodes reaches north.

Though Cecil Rhodes succeeded in monopolizing control of the diamond in-dustry under De Beers, he was much less successful in the much larger and more profitable gold industry that developed in the Transvaal from the mid-1880s onward. Locked out of access to the best gold finds by other mining magnates, Rhodes looked elsewhere to the north and the old gold mines of Zimbabwe, worked by Africans from the twelfth to the fifteenth centuries but largely abandoned thereafter. Zimbabwe was ruled by Lobengula, king of the Ndebele people who themselves had come to the area only in the 1840s, refu-gees first from Shaka's Zulu empire and then fleeing from Dutch trekkers and themselves conquering the Shona of old Zimbabwe. Lobengula had signed treaties with Europeans since the 1860s, permitting them to prospect for miner-als in exchange for paying him licensing fees. With demands for prospecting rights becoming incessant after the gold discoveries in the Transvaal, in 1888 Lobengula agreed, in return for a substantial payment, to grant a monopoly over mining to representatives of Cecil Rhodes. Though the treaty was for pros-pecting and mining rights only, it did grant to the licensees "full power to do all things that they may deem necessary to win and procure the same [metals and minerals], and to hold, collect, and enjoy the profits and revenues," terms which, like others in the treaty, could be subjected to a wide variety of interpretations.[26]

Know all men by these presents, that whereas Charles Dunell Rudd, of Kimberley; Rochfort Maguire, of London; and Francis Robert Thompson, of Kimberley, hereinafter called the grantees, have covenanted and agreed, and do hereby covenant and agree, to pay to me, my heirs and successors, the sum of one hundred pounds sterling, British currency, on the first day of every lunar month; and, fur-ther, to deliver at my royal kraal one thou-sand Martini-Henry breech-loading rifles, together with one hundred thousand rounds of suitable ball cartridge, five hundred of the said rifles and fifty thousand of the said car-tridges to be ordered from England forthwith and delivered with reasonable despatch, and the remainder of the said rifles and cartridges to be delivered as soon as the said grantees shall have commenced to work mining ma-chinery within my territory ; and further, to deliver on the Zambesi River a steamboat with guns suitable for defensive purposes upon the said river, or in lieu of the said steamboat, should I so elect, to pay to me the sum of five hundred pounds sterling, British currency.

On the execution of these presents, I, Lo Bengula, King of Matabeleland, Masho—naland, and other adjoining territories, in exercise of my sovereign powers, and in the presence and with the consent of my council of indunas, do hereby grant and assign unto the said grantees, their heirs, representatives, and assigns, jointly and severally, the com-plete and exclusive charge over all metals and minerals situated and contained in my king-doms, principalities, and dominions, together with full power to do all things that they may deem necessary to win and procure the same, and to hold, collect, and enjoy the profits and revenues, if any, derivable from the said met-als and minerals, subject to the aforesaid pay-ment; and whereas I have been much molested of late by divers persons seeking and desiring to obtain grants and concessions of land and mining rights in my territories, I do hereby authorise the said grantees, their heirs, representatives, and assigns, to take all necessary and lawful steps to exclude from my kingdom, principalities, and dominions all persons seeking land, metals, minerals, or

---

26. Lewis Michell, *The Life of the Rt. Hon. Cecil John Rhodes, 1853–1902*, vol. 2 (London: Edward Arnold, 1910), pp. 244–45.

mining rights therein, and I do hereby undertake to render them all such needful assistance as they may from time to time require for the exclusion of such persons, and to grant no concessions of land or mining rights from and after this date without their consent and concurrence; provided that, if at any time the said monthly payment of one hundred pounds shall be in arrears for a period of three months, then this grant shall cease and determine from the date of the last-made payment; and, further, provided, that nothing contained in these presents shall extend to or affect a grant made by me of certain mining

rights in a portion of my territory south of the Ramaquaban River, which grant is commonly known as the Tati Concession.

This, given under my hand this thirtieth day of October, in the year of our Lord 1888, at my royal kraal.

LO BENGULA X his mark

C.D. RUDD

ROCHFORT MAGUIRE

F. R. THOMPSON

Witnesses: Chas. D. HELM

J. F. DREYER

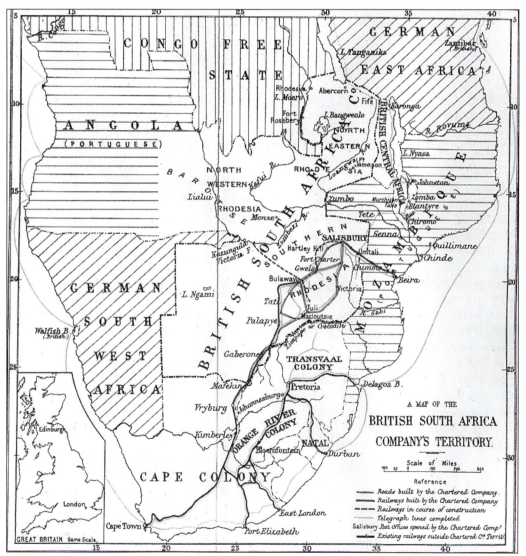

Territory owned by Cecil Rhodes's British South Africa Company in 1900. *Source: Handy Notes on S. Africa for the Use of Speakers and Others*, 4th edition (London: Imperial South African Association, 1901), frontispiece.

27. The imperialism of chartered companies.

The Berlin Conference only intensified the competitive rush for territory and fortune in Africa. National governments now took a much greater role in supporting the interests of their merchants than had been the case before 1870. The British government, in particular, awarded a series of royal "charters" to companies in West, East, and Southern Africa. These charters formally recognized the legality of the treaties made between merchant companies and African rulers, and allocated to the companies the power (within British law) to operate in Africa as though they were themselves sovereign states. Royal charters were awarded in 1886 to Sir George Goldie's Royal Niger Company, in 1888 to Sir William Mackinnon's British East Africa Company, and in 1889 to Cecil Rhodes's British South Africa Company. Goldie came from an Isle of Man family that had made its money in smuggling and then legitimated itself through landholding. Mackinnon, a Scotsman, had made a fortune in shipping. Rhodes had added to his diamond fortune by investing in the Transvaal gold mining industry. Each saw the enormous economic potential of monopolizing trade in their respective parts of Africa.[27]

Royal charter granted to the National African Company (re-named the Royal Niger Company in 1887), July 10, 1886.

1. The said National African Company Limited (in this our Charter referred to as the Company), is hereby authorized and empowered to hold and retain the full benefit of the several cessions aforesaid [the 343 treaties noted above], or any of them, and all rights, interests, authorities, and powers for the purposes of government, preservation of public order, protection of said territories, or otherwise of what nature or kind soever. . . .

12. The Company is hereby further authorized and empowered, subject to the approval of our Secretary of State, to acquire and take by purchase, cession, or other lawful means, other rights, interests, authorities, or powers of any kind or nature whatever, in, over, or affecting the territories, lands, or properties comprised in the several treaties aforesaid, or any rights, interests, authorities, or powers of any kind or nature whatever in, over, or affecting other territories, lands, or property in the region aforesaid [the basin of the Niger

river], and to hold, use, enjoy, and exercise the same for the purposes of the Company and on the terms of this our Charter. . . .

Royal charter granted to the Imperial British East Africa Company, September 3, 1888.

(The petition of William Mackinnon and others for a charter with powers much like those of the Royal Niger Company was granted on the following grounds:)

That his Highness the Sayyid Barghash Bin-Said, Sultan of Zanzibar and its East African Dependencies . . . granted and conceded to the Petitioners . . . all his powers, and the rights and duties of administration. . . .

That divers preliminary Agreements have been made on behalf of the Petitioners with Chiefs and tribes in regions which adjoin or are situate to the landward of the territories in the said Grants or Concessions . . . by which powers of government and administration such regions are granted or conceded to or for the benefit of the Petitioners.

That the Petitioners desire to carry into effect the said Grants, Concessions, and

---

27. Edward Hertslet, *The Map of Africa by Treaty*, vol. 1 (London: Her Majesty's Stationery Office, 1894), pp. 118–20, 177–80, 446–48.

Agreements . . . within the sphere reserved for British influence, and elsewhere, as we may be pleased, with the view of promoting trade, commerce, and good government in the territories and regions . . . if the said Grants, Concessions, Agreements, or Treaties can be carried into effect, the condition of the natives . . . would be materially improved, and their civilization advanced, and an organization established which would tend to the suppression of the Slave Trade in such territories, and the said territories and regions would be opened to the lawful trade and commerce of our subjects and of other nations.

That the possession by a British Company of the coast-line . . . would be advantageous to the commercial and other interests of our subjects in the Indian Ocean, who may otherwise become compelled to reside and trade under the government or protection of alien powers. . . .

Royal charter granted to the British South Africa Company, October 29, 1889.

6. The Company shall always be and remain British in character and domicile, and shall have its principal office in Great Britain, and the Company's principal representatives in South Africa and the Directors shall always be natural born British subjects, or persons who have been naturalized as British subjects by or under an Act of Parliament of Our United Kingdom. . . .

7. In case at any time any difference arises between any chief or tribe inhabiting any of the territories [the region of South Africa north of Bechuanaland and west of Portuguese East Africa] . . . that difference shall, if Our Secretary of State so require, be submitted by the Company to him for his decision, and the Company shall act in accordance with such decision. . . .

20. Nothing in this Our Charter shall be deemed to authorize the Company to set up or grant any monopoly of trade; provided that the establishment of or the grant of concessions for banks, railways, tramways, docks, telegraphs, waterworks, or any other similar undertakings or the establishment of any system of patent or copyright approved by Our Secretary of State, shall not be deemed monopolies for this purpose. . . .

22. The Company shall be subject to and shall perform and undertake all the obligations contained in or undertaken by Ourselves under any Treaty, Agreement, or Arrangement between Ourselves and any other State or Power whether already made or hereafter to be made. . . . The Company shall appoint all necessary officers to perform such duties, and shall provide such Courts and other requisites as may from time to time be necessary for the administration of justice. . . .

28. Voices of imperialism.

The scramble for Africa accelerated in the 1890s, with treaty-making always accompanied by the threat of armed force, and often by its use, particularly in the form of the maxim gun. Among the British, the leaders of this scramble were for the most part men who had first come to Africa as traders or as employees of the chartered companies. Such a background influenced their beliefs about the benefits of international commerce and European rule for African societies. Frederick Lugard, for example, went to East Africa as an employee of Mackinnon's British East Africa Company and on its behalf concluded treaties with African rulers (including Mwanga, the king of Uganda) by the terms of which the African leaders recognized the "sovereignty" of the company in exchange for its "protection." In the extract below from his published account of his East African exploits, Lugard stresses the economic benefits of Empire to

Britain and Africa alike, while in the extract from his private diary he describes the exact process by which he concluded a treaty with Mwanga on December 26, 1890. That trickery could be used to considerable effect is illustrated by the account of R. S. S. Baden-Powell (who later founded the Boy Scout movement) of how the British got the king of Asante, Prempeh I, to prostrate himself before their officers. Baden-Powell continues with a description of the second British torching in 20 years of the Asante capital, Kumasi.

While Mackinnon and his agent Lugard expanded British territorial control in East Africa primarily by treaty, Sir George Goldie relied more on armed force. In a somewhat breathless account of his conquests in northern Nigeria in early 1897, he shows his determination to break any form of resistance to British rule and to enforce complete submission.

That the exercise of armed force was not solely to be extended against African opponents but against anyone perceived to stand in the way of British Empire is made clear by the activities of Joseph Chamberlain, secretary of state for colonies, and his agents in South Africa at the end of the nineteenth century. Concerned that control of the South African gold industry, the largest in the world, not remain in the hands of the Voortrekker descendants who ruled the Transvaal Republic, Chamberlain corresponded with Sir Alfred Milner as to how British supremacy could be secured, even at the cost of war.[28]

(A). Frederick Lugard envisions empire in East Africa.

My aim . . . in these volumes, has been not so much to set forth a narrative of personal adventure, sport, and travel—a series of writing with which the public has been regaled by those who have far more to tell than I—but rather to place before thinking men subjects of more serious concern, both to ourselves in our dealings with Africa and to the subject races for whose welfare we have made ourselves responsible.

The rapid increase of population, the closing of the hitherto available outlets for emigration, as well as of the markets for our goods, and the sources of supply of our needs, indicate that the time is not far distant when the teeming populations of Europe will turn to the fertile highlands of Africa to seek new fields of expansion. It is possible, therefore, that British Central and British East Africa may be the embryo empires of an epoch already dawning—empires which, in the zenith of their growth and development, may rival those mighty dependencies which are now the pride of the Anglo-Saxon race. It behoves us, then, to take heed to the small beginnings of these great things, and in laying the foundations, to ensure that the greatness of the structure shall not suffer from lack of realisation on our part in the present.

There are many who have seemed to look on Africa as merely a field for romance and adventure—as a great blank continent on which explorers or adventurers were free to write their own names in capital letters. With the last decade of the nineteenth century I trust

---

28. (A), Frederick D. Lugard, *The Rise of Our East African Empire* (Edinburgh: William Blackwood and Sons, 1893), vol. 1, pp. viii–ix, 381–83, 395–97, 471, 473, 487–89; vol. 2, pp. 585, 591–92, and Margery Perham, ed., *The Diaries of Lord Lugard*, vol. 1 (Evanston, IL: Northwestern University Press, 1959; first published by Faber and Faber, London, 1959), pp. 40–42, reprinted with the permission of the estate of Margery Perham; (B), R. S. S. Baden-Powell, *The Downfall of Prempeh: A Diary of Life with the Native Levy in Ashanti, 1895–96* (London: Methuen and Company, 1896), pp. 19–22, 108–09, 123–31, 158–61; (C), C. W. Newbury, ed., *British Policy Towards West Africa, Select Documents, 1875–1914, with Statistical Appendices, 1800–1914* (Oxford: Clarendon Press, 1971), pp. 148–50, reprinted with the permission of Colin Newbury; (D), Cecil Headlam, ed., *The Milner Papers: South Africa, 1897–1899*, vol. 1 (London: Cassell & Company, 1931), pp. 525–28, 546–47, reprinted with the agreement of Cassell & Company.

Maxim automatic gun, 1887. *Source:* Henry M. Stanley, *In Darkest Africa, or the Quest, Rescue, and Retreat of Emin Governor of Equatoria,* vol. 2 (New York: Charles Scribner's Sons, 1890), p. 83.

that a new era has dawned for the African, and a new conception of our duties with regard to him has dawned upon ourselves. . . .

The "Scramble for Africa" by the nations of Europe—an incident without parallel in the history of the world—was due to the growing commercial rivalry, which brought home to civilised nations the vital necessity of securing the only remaining fields for industrial enterprise and expansion. It is well, then, to realise that it is for our *advantage*—and not alone at the dictates of duty—that we have undertaken responsibilities in East Africa. It is in order to foster the growth of the trade of this country, and to find an outlet for our manufactures and our surplus energy, that our far-seeing statesmen and our commercial men advocate colonial expansion.

Money spent in such extension is circulated for the ultimate advantage of the masses. It is, then, beside the mark to argue that while there is want and misery at home money should not be spent in Africa. It has yet to be proved that the most effective way of relieving poverty permanently, and in accordance with sound political economy, is by distributing half-pence in the street. If our advent in Africa introduces civilisation, peace, and good government, abolishes the slave-trade, and effects other advantages for Africa, it must not be therefore supposed that this was our sole and only aim in going there. How-

ever greatly such objects may weigh with a large and powerful section of the nation, I do not believe that in these days our national policy is based on motives of philanthropy only. Though these may be our *duties*, it is quite possible that here (as frequently if not generally is the case) advantage may run parallel with duty. There are some who say we have no *right* in Africa at all, "that it belongs to the natives." I hold that our right is the necessity that is upon us to provide for our ever-growing population—either by opening new fields for emigration, or by providing work and employment which the development of over-sea extension entails—and to stimulate trade by finding new markets, since we know what misery trade depression brings at home.

While thus serving our own interests as a nation, we may, by selecting men of the right stamp for the control of new territories, bring at the same time many advantages to Africa. Nor do we deprive the natives of their birthright of freedom, to place them under a foreign yoke. It has ever been the key-note of British colonial method to rule through and

F. D. Lugard. *Source:* F.D. Lugard, *The Rise of Our East African Empire: Early Efforts in Nyasaland and Uganda,* vol. 1 (Edinburgh: William Blackwood and Sons, 1893), frontispiece.

by the natives, and it is this method, in contrast to the arbitrary and uncompromising rule of Germany, France, Portugal, and Spain, which has been the secret of our success as a colonising nation, and has made us welcomed by tribes and peoples in Africa, who ever rose in revolt against the other nations named. In Africa, moreover, there is among the people a natural inclination to submit to higher authority. That intense detestation of control which animates our Teutonic races does not exist among the tribes of Africa . . . and if there is any authority that we replace, it is the authority of the Slavers and Arabs, or the intolerable tyranny of the "dominant tribe." . . . The experiment of an autonomous and civilised African state of freed negroes, such as was founded in "Liberia" in 1820 by the Washington Colonisation Society, and recognised an independent state by Europe in 1847, "can hardly be said to have been a success". . . .

[T]he question of the hostility of native tribes . . . is so important that it merits an additional word. The South African Company have the Matabeles [Ndebele] to deal with—an extremely powerful Zulu tribe of great organisation, who we are told are rapidly arming themselves with rifles. They have also had a collision with European neighbours in the Portuguese, and a similar collision with the Boers was narrowly avoided. The "British Central African Protectorate" is permeated by the slave-traders and their affiliated tribes, all armed with rifles and bitterly hostile, with whom the Administration is at chronic war, and who have hitherto proved themselves more than a match for its resources. There are also the fierce Angoni tribe, a tribe of Zulu origin. The Germans in like manner have tribes to deal with who are armed with thousands of rifles, and the whole country is full of arms. . . . The French have in West Africa powerful negro states, well armed, on their frontiers, such as Dahomey and others, and still more powerful opposition in Algeria. . . .

In the greater part at least of British East Africa there are no tribes to compare in power with any of these I have named. . . . There are no settlements of armed slave-traders and no savage tribes armed with rifles, as in the case of every other territory in Africa, and the natives almost without exception are well disposed.

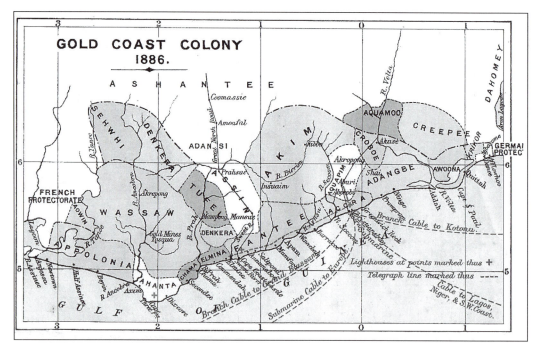

Gold Coast Colony, 1886. *Source:* J.J. Crooks, *Records Relating to the Gold Coast Settlements from 1754 to 1874* (Dublin: Browne and Nolan, Limited, 1923), frontispiece.

Another advantage which accrues to us in East Africa is the possession of at least three excellent harbours. Of these Mombasa is perhaps the finest natural port on the East African coast, and would form a most valuable coaling station for our fleet in these waters. But with its political importance we are not concerned here. With such a port at the base, and such an objective at the further point as . . . would be attained by communication with the lake and Nile waterways, surely the country offers indisputable natural advantages for commercial development?

Mr. Stanley has stated that we should be face to face with twelve millions of people as customers for our goods. Mr. Ravenstein's estimate of the population of British East Africa is 6½ millions, and probably if we extended our commerce to the shores of the lakes and the Nile, we should arrive at a total not far short of Mr. Stanley's estimate. Apart, however, from the wants of this native population are the requirements of alien immigrants. These form a very appreciable factor in the consumption of imports. . . .

Whether European colonisation in the true sense of the term be feasible or not, it remains beyond a doubt that extensive areas suitable for European exploitation similar to that in India and Nyasaland, where large plantations of tea, coffee, cotton, &c., are raised, or for stock-rearing and sheep-farming, as in Australia and Canada, are available, and also that East Africa is eminently suitable for Asiatic colonisation. . . .

The commercial value of East Africa is largely dependent on the labour available to develop its products. It has been said that the African is inherently lazy, and that he will do no more work than he is absolutely compelled to, and will relegate even that to his women. . . .

So far . . . as my personal experience goes, I have formed the following estimate: (1) No kind of men I have ever met with—including British soldiers, Afghans, Burmese, and many tribes of India—are more amenable to discipline, more ready to fall into the prescribed groove willingly and quickly, more easy to handle, or require so little compulsion as the African. (2) To obtain satisfactory results a great deal of system, division of labour, supervision, &c., is required. (3) On the whole, the African is very quick at learning, and those who prove themselves good at the superior class of work take pride in the results, and are very amenable to a word of praise, blame, or sarcasm. . . .

If . . . we accept the position that we go to Africa not merely for the good of the African, but for our own, it follows that, if the laziness of the natives should make it impossible for us to reap our advantage, we must find means to do it in spite of them. I have shown that in East Africa the population is restricted to certain areas, mainly through tribal wars and Masai raids. There are, therefore, large tracts of equally fertile country available for colonisation, without dispossessing or in any way incommoding the natives. Such colonies might consist of Africans—freed slaves, or the Sudanese from Equatoria, who would furnish labour. They might also consist of Asiatic immigrants. . . . .

From the overcrowded provinces of India especially, colonists might be drawn, and this would effect a relief to congested districts. From them we could draw labourers, both artisans and coolies, while they might also afford a recruiting ground for soldiers and police. The wants, moreover, of these more civilised settlers would . . . very greatly add to the imports, and the products of their industry to the exports of the country, thus giving a great impetus to trade. The African, too, is extremely imitative. The presence in his midst of a fully clothed people would be to him an example of decency which he would speedily imitate. His wants would become identical with theirs, and thus, while his status was improved, and a new encouragement given to trade, he would be compelled to exert himself and to labour in order to supply those wants. Moreover, the methods of agriculture, the simple implements of the Indian ryot, the use of the bullock, the sinking of wells, the system of irrigation and of manuring the soil, &c. &c., would soon be imitated by the African, and the produce of his land would thus be vastly multiplied. As the popu-

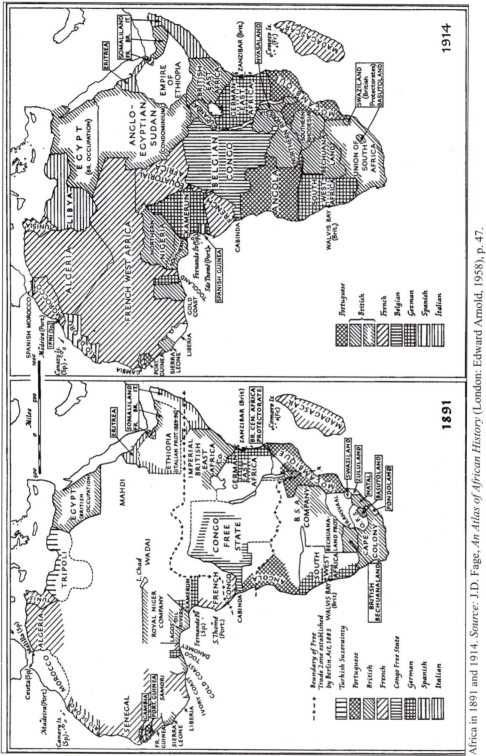

Africa in 1891 and 1914. *Source:* J.D. Fage, *An Atlas of African History* (London: Edward Arnold, 1958), p. 47.

lation increased, both by the introduction of these aliens and by the cessation of war, famine, small-pox, and the slave-trade—a result which would follow on a settled government—the African would be compelled to work for his living, not, as heretofore, by the compulsion of slave labour, but in order to prove himself with the requirements of his increasing necessities and improved status, and by that law of competition which compels the indolent to labour. . . .

[A]s long as our policy is one of free trade, we are compelled to seek new markets; for the old ones are being closed to us by hostile tariffs, and our great dependencies, which formerly were the consumers of our goods, are now becoming our commercial rivals. It is inherent in a great colonial and commercial empire like ours that we go forward or backward. To allow other nations to develop new fields, and to refuse to do so ourselves, is to go backward; and this is more deplorable, seeing that we have proved ourselves notably capable of dealing with native races, and of developing new countries at a less expense than other nations. We owe to the instincts of our ancestors, those vast and noble dependencies which are our pride and the outlets of our trade to-day; and we are accountable to posterity that opportunities which now present themselves of extending the sphere of our industrial enterprise are not neglected, for the opportunities now offered will never recur again. . . .

We have a prescriptive right in East Africa and its lakes. They were all discovered by British explorers: Victoria by Speke and Grant, Nyasa by Livingstone, Tanganyika by Burton, Albert by Baker, and Albert Edward by Stanley. The steamers (three) placed on Nyasa have all been brought by the British; so has the one on Tanganyika; and those on the Albert and the Nile were brought down by Baker when in the Khedive's service. Our missionaries first penetrated to Uganda in the footsteps of our explorers. Thus, by right of discovery and of missionary effort, we had the prior claim to Uganda, and the time has now come for us to assert or forgo entirely that claim.

Those few who have given voice to the arguments against retention have, so far as I am aware, altogether avoided dealing with the strong array of facts which I have endeavoured to present to my readers. Briefly they are these:

1. Fulfilment of pledges to Europe, under (1) the Berlin Act, (2) the Brussels Act.

2. Pledges to the natives, and responsibility for anarchy, &c., on evacuation.

3. Political importance of retaining our hold on the Nile valley, and of the ports on the coast.

4. Commercial necessity of finding new markets, &c.

5. Obligation as regards missionaries, French and English.

6. Check to slave-trade—by establishing a protectorate in the heart of Africa.

7. Reflex action on other African possessions caused by loss of prestige.

8. Uniformity of policy inaugurated by cession of Heligoland, &c.

9. Preponderance of public opinion in favour of retention.

10. Prescriptive rights.

[In the following text extracted from his diary entry for December 26, 1890, Lugard, who was then in the employ of the British East Africa Company, describes the process by which he made a treaty with Mwanga, the king of Uganda]

I was ready at 8 A.M. but no message came. 9 past and 9.30 or more, and I made up my mind they had changed and it was war. Then I saw the Durbar break up, and crowds and crowds coming out. They came to us, and soon I got a message that they [the main advisors of Mwanga] would come and sign here, and go to the King afterwards. All the biggest knobs came in (not a single gun of any sort among them) and I sat them down on a big tarpaulin at the tent door, and had the table and everything ready. There was much long speechifying, and then they said they would sign provided they were allowed to write a Codicil, and I would sign that and give it to them. This they wrote themselves; it was mainly that the treaty was to be null, and another made, if the messengers from the coast came with other news than mine. Also that a compact which they would not show me made between themselves was still to be binding. Its main provision was religious toleration for both sides, I believe. This I signed, and then there was much discussion as to whether they should sign now first, or take it first to the King. At last they said I was to go alone to the King and he would sign and then all would sign. It eventually ended in all following on, so De W. came with me, and three or four Askari. Grant in camp with orders to send all Sudanese and 4 batches of men to our assistance in case he heard firing, and hold the camp with the other 2 troops and the Maxim, which he was to use freely if required. For the chiefs still spoke of some bad men of whom they seemed much afraid. It appears as far as I can understand that there really is a rabble of whom the king and all are afraid. They are, I believe, a drunken bang-smoking lot of blackguards, probably not Christians of either sect, and it was they who threatened to shoot if the Treaty was signed on 23rd. As a protection I wanted the Kimbugwe and Katikiro to accompany me—they said they would but the little Kauta was the only one who stuck close by us all the time, and ordered back the rabble when we entered. He is a right good little fellow, one of the very best, if not *the* best in the country, and I am most glad he is a R.C. because now if I favour him I can't be accused of partiality to the Protestants.

We found the King in undress reclining on a mat. I had brought no chair thinking it was to be a quick affair, but I stood till one was brought me. De W. brought his, all the rest (King included) on the ground. The King said I professed friendship but had given him no present. I said I knew it, but had come in haste and brought nothing but food, the Maxim and cartridges. Bye the way, they have keenly taken stock of our loads, and I heard on arrival here all about it. I had no cloth, and nearly all boxes which they supposed were *ammunition*. They are really all nearly bead boxes but it has helped to add to their fear of us, for supposing them all to be ammunition they were of course very afraid of us. I have not undeceived them! I added that

Stokes was bringing me some loads and I wanted some canoes to fetch them from the South of the Lake, and in these were my presents for him. Then all the big chiefs came in one by one, till it was a full Durbar. Their Codicil was read to the King, and he at once asked if all the tributary states would still be compelled to pay tribute. I replied as before that I was a stranger and knew nothing of these States, that when I knew all about it we would see, that I had said nothing about it in the Treaty, one way or the other—this was merely a treaty of friendship with Uganda, and its tributary States, and did not touch the further question. I tried to turn the conversation by talking of the piece of Uganda lost which the Germans have taken, and told them that had they made a treaty with the British sooner they would not have lost it, but that even now I would write to Emin Pasha and see if I could get the tribute and if he refused would refer it to England. They would not be put off, however, and the King ordered them to add it to the Codicil. This was a poser, for it would considerably cripple my treaty to enter into such an obligation. So I got them to add, "and its tributary States" after the words "I Mwanga Sultan of Uganda," which of course meant nothing, or at least bound me to nothing.

Then the King told someone to sign for him. I would not have this, and insisted on his making a mark. He did it with a bad grace, just dashing the pen at the paper and making a blot, but I made him go at it again and make a cross, and on the 2nd copy he made a proper cross. Then one of the chiefs who could write wrote Mwanga's name opposite the mark, and "ilamu zake" as well and I was satisfied. Several of the head chiefs also signed, but it took about 10 minutes or ¼ hour per signature as they slowly formed each letter, and paused. At last the King left, and after one or two more signatures I left too, giving them their copy of the treaty and Codicil and taking mine. Need I say how delighted De W. and I were at our success! I had determined to arrive in Uganda by Xmas. I had not only done it but reached the capital, and spite of all trouble and opposition had got the Treaty made and signed within 12 hrs after

Xmas. Not a bad 8 weeks' work from Dagoretti to Mengo and treaty made and signed!

(B). R. S. S. Baden-Powell describes the downfall of the Asantehene, Prempeh, 1896.

[T]here exist more particular reasons for it [taking action against Asante] in the refusal of the king to carry out the provisions of the treaty of 1874.

The danger of allowing treaty contracts to be evaded is fairly well understood among European nations, but the results of slackness or leniency in their enforcement are none the less dangerous when the treaty has been made with an uncivilised potentate, since his neighbours are quick to note any sign of weakness or loss of prestige on the part of the white contracting party, and they in their turn gain courage to make a stand against the white ruler and his claims over them.

In Ashanti the abuse had been allowed to go on far too long. Natives near our border—ay, within it too—had seen year after year go by, and the Ashanti liberty taking the form of licence more and more pronounced, with little or no restraint beyond mild and useless remonstrance on our part. Naturally this raised the Ashantis once more in their estimation, while it lowered our prestige in a corresponding degree; and although the people were sufficiently knowing to see that under our government they were their own masters and were able to carry out any ideas of commerce that they might entertain, still they also saw that, as far as local indications went, the Ashantis were equal in power to the white men, and, as a natural consequence, they were much inclined at least to waver in their allegiance to us.

"Britons never will be slaves," and Britons are so peculiarly imbued with a notion of fair-play that they will not see anybody else in a state of slavery either, if they can prevent it.

Slaves in some parts of the world form the currency of the country; in others they are the beasts of burden and the machinery; often their lot is mercilessly hard, though not always. . . .

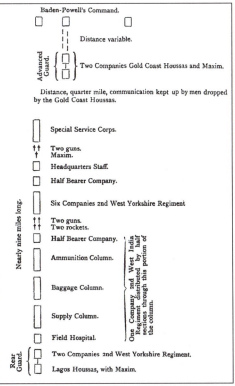

Baden-Powell's army column, 1895–1896. *Source:* R.S.S. Baden-Powell, *The Downfall of Prempeh: A Diary of Life with the Native Levy in Ashanti, 1895-96* (London: Methuen & Co., 1896), pp. 108-09.

But in no part of the world does slavery appear to be more detestable than in Ashanti. Slaves, other than those obtained by raids into neighbours' territory, have here to be smuggled through the various "spheres," French, German, and English, which are beginning to hem the country in on every side. . . .

They are not required for currency, since gold-dust is the medium here.

Nor are they required to any considerable extent as labourers, since the Ashanti lives merely on vegetables, which in this country want little or no cultivation.

And yet there is a strong demand for slaves. They are wanted for human sacrifice. Stop human sacrifice, and you deal a fatal blow to the slave trade, while you render raiding an unprofitable game. . . .

The levy, being now 860 strong, is able to find two flanking parties on by-roads to the town [Kumasi], in addition to its main party on the central road.

THE DOWNFALL, 20th January [1896].

. . . Six o'clock had been named as the hour for Prempeh and all his chiefs to be on the palaver-ground. This was done, well knowing that he might then be expected about seven, and it was desirable to make an early start with the ceremony, in order not to keep the white troops exposed to the sun in the middle of the day. Soon after seven o'clock the troops began to form on the parade-ground, but still no sign of any of the Ashantis coming; nor even was there any of the usual preliminary drumming that invariably goes on to summon all the retainers who usually form the procession.

Nearly two hours' grace had been given him; it looked as though Prempeh did not mean coming. The order was accordingly given for the Special Service Corps, assisted by the native levy, to surround the palace and the queen-mother's house, and to bring Prempeh and the queen to the Governor.

The native levy, in view of such course becoming necessary, had during the previous day cut away the bush adjoining the palace enclosure, and thus the cordon was enabled rapidly to take up its position to close every outlet.

In a very few minutes the king was carried forth in his state cradle with a small following, and, escorted by the troops, he proceeded hurriedly to the palaver-ground. The queen-mother, similarly escorted, followed shortly after, as well as all the chiefs. They were then marshalled in a line, with a limited number of attendants each, in front of the Governor, Mr. Maxwell, C.M.G., who was seated on a dais, together with Colonel Sir Francis Scott, K.C.B., and Colonel Kempster, D.S.O.

Submission of King Prempeh, January 20, 1896. *Source:* R.S.S. Baden-Powell, *The Downfall of Prempeh: A Diary of Life with the Native Levy in Ashanti, 1895-96* (London: Methuen & Co., 1896), facing p. 126.

A square of British troops was formed all round, backed by Houssas and the native levy.

Then the doom of the nation was pronounced in a set-scene, and amid dramatic incidents such as could not fail to impress both natives and Europeans alike.

Through the medium of interpreters—Vroom, Secretary for Native Affairs, acting for the Governor; Albert Ansah, for the king—the conditions of the treaty to be imposed upon the Ashantis were demanded of them.

The first of these was that Prempeh should render submission to the Governor, in accordance with the native form and custom signifying abject surrender. This is a ceremony which has only once before been carried out between the Ashantis and a British Governor, namely, Governor Rowe. On that occasion the king deputed officers of his court to perform the actual ceremony; but in this case it was insisted that the king must himself personally carry it out. Accordingly, with bad enough grace, he walked from his chair, accompanied by the queen-mother, and, bowing before Mr. Maxwell, he embraced his knees. It was a little thing, but it was a blow to the Ashanti pride and prestige such as they had never suffered before. Then came the demand for payment of the indemnity for the war. Due notice had been previously given, and the Ashantis had promised to pay it; but unless the amount, or a fair proportion of it, could now be produced, the king and his chiefs must be taken as guarantee for its payment.

The king could produce about a twentieth part of what had been promised. Accordingly, he was informed that he, together with his mother and chiefs, would now be held as prisoners, and deported to the Gold Coast.

The sentence moved the Ashantis very visibly. Usually it is etiquette with them to receive all news, of whatever description, in the gravest and most unmoved indifference; but here was Prempeh bowing himself to the earth for mercy, as doubtless many and many a victim to his lust for blood had bowed in vain to him, and around him were his ministers on their feet, clamouring for delay and reconsideration of the case. The only "man" among them was the queen.

In vain. Each chief found two stalwart British non-commissioned officers at his elbow, Prempeh being under charge of Inspector Donovan. Their arrest was complete

But there was still an incident coming to complete the scene. The two Ansahs, although they held a large hand in causing the trouble between the British and Ashantis, appear in their own country to have little or no influence with the people, and, indeed, were looked on with jealousy and suspicion. These were surveying the scene—their handiwork—with a somewhat curious look, half amused, half nonplussed, when the Governor added to his remarks the suggestion that the present might be a suitable occasion for the arrest of these two gentlemen on a charge of forgery; and before they had fully realised between them that the charge was actually being preferred against them, they found that Mr. Donovan had adroitly handcuffed them wrist to wrist, and the scene was complete.

During the performance of this act another had been quietly preparing behind the scenes. Parties of the native levy had been withdrawn from the parade-ground, and were added to the cordon already drawn round the palace. All was silent there, and all the many doors were locked. But a path from the jungle leading to the back door, also locked, brought one within sound of the buzz of many men talking within, and of the soughing of bellows of smelting fires. At the close of the palaver on the parade-ground, two companies of the West Yorkshire Regiment, under Captain Walker, were detailed to take possession of the palace, clear it of all people inside, and to collect and make an inventory of all property found inside.

One company was accordingly sent to stiffen the cordon of native levies, and with the other company I proceeded to effect an entrance by a back way, which I had previously reconnoitred. . . .

There could be no more interesting, no more tempting work than this. To poke about in a barbarian king's palace, whose wealth has been reported very great, was enough to

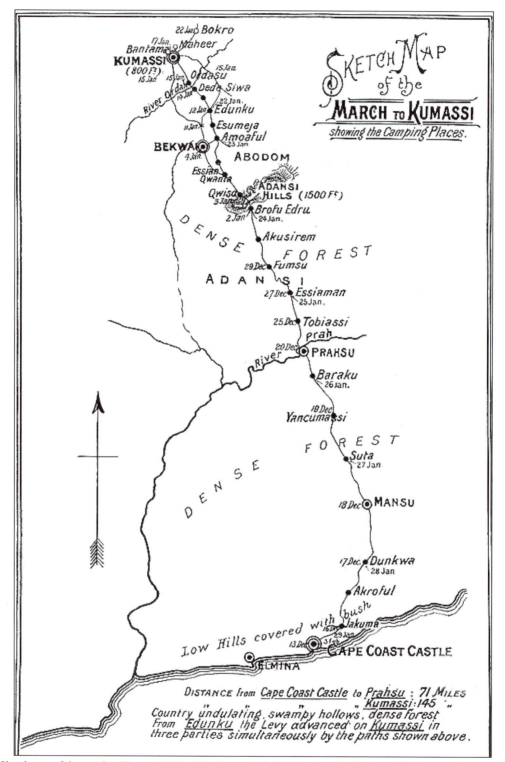

Sketch map of the march to Kumasi, 1895–1896. *Source:* R.S.S. Baden-Powell, *The Downfall of Prempeh: A Diary of Life with the Native Levy in Ashanti, 1895-96* (London: Methuen & Co., 1896), facing p. 15.

make it so. Perhaps one of the most striking features about it was that the work of collecting the treasures was entrusted to a company of British soldiers, and that it was done most honestly and well, without a single case of looting. Here was a man with an armful of gold-hilted swords, there one with a box full of gold trinkets and rings, another with a spirit-case full of bottles of brandy, yet in no instance was there any attempt at looting.

It need not be supposed that all the property found in the palace was of great value. There were piles of the tawdriest and commonest stuff mixed indiscriminately with quaint, old, and valuable articles, a few good brass dishes, large metal ewers, Ashanti stools, old arms, etc. But a large amount of valuables known to belong to the king had disappeared, probably weeks previously—such as his celebrated dinner service of Dutch silver, his golden hat, his golden chair of state, and, above all, the royal stool, the emblem, *par excellence*, of the King of Ashanti.

These were all probably hidden, together with his wives, in various hamlets in the remote bush. The "loot" which we collected was sold by public auction, excepting golden valuables, which were all sent home to the Secretary of State.

The term "palace" has merely been used to denote the residence of the king. In reality there is very little that is palatial about it. It consists of a collection of the usual wattle-and-daub huts, with high walls and enormous high-pitched thatched roofs; endless courts, big and little, succeed each other, with narrow entries between, and with little or no attempt at architectural design or ornamentation.

The foundations of the old palace, built on more substantial principles, and destroyed in the last campaign, are still to be seen in the centre of the present place in a disused court.

Finding so little of real value in the palace, it was hoped that some treasure might be discovered in the sacred fetish-houses at Bantama, the burial-place of the kings of Ashanti, about a mile out of Bantama. This place had also been piqueted, but all its priests

had disappeared previously, and when we broke in, only one harmless old man was found residing there. No valuables—in fact, little of any kind was found in the common huts that form the sacred place. In the big fetish building, with its enormous thatched roof, when burst open, we only found a few brass coffers—all empty! The door, which was newly sealed with mortar, showed no signs of having been quite freshly closed up, and it may therefore be inferred that the treasure had been removed some weeks previously.

Then, in accordance with orders, we set the whole of the fetish village in flames, and a splendid blaze it made. The great fetish-tree, in whose shade hundreds of victims have been sacrificed, was blown up with gun-cotton, as also were the great fetish-trees on the Kumassi parade-ground. Among the roots of these there lie the skulls and bones of hundreds, and possibly of thousands, of victims to the *regime* which to-day has so dramatically been brought to a close. . . .

From the foregoing it will have been deduced that the success and bloodless victory of the expedition was due to the rapidity and the completeness of the movements of the force; and that this rapidity was in its turn the result of a thoroughly planned and well-equipped organisation. But then arises the question, *Cui bono*? What is the good of this victory when you have won it? What return is there for the half million that will have been spent upon it ?

Inter alia, one may at once point out that it has, at any rate, put an end to the practice of human sacrifice, which, up till within three months ago, had gone on with all the unchecked force that it had ever enjoyed. Fetish superstition has an immense hold on the untutored children of the bush, and tradition and custom decreed that human sacrifice was the best form of propitiation of the fetish demons. Moreover, the men of the country have no kind of diversion or employment beyond very poor hunting and an occasional raid on a neighbouring tribe. Bloodlust, like many another vicious habit, rapidly takes root and grows on a man who is without other occupation. A bloody spectacle was naturally to the Ashantis a most attractive form of amusement, especially as at the same time it satisfied their superstition.

The popularity of human sacrifice was none the less great because it gave a direct impetus to the slave trade. As a rule, the victims of fetish sacrifice were slaves, and the supply had to be kept up to the demand. How great that demand was we may, perhaps, never know, but that it was little short of enormous may be guessed partly from the deposit of skulls and bones about the fetish groves, and partly from the fact that two streets in Kumassi consisted of the houses occupied by the official executioners. The suppression of this abuse has been one result of the expedition, and the disintegration of the Ashanti kingdom into its minor kingdoms will ensure its non-revival. This alliance of lawless chiefs into a common band, under the direction of the Kumassi king, has hitherto acted like a dam to a reservoir. Within five days' march of Kumassi, to the northward, the poisonous bush country comes to an end, and on beyond there lies the open country, rich and populous, which stretches thence to Timbuctoo. The natural outlet for this country's trade is by the Kumassi road to Cape Coast Castle and the sea. This is the reservoir which the Ashanti dam has kept closed up so long. In breaking down the Ashanti gang we have broken up the dam, and the stream which will now begin to flow should, in the near future, well repay the expenses of the machine with which it has been cut. An encouraging example lies to hand in the colony at Lagos, where, as a direct result of the Jebu campaign, the trade has in a single year leaped up to double what it was before.

The British prestige has, moreover, now extended its effect into the back country among tribes who were hitherto wavering with their future allegiance in the balance, and it may be inferred that they will not delay to come under our protectorate. This in its turn will mean the extension of our boundaries till they touch the Niger, and will thereby save the Gold Coast Colony from being shut out from up-country trade, as had been threat-

ened, by the junction of the two French forces in Dahomey and in Timbuctoo. Indeed, the colonial party of our friends across the Channel are just beginning to suspect that, using Prempeh as a nail to hang our cloak upon, we have quietly beaten them in the race for the Gold Coast Hinterland—that instead of Dahomey joining hands with the French Soudan, the Gold Coast will ere long have marched its boundary on to that of the Royal Niger Protectorate. In gaining this enlarged territory, we may very probably also gain the assistance of a ready-made force with which to hold it, namely, the army, horse and foot, of Samory.

Thus, in the course of a few weeks, an enormous change has been wrought in the history of this part of Africa, and the vista of a great future has been suddenly opened to the Gold Coast Colony. And yet this great result has been gained by the use of a mere handful of men, and it is only when one realises the magnitude of the result that one sees with something akin to awe how much might have been lost by a little mismanagement or by a single false move.

(C). Sir George Goldie reports to the British governor on his conquests in the Niger basin, February 18, 1897.

In view of the interest felt by your Government in the Ilorin question, I venture to trouble you with the following brief report, and I shall be obliged if you will forward a copy to the Secretary of State for the Colonies. I am, of course, preparing a full report for the Secretary of State for Foreign Affairs, who will doubtless communicate it to the Colonial Office, but this fuller report cannot be completed at once, and I shall take it home with me, as I am returning at once to London, having fully succeeded, and to an extent beyond my expectations, in the three expeditions which I came out to direct.

Believing that Ilorin would accede peacefully to my suggestions after the fall of Bida, and having received the written submission of the Emir Suliman, I only brought from Jebba one half of the troops, and less than half of the guns, with which the battle of Bida had been won. I knew, however, that I could not find an opposing force more than one-fourth that of Bida; and, moreover, that our troops, flushed with success, were fit to combat much larger numbers.

On the 14th instant, at the River Araibi, ten miles from the City of Ilorin, I learnt from my spies that the four Baloguns, or War Chiefs, had compelled the Emir to agree to fight, and that the whole Ilorin forces were drawn up near the River Oyon, three or four miles from Ilorin, and were advancing to meet us.

The battle commenced about 8 A.M. on the 15th inst. and lasted till the afternoon of the 16th. We were compelled to inflict very heavy losses on the enemy. The Balogun Alanamu, the most warlike of the four War Chiefs, has just told me that we killed over 200 horsemen; and as the foot soldiers were in the proportion of about six to one, it may be assumed that their total loss exceeded a thousand. We then bombarded the town (which unfortunately caught fire) and took possession of it, the Emir, four Baloguns and all other Chiefs flying dispersed to distant villages.

While the troops were occupied in stopping the conflagration, I took active steps to enter in communication with the Emir, who has always been most faithful to his treaty with the [Royal Niger] Company. Today, at noon, the Emir and four Baloguns with other Chiefs surrendered to us and came here to negotiate a new treaty, which was signed in the presence of all the troops and many spectators in the great square. The Emir recognises the entire power of the Company over all the Ilorin territory, and that he will govern in accordance with the directions given him from time to time; that he must not make war without consent of the Company; that he must accept such frontier between Ilorin and Lagos as may be directed.

I told the Emir and Baloguns that, pending Her Majesty's decision, the frontier must be that fixed by Captain Bower some time ago on behalf of Sir Gilbert Carter. I carefully abstained from holding out any hopes that this frontier line would be rectified, but I think it right to inform you that I reserve to myself the liberty to reopen this question with Her Majesty's Government.

The Emir and Baloguns were greatly concerned with the difficulty they would have, after their crushing defeat, in organising any government in the Ilorin territory. I told them, however, that the Company felt that any government is better than anarchy, that they were at liberty to take the steps taken by all governments to enforce order in the regions left under their authority; but that they must wait for one month before taking such steps in the southern portion lying to the north of the Lagos frontier and Odo Otin, so as to give me time to inform you of what had taken place and to give you time to issue instructions to your officials and troops, so that the approach of Ilorin horsemen to the neighbourhood of the Lagos frontier should not be mistaken for a renewal of hostilities.

There is no fear of such renewal for a generation to come. The Ilorin power is completely broken. The four Baloguns, Alanamu, Salu, Ajikobi, and Suberu, were far more humble and broken than the peaceful Emir Suliman, whom they had forced into war, and who behaved today with great dignity, although with a keen sense of the entirely new position created by our conquest of Ilorin.

I have arranged that some of our troops shall move frequently along the Ilorin side of the temporary Lagos frontier, so as to ensure order and the roads being kept open. No garrison will be left permanently in Ilorin City, but troops will visit it occasionally.

We leave here to-morrow to receive the submission of another Sokoto province, Lafiagi. . . .

I find to my regret, that the greater part of the City of Ilorin has been burnt.

(D). Joseph Chamberlain and Alfred Milner plan for war in South Africa, September 1899.

Chamberlain to Milner, September 2, 1899, CONFIDENTIAL.

I am very glad to have your letters (Aug. 2nd and 16th received) when you can find time to write. The situation changes hourly. This afternoon I have suggested a Cabinet to Lord Salisbury to arrange for an ultimatum. Just now (1 A.M.) I have a telegram from Reuter to say that the Transvaal Govt. has sent a favourable reply! May it be so! but after recent experiences I am very sceptical. The incident however illustrates the difficulty of revising or of elaborating a policy which may be hopeless before the letter reaches you. Accordingly I propose to confine myself to generalities.

In the first place then I hope you are satisfied by now that although in the light of information which is incomplete and of telegrams which always are inadequate to explain fully the meaning of the sender, I may occasionally differ from you, yet that I am in the fullest sense of the word loyal to you as I believe you are to me. We have both a very difficult part to play and the atmosphere here is very different from that of Cape Town. Just consider how it strikes the ordinary patriotic Englishman . . . He sees that if there is a war it will be a very big affair—the biggest since the Crimea—with no honour to be gained, if we are successful, and with many most unpleasant contingent possibilities.

These things influence the outside politician, but in addition we, who are inside, have other difficulties. The War Office is not an ideal institution. The other day they were ready " to the last button"—now they talk of four months before they can put an army corps to the front. Of the Treasury I will say nothing since you were yourself an ornament of that great department. . . . When I reflect on all these things I am really astonished at the progress we have made. It is a great thing to say that the majority of the people have, as I believe, recognized that there is a greater issue than the franchise or the grievances of the Uitlanders [English speakers resident in the Transvaal, most of them mine workers] at stake, and that our supremacy in S. Africa and our existence as a great Power in the world are involved in the result of our present controversy. Three months ago we could not—that is to say we should not have been allowed to—go to war on this issue—now—although still most unwillingly and with a large minority against us—we shall be sufficiently supported. But please bear all this in mind if we move more slowly than you think wise, and than would be wise if we had only Cape opinion to think of—and the interests of the British Empire in South Africa.

What is going to happen next? If the reply from the Transvaal is unsatisfactory I hope you will get a report from your Commissioners in a very few days. I cannot see why there should be any careful examination of existing laws in the Transvaal. I should expect your men to report that the offer of 5 years' retrospective franchise and 8 additional seats would give substantial and immediate representation, if all the conditions of registration, residence, etc., etc., were the same as, say, in the Orange Free State and the Cape Colony. They might add that it would be necessary to allow the new members to use their own language in the Raad [parliament]—that it would be advisable that the amount of representation given to the Rand [Witwatersrand] should be reconsidered in 5 years and increased in proportion to population and that these views should be embodied in a new Convention. Then shall we give Kruger one more chance by asking him to accept this Report and carry it out? At present I think we should. I can see clearly that the British in the Cape and in Natal are afraid that if he accepts at the last moment, he will do so with the intention of repudiating his obligations whenever we are otherwise engaged; and they would like us to increase our demands and send an ultimatum on other points such as Suzerainty, Disarmament, Federation, and I know not what which would certainly force a war. But can we do this yet? We must play this game out "selon les régles," and it seems to me to-day that we ought to exhaust the franchise proposals and get a clear report before, on the principle of the Sybilline books, laid down by Lord Salisbury, we ask for more.

If and when we ask for more it means war, and therefore, before we do this, we must have a sufficient force in S. Africa to defend ourselves during the time that will be required to get the full fighting forces into the country. And besides this we must have Parliamentary sanction for the despatch of a large force, which means discussions, some division of opinion and delay. But suppose the time has come to put forward fresh demands and to obtain, at the price of war, a final settlement. What are these fresh demands to be? Perhaps they will have been settled by the Cabinet before this reaches you. If not let me have your views at the time by telegraph as well as by letter.

Here is a list of things for which we might ask—all to be embodied in a new Convention—1. Explicit recognition of Suzerainty. 2. Foreign affairs to be conducted through H.M.G. 3. Acceptance of Judicial Come. of P[rivy] Council, with Transvaal judge added, to deal with all future questions of interpretation. 4. Franchise, etc., as in Cape Colony. 5. Municipal rights for gold Mining Districts. 6. All legislation since 1884 restricting rights and privileges of Uitlanders to be repealed. 7. Disarmament. 8. Indemnity for expenses incurred since refusal of Franchise proposals. 9. Federation of S. African Colonies and States. I give these as a list of possible demands, but whether it would be good policy to put all of them forward before the war may well be a question . . . .

Milner to Chamberlain, September 27, 1899, CONFIDENTIAL.

I have to thank you for your long and most interesting letter of Sept. 2nd. For want of time I will not discuss all the useful information it gives me. Much that you tell me I had more or less surmised, both from the actual course of our diplomacy and the natural indications in the Press and in private letters. As far as home opinion is concerned the management of the controversy has been perfect. Seeing how hopelessly the British people were dead to the real issues 4 months ago, it is wonderful where they stand to-day. Unfortunately, inevitably, the long dragging controversy which has enlightened public opinion at home, has done harm here. It has discouraged many of our best supporters, but, what is worse than that, it has given time for the Afrikander propaganda to produce more and more effect throughout the Colony and has consolidated the Afrikander party. There

is a good deal of actual plotting, but it is for the most part so cunningly concealed that one cannot lay hands upon it. In this respect the necessity of keeping on terms with Ministers has been a great weakness to me. It was necessary—otherwise I should have had something like an insurrection in parts of the Colony before now—but it has been a fearful hindrance to finding out the secret workings of the enemy, as the officials and police, who are mostly in sympathy with us, have been in many more or less intangible ways hampered and discouraged in following up indications of sedition. And all the time the two Republics have been arming and colloguing. Until lately the O.F.S. [Orange Free State] was very wavering, but as weeks passed, our patience which was misinterpreted there, gradually turned against us and finally the bulk of opinion swung over to that side, to which Steyn and Fischer had all along been trying to incline it.

But after all, these are not our greatest difficulties. At a pinch I always felt pretty certain that we should have Afrikanderdom solid against us *in feeling*. But if we were able to strike a decisive blow quickly, that would not mean so much in actual physical force. The O.F.S. people would fight halfheartedly and the Colonial Afrikanders, with a few exceptions, would sit still, though secretly hostile. But here comes in the military, or perhaps as you hint really the financial obstacle. Owing to the fact that, as I suppose for financial reasons, provisional arrangements for the immediate transport of a large force have not been made during all these months, the large force cannot begin to arrive for at least two months, and during that time the military task it will have to perform may grow to much greater proportions. Moreover, we have an even more pressing problem and that is how to get over the next 3 weeks, if, as now seems most probable, the Republics decide to have a dash at us. However, it is no use dwelling on immediate contingencies, which will be decided one way or the other before this reaches you. We are doing our best in the dilemma, which especially in this Colony is great, viz. whether [to] scatter our small force along the border in order to keep the enemy in check and prevent risings—at the risk of being cut up or invested in detail, or to keep it concentrated down here at the risk of losing hold of the great part of the Colony and of the lines of communication. On the whole I think the former course is the better. The other is too suggestive of fear.

29. Voices of resistance.

The establishment of European rule was never a straightforward matter, particularly because of the determined resistance of Africans. Such resistance meant that the process of conquest sometimes stretched over several decades. It also meant that indigenous people developed new ways of combining, often across regional and ethnic boundaries, to overthrow foreign rule. In the first selection, Ndansi Kumalo, an Ndebele chief and subject of Lobengula born around 1860, describes what happened when Cecil Rhodes and Lobengula disagreed about the terms of the treaty signed in 1888; Lobengula believed that he had only extended mineral rights to the diamond magnate, Rhodes thought that the entire territory had become his personal fiefdom (symbolized in the name he gave the country, Rhodesia). The events that Kumalo narrates took place in 1893 and ended with British conquest of the Ndebele and the suicide of Lobengula. Still, the British had to fight another even more violent war in 1896, ultimately dynamiting the caves in which African resisters fought to the last.

In an account from German Southwest Africa (present day Namibia), Hendrik Witbooi calls on a German officer to respect the autonomy of the local inhabitants. Witbooi, a leader of the Nama people, had fought against German encroachment in the early 1890s, forming an alliance with his long-term enemies, the Herero, in order to strengthen the forces of resistance. Though Witbooi soon concluded (after the death of many Nama women and children) a peace treaty with the Germans, he continued to complain about the way in which he and his people were treated, subjected to heavy taxation and forced labor. The refusal of the Germans to treat the people of Namibia as anything but a conquered and servile people eventually caused Witbooi to rise again in rebellion. In 1904, when he was 80 years old, he led a revolt of Nama and Herero against colonial rule. The Germans responded by waging a war of extermination, driving their opponents into the desert and sealing the wells behind them so that they could not have water, and placing the survivors in forced labor camps where most died. Witbooi was killed leading an attack on a German supply column. He was not alone. A 1911 census recorded only half as many Nama living as had been the case in 1900; only one-fifth as many Herero as a decade before.

Some Africans fought back with words, as did the brass traders in the Niger delta who in 1895 complained to the British government about the unfair way that the Niger Company treated them. Their petition directly challenges the arguments of exponents of commercial empire like Lugard that Europeans brought economic development to Africa and that the chartered companies sought to better the lot of backward people. The British government ignored the Brass merchants.

Jan Smuts, who fought with the Boers against the British, also had little doubt about what he considered motivated British imperialism–it was "the new forces of Capitalism" which he blamed. British greed for Boer gold resulted in the greatest casualty figures of any British colonial war in the nineteenth century: 20,000 British dead, 7,000 Boer men and 30,000 women and children (the women and children incarcerated in concentration camps which, because of poor sanitation and the lack of medical treatment, quickly turned into death camps), and at least 15,000 African fatalities, likewise mostly among people incarcerated as the British pursued a scorched earth policy.

In German East Africa (present day Tanzania), the very ways in which imperialism took practical form forced production of new crops for the export market, and harsh labor conditions on these new plantations (which meant little African land and labor devoted to growing their own food needs). It also led rapidly to widespread opposition that, as in Namibia, transcended old ethnic boundaries. From July 1905 until August 1907, Africans from more than 12 different ethnic groups, assumed by German colonial officials to be incapable of working together, organized a large-scale resistance movement covering more than 100,000 square miles (or at least a third of the colony). Led by a prophet-like figure, Kinjikitile Ngwale, who claimed to be possessed by a powerful ancestral spirit and to have a war "medicine," maji [water] maji, that could render European arms ineffective, the movement persisted long after the Germans hanged its leader in August 1905. African casualties in the war exceeded 120,000. Still, leaders of movements supporting African independence in the 1940s and 1950s looked back to the Maji Maji movement and its leader Kinjikitile as symbols of African defiance of European colonialism. [29]

(A). Ndansi Kumalo describes the defeat of Lobengula and the Ndebele, July-December 1893.

. . . When I first saw a white man I could not make it out and ran away. When we got used to them we would go with goats and sheep and buy European clothing. Later people used to take cattle and barter for beads and blankets.

We were terribly upset and very angry at the coming of the white men, for Lobengula had sent to the Queen in England and he was under her protection and it was quite unjustified that white men should come with force into our country. Our regiments were very distressed that we were not in a fit condition to fight for the king because of the smallpox. Lobengula had no war in his heart: he had always protected the white men and been good to them. If he had meant war, would he have sent our regiments far away to the north at this moment? As far as I know the trouble began in this way. Gandani, a chief who was

29. (A), Margery Perham, ed., *The Africans* (London: Faber and Faber, 1936), pp. 69–75, reprinted with the permission of the estate of Margery Perham; (B), Georg M. Gugelberger, ed., *Nama/Namibia: Diary and Letters of Nama Chief Hendrik Witbooi, 1884–1894* (Boston: Boston University African Studies Center, 1984), pp. 117–18, reprinted with the permission of the African Studies Center, Boston University; (C), C. W. Newbury, ed., *British Policy Towards West Africa, Select Documents, 1875–1914, with Statistical Appendices, 1800–1914* (Oxford: Clarendon Press, 1971), pp. 143–45, reprinted with the permission of Colin Newbury; (D), J. C. Smuts, *A Century of Wrong* (London: Review of Reviews, 1899?), issued by F. W. Reitz, with preface by W. T. Stead, pp. 89–98; (E), G. C. K. Gwassa and John Iliffe, eds., *Records of the Maji Maji Rising* (Dar es Salaam: East African Publishing House, 1967), Part 1, pp. 5–6, 8–10, 11–12, 25–26, reprinted with the permission of John Iliffe and the estate of G.C.K. Gwassa.

Colonial atrocity, Mashonaland, 1896. *Source:* Olive Shreiner, *Trooper Peter Halket of Mashonaland* (Boston: Roberts Brothers, 1897), frontispiece.

sent out, reported that some of the Mashona had taken the king's cattle; some regiments were detailed to follow and recover them. They followed the Mashona to Ziminto's people [Victoria district]. Gandani had strict instructions not to molest the white people established in certain parts and to confine himself to the people who had taken the cattle. The commander was given a letter which he had to produce to the Europeans and tell them what the object of the party was. But the members of the party were restless and went without reporting to the white people and killed a lot of Mashonas. The pioneers were very angry and said, "You have trespassed into our part." They went with the letter, but only after they had killed some people, and the white men said, "You have done wrong, you should have brought the letter first and then we should have given you permission to follow the cattle." The commander received orders from the white people to get out, and up to a certain point which he could not possibly reach in the time allowed. A force followed them up and they defended themselves.

When the pioneers turned out there was a fight at Shangani and Bembezi.

I was in the Matoppos and had not recovered from smallpox. I did not see Lobengula at this time for we were isolated. We sent a message to the King asking for permission to join with his forces; he agreed and we reorganized our regiment. The King agreed that we might come out of quarantine and told us to go to Gwelo's to fetch some of his cattle, but we could not; we were too weak. Only fourteen of our regiment went to try and recover the King's cattle and on the way they heard that they were too late. The white men were there and had seized the cattle. These fourteen incorporated themselves in Imbizo's regiment and fought at Bembezi, and two were killed. The next news was that the white people had entered Bulawayo; the King's kraal had been burnt down and the King had fled. Of the cattle very few were recovered; most fell into the hands of the white people. Only a very small portion were found and brought to Shangani where the King was, and we went there to give him any assistance we could. I could not catch up with the King; he had gone on ahead. Three of our leaders mounted their horses and followed up the King and he wanted to know where his cattle were. They said they had fallen into the hands of the whites, only a few were left. He said, "Go back and bring them along." But they did not go back again; the white forces had occupied Bulawayo and they went into the Matoppos. Then the white people came to where we were living and sent word round that all chiefs and warriors should go into Bulawayo and discuss peace, for the King had gone and they wanted to make peace. The first order we got was, "When you come in, come in with cattle so that we can see that you are sincere about it." The white people said, "Now that your King has deserted you, we occupy your country. Do you submit to us?" What could we do? "If you are sincere, come back and bring in all your arms, guns and spears." We did so.

I cannot say what happened to Lobengula, but the older people said, "The light has gone out. We can do no more. There is nothing left for us but to go back to our homes." All that we could hear was that the King had disappeared alone; no one knew where he went. It could not be that his body, alive or dead, should pass into the hands of his enemies. Our King was powerful and a great king; he was invincible against other tribes. He ruled right up to the Zambezi. He was just; and if, unfortunately, many innocent men were killed it was through the jealousy and cunning of others who sent false reports which the King believed. At the beginning Lobengula was loved by everybody, but later bitterness arose in the families which had suffered loss and there was a good deal of dissension. I remember a tragedy when two of my relatives were killed. They were at the King's kraal and he was annoyed with them. He fired towards them with a shot-gun to frighten them and the warriors took it as a sign to despatch them and clubbed them to death. When news came to their kraal the children fled, but their wives said, "Let us die with them." The King sent

them a message that it was a mistake. It all arose from a dispute over cattle.

So we surrendered to the white people and were told to go back to our homes and live our usual lives and attend to our crops. But the white men sent native police who did abominable things; they were cruel and assaulted a lot of our people and helped themselves to our cattle and goats. These policemen were not our own people; anybody was made a policeman. We were treated like slaves. They came and were overbearing and we were ordered to carry their clothes and bundles. They interfered with our wives and our daughters and molested them. In fact, the treatment we received was intolerable. We thought it best to fight and die rather than bear it. How the rebellion started I do not know; there was no organization, it was like a fire that suddenly flames up. We had been flogged by native police and then they rubbed salt water in the wounds. There was much bitterness because so many of our cattle were branded and taken away from us; we had no property, nothing we could call our own. We said, "It is no good living under such conditions; death would be better—let us fight." Our King gone, we had submitted to the white people and they ill-treated us until we became desperate and tried to make an end of it all. We knew that we had very little chance because their weapons were so much superior to ours. But we meant to fight to the last, feeling that even if we could not beat them we might at least kill a few of them and so have some sort of revenge.

I fought in the rebellion. We used to look out for valleys where the white men were likely to approach. We took cover behind rocks and trees and tried to ambush them. We were forced by the nature of our weapons not to expose ourselves. I had a gun, a breech-loader. They—the white men—fought us with big guns and Maxims and rifles.

I remember a fight in the Matoppos when we charged the white men. There were some hundreds of us; the white men also were many. We charged them at close quarters; we thought we had a good chance to kill them but the Maxims were too much for us. We drove them off at the first charge, but they returned and formed up again. We made a second charge, but they were too strong for us. I cannot say how many white people were killed, but we think it was quite a lot. I do not know if I killed any of them, but I know I killed some of their horses. I remember how, when one of their scouts fell wounded, two of his companions raced out and took him away. Many of our people were killed in this fight. I saw four of my cousins shot. One was shot in the jaw and the whole of his face was blown away—like this—and he died. One was hit between the eyes; another here, in the shoulder; another had part of his ear shot off. We made many charges but each time we were beaten off, until at last the white men packed up and retreated. But for the Maxims, it would have been different. The place where we have been making the film [Kumalo had been hired to perform as Lobengula in a British movie about Rhodes' conquest of the Ndebele] is the very place where my cousins were killed.

We were still fighting when we heard that Mr. Rhodes was coming and wanted to make peace with us. It was best to come to terms he said, and not go shedding blood like this on both sides. The older people went to meet him. Mr. Rhodes came and they had a discussion and our leaders came back and discussed amongst themselves and the people. Then Mr. Rhodes came again and we agreed at last to terms of peace.

So peace was made. Many of our people had been killed, and now we began to die of starvation; and then came the rinderpest and the cattle that were still left to us perished. We could not help thinking that these dreadful things were brought by the white people.

(B). Hendrik Witbooi to Theodor Leutwein, August 17, 1894.

Your Highness, dear Major Leutwein!

I received your long letter late last night. I take it from this letter of yours that you accuse me of various deeds. From this you seem to claim the right to condemn me to death as if I were a common criminal. You seem to try to reason with me by force of guns.

I. You accuse me of intending to attack Kirris. This is absolutely untrue.

II. You claim that I try to seduce people to do malicious things. This is blatantly untrue as well. You refer to Simon Kopper. You yourself have seen Simon Kopper and found out that he was quite against you long before I ever spoke to him. Why do you blame me for Kopper's present attitude? If Kopper's views have changed, what has that to do with me?

III. You say that I arrogantly claim to be ruler over certain territories and claim the sole right to sell such territories. I have this to give you for an answer: You white men, as well as the red men, know very well that this territory of which you speak has been my property since the death of my grandfather. The Red Nation attacked my grandfather without any cause. He conquered them. Later the same tribes attacked me as well. I con-

Hendrik Witbooi. *Source:* Georg M. Gugelberger, ed., *Nama/Namibia: Diary and Letters of Nama Chief Hendrik Witbooi, 1884-1894* (Boston: Boston University African Studies Center, 1984), back cover.

quered them a second time. This means that I have a double right to this territory. I have purchased these lands not with money, nor were they given to me as presents. Through bloodshed these lands came into my hands. This has been an old rule of war. You yourself indirectly acknowledge my right as proprietor to these lands by trying to take these lands away from me by force. Obviously you cannot see any other way of getting hold of these lands. If the said territory were not my own, why would you be attacking me? Again, I am not guilty of anything concerning this point.

IV. You claim that you are sorry that I do not accept German protection. You seem to think that I am guilty even of this. And therefore you seem to try to penalize me.

This is my answer: I have never in my life seen the German emperor and I am sure he has never seen me. Therefore it seems impossible that I could ever have hurt him.

God has made us rulers of some parts of the world. I don't think that one can call someone guilty if he wants to remain an independent ruler over his land and his people.

If you intend now to have me killed because of my love of independence, this is not shame or harm. If I have to die I shall die as an honest man defending my property and my rights.

What can be wrong with a man who refuses to be inferior to someone else? Why should I be condemned to death for things which are natural?

All the things you have said so far are constructs helpful for your own profit. You argue the way you do in order to appear to the rest of the world as a person who loves truth and rightful doings and to try to prove to this world that I have been wrong and guilty. But my dear friend! I must tell you that I have a clear conscience. I know that I have been innocent. I also know that you yourself are basically convinced of my innocence, but you seem to claim that strength and might precede truth and law. Since you have the guns, you force the right on your side. I fully agree with you in one thing: in comparison with you, we are nothing here. My dear friend!

You arrive with such forces and guns and you tell me that you intend to attack me.

I guess this time I shall be forced to defend myself against you. I shall do so not so much in my own name but in the name of the Lord. Trusting in His aid and strength I shall defend myself. You also say that you are against bloodshed and that you are innocent in the event that people shall be killed in the near future. You claim that everything has been my fault.

This is blatantly impossible. I must say that I am astonished how you can think up such things.

I have told you that I am fully in favor of peace and that I shall never be the one breaking such a peace. But you say that you intend to attack me. The responsibility for the innocent blood of my men and yours therefore cannot be mine since I am not the instigator of another war. Since it is not I who plans another attack, how can I be guilty for what you plan to do?

V. Once more I must ask you, dear friend, to accept the truthful and honest peace I have offered you. You yourself have called this a true peace.

Please do leave us alone and withdraw!

Call your troops back and withdraw. Please do withdraw! Please do so!

This is my very serious plea! I am your friend and Captain,

Hendrik Witbooi

(C). Memorandum, case of the Brass chiefs, June 8, 1895.

The Company which is now known as the Niger Company has done us many injuries . . . for some time after the Charter was granted they drove us away from our markets in which we and our forefathers had traded for generations, and did not allow us to get in our trust, or trade debts, some of which remain unpaid to this day. Neither will they permit the Ejoh or market people to come down and pay us.

In 1889, Major MacDonald, now our big Consul, came to us, and we told him of all these things, and he promised that he would lay our complaints before the Queen's Government. . . .

In 1891, he, Major MacDonald, came again and explained to us that it was the intention of the Queen's Government to send Consuls to these rivers and that we should then have a Consul of our own who would specially look after our interests. He pointed out to us that this could not be done without money, and explained how the money could be raised by means of duty, and asked whether we consented to pay these duties. At first we refused, because we could get no satisfactory answer about our markets; but eventually we signed, but begged the Major that he would do what he could to get some of our markets back for us. . . .

Since then we have seen the Major many times, and he has always told us to be patient, but latterly things have gone from bad to worse, and the markets that we have are quite insufficient to maintain us.

We thoroughly understand that all markets are free, and open to everybody, black and white man alike; and we are quite willing to trade side by side with the white man at those markets. We do not now ask for any exclusive privileges whatever, but only that we may be allowed to trade without molestation at the places we and our fathers have traded in days gone by.

We are willing to pay fair duties: but we cannot understand, however, if all markets are free and open to black and white man alike, why there are many villages or markets in the Niger where neither are allowed to go and trade.

We submit that, if we have to go to Akassa, a distance of nearly 40 miles, to pay our duties, and are only allowed to trade at certain places selected by the Niger Company called "ports of entry," and have to take out trade and spirit licences, and pay a very heavy duty going into the territories and a heavy duty coming out, it is the same thing as if we were forbidden to trade at all.

The Niger Company say, "We (the Company) have to do these things, why not you?"

We can only say that, with our resources, to carry out these Regulations and pay these duties means ruin to us.

The Niger Company are cleverer than we are. We humbly submit that we have a right, confirmed by our Treaty, to go and trade freely in the places we have traded at for all these generations. We are ready to pay to do so, but let us pay a fair duty, and conform to fair Regulations.

The duties and Regulations of the Company mean to us ruin; of this there is no doubt.

We do not deny that we have smuggled, but under the circumstances can this be wondered at?

We have suffered many hardships from the Company's Regulations. Our people have been fired upon by the Company's launches, they have been fired upon from the Company's hulks, our canoes have been seized and goods taken, sometimes when engaged in what white men call smuggling, and sometimes when not.

The "chop" canoes coming from the Ejohs have also been stopped.

Within the last few weeks the Niger Company has sent messengers to the Ejohs and other tribes with whom we have always traded and said that any of them who traded with us at all, or who paid us their debts, would be severely punished, and their villages burnt.

We have evidence to prove all this, which we would like to lay before the big man who has been sent by the Queen.

All these unjust things that have been done to us, the many times we have been told to be patient and have been so, and the wrongs which we consider we have suffered are now worse than ever, all these drove us to take the law into our own hands and attack the Company's factories at Akassa.

We know now we have done wrong, and for this wrong we have been severely punished; but we submit that the many unjust oppressions we have borne have been very great, and it is only in self-defence, and with a view to have our wrongs inquired into, that we have done this thing. We have frequently asked the Consuls that have been put over us . . . to tell us in what way we have offended the Queen to cause her to send this trouble on us.

Traders we are, have been, and always will be. The soil of our country is too poor to cultivate sufficient food for all our people, and so if we do not trade and get food from other tribes we shall suffer great want and misery.

We fervently hope and pray that some arrangements may be arrived at which will enable us to pursue our trade in peace and quietness.

Warri, his x mark
Karemma, ditto
Thomas Okea, ditto
Nathaniel Hardstone, ditto
Witnesses: H. L. Gallwey, Deputy Commissioner and Vice-Consul, Benin District

(D). Jan Smuts denounces British "Capitalism" and "Jingoism," 1899.

In this awful turning point in the history of South Africa, on the eve of the conflict which threatens to exterminate our people, it behoves us to speak the truth in what may be, perchance, our last message to the world. Even if we are exterminated the truth will triumph through us over our conquerors, and will sterilise and paralyse all their efforts until they too disappear in the night of oblivion.

Up to the present our people have remained silent; we have been spat upon by the enemy, slandered, harried, and treated with every possible mark of disdain and contempt. . . .

During this century there have been three periods which have been characterised by different attitudes of the British Government towards us. The first began in 1806, and lasted until the middle of the century. During this period the chief feature of British policy was one of utter contempt, and the general trend of British feeling in regard to our unfortunate people can be summarised by the phrase, "The stupid and dirty Dutch." But the hypocritical ingenuity of British policy was perfectly competent to express this contempt in accents which harmonised with the loftiest sentiments then prevailing. The wave of sentimental philanthropy then passing over the civilised world was utilised by the British Government in order to represent the Boers to the world as oppressors of poor peace-loving natives, who were also men and brethren eminently capable of receiving religion and civilisation. . . .

The fundamental sentiment which governed the policy of the second period was a feeling of regret at having made this mistake [granting in 1852 and 1854 settlers in the Orange Free State and the Transvaal possession of the lands they then occupied as a result of the Great Trek], coupled with the firm determination to set aside its results. These wild and useless tracts, which had been guaranteed to the Boers, appeared to be very valuable after the Boers had rescued them from barbarism, and opened them up for civilisation. It was felt that they ought to gleam amongst the jewels of Her Majesty's Crown, nothwithstanding the obstacle in the treaties that had been concluded with the Boers. As far as the means were concerned—they were, from the very exigency of inborn hypocrisy, partly revealed and partly concealed; the one differing from the other as light from darkness. The secret means consisted in arming the Kaffir tribes against us in the most incredible manner, and in inciting them to attack us in violation of solemn treaties and promises. If this policy succeeded the real objects and means could be suppressed, and England could then come forward and pose openly as the champion of peace and order, and as the guardian angel of civilisation in this part of the world. . . . The British succeeded in. . . . annexing the Diamond Fields—a flagrantly illegal act. . . .

The third period of our history is characterised by the amalgamation of the old and well-known policy of fraud and violence with the new forces of Capitalism, which had developed so powerfully owing to the mineral riches of the South African Republic. Our existence as a people and a State is now threatened by an unparalleled combination of forces. Arrayed against us we find numerical strength, the public opinion of the United Kingdom thirsting and shouting for blood and revenge, the world-wide and cosmopolitan power of Capitalism, and all the forces which underlie the lust of robbery and the spirit of plunder.

Our lot has become more and more perilous. . . . Every sea in the world is being furrowed by ships which are conveying British troops from every corner of the globe in order to smash this little handful of people. Even Xerxes, with his millions against little Greece, does not afford a stranger spectacle to the wonder and astonishment of mankind than this gentle and kindhearted Mother of Nations, as, wrapped in all the panoply of her might, riches, and exalted traditions, she approaches the little child grovelling in the dust with a sharpened knife in her hand. This is no War—it is an attempt at Infanticide. . . .

Nor will a Chamberlain be more fortunate in effecting the triumph of Capitalism, with its lust for power, over us.

If it is ordained that we, insignificant as we are, should be the first among all peoples to begin the struggle against the new-world tyranny of Capitalism, then we are ready to do so, even if that tyranny is reinforced by the power of Jingoism. . . .

[W]e now submit our cause with perfect confidence to the whole world. Whether the result be Victory or Death, Liberty will assuredly rise in South Africa like the sun from out the mists of the morning, just as Freedom dawned over the United States of America a little more than a century ago. Then from the Zambesi to Simon's Bay it will be "AFRICA FOR THE AFRICANDER."

(E). Memories of Maji Maji, 1905.

During the [cotton] cultivation there was much suffering. We, the labour conscripts, stayed in the front line cultivating. Then behind us was an overseer whose work it was to whip us. Behind the overseer was a jumbe [official, chief], and every jumbe stood behind his fifty men. Behind the line of jumbes stood Bwana Kinoo [a German settler named Steinhagen] himself. Then, behold death there! And then as you till the land from beginning to end your footprints must not be seen save those of the jumbe. And that Selemani, the overseer, had a whip, and he was extremely cruel. His work was to whip the conscripts if they rose up or tried to rest, of if they left a trail of their footprints behind

them. Ah, brothers, God is great—that we have lived like this is God's Providence! And on the other side Bwana Kinoo had a bamboo stick. If the men of a certain jumbe left their footprints behind them, that jumbe would be boxed on the ears and Kinoo would beat him with the bamboo stick using both hands, while at the same time Selemani lashed out at us labourers. . . .

They [the people] waited for a long period because they were afraid. How could one clan face the Germans alone and not be wiped out? There had to be many.

It is true they were ruled for a very long time before they rose in arms against the Germans. The problem was how to beat him really well. Who would start? Thus they waited for a long time because there was no plan or knowledge. Truly his practices were bad. But while there were no superior weapons should the people not fear? Everywhere elders were busy thinking, "What should we do?"

He [Kinjikitile] was taken by an evil spirit one day in the morning at about nine o'clock. Everyone saw it, and his children and wives as well. They were basking outside when they saw him go on his belly, his hands stretched out before him. They tried to get hold of his legs and pull him but it was impossible, and he cried out that he did not want [to be pulled back] and that they were hurting him. Then he disappeared in the pool of water. He slept in there and his relatives slept by the pool overnight waiting for him. Those who knew how to swim dived down into the pool but they did not see anything. Then they said, "If he is dead we will see his body; if he has been taken by a beast or by a spirit of the waters we shall see him returned dead or alive." So they waited, and the following morning, at about nine o'clock again, he emerged unhurt with his clothes dry and as he had tucked them the previous day. After returning from there he began talking of prophetic matters. He said, "All dead ancestors will come back; they are at Bokero's in Rufiji Ruhingo. No lion or leopard will eat men. We are all the Sayyid Said's, the Sayyid's alone." The song ran: "We are the Sayyid's family alone. Be it an Mpogoro, Mkichi, or Mmatumbi, we are all the Sayyid Said's." The lion was sheep, and the European was red earth or fish of the water. Let us beat him. And he caught two lions which he tethered with a creeper, and people danced Likinda before those two lions. They remained harmless. Then word of this new man spread afar. . . .

Njwiywila meant secret communication such as at a secret meeting. At that time if you listened to Njwiywila you paid one price. That was the meaning of Njwiywila. The message of Njwiywila was like this: "This year is a year of war, for there is a man at Ngarambe who has been possessed—he has Lilungu. Why? Because we are suffering like this and because . . . we are oppressed. . . . We work without payment. . . . This Njwiywila began at Kikobo amongst the Kichi, for they were very near Kinjikitile. It spread to Mwengei and Kipatimu and to Samanga. But the people of Samanga did not believe quickly. It spread quickly throughout Matumbi country and beyond. In the message of Njwiywila was also the information that those who went to Ngarambe would see their dead ancestors. The people began going to Ngarambe to see for themselves. . . .

It was like a wedding procession, I tell you! People were singing, dancing, and ululating throughout. When they arrived at Ngarambe they slept there and danced likinda, everyone in his own group. The following morning they received medicine and returned to their homes. . . .

The song of Mpokosi [a representative of Kinjikitile] during likinda was in the Ngindo language. He used to take his fly-switch and his calabash container for medicine, and he went around sprinkling them with medicine. It was like military drilling with muzzle-loaders, and under very strict discipline. Thus Mpokosi would say:

"Attention!

We are at attention.

What are you carrying?

We are carrying peas.

Peas? Peas of what type?

Creeping peas.

Creeping?

Creeping?"

And so on as they marched, until Mpokosi ordered:

"Attention!

Turn towards Donde country [inland].

(The warriors turned).

Turn towards the black water [the ocean].

(They obeyed).

Destroy the red earth.

Destroy!

Destroy?

Destroy!"

And so on as they advanced as if to shoot.

During that time they were dressed in their military attire called Ngumbalyo. Further, each one was told where to go for this type of drilling. Thus, all gathered at Nandete for this type of likinda. The song was entirely in riddles. Thus the question "what are you carrying?" meant "what do you want to do?" The answer "we are carrying peas" meant "we are carrying bullets," and they used peas in their guns during drilling. "Creeping peas" are those that creep, and it meant that they were marching to the battlefield. "Creeping, creeping"—that was walking, that is military marching. "Destroy the red earth"—that meant tear the European apart or destroy him. . . .

The District Officer let Fr. Johannes know that the sultans were to be hanged today. He could if necessary see for himself whether any of them wished to be baptised. (For Fr. Johannes had previously sought permission from the District Officer to baptise them if possible.) Fr. Johannes therefore went into the gaol, or rather into the passage between the gaols, in which the condemned men were lodged. They had just received sentence, and things in the gaol were therefore animated. Each still had commissions for his dependents to carry out. As soon as Fr. Johannes set foot in the place, some of those he knew came to him and asked him to undertake these commissions, which he said he was prepared to do. Then he asked some who had already received a certain amount of instruction at Peramiho, "Do you not wish to be baptised before you die?" They asked, "Can we do that?" When they were assured of this, many raised their hands and called out, "I want to be baptised, and I, and I!" A few who had not as yet received any instruction asked what this was all about. Fr. Johannes told them that if they would only be quiet he would explain it to them. Mputa [a paramount chief] himself then demanded silence, and Fr. Johannes instructed them briefly in the essential truths and on baptism and contrition. Then he asked who wanted to be baptised. Thirty-one men declared themselves ready for baptism, among them Sultan Mputa. Seventeen men, among whom were numbered a few Muslims, wished to know nothing of baptism. Despite exhortation, Mpambalyoto said briefly, I will die a pagan. Msimanimoto, a chief from the neighbourhood of Peramiho, also wanted to know nothing of baptism, for he protested that he would die blameless, he had done no wrong. Even those who had taken part in the attack on Kigonsera offered themselves for baptism, although they had not previously received instruction. Some—Fratera, for example—showed themselves especially pleased that they could still be baptised. One asked whether he would truly rise again. The District Officer had allowed half an hour, but not all had been baptised when this expired, so that he extended it slightly. When all were baptised, they were called out in threes and their hands bound. Then they were led out to the gallows, which were alongside the gaol, outside the boma. Some took leave of Fr. Johannes with the words, "Until we meet again." As he went out, Mputa, who showed genuine contrition, said in his bad Swahili, "But Kinjala led me astray."

The mood of the condemned men varied. Some cheered themselves with the fact that they could at least all die together. Kasembe declared: "Why should we fear to die? My father is dead, my mother is dead; now do I merely follow them." A few began to tremble somewhat as they were called out and bound. Others sat quietly by, and one could see from their behaviour that they were grieved and reluctant to die. On the whole, the business sat lightly on many, who chattered and laughed as at any other time. One asked Fr. Johannes for a pinch of snuff. Since he had none, he applied to Sergeant Leder, who stood watch, to get some from the guard. At this others also wanted snuff, but no more could be obtained. Some began to sing as they were led out. A few, however, cursed the District Officer especially. Mpambalyato declared that Chabruma would soon come to revenge them. Several asked Fr. Johannes to tell their families to bury them themselves, to buy cloth for the purpose and to wrap them in it. Bonjoli flatly demanded that Fr. Johannes should arrange it so that he was not hanged—from now on he would be true. Fratera prayed aloud the "Our Father" and "Hail Mary," and said, after he had been instructed, that at the end he would pray, "Jesus, Saviour, receive my spirit." For one the affair went on too long. He wanted to be led out before his turn. Fr. Johannes remained in the gaol until all had been led out, exhorting them to prayer and to a sense of contrition.

Thus many found at the end a merciful death, many who otherwise stood in grave peril of being lost eternally. God be thanked for it.

A vast crowd had naturally assembled outside to be witnesses of the "spectacle."

At evening the hanged men were buried in a large common grave.

PART 3
Colonialism and
Its Critics

Introduction

Once the European powers determined to enter the African continent itself and to conquer the people and societies with whom for so many years (centuries often) they had bartered and traded, they faced the question of how to rule these foreign cultures, and how to do so as cheaply as possible since the main rationale for empire at the end of the nineteenth century was profit. Force was always there to be used, but the high cost of maintaining standing armies and employing large numbers of European bureaucrats was more than most proponents of empire were prepared to countenance. Instead, imperialists sought to use Africans to administer the new colonial societies but always under the strict supervision of European overseers.

In Natal in the 1870s, at the very beginning of the "scramble," the British fashioned a model of rule—autocratic, hierarchical, and completely undemocratic—that they claimed mirrored "traditional" indigenous practice (despite the evidence to the contrary given by Cetshwayo, Part 2, document 22), and placed at its head as the all-powerful, unquestionable "Supreme Chief" none other than the governor of the colony (document 1). Elsewhere in Africa systems of "indirect" and "direct" rule differed somewhat in form, but the substance experienced by Africans was usually much the same. Colonialism was expressed by its masters in the language of command, and the only role allocated to and expected of Africans was obedience (documents 4, 5). Colonial rule rested also on a new class of Africans, very different from the "traditional" chiefs so favored in Natal. These were the people who had been attracted to Christianity. In mission schools, they learned the vernacular of their new masters and found employment as agents of the colonial state: as translators, clerks, and tax collectors (document 6).

Colonial officials adopted this combination of force and African intermediaries, because they wanted colonialism to pay—to pay enough to return a profit to the metropole and to pay enough to support the new structures of rule established to administer the colonies. To ensure profitability, the colonial authorities required Africans to grow cash crops for the export market rather than items for trade within Africa or food for their own sustenance; and to work on the new plantations established and for the new industries developed, many of them highly labor intensive such as tobacco in Tanganyika or gold mining in South Africa. To force people to engage in these economic activities on terms set by the employers and not open to negotiation (black workers in South Africa, for example, were not recognized in law as workers and therefore did not have the right to engage in collective bargaining), Europeans confiscated the land of Africans (especially in South Africa, southern Rhodesia, and Kenya), forced people to work on European and state-owned farms and roads (in French and Belgian territories as well as those of the

British), and imposed taxes at every possible opportunity (one of the favorites was a tax on African dogs) (documents 7, 14, 16, 17). The worst extreme was probably that of the Congo, the private domain of Belgium's King Leopold where Africans who failed to collect enough rubber had their hands chopped off as a warning to others to work faster (document 3).

Such atrocities and oppression did not go unopposed. It was often missionaries who enabled such opposition to reach a mass audience. Africans at mission stations learned to read and write and, from the late nineteenth century onward, established a vibrant indigenous press. Often these educated Africans traveled overseas, usually under missionary sponsorship, to obtain the higher education that they could not obtain on a continent where the colonial authorities established no universities open to blacks until the twentieth century. Many of these travelers went to the United States where, frequently attending universities for African Americans, they gained a sense of brotherhood with the descendants of former slaves and an appreciation that white rule did not necessarily lead to the improvements in society that had been promised by missionaries. People like John Chilembwe and John Dube returned to Africa determined to improve the lot of their fellow Africans: Chilembwe took the path of armed revolt and like so many of his peers was killed; Dube chose the politics of protest and petition and lived, though not without constant police harassment (documents 2, 7, 8). Aware of their shared oppression, blacks on both sides of the Atlantic demanded an end to racism and white oppression, calling for all peoples of African descent to join together in a movement for pan-African unity (documents 9, 10). Chilembwe called on the United States to pay reparations to African Americans for "250 years of unpaid slave labor" (document 2).

Growing consciousness of the repressive nature and the hypocritical justifications on which colonialism rested spurred the growth of new political movements in the 1910s and 1920s. These were led primarily by members of the new educated "elite," people who did not repudiate the West but who did denounce colonialism. They aimed to bring together people across ethnic and regional boundaries and combine them in movements that would gain strength from their mass membership (documents 7, 8, 11, 12, 13, 14). Perhaps the most successful, and distinctive, of these new movements was the Industrial and Commercial Workers Union in South Africa, where under the leadership of Clements Kadalie a combination of labor organization and messianic appeal produced a strong enough threat that colonial authorities did everything that they could to bring about (successfully) its demise (document 13).

Despite the successful repression of their indigenous opponents during the 1920s and the 1930s, in the 1940s colonial rulers found their ability to rule profoundly challenged. Africans, many of whom had battled Axis imperialism during World War II, returned home dismayed that the pro-democracy rhetoric of the West did not apply to their own communities after the war, and found that the levels of exploitation to which they were subjected were ever greater as European colonizers tried to re-build their war-torn economies on profits from their overseas possessions (documents 19, 20). People like the returned soldier Waruhui Itote and his near contemporaries Anton Lembede and Mugo Gatheru wanted freedom "now," not later, and they turned from the politics of petition to those of labor struggle and mass protest to achieve their goals (documents 21, 22, 23).

Though white settlers in South Africa, Southern Rhodesia, and Kenya, as well as the Belgians and the Portuguese, determined to strengthen white supremacy as a means of maintaining their economic privilege (documents 24, 25, 26, 27), officials in Britain and France realized, sometimes hesitantly, that the price of repression was beginning to exceed the profits of colonialism. In the 1950s, the British and the French began searching for ways to grant political autonomy to their colonial territories while at the same time securing the economic linkages that had made conquest so attractive in the first place and which ensured the continued presence of Europeans in Africa (document 23).

Formal colonialism ended for most Africans in the late 1950s and the early 1960s, but its conclusion was a costly business. The British hanged a thousand Kenyans before they let go. At much the same time that Kwame Nkrumah celebrated Ghana's independence—the first of any African country—with ringing cries of "Freedom! Freedom! Freedom!," Hendrik Verwoerd committed South Africa to another 40 years of race hatred (documents 29, 30). And Patrice Lumumba, the first president of the newly independent Congo, caught up in an international Cold War not of Africa's making, lost his life in a secessionist war encouraged by European and South African investors who feared losing the mineral riches of the country to a populist government (document 31).

Colonialism ended as it had begun, in false promises, boundless expectations, and blood.

1. Making colonialism appear "traditional."

The cost of rule was always of paramount concern to colonial officials. Having acquired empire in most instances for economic reasons, the colonial powers were not prepared to bear the heavy cost involved in employing large numbers of European administrators or maintaining expensive armies of occupation. Better to get Africans to rule themselves for less money. But that meant identifying, or, as was often the case, inventing "traditional" indigenous institutions through which Europeans could exercise their overrule.

For the British, the most pressing case in the latter half of the nineteenth century was that of the Zulu in southeastern Africa. Militarily powerful under the early kings, Shaka and Dingane, and capable of inflicting on the British their greatest defeat in a nineteenth century colonial war (Isandhlwana in 1879), the Zulu state remained potentially the most formidable challenge to British might, even after the defeat of King Cetshwayo's forces in the aftermath of Isandhlwana. Natal officials, primarily Theophilus Shepstone, who was in charge of "native affairs" in the colony from 1845 until 1876, fashioned an administrative structure in the mid-1870s which they claimed reflected tradi-tional African practices—a strictly hierarchical system headed by an all powerful "Supreme Chief" supposedly modeled on Shaka (in colonial practice the lieutenant-governor would act as Shaka)—but improved upon because of the introduction of formal trials (though with no jury). The system would be regulated by European administrators of native law, since foreigners were deemed more knowledgeable about African practices than were Africans themselves. The 1877 Natal Native Administration Law, modeled on systems of indirect rule developed in India and itself a model for later systems of "indirect" rule elsewhere in Africa, was enacted into law by none other than Sir Garnet Wolseley, recently arrived in South Africa as lieutenant-governor of Natal from his tri-umphal campaign against the Asante.[1]

NATIVE ADMINISTRATION LAW, No. 26, December 17, 1875.

Law: To make better provision for the Ad-ministration of justice among the Native Population of Natal, and for the gradual as-similation of Native Law to the Laws of the Colony. . . .

2. It shall be lawful for the Lieu-tenant-Governor for the time being to ap-point persons of European descent, who shall be called Administrators of Native Law, as also [Africans as] Native Chiefs or other Native Officers, to preside and exercise au-thority over and to administer justice among Natives living under Native Law, within such districts as may be hereafter determined, and the Lieutenant-Governor shall have power summarily to remove such Native Chiefs or other Native Officers, so appointed, and to appoint others in their stead.

3. Every Administrator of Native Law, or Native Chief, or other Native Officer so ap-pointed, shall have power to try and decide all civil disputes between native and native in the tribe or community placed under his charge, and within such limits as may from time to time be prescribed by the Lieutenant-Governor, except upon such cases as are hereinafter excepted, or may from time to time be excepted in manner hereinafter provided: Provided, however, that in all cases decided by any Native Chief or other Native Officer, a new trial may be had in conformity with such rules, of procedure as may be framed under the provisions of the 10th Sec-tion of this Law, before the Administrator of Native Law appointed over the district in which such Native Chief or other Native Of-ficer resides, and that every such Native Chief or other Native Officer shall within ten days after the decision of any such civil case, com-municate to the Administrator of Native Law having jurisdiction, the names of the plaintiff and defendant, the cause of the action, the decision arrived at, and the grounds of such decision; and each such officer is hereby re-quired to record the same.

4. In all such civil cases there shall be an appeal to the Native High Court in this Law specified.

5. All matters and disputes in the nature of civil cases between Natives living under Native Law shall be tried under the provi-sions of this Law and not otherwise, and ac-cording to Native Laws, customs, and usages for the time being prevailing, so far as the same shall not be of a nature to work some manifest injustice, or be repugnant to the settled principles and policy of natural eq-uity; except that all civil cases arising out of transactions in trade, or out of the owner-ship of or succession to land, shall be adjudi-cated upon according to the principles laid down by the ordinary Colonial Law in such cases; Provided always, that in the district or districts referred to in the proviso to Sec-tion____, of this Law, all matters and things

---

1. G. W. Eybers, ed., *Select Constitutional Documents Illustrating South African History, 1795–1910* (New York: George Routledge and Sons, 1918), pp. 247–51, 254–55.

required to be done and observed by an Administrator of Native Law appointed under this Law, may, and shall be done and observed by an Administrator of Native Law appointed under Ordinance 3, 1849, until appointments under this Law shall have been made therein.

6. Subject to the exceptions in this Law specified, all crimes and offences committed by Natives shall be tried before the ordinary Courts of Law in this Colony in the same manner as if they had been committed by persons of European descent: Provided, however, that the following classes of crime shall be excepted:

(a) All crimes and offences of a political character, which shall be tried at the discretion of the Attorney-General, either before the Supreme Court of the Colony or the Native High Court: Provided that the Native High Court shall not have the power of passing sentence of capital punishment.

(b) All homicides, assaults, or other injury to the person or property of any Native caused by or arising out of riots by Natives or faction fights between Natives, or in which any tribe or section of a tribe or community of Natives may have taken part, and which in the judgment of the Attorney-General may be more conveniently tried according to the provisions of Native Law.

(c) All crimes or offences with respect to which it has been or may hereafter be enacted by any Law that they shall be tried by Native Law or before any special Court. And all crimes and offences so excepted, except those for the trial of which special provision has been made, shall be tried by the Native High Court in this Law specified: Provided, always, that it shall be lawful for the Native High Court to remit the trial of any such assault or injury aforesaid to one or more Administrators of Native Law, and such Administrators of Native Law may thereupon try the case subject to an appeal to the Native High Court, whose decision shall in such case be final.

7. There shall be constituted a Court, to be termed the Native High Court, and such High Court shall be presided over by a judge specially appointed by the Lieutenant-Governor, and such judge shall sit as sole judge, or may be assisted, as occasion may require, by Administrators of Native Law, or Native Chiefs, or other Native Officers, as assessors, in manner hereafter to be provided; and such Court shall hear and try all appeal cases from the Courts of the Administrators of Native Law, all civil cases that may be brought before it under the provisions of this Law, and all criminal cases, the trial of which is in this Law specially reserved to such High Court.

8. [Judge to hold office during good behaviour.]

9. All appeals from the Native High Court shall be to a Court of Appeal, which shall be held to be, and shall be a branch of the Supreme Court of the Colony, and shall consist of the Chief justice or one of the Puisne [other than the Chief Justice] judges of the said Supreme Court, the Secretary for Native Affairs for the time being, and the judge of the Native High Court established under this Law; and the Court so constituted shall hear and determine all appeals that shall be brought before it under provisions of this Law. . . .

[Addendum, 1887]
THE SUPREME CHIEF

32. The Supreme Chief for the time being exercises in and over all Natives in the Colony of Natal all political power and authority, subject to the provisions of Section 7 of Law 44 of 1887.

33. The Supreme Chief appoints all Chiefs to preside over tribes, or sections of tribes; and also divides existing tribes into two or more parts, or amalgamates tribes or parts of tribes into one tribe, as necessity or the good government of the Natives may, in his opinion, require.

34. The Supreme Chief in Council may remove any Chief found guilty of any political offence, or for incompetency or other just cause, from his position as such Chief, and may also order his removal with his family and property, to another part of the Colony.

35. The Supreme Chief has absolute power to call upon Chiefs, District Headmen,

and all other Natives, to supply armed men or levies for the defence of the Colony, and for the suppression of disorder and rebellion within its borders, and may call upon such chiefs, District Headmen, and all other Natives to personally render such military and other service.

36. The Supreme Chief has power to call upon all Natives to supply labour for public works, or for the general needs of the colony. This call or command may be transmitted by any person authorised so to do, and each native so called upon is bound to obey such call, and render such service in person, unless lawfully released from such duty.

37. The Supreme Chief, acting in conjunction with the Natal Native Trust, may, when deemed expedient in the general public good, remove any tribe or tribes, or portion thereof, or any native, from any part of the Colony or Location, to any other part of the Colony or Location, upon such terms and conditions and arrangements as he may determine.

38. The orders and directions of the Supreme Chief, or of the Supreme Chief in Council, may be carried into execution by the Secretary for Native Affairs, or by the Administrators of Native Law, or by other officers authorised for the purpose, and in respect of all such acts the various officers so employed shall be regarded as the deputies or representatives of the Supreme Chief, or of the Supreme Chief in Council, as the case may be.

39. The Supreme Chief, in the exercise of the political powers which attach to his office, has authority to punish by fine or imprisonment, or by both, for disobedience of his orders or for disregard of his authority.

40. The Supreme Chief is not subject to the Supreme Court, or to any other court of Law in the Colony of Natal, for, or by reason of, any order or proclamation, or of any other act or matter whatsoever, committed, ordered, permitted, or done either personally or in council.

41. The Supreme Chief is, by virtue of his office, Upper Guardian of all orphans and minors in law.

42. The Supreme Chief has power to regulate and fix from time to time the least number of houses which shall compose a kraal. He may, in his discretion, permit of exceptions to any such general rule in special cases.

2. Africa for the African.

Christianity appealed to many Africans, but often in ways not intended by the European missionaries. It offered a body of thought and attendant language to criticize the ways in which colonialism was imposed and practiced. There was no basis in the Bible for the exclusion of Africans from the higher reaches of church and state as was practiced without exception throughout colonial Africa. There was no basis in the Christian message for the harsh treatment of African workers in the Belgian Congo rubber industry, the South African gold mines, or the tea and coffee plantations of East Africa. Indeed, African converts to Christianity became some of the most powerful critics of colonial hypocrisy.

One of the most notable of these critics was John Chilembwe, born around 1871 in present-day Malawi, the son of a Yao slave trader and a woman initially captured for trade. Chilembwe grew up to become the first convert of Joseph Booth, an Englishman who had become a born-again Christian while living in New Zealand and who then traveled as a missionary to Central Africa, following consciously in the footsteps of David Livingstone. Under the sponsorship of Booth, Chilembwe traveled to the United States in 1898 and studied at the Virginia Theological Seminary and College in Lynchburg, an institution established in 1890 "to prepare Christian preachers, teachers and workers for work among Negroes." After two years of study, Chilembwe returned to Nyasaland (as Malawi was then called) as a Baptist missionary and worked together with African American missionaries to establish an industrial school at which Africans could learn practical skills. Over time he became a strong critic of the ways in which Europeans treated Africans, particularly of the ways in which African land was forcibly taken and African workers cruelly treated. Chilembwe aimed his criticism especially at the Bruce Estates, a large cotton and coffee plantation owned by a family that had, with George Mackinnon, founded the British East Africa Company, and that was managed by a distant relative of David Livingstone.

In 1915, John Chilembwe, using biblical texts (Acts XX, 29–32) to justify forceful action, led an armed uprising against British colonial rule, ordering the beheading of Livingstone's relative and torching European-run mission stations. British retribution was harsh. Chilembwe was hunted down and killed; his body was buried in secret so that a grave would not provide a symbol for further resistance. While overall casualties were small compared with those of the Maji Maji uprising, Chilembwe too, despite British attempts at cover-up, served as a powerful symbol to later proponents of African independence.

The African Christian Union, first established in 1896 in Natal by Booth, was extended to Nyasaland by Chilembwe working with his mentor in 1897. The aim of the mission was to raise funds from local people in order to establish an industrial mission for Africans independent of the organizations run by European mission societies.[2]

African Christian Union Schedule, January 14, 1897.

Objects of the Society:

1. To unite together in the name of Jesus Christ such persons as desire to see full justice done to the African race and are resolved to work towards and pray for the day when the African people shall become an African Christian Nation.

2. To provide capital to equip and develop Industrial Mission Stations worked by competent Native Christians or others of the African race; such stations to be placed on a self-supporting and self-propagating basis.

3. To steadfastly demand by Christian and lawful methods the equal recognition of the African and those having blood relationship, to the rights and privileges accorded to Europeans.

4. To call upon every man, woman and child of the African race, as far as may be practicable, to take part in the redemption of Africa during this generation, by gift, loan, or personal service.

5. To specially call upon the Afro-American Christians, and those of the West Indies to join hearts and hands in the work either by coming in person to take an active part or by generous, systematic contributions.

6. To solicit funds in Great Britain, America and Australia for the purpose of restoring at their own wish carefully selected Christian Negro families, or adults of either sex, back to their fatherland in pursuance of the objects of the Union; and to organize an adequate propaganda to compass the work.

---

2. George Shepperson and Thomas Price, *Independent African: John Chilembwe and the Origins, Setting and Significance of the Nyasaland Native Rising of 1915* (Edinburgh: Edinburgh University Press, 1958; first paperback ed. 1987), pp. 541–43. Reprinted with the permission of George Shepperson.

7. To apply such funds in equal parts to the founding of Industrial Mission centres and to the establishing of Christian Negro settlements. . . .

9. [Misnumered in the original] To firmly, judiciously and repeatedly place on record by voice and pen for the information of the un-informed, the great wrongs inflicted upon the African race in the past and in the present, and to urge upon those who wish to be clear of African blood in the day of God's judge-ments, to make restitution for the wrongs of the past and to withstand the appropriation of the African's land in the present.

10. To initiate or develop the culture of Tea, Coffee, Cocoa, Sugar, etc. etc., and to establish profitable mining or other industries or manufactures.

11. To establish such transport agencies by land, river, lakes or ocean as shall give the African free access to the different parts of his great country and people, and to the gen-eral commerce of the world.

12. To engage qualified persons to train and teach African learners any department of Commercial, Engineering, nautical, pro-fessional or other necessary knowledge.

13. To mould and guide the labor of Africa's millions into channels that shall de-velop the vast God-given wealth of Africa for the uplifting and commonwealth of the people, rather than for the aggrandisement of a few already rich persons.

14. To promote the formation of Compa-nies on a Christian basis devoted to special aspects of the work; whose liability shall be limited, whose shares shall not be transfer-able without the society's consent; whose shareholders shall receive a moderate rate of interest only; whose profits shall permanently become the property of the Trustees of the African Christian Union, for the prosecution of the defined objects of the Union.

15. To petition the government of the United States of America to make a substan-tial monetary grant to each adult Afro-American desiring to be restored to African soil, as some recognition of the 250 years of unpaid slave labor and the violent abduction of millions of Africans from their native land.

16. To petition the British and other Eu-ropean governments holding or claiming Af-rican territory to generously restore the same to the African people or at least to make ad-equate inalienable native reserve lands, such reserves to be convenient to the locality of the different tribes.

17. To petition the British and other Eu-ropean governments occupying portions of Africa to make substantial and free grants of land to expatriated Africans or their descen-dents desiring restoration to their fatherland, such grants to be made inalienable from the African race.

18. To provide for all representatives, of-ficials or agents of the Union and its auxilia-ries, inclusive of the Companies it may promote modest, economical yet efficient and as far as may be, equable, maintenance, to-gether with due provision for periods of sick-ness, incapacity, widowhood or orphanage.

19. To print and publish literature in the interests of the African race and to furnish periodical accounts of the transactions of the Society and its auxiliary agencies, the same to be certified by recognized auditors and to be open to the fullest scrutiny of the Union's supporters.

20. To vest all funds, properties, products or other sources of income in the hands of Trustees, not less than seven in number, to be held in perpetuity in the distinct interest of the African race and for the accomplish-ment of the objects herein set forth in 21 clauses.

21. Finally, to pursue steadily and unswervingly the policy:

"AFRICA FOR THE AFRICAN"

and look for and hasten by prayer and united effort the forming of a united

AFRICAN CHRISTIAN NATION

By God's power and blessing and in His own time and way.

[Signed]

JOSEPH BOOTH, English missionary.

JOHN CHILEMBWE, Ajawa Christian Native.

ALEXANDER DICKIE, English missionary.

MORRISON MALINKA, Native Christian Chipeta Tribe.

Dated January 14th, 1897 at Blantyre, Nyassaland, East Central Africa.

3. Evidence of colonial atrocities in the Belgian Congo.

While conditions for African workers in South Africa and elsewhere in Africa were always harsh, seldom did they reach the horrendous conditions found in King Leopold's Congo. Indeed, the Belgian king's private preserve served as something of a welcome change of focus for other European colonizers, who could condemn Leopold's practices while deflecting attention from, for example, the appalling death rates in South African mines or the brutal treatment meted out to plantation workers in German East Africa. In 1903, Roger Casement, working on behalf of the British government, wrote a powerful exposé of the conditions that African rubber collectors had to endure. His descriptions (and accompanying photographs) of the mutilations inflicted by Leopold's employees on Africans to make them produce more rubber shocked the world and forced the king to hand control of his colony over to the Belgian government (which, however, continued to use forced labor). In an ironic postscript to the affair, Casement himself became a victim of imperialism. A fervent supporter of Irish nationalism, he was hanged by the British on August 3, 1916, for having negotiated with Germany for support for an armed uprising in Ireland.[3]

Casement's report on the Congo submitted to the Marquess of Lansdowne, December 11, 1903, noted on refugee tribes encountered.

The town of N * consists approximately of seventy-one K * houses and seventy-three occupied by L *. These latter seemed industrious, simple folk, many weaving palm fibre into mats or native cloth; others had smithies, working brass wire into bracelets, chains and anklets; some iron-workers making knives. Sitting down in one of these blacksmith's sheds, the five men at work ceased and came over to talk to us. I counted ten women, six grown-up men and eight lads and women in this one shed of L *. I then asked them to tell me why they had left their homes. Three of the men sat down in front of me, and told a tale which I cannot think can be true, but it seemed to come straight from their hearts. I repeatedly asked certain parts to be gone over again while I wrote in my note-book. The fact of my writing down and asking for names, etc., seemed to impress them, and they spoke with what certainly impressed me as being great sincerity.

I asked, first, why they had left their homes, and had come to live in a strange, far-off country among the K * where they owned nothing, and were little better than servitors. All, when this question was put, women as well, shouted out: "On account of the rubber tax levied by the Government posts."

3. *Correspondence and Report from His Majesty's Consul at Boma Respecting the Administration of the Independent State of the Congo*, Cd 1933 [Command Paper No. 1933] (London: Harrison and Sons, 1904), pp. 60–61.

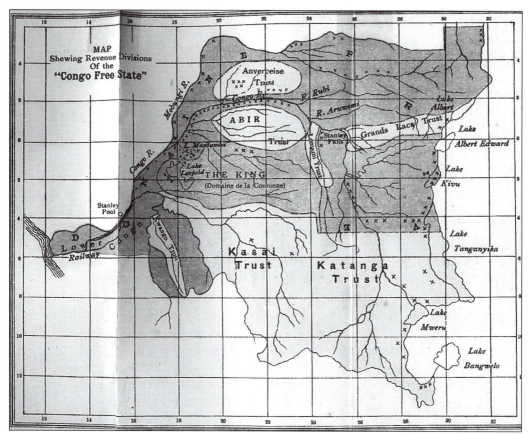

Revenue divisions of the Congo Free State, 1906. *Source:* E.D. Morel, *Red Rubber: The Story of the Rubber Slave Trade which flourished on the Congo for Twenty Years, 1890-1910*, new and revised edition (Manchester: The National Labour Press, 1920), facing p. 119.

. . . I asked, then, how this tax was imposed. One of them, who had been hammering out an iron collar on my arrival, spoke first. He said:—

"I am N.N. These two beside me are O.O. and P.P. all of us Y**. From our country each village had to take twenty loads of rubber. These loads were big; they were as big as this. . . ." (Producing an empty basket which came nearly up to the handle of my walking stick). "That was the first size. We had to fill that up, but as rubber got scarcer the white man reduced the amount. We had to take these loads in four times a month."

Q.: "How much pay do you get for this?"

A.: (entire audience): "We got no pay. We got nothing."

And then N.N., whom I asked again, said:—

"Our village got cloth and a little salt but not the people who did the work. Our Chiefs eat up the cloth; the workers got nothing. The pay was a fathom of cloth and a little salt for every basket full, but it was given to the Chief, never to the men. It used to take ten days to get the twenty baskets of rubber—we were always in the forest and then when we were late we were killed. We had to go further and further into the forest to find the rubber vines, to go without food, and our women had to give up cultivating the fields and gardens. Then we starved. Wild beasts—the leopards—killed some of us when we were working away in the forest, and others got lost or died from exposure and starvation and we begged the white man to leave us alone, saying we could get no more rubber, but the white men and their soldiers said: 'Go! You are only beasts yourselves, you are nyama (meat).' We tried, always going further into the forest, and when we failed and our rubber was short, the soldiers came to our towns and killed us. Many were shot, some had their ears cut off; others were tied up with ropes around their necks and bodies and taken away. The white men sometimes at the posts did not know of the bad things the soldiers did to us, but it was the white men who sent the soldiers to punish us for not bringing in enough rubber."

Here PP. took up the story from N.N.:—

"We said to the white man: 'We are not enough people now to do what you want us. Our country has not many people in it and we are dying fast. We are killed by the work you make us do, by the stoppage of our plantations, and the breaking up of our homes.' The white man looked at us and said: 'There are lots of people in Mputu' (Europe, the white man's country). 'If there are lots of people in the white man's country there must be many people in the black man's country.' The white man who said this was the chief white man at F.F *, his name was A.B., he was a very bad man. Other white men of Bula Matadi who had been bad and wicked were B.C., C.D., and D.E. These had killed us often, and killed us by their own hands as well as by their soldiers. Some white men were good. . . .

"These ones told them to stay in their homes, and did not hunt and chase them as the others had done, but after what they had suffered they did not trust more any one's word and they had fled from their country and were now going to stay here, far from their homes, in this country where there was no rubber."

Q.: "How long is it since you left your homes, since the big trouble you speak of?"

A.: "It lasted for three full seasons, and it is now four seasons since we fled and came into the K* country."

Q.: "How many days is it from N* to your own country?"

A.: "Six days of quick marching. We fled because we could not endure the things done to us. Our Chiefs were hanged and we were killed and starved and worked beyond endurance to get rubber."

Q.: "How do you know it was the white men themselves who ordered these cruel things to be done to you? These things must have been done without the white men's knowledge by the black soldiers."

A. (P.P.): "The white men told their soldiers: 'You kill only women; you cannot kill men. You must prove that you kill men.' So then the soldiers when they killed us" (here he stopped and hesitated, and then pointing to the private parts of my bulldog—it was lying asleep at my feet) he said: "then they cut off those things and took them to the white men, who said: 'It is true, you have killed men.'"

Q.: "You mean to tell me that any white man ordered your bodies to be mutilated like that and those parts of you carried to him?"

P.P., O.O., and all (shouting): "Yes! many white man. D.E. did it."

Q. "You say this is true? Were many of you so treated after being shot?"

All (shouting out): "Nkoto! Nkoto!" (Very many! Very many!)

There was no doubt. Their vehemence, their flashing eyes, their excitement was not simulated. Doubtless they exaggerated the numbers, but they were clearly telling me what they knew and loathed.

4. Frederick Lugard instructs his officials on how to implement indirect rule.

The most famous theoretician of British colonial rule was Frederick Lugard, the same man who had been so enthusiastic about commercial empire in East Africa and who went on to govern Britain's largest possession by far in West Africa, Nigeria, for most of the first three decades of the twentieth century. Lugard's name has become synonymous with the theory of indirect rule, the process by which a very few Europeans would supposedly use indigenous insti-

tutions and practices to rule vast numbers of Africans. Over time, the memoranda that Lugard wrote to his officers regarding their duties became a sort of "bible" of colonial practice. As the following extracts demonstrate, there are clear links to the ideas developed by Shepstone and implemented by Wolseley decades earlier in Natal. As with their system, also, though rule is meant to be "indirect," the governor is always given the powers of an autocrat, and in the final analysis, colonial control rests on a readiness to use armed force to crush all opposition.[4]

Memo. No. 1. Duties of Political Officers.

. . . 3. The British role here [Nigeria] is to bring to the country all the gains of civilisation by applied science (whether in the development of material resources, or the eradication of disease, &c.), with as little interference as possible with Native customs and modes of thought. Where new ideas are to be presented to the native mind, patient explanation of the objects in view will be well rewarded, and new methods may often be clothed in a familiar garb. Thus the object of Vaccination and its practical results may be sufficiently obvious, while the prejudice which exists among some Moslems may perhaps be removed by pointing out that it is a preventive of disease by contagion, no less than the circumcision enforced by their own law.

4. The term "Resident" implies duties rather of a Political or advisory nature, while the term "Commissioner" connotes names of ranks, functions of a more directly Administrative character. The former is therefore applicable to the Chief Government Officer in a Province of which large areas are under the immediate rule of a Paramount Chief, who, with Native Officials, himself administers a form of Government. The latter is more adapted to Provinces, or parts of Provinces, less advanced in civilisation, where the authority of the Native Chiefs is small, and a large measure of direct Administration must devolve upon the Protectorate Government. . . .

5. It is the duty of Residents to carry out loyally the policy of the Governor, and not to inaugurate policies of their own. The Governor, through the Lieutenant-Governor, is at all times ready and anxious to hear, and to give full and careful consideration to the views of Residents, but, when once a decision has been arrived at, he expects Residents to give effect to it in a thorough and loyal spirit, and to inculcate the same spirit in their juniors. This does not mean a rigid adherence to the letter of a ruling. Among such diverse races in widely varying degrees of advancement, it is inevitable and desirable that there should be diversity in the application of a general policy by the Resident, who knows the local conditions and feelings of his people. It does mean, however, that the principles underlying the policy are to be observed and the Resident in modifying their application will fully inform and obtain the approval of the Governor.

As I have said . . . we are all working not only with a common object but as parts of one organisation. The Government relies on its Administrative Officers to keep in close touch with Native opinion and feeling and to report for the information of the Governor. It is thus only that we can produce the best results, that the Governor and Lieutenant-Governors can keep in touch and gain information, and the Political Officer can count on support and on recognition of his work.

6. The degree to which a Political Officer may be called upon to act in an administrative capacity, will thus depend upon the influence and ability of the Native Chiefs in each part of the Province, though in every case he will endeavour to rule through the Native Chiefs.

---

4. Frederick Lugard, *Political Memoranda: Revision of Instructions to Political Officers on Subjects Chiefly Political and Administrative, 1913–1918,* 2nd edition (London: Waterlow and Sons, 1919), pp. 9–11, 166–67, 223–26, 254–56.

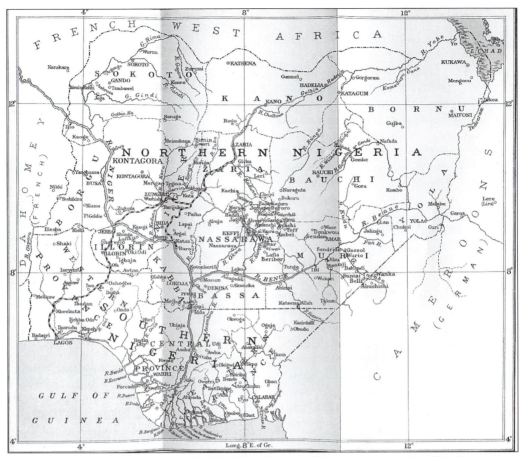

Nigeria, 1912. *Source:* A.J.N. Tremearne, *The Tailed Head-Hunters of Nigeria: An Account of an Official's Seven Years' Experiences in the Northern Nigerian Pagan Belt* . . . (London: Seeley, Service & Co. Limited, 1912), facing p. 336.

In those parts of Provinces which are under the immediate authority of a Chief of the first or of the second grade, the primary duty and object of a Political Officer will be to educate them in the duties of Rulers according to a civilised standard; to convince them that oppression of the people is not sound policy, or to the eventual benefit of the rulers; to bring home to their intelligence, as far as may be, the evils attendant on a system which holds the lower classes in a state of slavery or serfdom, and so destroys individual responsibility, ambition, and development amongst them; to impress upon them the advantage of delegating the control of districts to subordinate Chiefs, and of trusting and encouraging these subordinates, while keeping a strict supervision over them; to see that there is no favouritism in such appointments; and to inculcate the unspeakable benefit of justice, free from bribery and open to all. . . .

In districts where there is no Chief of the first or second grade, a Political Officer's functions become more largely Administrative, and among uncivilised Pagan tribes he must assume the full onus of Administration, to the extent to which time and opportunity permit. In such communities he will constantly endeavour to support the authority of the Chief, and encourage him to show initiative. If there is no Chief who exercises authority beyond his own village, he will encourage any village Chief of influence and character to control a group of villages, with a view to making him Chief of a district later if he shows ability for the charge. Native Court clerks or scribes, constables or couriers will never be allowed to usurp the authority of the Native Chief or Village Head….

Memo. No. 5. Taxation.

. . . 4. "Experience (I wrote) seems to point to the conclusion that in a country so fertile as this, direct taxation is a moral benefit to the people by stimulating industry and production. Hitherto the male population has been largely engaged in tribal war, and the men have depended on the labour of their women and the great fertility of the soil to supply their needs in food. Where taxes were formerly paid and have lapsed, it is stated that large areas have gone out of cultivation and the male population, deprived of the necessity for producing a surplus to pay their taxes, and of the pastime of war, have become indolent and addicted to drinking and quarrelling"....

5. [Direct taxation] . . . imposes on the freed slave, on the one hand, the obligation to render to the State, to which he owes his liberty, some portion, however small, of the labour or its equivalent which was formerly the sole property of his master, while the latter, deprived of the forced labour of his slaves, is compelled to lead a more useful life, either by personal effort, or by taking an active part in the labours of administration in return for a salary provided by means of taxation....

6. There is no civilised State in the world where direct taxation has not been found to be a necessity, and African communities which aspire to be regarded as civilised must share the common burden of civilisation....

7. Apart from the beneficial results of taxation described in the foregoing paragraphs . . . the immediate object of direct taxation is to provide a revenue....

Memo. No. 6. Slavery (Forced Labour, etc.).

. . . 11. Since slavery . . . stands condemned, why, it may be asked, was it not at once summarily abolished? If, however, slaves had been encouraged to assert their freedom unnecessarily in large numbers, or if those so asserting it, by leaving their masters without some good cause, had been indiscriminately upheld in their action by Political Officers, a state of anarchy and chaos would have resulted, and the whole social system of the Mohammedan States would, as I have said, have been dislocated. It might even have become necessary to legalise the institution under some other name, as was in effect done by the House Rule Proclamation in Southern Nigeria. . . .

Such a sudden repudiation of their obligations to their employers by the mass of the slave population would, moreover, have involved equal misery to the slaves and to their masters. The former would have had no immediate means of livelihood, while the latter would have been reduced to beggary, and to detestation of British rule which had brought this result about. The great cities would have been filled with vagrants, criminals, and prostitutes; indeed in the early days of British Administration the large majority of the criminal class consisted of runaway slaves.

Moreover, to abolish prematurely the almost universal form of labour contract, before a better system had been developed to take its place, would not only have been an act of administrative folly, but would have been an injustice to the masters, since domestic slavery is an institution sanctioned by the law of Islam, and property in slaves was as real as any other form of property among the Mohammedan population at the time that the British assumed the Government, a nullification of which would have amounted to nothing less than wholesale confiscation. This is equally true of either household or farm slaves, and it was very important that the latter should not leave their accustomed employment as agriculturists, and flock into the cities as "free" vagrants without means of subsistence. Residents were therefore instructed to discourage wholesale assertion of freedom, and where similar circumstances still exist the same course will be pursued. . . .

13. The introduction of a coin currency, and the enormous quantity put into circulation by the development of mining and trade, has greatly facilitated the employment of paid labour. Even the Native employer can now pay for his labour in cash. Payment in kind is always to be deprecated and discouraged for the employee so paid is unable to save his wages to purchase when and what he likes,

and is dependent on instalments as they become available at arbitrary rates. The conditions in fact approximate to the slavery system, and free labour will not readily engage except for a money wage.

But above all the Government rule that each labourer must be paid up fully in cash, at short intervals, and without the intermediary of any middleman or Chief, has done more than anything else to popularise the system of paid labour, and to create a free labour market....

15. These results, so far as they have been achieved, have only been won at the cost of unwearied patience and sympathetic counsel on the part of the Political Staff—and the task is by no means ended. It is still as necessary as ever, not merely to warn the ruling classes that slavery must eventually cease under British rule, but to explain to them the *practical* advantages of free labour.

One advantage to the master is that he is no longer responsible for the faults committed by his slave, or for his maintenance and that of his family in case of sickness. The labourer can no longer claim a share of the produce of the land, and is entitled to his day's wage and no more. Even the right of the freeman to terminate his contract when he pleases, on giving the agreed notice, produces no more inconvenience than the claim of the slave to run away, now that the master is unable to force him to return.

Another practical advantage of free labour to the master lies in the fact that, whereas the British Courts lend him no assistance in compelling his slave to do his proper day's work, or in punishing him if he runs away—while the legitimate assistance of the Native Courts is also strictly limited—he can, if he employs free labour, obtain the full assistance of the Administration in enforcing the contract, and punishing its breach, and it should be explained to him how he should enter into a contract enforceable at law. That slave owners were quick to recognise the advantage of free labour was shown by the voluntary emancipation of a large number of his slaves by the Sarkin Kwotto. . . .

Memo. No. 7. The Use of Armed Force.

. . . 12. When nearing the village where opposition is expected, the Political Officer will (if he can do so without too great risk to the envoy) send a message ahead, informing the people in unmistakable terms of the object of his visit, and what it is that they are required to do or to refrain from doing, and which has given rise to the advent of all armed force. . . .

If the terms are accepted, he will proceed with the troops to the village and meet the Chiefs there, subsequently withdrawing and awaiting the fulfillment of the pledges to the limit of the time allowed. He will meantime use every effort to get in touch with the Chiefs and people, and reassure them that no hostilities, will take place if the demands are met.

13. If, however, the message is ignored, or the attempt to get into communication has failed, and it is obvious that preparations are being made for resistance, the Civil Officer, after allowing time for the non-combatants to escape, will request the Officer Commanding the Patrol to advance and occupy the village.

Fire will not be opened until the party has been actually fired upon, or is beyond all possibility of doubt about to be attacked in force. Even then, the object will be to occupy the village—which will usually be found to have been deserted with the infliction only of such loss on the opponents as is necessary for the purpose, and fire discipline will be strictly maintained.

14. If the advance has been resisted, sufficient livestock and food will, if possible, be collected in and around the village to pay the fine demanded, and the Political Officer will again endeavour to get into communication with the Chiefs by means of any prisoner captured. He will repeat his ultimatum, and summon the Chiefs and Elders under a promise that their lives will be safe, and that they will not be carried off as prisoners, but will inform them that failure to obey the summons will result in the burning of the principal huts and of the seizure of food supplies for the troops. The Patrol will pay for its supplies

unless it has been wantonly attacked, but will *insist* on having them, and take them by force if necessary.

15. If this second summons is ineffectual, he will proceed to destroy the houses of the Chiefs and those of the persons or faction known to be implicated in the original outrages (if any) and of the ringleaders in the disturbance. If in spite of this resistance is maintained, he will request the Officer Commanding the Patrol to proceed to break down the opposition, and if this is of a determined character it will be necessary to inflict a severe blow, and thoroughly disperse the opponents. The party will remain in possession of the village, the Patrol being fed from local supplies, but no looting will ever be allowed.

This, in most cases, will have the desired effect, and the Chiefs will come in and comply with the demands. If, however, the people prefer to carry on active hostilities, the Officer Commanding the Patrol will search the surrounding bush and attack and destroy the "war-camps." Before leaving the place, sufficient livestock and food will, if possible, be collected to liquidate an increased fine. This, however, is rarely feasible, for such determined resistance will only be offered by a tribe which has been guilty of repeated crimes, and which has made every preparation for a fight by removing their belongings. In such a case it may be necessary before leaving to burn the entire village and destroy the crops. . . .

17. Experience has shown that where resistance is obstinate the only way to avoid the perpetration of crimes and recurrent expeditions, is to inflict sufficiently deterrent punishment. Uncivilised man regrettably only recognises force, and measures its potency by his own losses.

5. The French practice direct rule to enforce submission.

In apparent contrast to the British, the French believed in the direct administration of their colonial possessions: that is, ruling without the use of indigenous intermediaries other than the Africans who composed the bulk of their armies. This policy was clearly expressed by G. L. Angoulvant, governor of French West Africa, in a set of instructions that he wrote for civilian administrators in November 1906. Despite the stress on direct rule as distinct from indirect, many of Angoulvant's ideas about colonial rule would have found considerable support among his British contemporaries. Angoulvant argued that before the advent of European rule most Africans had lived in a perpetual state of subjugation and were largely unable (and incapable) of expressing their political views. For him, a necessary goal of colonial rule was to change completely the "Negro mentality." And a necessary start to such a revolutionary process would be the "suppression of all resistance," physical and mental, by Africans to their rulers.[5]

General instructions to civilian administrators, November 26, 1908.

One of the greatest difficulties we have encountered in establishing our influence lies in the natives' attitude of mind, or in short in the moral condition of the country. I do not refer to the northern regions, whose inhabitants have too many links with the Sudan not to share, from the mental and even intellectual point of view, in the relative but undeniable degree of civilisation of the sudanic

5. John D. Hargreaves, ed., *France and West Africa: An Anthology of Historical Documents* (London: Macmillan, 1969), pp. 200–06. Reprinted with the permission of Macmillan Publishers Ltd.

peoples. The peoples of these regions have been softened up by forced subjection to the yoke of black conquerors. They do not dispute our supremacy, which for them means an incomparable improvement in their moral and material condition.

Among the natives of the centre of the Colony and the lower Ivory Coast the previous state of anarchy, with the solid advantages it brought to savage peoples, is still all too persistent, and where it has ceased it has left deep traces; its gradual disappearance is causing too many regrets for there to be no after-effects. These are manifested by the survival of internal disputes, feuds and rivalries, which are too often translated into sudden attacks, fights between villages, or individual crimes. Order, which in this country should ideally develop through the sacrifices of particular liberties for the sake of the liberty of all, seems to the masses to mean painful, almost intolerable, interference with all their conscious aspirations. . . . The native is so incapable of reflection that he does not spontaneously compare the present with the past, does not consider that we have brought him peace, the right to circulate freely, to enrich himself by his labour and to enjoy its fruits. We are the masters, and so people whose power must be respected but whose actions, however full of justice and goodwill, arouse no affection.

To make ourselves understood we must totally change the Negro mentality. It is not those who lived through the periods of anarchy who will follow us, welcome us, and love us. If we had any illusions about this they would be destroyed by the way our favourites—those who have been able to serve us and earn our special interests—often hasten to profit from their position at the public expense. Let's face it; at present the native is still hostile to our institutions and indifferent to the efforts we are making to improve his miserable lot.

This is a sad conclusion but we must recognise it; even if it does not modify our aims it should dictate our actions. For a long time yet our subjects must be led to progress despite themselves, as some children are edu-

cated despite their reluctance to work. We must play the role of strong, strict parents towards the natives, obtaining through authority what persuasion would not gain.

The most urgent task is to check every sign of insubordination or ill-will. . . .

I was quickly struck, when talking with administrators or reading their reports, by the false ideas which natives have about our occupation. In many parts of the Colony they regard it as temporary, and do not hesitate to say so. Again, when making contact with certain tribes I was greatly astonished by the lack of deference in their chief's attitude towards us, and by the independence of character which even led them to try to discuss with us the advisability of our best-justified measures.

Henceforth I wish there to be no hesitation about the political attitude to be adopted. Our line of conduct must be uniform throughout the Colony, even though, in its present immaturity, the Colony is in a state of continuous evolution and may present, within a single region, radically different situations requiring different forms of action in matters of detail. Even if the exact methods of action cannot be defined, since they must follow the development of the country and adapt themselves to circumstances, they must nevertheless share one invariable inspiration, one fixed principle, namely the principle of authority.

This principle is derived from the purposes we pursue—purposes which I have already clearly stated in special instructions addressed to certain administrators, and which may be defined as follows. To subdue all hostile elements; to win over the waverers; to encourage the masses, who can always be drawn to our side by self-interest until one day they are drawn there by sympathy; in short, to establish our authority beyond dispute; and finally to express these results in such tangible ways as the full collection of taxes, the rendering of assistance by the natives in the creation of public fixed capital, and economic and social progress. . . .

What I want us to avoid, in this country where minds have still to be conquered, is making a display of fruitless sentimentalism. We ought not to start off by seeming to set great value on the natives' wishes; the essential thing is to follow, without weakening, the only road capable of leading us to our goal. Make no mistake, these wishes of the natives are essentially unproductive, and hindrances to progress. To respect them would mean deferring indefinitely the establishment of order.

In a new country where the natives have hitherto been guided almost exclusively by instinct, order cannot be secured without provoking misunderstandings and clashes. These originate with the bad elements, that is to say with the tiny minority which unfortunately commonly has the gift of leading the masses astray. The masses are then the first to deplore the consequences of these errors, and to repudiate the real authors.

The native policy to be followed in this country must therefore be, literally, benevolent but firm; its firmness will be shown by the suppression of all resistance (which does not mean that we may depart for a moment from the humane principles by which our colonial policy is inspired). If it is important to avoid abuses and excesses by individuals, to aim always to appeal to the native's reason and to win his goodwill, to use patience, diplomacy and forbearance, it is as dangerous to show weakness as it is unwise. It is desirable to avoid the use of force, but if it is used against us we must not be afraid to use it in our turn; I am determined to teach the natives a very sharp lesson whenever, wearying of our gentleness, they think they can flout our authority.

Although our policy is a benevolent one, it does not follow that this should mean exaggerated condescension towards the native or excessive respect for the interests of a few privileged ones, mostly chiefs. These are usually unworthy of respect since they owe their prestige to excesses at the expense of the masses, of whom they all too often lead us to lose sight.

It is futile to suppose that at the present time native policy can be based solely upon reciprocal sympathies. To believe this is to risk placing blind trust in people who will abuse it. The administrator must never drop his vigilance; in fact he will do well to be mistrustful for the most trifling symptoms may conceal broad and deep movements.

In short, I cannot repeat too often that the first condition for achieving anything practical and useful in our Colony is to establish our authority on unshakeable foundations. If there is the slightest crack, all our work will be at risk; hence we must not tolerate even the slightest breach in security. In native countries events may have extraordinary reverberations and the slightest incident, especially if troublesome for us, is at once blown up and misrepresented. Administrators must thus keep an attentive watch, and even eavesdrop. Demonstrations of impatience or disrespect for our authority, or any deliberate lack of goodwill must be suppressed without delay. Populations must be kept in suspense, held on the right lines by repeated visits from those whose mission it is to command them. It is essential that bad characters, who are generally the only instigators of disorders, should be isolated and eliminated.

Now I have indicated the attitude to be adopted towards the populations [at large] I can raise the question of native administration. . . . We may consider our purpose as almost fulfilled when we can administer with the help of native elements, instead of finding them in our way. This result has been achieved in the Northern districts. We must now bring it about in the forest zone and in Baoulé. . . .

Not that I have the slightest notion of attempting here any experiment in indirect administration. Except in a few northern districts the Ivory Coast does not have, among its own natives, any subjects capable of even roughly discharging the role of native official, of holding even the slightest fragment of public authority. Long years will be needed before we can find individuals who are at once relatively well educated, energetic, active, honest, loyal, ready to face the dangers involved for a native in exercising of power in his own country, and sufficiently disinterested to serve us as administrative auxiliaries, even at the price of close and continuing control.

We must thus confine ourselves to practising direct administration, which is in any case the most moral system in Negro countries, for it involves far fewer of those excesses which are the undeniable consequence of any participation by natives in public affairs. . . .

Some will doubtless think that innovations of the sort which I have outlined and will enlarge on later would gravely jeopardise an existing social order for which they do not believe we can safely substitute an or—ganisation made out of nothing.

On the contrary, I believe that we are in this country precisely in order to change the social order of the people now submitted to our laws. What this social order amounts to, among the forest-dwellers and the Baoulé, is permanent and general anarchy, resulting

from the absence of any authority and obstructing the realisation of any useful reform. . . . It is our mission to bring civilisation, moral and social progress, economic prosperity. We shall never succeed in this if we think ourselves obliged to preserve a deplorable situation where the weight of the past prevents any reform; or if we do succeed it will be at a speed out of keeping with the importance of the sacrifices we have made and the interests which are involved.

In colonial politics nothing is more dangerous than a conservative policy. Why make firm resolutions if they are to weaken in face of a situation which it was their very purpose to bring to an end? Why make such efforts if we doom them to failure in advance, condemning them to remain platonic on the pretext of respecting the customs and instincts of the natives?

6. A German school examination for African children.

In the 1860s, Edward Blyden (see Part 2, document 23) proposed a new university for Africa with a curriculum based on the teaching of classical languages, literature, and history (he was referring to Greece and Rome), combined with study of the Arab world, as well as the history and culture of African societies. Although the imperialists of the late nineteenth century argued that one of their chief goals in extending direct rule over African peoples was to "civilize" them, the following school examination illustrates the limits of colonial education in practice.[6]

A school examination administered to 55 pupils at Catholic and Protestant mission stations in German Togo in November 1909.

Saturday, November 20, 1909.
10–10.30 A.M. *Calligraphy.* A passage was written on the blackboard and the pupils had to copy it.
10.30–11 A.M. *Spelling.* The chairman of the commission dictated a simple passage from a short story, with which none of them was acquainted.

11–12 A.M. *Geography.* The following questions had been set as a task:

(a) The large states of Europe and their capitals.

(b) What are the names of Germany's most important mountains?

(c) What are the names of the most important rivers in Germany and in what direction do they run?

The last question was intended to show whether the pupils could not only reproduce the names mechanically, but could also visualize a map.

---

6. Bruce Fetter, ed., *Colonial Rule in Africa: Readings from Primary Sources* (Madison: University of Wisconsin Press, 1979), pp. 128–29.

3–4.30 P.M. *An Essay*. The subject set was: "What good things have the Europeans brought us?"

5.30–6 P.M. *Reading*. In addition to passages known to the pupils, they had to read aloud an unfamiliar article from a little book, called "Drei Kaiserbuchlein," out of the bookshop of the North German Mission.

Monday, November 22, 1909.
7.30–9 A.M. *Oral Arithmetic*. The questions were asked by the teachers themselves.
10–11 A.M. *Written Arithmetic*. One question each was chosen from amongst those proposed by the school associations:

(1) Multiply 118.92 by 67¼ and then divide the number obtained by 3,964.

(2) In 1906 Togo exported copra worth 8,000 marks. In 1907 11,000 marks' worth.

What was the increase per cent on the export of 1907?

(3) A labourer drinks brandy worth 0.25 marks a day. (a) How much does he pay for the brandy in a year? (b) How many days must he work for the brandy, if he earns 2 marks a day? (c) How many kgs of pork could he have bought with this sum, if pork costs 65 pfennige a kg?

From 11–12 and from 3–6 in the afternoon, *useful knowledge, grammar* and *translation* were examined.

Tuesday, November 23, 1909.
7–8 A.M. *History*. The task set was: The reign of emperor William I and the wars he had waged. Name those men who had specially supported his government.

From 8–11.30 A.M. the examinations in translation were completed.

7. The Natives Land Act, South Africa, 1913.

After the formal establishment of the Union of South Africa in 1910, under a constitution which in practice guaranteed that whites would remain in control of the state, the new government led by Boers, but working in league with the English-speaking owners of the gold mining industry, implemented legislation to protect their respective economic interests. The Mines and Works Act of 1911 formally introduced a legal color bar into the mining industry, preventing Africans from having jobs beyond the level of manual laborer and thereby helping ensure that labor costs would remain low. The Natives Land Act of 1913, discussed in draft form for several years before its passage, was much more far-reaching. It would set up the mechanism to allocate land in South Africa on the basis of race. An official government body, known popularly as the Beaumont Commission, determined the exact proportions of this allocation. Eighty-three percent of the land in South Africa—the best land as well the most—went to 20 percent of the population (the whites); the balance went to the Africans, who comprised 80 percent of the country's population. Africans were prohibited from owning or acquiring land in areas designated for whites. Nor could they legally lease or farm as sharecroppers on white land. Their only occupation, at least as recognized by law, would be as laborers. The introduction of the legislation spurred the formation of the South African Native National Congress (SANNC), a body that aimed to represent the concerns of all Africans in South Africa. (See document 8.) In this selection, the leaders of the SANNC express their objections to the new legislation. [7]

7. Thomas Karis and Gwendolen M. Carter, *From Protest to Challenge: A Documentary History of African Politics in South Africa, 1882–1964* (Stanford: Hoover Institution Press, 1972), vol. 1, Sheridan Johns, ed., *Protest and Hope, 1882–1934*, pp. 86–88. Reprinted with the agreement of the Hoover Institution Press.

Resolution against the Natives Land Act 1913 and the report of the Natives Land (Beaumont) Commission, October 2, 1916.

Having heard the main features of the Report of the Natives Land Commission on the Natives Land Act of 1913, and having learnt its principal recommendations, this meeting of the South African Native National Congress held at Pietermaritzburg, Natal, this 2nd day of October 1916, resolves:

I.

THAT looking to the interests and welfare of the Bantu people within the Union, the Report of the Natives' Land Commission presented to Parliament is disappointing and unsatisfactory, and fails to carry out the alleged principle of territorial separation of the races on an equitable basis for the following reasons:

THAT it confirms all our previous apprehensions prior to the passing of the Act: That it offers no alternative for the restriction of the free right to acquire land or interest in land: It recommends no practical or equitable remedy for the removal of the manifold objectionable disabilities imposed on the Natives by the Natives Land Act.

THAT it has failed to fulfill the official promises made to the Natives and also to satisfy their anticipations that the Report of the Commission would provide more land sufficient for occupation for themselves and their stock.

WHEREAS the land now demarcated or recommended by the Commission is inadequate for permanent settlement or occupation in proportion to the needs of the present and future Native population: And Whereas the said land is, in most parts, unsuitable for human habitation as also for agricultural or

Delegation to Great Britain of leaders of the South African Native National Congress protesting the 1913 Natives Land Act. *Source:* ANC Web site, <www.anc.org.za/ancdocs/history/images/sannc.html>, accessed June 26, 2000.

pastoral requirements, seeing that it has been studiously selected on the barren, marshy and malarial districts more especially in the Provinces of the Transvaal and the Orange Free State:

AND WHEREAS according to the evidence given before the Commission there is conflict of opinion amongst the whites as to the approval or disapproval of the principle of the Natives Land Act—the majority of the whites in the Northern Provinces are opposed to the Natives having the right to purchase land or acquire any interest in land in their own names: Nor are they in favour of any large tracts of land being granted to Natives for occupation or settlement except in the unsuitable districts as aforesaid.

BY REASON of these facts the Report of the Commission as presented for consideration by Parliament cannot be acceptable as a basis for the alleged intended territorial separation of the races or as a fair application of the alleged principles of the Act, on just and equitable lines.

ON THE OTHER HAND, while the ostensible aim of the Natives Land Act is that of territorial separation of the races, the evidence in the Report of the Commission shows that the ulterior object of the Government as well as the real desire of the white population of the country is:

To deprive the Natives as a people of their freedom to acquire more land in their own right: To restrict or limit their right to bargain mutually on even terms for the occupation of or settlement on land: To reduce by gradual process and by artificial means the Bantu people as a race to a status of permanent labourers or subordinates for all purposes and for all times with little or no freedom to sell their labour by bargaining on even terms with employers in the open markets of labour either in the agricultural or industrial centres: To limit all opportunities for their economic improvement and independence: To lessen their chances as a people of competing freely and fairly in all commercial enterprises.

THEREFORE this Congress, representing all the tribes of the Bantu Races within the Union, earnestly prays that Parliament unhesitatingly reject the Report of the Natives Land Commission and instantly withdraw the Natives Land Act 1913 from operation as a statute.

II.

With regard to ZULULAND it can only be pointed out as an acknowledged historical fact that the parcelling out of this territory into private farms for whites by the successive Colonial Governments was a breach of the Royal proclamation especially making this territory of Zululand a permanent reserve for the original owners. Having regard to the breaches of the aforesaid Royal proclamations and apart from the Natives Land Act 1913, this Congress urges Parliament to take the bold step of restoring the status quo in Zululand by proclaiming it a territory and a permanent place for the original owners thus securing an act of justice where it is due.

III.

FINALLY, this Congress begs to point out that the great bulk of the Native population in South Africa has no protection or any privilege under the Constitution of the Union, no legal safeguard of their interest and vested rights as subjects of the British Empire, no channel for any other intervention on their behalf in the redress of their just grievances, no recognised means whereby they can effectively make their legitimate objections felt on any proposed legislation in the Union Parliament; and that as things stand the Executive for the time being in its own initiative and their interest and that of their supporters may (without any previous consultation with the Natives and their Chiefs) impose any law on the Native people without let or hinderance and regardless of the principles of that law and its effects on the people concerned. Guided by these facts and by the light of political experiences in the past we cannot accept the projected solution of the land question. We regard the Natives Land Act as one-sided and as inconsistent with the ideals of fair Government by reason of the disabilities it imposes on the Native people of the Union, while the Report of the Lands Commission is based on the objections of the European people only. Consequently, instead of establishing good relationship it is creating friction and racial antipathies between the blacks and the whites.

That the welfare of this country depends upon its economic development while this Act is calculated to retard the law of supply and demand. The Act as designed is wrong in principle as violating the laws of nature that every man is a free agent and has a right to live where he chooses according to his circumstances and his inclinations. Any system therefore of settlement on land to be lasting and beneficial without the least injury to any section of the community can only be on natural lines, and not by means of artificial legislation. Further that partial territorial separation of the races already obtains in every sphere of life in the urban and rural places: and therefore this cannot effectively be met by retaining the Natives Land Act on the statute Book. We submit there should be no interference with the existing conditions and vested rights of the Natives, and there should be no removal or ejectment of *them* from their ancestral lands or from lands they have occupied for generations past: but they should have unrestricted liberty in every Province to acquire land wherever and whenever opportunity permits.

For these and diverse reasons this Congress consisting of delegates representing the various Native tribes of South Africa in declaring its unshakable opposition to the Natives Land Act 1913 reiterated all its former resolutions with respect thereto and hereby further resolves to employ all means within its power to secure the repeal of this mischievous Act and the nonenforcement of the Commission's Report.

In spite of our previous promises to desist from agitation in connection with the Natives Land Act 1913, and recognising the Act is still in operation with detrimental effects to our people, the Executive Committee is instructed to immediately inaugurate a campaign for the collection of funds for the purposes of this resolution and to educate the Bantu people by directing their attention towards this iniquitous law.

That this resolution be sent to the Governor-General, the Missionary Societies and other interested bodies, and to the Anti-Slavery and Aborigines Protection Society. That the Chief Executive appoint a deputation of three to place this resolution before the Union Government at the earliest opportunity and also to lay same before the Union Parliament next session.

8. The ANC in South Africa.

While colonial administrators such as Lugard (see document 4) and Angoulvant (see document 5) argued for continuing European tutelage until such time— usually viewed as being several centuries in the future—as Africans would be capable of ruling themselves, many Africans pushed for a much more accelerated process of change. In South Africa, people distressed by the post-South African War failure of the British to oppose the racially discriminatory policies of local officials and settlers, established a number of political organizations, the most significant of which was the South African Native National Congress (SANNC), formed in 1912 and renamed the African National Congress (ANC) in 1923. The principal founder of this organization was Pixley Seme, who grew up on a U.S. mission station in Natal and, through the assistance of a Congregationalist missionary (S. Pixley), traveled to the United States to attend high school in Massachusetts. Seme went on to obtain a B.A. from Columbia University in 1906 and then, after moving to Britain, studied law at Oxford Uni-

versity and was admitted to the London bar in 1910. He then returned to South Africa to practice as an attorney.

The first president of the organization was John L. Dube, a Zulu educated by U.S. missionaries in the 1870s and 1880s, who in 1887 traveled to the United States where he enrolled at Oberlin College. In the late 1890s, Dube spent another three years in the United States, studying theology at a seminary in Brooklyn. On his return to South Africa, he established a vocational school based on the model of Booker T. Washington's Tuskegee Institute, and later helped launch Natal's first African newspaper.

Under the influence of Seme and Dube, the SANNC aimed to represent the concerns of all Africans in South Africa but did not call for an immediate end to British colonial rule. Its leaders praised the benefits of British civilization, while arguing that Africans should not be deprived of all the rights and privileges of citizenship simply because of their color. The organization's constitution, drawn up in 1919, stressed the importance of mutual understanding between civilized peoples.[8]

Objects of the South African Native National Congress.

1. To form a National Vigilant Association and a deliberative Assembly or Council, without legislative pretentions.

2. To unite, absorb, consolidate and preserve under its aegis existing political and educational Associations, Vigilance Committees and other public and private bodies whose aims are the promotion and safeguarding of the interests of the aboriginal races.

3. To be the medium of expression of representative opinion and to formulate a standard policy on Native Affairs for the benefit and guidance of the Union Government and Parliament.

4. To educate Parliament and Provincial Councils, Municipalities, other bodies and the public generally regarding the requirements and aspirations of the native people; and to enlist the sympathy and support of such European Societies, Leagues, or Unions as might be willing to espouse the cause of right and fair treatment of coloured races.

5. To educate Bantu people on their rights, duties and obligations to the state and to themselves individually and collectively; and

to promote mutual help, feeling of fellowship and a spirit of brotherhood among them.

6. To encourage mutual understanding and to bring together into common action as one political people all tribes and clans of various tribes or races and by means of combined effort and united political organisation to defend their freedom, rights and privileges.

7. To discourage and contend against racialism and tribal feuds or to secure the elimination of racialism and tribal feuds; jealousy and petty quarrels by economic combination, education, goodwill and by other means.

8. To recommend, propose and lay before the Government for consideration and adoption laws for the benefit and protection of the Native races. And also to watch Bills introduced in Parliament for proposed legislation as well as in other bodies for legislation affecting Natives and to draft and present amendments thereto.

9. To agitate and advocate by just means for the removal of the "Colour Bar" in political education and industrial fields and for equitable representation of Natives in Parliament or in those public bodies that are vested with legislative powers or in those charged with the duty of administering matters affecting the Coloured races.

---

8. ANC Web site, <www.anc.org.za/ancdocs/history/const/constitution_sannc.html>. Accessed June 1, 2000.

10. To promote and advocate the establishment in Parliament and other public bodies of representatives to be under the control of and for the purpose of the Association.

11. To record all grievances and wants of native peoples and to seek by constitutional means the redress thereof, and to obtain legal advice and assistance for members of the Association and its branches and to render financial [aid] where necessary with the objects hereof.

12. To encourage and promote union of Churches free from all sectarian and denominational anomalies.

13. To establish or assist the establishment of national Colleges or Public Institutions free from denominationalism or State control.

14. To originate and expound the right system of education in all schools and colleges and to advocate for its adoption by State and Churches and by all other independent bodies in respect thereto.

15. To encourage inculcation and practice of habits of industry, thrift and cleanliness among the people and propagate the gospel of the dignity of labour.

16. To acquire land by purchase, lease exchange, gift or otherwise for erection of halls and other public buildings for the use and purposes of the Association.

17. To sell, dispose, manage, develop, let and deal in any way with all or any part of the property of the Association.

18. To borrow or raise money by mortgage or charge of all or any part of the property of the Association; and also to grant loans on security of mortgages in the manner hereinafter provided.

19. To establish a National Fund for the purposes of the Association either by means of voluntary contributions, periodical subscriptions, levies, contributions, charges or other payments; and to hold and manage all funds raised for the objects of the Association.

20. To [do] all and everything directly or indirectly to maintain and uplift the standard of the race morally and spiritually, mentally and materially, socially and politically.

21. AND GENERALLY, to do all such things as are incidental or conducive to the attainment of the above objects or any of them.

9. W. E. B. Du Bois describes an Atlantic world bounded by racial exploitation.

As did the African American missionaries who joined people like John Chilembwe in working to ameliorate the worst excesses of European rule in Africa, other African American critics of colonialism called attention to the economic exploitation of black people on both sides of the Atlantic. Perhaps the most prominent of these individuals was W. E. B. Du Bois, the first African American to earn a Ph.D. in the United States (from Harvard University). His The Souls of Black Folk, *a powerful indictment of the discrimination faced by African Americans in the South, found sympathetic readers throughout the world. In* The Negro, *published during World War I, Du Bois tackled the history of Africans in Africa, using the same written sources as European historians of the continent but focusing critically on the economic exploitation and political repression that he considered integral features of colonialism. Du Bois argued that black people everywhere should join together to resist the oppression to which they were subjected solely on the basis of their race.[9]*

9. W. E. B. Du Bois, *The Negro* (New York: Henry Holt and Company, 1915), pp. 232–42.

It is impossible to separate the population of the world accurately by race, since there is no scientific criterion by which to divide races. If we divide the world, however, roughly into African Negroes and Negroids, European whites, and Asiatic and American brown and yellow peoples, we have approximately 150,000,000 Negroes, 500,000,000 whites, and 900,000,000 yellow and brown peoples. Of the 150,000,000 Negroes, 121,000,000 live in Africa, 27,000,000 in the new world, and 9,000,000 in Asia.

What is to be the future relation of the Negro race to the rest of the world? The visitor from Altruria might see here no peculiar problem. He would expect the Negro race to develop along the lines of other human races. In Africa his economic and political development would restore and eventually outrun the ancient glories of Egypt, Ethiopia, and Yoruba; overseas the West Indies would become a new and nobler Africa, built in the very pathway of the new highway of commerce between East and West—the real sea route to India; while in the United States a large part of its citizenship (showing for perhaps centuries their dark descent, but nevertheless equal sharers of and contributors to the civilization of the West) would be the descendants of the wretched victims of the seventeenth, eighteenth, and nineteenth century slave trade.

This natural assumption of a stranger finds, however, lodging in the minds of few present-day thinkers. On the contrary, such an outcome is usually dismissed summarily. Most persons have accepted that tacit but clear modern philosophy which assigns to the white race alone the hegemony of the world and assumes that other races, and particularly the Negro race, will either be content to serve the interests of the whites or die out before their all-conquering march. This philosophy is the child of the African slave trade and of the expansion of Europe during the nineteenth century.

The Negro slave trade was the first step in modern world commerce, followed by the modern theory of colonial expansion. Slaves as an article of commerce were shipped as long as the traffic paid. When the Americas had enough black laborers for their immediate demand, the moral action of the eighteenth century had a chance to make its faint voice heard.

The moral repugnance was powerfully reinforced by the revolt of the slaves in the West Indies and South America, and by the fact that North America early began to regard itself as the seat of advanced ideas in politics, religion, and humanity.

Finally European capital began to find better investments than slave shipping and flew to them. These better investments were the fruit of the new industrial revolution of the nineteenth century, with its factory system; they were also in part the result of the cheapened price of gold and silver, brought about by slavery and the slave trade to the new world. Commodities other than gold, and commodities capable of manufacture and exploitation in Europe out of materials furnishable by America, became enhanced in value; the bottom fell out of the commercial slave trade and its suppression became possible.

The middle of the nineteenth century saw the beginning of the rise of the modern working class. By means of political power the laborers slowly but surely began to demand a larger share in the profiting industry. In the United States their demand bade fair to be halted by the competition of slave labor. The labor vote, therefore, first confined slavery to limits in which it could not live, and when the slave power sought to exceed these territorial limits, it was suddenly and unintentionally abolished.

As the emancipation of millions of dark workers took place in the West Indies, North and South America, and parts of Africa at this time, it was natural to assume that the uplift of this working class lay along the same paths with that of European and American whites. This was the *first* suggested solution of the Negro problem. Consequently these Negroes received partial enfranchisement, the beginnings of education, and some of the elementary rights of wage earners and property holders, while the independence of Liberia and Hayti was recognized. However, long before they were strong enough to assert the rights thus granted or to gather intelligence enough for proper group leadership, the new colonialism of the later nineteenth and twentieth centuries began to dawn. The new colonial theory transferred the reign of commercial privilege and extraordinary profit from the exploitation of the European working class to the exploitation of backward races under the political domination of Europe. For the purpose of carrying out this idea the European and white American working class was practically invited to share in this new exploitation, and particularly were flattered by popular appeals to their inherent superiority to "Dagoes," "Chinks," "Japs," and "Niggers."

This tendency was strengthened by the fact that the new colonial expansion centered in Africa. Thus in 1875 something less than one-tenth of Africa was under nominal European control, but the Franco-Prussian War and the exploration of the Congo led to new and fateful things. Germany desired economic expansion and, being shut out from America by the Monroe Doctrine, turned to Africa. France, humiliated in war, dreamed of an African empire from the Atlantic to the Red Sea. Italy became ambitious for Tripoli and Abyssinia. Great Britain began to take new interest in her African realm, but found herself largely checkmated by the jealousy of all Europe. Portugal sought to make good her ancient claim to the larger part of the whole southern peninsula. It was Leopold of Belgium who started to make the exploration and civilization of Africa an international movement. This project failed, and the Congo Free State became in time simply a Belgian colony. While the project was under discussion, the international scramble for Africa began. As a result the Berlin Conference and subsequent wars and treaties gave Great Britain control of 2,101,411 square miles of African territory, in addition to Egypt and the Egyptian Sudan with 1,600,000 square miles. This includes South Africa, Bechuanaland and Rhodesia, East Africa, Uganda and Zanzibar, Nigeria, and British West Africa. The French hold 4,106,950 square miles, including nearly all North Africa (except Tripoli) west of the Niger valley and Libyan Desert, and touching the Atlantic at four points. To this is added the Island of Madagascar. The Germans have 910,150 square miles, principally in Southeast and Southwest Africa and the Kamerun. The Portuguese retain 787,500 square miles in Southeast and Southwest Africa. The Belgians have 900,000 square miles, while Liberia (43,000 square miles) and Abyssinia (350,000 square miles) are independent. The Italians have about 600,000 square miles and the Spanish less than 100,000 square miles.

This partition of Africa brought revision of the ideas of Negro uplift. Why was it necessary, the European investors argued, to push a continent of black workers along the paths of social uplift by education, tradesunionism, property holding, and the electoral franchise when the workers desired no change, and the rate of European profit would suffer?

There quickly arose then the *second* suggestion for settling the Negro problem. It called for the virtual enslavement of natives in certain industries, as rubber and ivory collecting in the Belgian Congo, cocoa raising in Portuguese Angola, and diamond mining in South Africa. This new slavery or "forced" labor was stoutly defended as a necessary foundation for implanting modern industry in a barbarous land; but its likeness to slavery was too clear and it has been modified, but not wholly abolished.

The *third* attempted solution of the Negro sought the result of the *second* by less direct methods. Negroes in Africa, the West Indies, and America were to be forced to work by land monopoly, taxation, and little or no education. In this way a docile industrial class working for low wages, and not intelligent enough to unite in labor unions, was to be developed. The peonage systems in parts of the United States and the labor systems of many of the African colonies of Great Britain and Germany illustrate this phase of solution. (Footnote text: The South African natives, in an appeal to the English Parliament, show in an astonishing way the confiscation of their land by the English. They say that in the Union of South Africa 1,250,000 whites own 264,000,000 acres of land, while the 4,500,000 natives have only 21,000,000 acres. On top of this the Union Parliament has passed a law making even the future purchase of land by Negroes illegal save in restricted areas!) It is also illustrated in many of the West Indian islands where we have a predominant Negro population, and this population freed from slavery and partially enfranchised. Land and capital, however, have for the most part been so managed and monopolized that the black peasantry have been reduced to straits to earn a living in one of the richest parts of the world. The problem is now going to be intensified when the world's commerce begins to sweep through the Panama Canal.

All these solutions and methods, however, run directly counter to modern philanthropy, and have to be carried on with a certain concealment and half-hypocrisy which is not only distasteful in itself, but always liable to be discovered and exposed by some liberal or religious movement of the masses of men and suddenly overthrown. These solutions are, therefore, gradually merging into a *fourth* solution, which is to-day very popular. This solution says: Negroes differ from whites in their inherent genius and stage of development. Their development must not, therefore, be sought along European lines, but along their own native lines. Consequently the effort is made to-day in British Nigeria, in the French Congo and Sudan, in Uganda and Rhodesia to leave so far as possible the outward structure of native life intact; the king or chief reigns, the popular assemblies meet and act, the native courts adjudicate, and native social and family life and religion prevail. All this, however, is subject to the veto and command of a European magistracy supported by a native army with European officers. The advantage of this method is that on its face it carries no clue to its real working. Indeed it can always point to certain undoubted advantages: the abolition of the slave trade, the suppression of war and feud, the encouragement of peaceful industry. On the other hand, back of practically all these experiments stands the economic motive—the determination to use the organization, the land, and the people, not for their own benefit, but for the benefit of white Europe. For this reason education is seldom encouraged, modern religious ideas are carefully limited, sound political development is sternly frowned upon, and industry is degraded and changed to the demands of European markets. The most ruthless class of white mercantile exploiters is allowed large liberty, if not a free hand, and protected by a concerted attempt to deify white men as such in the eyes of the native and in their own imagination. (Footnote text: The traveler Glave writes . . . "Formerly [in the Congo Free State] an ordinary white man was merely called 'bwana' or 'Mzunga'; now the merest insect of a pale face earns the title of 'bwana Mkubwa' [big master]")

White missionary societies are spending perhaps as much as five million dollars a year in Africa and accomplishing much good, but at the same time white merchants are sending at least twenty million dollars' worth of European liquor into Africa each year, and the debauchery of the almost unrestricted rum traffic goes far to neutralize missionary effort.

Under this last mentioned solution of the Negro problems we may put the attempts at the segregation of Negroes and mulattoes in the United States and to some extent in the West Indies. Ostensibly this is "separation" of the races in society, civil rights, etc. In practice it is the subordination of colored people of all grades under white tutelage, and their separation as far as possible from contact with civilization in dwelling place, in education, and in public life.

On the other hand the economic significance of the Negro to-day is tremendous. Black Africa to-day exports annually nearly two hundred million dollars' worth of goods, and its economic development has scarcely begun. The black West Indies export nearly one hundred million dollars' worth of goods; to this must be added the labor value of Negroes in South Africa, Egypt, the West Indies,

North, Central, and South America, where the result is blended in the common output of many races. The economic foundation of the Negro problem can easily be seen to be a matter of many hundreds of millions to-day, and ready to rise to the billions tomorrow.

Such figures and facts give some slight idea of the economic meaning of the Negro to-day as a worker and industrial factor. . . .

What do Negroes themselves think of these their problems and the attitude of the world toward them? First and most significant, they are thinking. There is as yet no great single centralizing of thought or unification of opinion, but there are centers which are growing larger and larger and touching edges. The most significant centers of this new thinking are, perhaps naturally, outside Africa and in America: in the United States and in the West Indies; this is followed by South Africa and West Africa and then, more vaguely, by South America, with faint beginnings in East Central Africa, Nigeria, and the Sudan.

The Pan-African movement when it comes will not, however, be merely a narrow racial propaganda. Already the more far-seeing Negroes sense the coming unities: a unity of the working classes everywhere, a unity of the colored races, a new unity of men. The proposed economic solution of the Negro problem in Africa and America has turned the thoughts of Negroes toward a realization of the fact that the modern white laborer of Europe and America has the key to the serfdom of black folk, in his support of militarism and colonial expansion. He is beginning to say to these workingmen that, so long as black laborers are slaves, white laborers cannot be free. Already there are signs in South Africa and the United States of the beginning of understanding between the two classes.

In a conscious sense of unity among colored races there is to-day only a growing interest. There is slowly arising not only a curiously strong brotherhood of Negro blood throughout the world, but the common cause of the darker races against the intolerable assumptions and insults of Europeans has already found expression. Most men in this world are colored. A belief in humanity means a belief in colored men. The future world will, in all reasonable probability, be what colored men make it. In order for this colored world to come into its heritage, must the earth again be drenched in the blood of fighting, snarling human beasts, or will Reason and Good Will prevail? That such may be true, the character of the Negro race is the best and greatest hope; for in its normal condition it is at once the strongest and gentlest of the races of men: "Semper novi quid ex Africa!"

10. An appeal for the equal treatment of Africans and people of African descent.

W. E. B. Du Bois, joined by other black leaders from the United States, the Caribbean, and Africa, attended the peace treaty negotiations held in Versailles in 1919 at the conclusion of World War I. None of the European powers present (including the United States) accepted the arguments of Du Bois and his colleagues that representatives of colonized people should participate officially in the negotiations, nor did they agree to turn over the former colonies of Germany to an international organization rather than dividing them up among the other colonial powers. Germany's colonial possessions were apportioned between Britain and France. Du Bois and his colleagues, however, passed a series of resolutions that likely influenced the newly formed League of Nations' decision to establish a Mandate Commission, an international body responsible for overseeing the treatment of the former colonial subjects of Germany. Their presence at the negotiations, and their unity on behalf of oppressed people of color on both sides of the Atlantic, also demonstrated the potential for a pan-African movement.[10]

Resolutions of the Pan African Congress, Paris, February 1919.

The resolutions of the Congress asked in part:

A. That the Allied and Associated Powers establish a code of law for the international protection of the natives of Africa, similar to the proposed international code for labor.

B. That the League of Nations establish a permanent Bureau charged with the special duty of overseeing the application of these laws to the political, social, and economic welfare of the natives.

C. The Negroes of the world demand that hereafter the natives of Africa and the peoples of African descent be governed according to the following principles;

1. The Land: the land and its natural resources shall be held in trust for the natives and at all times they shall have effective ownership of as much land as they can profitably develop.

2. Capital: the investment of capital and granting of concessions shall be so regulated as to prevent the exploitation of the natives and the exhaustion of the natural wealth of the country. Concessions shall always be limited in time and subject to State control. The growing social needs of the natives must be regarded and the profits taxed for social and material benefit of the natives.

3. Labor: slavery and corporal punishment shall be abolished and forced labor except in punishment for crime, and the general conditions of labor shall be prescribed and regulated by the State.

4. Education: it shall be the right of every native child to learn to read and write his own language, and the language of the trustee nation, at public expense, and to be given technical instruction in some branch of industry. The State shall also educate as large a number of natives as possible in higher technical and cultural training and maintain a corps of native teachers.

5. The State: the natives of Africa must have the right to participate in the government as fast as their development permits, in conformity with the principle that the government exists for the natives, and not the natives for the government. They shall at once be allowed to participate in local and tribal government, according to ancient usage, and this participation shall gradually extend, as education and experience proceed, to the higher offices of State; to that end, in time, Africa be ruled by consent of the Africans.... Whenever it is proven that African natives are not receiving just treatment at the hands of any State or that any State deliberately excludes its civilized citizens or subjects of Negro descent from its body politic and cultural, it shall be the duty of the League of Nations to bring the matter to the notice of the civilized World.

11. Harry Thuku explains why he formed a political movement for all East Africans.

Harry Thuku was born in what is present day Kenya in 1895 and was educated at a school run by U.S. missionaries. As a teenager, he moved to Nairobi and worked as a clerk. His employment in Nairobi made him aware that he was part of a larger community than his own Gikuyu people and that it was a multi-ethnic community. ("Gikuyu" is the indigenous spelling of the more com-

---

10. W. E. B. Du Bois, *The World and Africa: An Inquiry into the Part which Africa Has Played in World History* (New York: International Publishers, 1965), pp. 11–12.

mon term "kikuyu.") In many ways, this transformation was a typical experi-
ence for members of the newly emerging elite class of missionary-educated
Africans. Thuku was also representative of this first generation coming of age
under colonialism in his perception and condemnation of the daily practices of
white settler rule, practices which seemed contrary to the claims of upliftment,
civilization, and development emanating from the distant imperial capital of
London. In 1921, Thuku established the East Africa Association, a political
organization to represent Africans throughout British East Africa. He was mo-
tivated in particular by British legislation, passed in a period from 1915 to
1920, that dispossessed Africans of most of their land, restricted lease-holding
to Europeans, and began the process of placing Africans in rural reserves (usu-
ally on the poorest of land), a policy already implemented in South Africa. For
his attempts to develop a political movement, Thuku was arrested by the Brit-
ish in 1922 and kept in prison until 1930, again an experience that was com-
mon for those Africans who attempted to resist colonialism through peaceful
means during the first half of the twentieth century.[11]

I can tell you how I know I was born in 1895; my elder brother, who died recently, was circumcised in that year. My father's village was here on the site of my house, and this brother, Kigume, was circumcised just a few yards away beyond my present hedge; in fact it was on the land of one of my father's tenants. But the reason I know my year of birth was that later on my mother told me that she could not attend the ceremony, even though it was close by, because she had just delivered me and had no strength to go. And I have since then found out from the books of government officers that my brother's age-set, Mutung'u, was circumcised in 1895.

My father's village was about two miles from Kambui Hill, on one of the ridges between the Chomba River and the Mukuyu. In his compound there were the huts of his four wives, the eldest wife being nearest his hut, and my mother, Wanjiku, furthest from the centre. According to the custom of my clan, Anjiru, the village entrance faced south, just like my present house; I am not sure why this is, for other Kikuyu clans, such as Achera, and my wife's clan, Agachiku, actually face north. My father's cattle stayed some distance from his village in a *manyatta* (kraal), but

each night the sheep and the goats returned; they all knew their way to the huts of the various wives.

My mother was also a cultivator, and grew her maize, beans, and sweet potatoes along with delicious arrowroot, on a small patch behind my house. As soon as I was able to walk a little I would accompany my elder brothers—it would not be very far, but we loved to go, just as my children now cry to go and herd, when I want them to go to school. I used also to accompany my mother to her little patch where my coffee now grows. Indeed I buried her when she died in 1934 right in her old garden. She was very old. But with us children she was very kind, showing it in many ways; she never punished or beat any of the children including myself. Also she had a lot of food for us, since she was a good cultivator. In this work she was much helped by these unpaid female labourers we call *ndungata*. They would work on the land of a rich man, getting their food supplied, and gradually acquire goats and sheep of their own. You know, I remember a woman who died just a few years ago who had been one of my mother's *ndungata*.

Kairianja, my father, died in 1899, when I was only four years old; so Kigume became

11. Harry Thuku, *Harry Thuku: An Autobiography* (Nairobi: Oxford University Press, 1970), pp. 1–3, 5–6, 8–9, 11, 14–15, 16, 18–20, 22–23, 29–30, 32, 33–34. Reprinted with the permission of Oxford University Press, Eastern Africa.

the *muramati* of all our land and property. At this time Kigume used to do a little work for a European who had quietly slipped on to our land. We did not know he was coming to stay, since he had just built a little mud and grass house where the present manager of Mchana Estate lives. The Kikuyu gave him the nickname Kibara for he was always beating people, but he did not seem to do much actual planting; he did not plant any crops or coffee, and did not come into any Kikuyu village—I think because he was afraid probably. But anyway I did go sometimes to take food to my brother who was working with him. No one thought that Kibara had come permanently. In fact it was only in 1915 that some of us finally heard that this part of our land had been sold to a Mr. Noon, one of the government transport officers, who I happened to know quite well. Then our people, including Waweru, the chief, were asked to move a little further west. Of course it was government policy to sell land without telling the occupiers. Then later the new "owner" would come along and say, "This land is mine; I bought it from government." Naturally the people were afraid of government. And if you asked these early white settlers and government people how they had sold off our land they would reply, "You have no land. The land belongs to God. God has given it to the white man, and they have it now." Indeed I remember one man told me he had gone to see Mr. Ainsworth, the Commissioner in Nairobi, and after protesting about land sales, Ainsworth had told him that amongst the Kikuyu, land belonged to the *hiti* (hyena)!

When I was about five, the government had made a large encampment with Nubian soldiers near Ruiru, which was about seven miles from my home. And there they had brought some Amerikani (cotton cloth) for people to buy. One day I had been given one rupee by my brother and I went along with some other boys to buy my first cloth. I bought it and wore it like a Maasai, over my shoulder. But the first European I saw with my eyes was in 1902. It was Mr. Knapp of the Gospel Missionary Society (GMS) who

had come to the village of my cousin, Mburu, just beneath our village. I and some other small boys heard there was to be a white man speaking, so we went along. His Kikuyu was very poor, but we were so interested in him that when he asked us to pray, we looked through our fingers just to see him.

Eventually, he had discussions with the elders of our clan about land for a mission station, and it was agreed to give the mission one hundred acres. Included in that was Kambui Hill which had also belonged to our family. It was there that my oldest brother, Njongoro, had had his village, but he had died earlier at the turn of the century. . . .

I got my name Thuku from my grandfather on my mother's side. Originally he had been called Karanja, but then the Arabs came into the country selling that brass wire in exchange for elephant tusks. They called it *ruthuku*. So my grandfather took that name and forgot his first one, and I in turn was given it later.

I have nothing belonging to my mother or my father except my mother's photograph. Some people when they became Christians, including myself, were no longer interested in Kikuyu things. The man, however, who kept some things of Kikuyu tradition was Kenyatta. But I was not interested. I did not have to destroy anything when I became a Christian because I did not own anything— not even a snuff box! And these were the commonest things that I saw being thrown on the fire at the mission when I was a boy. The Gospel Mission did not order people to destroy such things; it simply preached that witchcraft, greasing the body, and wearing ornaments were not God's way. But people did not throw their necklaces and bracelets on the mission fires, only snuff boxes and the things the witchdoctor used for doctoring people....

In 1908, when I had been at the mission one year, two important things happened. First, I was baptized—they gave me the name Harry—and I had to go completely under water in a deep pool in the Mukuyu River. With baptism, my mother and brother did not seem to mind at all; they did not object certainly. . . .

I did not get any political education from the missionaries, for they did not discuss political matters with us. But I found out later that they fought for us out of our presence amongst other Europeans. I have said that Dr. Henderson fought for African rights, and he was certainly a very fearless man. I know this because of evidence that he gave to a Commission; the settlers wanted to take all Kikuyu lands, and some suggested, with Lord Delamere's encouragement, that the Kikuyu should be moved three hundred miles to the north. Now, Dr. Henderson was on this commission at the time, and when he gave his evidence, I remember he said: "If you interfere or try to move the Kikuyu people from their land completely, all Europeans in Kikuyu country will be killed in one night". . . .

My time in the mission came to an end in 1911, and I set off for employment in Nairobi. . . .

You know, there were only two churches in Nairobi for Africans at that time, the CMS and the Roman Catholics (RC). At that time the Catholics were all Italian and French fathers (the Italians north of the Chania River, and the others nearer Nairobi). Funnily enough the Catholics were always trying to sow hatred between the RC and the CMS mission boys, and one father I remember even refused to come into Mr. Knapp's house. The Catholic policy was only to teach Africans religion, but no fuller education. So there were no Catholics working in those days in government offices in Nairobi; instead almost everybody was CMS. Indeed I only remember that I knew one Catholic friend, a man Matthew who worked with me in my second job. But later on when I founded the East African Association, there were no Catholic members—although there were many Muslims. I think this was because the Italian and French fathers did not give Africans good English, and also because they taught their students that it was a sin to take part in politics. When there were political troubles in Nairobi after my arrest in 1922, they thought this showed their policy had been right. For

they wrote in their mission newspaper published in Nyeri, "You British people, you have made a mistake. You sharpened a knife which is now cutting you." They meant the knife of education. . . .

Several of my friends, including Josiah Njonjo, were at that time working on the newspaper, the *Leader* of British East Africa; so in 1914 I joined these boys and was given the job of composing type. Later I was taught to print, and I spent my time between those two jobs of compositor and machine man. Of course some people did not think it a very honourable position, but looking back I can see I was rather lucky to be there. All my further education, or self-education, I gained from there. Whenever there were words or phrases I did not understand, I consulted Goan or Indian friends working there.

And beyond this, when the war came to East Africa, I was also taught by a military sergeant how to print maps and sketches of war positions. This was a special skill, and as only the sergeant and I knew how to do it, the *Leader* did not allow me to go and fight in the East Africa Campaign. Also I read many of the articles that the settlers wrote to the *Leader* (the paper was strongly in favour of the white settlers), and when I saw something there about the treatment of Africans, it entered into my head and lay quiet until later on.

While I was at the *Leader*, I used to get a monthly wage of 46 rupees, and usually 12 rupees out of this I spent on my lodgings. At the time, I lived in River Road, in one room in various Asians' houses. I did not have any transport, so it was easier to live in River Road than over at Pangani village. River Road was also the place where many of the first government African clerks lived, and these came from Freretown and Rabai at the Coast, or from Buganda. This was why most of my friends at this time were Coast men, all good Swahili speakers, and it was how I got a grasp of good pronunciation. . . .

It was at the *Leader*, from about 1915, that I first began to think seriously about some of our troubles as Africans—especially this question of forced labour. Before then only men had been made to work, but at about that time women and girls too were compelled to go out to work. This was what happened: a settler who wanted labour for his farm would write to the D.C. [District Commissioner] saying he required thirty young men, women or girls for work on his farm. The D.C. sent a letter to a chief or headman to supply such and such a number, and the chief in turn had his tribal retainers to carry out this business. They would simply go to people's houses—very often where there were beautiful women and daughters—and point out which were to come to work. Sometimes they had to work a distance from home, and the number of girls who got pregnant in this way was very great. . . .

1916 was the year I first began meeting Koinange—old Chief Koinange—and later on when I was living in Pangani itself, he once came to my single room and spent the night there. We discussed many matters, and I saw he was quite fearless. He was very opposed to what had happened with Kikuyu land, and the government had done a very stupid thing over his own land. A road divided it in two, and the government had declared that on one side of the road was European, and on the other African land. Yet it was across the road from Koinange's house that both his father's and grandfather's graves were. And every morning when Koinange got up he would look across the road at the European coffee which he was not allowed to grow. . . .

The War ended, and after it, things began to warm up in the British East Africa Protectorate (that was Kenya's old name). First there were many thousands of porters who came back from very very difficult conditions in the East Africa Campaign, and found that they would not get any gratuity. Instead the government under General Northey decided that the white soldiers, and especially the officers, should be rewarded. So they alienated many thousands of acres in the area round Kericho for a Soldier Settlement Scheme. Also in my own Kiambu area, more land was taken at this time and given to white settlers. However, I want to make one thing clear about this land business; back at that time

we Africans who were a little educated were not saying that all Europeans should leave the country, or that we should get self-government. There was no idea of that. What we objected to was that the Europeans did not treat us as we had treated the Dorobos. I mean, we bought our land from the Dorobo according to agreed prices, and as I said earlier, we planted *itoka* lilies to confirm these sales. We did not simply claim land without the Dorobo knowing anything about it. And I am not saying that one or two Europeans did not do things in a proper manner. Take the way Mr. Krieger bought his farm from a Kikuyu, Gichinga, just nearby here at Thembigwa. He paid him 70 female goats in the presence of Mr. Knapp, and I always told my people that they should not fight to get that piece back, for it was not taken secretly or by force. . . .

The second thing that was making Africans angrier after the War was this thing called *kipande*. This was Swahili for a container in which a registration paper was carried. Now General Northey, Kenya's Governor after the War, decided in 1919 to implement the recommendations of an earlier committee which had suggested that Africans be registered. The ordinary people did not understand what this registration was, but even more educated ones like me did not oppose it to begin with, for we knew that many countries asked their citizens to register. So we did not object until we found out that it was a very different business in Kenya. First of all you had to wear this quite heavy metal box round your neck on a string all the time; then in the columns on the paper inside there were many things that were against Africans. There was one space where the employer had to sign when he engaged you and also when you left. You could not leave employment without permission, and if you did, you could be taken to the D.C.'s court. Also, no other employer would take you if the space for discharge was not filled up. Another thing in the early kind of *kipande* was a space for remarks; and here, if an employer did not like you, he could spoil your name completely by putting "lazy," "disobedient," or "cheeky." That column made me very angry. *Kipande* was only for Africans; and in 1919, at that old building still standing opposite Nairobi General Post Office, I collected my one [kipande].

There was also the question of rising tax for Africans. It kept on going up even though we did not see anything like schools or clinics which we get nowadays for our high taxes. The reason for it was to pull African workers out of their houses to work for the European settlers; you see, they could not get the money to pay their tax unless they left their homes and worked for some months. . . .

The final thing was when we heard that the settlers were going to reduce African wages by one third. Many of us got very angry, and we called a meeting in Pangani on 7 June 1921 to see if we could form a Young Kikuyu Association. The reason we called it "Young" was this. For a long time in Nairobi I had known Baganda people. There was one Muganda called Ssentongo who had his own newspaper, *Sekanyolya*, and there were clerical workers. Then there was a Buganda football team which used to come through and play us in Nairobi. Indeed a little later on it was through football that I met Prince Suna of Buganda—he was the uncle of Kabaka Daudi Chwa. He had come to Nairobi accompanying his team; his secretary came and found me, and Suna and I had our photograph taken together. From some of these people I learnt that they had a body called the Young Baganda Association in their country. "Does that mean," I asked them, "that only young people can join it?" "No!" they told me, "even men of seventy years old, for it is the Association which is young and not the members!" So we thought of doing the same. . . .

Once I got back to Nairobi, I began to have discussions with my friends. We saw clearly that if we sent anything coming from the Kikuyu tribe alone, we would carry no weight. But if we could show that it came from all tribes—the Maasai, the Kamba etc., then we should have a great voice. At the same time, over the next few days, we continued our discussions for the proper name for our Association, and finally decided that we

should change it from the Young Kikuyu to the East African Association (EAA), so that anyone in the whole area could join. This we agreed in committee on 1 July.

To acquaint the people of Nairobi with our plans, I called a meeting on Sunday, 10 July, 1921, for all Africans. The site was where the present Arya Samaj Girls' School is, near Ngara Road, and we had an attendance of about 2,000. I was voted into the Chair, and we had a long discussion on our grievances. I do not remember all the speakers, but I do remember two men in particular—how powerfully James Mwanthi from Kamba country spoke; and also how a Luo, Abednego, jumped up on the table and gave a fiery speech. By the end we had passed a number of resolutions on the Indians, forced labour, taxation and education, and the mass meeting agreed that we should send the substance of our resolutions direct to the Colonial Office in London. . . .

Within Kenya itself, the EAA had by now many members from different tribes. The Maasai had been in it from the beginnings with people like Haikoko, the chauffeur of Mr. Jeevanjee. Then there were my very close Kamba friends, Ali Kironjo [Kilonzo], James Mwanthi, and Mohamed Sheikh, who helped us to spread out into Kamba country. We had a few Luo (we called them Kavirondo then), and even some Nandi. What all of us wanted was to show people that we were all one family and that there was no difference between all the tribes of Kenya.

Once, for instance, I went to hold a meeting at Waiganjo's place, Ng'enda; it was deep in Kikuyu country. But in order to show the Kikuyu that there were many other people in Kenya, I deliberately took along Juma Mnandi (a Nandi who was a gardener in Government House), Samuel Okoth the Kavirondo pastor, and Ali Kironjo, the Kamba Muslim. . . .

I was very delighted to be travelling to the meeting at Ng'enda, because I was accompanied by the school teacher, Samuel Okoth, a Christian from Maseno, and two Moslems, their names were Abdulla Tairara and Ali Kironjo. We were very pleased at our trip for we travelled as brothers. And I saw no difference between the Kavirondo and the man from Kikuyu, or even between the Christian believer and the believer in Islam. I was pleased too in that we fulfilled the command of our Lord God—that you should love your neighbour as yourself. . . .

The chiefs, as I said, had been continuing to preach against us. So this time we decided to follow them up by car. None of us drove, so we hired an Indian taxi (the driver was in Nairobi until quite recently) and set off. All the main members went along, including Waiganjo, Muchuchu and Tairara. And we toured a number of places like Wangindu and Kiguoya's. Everywhere I gave advice to carry on underground if the Association was stopped and I was arrested. . . .

We returned to Nairobi and paid about 1,300 rupees for the hire of the car. But I knew that chiefs and missionaries had been collecting affidavits against me, and I suppose I was not really surprised when at 6 o'clock on 14 March I was arrested. . . .

Soon fifty members of the Association had been arrested, and the government decided to deport three of us—Waiganjo, Mugekenyi and me. I think they felt that if they left either of those free, the movement would continue. As it was, Waiganjo heard that they were looking for him, and as he was a fearless man, he rode his mule right into the D.C.'s compound at Kiambu, and said, "I understand you are looking for me." He was arrested.

12. Creating a national movement for all West Africans.

In 1919, the same year that W. E. B. Du Bois (see document 9) was presenting the grievances of colonial people at Versailles, that the African National Congress (ANC) (see document 8) was agreeing upon a constitution for a body to represent all "native peoples" in southern Africa, and that Harry Thuku (see document 11) was becoming increasingly appalled by the racist treatment meted out to Africans in British East Africa, representatives from all the British colonial possessions in West Africa met to form a political organization of their own, the National Congress for British West Africa. The members of this new organization, most of them merchants and missionary-educated professionals (doctors, lawyers), petitioned the British government to allow Africans to elect their own political representatives, especially to the administrative bodies that determined the type and amount of taxes levied in colonial territories. They objected also to the re-partitioning of Africa that they saw taking place at Versailles. Their requests were ignored by the British government. [12]

Petition of the National Congress of British West Africa, October 19, 1920.

To his most Gracious Majesty George the Fifth, King of Great Britain and Ireland, and the Dominions Beyond the Seas in Council. The Humble Petition of the National Congress of British West Africa by its Delegates now in London,

Sheweth:

That your Petitioners are the accredited representatives of the National Congress of British West Africa, which was brought into being after the first Conference of Africans of British West Africa [held in Accra, March 1919, with delegates from Ghana, Nigeria, Sierra Leone, and Gambia], for the purpose of continuing and perpetuating the work of the Conference.

---

12. George Metcalfe, ed., *Great Britain and Ghana: Documents of Ghana History, 1807–1957* (Legon: University of Ghana, 1964), pp. 583–85.

That your Petitioners would respectfully seize the opportunity of expressing their loyalty, devotion, and attachment to Your Majesty's person and throne and would further beg to refer to the sentiment of the Conference in one of its Resolutions, to the effect "That this Conference desires to place on record the attachment of the peoples of British West Africa to the British Empire, and their unfeigned loyalty and devotion to the throne and person of His Majesty the King-Emperor, and direct that copies of these Resolutions be forwarded in due course to His Majesty's Principal Secretary of State for the Colonies and to each of the Governors of the several Dependencies." Further it may be noted that the policy of the Congress is "to preserve strictly and inviolate the connection of the British West African Dependencies with the British Empire and to maintain unreservedly all and every right of free citizenship of the Empire and the fundamental principle that taxation goes with effective representation." . . .

That your Petitioners desire to bring to the notice of Your Majesty, that the administrations of the several British West African Dependencies are composed of Executive and Legislative Councils. The Members of the Executive Councils are all Government officials who also, together with Members nominated by the Governors, compose the Legislative Councils. As such the nominated members do not really represent the people, and they are not directly in touch with them. . . .

That apart from the fact that the National Congress of British West Africa represents substantially the intelligentsia and the advanced thought of British West Africa, and that the principles it stands for are some of those fundamental ones that have always actuated communities that have arrived at the stage of national consciousness, it also represents the bulk of the inhabitants of the various indigenous communities and with them claims, as sons of the soil, the inherent right to make representations [as] to existing disabilities, and to submit recommendations for the necessary reforms.

That your Petitioners would respectfully beg leave to point out that in asking for the franchise, the people of British West Africa are not seeking to copy a foreign institution. On the contrary, it is important to notice that the principle of electing representatives to local councils and bodies is inherent in all the [political] systems of British West Africa, which are essentially democratic in nature, as may be gathered from standard works on the subject.

That, further, according to the African system, no Headman, Chief, or Paramount Ruler has an inherent right to exercise Jurisdiction unless he is duly elected by the people to represent them, and that the appointment to political offices also entirely depends upon the election and the will of the people.

That such being the British West African system of representation the arrangement by which the Governor of a Crown Colony nominates whom he thinks proper to represent the people, cannot but strike them as a great anomaly and does constitute a grievance and a disability which they now respectfully pray may be remedied. . . .

That in order that Your Majesty may appreciate how detrimentally the present system of appointment to the Legislative Councils by Government nomination works, attention is respectfully drawn to the passage of the Palm Kernels Ordinance against the will of the people. . . .

That your Petitioners, therefore, humbly pray your Majesty to grant an amendment of the existing letters patent for the several British West African Dependencies whereby the present system of Government may be altered so as to provide for the reconstruction of the several Legislative Councils by giving the people the right of electing one-half of the Members thereof, and by the constitution of Houses of Assembly which shall be composed of the Members of the Legislative Council besides six other financial representatives elected by the people, who shall have the power of imposing all taxes and of discussing freely and without reserve the items on the annual estimates of revenue and expenditure prepared by the Governors in the Executive Council and approving of them. . . .

That your Petitioners would respectfully submit that the time has come for the establishment of Municipal Corporations in all the principal towns of British West Africa with full power of local self-government, and that the people may have the power of electing four-fifths of the Members thereof and the remaining one-fifth nominated by the Government, such elected and nominated members having the power of electing the Mayor of the Corporation, who, however, must be an elected member.

That your Petitioners desire the establishment of a British West African University, and are prepared to promote the necessary funds for its establishment, supported by Government subsidies.

That in the opinion of your Petitioners the time has arrived for the introduction of Emigration Laws so as to keep out "undesirables," and the opinion of Your Majesty's Government is invited as to whether Syrians are not "undesirables". . . .

That your Petitioners view with marked disfavour the scheme of the Empire Resources Development Committee, and regret that British publicists should be found capable of advocating a policy which, if adopted, would bring Imperial Britain on a par with pre-war German attitude with regard to African Proprietary rights. In this connection, it is submitted that the principle of Trusteeship may easily be made to operate detrimentally to African proprietary rights, and that the people are well able to control their own lands and to watch and protect their proprietary interests. . . .

That Your Majesty's Petitioners view with grave alarm the right assumed by the European Powers of exchanging or partitioning African countries between them without regard to the wishes of the people, and beg leave respectfully to request that the partitioning of Togoland between the English and the French be reconsidered. . . .

Signed for and on behalf of the National Congress of British West Africa.

T. Hutton-Mills, Barrister-at-Law, President

Casely Hayford, M.B.E., M.L.C., Barrister-at-Law, Vice President and Gold Coast Delegate

Edward Francis Small, Gambia Delegate

Henry Maurice Jones, Merchant, Gambia Delegate

Fred. W. Dove, Merchant, Sierra Leone Delegate

H. C. Bankole-Bright, Physician and Surgeon, Editor "Aurora," Secretary London Committee, Delegate Sierra Leone

H. Van Hien, Merchant, Treasurer, Gold Coast Delegate

J. Egerton-Shyngle, Barrister-at-Law, Nigeria Delegate

Chief Oluwa, of Lagos, Nigeria Delegate

13. Organizing African workers.

While the African National Congress (ANC) focused primarily on representing the urban, newly educated professional classes, Clements Kadalie aimed at developing a trade union movement for the people he regarded as the most oppressed by colonialism: "workers." Kadalie was born in Nyasaland around 1896 and schooled by his uncle (a brother of the first prime minister of independent Malawi, Hastings Banda) and later on at a mission station.

He worked as a clerk in Portuguese East Africa and in Rhodesia before coming to South Africa, where in 1919 he established the Industrial and Commercial Workers Union (ICU) to represent the African dock workers. All African workers in South Africa were excluded from the legal definition of "worker"

*under South African law and therefore were not entitled to be formally repre-
sented in contract or wage negotiations. Despite this obstacle, the ICU grew
enormously in the early to mid-1920s, benefiting from Kadalie's charisma as a
public speaker and his readiness to develop the organization into a movement
that aimed to unite all Africans opposed to racial segregation, and to challenge
the ruling order by threatening strike action rather than the petitions relied
upon by the ANC. Though the ICU claimed a membership of 100,000 by 1928
(when the ANC had only a few thousand dues-paying members), it collapsed
because of a combination of internal conflicts and police action. The fundamental problem for people who adopted the same approach as Kadalie was
that while direct challenges to the ruling system engendered a great deal of
popular support, the readiness of the South African state (like that of every
other colonial ruler in Africa) to use force to repress opposition, and its monopoly of arms, meant that the challenge could not succeed without unacceptable levels (to the protestors) of bloodshed. Kadalie was charged with "promoting
racial hostility" under legislation introduced in 1927, and thereafter became
an increasingly marginal figure in South African politics. For a time though,
his was the most eloquent voice opposing racial discrimination in South Africa.*[13]

Industrial and Commercial Workers' Union of South Africa program for 1928.

Opponents of the I.C.U. have frequently asserted that the Organisation is not a trade
union in the sense that the term is generally
understood in South Africa, but that it is a
kind of pseudo-political body. The ground
on which this assertion has been based is the
fact that I.C.U. has concentrated its attention on matters in which the issues involved
have not been "purely economic" whilst these
"purely economic" issues have been very
largely neglected.

The new constitution, which was adopted
at the Special Congress at Kimberley in December last, definitely establishes the I.C.U.
as a trade union, albeit one of the native workers whose rights of organisation are only now
earning recognition. In these circumstances
it has become necessary for the organisation
to have a clearly defined economic
programme, corresponding to the interests
of the membership at large. At the same time
it must be clearly understood that we have

no intention of copying the stupid and futile
"Non-political" attitude of our White contemporaries. As Karl Marx said, every economic question is, in the last analysis, a
political question also, and we must recognise
that in neglecting to concern ourselves with
current politics, in leaving the political machines to the unchallenged control of our class
enemies, we are rendering a disservice to
those tens of thousands of our members who
are groaning under oppressive laws and who
are looking to the I.C.U. for a lead.

In the past, the officers of the I.C.U. in
the field have had no definite programme to
follow, and this has resulted not merely in
confusion of ideas, but it has led to the dis-
semination of conflicting politics. This being
so, I make no apology for introducing the
subject of an Economic and Political
Programme for the Organisation at this stage.
The I.C.U. is a homogeneous national
organisation. As such it must have a national
policy, consonant with the terms of its constitution, which will serve as a programme of
action by which its officials will be guided in

13. Thomas Karis and Gwendolen M. Carter, eds., *From Protest to Challenge: A Documentary History of African Politics in South Africa, 1882–1962* (Stanford: Hoover Institution Press, 1972), vol. 1. Sheridan Johns, ed., *Protest and Hope, 1882–1934*, pp. 331–33. Reprinted with the agreement of the Hoover Institution Press.

their work. The framing of such a policy or programme is essentially the work of Congress, and I propose to give here the broad outlines for a programme, which I trust will serve as a basis of discussion. In view of what I said above it will be realised that it is not necessary to divide the programme into political and economic sections, the two being closely bound up with each other.

I will further preface the proposals I have to make by remarking that our programme must be largely of an agrarian character, for the reason that the greater proportion of our membership comprises rural workers, landless peasants, whose dissatisfaction with conditions is with good reason greater than that of the workers in urban areas. These conditions are only too well known to you to require any restatement from me. The town workers must not, however, be neglected. More attention must in the future be given to their grievances, desires and aspirations if their loyalty to the I.C.U. is to be secured. At the present stage of our development it is inevitable that our activities should be almost entirely of an agitational character for we are not recognised as citizens in our own country, being almost entirely disfranchised and debarred from exercising a say in state affairs closely affecting our lives and welfare. Our programme will therefore be almost entirely agitational in character.

I now detail my proposals, as follows:

(1) WAGES: A consistent and persistent agitation for improved wages for native workers must be conducted by all branches of the Union. The agitation must be Union-wide, and regard must always be had to local conditions and circumstances. Improvements, however small in themselves, must be welcomed and made the basis on which to agitate for further advances. Every endeavour should be made to enter into friendly negotiations with farmers' associations, employers' organisations and individual employers in the towns, with a view to securing improvements. If no results are obtained branch secretaries should, wherever practicable, invoke the aid of the Wage Board. In this connection a study of the Wage Act, 1925, is urged.

As an immediate objective, a minimum wage of £5 per month (plus food and housing in country districts) should be striven for. The reasonableness of this claim cannot be disputed by anyone. The attainment of this admittedly low rate, which it must be said few native workers are receiving, is not to be regarded as an end in itself, but as a stepping stone to the ultimate achievement of the full economic rights of the native workers.

(2) HOURS: Insistence should be made on a maximum working day of eight hours and a working week of 5½ days for town and country workers alike. This demand will have the support of all right-thinking and justice-loving people, and members who refuse to exceed this working-time should be given every possible support and encouragement.

(3) ILLEGAL PRACTICES: Illegal practices by employers, such as withholding wages, seizing stock, etc. should be reported to the local Magistrate and Native Affairs Department, with fullest particulars. Any refusal by these officials to deal with complaints, or failure to secure satisfaction for the members concerned should be reported to the Head Office of the Organisation for submission to the higher authorities.

(4) THE FRANCHISE: The proposal of the present government to withdraw the very limited franchise granted to Natives in the Cape Province should be unequivocally condemned at every public gathering of the I.C.U. Further, on the principle: "No taxation without representation" an extension of the franchise to Natives should be demanded. We would suggest that a monster petition be organised by the I.C.U. against the present reactionary proposal and presented to Parliament during the present session.

In the event of the Bill being passed and the franchise being withdrawn a protest should be made by means of a mammoth petition calling into question the necessity and legality of taxing and legislating for sections of the population and citizens without granting them the same representation as provided for the Europeans, at the same time asking for tangible and unbiased reasons why the

Natives should not refuse to pay taxes without representation.

(5) PASS LAWS: The Pass Laws are a legal expression of Native enslavement, corresponding with the dark days of Tzarist Russia. They manufacture criminals and possess no moral or ethical justification. It is therefore the duty of the I.C.U. to oppose them by every possible means at its disposal. I would propose that the government be petitioned to suspend the Pass Laws for, say, a period of six months. If, during that period it is found that there has been no increase of lawlessness among the Natives, but that they are just as law-abiding without passes as with them, then the Government should be asked to repeal the Pass Laws in their entirety as there will no longer be any reason or justification, either real or imaginary, for their continuance.

In the event of the government refusing to comply with such a petition, Congress should fix a day of national protest against the Pass Laws, to be marked by mass demonstrations at which all natives should be asked to hand in their passports, the same to be burned in public, by the demonstrations. In addition, those assembled should be pledged by solemn resolution to refuse to carry any further passports or to give any further recognition to the Pass Laws.

(6) LAND: The total area of land set aside for exclusive native occupation in the Union is notoriously inadequate. Parliament should be petitioned through one or more of its members to increase the Native reserves so as to make provision for the landless native farmers. The assistance of labour organisations overseas should be invoked in this matter. In addition, an agitation should be started against the laws prohibiting native squatting.

(7) FREE SPEECH: Vigorous propaganda must be carried on against those provisions in the Native Administration Act which place restrictions on the right of free speech. Ostensibly these provisions are designed to prevent the stirring-up of hostility between the white and black races. Actually they are intended to limit the opportunities for trade union propaganda and organisation among the native workers. These provisions must therefore be strenuously fought against and their legality challenged where wrongful arrests are carried out. In this connection, no opportunity must be lost of stressing the fact that the I.C.U. is not an anti-European organisation, and that where it has occasion to criticise Europeans it is on grounds of their actions (usually as employers of labour) towards the natives and not on account of the colour of their skins.

(8) PROPAGANDA: Members must be kept fully informed of the activities of the organisation and of all happenings affecting their interests. For this purpose regular members' meetings must be called by Branch Secretaries and the speeches made thereat must not, as heretofore, be of a vague or general agitational character but must deal with concrete and immediate problems. Every endeavour must be made to stimulate a direct personal interest in the affairs of the organisation and to this end questions and discussions by the audience must be encouraged.

The "Workers Herald," our official organ, must be further popularised among the members. If every member bought the paper its circulation could be easily quadrupled and more. The paper could be made to possess an interest for each district if Branch Secretaries would take the trouble to contribute notes concerning local happenings with their comments thereon.

(9) NEW RECRUITS: There are large numbers of native workers to whom the I.C.U. is scarcely known. I refer to the workers on the Witwatersrand gold mines, the Natal Coal Mines and the Railways. Branch Secretaries in these areas should make every endeavour to rope these men in as members of the I.C.U. as they would be an undoubted source of strength. The good work commenced some years ago among Dock Workers has unfortunately been discontinued very largely. Renewed efforts must be made during the ensuing year to bring the strayed ones back to the fold.

(10) REPRESENTATION ON PUBLIC BODIES: It was decided at a previous Congress that advantage be taken of the laws governing Provincial Council elections in the Cape to run official I.C.U. candidates. Native Parliamentary voters are qualified to enter the Cape Provincial Council, and definite steps should be taken to select candidates to stand on behalf of the I.C.U. in Cape constituencies where there is a possibility of securing a fair vote at least. An instruction should be issued to the National Council accordingly, and full preparations should be made by the branch or branches concerned for a thorough election campaign in the next Cape Provincial Council elections. Propaganda must be the main consideration, although every effort must be made to secure the return of any candidates put up. The question of candidates in the Parliamentary General Elections forms a separate item on the agenda. In submitting the above outline, I trust that delegates will see with me the urgent necessity for a national policy for the organisation. Once a policy is adopted, and a programme arranged, it must not be allowed to remain on paper, and every official will be expected to do his utmost to translate the same into practice. Only in this way can the organisation grow and become an effective agency for liberating the African workers from the thraldom of slavery.

14. Charlotte Maxeke describes the impact of colonialism on women and the family.

While Clements Kadalie focused primarily on the concerns of African male workers, other critics of European rule drew attention to the way in which colonialism had a particularly harsh impact on women. Charlotte Maxeke, born in South Africa in 1874, and educated by missionaries, had traveled overseas with a choral group in the 1890s visiting Great Britain, Canada, and the United States. She became the first African woman to earn a bachelor's degree, graduating from Wilberforce University in 1905. Upon her return to South Africa, she founded the Women's League of the African National Congress. In a speech given in 1930 at Fort Hare, a university college established by the South African government for blacks only, Maxeke describes the ways in which the loss of land and the development of migrant labor had a profound impact on African family life.[14]

Charlotte Maxeke, "Social Conditions among Bantu Women and Girls," Fort Hare 1930.

In speaking of Bantu women in urban areas, the first thing to be considered is the Home, around which and in which the whole activity of family life circulates. First of all, the Home is the residence of the family, and home and family life are successful only where husband and wife live happily together, bringing up their family in a sensible way, sharing the responsibilities naturally involved in a fair and wholehearted spirit. The woman, the wife, is the keystone of the household: she holds a position of supreme importance, for is she not directly and intimately concerned with the nurturing and upbringing of the *children* of the family, the future generation? She is their first counsellor, and teacher; on her rests the responsibility of implanting in the flexible minds of her young, the right principles and

---

14. Thomas Karis and Gwendolen M. Carter, eds., *From Protest to Challenge: A Documentary History of African Politics in South Africa, 1882–1962* (Stanford: Hoover Institution Press, 1972), vol. 1. Sheridan Johns, ed., *Protest and Hope, 1882–1934*, pp. 344–46. Reprinted with the agreement of the Hoover Institution Press.

teachings of modern civilisation. Indeed, on her rests the failure or success of her children when they go out into life. It is therefore essential that the home atmosphere be right, that the mother be the real "queen" of the home, the inspiration of her family, if her children are to go out into the world equipped for the battles of life.

There are many problems pressing in upon us Bantu, to disturb the peaceful working of our homes. One of the chief is perhaps the stream of Native life into the towns. Men leave their homes, and go into big towns like Johannesburg, where they get a glimpse of a life such as they had never dreamed existed. At the end of their term of employment they receive the wages for which they have worked hard, and which should be used for the sustenance of their families, but the attractive luxuries of civilisation are in many instances too much for them, they waste their hard earned wages, and seem to forget completely the crying need of their family out in the veld.

The wife finds that her husband has apparently forgotten her existence, and she therefore makes her hard and weary way to the town in search of him. When she gets there, and starts looking round for a house of some sort in which to accommodate herself and her children, she meets with the first rebuff. The Location Superintendent informs her that she cannot rent accommodation unless she has a husband. Thus she is driven to the first step on the downward path, for if she would have a roof to cover her children's heads a husband must be found, and so we get these Poor women forced by circumstances to consort with men in order to provide shelter for their families. Thus we see that the authorities in enforcing the restrictions in regard to accommodation are often doing Bantu society a grievous harm, for they are forcing its womanhood, its wedded womanhood, to the first step on the downward path of sin and crime.

Many Bantu women live in the cities at a great price, the price of their children; for these women, even when they live with their husbands, are forced in most cases to go out and work, to bring sufficient into the homes to keep their children alive. The children of these unfortunate people therefore run wild, and as there are not sufficient schools to house them, it is easy for them to live an aimless existence, learning crime of all sorts in their infancy almost.

If these circumstances obtain when husband and wife live together in the towns, imagine the case of the woman, whose husband has gone to town and left her, forgetting apparently all his responsibilities. Here we get young women, the flower of the youth of the Bantu, going up to towns in search of their husbands, and as I have already stated, living as the reputed wives of other men, because of the location requirements, or becoming housekeepers to men in the locations and towns, and eventually their nominal wives.

In Johannesburg, and other large towns, the male Natives are employed to do domestic work, in the majority of instances, and a female domestic servant is a rarity. We thus have a very dangerous environment existing for any woman who goes into any kind of domestic service in these towns, and naturally immorality of various kinds ensues, as the inevitable outcome of this situation. Thus we see that the European is by his treatment of the Native in these ways which I have mentioned, only pushing him further and further down in the social scale, forgetting that it was he and his kind who brought these conditions about in South Africa, forgetting his responsibilities to those who labour for him and to whom he introduced the benefits, and evils, of civilisation. These facts do not sound very pleasant I know, but this Conference is, according to my belief, intended to give us all the opportunity of expressing our views, our problems, and of discussing them in an attitude of friendliness and fairmindedness, so that we may perhaps be enabled to see some way out of them.

Then we come to the *Land Question.* This is very acute in South Africa, especially from the Bantu point of view. South Africa in terms of available land is shrinking daily owing to increased population, and to many other economic and climatic causes. Cattle diseases have crept into the country, ruining many a stock farmer, and thus Bantu wealth is gradually decaying. As a result there are more and more workers making their way to the towns and cities such as Johannesburg to earn a living. And what a living! The majority earn about £3 10s. per month, out of which they must pay 25s. for rent, and 10s. for tram fares, so I leave you to imagine what sort of existence they lead on the remainder.

Here again we come back to the same old problem that I outlined before, that of the woman of the home being obliged to find work in order to supplement her husband's wages, with the children growing up undisciplined and uncared for, and the natural following rapid decay of morality among the people. We find that in this state of affairs, the woman in despair very often decides that she cannot leave her children thus uncared for, and she therefore throws up her employment in order to care for them, but is naturally forced into some form of home industry, which, as there is very little choice for her in this direction, more often than not takes the form of the brewing and selling of skokiaan [African beer]. Thus the woman starts on a career of crime for herself and her children, a career which often takes her and her children right down the depths of immorality and misery.

The woman, poor unfortunate victim of circumstances, goes to prison, and the children are left even more desolate than when their mother left them to earn her living. Again they are uncared for, undisciplined, no-one's responsibility, the prey of the undesirables with whom their mother has come into contact in her frantic endeavour to provide for them by selling skokiaan. The children thus become decadent, never having had a chance in life. About ten years ago, there was talk of Industrial schools being started for such unfortunate children, but it was only talk, and we are to-day in the same position, aggravated by the increased numbers steadily streaming in from the rural areas, all undergoing very similar experiences to those I have just outlined.

I would suggest that there might be a conference of Native and European women, where we could get to understand each others point of view, each others difficulties and problems, and where, actuated by the real spirit of love, we might find some basis on which we could work for the common good of European and Bantu womanhood.

Many of the Bantu feel and rightly too that the laws of the land are not made for Black and White alike. Take the question of permits for the right to look for work. To look for work, mark you! The poor unfortunate Native, fresh from the country does not know of these rules and regulations, naturally breaks them and is thrown into prison; or if he does happen to know the regulations and obtains a pass for six days, and is obliged to renew it several times, as is of course very often the case, he will find that when he turns up for the third or fourth time for the renewal of his permit, he is put into prison, because he has been unsuccessful in obtaining work. And not only do the Bantu feel that the law for the White and the Black is not similar, but we even find some of them convinced that there are two Gods, one for the White and one for the Black. I had an instance of this in an old Native woman who had suffered much and could not be convinced that the same God watched over and cared for us all, but felt that the God who gave the Europeans their life of comparative comfort and ease, could not possibly be the same God who allowed his poor Bantu to suffer so. As another instance of the inequalities existing in our social scheme, we have the fact of Natives not being allowed to travel on buses and trams in many towns, except those specially designed for them.

In connection with the difficulty experienced through men being employed almost exclusively in domestic work in the cities, I would mention that this is of course one of the chief reasons for young women, who should rightly be doing that work, going rapidly down in the social life of the community; and it is here that joint service councils of Bantu and White women would be able to do so much for the good of the community. The solution to the problem seems to me to be to get women into service, and to give them proper accommodation, where they know they are safe. Provide hostels, and club-rooms, and rest rooms for these domestic servants, where they may spend their leisure hours, and I think you will find the problem of the employment of female domestic servants will solve itself, and that a better and happier condition of life will come into being for the Bantu.

If you definitely and earnestly set out to lift women and children up in the social life of the Bantu, you will find the men will ben-efit, and thus the whole community, both White and Black. Johannesburg is, to my knowledge, a great example of endeavour for the uplift of the Bantu woman, but we must put all our energies into this task if we would succeed. What we want is more co-opera-tion and friendship between the two races, and more definite display of real Christianity to help us in the solving of these riddles. Let us try to make our Christianity practical.

15. Education in the United States of America.

Colonial officials preferred that Africans not go overseas for higher education because they would likely be influenced by people that the officials considered radical, such as W. E. B. Du Bois (see document 9). Cases like that of John Chilembwe (see document 2), for example, convinced colonial officials of the potentially subversive nature of U.S. education. Yet the limited development of local universities—a few only in British territories, none in Portuguese or French-ruled areas—and the long-term linkages that existed between Africa and Afri-can American communities in the United States, meant that large numbers of Africans continued to go overseas for their higher education. Nnamdi Azikiwe was one such individual. He studied at Lincoln University where one of his classmates was Thurgood Marshall, and continued his education at Howard University and later, at the graduate level, at the University of Pennsylvania. He became the leader of the independence movement in Nigeria during the 1940s and 1950s, the first African governor general of that country in 1960, and its first president when Nigeria became a republic in 1963. In his autobi-ography, he reflects on the decade that he spent living in the United States, a country that both shocked and impressed him.[15]

Nnamdi Azikiwe's memories of nine years spent in the United States.

On the eve of my sixtieth birthday in 1964, "Peter Pan," the satirical columnist of the *Daily Times*, asked me whether there were any events that haunted me and which had registered unfavourable impressions on my memory during my nine years' sojourn in the United States. . . .

As far as the unfavourable impressions were concerned, I replied that four lynchings had shocked me. With the aid of the maga-zine *Fact*, I was able to recollect the details of these macabre holocausts. In December 1925, two months after my arrival in the United States, Lindsay Coleman, a Negro, was tried by a Circuit Court for alleged mur-der of a plantation manager. He was found not guilty by a jury in Clarksdale, Mississippi; nevertheless he was lynched.

In June 1926, Albert Blades, a twenty-two-year-old Negro, was lynched, by hanging and burning, because he was suspected of having criminally assaulted a small white girl. The official physicians who examined the girl ex-onerated the Negro and declared that the girl was never attacked but was merely startled

---

15. Nnamdi Azikiwe, *My Odyssey: An Autobiography* (London: C. Hurst and Company, 1970), pp. 193–97.

by the presence of a black man. This happened in Osceola, Arkansas.

In November 1927, at Columbia, Tennessee, a Negro named Henry Choate was accused of attacking a white girl. It was Armistice Day and the court-house where he was to be tried was festooned with flags and bunting. A mob of white men transformed the balcony of the court into a gallows, wrested him from the police and lynched him without a fair trial.

In October 1933 a crowd of 3,000 white men, women and children in Princess Anne, Maryland, overpowered fifty policemen, smashed the doors of a prison cell, dragged out and lynched George Armwood, aged twenty-four, in one of the wildest lynching orgies ever staged in America. He was accused of attacking an aged white woman; and without giving him a fair chance to defend himself or to be tried by a lawfully constituted court, the mob took the law into their hands. The lynching was especially ghastly because one white boy, aged eighteen years, was reported by the *New York Times* of October 19, 1933, to have slashed off Armwood's ear with a knife.

On the favourable impressions, the victory of Franklin Delano Roosevelt in the presidential elections of 1932, and the introduction of the "New Deal" reinforced my faith in the ultimate emergence of the United States as a moral force in the twentieth-century world. Roosevelt's policy was radical, because with imagination and confidence he courageously departed from the beaten path of the traditional capitalist practice of leaving private entrepreneurs to determine the factors for employing labour on an inequitable basis of the "law" of supply and demand. The "New Deal" was designed to deploy public funds to create employment opportunities in public works and other units of the public sector, so that the unemployed would be kept employed. This philosophy laid a solid foundation for the elaborate machinery of social security introduced later to guarantee the welfare of what Roosevelt and his "brains trust" characterised as "the Forgotten Man."

These unfavourable and favourable impressions combined to mould my ideas and construct in my mind the image of America which has lingered. On the one side of the balance sheet, we have an America saturated with racial intolerance, bigotry and lawlessness. This was a passing phase in the saga of American history, in spite of the colourful roles of certain American politicians. The fact that successive administrations tightened the screw on the law enforcement agencies, compelling them to perform their sworn duties and protect the lives and properties of American citizens, was a clear indication that the era of unbridled fanaticism and anarchy was in process of becoming an unlamented closed chapter in American history.

On the other side of the balance sheet, we have a great and sprawling country, peopled by self-reliant, hard-working, and philanthropic go-getters, descendants of hardy pioneers who defied the elements in order to crystallise democracy as a way of life. If we examine more closely the adjectives I have employed to describe this species of humanity, we should be able to appreciate the soul of the real American.

Self-reliance has enabled Americans to build the mightiest nation on the face of the earth. Hard work has enabled them to establish the highest standard of living and remuneration for work in the whole world. Philanthropy demonstrates the humanistic philosophy of these pioneers and the spiritual nature of their make-up as fellow human beings, thus justifying the exodus of the "Pilgrim Fathers" in the seventeenth century, who defied the dangers of the Atlantic, fervently believing that, although their ancestors were "chained in prisons dark," yet they did not mortgage their conscience to the forces of oppression, intolerance and inhumanity.

Go-getting is an American trait. It implies the exercise of initiative and enterprising ability. Hardy pioneering means an adventurous spirit that ignores all hazards. It is an exemplification of willpower that is resolute, undaunted and irresistible. Democracy is the legacy bequeathed to those who are now privileged to live as full-fledged citizens of the fifty states comprising the United States of America. It means living in an atmosphere in which the state concedes to the citizen certain fundamental freedoms and basic rights: the freedom to life, the freedom of speech, the freedom of the press, the freedom to acquire and possess property, the freedom of movement, the freedom of peaceful assembly and the freedom of association. Protection of these basic freedoms is guaranteed under the provisions of a written constitution, which can not be abridged, denied or violated excepting under due process of law.

If such a country is described as "God's country," the exaggeration can be excused. But deep in my heart I can honestly confess that the United States of America impressed me as a haven of refuge for the oppressed sections of humanity in Europe, Africa, Asia and the rest of the world. It is only in the United States that any human being can live in a free environment which will give that individual full scope to develop his personality to the full, in spite of the vagaries of human life, some of which I have spotlighted above.

Therefore, if one should ask me why tears tickled down my cheek as the *Aquitania* sailed away [in 1933] from the shores of the United States of America, my simple reply would be that, despite the fact that some people who

looked like me were fed "with bread of bitterness" by a microscopic section of the backward elements of this progressive and philanthropically-minded segment of human society, this great country is still the bulwark of liberty and the haven of the children of God. Don't blame me for calling it "God's country." In the words of Louis F. Benson:

"Who shares his life's pure pleasures

And walks the honest road,

Who trades with heaping measures

And lifts his brother's load,

Who turns the wrong down bluntly

And lends the right a hand,

He dwells in God's own country,

And tills the holy land."

I lived in the United States for close on nine years. My life is a testimonial that Americans shared life's pleasures and walked the honest road with me. They traded with heaping measures and lifted the heavy load off my shoulders. They turned the wrong of inhumanity down bluntly and lent a helping hand to the forces of righteousness. Surely, people of this nature dwell in God's country and till the holy land. I am a living witness.

16. Colonial rule equals taxes and forced labor.

Despite imperial rhetoric about their civilizing mission to uplift African peoples, the main aspects of colonialism experienced by all Africans on a daily basis were the constant demands made by Europeans for taxes and labor. Geoffrey Gorer here describes the practices of colonialism that he witnessed while making an extended tour through French West Africa in 1934. Gorer, a young man at the time and not yet embarked on a career, was led in his travels by Féral Benga, an African dancer with the Folies Bergères, who invited the author to accompany him on a trip to study dance in West Africa. Gorer later moved to the United States where he studied anthropology briefly with Ruth Benedict and Margaret Mead. Benga returned to France where, after a period underground during the Nazi occupation, he eventually opened a café catering to Africans resident in Paris.[16]

---

16. Geoffrey Gorer, *Africa Dances: A Book about West African Negroes* (New York: W. W. Norton, 1962; first published 1935), pp. 92–97.

Taxes

"The idea of colonization becomes increasingly more repugnant to me. To collect taxes, that is the chief preoccupation. Pacification, medical aid, have only one aim: to tame the people so that they will be docile and pay their taxes. What is the object of tours, sometimes accompanied by bloodshed? To bring in the taxes. What is the object of studies? To learn how to govern more subtly so that the taxes shall come in better. I think of the Negroes of the A.O.F. [French West Africa] who paid with their lungs and their blood in the 1914–1918 war to give to the least "nigger" among them the right to vote for M. [Blaise] Diagne; of the Negroes of the A.E.F. [French Equatorial Africa] who are the prey of the big concessionary companies and the railway builders. . . ." So writes Michel Leiris in the diary which he kept while working for the Griaule ethnographical expedition. It is, at least as far as concerns French West Africa, a judgment which it is difficult to quarrel with. (Except that the Negroes did not even get the right to vote for M. Diagne by the sacrifice of their lungs and blood; they had had that for several years before. The victims of the 1914–1918 war were simply blood sacrifices on the altars of the white fetishes Gloire and Patrie; they didn't get any more out of the transaction than sacrificial animals usually do.)

All Negroes, with the exception of a few town dwellers, are subject to taxation in two forms—"capitation" or head-tax, and "prestation," which is defined by Larousse as "a local tax used for the upkeep of roads in the neighborhood, payable either in money or work." As far as I know this latter is assessed everywhere except in the towns at twenty francs a head; but except as a favor Negroes are not allowed to pay in money; they have to work off the tax under conditions which I shall describe in the next section.

The amount and incidence of the head-tax varies with each district. In the most favored it is only levied on all males over the age of fifteen; in the majority on all people over that age; in the most unfortunate on all people. The amount varies between six and fifty francs a year. It is usually the smallest sums which are the hardest to pay, for the taxes are assessed more or less according to the richness of the country; if they are under fifteen francs a head it is a pretty safe bet that there is no work to be found in the district and no produce which can be sold.

The district administrator is instructed from Dakar of the amount of taxes he has to collect—a sum usually calculated on the last census figures; the administrator is made responsible for seeing that the stipulated amount is brought in. He in turn assigns to the *chefs de canton* the sum for which each is responsible in his district, and they in their turn tell each village chief how much his village must contribute. The village chief is personally responsible for the taxes of the entire village; if he is unable to get enough out of the villagers he has to make up the sum himself; if the village does not pay to the full the administration takes a hand, and the village chief is the first to suffer. The village chiefs will consequently go to almost any lengths to collect the required sum, and it is on them that the chief onus is thrown.

If the money can be earned, either by selling produce or labor, the tax is not unduly hard. Moreover the census figures—which were, I think, last taken in 1931—then probably bear a reasonable relation to the population. But the districts which fulfil these conditions are almost exclusively situated within a hundred miles or so of the coast—that is to say the forest region of the Ivory Coast, with its numerous and flourishing coffee plantations, the banana area of New Guinea, and at any rate until the slump in Senegal and lower Dahomey, with groundnuts and palms respectively. But between this prolific band and the Sahara to the north there is a large area of savannah, save on the banks of the Niger indifferently watered, which can produce little beyond the food needed to support a scanty population. It is this very extensive region on which the taxation falls hardest. There is no money to be earned locally; except for rice or cotton in a few small areas there is no exportable product; however moderate the tax, it is almost impossible for the natives to acquire any money unless they go south to seek work. A considerable number do this, and all do not return, which is one of the numerous reasons why the census figure is in most districts far higher than the present population—in Bodi in North Dahomey, for instance, the 1926 census figures on which the tax is collected give the population as three thousand: according to a native estimate it is now six hundred, a statement which the number of abandoned huts confirmed—and consequently the tax which is demanded of the village works out at far more per head than the official figure. To pay the sum required is almost an impossibility; and there are numerous cases of unscrupulous administrators and/or *chefs de canton* demanding the tax two or three times in the year. There is no redress against this, except a personal appeal to the governor; and that is made very difficult.

When a village fails to pay its taxes the administration steps in brutally and ruthlessly. When punitive measures are taken, as they frequently are, the administrator himself is never present, and therefore has a complete alibi; he sends his Negro soldiers—naturally always of a different race to the people they are sent out against, most usually Bambara—with instructions to collect the money. It is axiomatic that no one treats servants so badly as a servant set in authority; no one could be more heartlessly brutal to the Negroes than the uniformed Negroes who act for the administrators. This employment of Negroes for the dirty work serves a double aim; it keeps lively the interracial hatred which is so essential for colonies where the subject races are more numerous than the colonizers, and it enables the administration to deny forthright the more inhuman practices in which they tacitly acquiesce, or should the facts be irrefutable, to lay the blame on the excessive zeal of their subordinates.

I heard on my journey a very great number of stories nauseatingly horrible, but obviously unproved. I shall only tell of those incidents which I know to be true, either from personal experience or from abundant evidence. I am not indicating the district exactly

for fear of getting my informants into trouble. None of the cases are exceptional.

A village in the southern Sudan was unable to pay the taxes; the native guards were sent, took all the women and children of the village, put them into a compound in the center, burned the huts, and told the men they could have their families back when the taxes were paid.

In North Dahomey two men who had not paid their taxes fully (they were twenty-five francs short of the hundred at the proper date) were flogged with the *chacoute* (a heavy leather whip) in front of the assembled village until they fainted, were taken to prison without medical attention where they had to work for fifty days, and were then sent back with the remainder of the tax still owing. I spoke to one of the men in question and saw his back covered with suppurating sores.

In a village in the northern Ivory Coast, the chief's son had been taken as hostage until the tax was paid. The chief had not seen his son for nearly two years. Incidentally this practice of hostage-taking is very common; and I cannot remember how many times I have been offered young girls and boys to enjoy or keep as servants for the price of the head-tax.

The following letter was received by the servant of a doctor from his father: "Envoie vite 30 francs pour impôt. Ils nous avons pris tout le bétail et tout le mil et nous crevons de faim." (Send thirty francs for taxes at once. They have taken all our animals and millet and we are starving.) In a village in the Upper Volta, people were collecting winged ants; they explained that they had nothing to eat, for the whole of their livestock and grain had been taken for taxes.

In the whole of the western Ivory Coast flogging with the *chacoute*—legally nonexistent—and imprisonment follow unpunctuality in taxpaying.

On the way to Abengourou in the Ivory Coast, though not in that *cercle*, I was stopped by a native guard who mistook my car for the administrator's. The guard was slightly wounded in the head and had with him the most miserable man I have ever seen. He was naked with his genitals much swollen, his belly puffed and bruised, his eyes closed and bloody, and blood pouring from his nearly toothless mouth. His hands were tied, but he could barely stand, much less run away. The guard explained that the man was behindhand with his taxes; he had therefore gone to fetch him to work on the road, and the man had refused on the ground that if he left his plantation at such a critical moment he would never be able to pay taxes. He had tried to resist, slightly wounding the guard, who thereupon "lui avait foutu dans la gueule." He was obviously very pleased with himself and waited anxiously for my commendation. I told him that he deserved the legion of honor.

Labour Service

"Forced labor" and "prison labor" were a few years ago the two most popular anti-Bolshevik war cries; with Russia's increasing respectability they have now become rather old-fashioned; but they are very adequate descriptions of how nine-tenths of the public work in the French West African colonies are performed. Fifty centimes—one penny at the normal rate of exchange—is considered the proper rate of remuneration for a ten-hour working day; and the "prestation" or work tax, fines, and arrears of taxes are worked off at that rate. Consequently every adult male Negro—in some districts also women and children—does at least forty days' work for the state, chiefly road making, and if it happens that he has to make roads when he should be cultivating his fields, that is just too bad. The more conscientious administrators try to avoid this contingency, but the fields have to be worked during the rainy season, which is also the time when the roads need the most attention.

Except in the districts where there are railways, the roads in French West Africa are reasonably plentiful and good. They have been built and kept in repair by unpaid laborers working without any tools except the short-handled hatchet which is the Negro's sole agricultural instrument. The roads are made of earth and in the southern part of the colony the sod is laterite, which makes a par-

ticularly good and hard surface. The best roads are slightly raised above the surrounding country, on account of the rains; the earth to make them up is scooped out of the neighboring land with these hatchets into wicker baskets which are then carried on to the road and dumped. The surface is smoothed by having mud poured on to it which is beaten by women standing in serried lines holding pieces of wood and beating the earth to the time given out by the forewoman. They keep this up for ten hours, continually stooping, many of them pregnant or with babies strapped to their backs. . . .

Except in the case of a couple of bridges being built by private contractors, I did not see any instruments of any sort being used in public works in French West Africa. Albert Londres has already described the building of the Congo-Océan railway, where each sleeper literally represents a Negro life, and where the only instruments he found were one hammer and one pickaxe for making tunnels, and I have no reason to believe that conditions are better in French West Africa. Negroes cost far less than shovels, not to mention cranes. I did not see any railway building, but the Thiess-Niger line is so bad that part of it will have to be relaid shortly; still, after the strike of 1925 the government may take a few more precautions.

In the forest regions of the Ivory Coast there is a great deal of work to be done with woodcutting and plantations and a very sparse population; consequently workers have to be recruited elsewhere, and particularly among the Mossi of the Upper Volta (now part of the Ivory Coast) who were by far the most populous tribe of the savannah; this is done both by public and private enterprise. On several occasions the administration have settled large groups of the Mossi in the Ivory Coast—sixty thousand have been moved to the neighborhood of Yammossoukro, in the middle of the forest, this year; but the Negroes support the changed climatic and dietary conditions so badly—not to mention hard work on inadequate pay—that something like half die in the first year. Private woodcutters and planters can also get permission to go and recruit the men they need; the local administrator merely tells the chiefs that so many men are required and are to be delivered at such a place and date. The men cannot refuse to go.

When men are working away from their village, they are meant to be fed and housed.

What is more they sometimes are, though in more than one case that I have seen the Society for the Prevention of Cruelty to Animals would have prosecuted me if I had given a dog the same quantity and quality of food and shelter.

17. Colonial rule equals police harassment.

Control of labor was a keystone of colonial policy in Africa. In South Africa, this control took the form of the hated pass; in Kenya it was the "kipande." Rural peasants and urban workers were the principal victims of this system, but it also affected educated Africans such as Mugo Gatheru. Gatheru, born in 1925, was the son of a "squatter" in the area of Kenya designated by colonial officials as the white highlands (where only Europeans could own the land). He learned to read and write at missionary schools and became the editor of a newspaper. For men of his emerging class, the affront of being stopped and having to produce evidence that he was not an "idler" and should not be sent to a rural "reserve" or forced to work for a European employer was especially grating. Gatheru became a thorn in the side of the British. In 1951, he traveled to the United States and enrolled at Lincoln University. Despite being subjected to investigation by the FBI and the INS as a suspected communist (the U.S. authorities were following up on a request to investigate made by British colonial officials), Gatheru remained in the United States throughout the 1950s, earning a B.A. from Lincoln and an M.A. from New York University before returning to independent Kenya in the 1960s. The following excerpt is from Gatheru's autobiography.[17]

What was the Kipande system?

The Kipande system was officially introduced in Kenya in 1921. Every male African above sixteen years of age had to be registered, finger-printed, and issued with a registration certificate—Kipande. Kipande was different from the passport, the birth certificate, the identity cards in Britain, or social security numbers in the United States of America.

In Kenya a policeman could stop an African on the road or in the street and demand that he produce his Kipande—regardless of whether the African concerned was as wise as Socrates, as holy as St. Francis, or as piratical as Sir Francis Drake.

Kipande was also used to prevent the African labourer escaping distasteful employment or from unjust employers who had power to have him arrested and then fined, imprisoned, or both. When Kenyatta took over the leadership of the Kenya African Union from James Gichuru he announced publicly that the Africans had carried "Vipande" (plural for Kipande) long enough and that they should burn them if the Kenya Government refused to repeal the ordinance which had instituted the system. The alternative, Kenyatta explained, was for the Kenya Government to issue Vipande to all the races of Kenya—the Europeans, the Asians, and the Africans. The Africans, at that time, were

---

17 R. Mugo Gatheru, *Child of Two Worlds: A Kikuyu's Story* (New York: Frederick A. Praeger, 1964), pp. 88–95.

seriously prepared to take action, illegal if necessary, to abolish Vipande whether the Government liked it or not. Mass meetings were held all over Kenya at which a lot of money was collected to buy wood for a big fire at the centre of Nairobi city on which all the Africans would burn their Vipande. This was to be an historic fire!

Quickly and wisely the Kenya Government promised the African leaders that the Kipande system would be repealed forthwith and that a system of identity cards for all the races in Kenya would replace it.

The Africans welcomed the government promise and in 1950 the Kipande system was abolished. But the scars of Kipande remained. In the thirty years of its existence Kipande caused great humiliation and hardship and was a constant grievance among my people. It cannot be said that the British Government knew nothing of this: when sending Kenyatta to England on various occasions from 1929 onwards the Africans instructed him to speak not only about the thorny problems of land but also to protest about Kipande.

A well-known missionary, and one of the few well-wishers of the Kenya Africans among the Europeans there, complained in a letter to the London *Times* of June 1938 that not less than 50,000 Africans in Kenya had been jailed since 1920 for failure to produce Vipande—an average of 5000 Africans per year!

When the Kenya Government announced officially in 1948 that the Kipande system would be abolished the Kenya settlers, as was expected, resisted strongly. The instrument which they had used so long in keeping the African labourers in a state of serfdom was now being lifted. They accused the Government of yielding to "African agitators" and "irresponsible demagogues"! The settlers did not stop to ask themselves what would be the effect of the frustrated anger of the Kenya Africans. They did not understand that no human being, of whatever nationality, can keep on indefinitely without breaking through such frustration. After all, the Kenya Africans had carried their Vipande on their persons from 1921 to 1950, and yet the Kipande was only one of innumerable grievances.

The Europeans and the Asians were free from having Vipande. The psychological effect of the Kipande system was equal to that of an African calling a European "Bwana" instead of "Mr.," or of a European calling a seventy-year-old African "boy," or referring to "natives" without a capital "N," or "native locations" in the city instead of "African sections."

The Africans were constantly worried by these passes. I remember full well that, whenever my father mislaid his Kipande he was as much worried and unhappy as if he had been an important government official accused of accepting a vicuna coat from a private citizen!

There were also numerous other passes which were equally insulting, and principally the so-called "The Red-Book" issued by the Labour Exchange and which every African domestic servant was required to carry. In the Red-Book the character of the African concerned, the amount of pay he was receiving, and the cause of dismissal were to be recorded.

I remember well one afternoon when I was walking with Muchaba who had been my chief aide during my *irua* or circumcision ceremony. We were in Pangani, one of the sections of Nairobi, when we heard a voice far away call "Simama" or "Halt!" We did not pay too much attention since we were discussing family matters. Suddenly, we heard another voice shouting loudly: "You! Stop there!" We looked back and saw two policemen hurrying towards us. We suddenly had butterflies in our stomachs. We stopped and waited for them and, as they were approaching us, I whispered to Muchaba:

"Do you have your Kipande with you?"
"No, I don't have it," he replied. "I don't have mine either."

"We'll catch hell now," Muchaba said. The two policemen came up to us.

"Why didn't you stop at once when we called you?" the first one asked. And the second one, sarcastically:

"Who do you think you are?" even before we had a chance to reply.

"At first we didn't know you were calling to us, sirs," Muchaba said. "We are very sorry."

"No, you look like law breakers, like most of the Kikuyu," one policeman said.

"Show us your Kipande quickly!" the second one demanded. "I don't have mine. I have just forgotten it," Muchaba replied.

"Where?"

"Where I work," Muchaba said.

"Where and for whom do you work?" asked the policeman.

"I work for a European lady just near the Fair View Hotel."

"What do you do?"

"I am a cook," Muchaba replied.

"Do you have any other pass as an identification?" asked the policeman.

"No. But I can give you my employer's address and the telephone number if you like," Muchaba said.

"Idiot!" shouted the policeman. "How stupid can you get? Do you expect us to make telephone calls for all criminals we arrest without their Vipande? We are not your telephone operators."

"What can I do then?" asked Muchaba.

"Carry your Kipande with you,"' replied the policeman. "Incidentally, who is this fellow here with his arms folded like a great bwana. Do you have your Kipande?" They turned to me.

"No, I don't have it. I have never had a formal Kipande," I said.

"What!" they both exclaimed thunderously.

"When I joined the Medical Department in 1945 the Senior Medical Officer sent me to the Labour Exchange to obtain my Kipande but I found out that the copies of the formal Kipande were exhausted. I was given an emergency certificate and told to get a formal Kipande later on," I explained.

"Are you still in the Medical Department?" they asked.

"No, I am working for the Kenya African Union as an assistant editor," I said.

"Where do you live?" they asked.

"Kaloleni," I replied.

"Just because you are working for that trouble-making KAU you think you don't have to carry Kipande?"

"No, that is not the reason. I just forgot my emergency certificate. I don't think that KAU is trouble making. We fight for the rights of everyone in Kenya, including the police," I said.

They looked at each other, confused. "Do you have any other papers as identification?" they asked.

"I have some papers with the letter-heading of the Kenya African Union."

"We are not interested in letter-heads. We want official documents. Any fool can produce letter-heads."

This comedy finally ended and they decided to take us to the police station.

We walked in front of them and they followed us. As we were walking I tried to get a handkerchief from my pocket to blow my nose. One policeman thought that I was insulting him by putting my hands in my pocket like a big bwana and hit me on my shoulder with his truncheon. He hit me hard. I tried to explain to him that my nose was running but I saw he was ready to hit me again, and so I kept quiet. Muchaba said nothing.

As we approached the police station I heard somebody calling:

"Hey you, that's Mr. Mathu's man. What did he do?"

Muchaba and I were afraid to look back in case we should be hit again. The two policemen answered the call and then suddenly told us to stop. We turned round and saw two other policemen coming towards us. I recognized one of them. He was my classmate at Kambui Primary School and he knew both Muchaba and I full well. We were relieved and happy! The four policemen conferred together and the one who knew us explained to his colleagues that we must have been telling the truth, and that we should not be arrested. Two of them agreed but the third still wanted to go to the police station.

At last they let us go but by then Muchaba was very late in returning to his work. His employer was very, very angry, as her dinner was late. Muchaba had not telephoned and she had no idea where to find him.

I advised Muchaba to take a taxi but there was none in sight. It was getting too late. Finally he took a bus and, when he arrived at his employer's home, he found her waiting near the gate holding a pen.

"Bring your Red-Book right away. You have no job now. You are entirely unreliable, a lazy, untrustworthy African. I hate you bloody niggers," she said.

Muchaba had no chance to explain anything. He was told to pack up his belongings and leave at once. He had some heavy luggage and couldn't move it all at once and so he took it bit by bit to the nearest street. Finally he took a taxi and came to my place. I took a chance and let him stay with me for the night! If the police had knocked me up in the night and found him with me, both of us would have been in trouble.

That evening, as he had never learnt to read or write English, Muchaba asked me to tell him what had been written in his Red-Book. I knew Muchaba very well to be a sensitive and intelligent man and was sickened to read: "He is quick in his work; he likes sweet things and may steal sugar if he has a chance; sometimes his thinking is like that of an eleven-year-old child." When Muchaba heard this he was so angry that he burnt the book. I cannot blame him for this but it put him in serious difficulty as no one would give him another job unless he produced the book, even this one with its permanent defamatory record. It was more than a month before the Labour Exchange agreed to issue Muchaba with a new book (I can only liken the process to that when one loses a passport), and then he was able to get another job working as a cook for a wealthy Indian businessman.

Muchaba's story can also illustrate the considerable licence allowed by their superiors to the ordinary police force, at that time largely illiterate, which in itself contributed to the atmosphere of European superiority and power which sapped the resistance of the unorganized African population.

In the evenings the police could knock on the door of any African in the African locations and demand to know how many people were sleeping there, how many had Kipande, and proof of where they were working. This could have happened to any African rooming place, and almost always the police called about eleven o'clock or midnight.

In some cases, a man and his wife might be sleeping peacefully but they had to open the door quickly. Police would then ask the man to produce Kipande and to say where he was working. They would search everywhere with their flash-lights and, if they were satisfied, would leave the place without even saying sorry to the couple they had awakened.

I remember full well when the police knocked up one of my uncles at about 12.45 A.M. When three policemen entered the room my uncle and his wife were trying to fix their pyjamas. One of the policemen shouted:

"How many people do you have in this room, eh?"

"Only my wife and myself, sir."

"How many people do you usually accommodate?" the second policeman demanded.

"None at all except my wife."

"My wife, my wife," the third policeman shouted. "How do we know she isn't just a prostitute from Manjengo eh?"

"No! No! You have it all wrong. This is my own legal wife and if you insist on disagreeing with me please take me to the police station," Uncle protested vehemently. His pride and dignity were badly shaken. Utterly hurt.

The three policemen left. They had caused great upset and inconvenience to my uncle and his wife but he had no remedy. He could not sue the Police Department which could always say, "They did this in the course of their duty to uproot undesirable natives": an excuse invariably accepted by their superiors.

I would illustrate the general attitude of their superiors to the police by quoting from *The Report on the Committee on Police Terms of Service*, 1942, which among other things says:

> The evidence submitted to us indicates that, in general, the illiterate African makes a better policeman than a literate African. The latter is less amenable to discipline and is reluctant to undertake the menial tasks which sometimes fall to the lot of ordinary constables. That being so, it seems to us that the policy of recruiting literates should be pursued with great caution, and that no special inducements by way of salary are necessary. In fact, we venture to go so far as to recommend the abolition of literacy allowance for new entrants.

In the rural area it was difficult for me to realize that the Africans were always accorded the last treatment. The city life taught me this.

It could well be asked why the Africans submit to the unjust domination of the police and the system of Kipande. For once the answer is quite simple: lack of good organization, one virtue of their civilization which the Europeans were not eager to pass on, and the determination of the Europeans to preserve their privileged system at any price. Thus, in 1943, there was only one African representative in the Kenya Legislative Council, none in the Executive Council, and in 1946 two were nominated in the City Council with no real voice in civic affairs. There was no effective organization to correlate the grievances of the Africans and present them with any force. Certainly neither the European settlers nor the British Colonial Government felt any inclination to remedy the appalling and obvious defects in the system which they had created, for which they were responsible, and which only they were strong enough to change.

18. Colonial rule equals censorship.

All colonial regimes kept a strict control over African speech. In every colony, whether British or French or Portuguese, criticism of the colonial administration was never acceptable and was always subject to criminal penalty. Frequently, critical comments, whether spoken or written, were deemed seditious on the grounds that they would promote hostility between the races, a legal labeling process that was never applied to settler comments on Africans. Censorship became a major source of conflict between African and European, especially because of the huge growth of the African press. While African-run newspapers had been in existence since the middle of the nineteenth century, many of these had been published under the auspices of missionary societies. From the 1920s onward, however, new publications emerged throughout Africa which took as their main subject matter the suffering of Africans under colonialism and the need for a swift movement toward independence.

One of the leaders of this critical journalism was Nnamdi Azikiwe who, after leaving the United States, went to Ghana where he became editor of the African Morning Post. On May 15, 1936, Azikiwe published a mocking article written by a prominent local opponent of British rule, Wallace Johnson. Azikiwe was arrested and charged with publishing a seditious document. Found guilty at first, with that judgement upheld all the way up through the British judicial system to the Privy Council in London, Azikiwe was later found not guilty on a technicality—that the prosecution had not proved that he was the editor of the newspaper on the exact day that the article appeared. Azikiwe left Ghana in 1937 and returned to Nigeria where he became a leader in the independence movement. The following extract from Azikiwe's autobiography reproduces the offending passage by Johnson and then lists the Privy Council's grounds for at first upholding his conviction.[18]

Personally, I [Wallace Johnson] believe the European has a God in whom he believes and whom he is representing in his churches all over Africa. He believes in the god whose name is spelt *deceit*. He believes in the god whose law is Ye strong, you must weaken the weak. Ye 'civilised' Europeans, you must 'civilise' the 'barbarous' Africans with machine guns. Ye 'Christian' Europeans, you must 'christianise' the 'pagan' Africans with bombs, poison gases, etc.

"In the colonies the Europeans believe in the god that commands 'Ye administrators …' (meaning to include therein the Government of the Gold Coast) '. . . Sedition Bill' (meaning to include therein the Criminal Code Amendment Ordinance No. 21 of 1934 of the Gold Coast) '. . . to keep the African gagged. Make Forced Labour Ordinance of the Gold Coast to work the Africans as slaves. Make Deportation Ordinance' (meaning to include therein the Kofi Sechere Detention and Removal Ordinance No. 1 of 1936) '. . . to send the Africans to exile whenever they dare to question your authority.'

"Make an ordinance to grab his money so that he cannot stand economically. Make Levy Bill (meaning to include therein the Native Administration Ordinance No. 25 of 1936 of the Gold Coast Colony) to force him to pay taxes for the importation of unemployed Europeans to serve as Stool Treasurers. Send detectives to stay around the house of any African who is nationally conscious and who is agitating for national independence and if possible to round him up in a 'criminal frame-up' (meaning thereby a criminal charge in which the evidence is fabricated) 'so that he could be kept behind the bars' (meaning thereby prison).

Among the definitions of "A seditious intention" then operative in colonial law were the following:

1. To bring into hatred or contempt or to excite disaffection against the person of His Majesty, his heirs or successors of the Government of the Gold Coast as by law established; or

2. To bring about a change in the sovereignty of the Gold Coast; or

3. To excite His Majesty's subjects or inhabitants of the Gold Coast to attempt to procure the alteration, otherwise than by lawful means, of any matter in the Gold Coast as by law established; or

4. To bring into hatred or contempt or to excite disaffection against the administration of justice in the Gold Coast; or

5. To raise discontent or disaffection among His Majesty's subjects or inhabitants of the Gold Coast; or

6. To promote feelings of ill-will and hostility between different classes of the population of the Gold Coast.

19. The impact of World War II.

World War II had a major impact on Africa in a variety of ways. On the continent it emphasized Great Britain's dependence on certain critical agricultural products, such as vegetable oils, to sustain its beleaguered economy. This dependence did not end with the war but was intensified in major agricultural campaigns such as a disastrous groundnut scheme in southern Tanganyika (mainland Tanzania) in 1947 which only aggravated colonial demands for taxes and labor. The other major impact was on the men who enlisted in the colonial armies of the French and the British and who fought against fascism

---

18. Nnamdi Azikiwe, *My Odyssey: An Autobiography* (London: C. Hurst and Company, 1970), pp. 262–64.

in both the European and the Asian theaters of action. For soldiers of the King's African Rifles, composed of troops from Kenya, Uganda, Tanganyika, and Nyasaland, this meant that they were trained in Ceylon (Sri Lanka), fought against the Japanese in Burma (Myanmar), occupied Vichy French Madagascar, and, in some cases, were stationed in Mauritius after the war. Even before the war, some had fought in the 1930s against the Italians in Somalia.

Waruhui Itote was born in 1922. Schooled at a Church of Scotland mission, he went to Nairobi at the age of 17 and worked at a grinding machine. In 1939 he started a vegetable business with the help of some friends. Since the business was not going well, and British officials told young African men that "unless we joined up and helped the Government, Kenya would be occupied by Germans and Italians," Itote enlisted in 1941. For African men such as him, their war experiences showed them how much Britain depended on the support and loyalty of African colonial troops to defend its empire, and showed them also that the supposedly invincible British could be defeated by people of "color" (the Japanese). A secondary influence were the close connections between East Africa and India, with respect to the presence of Indian communities on the continent (so favored by Frederick Lugard), the role of India in fighting the Japanese in World War II, and the powerful symbol of the Indian campaign for self-rule that led to their independence in 1947. In common with many of the African men who served overseas during the war, Waruhui Itote carried his experiences back home and eventually translated them into direct military action for the liberation of Kenya during the Mau Mau movement of the 1950s.[19]

The first time I ever thought of myself as a Kenyan was in 1943, in the Kalewa trenches on the Burma Front. I'd spent several evenings talking to a British soldier, and thought we had become friends. But I was rather surprised one evening when, after we had been talking for a while, he said, "You know, sometimes I don't understand you Africans who are out here fighting. What do you think you are fighting for?"

I didn't have to reflect much on that question—we had all had it drilled into our heads many times.

"I'm fighting for the same thing as you are, of course," I told him.

"In a funny way," he said, "I think you're right—and I'm not sure that's such a good idea."

I asked him to explain this.

"Look," he began, "I'm fighting for England, to preserve my country, my culture, all those things which we Englishmen have built up over the centuries of our history as a nation; it's really my 'national independence' that I'm fighting to preserve. And, I suppose, all that goes with it, including the British Empire. Does it seem right to you, that you should be fighting for the same things as I?"

I did not know how to answer this, so I said, "I doubt it, I don't think so."

"You'd better not think so," he replied. "Naturally, we're all fighting to protect not only our own countries but the whole world against Fascism and dictatorship; we know that. But I can't see why you Africans should fight to protect the Empire instead of fighting to free yourselves. Years from now, maybe, your children will fight a war to preserve the national independence of your country, but before that it's up to you to see that they get an independence in the first place, so they can preserve it later!"

---

19. Waruhui Itote (General China), *"Mau Mau" General* (Nairobi: East African Publishing House, 1967), pp. 9–12, 23–25.

He turned away for a moment, and then turned back for a last word before leaving me alone.

"At least if I die in this war," he said softly, "I know it will be for my country. But if you're killed here, what will your country have gained?"

A week later he was killed, in Burma and far from home, but still a link in the defence and preservation of his own Britain. What he'd told me never left my mind. At first I could only ease the conflicts in my head by thinking of myself simply and purely as a mercenary, fighting for a foreign power which just happened to be our colonial ruler. But being a mercenary seemed cheap and second-rate, especially when there were more worthy causes much nearer my own home.

The following year I was at the Calcutta Rest Camp, where I met a tall and powerful Negro from the American South. An English-speaking Tanganyikan, Ali, was with me and the three of us started chatting. "What's your real name?" I asked the Negro, when I read the name "Stephenson" on his American Army bush jacket.

"What do you mean, 'real name'? That's my name right here, 'Stephenson'," he replied.

I explained that I meant his African name. Since he was a black man like the rest of us, he must have an African name somewhere in his background.

"If I had an African name," he said, "it must have been lost a long time ago, probably on the slave ship that brought one of my grandfathers to America. . . ."

"What about your tribe?" Ali asked him. "Can't you even remember that?"

Stephenson shook his head, looking round at the handful of other African soldiers who had gathered at the interesting sound of our conversation.

"You guys," he said very clearly, "are all looking at me as though I'm some freak, something strange, just because I don't have an African name. Well, I got this way because somewhere, a long time ago, some Arabs shipped my people to America, and after that we all grew up in a Christian country. But the same thing can happen to people when the Christians come to them—you don't have to be taken to England to lose not only your names but your whole way of life as well. You can lose it right out from under you in your own country! Right now you're being baptized as Christians generation after generation; one day you'll all wake up and think that you *are* Christians. Won't this make it easy for the white men to keep on ruling you? Some of you will believe it when you're told that the white way of life, the white religions, everything white is the best thing for Africans to believe in and follow. Then who will be willing to fight for your freedom?"

He must have seen that his conversation was turning into a speech, and I thought for a moment he was going to break off out of embarrassment. But we were all somehow held by his words, and fortunately, I think for all of us, he didn't stop. Instead he told us about the colour-bar in America, a fact, he said, which screamed at him in hotels, cinemas, buses and shops even though all Americans, from Roosevelt downwards, denied there was such a thing. America was a great nation, he said, but eaten away inside by racial discrimination; a nation of two standards and two faces, seemingly lacking the capacity to heal itself.

"We Negroes in America are always being told that it is the land of freedom," he continued, "that we have nothing to worry about as long as we work hard. So we go along, suffering for decades. And you'll be misled in the same way after this war, I'm sure. The British or whoever rules your countries will tell you that nothing is wrong, that you should leave everything to them and not worry. I don't know how much you've suffered in the past, but I know you'll suffer in the future if you don't have your own freedom."

I was listening very closely to all this, for it had called up in me memories of that other strange conversation I had had in Burma.

"All I can say," Stephenson went on, "is that you shouldn't be misled by white Christians who tell you they are superior with their holy names and their holy way of life. Jerusalem isn't in heaven, you know, it's just in Palestine and people are fighting there with bombs and shells, dying in the so-called Holy Places."

This rather shocked me, for I had always believed Jerusalem to be in Heaven. "White Christians are fighting each other right now, so don't you worry when they tell you not to fight for your own freedom," Stephenson told us, almost with a shout. "But the whites who are fighting now will be heroes in their own countries forever and amen, while you Africans will be heroes for a day and then you'll be forgotten. If you want to be heroes, why don't you fight for your own countries?"

Stephenson's speech and the long talks I had with him over the next few days were like being in school again. He was fond of talking about history, and especially about wars and revolutions—his favourite example was Haiti, where black men had fought and won their freedom from Napoleon, despite claims that they could never succeed. Before we parted, Stephenson told me he liked my "guts" and that he would make arrangements for me to get to America, where I could find the education I would need to help my people. His promise was sincere, but the fortunes of war never brought us together again, and what was then a big part of my dreams never came true. Still, he had been a good teacher at an important moment in my life.

I was still in Calcutta when I lost my way in a subway and asked a passing Indian lady for directions. It turned out that her family had been in Tanganyika for many years and she herself spoke Swahili. She invited me to her home for a meal and I was only too glad to accept the chance of some conversation about Africa. Her husband was particularly interested in knowing what my fighting experiences had been, and what the war in Burma was like. We were taking tea when our conversation turned to political topics, in which, after my talks with Stephenson, I had begun to take a great interest. I was anxious to hear what somebody who knew Africa would have to say about our situation there.

"While you're here in India," the man was telling me, "you ought to pay attention to what we are doing, because you might learn something to help your own countries. We Indians are fighting for others in this war, but in return we've received a promise of Independence when it ends. I have seen many Africans fighting alongside our men, but I haven't heard what demands you've made for the end of the war?"

I certainly didn't know of any myself, and said so. "So you mean," he asked, "when the British in Kenya came and told you to fight, you just got up without a word and went?" I had to admit that was more or less the case, except of course that we had been told our country was threatened with invasion by the Germans and Italians, whom we could only imagine to be the worst monsters on earth.

"You should have demanded Independence as your minimum price for fighting," he said.

"But," I interrupted, "Europeans have all the land and schooling, and Africans have no factories or anything else to support themselves. How could we begin to run our own country right now?" My background on such topics was limited, and I could only feel a sense of wonder at the whole idea.

"If you must have them," the Indian replied, "you can keep all the Europeans you need after Independence—we will even be doing that for a while here in India. But at least you will have your say in what goes on, instead of being always at the mercy of foreigners. And it won't take long before you are running everything yourselves. If you remember, you were colonized in the first place because you had no education and no weapons to match the Europeans. Now some of you have got education, and some of you know how to use European weapons and can get them if necessary—is there anything else you have to wait for?"

Conversations like this continued throughout my stay in Calcutta. My new friends took a great interest in me, and often talked about the things we servicemen could do for ourselves once we were back in our home countries. Co-operatives were important, they told me, for a hundred ex-service-men with gratuities could get rich much faster than one man alone, struggling against large organizations. Unity and trust seemed to my Indian friends to be the most important elements in any kind of social or political activity, and they transmitted to me a high regard for co-operation, as well as a deepening awareness that I personally wanted to play an active part in bringing Independence to my people. . . .

I join the K.A.R. [Kenya African Rifles]

In 1941 Gachehe joined the army and Gakunga went to Kisumu. There was also some trouble with the money in our business and we agreed to close it down. Late in 1941 I decided to go into the army and on the second of January, 1942, I enlisted at Langata Camp, on the edge of the Nairobi Game Park. After three months Depot training at Ruiru, and a similar period at Nanyuki and Yatta, I was posted to 36 KAR [Kenya African Rifles] at Moshi in Tanganyika. In the full battalion there were only nine Kikuyu and since we constituted one-fifth of Kenya's population this seemed curious. Although most Europeans condemned us as bad and disloyal people, it is more likely that they saw us as the greatest threat to their dominant position and to the strange feudal society they had created in Kenya.

Life in the Army training depot quickly revealed some of the humiliating absurdities of colour discrimination. There was a large difference between the pay packets of European and African corporals, although both of them had the same responsibilities. We shared the same chances of death and salvation, but used separate messes and separate lavatories.

From Moshi we were drafted to Ceylon, and travelled there in a troopship. It is probably difficult for others to understand how surprised we were to find ourselves doing P.T. in a house moving on water. New experiences were crowding in on me. When we were two days out from Ceylon the alarm was sounded as a practice, but one young Tanganyikan

thought it was the real thing and jumped into the sea with his lifebelt on. We were astounded at the speed with which a destroyer rushed in like a hawk and plucked him out of the water. To us it was miraculous to watch.

After completing some rigorous training manoeuvres in Ceylon we left on 12 July, 1943 by ship, rail and road for the Burma Front. We were to relieve a section of the Indian Army that had been severely battered. Just before we reached the India/Burma border I was promoted to full corporal.

The Japanese knew how to fight, especially in the jungle. Their snipers always fired on our leaders, the officers, the sergeants and corporals, and so we removed all arm chevrons and wore wristbands of rank in their place. We developed extra instincts for danger. The Europeans covered their faces with black boot polish, for no one wanted to stick out in any way. We all wanted to merge into one anonymous group.

I learnt many useful things about the spirit of men under the strain of fighting. In a crisis, the calibre and aspect of the leaders is all important. The Indians we replaced had poor officers and they were steadily defeated. Our colonel and his subordinates were excellent and we held our line, though at a heavy cost in men's lives and bodies. The Japanese split up into small groups and, as a result, greatly increased their effectiveness in this type of country. A group of three or four people can easily achieve the same results as a full company by rapid movement and careful shooting. The Japanese knew how to conceal themselves. They dug pits well behind our lines, camouflaged them with living grass, and used them as ammunition dumps and food stores and also as shelters. In order to survive anything at all a soldier must carry enough food and ammunition. Once he has lost either of these he becomes useless.

It was always raining in the Burma forests and we never changed our clothes. Leeches presented a problem that was never really solved. Food and other supplies were dropped by parachute, including the very welcome bottles of rum issued to warm us up spiritually as well as physically. I saw elephants being used to carry ammunition. The jungle trees were soft and not at all like those in our Kenya forests. They were easily chopped down with a panga [machete] and we used them to make a surface on the forest tracks for our transport. I was so busy merely surviving that I did not think much about Kenya and home at this time, although I used to send back the usual stereotyped letter-forms.

As the battle went on we suffered severe casualties and when we reached Kalewa we were relieved by another battalion. At one stage, morale dropped very low indeed and none of us could see any end to it at all but death. Many started malingering. Thomas, a Masai friend from Tanganyika, wanted to shoot himself through the middle of his hand so as to be returned home. I dissuaded him by pointing out that if he did this, even if he went back to Tanganyika, he would be crippled and poor, whereas by sticking it out he had at least an even chance of surviving intact.

During the see-saw Kalewa battle we were told to dig a slit-trench, but as soon as it was finished we were told to leave it and advance. After half a mile we stopped, buckled to and dug another slit-trench; as soon as we had made this one snug and comfortable we upped sticks again and advanced another half-mile, only to go through the whole rigmarole of digging and abandoning once more. By this time people were getting fed up and Private Masood showed his feelings by relieving himself in his trench and not even bothering to cover it up with earth. Many others followed his lead as we jerked our way forward. But then we had to retreat and when the Japanese airplanes strafed us we had to use our former trenches, muck and all! This taught me that if you have built something good, it is not right to destroy it, because you do not know when you will need it later.

After this no askari [African soldier] was ever angry again at being told to dig trenches. We all saw their importance in saving our lives. Even we corporals found it easier from then on. There was no more talk of "I've fifty

rounds of ammunition and you've fifty rounds of ammunition, however many stripes you may have. Let's see who's who."

In Ceylon we were taught to swim and it seemed a complete waste of time. But when we crossed the Chindwin River, and saw boats capsize under bombing attacks and swimmers saving not only themselves but many others as well, we revised our opinions. We slowly realized that whenever anyone was instructing us we must listen carefully. We could never know when the lesson would come in useful.

In 1944 we returned to India from the Kalewa battlefront. I took back with me many lasting memories. Among the shells and bullets there had been no pride, no air of superiority from our European comrades-in-arms. We drank the same tea, used the same water and lavatories, and shared the same jokes. There were no racial insults, no references to "niggers," "baboons" and so on. The white heat of battle had blistered all that away and left only our common humanity and our common fate, either death or survival.

I had learnt much, too, about military organization. I was now familiar with the procedure and conduct of pre-battle meetings. I realized the importance of establishing a Headquarters in every camp as a centre for communications, reports, records, discipline and control. Information, not only about the enemy, but also about your own forces and their positions, is crucially important in war, especially in guerilla fighting.

Perhaps most important, I had become conscious of myself as a Kenya African, one among millions whose destinies were still in the hands of foreigners, yet also one who could see the need and the possibility of changing that situation.

Late in 1944 we returned to Nairobi and at the Railway Station our troop-train was met by Eliud Mathu, the first nominated African member of the Kenya Legislative Council. The military bands were playing and beautifully dressed European ladies chattered while they served us with tea and cakes on the platform. This was a very surprising thing, because we knew that, the next day, if we so much as looked at one of them in the Nairobi streets we would be arrested. But today we were heroes and they were grateful. Their tea and cakes nearly choked me.

When I went home on leave I found my darling Leah had been very worried and frightened, for people had said I was dead and many men had offered to marry her. However, she had remained faithful and our baby boy, Itote, had now grown very big. Leah was beside herself with joy at seeing me and we were very happy during our short time together.

On my return from leave in 1945 1 was posted to the 3rd KAR Depot at Jinja, Uganda. I met and talked with many Baganda there. They told me that they had their own king, and I even saw the police giving tax money to the Kabaka, not to a European District Commissioner. We discussed these things with the other Kikuyu in the battalion and talked about the Kikuyu Central Association which had been proscribed in 1940 and about the iniquitous Carter Land Commission Report and of our leaders' attempts to get it revised. We talked about our great leader, Jomo Kenyatta, who had been fighting for us for so many years in England. It was time he came back to lead us, like Moses, into the Promised Land.

The KAR had been sent to Uganda because of some unrest there. I particularly remember one Muganda called Musa. We were drinking "Mwenge" at his house one day when he gave us a strong lecture.

"Why have you come here to plague us?" he asked, "and to punish us for trying to get our freedom? Why aren't you helping your own people to get theirs? The leaders of your Kikuyu Central Association were all deported and you do nothing. You have a duty to fight until you have made Kenyatta your Kabaka and until your taxes go to him, not to the English. You should be making your own armies and your own roads and building schools for your own kind of education. If you don't fight for Kenyatta to become your Kabaka you will be a useless lot of people. Are you Kikuyu just a collection of women?"

20. The dream of the warrior.

Mugo Gatheru's dream reveals the kind of class consciousness that developed among educated Africans (who were overwhelmingly male) after World War II. Full of contradictions, colonialism had enabled men like Gatheru to imagine a better life for themselves and their people while at the same time denying them the right to effect such change in practice. Frustration was a major force in post-World War II nationalism among these elites, and the possibility of bringing about rapid and forceful change was attractive. Yet the rhetoric of such dreams reflected often another contradiction: that between members of the elite's visions of a liberated nation and their hopes for their own class position within a free Africa.[20]

Day after day, as I lived and worked in Nairobi, my mind would drift into "The Dream of the Warrior," a fable I made up in which the main character was a Kikuyu boy named Gambuguatheru, a disguised form of my own name. My dream was, to me, also a kind of "revelation," in which it was "re- vealed" to me that it is wrong to think that heroism can be displayed in warfare only, though many people cling to that idea. A true hero may also display his mettle in fighting against the wrong deeds or ideas of those around him, just as much as in actual warfare. And so I kept on dreaming.

20. R. Mugo Gatheru, *Child of Two Worlds: A Kikuyu's Story* (New York: Frederick A. Praeger, 1964), pp. 101–04.

Gambuguatheru, of my dream, was a boy when the white men came. He became so curious to know who they were and what they wanted in his country that he was determined to go and question a European. One evening he told his father of his intent, and his father was so astonished at his son's daring that he would not allow him to sleep alone in his room for fear he might escape and go out to accomplish this dangerous mission. Next morning his father, still determined to dissuade Gambuguatheru, told him how the white men could shoot black men at a great distance and how they could make a box (gramophone) speak, but Gambuguatheru was still determined.

At noon he went to a certain missionary station and there he found an English missionary. He was told by the missionary that the sole aim of the white men was to preach the gospel. After receiving several presents he returned to his home. The whole family was amazed to hear of the boy's adventure since he was the first among them to talk to a white man. And he had returned unharmed.

In spite of his father's opposition to any more contact between his son and the missionary and the latter's plan to spread the new gospel, Gambuguatheru decided to take the leadership of his people so that their ignorance of the foreigners might not cause them loss in trade or menace their control of their country. How to do that was a serious problem. People began to fear him for his queer behaviour, but his personality was such that once he began talking people gathered round him to listen. In this way he was able to make most of the people trust him.

During this time there was a belief that if one wrote a letter trying to contact a European, or if one invented something like a machine, one's hands would be cut off by the white men. Gambuguatheru wanted to prove the truth or falsity of this belief so that he could rid his country of apprehension if it was false. "But what shall I write about?" he wondered. At last an idea struck him. He saw that the country was desperately in need of education and he wanted men and women to come who would concentrate only on educating his people. After much thinking and hesitation he wrote the letter and gave it to the missionary, who posted it for him to England. After a year he got a reply which promised him that he would get the men he wanted in a few months' time. And nothing was said about cutting off his hands for having written the letter.

Gambuguatheru then decided to turn to matters concerning the administration of his country. Already some administrative centres had been established in different parts of the country. He learned that the Europeans staying in these centres were called District Commissioners. They had already begun giving orders to the people around them. He very well knew that these District Commissioners would not agree to train him so that he could become a District Commissioner too since he would be trying to be their equal. So taking his spear and club he went out to go to the Governor to demand such training.

At the Governor's gate he was stopped from entering by gate-keepers. He was so dusty that they could not believe that such a man was entitled to talk to the Governor. Fortunately, the Governor happened to be walking round his garden and saw him. Gambuguatheru at once left the gate-keepers and ran to the nearest side of the garden. Then, speaking the bad English he had picked up from the missionaries, he shouted to the Governor. It was a wonder to hear an African talking to the Governor on such a subject in so loud and peremptory a manner!

Although he was the dirtiest man the Governor had ever seen, Gambuguatheru was admitted. It was arranged that he should be trained as a District Commissioner. The training took two years, after which he returned to his home and was made a D.C. He found that his people had abandoned all their old customs and copied the foreign ones. He was not impressed by all this. Within six months he had made his people see the mistake of giving up all their customs, so that it was easy for him to introduce subjects like African pottery, painting, the blacksmith's craft, and carving in the schools. Later, he established a school teaching only old things and trying to improve them by applying foreign methods where necessary.

The results of this school were so successful that years afterwards it was one of the biggest and most liked in Kikuyuland. After Gambuguatheru's death his statue was placed at the gate of the school, and the following words written on it:

A HERO HE WAS INDEED! IN BOTH THOUGHT

AND DEED. HE NEVER LEFT ANYTHING

UNDONE IF HE KNEW IT SHOULD BE DONE.

Now that I have had a college education I recognize that in this daydream, which I used to imagine at the age of twenty, my unconscious mind had condensed and disguised all sorts of ideas and images that I was getting from my reading and from the new experiences I was having in the big city of Nairobi. Now, for the first time in my life I was beginning to get interested in "politics"—those serious affairs that were affecting all Kenya Africans. My image of myself and of what the country needed was not yet clear. The vision of myself in the dream was A SORT OF COMBINED IMAGE OF "The Educated Ones"—that very small group of Kenya Africans who had been away to colleges and universities overseas and who were the acknowledged leaders among the Africans. Of these, three stood out above all the rest, Jomo Kenyatta, Mbiyu Koinange, and Eliud Wambu Mathu. To understand my dream, one needs to understand them.

21. Freedom in our lifetime.

World War II escalated economic and political tensions in South Africa. The demands of war production led to a huge expansion of African urbanization. Segregated areas such as Soweto (South West Townships) were built by the government to house the new immigrants, and the pass law was strictly enforced to maintain the supply and circulation of cheap black labor on which the country's industries depended. In this context of urban expansion and impoverishment, the African National Congress (ANC) took the lead as the prime political representative of African frustrations, especially in the person of younger people such as Anton Lembede and Nelson Mandela who were more ready to demand immediate action than were their elders.

Lembede was born in 1914, the son of a farm laborer. Educated initially by his mother, he later won scholarships that enabled him to train as an elementary school teacher. Subsequently, while teaching full time, he secured a B.A., a law degree, and an M.A. in philosophy. Along with Mandela, he was a founder of the ANC's Youth League and became its first president in 1944. A fervent anti-communist, Lembede believed that contrary to its past policy of aiming to work with representatives of all groups opposed to racial discrimination in South Africa, the ANC should focus primarily on the concerns of Africans since they were the majority of the population and the segment most affected by colonialism. He also argued against past policies of petitioning and sending letters of protest, and argued that the ANC should take much more forceful steps to achieve its goals. He advocated strikes, boycotts, and stay-at-homes. Lembede died prematurely of natural causes in 1947, working at the time on a doctorate in law. His Africanist ideas lost favor in the ANC after his death, but reappeared in the Pan-Africanist Congress formed in 1958.[21]

Anton Lembede outlines the policy of the African National Congress Youth League, May 1946.

The history of modern times is the history of nationalism. Nationalism has been tested in the people's struggles and the fires of battle and found to be the only effective weapon, the only antidote against foreign rule and modern imperialism. It is for that reason that the great imperialistic powers feverishly endeavour with all their might to discourage and eradicate all nationalistic tendencies among their alien subjects; for that purpose huge and enormous sums of money are lavishly expended on propaganda against nationalism which is dubbed, designated, or dismissed as "narrow," "barbarous," "uncultured," "devilish" etc. Some alien subjects become dupes of this sinister propaganda and consequently become tools or instruments of imperialism for which great service they are highly praised, extolled and eulogised by the imperialistic power and showered with such epithets as "cultured," "liberal," "progressive," "broadminded" etc.

All over the world nationalism is rising in revolt against foreign domination, conquest and oppression in India, in Indonesia, in Egypt, in Persia and several other countries. Among Africans also clear signs of national awakening, national renaissance, or rebirth are noticeable on the far-off horizon.

A new spirit of African nationalism, or Africanism, is pervading through and stirring the African society. A young virile nation is in the process of birth and emergence. The national movement imbued with and animated by the national spirit is gaining strength and momentum. The African National Congress Youth League is called upon to aid and participate in this historical process. African nationalism is based on the following cardinal principles:

1. *Africa is a blackman's country.* Africans are the natives of Africa and they have inhabited Africa, their Motherland, from times immemorial; Africa belongs to them.

2. *Africans are one.* Out of the heterogeneous tribes, there must emerge a homogeneous nation. The basis of national unity is the nationalistic feeling of the Africans, the feeling of being Africans irrespective of tribal connection, social status, educational attainment or economic class. This nationalistic feeling can only be realised in and interpreted by [a] national movement of which all Africans must be members.

3. *The Leader of the Africans will come out of their own loins.* No foreigner can ever be a true and genuine leader of the African people because no foreigner can ever truly and genuinely interpret the African spirit which is unique and peculiar to Africans only. Some foreigners Asiatic or European who pose as African leaders must be categorically denounced and rejected. An African must lead Africans. Africans must honour, venerate and find inspiration from African heroes of the past: Shaka, Moshoeshoe, Makana, Hintsa, Khama, Mzilikazi, Sekhukhuni, Sobhuza and many others.

4. *Cooperation between Africans and other non-Europeans on common problems and issues may be highly desirable.* But this occasional cooperation can only take place between Africans as a single unit and other non-European groups as separate units. Non-European unity is a fantastic dream which has no foundation in reality.

5. *The divine destiny of the African people is National Freedom.* Unless Africans achieve national freedom as early as possible they will be confronted with the impending doom and imminent catastrophe of extermination; they will not be able to survive the satanic forces, economic, social and political unleashed against them. Africans are being mowed

21. Thomas Karis and Gwendolen M. Carter, eds., *From Protest to Challenge: A Documentary History of African Politics in South Africa, 1882–1962* (Stanford: Hoover Institution Press, 1972), vol. 2, Thomas Karis, ed., *Hope and Challenge, 1935–1952*, pp. 317–18. Reprinted with the agreement of the Hoover Institution Press.

down by such diseases as tuberculosis, typhus, venereal diseases etc. Infantile mortality is tremendously high. Moral and physical degeneration is assuming alarming dimensions. Moral and spiritual degeneration manifests itself in such abnormal and pathological phenomena as loss of self confidence, inferiority complex, a feeling of frustration, the worship and idolisation of white men, foreign leaders and ideologies. All these are symptoms of a pathological state of mind.

As a result of educational and industrial colour bars, young African men and women are converted into juvenile delinquents.

Now the panacea of all these ills is National Freedom, in as much as when Africans are free, they will be in a position to pilot their own ship and, unhampered, work toward their own destiny and, without external hindrance or restriction devise ways and means of saving or rescuing their perishing race.

Freedom is an indispensable condition for all progress and development. It will only be when Africans are free that they will be able to exploit fully and bring to fruition their divine talent and contribute something new towards the general welfare and prosperity of Mankind; and it will only be then that Africans will enter on a footing of equality with other nations of the world into the commonwealth of nations; and only then will Africans occupy their rightful and honourable place among the nations of the world.

6. *Africans must aim at balanced progress or advancement*. We must guard against the temptation of lop-sided or one-sided progress. Our forces as it were, must march forward in a coordinated manner and in all theatres of the war, socially, educationally, culturally, morally, economically, and politically. Hence the Youth League must be all inclusive.

7. *After national freedom, then socialism*. Africans are naturally socialistic as illustrated in their social practices and customs. The achievement of national liberation will therefore herald or usher in a new era, the era of African socialism. Our immediate task, however, is not socialism, but national liberation.

Our motto: *Freedom in Our Life Time*.

22. Women and men on strike.

In the immediate aftermath of World War II, colonial Africa was racked by labor conflict. Africans like Waruhui Itote had volunteered in large numbers to fight with the allies and had listened to the anti-Axis rhetoric that the war was being fought to keep the world free of Nazi aggression and to liberate the peoples conquered by the Germans, the Italians, and the Japanese. Yet after the war, none of the European powers extended this essentially anti-colonial rhetoric to their own empires. Instead they sought to rebuild their war-torn economies by imposing greater production targets and labor demands on their subject peoples. Africans responded with a series of massive strikes—in South Africa, Kenya, Senegal, Ghana, and elsewhere—that demonstrated that they would not passively accept these new demands. Perhaps the most famous of these strikes, both because of its magnitude and because of its celebration in a novel by the Senegalese author Sembene Ousmane, took place in Senegal and extended over a period of six months. In this extract from the novel, God's Bits of Wood, *the strike, and particularly the role of women in its organization and success, serves as an opportunity to discuss issues of women and men, of army camps, of the early slave port of Gorée, and of demon possession and illegitimate children.*[22]

22. Sembene Ousmane, *God's Bits of Wood* (London: Heinemann, 1985; first published in 1960 as *Les Bouts de Bois de Dieu*), pp. 184–202. Reprinted with the permission of Heinemann Educational Publishers, a division of Reed Educational & Professional Publishing.

The crowd had preceded the delegates to the Place Aly N'Guer. Weary with the long hours of waiting, first at the union building and then before the offices of the company, most of them were sitting on the dusty ground, but others gathered in little animated groups, discussing the events of the day, while the sun blasted their sweaty shoulders and arms and skulls with the last of that day's fires. Penda, Dieynaba, and Mariame Sonko tried as best they could to maintain some semblance of order among the excited women, but it was not until the delegation arrived and took up its position at the center of the square that the clamor finally subsided.

Lahbib spoke first. He gave them all of the details of the meeting with Dejean and his associates, but he was a bad speaker and he knew it, so he performed his duty as rapidly as possible and turned the platform over to Bakayoko. The trainman waited until the murmurs which had followed Lahbib's account died down. His voice was clear and distinct and could be heard at the farthest corners of the square. Since they already knew what had happened that afternoon, he spoke first of other things, beginning with a brief history of the events which had brought the [railway] line into being, and then speaking of the strike of September 1938 and of the men who had died in it. He knew that he would provoke the anger of the crowd when he concluded, "And now they refuse to give us what we are asking for, on the pretext that our wives and our mothers are concubines, and we and our sons are bastards!"

Again he had to wait for silence, and then he said, "Well, we are not going to give in to them and go back to work! And it is here that this strike must be won! In every town I have visited in these past months I have been told, 'If Thiès can hold out, we will hold out.' Workers of Thiès, it is here, in this city, that there is a Place du Premier Septembre, in honor of the men who died in 1938, and it is in their name that you must hold out now. You know that there is support for you everywhere—from Kaolack to Saint-Louis, from Guinea to Dahomey, and even in France itself. The time when we could be beaten by

dividing us against ourselves is past. We will maintain the order for an unlimited strike, and we will continue to maintain it until we have won!"

Shouts and roars of approval came back to him from the crowd, where even the few who had remained seated were standing now and waving their fists with the others. But in the midst of this unleashed tumult, a little group of women managed to make its way through the crush and approach the delegates. Bakayoko saw them and raised his arms, calling for silence.

"Our gallant women have something to say to us," he cried. "They have the right to be heard!"

It was Penda who addressed them, hesitantly at first, but gathering assurance as she spoke.

"I speak in the name of all of the women, but I am just the voice they have chosen to tell you what they have decided to do. Yesterday we all laughed together, men and women, and today we weep together, but for us women this strike still means the possibility of a better life tomorrow. We owe it to ourselves to hold up our heads and not to give in now. So we have decided that tomorrow we will march together to Dakar."

For a moment Penda's voice was lost in a confused murmuring that linked astonishment and misgiving, and then she spoke again, more firmly.

"Yes—we will go together to Dakar to hear what these *toubabs* have to say and to let them see if we are concubines! Men, you must allow your wives to come with us! Every woman here who is capable of walking should be with us tomorrow!"

Again there was murmuring and shouting, and some applause, but there were also cries of remonstrance and protest. Bakayoko took Penda by the arm,

"Come to the union office with us," he said. "Your idea is good, but you can't start on something like this without thinking it over carefully."

As they crossed the square, through the gradually scattering crowd, they passed dozens of little groups discussing this new development. It was the first time in living memory that a woman had spoken in public in Thiès, and even the onslaught of night could not still the arguments.

The discussion at the union office was no less heated. Balla expressed the opinion of many when he said. "I'm against letting the women go. It's normal that they should support us; a wife should support her husband, but from that to a march on Dakar. . . . No, I vote against it. The heat or their anger or something his gone to their heads! Lahbib, would you take the responsibility for letting the women go?"

"We can't possibly listen to everyone's ideas or opinions about it. If you wish, we can take a vote."

Bakayoko interrupted the argument that threatened to break out. "We have no right to discourage anyone who wants to strike a blow for us," he said brutally. "It may be just that blow that is needed. If the women have decided, all that is left for us to do is to help them. I move that the delegates from Dakar leave immediately to warn the local committee of their arrival. You're from Dakar, aren't you?" he asked, speaking to Beaugosse for the first time. "How long do you think it will take them to get there?"

"I've never gone to Dakar on foot," Beaugosse answered, "but I don't think it is anything for women to try. Besides, there is no water there; when I left, Alioune and all the other men were scouring the city for a cask or even a bottle of water—which is what the women should be doing. Instead of that, they have been battling troops in the streets and starting fires. Now the soldiers and the militia are patrolling everywhere. You would be sending those women straight into the jaws of a lion.'"

"You can keep your French for yourself," Bakayoko said. "The men will understand you better if you speak their language. As for the men in Dakar looking for water for their families, the time when our fathers would have considered that demeaning is past. If all the workers thought like you, we might as well say good-by to the strike and to all the months of sacrifice."

"All right, Bakayoko," Lahbib said. "Calm down, and let's get back to practical matters. If the women have decided to go, we must help them and prepare an escort for them. We'll have to do something about the children, too—at least about those whose mothers will be leaving. I suggest that we try to find some trucks and send them into the villages in the brush country. Everyone here has relatives in the villages. As for you, Penda, you will have to be sure that the men who come with you do not bother the women; and if you find that this march is too hard for the women, stop them and make them turn back. There will be no shame in that, and no one will hold it against you."

If the truth be told, although Bakayoko, with his manner of disregarding destiny or bending it to his will, was the soul of this strike, it was Lahbib, the serious, thoughtful, calm, and modest Lahbib, who was its brain. Lahbib counted each one of God's bits of wood, weighed them, and balanced them, but the strength that was in them came from Bakayoko.

While the men discussed the measures to be taken at the union office, the women prepared for their departure. An inky night flowed through the city, somber and viscid, as if the heavens had decanted a layer of crude oil across the earth. The cries and shouts that pierced the darkness were like fitful flashes of lightning, but the ceaseless sound of the tam-tams seemed to carry with it a promise that dawn would come.

The compound of Dieynaba, the market woman, had been turned into the major place of assembly, although she herself was not to leave because Gorgui was dying. Shadows came and went in the courtyard, challenging and calling to each other; the squalling of children and the excited chattering and laughter of the old women who were being left at home added to the hubbub and confusion, but at the same time there was a steady trampling of purposeful feet, like the sounds of a legion lifting camp.

Another group was making ready in the Place du Premier Septembre, just across from the militiamen who stood guard in front of the police station. Prevented by their orders from talking with the women, and uneasy in the flickering light of the lanterns they had brought from the guardhouse, they watched this gathering of shadows without knowing quite what to do, but there were some among them who listened to the drums and knew what was in the air.

At last, toward two o'clock in the morning, when a few venturesome stars had succeeded in stabbing through the obscurity, the two groups came together. A cloud of white dust, pushed up and out by a lazy wind, rose to the sky and a meeting with the darkness.

"Now we are leaving!" Penda cried. Like so many echoes, hundreds of voices answered her. "Now we are leaving . . . leaving . . . leaving. . . . "Preceded, accompanied, and followed by the beating of the drums, the cortège moved out into the night.

At the first light of morning, some of the men who had gone out with the women to speed them on their way turned and went back to Thiès.

"Do you think they will get there safely?" Bakary asked. The bowl of Bakayoko's pipe glowed briefly in the gray dawn. "Yes, Uncle," he said, "We have faith in them."

To observe the ceremony of the women's departure properly, Bakary had girded his arms with amulets and fetishes. His upper arms were completely covered by circlets of red, black, and yellow leather, and his forearms with bracelets made of antelope horns edged with horsehair or covered with red cloth sewn with *cauris,* the little shells which once had been used as money. On the index finger of his right hand he wore an enormous ring of raw metal. He had sworn that none of these charms would leave his body until the women's journey had ended. . . .

Ever since they left Thiès, the women had not stopped singing. As soon as one group allowed the refrain to die, another picked it up, and new verses were born at the hazard of chance or inspiration, one word leading to another and each finding, in its turn, its rhythm and its place. No one was very sure any longer where the song began, or if it had an ending. It rolled out over its own length,

like the movement of a serpent. It was as long as a life. . . .

The sun was behind them, beating ever harder on their backs, but they paid no attention to it; they knew it well. The sun was a native.

Penda, still wearing her soldier's cartridge belt, marched at the head of the procession with Mariame Sonko, the wife of Balla, and Maimouna, the blind woman, who had joined them in the darkness without being noticed by anyone. Her baby was strapped across her back with an old shawl.

The men of the little escort group followed at some distance behind the women, and several of them had brought bicycles in the event that they should be needed. Boubacar had strung a necklace of cans and gourds filled with water from the framework and handlebars on his. Samba N'Doulougou was perched like a scrawny bird on an elegant English machine. His rump beat irregularly against the saddle, and his feet parted company with the pedals at every turn.

They were traveling across a countryside laid waste by the dry season. The torrents of the sun had struck at the hearts of even the grasses and the wild plants and drained away their sap. The smallest leaves and stalks leaned toward the earth, preparing to fall and die. The only things that seemed alive were the thorny plants that thrived on drought and, far off toward the horizon, the lofty baobabs, to whom the comings and goings of seasons meant nothing. The soil was ridged and caked in an unwholesome crust, but it still bore traces of ancient cultivation; little squares of earth pierced by stumps of millet or corn, standing like the teeth of a broken comb. Once, a line of thatched roofs had been drawn here, against the bosom of a rich, brown earth; and countless little pathways—coming from no one knew where, going no one knew where—crossed this master road, and the hundreds of feet that trod them raised a cloud of reddish dust, for in those days there was no asphalt on the road from Dakar.

Quite early on the first night they came to a village. The inhabitants, bewildered at the sight of so many women, plied them with questions. But their hospitality was cordial, although a little ceremonious because of their surprise at such an event. At dawn, their thirst assuaged, their stomachs calmed, their feet still sore, they left again, to a concert of compliments and encouragement. Two hours later they passed the bus to Thiès, and some of the women performed a little dance in the road, to acknowledge the cheers and waving of the travelers. Then they took up their march again.

And the second day was very much like the first. . . .

It was during the next stage of the march that the crisis occurred which seemed certain to bring about the failure of the whole enterprise.

It had not been easy to rouse the women, who groaned and complained bitterly, pressing their hands against their aching limbs and backs, trying to rid themselves of the stiffness brought on by an hour's rest. Penda tried to cheer them up by joking with the group of younger girls.

"Be sure you don't let the men get too close to you. I don't want to have to answer to your families when your bellies start to swell!"

"We haven't done anything," Aby said indignantly.

"And I suppose if you did you would come and tell me about it right away, hé?" But no one was in a mood to laugh. Water had become the only thing they thought about. The few cans Boubacar's men brought back had been enough to supply only a few drops to each person.

"I'm as filthy as a pig," one woman said, displaying the scales of dried sweat, raked with dust, that had formed on her legs.

"I'd like to get in the water and stay in it, like a fish!" "When I get to Dakar. I'm going to do nothing but drink for the first hour!"

"Those beautiful, well-scrubbed boys in Dakar won't be interested in our dirty bodies!"

Little by little, however, the column reformed. There was no laughter or singing now, but a curious new thing seemed to have come to them: the sort of hope, or instinct, that will guide an animal searching for a new place to graze.

More and more often now, Penda left her own group and walked back along the length of the column, gathering in the stragglers, stopping to talk to the old and the more feeble, encouraging them to go on. On one such journey she heard Awa talking to a group of her friends, in a loud, frightened voice.

"I swear to you, there are evil spirits among us. My dream came back while we were resting—but I've taken precautions; they won't want me." Saying this, she untied a corner of her skirt, which she had made into a large knot. "Before we left, I covered myself with salt and every now and then I eat a little of it. That way, when the *deumes* come to devour me, they will find that they don't want me."

Several of the others held out their hands eagerly, and Awa gave them each a pinch of salt. In their fatigue and discouragement, the women were beset again by all the fears instilled in them by age-old legends. The sky itself seemed to threaten them; little clouds the color of Dahomey ivory, bordered in dark gray, raced across the horizon, throwing the bony fingers of the cade trees into stark relief.

"You are right, Awa," one of the women said. "We must be very careful. These offshoots of hell can change themselves into grains of dust, or into ants or thorns, or even into birds. I'm going to warn my sister."

"You're a bunch of fools," Penda said angrily, "and you ought to. . . . "

But she was interrupted by a piercing, disjointed shriek, followed by the sound of hysterical screaming from the rear of the column. She began to run in that direction, and a few of the more curious among the other women followed her, but most of them remained frozen where they were, and some even fled in the opposite direction.

Séni was rolling in the dust in the middle of the road, her limbs writhing horribly, her back arched and twisted in convulsions. Her skirt had been torn off, a slimy foam dribbled from her mouth, and her eyes had rolled back into her head until only the whites stared out.

"I told you!" Awa cried. "It's a *deume* who is devouring her! We've got to find it!"

The great orbs of her eyes, rolling in terror, suddenly came to rest on the tiny figure of Yaciné, seated by the side of the road a few feet away. The old woman had cut her big toe, and since it was bleeding profusely, she was trying to bring her foot up to her mouth to suck the blood away.

"There she is! There she is!" Awa screamed. "Look—she is sucking Séni's blood through her feet!"

Twenty mouths screamed with her now. "There she is! There is the *deume*! Catch her, catch her!"

Yaciné leaped to her feet, panic-stricken, and tried to run, but she was caught in an instant. A dozen hands seized her roughly, and others hurled branches and stones at her.

"You've all gone mad!" Penda shouted, trying to protect the old woman, whose face had been gashed by a stone and was beginning to bleed.

Awa was still screaming hysterically. "I told you so! I told you so! We have a *deume*, and Séni is going to die!"

"*Fermez vos gueules!*" Without realizing it, Penda had spoken in French. "You're the ones who are *deumes*! Let this woman go, or I'll eat you alive myself! Mariame! Go get Boubacar and the men and bring Maimouna, too!"

She succeeded at last in freeing Yaciné, half dead with fright, her clothing almost torn from her body. Séni was lying on her back in the road, surrounded by a circle of women. Her legs were straight and stiff, and her teeth were chattering violently.

Boubacar arrived, followed by five or six men on bicycles, one of them carrying Maimouna behind him. She leaned over the prostrate woman, her fingers moving swiftly over her face and feeling for her pulse.

"It isn't serious," she said. "It's just the heat. She'll have to inhale some urine."

"All right, some of you sluts go and piss!" Penda cried.

Some of the women climbed over to the other side of the embankment, and Maimouna followed them. She came back a few minutes later, carrying some clods of humid earth. Seating herself in the road, she kneaded them into little balls, which she passed back and forth under Séni's nostrils, while Penda held up the unconscious woman's head.

In all this time, Awa never once stopped shouting. "There are others! I tell you, there are others! Séni is going to die—I can smell the odor of death from her already. They brought us out here because it would be easier to devour us here—it's just like it was in my dream!"

Penda could no longer control herself. She rested Séni's head on the knees of the blind woman and hurled herself at Awa.

"Now, you are going to be quiet!" Her fists were as hard as a man's, and she hammered at the other woman's face and stomach until she stumbled and fell against the foot of a tree, screaming with pain and fear.

Then, her anger drained out of her by this explosion of physical energy, Penda walked over to the giant smith, who had been watching her in amazement.

"Boubacar, some of the men will have to carry the women who are sick," she said, pointing at Awa, the weeping Yaciné, and Séni, who was now sitting up, with her head resting calmly on Maimouna's shoulder, next to that of the baby sleeping on her mother's back.

The men lifted her from the ground and installed her on the seat of a bicycle, where they could support her as they pushed it along. Boubacar took Awa on his powerful back, and the column formed up once again.

. . .

The ranks of the original column from Thiès had been swollen by women from the villages, and by a delegation from Rufisque; and a large group of men had reinforced the escort. The women sang again and laughed and joked.

"We will surely see some beautiful houses at Dakar."

"But they are not for us; they are only for the *toubabs*."

"After the strike we will have them, too."

"After the strike I am going to do what the wives of the *toubabs* do, and take my husband's pay."

"And if there are two of you?"

"We'll each take half, and that way he won't have anything left to spend on other women. We will have won the strike, too!"

"The men have been good, though. Did you see how the smith was sweating while he was carrying Awa?"

"Bah! For once he had a woman on his back. They have us on our backs every night!"

In the last miles before they reached their goal they passed a point from which they could see the island of Gorée, a tiny black dot in the green expanse of the ocean; they saw the vast Lafarge cement factories and the remains of an American army camp. As they approached the first buildings of Dakar's suburbs, a breathless boy on a bicycle raced up to meet them, leaping off his machine in front of the little group at the head of the column.

"There are soldiers on the road at the entrance to the city." he gasped. "They say that the women from Thiès will not be allowed to pass."

The laughter and the singing stopped abruptly, and there was silence. A few of the women left the road and took shelter behind the walls, as if they expected the soldiers to appear at any minute; but the bulk of the column stood firm. Penda climbed up on a little slope.

"The soldiers can't eat us!" she cried. "They can't even kill us; there are too many of us! Don't be afraid—our friends are waiting for us in Dakar! We'll go on!"

The long, multi-colored mass began to move forward again. Maimouna, who was walking a little behind Penda, suddenly felt a hand on her arm.

"Who is it?"

"It's me."

"You, Samba? What's the matter?"

"There are soldiers. . . ."

"Yes, I heard."

Samba N'Doulougou did not understand too clearly what force it was that had com-

pelled him to come here now and seek out this woman whose body he had enjoyed one night. Was it pity for the weak and infirm, or was it for the mother and the child? He remembered the shame he had lived with for months as he watched her working in the sun while her belly grew large with the child, his child. And he remembered the way he had tried to alter his voice so she would not recognize him.

"Give me the child," he said. "It will be easier for me to avoid the soldiers."

"You want your child?" the blind woman said.

"The soldiers are going to be there. . . ."

"And after that? . . . A father may die while a woman is big with child, but that does not prevent the child from living, because the mother is there. It is up to me to protect this child. Go away now. After I get to Dakar you will never see me again; and I have never seen you. No one knows who is the father of this child—you can sleep peacefully, and your honor will be safe. Now go back to the men."

Just outside the big racecourse of the city, the column confronted the red tarbooshes of the soldiers. A black non-commissioned officer who was standing with the captain commanding the little detachment called out to them.

"Go back to Thiès, women! We cannot let you pass!"

"We will pass if we have to walk on the body of your mother!" Penda cried.

And already the pressure of this human wall was forcing the soldiers to draw back. Reinforcements began to appear, from everywhere at once, but they were not for the men in uniform. A few rifle butts came up menacingly and were beaten down by clubs and stones. The unnerved soldiers hesitated, not knowing what to do, and then some shots rang out, and in the column two people fell—Penda and Samba N'Doulougou.

But how could a handful of men in red tarbooshes prevent this great river from rolling on to the sea?

23. Colonial officials take note of African discontent.

Less celebrated than the strike in French West Africa, but no less significant for the end of colonialism, were the labor struggles (or "disturbances" in colonial parlance) that brought production to a halt in the Gold Coast for much of 1948. As the following excerpt from an official investigation into unrest indicates, British colonial officials concluded that political, economic, and social forces were all at play, and that these different factors were closely interrelated. Indeed, so powerful was the challenge to colonialism, particularly its ability to produce cheap goods for a European market (the very rationale of Empire), that from this time onward British officials in London (though not the local white settlers in Africa) began to consider policies that might enable them to disengage themselves politically from their possessions in West and East Africa while still maintaining a close economic relationship. To pursue that approach, the British realized that they would have to identify potential leaders in Africa with whom they felt they could work and to whom could be given the responsibility for self-government. Unfortunately for the British, as for other colonial powers, their choices of responsible leaders often were viewed as collaborators by Africans calling for immediate and unfettered independence.[23]

Report of the commission of enquiry into disturbances on the Gold Coast, 1948.

. . . In the main, the underlying causes may be divided into three broad categories: political, economic and social. There is often no clear dividing line between them and they are frequently interrelated. . . . The remedy for the distrust and suspicion with which the African views the European, and which is to-day poisoning life in the Gold Coast, demands an attack on all three causes. None of them may be said to take precedence. . . . These may be summarised as follows:

A. Political.

(1) The large number of African soldiers returning from service with the Forces, where they had lived under different and better conditions, made for a general communicable state of unrest. Such Africans by reason of their contacts with other peoples, including Europeans, had developed a political and national consciousness. The fact that they were disappointed with conditions on their return, either from specious promises made before demobilisation or a general expectancy of a golden age for heroes, made them the natural focal point for any general movement against authority.

(2) A feeling of political frustration among the educated Africans who saw no prospect of ever experiencing political power under existing conditions and who regarded the 1946 Constitution as mere window-dressing designed to cover, but not to advance, their natural aspirations.

(3) A failure of the Government to realise that, with the spread of liberal ideas, increasing literacy and a closer contact with political developments in other parts of the world, the star of rule through the Chiefs was on the wane. The achievement of self-government in India, Burma and Ceylon had not passed unnoticed on the Gold Coast.

(4) A universal feeling that Africanisation was merely a promise and not a driving force in Government policy, coupled with the suspicion that education had been slowed up,

---

23. G. E. Metcalfe, ed., *Great Britain and Ghana: Documents of Ghana History, 1807–1957* (Legon: University of Ghana, 1964), pp. 682–83.

and directed in such a way as to impede Africanisation.

(5) A general suspicion of Government measures and intentions reinforced by a hostile press and heightened by the general failure of the Administration in the field of Public Relations.

(6) Increasing resentment at the growing concentration of certain trades in the hands of foreigners, particularly at the increase in the number of Syrian merchants.

B. Economic.

(1) The announcement of the Government that it would remain neutral in the dispute which had arisen between the traders and the people of the Gold Coast over high prices of imported goods and which led to the organised boycott of January–February, 1948.

(2) The continuance of war-time control of imports, and the shortage and high prices of consumer goods which were widely attributed to the machinations of European importers.

(3) The alleged unfair allocation and distribution of goods in short supply, by the importing firms.

(4) The Government's acceptance of the scientists' finding that the only cure for Swollen Shoot disease of cocoa was to cut out diseased trees, and their adoption of that policy, combined with allegations of improper methods of carrying it out.

(5) The degree of control in the Cocoa Marketing Board, which limited the powers of the farmers' representatives to control the vast reserves which are accumulating under the Board's policy.

(6) The feeling that the Government had not formulated any plans for the future of industry and agriculture, and that, indeed, it was lukewarm about any development apart from production for export.

C. Social.

(1) The alleged slow development of educational facilities in spite of a growing demand, and the almost complete failure to provide any technical or vocational training.

(2) The shortage of housing, particularly in the towns, and the low standards of houses for Africans as compared with those provided for Europeans.

(3) The fear of wholesale alienation of tribal lands leaving a landless peasantry.

(4) Inadequacy of the legal powers of Government necessary to deal with speeches designed to arouse disorder and violence. . . .

24. Hendrik Verwoerd explains apartheid.

While British officials in Ghana, Kenya, and elsewhere in Africa considered how colonies might be moved toward political independence without breaking the economic ties that bound African producers to European markets, in South Africa a newly triumphant Afrikaner nationalist movement took power in the parliamentary election of 1948 (in which whites comprised over 90 percent of the electorate, and of those voters, Afrikaners about two-thirds) and took steps to ensure that racial discrimination was strengthened, not weakened. The policy associated with the Afrikaner nationalists, and which they practiced for the next half century throughout South Africa, was apartheid (apartness): the policy of favoring racial separation and, ultimately, the removal of all peoples of color from South Africa (Africans to other parts of Africa, Indians to India, Chinese to China) so that it could be literally a white man's country. For white South Africans, the loss of political power and economic domination was not a scenario that they cared to face, even if it appeared to make little sense to call a country white in which more than 80 percent of the population was black, and to plan for the removal of the very workforce that made possible the enormously high standard of living enjoyed by white settlers (English-speaking and Afrikaner alike).

The most prominent spokesman for this extreme policy of racial separation was Hendrik Verwoerd, born in Amsterdam in 1901 but living in South Africa from 1903 onward. Interested at first in following a career in theology, Verwoerd switched his university studies to psychology and philosophy and in the 1920s became a professor first of applied psychology and philosophy and later of sociology and social work. Attracted to Afrikaner nationalist politics, he became a newspaper editor in the 1930s and then entered parliament in 1948. He was minister of native affairs 1950–1958, and then prime minister from 1958 until his assassination in 1966 (stabbed to death in the House of Assembly by a parliamentary messenger).[24]

Address of Hendrik Verwoerd, Minister of Native Affairs, to the Native Representative Council, December 5, 1950.

Next, I wish to accede to the wish which, I understand, has long been felt by members of this council, namely that a member of the Government should explain the main features of what is implied by the policy of Apartheid.

Within the compass of an address I have, naturally, to confine myself to the fundamentals of the Apartheid policy and to the main steps following logically from the policy. Further details and a fuller description of the reasons and value of what is being planned will have to remain in abeyance today. Properly understood, however, these main features will elucidate what will be done and how this will be as much in the interests of the Bantu as in those of the European.

As a premise, the question may be put: Must Bantu and European in future develop as intermixed communities, or as communities separated from one another in so far as this is practically possible? If the reply is "intermingled communities," then the following must be understood. There will be competition and conflict everywhere. So long as the points of contact are still comparatively few, as is the case now, friction and conflict will be few and less evident. The more this intermixing develops, however, the stronger the conflict will become. In such conflict, the Europeans will, at least for a long time, hold the stronger position, and the Bantu be the defeated party in every phase of the struggle. This must cause to rise in him an increasing sense of resentment and revenge. Neither for the European, nor for the Bantu, can this, namely increasing tension and conflict, be an ideal future, because the intermixed development involves disadvantage to both.

H. F. Verwoerd. © *Bettmann/CORBIS.*

24. A.N. Pelzer, ed., *Verwoerd Speaks: Speeches 1948–1966* (Johannesburg: APB Publishers, 1966), pp. 23–29.

Perhaps, in such an eventuality, it is best frankly to face the situation which must arise in the political sphere. In the event of an intermixed development, the Bantu will undoubtedly desire a share in the government of the intermixed country. He will, in due course, not be satisfied with a limited share in the form of communal representation, but will desire full participation in the country's government on the basis of an equal franchise. For the sake of simplicity, I shall not enlarge here on the fact that, simultaneously with the development of this demand, he will desire the same in the social, economic and other spheres of life, involving in due course, intermixed residence, intermixed labour, intermixed living, and, eventually, a miscegenated population—in spite of the well-known pride of both the Bantu and the European in their respective purity of descent. It follows logically, therefore, that, in an intermixed country, the Bantu must, in the political sphere, have as their object equal franchise with the European.

Now examine the same question from the European's point of view. A section of the Europeans, consisting of both Afrikaans- and English-speaking peoples, says equally clearly that, in regard to the above standpoint, the European must continue to dominate what will be the European part of South Africa. It should be noted that, notwithstanding false representations, these Europeans do not demand domination over the whole of South Africa, that is to say, over the Native territories according as the Bantu outgrow the need for their trusteeship. Because that section of the European population states its case very clearly, it must not be accepted, however, that the other section of the European population will support the above possible future demand of the Bantu. That section of the European population (English as well as Afrikaans) which is prepared to grant representation to the Bantu in the country's government does not wish to grant anything beyond communal representation, and that on a strictly limited basis. They do not yet realize that a balance of power may thereby be given to the non-European with which an attempt may later be made to secure full and equal franchise on the same voters' roll. The moment they realize that, or the moment when the attempt is made, this latter section of the European population will also throw in its weight with the first section in the interests of European supremacy in the European portion of the country. This appears clearly from its proposition that, in its belief on the basis of an inherent superiority, or greater knowledge, or whatever it may be, the European must remain master and leader. The section is, therefore, also a protagonist of separate residential areas, and of what it calls separation.

My point is this that, if mixed development is to be the policy of the future in South Africa, it will lead to the most terrific clash of interests imaginable. The endeavours and desires of the Bantu and the endeavours and objectives of all Europeans will be antagonistic. Such a clash can only bring unhappiness and misery to both. Both Bantu and European must, therefore, consider in good time how this misery can be averted from themselves and from their descendants. They must find a plan to provide the two population groups with opportunities for the full development of their respective powers and ambitions without coming into conflict.

The only possible way out is the second alternative, namely, that both adopt a development divorced from each other. That is all that the word apartheid means. Any word can be poisoned by attaching a false meaning to it. That has happened to this word. The Bantu have been made to believe that it means oppression, or even that the Native territories are to be taken away from them. In reality, however, exactly the opposite is intended with the policy of apartheid. To avoid the above-mentioned unpleasant and dangerous future for both sections of the population, the present Government adopts the attitude that it concedes and wishes to give to others precisely what it demands for itself. It believes in the supremacy (baasskap) of the European in his sphere but, then, it also believes equally in the supremacy (baasskap) of the Bantu in his own sphere. For the European child it wishes to create all the possible opportunities for its own development, prosperity and national service in its own sphere; but for the Bantu it also wishes to create all the opportunities for the realization of ambitions and the rendering of service to *their* own people. There is thus no policy of oppression here, but one of creating a situation which has never existed for the Bantu; namely, that, taking into consideration their languages, traditions, history and different national communities, they may pass through a development of their own. That opportunity arises for them as soon as such a division is brought into being between them and the Europeans that they need not be the imitators and henchmen of the latter.

The next question, then, is how the division is to be brought about so as to allow the European and the Bantu to pass through a development of their own, in accordance with their own traditions, under their own leaders in every sphere of life.

It is perfectly clear that it would have been the easiest—an ideal condition for each of the two groups—if the course of history had been different. Suppose there had arisen in Southern Africa a state in which only Bantu lived and worked, and another in which only Europeans lived and worked. Each could then have worked out its own destiny in its own way. This is not the situation today, however, and planning must in practice take present day actualities of life in the Union into account. We cannot escape from that which history has brought in its train. However, this easiest situation for peaceful association, self-government and development, each according to its own nature and completely apart from one another, may, in fact, be taken as a yardstick whereby to test plans for getting out of the present confusion and difficulties. One may, so far as is practicable, try to approach this objective in the future.

The realities of today are that a little over one-third of the Bantu resides, or still has its roots, in what are unambiguously termed Native territories. A little over a third lives in the countryside and on the farms of Europeans. A little less than a third lives and works in the cities, of whom a section have been detribalized and urbanized. The apartheid policy takes this reality into account.

Obviously, in order to grant equal opportunities to the Bantu, both in their interests as well as those of the Europeans, its starting-point is the Native territories. For the present, these territories cannot provide the desired opportunities for living and development to their inhabitants and their children, let alone to more people. Due to neglect of their soil and over-population by man and cattle, large numbers are even now being continuously forced to go and seek a living under the protection of the European and his industries. In these circumstances it cannot be expected that the Bantu community will so provide for itself and so progress as to allow ambitious and developed young people to be taken up by their own people in their own national service out of their own funds. According as a flourishing community arises in such territories, however, the need will develop for teachers, dealers, clerks, artisans, agricultural experts, leaders of local and general governing bodies of their own. In other words, the whole superstructure of administrative and professional people arising in every prosperous community will then become necessary. Our first aim as a Government is, therefore, to lay the foundation of a prosperous producing community through soil reclamation and conservation methods and through the systematic establishment in the Native territories of Bantu farming on an economic basis.

The limited territories are, however, as little able to carry the whole of the Bantu population of the reserves of the present and the future—if all were to be farmers—as the European area would be able to carry all the Europeans if they were all to be farmers, or as England would be able to carry its whole population if all of them had to be landowners, farmers and cattle breeders. Consequently, the systematic building up of the Native territories aims at a development precisely as in all prosperous countries. Side by side with agricultural development must also come an urban development founded on industrial growth. The future Bantu towns and cities in the reserves may arise partly in conjunction with Bantu industries of their own in those reserves. In their establishment Europeans must be prepared to help with money and knowledge, in the consciousness that such industries must, as soon as is possible, wholly pass over into the hands of the Bantu.

On account of the backlog, it is conceivable, however, that such industries may not develop sufficiently rapidly to meet adequately the needs of the Bantu requiring work. The European industrialist will, therefore, have to be encouraged to establish industries within the European areas near such towns and cities. Bantu working in those industries will then be able to live within their own territories, where they have their own schools, their own traders, and where they govern themselves. Indeed, the kernel of the apartheid policy is that, as the Bantu no longer need the European, the latter must wholly withdraw from the Native territories.

What length of time it will take the Bantu in the reserves to advance to that stage of self-sufficiency and self-government will depend on his own industry and preparedness to grasp this opportunity offered by the apartheid policy for self-development and service to his own nation. This development of the reserves will not, however, mean that all Natives from the cities or European countryside will be able, or wish, to trek to them. In the countryside there has, up to the present, not been a clash of social interests. The endeavour, at any rate for the time being, must be to grant the Bantu in town locations as much self-government as is practicable under the guardianship of the town councils, and to let tribal control of farm Natives function effectively. There the residential and working conditions will also have to enjoy special attention so that the Bantu community finding a livelihood as farm labourers may also be prosperous and happy. Here the problem is rather how to create better relationships, greater stability, correct training and good working conditions. Apart from the removal of black spots (like the removal of white spots in the Native areas), the policy of apartheid is for the time being, not so much an issue at this juncture, except if mechanization of farming should later cause a decrease in non-European labourers.

Finally, there are the implications of the apartheid policy in respect of European cities. The primary requirement of this policy is well known, namely, that not only must there be separation between European and non-European residential areas, but also that the different non-European groups, such as the Bantu, the Coloured, and the Indian, shall live in their own residential areas. Although considerable numbers of Bantu who are still rooted in the reserves may conceivably return thither, particularly according as urban and industrial development take place, or even many urbanized Bantu may proceed thence because of the opportunities to exercise their talents as artisans, traders, clerks or professionals, or to realize their political ambitions—large numbers will undoubtedly still remain behind in the big cities. For a long time to come, this will probably continue to be the case.

For these Bantu also the Apartheid policy and separate residential areas have great significance. The objective is, namely, to give them the greatest possible measure of self-government in such areas according to the degree in which local authorities, who construct these towns, can fall into line. In due course, too, depending on the ability of the Bantu community, all the work there will have to be done by their own people, as was described in connection with the reserves. Even within a European area, therefore, the Bantu communities would not be separated for the former to oppress them, but to form their own communities within which they may pursue a full life of work and service.

In view of all this, it will be appreciated why the Apartheid policy also takes an interest in suitable education for the Bantu. This, in fact, brings in its train the need for sufficiently competent Bantu in many spheres. The only and obvious reservation is that the Bantu will have to place his development and his knowledge exclusively at the service of his own people.

Co-operation in implementing the apartheid policy as described here is one of the greatest services the present leader of the Bantu population can render his people. Instead of striving after vague chimeras and trying to equal the European in an inter-mingled community with confused ideals and inevitable conflict, he can be a national fig-ure helping to lead his own people along the road of peace and prosperity. He can help to give the children and educated men and women of his people an opportunity to find employment or fully to realize their ambitions within their own sphere or, where this is not possible, as within the Europeans' sphere, employment and service within segregated areas of their own.

I trust that every Bantu will forget the misunderstandings of the past and choose not the road leading to conflict, but that which leads to peace and happiness for both the separate communities. Are the present lead-ers of the Bantu, under the influence of Com-munist agitators, going to seek a form of equality which they will not get? For in the long run they will come up against the whole of the European community, as well as the large section of their own compatriots who prefer the many advantages of self-govern-ment within a community of their own. I can-not believe that they will. Nobody can reject a form of independence, obtainable with everybody's co-operation, in favour of a fu-tile striving after that which promises to be not freedom but downfall.

25. Nelson Mandela's "No Easy Walk to Freedom."

Nelson Mandela (born 1918) was one of the founding members of the African National Congress's Youth League and in 1950 became its president. A lawyer by training, he organized the ANC's "Defiance Campaign" in 1952, in col-laboration with other anti-apartheid organizations, to demonstrate the futility of apartheid by encouraging massive popular noncompliance with the policy. Thousands burned their passes, refused to travel on segregated forms of trans-port, and ignored signs enforcing the color bar (such as indicating separate entrances for each race into post offices, law courts, as well as different parks, beaches, and other public facilities). The National Party government responded by arresting thousands of protestors, including Mandela and most of the lead-ers of the ANC. Mandela, along with several others, was charged under the terms of the Suppression of Communism Act (which made it legally possible to define as a communist anyone who encouraged "feelings of hostility between the European and the non-European races of the Union," and who aimed at "bringing about any political, industrial, social, or economic change within the Union by the promotion of disturbance or disorder"). Mandela was convicted and initially given a suspended sentence but then, under new legislation en-acted to deal with the protest movement, he was banned from participating in any public activities in South Africa. The speech reproduced below was the last that he was able to give publicly before his banning order went fully into ef-fect.[25]

25. Thomas Karis and Gwendolen M. Carter, eds., *From Protest to Challenge: A Documentary History of African Politics in South Africa, 1882–1962* (Stanford: Hoover Institution Press, 1972), vol. 3, Thomas Karis and Gail M. Gerhart, eds., *Challenge and Violence, 1953–1964*, pp. 106–15. Reprinted with the agreement of the Hoover Institu-tion Press.

Presidential address by Nelson Mandela to the ANC (Transvaal branch), September 21, 1953.

Since 1912 and year after year thereafter, in their homes and local areas, in provincial and national gatherings, on trains and buses, in the factories and on the farms, in cities, villages, shanty towns, schools and prisons, the African people have discussed the shameful misdeeds of those who rule the country. Year after year, they have raised their voices in condemnation of the grinding poverty of the people, the low wages, the acute shortage of land, the inhuman exploitation and the whole policy of white domination. But instead of more freedom repression began to grow in volume and intensity and it seemed that all their sacrifices would end up in smoke and dust. Today the entire country knows that their labours were not in vain for a new spirit and new ideas have gripped our people. Today the people speak the language of action: there is a mighty awakening among the men and women of our country and the year 1952 stands out as the year of this upsurge of national consciousness.

In June, 1952, the African National Congress and the South African Indian Congress [SAIC], bearing in mind their responsibility as the representatives of the downtrodden and oppressed people of South Africa, took the plunge and launched the Campaign for the Defiance of the Unjust Laws. Starting off in Port Elizabeth in the early hours of June 26 and with only thirty-three defiers in action and then in Johannesburg in the afternoon of the same day with one hundred and six defiers, it spread throughout the country like wild fire. Factory and office workers, doctors, lawyers, teachers, students and the clergy; Africans, Coloureds, Indians and Europeans, old and young, all rallied to the national call and defied the pass laws and the curfew and the railway apartheid regulations. At the end of the year, more than 8,000 people of all races had defied. The Campaign called for immediate and heavy sacrifices. Workers lost their jobs, chiefs and teachers were expelled from the service, doctors, lawyers and businessmen gave up their practices and businesses and elected to go to jail. Defiance was a step of great political significance. It released strong social forces which affected thousands of our countrymen. It was an effective way of getting the masses to function politically; a powerful method of voicing our indignation against the reactionary policies of the Government. It was one of the best ways of exerting pressure on the Government and extremely dangerous to the stability and security of the State. It inspired and aroused our people from a servile community of yesmen to a militant and uncompromising band of comrades-in-arms. The entire country was transformed into battle zones where the forces of liberation were locked up in immortal conflict against those of reaction and evil. Our flag flew in every battlefield and thousands of our countrymen rallied around it. We held the initiative and the forces of freedom were advancing on all fronts. It was against this background and at the height of this Campaign that we held our last annual provincial Conference in Pretoria from the 10th to the 12th of October last year. In a way, that Conference was a welcome reception for those who had returned from the battlefields and a farewell to those who were still going to action. The spirit of defiance and action dominated the entire conference.

Today we meet under totally different conditions. By the end of July last year, the Campaign had reached a stage where it had to be suppressed by the Government or it would impose its own policies on the country.

The government launched its reactionary offensive and struck at us. Between July last year and August this year forty-seven leading members from both Congresses in Johannesburg, Port Elizabeth and Kimberley were arrested, tried and convicted for launching the Defiance Campaign and given suspended sentences ranging from three months to two years on condition that they did not again participate in the defiance of the unjust laws. In November last year, a proclamation was passed which prohibited meetings of more than ten Africans and made it an offence for any person to call upon an African to defy. Contravention of this proclamation carried a penalty of three years or a fine of three hundred pounds. In March this year the Government passed the so-called Public Safety Act which empowered it to declare a state of emergency and to create conditions which would permit of the most ruthless and pitiless methods of suppressing our movement. Almost simultaneously, the Criminal Laws Amendment Act was passed which provided heavy penalties for those convicted of Defiance offences. This Act also made provision for the whipping of defiers including women. It was under this Act that Mr. Arthur Matiala who was the local [leader] of the Central Branch during the Defiance Campaign, was convicted and sentenced to twelve months with hard labour plus eight strokes by the Magistrate of Villa Nora. The Government also made extensive use of the Suppression of Communism Act. You will remember that in May last year the Government ordered Moses Kotane, Yusuf Dadoo, J. B. Marks, David Bopape and Johnson Ngwevela to resign from the Congresses and many other organisations and were also prohibited from attending political gatherings. In consequence of these bans, Moses Kotane, J. B. Marks, and David Bopape did not attend our last provincial Conference. In December last year, the Secretary-General, Mr. W. M. Sisulu, and I were banned from attending gatherings and confined to Johannesburg for six months. Early this year, the President-General, Chief Luthuli, whilst in the midst of a national tour which he was prosecuting with remarkable energy and devotion, was prohibited for a period of twelve months from attending public gatherings and from visiting Durban, Johannesburg, Cape Town, Port Elizabeth and many other centres. A few days before the President-General was banned, the President of the S.A.I.C., Dr. G. M. Naicker, had been served with a similar notice. Many other active workers both from the African and Indian Congresses and from trade union organisations were also banned.

The Congresses realised that these measures created a new situation which did not prevail when the Campaign was launched in June 1952. The tide of defiance was bound to recede and we were forced to pause and to take stock of the new situation. We had to analyse the dangers that faced us, formulate plans to overcome them and evolve new plans of political struggle. A political movement must keep in touch with reality and the prevailing conditions. Long speeches, the shaking of fists, the banging of tables and strongly worded resolutions out of touch with the objective conditions do not bring about mass action and can do a great deal of harm to the organisation and the struggle we serve. The masses had to be prepared and made ready for new forms of political struggle. We had to recuperate our strength and muster our forces for another and more powerful offensive against the enemy. To have gone ahead blindly as if nothing had happened would have been suicidal and stupid. The conditions under which we meet today are, therefore, vastly different. The Defiance Campaign together with its thrills and adventures has receded. The old methods of bringing about mass action through public mass meetings, press statements and leaflets calling upon the people to go to action have become extremely dangerous and difficult to use effectively. The authorities will not easily permit a meeting called under the auspices of the A.N.C., few newspapers will publish statements openly criticising the policies of the Government and there is hardly a single printing press which will agree to print leaflets calling upon workers to embark on industrial action for fear of prosecution under the Suppression of Communism Act and similar measures. These developments require the evolution of new forms of political struggle which will make it reasonable for us to strive for action on a higher level than the Defiance Campaign. The Government, alarmed at the indomitable upsurge of national consciousness, is doing everything in its power to crush our movement by removing the genuine representatives of the people from the organisations. According to a statement made by [C. R.] Swart [minister of justice] in Parliament on the 18th September, 1953, there are thirty-three trade union officials and eighty-nine other people who have been served with notices in terms of the Suppression of Communism Act. This does not include that formidable array of freedom fighters who have been named and blacklisted under the Suppression of Communism Act and those who have been banned under the Riotous Assemblies Act.

Meanwhile the living conditions of the people, already extremely difficult, are steadily worsening and becoming unbearable. The purchasing power of the masses is progressively declining and the cost of living is rocketing. Bread is now dearer than it was two months ago. The cost of milk, meat and vegetables is beyond the pockets of the average family and many of our people cannot afford them. The people are too poor to have enough food to feed their families and children. They cannot afford sufficient clothing, housing and medical care. They are denied the right to security in the event of unemployment, sickness, disability, old age and where these exist, they are of an extremely inferior and useless nature. Because of lack of proper medical amenities our people are ravaged by such dreaded diseases as tuberculosis, venereal disease, leprosy, pelagra, and infantile mortality is very high. The recent state budget made provision for the increase of the cost-of-living allowances for Europeans and not a word was said about the poorest and most hard-hit section of the population—the African people. The insane policies of the Government which have brought about an explosive situation in the country have definitely scared away foreign capital from South Africa and the financial crisis through which the country is now passing is forcing many industrial and business concerns to close down, to retrench their staffs and unemployment is growing every day. The farm labourers are in a particularly dire plight. You will perhaps recall the investigations and exposures of the semi-slave conditions on the Bethal farms made in 1948 by the Reverend Michael Scott and a *Guardian* correspondent; by the *Drum* last year and the *Advance* in April this year. You will recall how human beings, wearing only sacks with holes for their heads

and arms, never given enough food to eat, slept on cement floors on cold nights with only their sacks to cover their shivering bodies. You will remember how they are woken up as early as 4 A.M. and taken to work on the fields with the indunas sjamboking [whipping] those who tried to straighten their backs, who felt weak and dropped down because of hunger and sheer exhaustion. You will also recall the story of human beings toiling pathetically from the early hours of the morning till sunset, fed only on mealie [corn] meal served on filthy sacks spread on the ground and eating with their dirty hands. People falling ill and never once being given medical attention. You will also recall the revolting story of a farmer who was convicted for tying a labourer by his feet from a tree and had him flogged to death, pouring boiling water into his mouth whenever he cried for water. These things which have long vanished from many parts of the world still flourish in S. A. today. None will deny that they constitute a serious challenge to Congress and we are in duty bound to find an effective remedy for these obnoxious practices.

The Government has introduced in Parliament the Native Labour (Settlement of Disputes) Bill and the Bantu Education Bill. Speaking on the Labour Bill, the Minister of Labour, Ben Schoeman, openly stated that the aim of this wicked measure is to bleed African trade unions to death. By forbidding strikes and lockouts it deprives Africans of the one weapon the workers have to improve their position. The aim of the measure is to destroy the present African trade unions which are controlled by the workers themselves and which fight for the improvement of their working conditions in return for a Central Native Labour Board controlled by the Government and which will be used to frustrate the legitimate aspirations of the African worker. The Minister of Native Affairs, Verwoerd, has also been brutally clear in explaining the objects of the Bantu Education Bill. According to him the aim of this law is to teach our children that Africans are inferior to Europeans. African education would be taken out of the hands of people who taught equality between black and white. When this Bill becomes law, it will not be the parents but the Department of Native Affairs which will decide whether an African child should receive higher or other education. It might well be that the children of those who criticise the Government and who fight its policies will almost certainly be taught how to drill rocks in the mines and how to plough potatoes on the farms of Bethal. High education might well be the privilege of those children whose families have a tradition of collaboration with the ruling circles.

The attitude of the Congress on these bills is very clear and unequivocal. Congress totally rejects both bills without reservation. The last provincial Conference strongly condemned the then proposed Labour Bill as a measure designed to rob the African workers of the universal right of free trade unionism and to undermine and destroy the existing African trade unions. Conference further called upon the African workers to boycott and defy the application of this sinister scheme which was calculated to further the exploitation of the African worker. To accept a measure of this nature even in a qualified manner would be a betrayal of the toiling masses. At a time when every genuine Congressite should fight unreservedly for the recognition of African trade unions and the realisation of the principle that everyone has the right to form and to join trade unions for the protection of his interests, we declare our firm belief in the principles enunciated in the Universal Declaration of Human Rights that everyone has the right to education; that education shall be directed to the full development of human personality and to the strengthening of respect for human rights and fundamental freedoms. It shall promote understanding, tolerance and friendship among the nations, racial or religious groups and shall further the activities of the United Nations for the maintenance of peace. That parents have the right to choose the kind of education that shall be given to their children.

The cumulative effect of all these measures is to prop up and perpetuate the artificial and decaying policy of the supremacy of the white men. The attitude of the government to us is that: "Let's beat them down with guns and batons and trample them under our feet. We must be ready to drown the whole country in blood if only there is the slightest chance of preserving white supremacy."

But there is nothing inherently superior about the herrenvolk idea of the supremacy of the whites. In China, India, Indonesia and Korea, American, British, Dutch and French Imperialism, based on the concept of the supremacy of Europeans over Asians, has been completely and perfectly exploded. In Malaya and Indo-China British and French imperialisms are being shaken to their foundations by powerful and revolutionary national liberation movements. In Africa, there are approximately 190,000,000 Africans as against 4,000,000 Europeans. The entire continent is seething with discontent and already there are powerful revolutionary eruptions in the Gold Coast, Nigeria, Tunisia, Kenya, the Rhodesias and South Africa. The oppressed people and the oppressors are at loggerheads. *The day of reckoning* between the forces of freedom and those of reaction is not very far off. I have not the slightest doubt that when that day comes truth and justice will prevail.

The intensification of repressions and the extensive use of the bans is designed to immobilise every active worker and to check the national liberation movement. But gone forever are the days when harsh and wicked laws provided the oppressors with years of peace and quiet. The racial policies of the Government have pricked the conscience of all men of good will and have aroused their deepest indignation. The feelings of the oppressed people have never been more bitter. If the ruling circles seek to maintain their position by such inhuman methods then a clash between the forces of freedom and those of reaction is certain. The grave plight of the people compels them to resist to the death the stinking policies of the gangsters that rule our country.

But in spite of all the difficulties outlined above, we have won important victories. The general political level of the people has been considerably raised and they are now more conscious of their strength. Action has become the language of the day. The ties between the working people and the Congress have been greatly strengthened. This is a development of the highest importance because in a country such as ours a political organisation that does not receive the support of the workers is in fact paralysed on the very ground on which it has chosen to wage battle. Leaders of trade union organisations are at the same time important officials of the provincial and local branches of the A.N.C. In the past we talked of the African, Indian and Coloured struggles. Though certain individuals raised the question of a united front of all the oppressed groups, the various non-European organisations stood miles apart from one another and the efforts of those for co-ordination and unity were like a voice crying in the wilderness and it seemed that the day would never dawn when the oppressed people would stand and fight together shoulder to shoulder against a common enemy. Today we talk of the struggle of the oppressed people which, though it is waged through their respective autonomous organisations, is gravitating towards one central command.

Our immediate task is to consolidate these victories, to preserve our organisations and to muster our forces for the resumption of the offensive. To achieve this important task the National Executive of the A.N.C. in consultation with the National Action Committee of the A.N.C. and the S.A.I.C. formulated a plan of action popularly known as the "M" Plan and the highest importance is [given] to it by the National Executives. Instructions were given to all provinces to implement the "M" Plan without delay.

The underlying principle of this plan is the understanding that it is no longer possible to wage our struggle mainly on the old methods of public meetings and printed circulars. The aim is:

(1) to consolidate the Congress machinery;

(2) to enable the transmission of important decisions taken on a national level to every member of the organisation without calling public meetings, issuing press statements and printing circulars;

(3) to build up in the local branches themselves local Congresses which will effectively represent the strength and will of the people;

(4) to extend and strengthen the ties between Congress and the people and to consolidate Congress leadership.

This plan is being implemented in many branches not only in the Transvaal but also in the other provinces and is producing excellent results. The Regional Conferences held in Sophiatown, Germiston, Kliptown and Benoni on the 28th June, 23rd and 30th August and on the 6th September, 1953, which were attended by large crowds, are a striking demonstration of the effectiveness of this plan, and the National Executives must be complimented for it. I appeal to all members of the Congress to redouble their efforts and play their part truly and well in its implementation. The hard, dirty and strenuous task of recruiting members and strengthening our organisation through a house-to-house campaign in every locality must be done by you all. From now on the activity of Congressites must not be confined to speeches and resolutions. Their activities must find expression in wide scale work among the masses, work which will enable them to make the greatest possible contact with the working people. You must protect and defend your trade unions. If you are not allowed to have your meetings publicly, then you must hold them over your machines in the factories, on the trains and buses as you travel home. You must have them in your villages and shantytowns. You must make every home, every shack and every mud structure where our people live, a branch of the trade union movement and *never surrender.*

You must defend the right of African parents to decide the kind of education that shall be given to their children. Teach the children that Africans are not one iota inferior to Europeans. Establish your own community schools where the right kind of education will be given to our children. If it becomes dangerous or impossible to have these alternative schools, then again you must make every home, every shack or rickety structure a centre of learning for our children. Never surrender to the inhuman and barbaric theories of Verwoerd.

The decision to defy the unjust laws enabled Congress to develop considerably wider contacts between itself and the masses and the urge to join Congress grew day by day. But due to the fact that the local branches did not exercise proper control and supervision, the admission of new members was not carried out satisfactorily. No careful examination was made of their past history and political characteristics. As a result of this, there were many shady characters ranging from political clowns, place-seekers, splitters, saboteurs, agents-provocateurs to informers and even policemen, who infiltrated into the ranks of Congress. One need only refer to the Johannesburg trial of Dr. Moroka and nineteen others, where a member of Congress who actually worked at the National Headquarters, turned out to be a detective-sergeant on special duty. Remember the case of Leballo of Brakpan who wormed himself into that Branch by producing faked naming letters from the Liquidator, De Villiers Louw, who had instructions to spy on us. There are many other similar instances that emerged during the Johannesburg, Port Elizabeth and Kimberley trials. Whilst some of these men were discovered there are many who have not been found out. In Congress there are still many shady characters, political clowns, place-seekers, saboteurs, provocateurs, informers and policemen who masquerade as Progressives but who are in fact the bitterest enemies of our organisation. Outside appearances are highly deceptive and we cannot classify these men by looking at their faces or by listening to their sweet tongues or their vehement speeches demanding immediate action. The friends of the people are distinguishable by the ready and disciplined manner in which they rally behind their organisation and their readiness to sacrifice when the preservation of the organisation has become a matter of life and death. Similarly, enemies and shady characters are detected by the extent to which they consistently attempt to wreck the organisation by creating fratricidal strife, disseminating confusion and undermining and even opposing important plans of action to vitalise the organisation. In this respect it is interesting to note that almost all the people who oppose the "M" Plan are people who have consistently refused to respond when sacrifices were called for, and whose political background leaves much to be desired. These shady characters by means of flattery, bribes and corruption, win the support of the weak-willed and politically backward individuals, detach them from Congress and use them in their own interests. The presence of such elements in Congress constitutes a serious threat to the struggle, for the capacity for political action of an organisation which is ravaged by such disruptive and splitting elements is considerably undermined. Here in South Africa, as in many parts of the world, a revolution is maturing: it is the profound desire, the determination and the urge of the overwhelming majority of the country to destroy for ever the shackles of oppression that condemn them to servitude and slavery. To overthrow oppression has been sanctioned by humanity and is the highest aspiration of every free man. If elements in our organisation seek to impede the realisation of this lofty purpose then these people have placed themselves outside the organisation and must be put out of action before they do more harm. To do otherwise would be a crime and a serious neglect of duty. We must rid ourselves of such elements and give our organisation the striking power of a real militant mass organisation.

Kotane, Marks, Bopape, Tloome and I have been banned from attending gatherings and we cannot join and counsel with you on the serious problems that are facing our country. We have been banned because we champion the freedom of the oppressed people of our country and because we have consistently fought against the policy of racial discrimination in favour of a policy which accords fundamental human rights to all, irrespective of race, colour, sex or language. We are exiled from our own people for we have uncompromisingly resisted the efforts of imperialist America and her satellites to drag the world into the rule of violence and brutal force, into the rule of the napalm, hydrogen and the cobalt bombs where millions of people will be wiped out to satisfy the criminal and greedy appetites of the imperial powers. We have been gagged because we have emphatically and openly condemned the criminal attacks by the imperialists against the people of Malaya, Vietnam, Indonesia, Tunisia and Tanganyika and called upon our people to identify themselves unreservedly with the cause of world peace and to fight against the war policies of America and her satellites. We are being shadowed, hounded and trailed because we fearlessly voiced our horror and indignation at the slaughter of the people of Korea and Kenya. The massacre of the Kenya people by Britain has aroused world-wide indignation and protest. Children are being burnt alive, women are raped, tortured, whipped and boiling water poured on their breasts to force confessions from them that Jomo Kenyatta had administered the Mau

Mau oath to them. Men are being castrated and shot dead. In the Kikuyu country there are some villages in which the population has been completely wiped out. We are prisoners in our own country because we dared to raise our voices against these horrible atrocities and because we expressed our solidarity with the cause of the Kenya people.

You can see that "there is no easy walk to freedom anywhere, and many of us will have to pass through the valley of the shadow (of death) again and again before we reach the mountain tops of our desires.

"Dangers and difficulties have not deterred us in the past, they will not frighten us now. But we must be prepared for them like men in business who do not waste energy in vain talk and idle action. The way of preparation (for action) lies in our rooting out all impurity and indiscipline from our organisation and making it the bright and shining instrument that will cleave its way to (Africa's) freedom." [The sentences quoted by Mandela are from the speeches of Jawaharlal Nehru].

26. Jomo Kenyatta in court.

The British sought to decolonize Africa on their own terms. They were not prepared to be forced out. The situation was even more complicated when the colony had a significant white settler population, as in South Africa, Southern Rhodesia, and Kenya, because those settlers saw themselves as the natural inheritors of imperial dominion, not the Africans who provided their labor force. In Kenya in the early 1950s, some African opponents of the colonial regime, primarily people suffering from severe loss of land due to the encroachment of white settlers, went into the forest on the side of Mt. Kenya and formed what became known among Europeans as the Mau Mau movement (and among Africans as the Land and Freedom Army). Mau Mau is arguably the most highly contended political movement in the history of modern Africa. So hotly disputed is its meaning and heritage among Kenyans and historians, that not a single monument has ever been erected in commemoration of the movement in Kenya. So although its intimate connection to the history of anti-colonial liberation and, consequently, to nationalism in Kenya is evident, just how that relationship should be interpreted remains unresolved, especially at the level of national politics.

Whatever else we do know about Mau Mau, it is certain that Jomo Kenyatta (c.1894–1978), who like Azikiwe and other African leaders of his generation

had spent an extended time overseas before returning to lead an independence movement in his country, was not its leader nor even directly involved in the movement. But as the leader of the Kenya African Union (KAU), deemed "radical" by the British, he represented all that was dangerous and feared in Africans by the closed community of white settlers in Kenya. Moreover, with Nkrumah he had participated in organizing the 5th Pan-African Congress held at Manchester, England, an occasion when Africans from throughout the continent had joined together to denounce colonialism and call for immediate independence. In the early 1950s, when Nkrumah had just been released from an extended period of imprisonment for demanding self-rule for Ghana and Nelson Mandela and other leaders of the African National Congress (ANC) were being criminally prosecuted for creating race hostility because they protested against apartheid, Kenyatta was brought to trial as the head of Mau Mau and charged with every heinous crime that settler imagination and the colonial authorities could conjure up. Despite, perhaps because of, the eloquent statement that he made at his trial, Kenyatta was convicted and sentenced to seven years of hard labor and exile in a remote part of the barren north of Kenya. At least Kenyatta kept his life. British repression of Mau Mau was as severe as any taken by a colonizer on a colonized people, with tens of thousands of Africans forced off their land and into guarded encampments and more than 1,000 hanged, perhaps the largest judicially organized process of mass execution in Africa's colonial history. Though the Land and Freedom Army was defeated militarily by the mid-1950s, Kenyan opposition to colonial rule could not be repressed. Faced by the mounting costs of staying in control, the British government decided that imperial interests would best be served by granting Kenya independence with the understanding that British economic interests would be protected. In one of the jolting compromises of the end of colonialism British politicians had to accept their old nemesis, Kenyatta, as the first prime minister of independent Kenya in 1963.[26]

The principal examination of Jomo Kenyatta, on trial, January 26, 1953, charged with leading the Mau Mau movement at Kapenguria (West Kenya) [The testimony of Kenyatta].

The East African Association in 1921, with which I sympathised, opposed such things as forced labour of both African men and women, and the Registration Certificate introduced soon after the war. It was also concerned about land, and that people should have better wages, education, hospitals and roads. The Association worked by constitutional means, making representations to the Government in the most peaceful way we possibly could.

The Kikuyu Central Association, from about 1925 onwards, pursued the same aims and objects, but by 1928 more grievances were added. Most of us had become aware of the Crown Lands Ordinance of 1915, which said something like: "all land previously occupied by native people becomes the property of the Crown, and the Africans or natives living thereon become tenants at the will of the Crown." When we realised this, we started a demand for its abolition, on the grounds that it was unfair for our people, because we were not informed of its enactment and had no say in its provisions.

We were also protesting against the country's status being changed to that of a

26. Jomo Kenyatta, *Suffering without Bitterness* (Nairobi: East African Publishing House, 1968), pp. 24–28.

Colony, instead of a Protectorate. We knew the Africans would have less legal claim to their territory in a Colony than in a Protectorate, since the latter would be guided by the British Government until we could be left to our own affairs. We were told that everybody would have rights in a Colony, but Africans would have the least rights.

If you woke up one morning and found that somebody had come to your house, and had declared that house belonged to him, you would naturally be surprised, and you would like to know by what arrangement. Many Africans at that time found that, on land which had been in the possession of their ancestors from time immemorial, they were now working as squatters or as labourers.

I became a member of the Kikuyu Central Association in 1928, after the visit of the Hilton Young Commission which came to investigate land problems in Kenya. My people approached me saying they would like me to represent them, so I left Government service and joined the KCA. I immediately started a paper—the first newspaper in this part of the world published by Africans—called "Muigwithania" ["He who brings together"].

The KCA sought the redress of grievances through constitutional means: by making representations to the Government of Kenya, to various Commissions, and to the home Government, in England.

In 1929, I was asked if I could go to England to represent my people. By then our demands had increased, to include direct representation of the African people in Legislative Council. We were told when we approached the Government: "Well, you know, we have no objection to you coming to Legislative Council or any other place of Government, providing you have education." We badly wanted to educate our children, so another reason why I went to Europe was to seek ways and means of establishing our schools.

When I arrived in London, I prepared my case, sent a memorandum to the Secretary of State—then Lord Passfield—and made contact with Members of Parliament. There were many negotiations. A White Paper was then published saying, in essence, that the Government has decided no more African land would be taken away from them, and what was left to them would remain their land for ever. I think this reaffirmed as well another declaration—by the Duke of Devonshire in 1923—to the effect that: "Kenya is an African territory and the African interest must be paramount, and whenever the interests of the African people and those of the immigrant races conflict, the African interests will always prevail."

I think this 1930 White Paper was known as: "Native Policy in East Africa." But I have been placed at a great disadvantage because I cannot get my papers to present my case, so I have to rely on what I can remember. All my documents and files were taken away. . . . (*Note: Mzee Kenyatta's personal files and documents were never returned to him by the Administration or the Police. An exhaustive search since Independence has proved fruitless, and the assumption can only be that they were destroyed.*)

While in Europe, I had published the correspondence as between the KCA and the Secretary of State. I also had the opportunity of going to meet the Archbishop of Canterbury, and went to Edinburgh for an interview with the Moderator of the Church of Scotland.

Speaking to a Committee of the House of Commons, I said we could take some of the good European and Indian customs, and those of our customs which were good, and see how we could build a new kind of society in Kenya.

Whereas formerly it had been illegal for us to establish a school, we were now given permission by the Government to do so, if we could find land to build on, find the money to build, and find money to pay teachers. From about 1930, the Kikuyu Independent Schools Association and the Karinga ISA came into being. When I came back, I found they had over 300 schools educating more than 60,000 children, with no financial help at all from the Government.

I went to Europe again in 1931 and stayed till 1946, when I found the KCA had been proscribed. I saw the Governor (Note: the late Sir Philip Mitchell) . . . twice on this question, and had interviews with the Chief Native Commissioner several times to investigate the position. The Governor told me the matter would be reconsidered. He said he himself could see no reason why the Association should not start functioning, but he left the matter to his officials and to the Member of Legislative Council representing African interests. The Chief Native Commissioner said some people had behaved rashly and got themselves into trouble, so the matter was dropped.

Our files show that the KCA was a constitutional organization, but the Police are keeping them.

Early in 1947, when I was very busy in the activities of schools, I came to know about and joined the Kenya African Union. At the annual meeting in June, I was elected as President. The aims of KAU were to unite the African people of Kenya; to prepare the way for introduction of democracy in Kenya; to defend and promote the interests of the African people by organizing and educating them in the struggle for better working and social conditions; to fight for equal rights for all Africans and break down racial barriers; to strive for extension to all African adults of the right to vote and to be elected to parlia-mentary and other representative bodies; to publish a political newspaper; to fight for freedom of assembly, press and movement.

To fight for equal rights does not mean fighting with fists or with a weapon, but to fight through negotiations and by constitutional means. We do not believe in violence at all, but in discussion and representation.

We feel that the racial barrier is one of the most diabolical things that we have in the Colony, and we see no reason at all why all races in this country cannot work harmoniously together without any discrimination. If people of goodwill can come together, they can eliminate this evil. God put everybody into this world to live happily, and to enjoy the gifts of Nature that God bestowed upon mankind. During my stay in Europe—and especially in England—I lived very happily, and made thousands of good friends. I do not see why people in this country cannot do the same thing. To my mind, colour is irrelevant.

Some time ago, I invited about 40 Europeans to meet me, and spent a whole day with them at our school at Githunguri. One of them said they expected to be chased away; then he apologised for the hatred that he had felt for us, and for believing that we hated the Europeans. That was a common attitude of many settlers who had never met me. I told him I was just an ordinary man, striving to fight for the rights of my people, and to better their conditions, without hating anybody.

27. Mau Mau's daughter.

The Mau Mau movement involved virtually the entire Gikuyu people, whether as forest fighters, colonial soldiers, loyalist chiefs, urban dwellers who carried messages and materials from Nairobi into the reserves and forests, or rural villagers. Although men were at the center of the armed struggle, women and children played a critical role as messengers and carriers of provisions to the men hidden away in the forests. Some of these women and children, like Wambui Otieno (her excerpt follows), were progressively drawn into the conflict through their experience of the abuse and exploitation to which people were subjected in the reserves, and they participated in the oath-taking that bound them and their brothers together in the armed struggle.[27]

27. Wambui Waiyaki Otieno, *Mau Mau's Daughter: A Life History*, edited with an introduction by Cora Ann Presley (Boulder: Lynne Rienner Publishers, 1998), pp. 32–37. Copyright © 1998 by Virginia Edith Wambui Waiyaki Otieno. Reprinted with the permission of Lynne Rienner Publishers Inc.

As a sixteen-year-old schoolgirl, I did not know much about being a freedom fighter, although I read such newspapers as the *East African Standard* and *Daily Chronicle* and knew about Jomo Kenyatta's pronouncements. I had read his book *Facing Mount Kenya* [published in 1938] and Kenyatta himself was a frequent visitor to our home. He and the late Mbiyu Koinange would come and lie on the grass outside our house and have discussions with my father for hours on end. But, as children, we did not know what they were discussing. By the time the State of Emergency was declared, I had already taken my first Mau Mau oath, albeit unknowingly. This happened during one of the school holidays in 1952. I had assumed the oath to be associated with the Girl Guide movement, of which I was a member. A cousin named Timothy Chege took me and another woman to a place called Gaitumbi. She worked on our farm and was related to my mother. Both were aware of my intense resentment of the brutal treatment my great-grandfather Waiyaki wa Hinga had suffered at the hands of the colonialists [according to Gikuyu—or Kikuyu— memories, Hinga was buried alive by the British in 1892; the British claimed to the contrary that he had committed suicide], for I had openly said that I was prepared to avenge him.

I was told very little when we arrived at Gaitumbi. I was asked whether I was menstruating. (I later learned that a menstruating woman was disqualified from taking the oath at that time, as menstruation was regarded as dirty and a cause of misfortune.) I answered "No," and in turn received a hard slap, the purpose of which was not clear to me. I was then ordered to shed all my clothes except my bra and knickers. I was led into a poorly lit room where a group of people were casually sitting. On one side were two sugarcane poles standing erect with their tips tied to form an arch. The poles were tall enough for a person to walk underneath. Each initiate was told to walk through the arch seven times. Then I was tied to the other initiates with a long goatskin, which I later learned was called "Rukwaro." In a single line, we

again walked through the two poles seven times. After that an old man brought a calabash and told each of us to drink a mouthful of a concoction of blood and soil. I nearly threw up because it smelled like goat's intestines. However, I remembered the words of my mother's relative—freedom would not come easily. Kenyatta's similar sentiments had appeared in the newspapers on many occasions. I therefore forced myself to swallow everything. Then I took the oath of allegiance. Repeating carefully after an instructor, I swore to:

1. Fight for the soil of Gikuyu [Kikuyu] and Mumbi's children, which had been stolen from them by the whites.

2. If possible, get a gun from a white or a black collaborator and any other valuables or money to help strengthen the movement.

3. Kill anyone who was against the movement, even if that person was my brother.

4. Never reveal what had just happened or any other information disclosed to me as a member of the movement, but always to do my utmost to strengthen the movement; and if I didn't keep my words, may the oath kill me.

This ceremony took place a few months before the Emergency was declared.

The State of Emergency kept me from studying abroad. I left school in 1953 and was supposed to join my elder sister and brothers who were studying in England, but because of the state of affairs in the country I couldn't leave. Finding myself with more time on my hands, I became even more eager to learn about freedom activities and followed them more closely. I continued helping with the farm and house chores and became friendly with a woman farmworker to whom I often related matters concerning freedom-fighting activities. I told her of my indignation that Waiyaki had been brutally murdered by the whites and that Kinyanjui wa Gathirimu, the black collaborator, had been rewarded for his betrayal of our people with the office of paramount chief. She would talk to me about politics and I realized she knew more about Mau Mau than I did. Finally she trusted me enough to reveal her knowledge of the movement. She said that by joining it, I would assist in getting rid of colonialists and their black collaborators. I had not revealed to her that I had already taken the oath. I felt that I still did not really belong to the movement, despite having taken the oath. However, now that I was no longer in school, I wanted to participate more in its activities. So we made a plan. One night when everyone else was asleep, I sneaked out through the window. She and other members of Mau Mau were waiting for me. Together, we went again to Gaitumbi, to the homestead of a man called Mumira, where I took my second oath, which was similar to the one I had taken two years earlier.

Shortly after this oath-taking, there occurred an incident that left me with a terrible feeling of guilt. One night at home we heard gunshots outside. My mother began to open a window to peep out. I already know that an attack on the Kinoo Home Guard post was under way and had marked our gate with a special sign so the Mau Mau would know that our home helped the movement. Although I knew we would be left alone, I feared that a stray bullet might hit my mother, so I went after her, closing the windows. I was wrestling with her as she opened one window after another. She was puzzled by my strange behavior, but I did not explain because I was under oath. My real worry was that she might get hurt. Later I learned that was exactly what had happened to my uncle, Muchugia Wambaa, whose ear was injured. I protested to the Mau Mau War Council because, with the help of my cousin Chege, I had marked all my close relatives' homes as "safe." I could do this honestly because my relatives had not collaborated with the colonists.

After the attack on the Kinoo Home Guard post, I took my second oath at Kinoo in the bush near a river (I considered the first two oaths to be one oath). I took the third oath at Waithaka, at the home of Wairimu wa Wagaca, who was called "Nyina wa Andu" (mother of the people), a very determined freedom fighter. The other oaths I took varied according to reasons for taking them or

actions one was supposed to complete after taking them. Some were meant to strengthen previous ones, while others like Kindu or Mbatuni (battalion or platoon) were very serious and were administered only to the real fighters and scouts. I took Mbatuni voluntarily and felt more commitment to Mau Mau thereafter, convinced it was the only way Kenya could be free. The oath made believers keep secrets. Above all, it brought unity to Mau Mau's members. Through certain signs and modes of greeting, we were able to identify one another. We also had a code of regulations that we adhered to. I took nine oaths altogether during my time as a Mau Mau.

From 1952 to 1954, the government was on the defensive against Mau Mau. On April 23, 1954, two years after the State of Emergency had been declared, government forces began Operation Anvil. The following day my father was arrested and detained at Langata Camp. He was later moved to the camp at Mackinnon Road and finally detained at Camp No. 6 in Manyani. From there he wrote us a letter that read; "I am in Manyani Camp. I am keeping well. I have sent this letter with an officer who will collect my clothes. Yours, T.W. Munyua."

Matters worsened as the State of Emergency continued. People were arrested arbitrarily by the panicked colonial ad–ministration. All it took was a little suspicion for one to be branded a Mau Mau. This also encouraged black collaborators to accuse people of being Mau Mau with little or no proof. I personally knew many people who got into trouble yet who had nothing whatsoever to do with our movement. It became increasingly difficult not to take sides. Despite all this, I felt as determined as ever. In my mind I had no doubt that I was fighting for a just cause, and I owe my gratitude to the late Muiruri Waiyaki, my cousin, who helped me survive those early trying days. He inspired me and boosted my morale during the lengthy hours I spent with him. I felt a great sense of loss when he was captured at Kahawa and hanged by court order. May God rest his soul in peace.

My fighting spirit was aroused to a frenzy one day when my mother was almost hit on the head by a European called Peter. The incident took place when I was in our homestead garden near Kiharu River. As I came up the path, I immediately sensed something had happened. My mother's unsteady gait and the way she carried herself brought tears to my eyes. I suggested that we lodge a complaint with the district officer at Kikuyu, but she was hesitant. She said we must exercise caution. "Times are bad," she said. However, I was not going to let the matter end there. If she was not prepared to do something about it, then I was. My mother suggested she go to Thogoto Mission to inform Reverend MacPherson. I had no time for that suggestion. To me, they were all colonialists, and indeed they were. Without informing her, I hurriedly dressed, took fifty cents for bus fare from her drawer, and left.

When I arrived at the district officer's office, I encountered a disgusting sight. The body of a Mukurinu preacher who had been killed near Muguga had been brought and put on public display. The Europeans had removed his turban to reveal his dreadlocks, and to the ignorant public was a convincing Mau Mau terrorist. There was a queue of people waiting for travel passes. I jumped to the head of the queue and stormed into the DO's [District Officer] office. Mr. Martin, the assistant DO, was not amused by the intrusion.

But I was in no mood for compromise. He shouted at me and I shouted back. I intended to make as much of a scene as possible. My anger at my mother's treatment was so great that I did not care if they killed me for confronting them. The Home Guards cocked their rifles menacingly at me, and I dared them to shoot me. I was too angry to care. But their commander, Kiarie wa Wambari, did not give the order to fire. The senior DO, Mr. Kemble, ordered that I be taken to his office, and he asked me to compose myself so that we could discuss the matter rationally. I left his office only after he had agreed to have Peter removed from the Kinoo Home Guard post. Luckily, as I walked out I met Senior Chief Josiah Njonjo Mugane and a police officer, Eli John, who assisted in seeing that Peter was removed from that area. Peter was a lunatic who, when he could not find an excuse to shoot at Africans, would ask for sheep or goats to be brought to him so he could mow them down with his gun, after which he would calm down.

Meanwhile, investigations were going on concerning my father, who was still in detention. Special policemen from the Criminal Investigation Division (C.I.D.) visited our home many times at night in a futile search for evidence to prove his role in Mau Mau. Finally they had to release him. I owe my gratitude to Peter Okola, who saved my life during those searches, as I could not resist battling with the colonial police. Okola, who had worked with my father on the police force, became the director of intelligence after independence. During my father's absence from home, our family suffered many hardships. For lack of money, my brothers in England had to discontinue their education. My mother took risky train trips to Nairobi to collect rent from our house, No. 490 in Pumwani. She traveled without a pass and would have gotten into much trouble had she been discovered. We also felled black wattle trees and sold the wood and bark to Muguga Ginnery to supplement our income. Through all these hardships, I was active in the movement, surprisingly quite unknown to my mother. She was so innocent in her pursuit of Christianity that she became almost oblivious to what was happening around her. Still, to be on the safe side, I adopted my nickname "Wagio" (which I later changed to "Msaja"), so that my real name would not filter back and connect me with Mau Mau activities.

28. The Freedom Charter.

Unlike Anton Lembede, Nelson Mandela did not embrace wholeheartedly the Africanist philosophy. He thought that South Africa belonged to all who lived within its boundaries and that it should be a multi-racial state in which all residents would receive equal access to the political process and equal treatment before the law. The fullest expression of this point of view was developed at the Congress of the People held in 1955, a mass meeting of representatives of all South Africans opposed to apartheid. The National Party government responded to this show of unity with police raids on the Congress and interrogations of all the participants. A year later, in December 1956, the government ordered the arrest of more than 150 people, most of them participants in the meeting of the Congress, and put them on trial for high treason (a death penalty charge). The core of the government's case was that the Congress members, by calling for racial equality, demonstrated "hostile intent" which was, under South African law, a treasonable offence. After a very lengthy trial that prevented most of those accused from engaging in political action for almost half a decade, the courts in 1960 found the defendants not guilty on the ground that the prosecution had failed, despite its promises to the contrary, to prove that the African National Congress (ANC) had ever adopted a policy of violence.[28]

"Freedom Charter," adopted by the Congress of the People, June 26, 1955.

PREAMBLE

We, the people of South Africa, declare for all our country and the world to know:

That South Africa belongs to all who live in it, black and white, and that no government can justly claim authority unless it is based on the will of the people;

That our people have been robbed of their birthright to land, liberty and peace by a form of government founded on injustice and inequality;

That our country will never be prosperous or free until all our people live in brotherhood, enjoying equal rights and opportunities;

That only a democratic state, based on the will of the people, can secure to all their birthright without distinction of colour, race, sex or belief;

And therefore, we the people of South Africa, black and white, together—equals, countrymen and brothers—adopt this FREEDOM CHARTER. And we pledge ourselves to strive together, sparing nothing of our strength and courage, until the democratic changes here set out have been won.

THE PEOPLE SHALL GOVERN!

Every man and woman shall have the right to vote for and stand as a candidate for all bodies which make laws;

All the people shall be entitled to take part in the administration of the country;

The rights of the people shall be the same regardless of race, colour or sex;

All bodies of minority rule, advisory boards, councils and authorities shall be replaced by democratic organs of self-government.

---

28. ANC Web site, <www.anc.org.za/ancdocs/history/charter.html>. Accessed June 1, 2000.

ALL NATIONAL GROUPS SHALL HAVE EQUAL RIGHTS!

There shall be equal status in the bodies of the state, in the courts and in the schools for all national groups and races;

All national groups shall be protected by law against insults to their race and national pride;

All people shall have equal rights to use their own language and to develop their own folk culture and customs;

The preaching and practice of national, race or colour discrimination and contempt shall be a punishable crime;

All apartheid laws and practices shall be set aside.

THE PEOPLE SHALL SHARE IN THE COUNTRY'S WEALTH!

The national wealth of our country, the heritage of all South Africans, shall be restored to the people;

The mineral wealth beneath the soil, the banks and monopoly industry shall be transferred to the ownership of the people as a whole;

All other industries and trades shall be controlled to assist the well-being of the people;

All people shall have equal rights to trade where they choose, to manufacture and to enter all trades, crafts and professions.

THE LAND SHALL BE SHARED AMONG THOSE WHO WORK IT!

Restriction of land ownership on a racial basis shall be ended, and all the land re-divided amongst those who work it, to banish famine and land hunger;

The state shall help the peasants with implements, seed, tractors and dams to save the soil and assist the tillers;

Freedom of movement shall be guaranteed to all who work on the land;

All shall have the right to occupy land wherever they choose;

People shall not be robbed of their cattle, and forced labour and farm prisons shall be abolished.

ALL SHALL BE EQUAL BEFORE THE LAW!

No one shall be imprisoned, deported or restricted without fair trial;

No one shall be condemned by the order of any Government official;

The courts shall be representative of all the people;

Imprisonment shall be only for serious crimes against the people, and shall aim at re-education, not vengeance;

The police force and army shall be open to all on an equal basis and shall be the helpers and protectors of the people;

All laws which discriminate on the grounds of race, colour or belief shall be repealed.

ALL SHALL ENJOY HUMAN RIGHTS!

The law shall guarantee to all their right to speak, to organise, to meet together, to publish, to preach, to worship and to educate their children;

The privacy of the house from police raids shall be protected by law;

All shall be free to travel without restriction from countryside to town, from province to province, and from South Africa abroad;

Pass laws, permits and all other laws restricting these freedoms shall be abolished.

THERE SHALL BE WORK AND SECURITY!

All who work shall be free to form trade unions, to elect their officers and to make wage agreements with their employers;

The state shall recognise the right and duty of all to work, and to draw full, unemployment benefits;

Men and women of all races shall receive equal pay for equal work;

There shall be a forty-hour working week, a national minimum wage, paid annual leave, and sick leave for all workers, and maternity leave on full pay for all working mothers;

Miners, domestic workers, farm workers and civil servants shall have the same rights as all others who work;

Child labour, compound labour, the tot [whereby some workers were paid in measures of liquor rather than cash] system and contract labour shall be abolished.

THE DOORS OF LEARNING AND OF CULTURE SHALL BE OPENED!

The government shall discover, develop and encourage national talent for the enhancement of our cultural life;

All the cultural treasures of mankind shall be open to all, by free exchange of books, ideas and contact with other lands;

The aim of education shall be to teach the youth to love their people and their culture, to honour human brotherhood, liberty and peace;

Education shall be free, compulsory, universal and equal for all children;

Higher education and technical training shall be opened to all by means of state allowances and scholarships awarded on the basis of merit;

Adult illiteracy shall be ended by a mass state education plan;

Teachers shall have all the rights of other citizens;

The colour bar in cultural life, in sport and in education shall be abolished.

THERE SHALL BE HOUSES, SECURITY AND COMFORT!

All people shall have the right to live where they choose, to be decently housed, and to bring up their families in comfort and security;

Unused housing space to be made available to the people;

Rent and prices shall be lowered, food plentiful and no one shall go hungry;

A preventive health scheme shall be run by the state;

Free medical care and hospitalisation shall be provided for all, with special care for mothers and young children;

Slums shall be demolished and new suburbs built where all shall have transport, roads, lighting, playing fields, crêches and social centres;

The aged, the orphans, the disabled and the sick shall be cared for by the state;

Rest, leisure and recreation shall be the right of all;

Fenced locations and ghettos shall be abolished, and laws which break up families shall be repealed.

THERE SHALL BE PEACE AND FRIENDSHIP!

South Africa shall be a fully independent state, which respects the rights and sovereignty of all nations;

South Africa shall strive to maintain world peace and the settlement of all international disputes by negotiation—not war;

Peace and friendship amongst all our people shall be secured by upholding the equal rights, opportunities and status of all;

The people of the protectorates— Basutoland, Bechuanaland and Swaziland— shall be free to decide for themselves their own future;

The right of all the peoples of Africa to independence and self-government shall be recognised, and shall be the basis of close cooperation.

Let all who love their people and their country now say, as we say here: "THESE FREEDOMS WE WILL FIGHT FOR, SIDE BY SIDE, THROUGHOUT OUR LIVES, UNTIL WE HAVE WON OUR LIBERTY."

29. Freedom! Freedom! Freedom!

On March 6, 1957, Ghana became the first colony in Africa to win its independence. The leader of the independence movement was Kwame Nkrumah, a very different type of person from the type of collaborator that the British hoped would lead an independent Ghana. Nkrumah, like Azikiwe, had studied in the United States and had also graduated from Lincoln University. He was a strong proponent of the pan-African ideas of W. E. B. Du Bois and of Marcus Garvey (who had led a back-to-Africa movement in the United States during the 1920s). Despite subjecting him to lengthy periods of detention, the British were not able to undermine Nkrumah's leadership of the Ghanaian independence movement.

The most symbolic moment for the end of colonial rule always came at midnight on the eve of independence, as the flag of the old imperial power was lowered and that of the new state raised. This extract is from the speech that Nkrumah gave to the people gathered at the flag ceremony, among them thousands of Ghanaians, representatives of many foreign nations, and numerous dignitaries from Britain including Queen Elizabeth. For Nkrumah, this occasion symbolized the end of empire.[29]

At long last the battle has ended! And thus Ghana, your beloved country, is free for ever. And here again, I want to take the opportunity to thank the chiefs and people of this country, the youth, the farmers, the women, who have so nobly fought and won this battle. Also I want to thank the valiant ex-servicemen who have so co-operated with me in this mighty task of freeing our country from foreign rule and imperialism! And as I pointed out at our Party conference at Saltpond, I made it quite clear that from now on, today, we must change our attitudes, our minds. We must realise that from now on we are no more a colonial but a free and independent people! But also, as I pointed out, that entails hard work. I am depending upon the millions of the country, the chiefs and people to help me to reshape the destiny of this country. We are prepared to make it a nation that will be respected by any nation in the world. We know we are going to have a difficult beginning but again I am relying upon your support, I am relying upon your hard work, seeing you here in your thousands, however far my eye goes. My last warning to you is that you ought to stand firm behind us so that we can prove to the world that when the African is given a chance he can show the world that he is somebody. We are not waiting; we shall no more go back to sleep any more. Today, from now on, there is a new African in the world and that new African is ready to fight his own battle and show that after all the black man is capable of managing his own affairs. We are going to demonstrate to the world, to the other nations, young as we are, that we are prepared to lay our own foundation.

As I said in the Assembly just a few minutes ago, I made a point that we are going to see that we create our own African personality and identity; it is the only way in which we can show the world that we are masters of our own destiny. But today may I call upon you all; at this great day let us all remember

Kwame Nkrumah. *Source:* Kwame Nkrumah, *Africa Must Unite* (New York: Frederick A. Praeger, Inc., 1963), frontispiece.

29. Kwame Nkrumah, *I Speak of Freedom: A Statement of African Ideology* (New York: Frederick A. Praeger, 1961), pp. 106–08. Reprinted with the permission of Heinemann Educational Publishers, a division of Reed Educational & Professional Publishing Ltd.

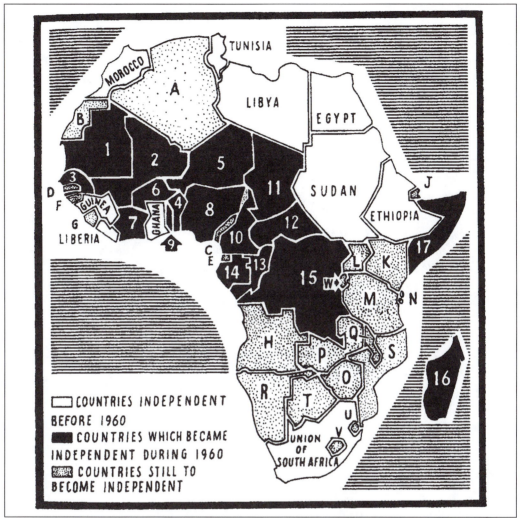

Africa, 1960. *Source:* Kwame Nkrumah, *Africa Must Unite* (New York: Frederick A. Praeger, Inc., 1963), facing p. xii.

that nothing in the world can be done unless it has the support of God. We have done with the battle and we again re-dedicate ourselves in the struggle to emancipate other countries in Africa, for our independence is meaningless unless it is linked up with the total liberation of the African continent.

Let us now, fellow Ghanaians, let us now ask for God's blessing, and in your tens of thousands, I want to ask you to pause for one minute, and give thanks to Almighty God for having led us through obstacles, difficulties, imprisonments, hardships and sufferings to have brought us to the end of our trouble today. One minute silence—Ghana is free forever! And here I will ask the band to play the Ghana national anthem.

Here the Ghana national anthem was played.

I want simply to thank those who have come from abroad to witness this occasion. Here I wish I could quote Marcus Garvey. Once upon a time, he said, he looked through the whole world to see if he could find a government of a black people. He looked around, he did not find one, and he said he was going to create one. Marcus Garvey did not succeed. But here today the work of Rousseau, the work of Marcus Garvey, the work of [John] Aggrey, the work of Casely Hayford, the work of these illustrious men who have gone before us has come to reality at this present moment. And so we thank all of you and I am going to ask the band to play again, because it must sink in and make us realise that from today, we are no more a colonial people. This time, the national anthem is going to be played in honour of the foreign states who are here with us today to witness this occasion and I want you all, those who have hats on, to take off your hats and let the band play our national anthem. And from now on that national anthem is the national anthem of Ghana to be played on all occasions.

The national anthem was played, and played again amid cries of Freedom! Freedom! Freedom!

30. Verwoerd reaffirms South Africa's commitment to white supremacy.

While Nkrumah celebrated African independence in Ghana, Hendrik Verwoerd (see also document 24) reflected on history as he spoke in 1958 about the need for white South Africans to defend their ideals in a world increasingly hostile to the continuance of legalized racial discrimination. Verwoerd chose as the occasion for his reflections the 120th anniversary of the battle of Blood River, when an armed force of Voortrekkers had avenged the death of their leader Piet Retief by massacring thousands of Dingane's Zulu subjects. For Verwoerd, and for many other whites in South Africa, Blood River symbolized the triumph of civilization over savagery and the power of Europeans fighting with the Christian God on their side. Indeed, commemoration of the battle had become an increasingly popular event for whites in the twentieth century, providing an opportunity for stirring speeches about the need to stand together to face the forces of darkness. For Verwoerd and his followers, the move to independence in the rest of Africa made the struggle to maintain white rule in South Africa more difficult and more important than ever.[30]

Speech delivered at Blood River, December 16, 1958.

Dear friends, I want to speak of then and now.

If we review the spirit of the world at the time of the Voortrekkers, we find that it was a period of commotion in the minds of men. A spiritual current was then flowing over the world which created a new atmosphere spreading its influence even as far as here in the southern part of Africa. We all know how a spirit of emancipation arose among humanity during the French Revolution, a spirit of freedom and brotherhood and equality of all people. It originated from the circumstances of the Europe of that time and was then wrongly applied to the outside world which was different.

The application of the idea of freedom, equality and fraternity of all people gave rise to violent disputes and strife and revealed the prevailing misconception regarding the life of people in other countries under different circumstances. In Europe they wrote about the "noble savage" while the human being among them, the European in his civilisation of that time, went unregarded. In that spirit the white men who were engaged in civilising countries and saving the savage from himself and from the oppressor among his own ranks, were described as oppressors.

The same happened to our own nation and the Voortrekkers.. Gross misrepresentations were prevalent in Europe regarding our

---

30. A. N. Pelzer, ed., *Verwoerd Speaks: Speeches 1948–1966* (Johannesburg: APB Publishers, 1966), pp. 206–11.

people and the deeds performed here. From those countries foreign missionaries, the Phillips's and the Van der Kemps, animated by the spirit which had spread over Europe, came to an area which they did not know. They brought not only the Gospel, but also the disturbance of misunderstanding. They rendered a disservice not only to the white man who at that time was penetrating the interior with the Bible in the hand, but also to the heathens by inciting them against the white man with all his goodwill and his knowledge of conditions here. They complicated matters and much of the blood which was spilt, and the strife engendered were the result of well-intentioned but misplaced transmission of a spirit which, in the circumstances of that time, did not fit here.

That spirit was not directed against the Afrikaner forefathers only but against all white men. The English-speaking people also realised that the Christianising process was necessary for Africa and that the supremacy of the white man was necessary in order to bring and extend civilisation and Christianity here in South Africa.

In the midst of all this the conduct of the Voortrekkers was characterised by three definite mental attitudes. The one was symbolised by the readiness of Piet Retief even when his people had found an unclaimed area, nevertheless to acquire it by proper negotiations. Piet Retief was prepared to enter into an agreement with Dingaan. He was prepared to trust and co-operate. He placed the lives of his small group of companions at the mercy of the barbarian. The white man's trust, the white man's honest sincerity, the white man's preparedness to negotiate, the readiness to grant suitable rights, each in its kind and place, were all symbolised in that act of Piet Retief. From the events at Murder Hill we also see that the people gathered there were not prepared to have a part in the suicide of a nation. They were not prepared to give way or to mix. They were prepared to remain or to trek to the Transvaal if necessary, but wherever they went, they were prepared to fight until victory was won, to struggle in order to help in building a nation. Whether the

Voortrekker was journeying or fighting and whether he put his hand to the plough when left in peace, he was always busy building his nation. He was never prepared to break up, to destroy or to lose.

It was characteristic of that struggle that the Voortrekker always had his wife and child with him. It was not a struggle of men only. It was a struggle of the whole family—man, woman and child—side by side to safeguard the future of their posterity and to preserve the purity of the blood of the nation. Had only men surged into a country, there would perhaps not have been a white nation today. Because it was a family trek and because the unity of the family was the basic bond of the democratic government of the states established, order and peace could soon be found there. It was the family that trekked, the family that fought, the family that built.

That is what happened then. What is the position today?

There is a remarkable similarity. Is it not so that today a liberalistic current very similar to that of 120 years ago is again moving across the world? A spirit which originates from World War II, perhaps even from World War I; a spirit engendered by the experience of the people elsewhere and by their self-interest; a spirit of liberalism which causes the white states to become so divided among themselves that each, with a view to the success of its aims, tries to obtain the support of the non-white world—whether in Asia or in Africa; a spirit not born from the highest moral considerations, as it is frequently represented to be. If it were, then it would not look down so damningly upon the fellow white man in other parts of the world but could be as equally understanding towards him as it is towards the black man.

It is peculiar that the world spirit, just like then, is not directed against the Afrikaner, but against all whites. That spirit is permeated with glorification of the noble savage. Everything that the non-white says or does, is good or is glossed over. If he acts roughly or foolishly it is described as merely characteristic of the transition period. But if the white man by standing firm has to ensure that civilisation is preserved, then it is oppression and he is maligned. The world spirit is also directed at all the colonial powers in Africa, whether it be the Portuguese or the British or the Belgians or the French, and whether it be the South Africans. Whoever brought civilisation here, whoever saved the people from mutual extinction, whoever provided shelter and food to greater masses than the country could carry previously goes unthanked for the life, for the prosperity, for the knowledge, and for the Divine enrichment of Primitive minds. It is also peculiar that once more foreign preachers have come to carry the misconceptions further—the Huddlestons, the Collins's, the Scotts, the De Blanks—people perhaps with good intentions, people infused with the spirit of Europe which has been imbibed by them, some even animated by a spirit proceeding from the abject Communism. In this country where we as a Christian nation with knowledge of our history and of the nature of the Bantu people and the level of their development try to do what is right and good and Christianlike, we are condemned by mouths which should have come and learned before they talked.

They do not observe that, just like 120 years ago, there are the clearest evidences of our preparedness to let fairness and justice prevail. I have referred to the manner in which Piet Retief was prepared to enter into an agreement. I add thereto that after that Murder Hill episode, Andries Pretorius, who had come to mete out punishment for the misdeed, while on the way still sent a message to Dingaan saying that if he should show repentance the Voortrekkers would yet be forgiving and not carry the warfare to extremes. Because the message was regarded with contempt, the battle at Blood River had to take place.

Even so the white man is today prepared in all kinds of ways to have justice done to the Bantu. It is the policy of South Africa to grant rights to the non-white in his own community and in his own area where it is fitting.

Again it is the white people of South Africa, who know the conditions, who have designed and now follow the only method which can bring peace and do justice to all. But they are not supported therein by those who come from outside and do not understand it. These have already accepted as unavoidable the disappearance of the white race. When it is said in Europe and also by some in our own country that the solution of this struggle is to be found in the merger of all people—so-called integration—it is not realised that this is not unification. All that will happen is the destruction of the white race. Not integration,. but disintegration—disintegration of the white race, of the civilisation and of the religion which we inherited, will be the only result. Therefore, even though we cannot trek any more, we say like the Voortrekker of yore, "we can still struggle." And we shall fight even though we have to perish. We shall keep on fighting for the survival of the white man at the southern tip of Africa and the religion which has been given to him to spread here. And we shall do it just as they did! Man, woman and child. We shall fight for our existence and the world must know it. We cannot do otherwise. Like Luther during the Reformation we are standing with our backs to the wall. We are not fighting for money or possessions. We are fighting for the life of our people.

But we are not fighting for our people only. I am deeply convinced in my soul that we are fighting for the survival of white civilisation. If ever a struggle between East and West were to come, if Africa ever were to throw in its weight somewhere—and it would be a decisive weight—then the weight of Africa would be on the side of the white man and the Western nations only if the idea for which we as a nation stand can remain victorious. The white man at the southern point of Africa is an outpost of white civilisation and as such the advance-guard of its forces, located where the first attacks are to come. We know that we are a small nation but we also know that we have in us the steel and the strength which resulted in the triumph of Blood River. When you are in the forward lines and see the danger coming, you are entitled to send messages to the armies in the rear who are still sheltering behind you.

Hence we send this message to the outside world and say to them once again that there is but one way of saving the white races of the world. And that is for the white and the non-white in Africa each to exercise his rights within his own areas.

We are fighting with all that is within us because we know that we are a nation in the making. We know that we are not yet half-way up the mast. We know that we are still foundation layers just like the heroes of Blood River. We also know that we are ordinary people with many weaknesses. But we know that those who are making history, like they did and we are doing now, are doing so with a young nation still in the spring-time of its life. If the foundations are laid right, the walls can be built strongly. And the foundations that we lay we are endeavouring to lay solidly and securely. We are trying to dig down through the clay to the gravel and bed-rock so that the nation of South Africa may exist to remote times in the future. That is why we are not allowing ourselves to be driven to rashness or to panic. That is why we are building on the only rock of nations, namely the faith and the same helping hand which gave our forefathers the victory of Blood River. We are building in faith, we are building with power because we know that we have not been planted here aimlessly. Why should Whites have been led to the southern tip of Africa three hundred years ago? Why was half of the country unoccupied, why could small numbers of people increase so much and become spread over the whole country? Why could they, in spite of their Moordkrans and Italeni [defeats], also gain their Blood River? Why could they go through their wars of independence and, win or lose, yet survive as a nation? Why was this all given to us if there is no purpose in it? And I believe this to be the purpose—that we should be an anchor and a stay for Western civilisation and for the Christian religion. Western civilisation and the white races are also going through a crisis, even though they do not notice it. Never before in history, at any rate the history of the past two thousand years, has the position of the white races been so perilous. They are in danger not because of their lack of knowledge or power, but on account of that which is going on in their own spirit: their inner weakening and wrong conception of what their task is on earth. And there sometimes have to be small groups that offer resistance; a resistance that can be extended until it embraces the whole pattern of nations.

Perhaps it was intended that we should have been planted here at the southern point within the crisis area so that from this resistance group might emanate the victory whereby all that has been built up since the days of Christ may be maintained for the good of all mankind. May you have the strength, people of South Africa, to serve the purpose for which you have been placed here!

31. Patrice Lumumba writes his last letter to his wife.

The most rapid pull-out by a colonial power from Africa was made by the Belgians in 1960s when, in the course of little more than a few months, they moved from a claim that they would continue to rule the country for the forseeable future to complete abandonment of their prized possession. Growing demonstrations, and the refusal of the bulk of the population to accept attempts that the Belgians were making to identify a collaborationist group, propelled the colonialists out of the country, but not before they had attempted to secure their economic interests in the mineral-rich southeastern province of Katanga. Belgian and South African investors encouraged the regional leader of Katanga, Moise Tshombe, to organize a secessionist movement. At the same time, the Congo became swept up in the Cold War as Soviet and U.S. diplo-

mats competed to incorporate this potentially rich and strategically situated country into their respective spheres of influence.

Caught up in these contradictory forces was Patrice Lumumba, who had led the movement for independence and who became the first president of an independent Congo. Perceived as anti-Belgium by the Belgians, as too pro-socialist by South African business leaders (who feared nationalization of their Katangan mining companies), as pro-Communist by the United States, and as too intransigent in his opposition to Katangan secession by the leaders of the United Nations, Lumumba became increasingly isolated. In November 1960, he was arrested by soldiers loyal to then-Colonel Mobutu (later the dictator of Zaire for nearly 40 years, Mobutu Sese Seko), and in January 1961, was secretly handed over, along with two of his political allies, to Moise Tshombe. Lumumba and his companions were never again seen alive. His death was officially announced by the Katangans on February 13, 1961. It is widely believed that he was tortured to death by Belgian mercenaries employed by Tshombe.

Before he was handed over to Tshombe, Lumumba wrote this letter to his wife not knowing whether or not she would receive it.[31]

My dear wife,

I am writing these words not knowing whether they will reach you, when they will reach you, and whether I shall still be alive when you read them. All through my struggle for the independence of my country. I have never doubted for a single instant the final triumph of the sacred to which my companions and I have devoted all our lives. But what we wished for our country, its right to an honourable life, to unstained dignity, to independence without restrictions, was never desired by the Belgian imperialists and their Western allies, who found direct and indirect support, both deliberate and unintentional, amongst certain high officials of the United Nations, that organisation in which we placed all our trust when we called on its assistance.

They have corrupted some of our compatriots and bribed others. They have helped to distort the truth and bring our independence into dishonour. How could I speak otherwise? Dead or alive, free or in prison by order of the imperialists, it is not I myself who count. It is the Congo, it is our poor people for whom independence has been transformed into a cage from beyond whose confines the outside world looks on us, sometimes with kindly sympathy, but at other times with joy and pleasure. But my faith will remain unshakeable. I know and I feel in my heart that sooner or later my people will rid themselves of all their enemies, both internal and external, and that they will rise as one man to say No to the degradation and shame of colonialism, and regain their dignity in the clear light of the sun.

We are not alone. Africa, Asia and the free liberated people from all corners of the world will always be found at the side of the millions of Congolese who will not abandon the struggle until the day when there are no longer any colonialists and their mercenaries in our country. As to my children, whom I leave and whom I may never see again, I should like them to be told that it is for them, as is it for every Congolese, to accomplish the sacred task of reconstructing our independence and our sovereignty: for without dignity there is no liberty, without justice there is no dignity, and without independence there are no free men.

Neither brutality, nor cruelty nor torture will ever bring me to ask for mercy, for I pre-

---

31. Patrice Lumumba, with a foreword and notes by Colin Legum, translated by Graham Heath, *Congo My Country* (London: Pall Mall Press with Barrie and Rockliff, 1962; first published in French in 1961 as *Le Congo—Terre d'Avenir— Est-il Menacé?*), pp. xxiii–xxiv.

Patrice Lumumba in the hands of General Mobutu's men, 1960. © *Bettmann/CORBIS.*

fer to die with my head unbowed, my faith unshakeable and with profound trust in the destiny of my country, rather than live under subjection and disregarding sacred principles. History will one day have its say, but it will not be the history that is taught in Brussels, Paris, Washington or in the United Nations, but the history which will be taught in the countries freed from imperialism and its pup-

pets. Africa will write her own history, and to the north and south of the Sahara, it will be a glorious and dignified history.

Do not weep for me, my dear wife. I know that my country, which is suffering so much, will know how to defend its independence and its liberty. Long live the Congo! Long live Africa!

Patrice

PART 4
The Contradictions of Post-Colonial Independence

Introduction

In the second half of the twentieth century, Africa experienced violent and ongoing struggle throughout the continent—in the last European colonies (Angola, Mozambique, Guinea-Bissau), in the remnant settler regimes (South Africa, Southern Rhodesia), and in many of the newly independent states (Ghana, Nigeria, Zaire/Congo, Liberia, Rwanda, Sierra Leone, among others). By the end of the century, every country was finally politically independent, but most were deeply troubled economically with little apparent hope for improvement in the daily lives of most Africans.

At the outset of the independence period, African leaders had tried to assess the obstacles they would face in creating nations from colonies and to fashion goals and strategies that could help Africans realize the wealth and potential of their continent after centuries of exploitation. The problems were grave, for despite colonial administrative policies that used some traditional authorities to implement colonial rule, few of the newly independent states inherited national networks of administration, communication, or transportation. The senior officials responsible for running these countries, Europeans, were withdrawn at independence. Trade with the former colonial powers continued, however, in most cases still under the control of privately owned European companies. And even when the local companies were nationalized in states that adopted socialism, the cash crops to which people had been required to devote their land and labor still had to be sold in a world market where prices fluctuated greatly. African leaders inherited the remnants of a colonial system of administration, geared to rule from the top down without regard for the needs or opinions of the ruled. Moreover, fragile export economies—cocoa in Ghana, coffee in Rwanda (accounting for 75 percent of the country's foreign earnings), and even gold in South Africa—made political stability difficult to achieve. A fall in world prices could easily precipitate violence, as the collapse in cocoa prices did in the mid-1960s for Ghana, the decline in the price of gold did in the 1980s for South Africa, or the fall in coffee prices did in the late 1980s for Rwanda.

As Frantz Fanon observed even before the advent of independence, the colonial system created serious economic, political, and social problems that continued well into the independence period; was independent Africa to be a place where freedom reigned or a place of continued dependence on the West (document 1)? Kwame Nkrumah believed that only the unification of all countries on the African continent into a federally unified state would enable Africans to channel the continent's enormous economic resources into rebuilding societies for the benefit of their members rather than the profit of multinational corporations (document 2). Julius Nyerere argued that Africans should aim for self-sufficiency by developing indigenous models of socialism and creating their own forms of democracy different from those of the West (document 3). Yet, in the post-colonial situation, or under "neo-colonialism" as Fanon and others called the psychological and political twilight zone between oppression and freedom, only the middle classes or petty bourgeoisie would likely reap the benefits of independence, as they had under colonialism, trained to serve an exploitative system. Indeed, Amílcar Cabral argued that the petty bourgeoisie would necessarily have to commit class "suicide" to break the bonds of colonialism before Africans could really free themselves politically (document 7).

But in the early 1960s not all were yet free. The Portuguese remained firmly entrenched in their colonial possessions, arguing that they were better able to bring about reform than their African subjects (document 5). White settlers in South Africa and Southern Rhodesia likewise claimed that continued policies of racial separation and white supremacy were necessary for the upliftment of Africans and for the defense of democracy in Africa against the predatory aims of the Soviet Union. Such hypocrisy was rejected by people like Cabral, Eduardo Mondlane, and Nelson Mandela, who, in light of the fact that Africans were not permitted any political rights (certainly not the right to vote) within the states that remained under European rule, nor could they protest peacefully without risk of arrest and banning, adopted policies of armed struggle (documents 4, 6, 7).

By the end of the first decade of Africa's independence, many of the expectations of a post-colonial era of freedom had died. Armed struggle began in the Portuguese colonies, in South Africa, and in Southern Rhodesia, and continued through the 1970s. For Southern Rhodesia/Zimbabwe it ended in 1980 with the negotiated victory of Robert Mugabe's revolutionary forces. For South Africa, it continued until the release of Nelson Mandela and the unbanning of the African National Congress (ANC) in 1990. For Angola and Mozambique, war brought about the fall of the Portuguese dictatorship in 1974, but internecine struggles have continued to ravage their countrysides, especially that of Angola where after nearly 40 years of fighting, peace seems almost unimaginable. The states that had become independent around 1960 entered a destructive cycle of civil wars and armed conflict that continues in many cases unabated into the twenty-first century. Ghana, one of the richest former colonies, saw the military overthrow of the charismatic Nkrumah while Nigeria, the most populous former colony, fell apart in coups and civil war and was brought together only at the expense of democracy. Deploring the premature death of such high hopes, African writers watched and recorded as the tragedies unfolded. Chinua Achebe, Africa's foremost novelist, chronicled the unraveling of Nigeria in a brilliant series of novels, detailing the transformation of colonial bureaucrats into successful power brokers, confirming Cabral's worst fears about the petty bourgeoisie at independence (documents 8, 9). Throughout Africa, ordinary people suffered under autocratic rule, in Ethiopia and Malawi as well as Angola and South Africa (documents 11, 13).

Outside intervention added to political instability. This intervention was a problem especially in southern Africa where to uphold white supremacy the apartheid government sent invasion forces and bomb and assassination squads (all the while denying that it was doing so) into Mozambique, Angola, Zimbabwe, and Zambia, while continuing militarily to occupy Namibia (where Hendrik Witbooi had fought against the Germans) in defiance of the United Nations which, under international law, had final authority for administering the former German colony. (See Part 2, document 29[B].) The French seldom hesitated to interfere in the politics of their former colonies, sending expeditionary forces to help those they deemed the "legitimate" authorities— usually former colonial collaborators—who so long as they favored French strategic and economic interests could reign as despots with metropolitan approval. More often the outside interference was less obvious, and all the more pernicious for being so disguised, in the form of underhand business relations between European and South African business investors, and dictators such as Mobutu Sese Seko of Zaire.

But despite all these impediments to freedom and democracy, people continued to struggle for liberation and against white rule and the legacy of colonialism. The leaders of the "black consciousness" movement in South Africa, particularly Steve Biko, argued that Africans first had to break the psychological bonds of colonialism to free themselves completely (document 10). Though Biko was later beaten to death in police custody, his message was taken up by thousands of young people who rose in protest against apartheid in Soweto in 1976 and, despite suffering torture and often death, continued to resist with support from throughout the black community of South Africa (documents 14, 15, 16). In Malawi, the poet Jack Mapanje took up the fire lit by John Chilembwe (see Part 3, document 2) and fought against the dictatorship of Hastings Banda and, though subjected to lengthy imprisonment, found the answer scratched in the walls of Mikuyu prison: resistance would never cease so long as people lived (document 21).

But the end of the twentieth century and the beginning of the twenty-first is still marked by too many reminders of the harsh legacy of colonialism. In Rwanda, for example, where in the course of a few months in 1994 a million people were killed by their immediate neighbors, a genocide took place that had ethnic dimensions but which arose, more than from any other causes, as a result of the divide and rule policies favored by the Belgians during the colonial era, French interference in the post-colonial period, and the dependence of the country's economy on a single export crop for its stability (or lack thereof). In Sierra Leone in 2000, where civil war has all but destroyed the country, "rebels" fight the government for control of the diamond industry, and child soldiers, their parents killed by the rebels in order to acquire and train a force of barely teenage soldiers, cut off the hands of people to intimidate them and prevent them from supporting the duly elected government. Such dismemberment for a supposedly precious stone is reminiscent of the atrocity photographs collected by Roger Casement to illustrate how King Leopold of Belgium made Africans collect rubber faster (see Part 3, document 3), and reminds us of how the scramble for Africa really took on steam only after the first discovery of diamonds in South Africa 130 years ago. In 2000 also, riots have been reported in northern Nigeria, with northern Muslims blamed for the killing of several hundred southern Christians, reminding us again of the problems of building a nation state from communities that did not necessarily have anything in common—politically, economically, and so-cially—at the time of conquest.

A new generation of leaders has emerged in Africa, many raised under independence without the experience of colonialism and others re-emergent after years of exile or imprisonment. Younger leaders such as Jerry Rawlings in Ghana and Yoweri Museveni in Uganda place much of the blame for Africa's problems on the shoulders of their African predecessors, accusing them of corruption and pointing out the need for bigger and better systems of rule throughout Africa (documents 17, 18). Yet there is often little new in their pronouncements despite their assertions to the contrary. While rejecting the generation of the 1960s, these new leaders often echo the analyses of Cabral and Nkrumah, with the difference that they now blame Africans rather than Europeans for creating Africa's problems, and see in the "free market" a bet-ter solution for economic development than the socialism so favored by their predecessors. Older leaders, nearly returned from the dead such as Nelson Mandela, becoming the first president of post-apartheid South Africa after spending 27 years in prison, or Olesegun Obasanjo, elected president of Ni-geria in 1999 after almost four decades of military rule (a short period of which Obasanjo himself administered in the 1970s), strike a different chord. They strive to remind Africans, all Africans, that theirs is a continent and a culture worth saving, building, and sharing. Still seeking uniquely African solutions, these elder statesmen ask Africans to look within their own societ-ies for answers, not blame, and for the strength to rebuild African communi-ties not only to imitate the past but also to move into a future of progress (documents 19, 23).

~ ~ ~

1. Frantz Fanon discusses the limits of African independence.

As independence approached for most African countries, an important ques-tion was what relationship these sovereign nations should have with their former colonizers. Was it wise to sever all ties, or even possible to do so? Was it pos-sible to develop a new cooperative relationship given the economic exploitation common to colonialism? Did continued contact and economic interaction threaten the viability of the new states? As the expansion and intensification of the Cold War threatened to draw Africa into the calculations of global strate-gists, African politicians had to face these crucial issues immediately upon independence. The former colonizers, such as England, France, Belgium, and Portugal, wanted to foster close economic association and to keep their former colonial possessions within their sphere of influence. However, this form of continued colonialism, known as "neo-colonialism" in Africa, did not provide much advantage for the inhabitants of the newly independent states. Only poli-ticians and the small middle class were able to secure much (and often consid-erable) profit from continued dependence on the West. Thus, within each country conflicting interests battled for control of these new states and their attendant resources, too often leading to military coups, popular resistance, and civil war; conflicts that continue to the present day.

Frantz Fanon (1925–1961) was Africa's most prominent theoretician of revolution/independence and its attendant difficulties. Born in Martinique (Caribbean), he studied medicine in France, specializing in psychiatry. He accepted a post as psychiatric physician at a hospital just outside Algiers, Algeria, in a country just commencing a mass-based anti-colonial war. In this position, Fanon observed the psychological effects of colonialism and revolution. In this selection from his numerous works, Fanon deals with the questions mentioned above concerning African independence and the relationship between former colonizer and former colonized. He examines the demands made by Western countries on Africa, and the compromises that will inevitably have to be made by the leaders of the new states. Such compromises, he notes, would lead to further friction within those societies that had just—as in Nkrumah's words—celebrated their entry into a new era of "freedom."[1]

First truths on the colonial problem.

The twentieth century, when the future looks back on it, will not only be remembered as the era of atomic discoveries and interplanetary explorations. The second upheaval of this period, unquestionably, is the conquest by the peoples of the lands that belong to them.

Jostled by the claims for national independence by immense regions, the colonialists have had to loosen their stranglehold. Nevertheless, this phenomenon of liberation, of triumph of national independence, of retreat of colonialism, does not manifest itself in a unique manner. Every former colony has a particular way of achieving independence. Every new sovereign state finds itself practically under the obligation of maintaining definite and deferential relations with the former oppressor.

The parties that lead the struggle against colonialist oppression, at a certain phase of the combat, decide for practical reasons to accept a fragment of independence with the firm intention of arousing the people again within the framework of the fundamental strategy of the total evacuation of the territory and of the effective seizure of all national resources. This style, which has taken form on a succession of occasions, is today well known. On the other hand, there is a whole opposite dialectic which, it seems, has not received sufficient attention.

A first condition: "The rights" of the former occupant.

Some decades ago, the colonialist rulers could indefinitely propound the highly civilizing intentions of their countries. The concessions, the expropriations, the exploitation of the workers, the great wretchedness of the peoples, were traditionally conjured away and denied. Afterwards, when the time came to withdraw from the territory, the colonialists were forced to discard their masks. In the negotiations on independence, the first matters at issue were the economic interests: banks, monetary areas, research permits, commercial concessions, inviolability of properties stolen from the peasants at the time of the conquest, etc. . . . Of civilizing, religious, or cultural works, there was no longer any question. The time had come for serious things, and trivialities had to be left behind. Such attitudes were to open the eyes of men struggling in other regions of the world.

The actual rights of the occupant were then perfectly identified. The minority that

---

1. Frantz Fanon, *Toward the African Revolution*, trans. Haakon Chevalier (New York: Grove Press, 1964), pp. 121–26. © 1964 by Monthly Review Press. Reprinted with the permission of the Monthly Review Press.

came from the mother country, the university missions, technical assistance, the friendship affirmed and reaffirmed, were all relegated to a secondary level. The important thing was obviously the real rights that the occupant meant to wrench from the people, as the price for a piece of independence.

The acceptance of a nominal sovereignty and the absolute refusal of real independence—such is the typical reaction of colonialist nations with respect to their former colonies. Neo-colonialism is impregnated with a few ideas which both constitute its force and at the same time prepare its necessary decline.

In the course of the struggle for liberation, things are not clear in the consciousness of the fighting people. Since it is a refusal, at one and the same time, of political non-existence, of wretchedness, of illiteracy, of the inferiority complex so subtly instilled by oppression, its battle is for a long time undifferentiated. Neo-colonialism takes advantage of this indetermination. Armed with a revolutionary and spectacular good will, it grants the former colony everything. But in so doing, it wrings from it an economic dependence which becomes an aid and assistance program.

We have seen that this operation usually triumphs. The novelty of this phase is that it is necessarily brief. This is because it takes the people little time to realize that nothing fundamental has changed. Once the hours of effusion and enthusiasm before the spectacle of the national flag floating in the wind are past, the people rediscover the first dimension of its requirement: bread, clothing, shelter.

Neo-colonialism, because it proposes to do justice to human dignity in general, addresses itself essentially to the middle class and to the intellectuals of the colonial country.

Today, the people no longer feel their bellies at peace when the colonial country has recognized the value of its elites. The people want things really to change and right away.

Thus it is that the struggle resumes with renewed violence.

In this second phase, the occupant bristles and unleashes all his forces. What was wrested by bombardments is reconverted into results of free negotiations. The former occupant intervenes, in the name of duty, and once again establishes his war in an independent country.

All the former colonies, from Indonesia to Egypt, without forgetting Panama, which have tried to denounce the agreements wrung from them by force, have found themselves obliged to undergo a new war and sometimes to see their sovereignty again violated and amputated.

The notorious "rights" of the occupant, the false appeal to a common past, the persistence of a rejuvenated colonial pact, are the permanent bases of an attack directed against national sovereignty.

A second obstacle: The zones of influence.

The concern to maintain the former colony in the yoke of economic oppression is obviously not sadism. It is not out of wickedness or ill-will that such an attitude is adopted. It is because the handling of their national riches by the colonized peoples compromises the economic equilibrium of the former occupant. The reconversion of the colonial economy, the industries engaged in processing raw materials from the underdeveloped territories, the disappearance of the colonial pact, competition with foreign capital, constitute a mortal danger for imperialism.

For countries like Great Britain and France there arises the important question of zones of influence. Unanimous in their decision to stifle the national aspirations of the colonial peoples, these countries wage a titanic struggle for the seizure of world markets. The economic battles between France, England, and the United States, in the Middle East, in the Far East, and now in Africa, give the measure of imperialist voracity and bestiality. And it is not an exaggeration to say that these battles are the direct cause of the strategies which, still today, shake the newly independent states. In exceptional circumstances, the zones of influence of the pound sterling, of the dollar, and of the franc, are converted and become, by a conjurer's trick, the Western world. Today in Lebanon and in Iraq, if we are to believe Mr. [Andre] Malraux, it is *homo occidentalis* who is threatened.

The oil of Iraq has removed all prohibitions and made concrete the true problems. We have only to remember the violent interventions in the West Indian archipelago or in Latin America every time the dictatorships supported by American policy were in danger. The Marines who today are being landed in Beirut are the brothers of those who, periodically, are sent to reestablish "order" in Haiti, in Costa Rica, in Panama. The United States considers that the two Americas constitute a world governed by the Monroe Doctrine whose application is entrusted to the American forces. The single article of this doctrine stipulates that America belongs to the Americans, in other words, to the State Department.

Its outlets having proved insufficient, it was inevitable that America would turn to other regions, namely the Far East, the Middle East, and Africa. There ensued a competition between beasts of prey; its creations are: the Eisenhower doctrine against England in the Middle East; support for Ngo Dinh Diem against France in Indochina; Economic Aid Commission in Africa announced by the presidential voyage of Mr. [Richard] Nixon, against France, England, and Belgium.

Every struggle for national liberation must take zones of influence into account.

The cold war.

This competitive strategy of Western nations, moreover, enters into the vaster framework of the policy of the two blocs, which for ten years has held a definite menace of atomic disintegration suspended over the world. And it is surely not purely by chance that the hand or the eye of Moscow is discovered, in an almost stereotyped way, behind each demand for national independence, put forth by a colonial people. This is because any difficulty that is put in the way of the supremacy of the

West in any given section of the world is a concrete threat to its economic power, to the range of its military strategic bases, and represents a limiting of its potential.

Every challenge to the rights of the West over a colonial country is experienced both as a weakening of the Western world and as a strengthening of the Communist world.

Today an island like Cyprus, which has almost no resources of its own and which has a population of barely half a million people, is the object of violent rivalries. And even NATO, an organization designed to parry a Soviet invasion, is being endangered by the problem to which the isle of Cyprus gives rise.

The third bloc.

The position taken by a few newly independent countries, which are determined to remain outside the policy of the coalitions, has introduced a new dimension into the balance of forces in the world. Adopting the so-called policy of positive neutralism, of non-dependence, of non-commitment, of the third force, the underdeveloped countries that are awakening from a long slumber of slavery and of oppression, have considered it their duty to remain outside of any warlike involvement, in order to devote themselves to the urgent economic tasks, to staving off hunger, to the improvement of man's lot.

And what the West has in truth not understood is that today a new humanism, a new theory of man is coming into being, which has its root in man. It is easy to regard President [Jawaharlal] Nehru as indecisive because he refuses to harness himself to Western imperialism, and Presidents [Gamal Abdel] Nasser or Sukarno as violent when they nationalize their companies or demand the fragments of their territories that are still under foreign domination. What no one sees is that the 350 million Hindus, who have known the hunger of British imperialism, are now demanding bread, peace, and well-being. The fact is that the Egyptian *fellahs* and the Indonesian boys, whom Western writers like to feature in their exotic novels, insist on taking their own destiny into their hands and refuse to play the role of an inert panorama that had been reserved for them.

The prestige of the West.

And we here touch upon a psychological problem which is perhaps not fundamental but which enters into the framework of the dialectics that is now developing. The West, whose economic system is the standard (and by virtue of that fact oppressive), also prides itself on its humanist supremacy. The Western "model" is being attacked in its essence and in its finality. The Orientals, the Arabs, and the Negroes, today, want to present their plans, want to affirm their values, want to define their relations with the world. The negation of political *beni-oui-ouism* [yes-man-ism] is linked to the refusal of economic *beni-oui-ouism* and of cultural *beni-oui-ouism*. It is no longer true that the promotion of values passes through the screen of the West. It is not true that we must constantly trail behind, follow, depend on someone or other. All the colonial countries that are waging the struggle today must know that

the political independence that they will wring from the enemy in exchange for the maintenance of an economic dependency is only a snare and a delusion, that the second phase of total liberation is necessary because required by the popular masses, that this second phase, because it is a capital one, is bound to be hard and waged with iron determination, that, finally, at that stage, it will be necessary to take the world strategy of coalition into account, for the West simultaneously faces a double problem: the communist danger and the coming into being of a third neutral coalition, represented essentially by the underdeveloped countries.

The future of every man today has a relation of close dependency on the rest of the universe. That is why the colonial peoples must redouble their vigilance and their vigor. A new humanism can be achieved only at this price. The wolves must no longer find isolated lambs to prey upon. Imperialism must be blocked in all its attempts to strengthen itself. The peoples demand this; the historic process requires it.

2. Nkrumah on pan-Africanism as an answer to neo-colonialism.

In 1957, Kwame Nkrumah became the first African politician to lead his country (Ghana) to independence and freedom from colonialism. But four years later, as he argued in his 1961 book, I Speak of Freedom: A Statement of African Ideology, *independence did not come unencumbered by continuing links to the West. Though Africa as a continent was rich in minerals and agricultural products, most of its people lived in poverty, producing goods for sale to the West at prices usually too low to sustain local development. Though the United States provided in many ways a model of democracy, Cold War politics meant that it, like the former colonial powers, intervened in African politics (though through its aid policies rather than the military means still adopted on occasion by the French). Nkrumah believed that the solution to these economic and political problems lay in African unity, in a practical realization of the pan-African ideals to which he had always held. Such ideals engendered considerable opposition within Ghana and from the outside world. He survived several assassination attempts and was routinely condemned by the West, especially the United States, for appearing too be to close to the camp of the Soviet Union. Becoming increasingly withdrawn while pursuing a cult of the personality in which his image appeared in public places throughout Ghana, he was over-thrown in February 1966 by a coup led by members of the armed forces. The document below reprints in full Nkrumah's preface to* I Speak of Freedom.[2]

The movement for independence in Africa which gained momentum after the Second World War has spread like a prairie fire throughout the length and breadth of Africa. The clear, ringing call for freedom which the eight independent states of Africa sounded in Accra in April 1958, followed by the All-African People's Conference in December of that year, stirred up the demand for independence from Conakry to Mogadishu, from Fort Lamy to Leopoldville. The "wind of change" has become a raging hurricane, sweeping away the old colonialist Africa. The year 1960 was Africa's year. In that year alone, seventeen African States emerged as proud and independent sovereign nations. Now the ultimate freedom of the whole of Africa can no more be in doubt.

For centuries, Europeans dominated the African continent. The white man arrogated to himself the right to rule and to be obeyed by the non-white; his mission, he claimed, was to "civilise" Africa. Under this cloak, the Europeans robbed the continent of vast riches and inflicted unimaginable suffering on the African people.

All this makes a sad story, but now we must be prepared to bury the past with its unpleasant memories and look to the future. All we ask of the former colonial powers is their goodwill and co-operation to remedy past mistakes and injustices and to grant independence to the colonies in Africa.

The new African nations from the very nature of things cannot but be economically weak at the early stages of nationhood as compared with the older and long established nations of the world. The long dependence on European and American financial and technical expertise has prevented the growth of local capital and the requisite technical knowledge to develop their resources. They need economic help, but in seeking outside aid they lay themselves open to a grave new danger which not merely threatens but could even destroy their hard-won freedom.

It is unreasonable to suppose that any foreign power, affluent enough to give aid to an African state, would not expect some measure of consideration or favour from the state receiving the aid. History has shown how one colonial empire in liquidation can easily be replaced by another, more insidious, because it is a disguised form of colonialism. The fate of those territories in Europe and North Africa which once formed the Turkish Empire is a warning to Africa today. It would be a tragedy if the initial weakness of the emergent African nations should lead to a new foreign domination of Africa brought about by economic forces.

It may be argued that the existence of the United Nations Organisation offers a guarantee for the independence and the territorial integrity of all states, whether big or small. In actual fact, however, the UN is just as reliable an instrument for world order and peace as the Great Powers are prepared to allow it to be. The present division of the world into rival blocs, and the dictates of power politics, offer little hope that this international body will ever become an effective instrument for world peace. Recent events in the Congo have not helped to foster confidence in the UN in the face of Great Power interests. Patrice Lumumba, democratically elected Prime Minister of the Congo Republic, who himself invited the UN to the Congo, was murdered along with two of his Ministers because the UN failed in its mission to maintain law and order.

It is clear that we must find an African solution to our problems, and that this can only be found in African unity. Divided we

---

2. Kwame Nkrumah, *I Speak of Freedom: A Statement of African Ideology* (New York: Frederick A. Praeger, 1961), pp. ix–xii. Reprinted with the permission of Heinemann Educational Publishers, a division of Reed Educational & Professional Publishing Ltd.

are weak; united, Africa could become one of the greatest forces for good in the world. Although most Africans are poor, our continent is potentially extremely rich. Our mineral resources, which are being exploited with foreign capital only to enrich foreign investors, range from gold and diamonds to uranium and petroleum. Our forests contain some of the finest woods to be grown anywhere. Our cash crops include cocoa, coffee, rubber, tobacco and cotton. As for power, which is an important factor in any economic development, Africa contains over 40% of the total potential water power of the world, as compared with about 10% in Europe and 13% in North America. Yet so far, less than 1% has been developed. This is one of the reasons why we have in Africa the paradox of poverty in the midst of plenty, and scarcity in the midst of abundance.

Never before have a people had within their grasp so great an opportunity for developing a continent endowed with so much wealth. Individually, the independent states of Africa, some of them potentially rich, others poor, can do little for their people. Together, by mutual help, they can achieve much. But the economic development of the continent must be planned and pursued as a whole. A loose confederation designed only for economic co-operation would not provide the necessary unity of purpose. Only a strong political union can bring about full and effective development of our natural resources for the benefit of our people.

The political situation in Africa today is heartening and at the same time disturbing. It is heartening to see so many new flags hoisted in place of the old; it is disturbing to see so many countries of varying sizes and at different levels of development, weak and, in some cases, almost helpless. If this terrible state of fragmentation is allowed to continue it may well be disastrous for us all.

There are at present some 28 states in Africa, excluding the Union of South Africa, and those countries not yet free. No less than nine of these states have a population of less than three million. Can we seriously believe that the colonial powers meant these coun-

tries to be independent, viable states? The example of South America, which has as much wealth, if not more than North America, and yet remains weak and dependent on outside interests, is one which every African would do well to study.

Critics of African unity often refer to the wide differences in culture, language and ideas in various parts of Africa. This is true, but the essential fact remains that we are all Africans, and have a common interest in the independence of Africa. The difficulties presented by questions of language, culture and different political systems are not insuperable. If the need for political union is agreed by us all, then the will to create it is born; and where there's a will there's a way.

The present leaders of Africa have already shown a remarkable willingness to consult and seek advice among themselves. Africans have, indeed, begun to think continentally. They realise that they have much in common, both in their past history, in their present problems and in their future hopes. To suggest that the time is not yet ripe for considering a political union of Africa is to evade the facts and ignore realities in Africa today. The greatest contribution that Africa can make to the peace of the world is to avoid all the dangers inherent in disunity, by creating a political union which will also by its success, stand as an example to a divided world. A union of African states will project more effectively the African personality. It will command respect from a world that has regard only for size and influence. The scant attention paid to African opposition to the French atomic tests in the Sahara, and the ignominious spectacle of the UN in the Congo quibbling about constitutional niceties while the Republic was tottering into anarchy, are evidence of the callous disregard of African Independence by the Great Powers.

We have to prove that greatness is not to be measured in stock piles of atom bombs. I believe strongly and sincerely that with the deep-rooted wisdom and dignity, the innate respect for human lives, the intense humanity that is our heritage, the African race, united under one federal government, will emerge not as just another world bloc to flaunt its wealth and strength, but as a Great Power whose greatness is indestructible because it is built not on fear, envy and suspicion, nor won at the expense of others, but founded on hope, trust, friendship and directed to the good of all mankind.

The emergence of such a mighty stabilising force in this strife-worn world should be regarded not as the shadowy dream of a visionary, but as a practical proposition, which the peoples of Africa can, and should,

translate into reality. There is a tide in the affairs of every people when the moment strikes for political action. Such was the moment in the history of the United States of America when the Founding Fathers saw beyond the petty wranglings of the separate states and created a Union. This is our chance. We must act now. Tomorrow may be too late and the opportunity will have passed, and with it the hope of free Africa's survival.

3. Julius Nyerere argues for African democracy, self-reliance, and socialism.

While Kwame Nkrumah was the most prominent spokesman for pan-Africanism in the early 1960s, Julius Nyerere(1922–1999), who in 1961 became the first prime minister of Tanganyika (and in 1964, the first president of Tanzania when Tanganyika joined with Zanzibar to form a republic), articulated a vision of a socialist Africa, one that did not follow foreign models but was distinctly indigenous, in which all commercial enterprises would be nationalized and active steps taken by the state to reduce inequalities of income between the poor and the rest of society. Tanzania, he argued, could be self-reliant economically, should develop a special form of African socialism rather than borrow foreign models, and was inherently democratic. In the selections below, Nyerere, known among Tanzanians as "Mwalimu" or teacher, argues that African democracy could flourish without an "official opposition" (as the West constantly demanded in its evaluation of whether or not democracy had been achieved in Africa). Africa, he contended, did not have to follow Western models because Africans were, within their small-scale village communities, traditionally, indeed naturally, democratic. The second selection recounts Nyerere's own discussion of the significance of his Arusha Declaration of February 5, 1967. The declaration was regarded by many at the time as a blueprint for the development of African independence under socialism. At a teach-in held at Dar es Salaam University College in August 1967, after explaining that Arusha was "a declaration of intent, no more than that," Nyerere goes on to describe in plain language how he felt the intentions of the declaration could be achieved.[3]

(A). The African and democracy.

By the end of this present decade the whole of the African continent will have freed itself from colonial rule. The African nationalist

claims that the end of colonialism will mean the establishment of democracy. His present rulers, who have themselves shown little respect for democracy, are equally convinced that the African is incapable of maintaining a

---

3. (A), Julius Nyerere, "The African and Democracy," in *Africa Speaks*, eds. James Duffy and Robert A. Manners (Princeton: D. van Nostrand and Company, 1961), pp. 28–34; (B), Mwalimu Julius K. Nyerere, *The Arusha Declaration Teach-in* (Dar es Salaam: Information Services; [1967]), pp. 4–11.

democratic form of government. They prophesy that the end of colonialism will lead to the establishment of dictatorships all over the African continent. This debate over the ability or inability of the African to be a democrat rages whenever the words "Africa" and "Democracy" are mentioned together.

I have chosen to join the debate, in this article, not because I want to take sides but because I believe the debaters have not bothered to define their terms. If they had done so, and particularly if they had cared to analyse the term "democracy," they would probably have discovered that their conceptions of democracy were totally different; that they were, in fact, wasting their time by arguing at cross purposes.

I think one of the first things one should beware of, in thinking of "democracy," is the tendency to confuse one's own personal picture of it—a picture which, if examined, will usually be found to include the "machinery" and symbols of democracy peculiar to the society with which one happens to be familiar—with democracy itself.

More than one attempt has been made to define democracy; probably the best, and certainly the most widely quoted, is that of Abraham Lincoln: "Government of the People, by the People, for the People." But I think the easiest way to eliminate the inessentials is to start by ignoring all such definitions and simply remember that the word means no more than "Government by the People." Now, if the ruling of a country is to be in the hands of the people of the country, the people must have some means of making their voice heard. It is obvious that not all of them can take a personal part in the actual legislation and policy-making, so it is necessary for them to choose from among themselves a certain number of individuals who will "represent" them, and who will act as their spokesmen within the government. This may seem so elementary as to need no such elaborate explanation as I have given it here; but is it? If it is, why do so many people claim that "Africans cannot maintain democratic government in their own countries once they become independent"? And why do they always explain their doubts by saying that "Of course no African government will tolerate an Opposition"?

I do not think anybody, at this stage of our history, can possibly have any valid reason for claiming that the existence of an Opposition is impossible in an independent African state; but, even supposing this were true, where did the idea of an organization opposition as an essential part of democratic government come from? If one starts, as I have suggested, from the purely etymological definition of democracy it becomes clear that this idea of "for" and "against," this obsession with "Government" balanced by "Official Opposition," is in fact something which, though it *may* exist in a democracy, or *may not* exist in a democracy, is not essential to it, although it happens to have become so familiar to the Western world that its absence immediately raises the cry "Dictatorship."

To the Ancient Greeks, "democracy" meant simply government by discussion. The people discussed, and the result was a "people's government." But not all the people assembled for these discussions, as the textbooks tell us; those who took part in them were "equals" and this excluded the women and the slaves.

The two factors of democracy which I want to bring out here are "discussion" and "equality." Both are essential to it, and both contain a third element, "freedom." There can be no true discussion without freedom, and "equals" must be equal in freedom, without which there is no equality. A small village in which the villagers are equals who make their own laws and conduct their own affairs by free discussion is the nearest thing to pure democracy. That is why the small Greek state (if one excludes the women and slaves) is so often pointed out to us as "democracy par excellence."

These three, then, I consider to be essential to democratic government: discussion, equality, and freedom—the last being implied by the other two. Those who doubt the African's ability to establish a democratic society cannot seriously be doubting the African's ability to "discuss." That is the one thing which is as African as the tropical sun. Neither can they be doubting the African's sense of equality, for aristocracy is something foreign to Africa. Even where there is a fairly distinct African aristocracy-by-birth, it can be traced historically to sources outside this continent. Traditionally the African knows no "class." I doubt if there is a word in any African language which is equivalent to "class" or "caste"; not even in those few societies where foreign infiltration has left behind some form of aristocracy is there such a word in the local languages. These aristocrats-by-birth are usually referred to as "the great" or "the clever ones." In my own country, the only two tribes which have a distinct aristocracy are the Bahaya in Buboka, and the Baha in the Buha districts. In both areas the "aristocrats" are historically foreigners, and they belong to the same stock.

The traditional African society, whether it had a chief or not and many, like my own, did not, was a society of equals and it conducted its business through discussion. Recently I was reading a delightful little book on Nyasaland by Mr. Clutton-Brock; in one passage he describes the life of traditional Nyasa, and when he comes to the Elders he uses a very significant phrase: "They talk till they agree."

"They talk till they agree." That gives you the very essence of traditional African democracy. It is rather a clumsy way of conducting affairs, especially in a world as impatient for results as this of the twentieth century, but discussion is one essential factor of any democracy; and the African is expert at it.

If democracy, then, is a form of government freely established by the people themselves; and if its essentials are free discussion and equality, there is nothing in traditional African society which unfits the African for it. On the contrary, there is everything in his tradition which fits the African to be just what he claims he is, a natural democrat.

It was possible for the ancient Greeks to boast of "democracy" when more than half the population had no say at all in the conduct of the affairs of the State. It was possible for the framers of the Declaration of Independence to talk about "the inalienable rights of Man" although they believed in exceptions; it was possible for Abraham Lincoln to bequeath to us a perfect definition of democracy although he spoke in a slave-owning society; it was possible for my friends the British to brag about "democracy" and still build a great Empire for the glory of the Britons.

These people were not hypocrites. They believed in democracy. It was "government by discussion" which they advocated, and it was discussion by equals; but they lived in a world which excluded masses of human beings from its idea of "equality" and felt few scruples in doing so. Today, in the twentieth century, this is impossible. Today the Hungarys, the Little Rocks, the Tibets, the Nyasalands, and the Bantustans must be explained away somehow. They are embarrassing in this century of the Universal Declaration of Human Rights. Man, the ordinary man and woman in the street or in the "bush," has never had such a high regard for himself; and the demi-gods who try to treat him as their inferior are conscious of his power—this power frightens them, and they are forced to try to explain away their crimes. Today the "people," whose right it is to govern themselves, cannot exclude any sane, law-abiding adult person.

There is no continent which has taken up the fight for the dignity of the common man more vigorously than Africa. In other countries men may shout "One Man, One Vote" with their tongues in their cheeks; in Africa the nationalist leaders believe in it as a fundamental principle, and the masses they lead would accept nothing less. "Equal Pay for Equal Work" is a catch-phrase in many countries which practise nothing of the kind; in Africa the leaders believe sincerely in the basic justice of this, and again their followers expect nothing less. In many countries which claim to be democracies the leaders come from an aristocracy either of wealth or of birth; in Africa they are of the common people, for if ever there was a continent where no real aristocracy has been built, whether of birth or of wealth, that continent is Africa.

Tradition has failed to create it, and the spirit of the twentieth century will make it almost impossible for it to grow now. Indeed, it is one way of discovering the widely different conceptions we may have of "democracy" to listen to those people who would like to build a middle class in Africa "as a safeguard for Democracy"! To them, democracy is government by the middle class, albeit the masses may play their part in electing that government.

Add, then, to the African tradition her lack of an aristocracy and the presence of a moral concept of human dignity on which she is waging her struggle for independence, and place these in the setting of this century of the Declaration of Human Rights, and it becomes difficult to see how anybody can seriously doubt the African's fitness for democracy.

I referred earlier in this article to the "machinery" and the symbols of democratic government. Many of the critics of African democracy are to be found in countries like Britain or the United States of America. These critics, when they challenge our ability to maintain a democratic form of government, really have in mind not democracy but the particular form it has taken in their own countries, the two-party system, and the debate conducted between the Government party and the opposition party within the parliament buildings. In effect, they are saying: "Can you imagine an African Parliament with at least two political parties holding a free debate, one party being 'for' and one 'against' the motion?"

Ghana and Nigeria would be understandably annoyed with me if I were to answer such critics by saying that I *can* "imagine" such countries; for they exist, and they are not figments of my "imagination."

But let us suppose they did not exist. To the Anglo-Saxon in particular, or to countries with an Anglo-Saxon tradition, the two-party system has become the very essence of democracy. It is no use telling an Anglo-Saxon that when a village of a hundred people have sat and talked together until they agreed where a well should be dug they have practiced democracy. The Anglo-Saxon will want to know whether the talking was properly organized. He will want to know whether there was an organized group "for" the motion, and an equally well organized group "against" the motion. He will also want to know whether, in the next debate, the same group will be "for" and the same group "against" the next motion. In other words, he will want to know whether the opposition was organized and therefore *automatic*, or whether it was spontaneous and therefore *free*. Only if it was automatic will he concede that it was democracy!

In spite of its existence in Ghana and Nigeria, however, I must say that I also have my own doubts about the suitability for Africa of the Anglo-Saxon form of democracy. Let me explain:

In his own traditional society the African has always been a free individual, very much a member of his community, but seeing no conflict between his own interests and those of his community. This is because the structure of his society was, in fact, a direct extension of the family. First you had the small family unit; this merged into a larger "blood" family which, in its turn, merged into the tribe. The affairs of the community, as I have shown, were conducted by free and equal discussion, but nevertheless the African's mental conception of "government" was personal—not institutional. When the word government was mentioned, the African thought of the chief; he did not, as does the Briton, think of a grand building in which a debate was taking place.

In colonial Africa this "personal" conception of government was unchanged, except that the average person hearing government mentioned now thought of the District Commissioner, the Provincial Commissioner, or the Governor.

When, later, the idea of government as an institution began to take hold of some African "agitators" such as myself, who had been reading Abraham Lincoln and John Stuart Mill, and we began demanding institutional government for our own countries, it was the very people who had now come to symbolize "Government" in their persons who resisted our demands—the District

Commissioners, the Provincial Commissioners, and the Governors. Not until the eleventh hour did they give way; and free elections have taken place in most of our countries almost on the eve of independence.

The new nations of the African continent are emerging today as the result of their struggle for independence. This struggle for freedom from foreign domination is a patriotic one which necessarily leaves no room for difference. It unites all elements in the country so that, not only in Africa but in any other part of the world facing a similar challenge, these countries are led by a nationalist movement rather than by a political party or parties. The same nationalist movement, having united the people and led them to independence, must inevitably form the first government of the new state; it could hardly be expected that a united country should halt in mid-stream and voluntarily divide itself into opposing political groups just for the sake of conforming to what I have called the "Anglo-Saxon form of democracy" at the moment of independence. Indeed, why should it? Surely, if a government is freely elected by the people, there can be nothing undemocratic about it simply because nearly all the people rather than merely a section of them have chosen to vote it into power.

In these circumstances, it would be surprising if the pattern of democracy in Africa were to take—at any rate for the first few years—the shape familiar to Anglo-Saxon countries. It would be illogical to expect it to; but it is unjust to African democrats to assume, therefore, that their own pattern of democratic government is less dedicated to the preservation of the rights and freedom of the individual, an assumption too often made by the very people who have delayed the establishment of democratic institutions on this continent.

I have already suggested that the nearest thing to pure democracy would be a self-governing village in which all affairs were conducted by free discussion. But I have also said that the government of a nation must necessarily be government by "representation"; therefore there must be elections and discussion-houses or parliaments. As a matter of fact, in Africa the actual parliament buildings are necessary rather for reasons of prestige than for protection against the weather. (Our weather is quite predictable!)

The two essentials for "representative" democracy are the freedom of the individual, and the regular opportunity for him to join with his fellows in replacing, or reinstating, the government of his country by means of the ballot-box and without recourse to assassination. An organized opposition is *not* an essential element, although a society which has no room and no time for the harmless eccentric can hardly be called "democratic." Where you have those two essentials, and the affairs of the country are conducted by free discussion, you have democracy. An organized opposition may arise, or it may not; but whether it does or it does not depends entirely upon the choice of the people themselves and makes little difference to free discussion and equality in freedom.

(B). Mwalimu Julius K. Nyerere, "The Arusha Declaration Teach-in," August 5, 1967.

Meaning of self-reliance.

What, then, is the meaning of self-reliance, and what are its implications for our future policies? First and foremost, it means that for our development we have to depend upon ourselves and our own resources. These resources are land, and people. Certainly we have a few factories, we have a small diamond mine, and so on. But it is important to realise that when measured in 1960 prices out of a gross domestic product estimated at Shs. [Tazanian shillings] 4,646 million in 1966, some Shs. 2,669 million—that is, more than 57%—was the direct result of agricultural activities. Only Shs. 321 million was the combined result of mining and manufacturing; that is to say that all the mining and manufacturing of Tanzania produced last year less than 7% of the gross domestic product.

The only thing we certainly do not have is money searching for investment opportunities. The per capita income in terms of 1966 prices, was about Shs. 525/- last year. That does not allow very much to be withdrawn from current consumption and invested in development. Indeed, we did very well last year to find Shs. 135 million (that is, about Shs. 14/- per person) from internal resources for development.

But to provide one job in a highly mechanised industry can cost Shs. 40,000/- or more. To build the oil refinery cost more than Shs. 110 million. To build a modern steel mill would cost rather more than that.

Agriculture mainstay.

On the other hand, it is possible to double the output of cotton on a particular acre by spending Shs. 130/- on fertiliser and insecticide; it is possible to double a farmer's acreage under crops by the provision of ox-plough at a cost of Shs. 250/- or less, and so on. In other words, whereas it is possible to find the sort of investment capital which can bring great increases in agricultural output from our present resources, it is not possible for us to envisage establishing heavy industries, or even very much in the way of light industries, in the near future.

To be realistic, therefore, we must stop dreaming of developing Tanzania through the establishment of large, modern industries. For such things we have neither the money nor the skilled man-power required to make them efficient and economic. We would even be making a mistake if we think in terms of covering Tanzania with mechanised farms, using tractors and combine-harvesters.

Once again, we have neither the money, nor the skilled man-power, nor in this case the social organisation which could make such investment possible and economic. This is not to say that there will be no new modern industries and no mechanised farms. But they will be the exception, not the rule, and they will be entered upon to meet particular problems. They are not the answer to the basic development needs of Tanzania.

Future in agriculture.

This is what the Arusha Declaration makes clear in both economic and social terms. Our future lies in the development of our agriculture, and in the development of our rural areas. But because we are seeking to grow from our own roots and to preserve that which is valuable in our traditional past, we have also to stop thinking in terms of massive agricultural mechanisation and the proletarianisation of our rural population.

We have, instead, to think in terms of development through the improvement of the tools we now use, and through the growth of co-operative systems of production. Instead of aiming at large farms using tractors and other modern equipment and employing agricultural labourers, we should be aiming at having ox-ploughs all over the country.

The jembe will have to be eliminated by the ox-plough before the latter can be eliminated by the tractor. We cannot hope to eliminate the jembe by the tractor. Instead of thinking about providing each farmer with his own lorry, we should consider the usefulness of oxen-drawn carts, which could be made within the country and which are appropriate both to our roads and to the loads which each farmer is likely to have.

Instead of the aerial spreading of crops with insecticide, we should use hand-operated pumps, and so on. In other words, we have to think in terms of what is available, or can be made available, at comparatively small cost, and which can be operated by the people. By moving into the future along this path, we can avoid massive social disruption and human suffering.

Small industries.

At the same time we can develop small industries and service stations in the rural areas where the people live, and thus help to diversify the rural economy. By this method we can achieve a widespread increase in the general level of people's income, instead of concentrating any economic improvement in the hands of a few people.

Such capital as we do have will make the widest possible impact by being invested in fertilisers, in credit for better breeding stock, in improved instruments of production, and other similar things. These, although small in themselves, can bring a great proportionate increase in the farmers' income.

This does not mean that there will be no new investment in towns, or that there will be no new factories. When you have large numbers of people living together, certain public services are essential for public health and security reasons. It would be absurd to pretend that we can forget the towns, which are in any case often a service centre for the surrounding rural areas.

Factory sites.

Factories which serve the whole country also have to be sited in places which are convenient for transport and communications. For example, if we had put the Friendship Textile Mill in a rural area, we would have had to invest in special road building etc. for it to be of any use, and in any case the number of its workers would soon mean that a new town had grown up in that place.

But even when we are building factories which serve the whole nation, we have to consider whether it is necessary for us to use the most modern machinery which exists in the world. We have to consider whether some older equipment which demands more labour, but labour which is less highly skilled, is not better suited to our needs, as well as being more within our capacity to build.

There are, however, two respects in which our call for self-reliance has been widely misunderstood or deliberately misinterpreted. The doctrine of self-reliance does not imply isolationism, either politically or economically. It means that we shall depend on ourselves, not on others.

Trade with others.

But this is not the same thing as saying we shall not trade with other people or co-operate with them when it is to mutual benefit. Obviously we shall do so. We shall have to continue to sell enough of our goods abroad to pay for the things we have to acquire. Up to now Tanzania has always done this; indeed, we have had a surplus of our balance of payment for many years. But the things we sell are the products of our agriculture, and this is likely to continue to be the case despite the problem of commodity prices in the world.

The things we import will increasingly have to be the things which are essential for our development, and which we cannot produce ourselves. Up to now we have been importing many things which a little effort would enable us to provide for ourselves, such as food, as well as luxury items which simply arouse desires among our people which could never be satisfied for more than a tiny minority.

Self-reliance, in other words, is unlikely to reduce our participation in international trade, but it should over time change its character to some extent. We should be exporting commodities after at least some preliminary processing, and we should be importing the things which we cannot produce and which are necessary for the development and the welfare of our whole people.

Tanzania wants capital assistance.

The other thing which is necessary to understand about self-reliance is that Tanzania has not said it does not want international assistance in its development. We shall continue to seek capital from abroad for particular projects or as a contribution to general development. It is clear, for example, that if we are to achieve our ambition of getting a railway which links Tanzania and Zambia, we shall have to obtain most of the capital and the technical skill from overseas.

Overseas capital will also be welcome for any project where it can make our own efforts more effective—where it acts as a catalyst for Tanzanian activity. It is for this reason that the Government has made it clear that we shall welcome outside participation—whether private or Government—in establishment of many different kinds of factories, especially those which produce consumption goods or process our crops and raw materials.

Capital assistance for education of all kinds is another of the many fields in which outside assistance can be valuable, provided it is linked to our capacity to meet the recurrent costs. The important thing, however, is that we in Tanzania should not adopt an attitude that nothing can be done until someone else agrees to give us money.

There are many things we can do by ourselves, and we must plan to do them. There are other things which can become easier if we get assistance, but these we should reckon on doing the hard way, by ourselves, only being thankful if assistance is forthcoming.

Expatriates as well.

But it is not only capital which we must welcome from outside, it is also men. Few things make me more angry than a refusal to accept and to work with people from other countries whose participation can make all the difference between our plans succeeding or failing. It is not being self-reliant to refuse to carry out the directions of a foreign engineer, a foreign doctor, or a foreign manager; it is just being stupid. It is absolutely vital that Tanzanians should determine policy; but if the implementation of a particular policy requires someone with good educational qualifications or long experience, it is not very sensible to allow that policy to fail through pride.

We must look at this question of employing expatriates scientifically and without prejudice; we must assess the interests of our development as a whole, not the interests of a particular person who feels that he would like the high post concerned but is neither ready for it nor prepared to go on learning from someone else.

No false pride in this matter.

Let us take note of the fact that the developed countries have no false pride in this matter. Western Europe and North America recruit trained people from countries like India and Pakistan, and West European countries complain bitterly about what they call the "brain drain" caused by the richer United States offering high incomes to educated and skilled people.

It has been alleged that the United States has saved itself billions of dollars by attracting workers on whose education it has not spent one cent. Yet while wealthy and developed countries adopt this kind of attitude, we in Tanzania appear to rejoice when we lose a trained person to Europe or North America.

We rejoice on the grounds that it provides us with an opportunity for Africanisation, or for self-reliance! Anyone would think that we have a problem of unemployed experts. It is time that we outgrew this childishness; and we must do so quickly if we intend to tackle this problem of modern development really seriously.

Socialism.

What, then, of socialism—the other aspect of the Arusha Declaration? First, it is important to be clear that nationalisation of existing industries and commercial undertakings is only a very small part of the socialism which we have adopted. The important thing for us is the extent to which we succeed in preventing the exploitation of one man by another and in spreading the concept of working together co-operatively for the common good instead of competitively for individual private gain. And the truth is that our economy is now so under-developed that it is in growth that we shall succeed or fail in these things.

The nationalisation of the banks, of insurance, and of the few industries affected, was important; but much more important is whether we succeed in expanding our economy without expanding the opportunities and the incentives for human exploitation.

Once again this really means that socialism has to spread in the rural areas where our people live. In this we have an advantage over many other countries, just because of our lack of development. Up to now exploitation in agriculture is very limited; the greater part of our farming is still individual peasant farming, or family farming. But although this is not capitalist, neither is it very efficient or productive in comparison with what it could be.

Indeed, it is true that where people work together in groups—and that is mostly in those restricted sectors of capitalist farming—there is often a greater output per worker and per acre. Our objective must be to develop in such a manner as to ensure that the advantages of modern knowledge and modern methods are achieved, but without the spread of capitalism.

Human equality—the essence of socialism.

Socialism, however, is not simply a matter of methods of production. They are part of it but not all of it. The essence of socialism is the practical acceptance of human equality. That is to say, man's equal rights to a decent life before any individual has a surplus above his needs; his equal right to participate in Government; and his equal responsibility to work and contribute to the society to the limit of his ability.

In Tanzania this means that we must safeguard and strengthen our democratic procedures; we must get to the position where every citizen plays an active and direct role in the government of his local community, at the same time as he plays a full role in the government of his own country. It also means that we have to correct the glaring income differentials which we inherited from colonialism, and ensure that the international imbalance between the wages of factory and service workers on the one hand, and of agricultural workers on the other, is not reproduced within our own nation. We have, in other words, to ensure that every person gets a return commensurate with the contribution he makes to the society.

But at the same time we have to make dignified provision for those whose age or disability prevents them from playing a full role in the economy. We have also to spread—although it can only be done gradually—equality of opportunity for all citizens, until every person is able to make the kind of contribution to our needs which is most within his capacity and his desires. But, most of all, we have to reactivate the philosophy of cooperation in production and sharing in distribution which was an essential part of traditional African society.

4. The African National Congress (ANC) adopts a policy of violence.

After the Sharpeville massacre of March 31, 1960, when members of the South African police shot dead (mostly in the back) 69 Pan Africanist Congress (PAC) members demonstrating peacefully against the pass laws, Hendrik Verwoerd's government declared both the PAC and the ANC illegal organizations and sentenced their leaders to terms of imprisonment. (Robert Sobukwe of the PAC got three years' hard labor, later extended administratively to another nine years; Albert Luthuli, president of the ANC, went to prison for a year and was banned from speaking in public until his death.) Nelson Mandela went underground and formed a new militant wing of the ANC, Umkonto We Sizwe (Spear of the Nation). Having fought against segregation and apartheid by nonviolent means ever since its formation in 1912, the ANC considered that it had been forced into a corner. It adopted a policy of armed struggle and pursued this policy through the 1960s, 1970s, and 1980s. In a pamphlet issued on December 16, 1961 (the same day Verwoerd had chosen three years earlier to make his speech in defense of white supremacy—Part 3, document 30), Umkonto We Sizwe announced that it was beginning a campaign of sabotage directed at strategically significant targets (police stations, prisons, railways, power transmission lines, etc.).[4]

4. ANC Web site, <www.anc.org.za/ancdocs/history/manifesto-mk.html>. Accessed June 1, 2000.

Flyer issued under the command of Umkonto we Sizwe, December 16, 1961.

Units of Umkonto We Sizwe today carried out planned attacks against Government installations, particularly those connected with the policy of apartheid and race discrimination.

Umkonto We Sizwe is a new, independent body, formed by Africans. It includes in its ranks South Africans of all races. It is not connected in any way with a so-called "Committee for National Liberation" whose existence has been announced in the press. Umkonto We Sizwe will carry on the struggle for freedom and democracy by new methods, which are necessary to complement the actions of the established national liberation organizations. Umkonto We Sizwe fully supports the national liberation movement, and our members, jointly and individually, place themselves under the overall political guidance of that movement.

It is, however, well known that the main national liberation organizations in this country have consistently followed a policy of non-violence. They have conducted themselves peaceably at all times, regardless of Government attacks and persecutions upon them, and despite all Government-inspired attempts to provoke them to violence. They have done so because the people prefer peaceful methods of change to achieve their aspirations without the suffering and bitterness of civil war. But the people's patience is not endless.

The time comes in the life of any nation when there remain only two choices: submit or fight. That time has now come to South Africa. We shall not submit and we have no choice but to hit back by all means within our power in defence of our people, our future and our freedom.

The Government has interpreted the peacefulness of the movement as weakness; the people's non-violent policies have been taken as a green light for Government violence. Refusal to resort to force has been interpreted by the Government as an invitation to use armed force against the people without any fear of reprisals. The methods of Umkonto We Sizwe mark a break with that past.

We are striking out along a new road for the liberation of the people of this country. The Government policy of force, repression and violence will no longer be met with non-violent resistance only! The choice is not ours; it has been made by the Nationalist Government which has rejected every peaceable demand by the people for rights and freedom and answered every such demand with force and yet more force! Twice in the past 18 months, virtual martial law has been imposed in order to beat down peaceful, non-violent strike action of the people in support of their rights. It is now preparing its forces—enlarging and rearming its armed forces and drawing white civilian population into commandos and pistol clubs—for full-scale military actions against the people. The Nationalist Government has chosen the course of force and massacre, now, deliberately, as it did at Sharpeville [March 21, 1960].

Umkonto We Sizwe will be at the front line of the people's defence. It will be the fighting arm of the people against the Government and its policies of race oppression. It will be the striking force of the people for liberty, for rights and for their final liberation! Let the Government, its supporters who put it into power, and those whose passive toleration of reaction keeps it in power, take note of where the Nationalist Government is leading the country!

We of Umkonto We Sizwe have always sought—as the liberation movement has sought—to achieve liberation, without bloodshed and civil clash. We do so still. We hope—even at this late hour—that our first actions will awaken everyone to a realization of the disastrous situation to which the Nationalist policy is leading. We hope that we will bring the Government and its supporters to their senses before it is too late, so that both Government and its policies can be changed before matters reach the desperate stage of civil war. We believe our actions to be a blow against the Nationalist preparations for civil war and military rule.

In these actions, we are working in the best interests of all the people of this country—black, brown and white—whose future happiness and well-being cannot be attained without the overthrow of the Nationalist Government, the abolition of white supremacy and the winning of liberty, democracy and full national rights and equality for all the people of this country.

We appeal for the support and encouragement of all those South Africans who seek the happiness and freedom of the people of this country.

Afrika Mayibuye!

Issued by command of Umkonto We Sizwe.

5. "The Civilized Man's Burden."

Unlike the other colonial powers in Africa, Portugal, ruled by the dictator António de Oliveira Salazar from 1933 until his death in 1968, saw no benefit for colonizer or colonized in ending its empire. Africans needed, according to Salazar, leadership and expertise to develop to their full capacity. It need not be white leadership and expertise, but it did have to be civilized. While a few Africans met Salazar's measure of civilized, it was not nearly enough to govern their own societies. Pursuing continent-wide unity as proposed by Kwame Nkrumah (document 2) would, in Salazar's view, only lead to the domination of sub-Saharan Africa by the "Arab" north, while attempts to forge a distinctly African path as described by Nyerere (document 3) would lead inevitably to "black racism." With most of Africa either independent or on the verge of becoming so, and armed struggle beginning in South Africa, Salazar spoke in 1963 of the determination of the Portuguese to retain their empire, while stressing at the same time that Portuguese colonialism was unlike that of the other European powers in that it was a multi-racial enterprise in which qualified Africans could work side-by-side with Europeans. In a line often adopted by supporters of continued colonial and/or white rule in the latter half of the twentieth century, Salazar argued that those people demanding immediate independence in Portuguese territories were not true patriots but were really the pawns of outside provocateurs, especially of the Soviet Union.[5]

The Civilized Man's Burden.

The aspirations of the African peoples do not differ from those of the majority of communities spread throughout the world, which even today yearn for liberation from the cycle of underdevelopment in which they find themselves. Their objectives thus coincide with the problems of governance in their respective countries or territories. And, as is the case everywhere, when such problems are not solved, or when the pace of their solution fails to attain the rhythm desired by the people, governments immediately are faced with a political crisis because doubts are cast upon the effectiveness of the institutions and the competence of the bureaucracy. This phenomenon is all the more frequent the lower the technical level of the particular community, and this level, in turn, derives essentially from the degree of autonomous economic development that has been reached, since instruction and education are not to be extracted from the soil or plucked from trees,

---

5. Ronald H. Chilcote, *Emerging Nationalism in Portuguese Africa: Documents* (Stanford: Hoover Institution Press, 1972), pp. 2–4. Reprinted with the agreement of the Hoover Institution Press.

like fruit growing spontaneously. They are acquired by work. It seems, therefore, that there is no way out from the cycle of under-development other than through the toil of the peoples concerned, since programs of mass culture imposed by aliens and, offered as gifts to boot, will fail to overcome the material obstacles which such programs encounter and which prevent the attainment of spectacular results. If this notion is true— and I cannot see that anywhere on the globe or at any time in history it has been proved otherwise—it would seem that the criterion for African development ought not to ignore the need for entrusting the responsibilities of administration to those best qualified to assume them, and for ensuring the active support of a political sovereignty whose interest is to foster the progress of all.

This, however, has not been the general opinion. Rather, has it been held that the solution to the problems will be better and will be found if the responsibilities of government in all the African territories are transferred to the local inhabitants, the contention being that human societies completely fulfill themselves only when they become arbitrary mistresses of their own destinies. This theory has been given the name of self-determination, and the movement directed to its achievement has come to be regarded as a natural force described as "the Tide of History."

I do not propose to raise certain doubts, the first of which would be whether this doctrine, in practice, has sufficiently taken into account what to our mind should have been its chief justification—that is, the welfare of the interested parties. Nor will I seek answers to certain queries, such as who has been gaining most from the "wind of change," and whether the doctrine is at all times being applied; or whether, on the contrary, the international community has been apathetically witnessing flagrant derogations of its principle. I shall confine myself to stating our opinion.

Through a long tradition of association, we have come to know the virtues and the capacities of some outstanding African tribes. Hence we do not doubt their leaders' being

fit for command, which in the Portuguese case they share and have always shared during our common history. But we do not consider—and experience is confirming our conviction—that these elites exist in sufficient numbers in all fields and at all levels. It is so in the administration of government as well as in private enterprise, without which the official administration would be pointless. Now the aforementioned insufficiency prevents them from assuming entirely on their own the complex management of public affairs under modern conditions. This seems to be proved by the fact that, in certain lands, an experiment is being carried out which appears to us to militate against the real autonomy of the peoples concerned. Thus, while sovereign power is made over to local inhabitants, basic economic enterprises and initiatives remain—and this under the most favorable circumstances—in the hands of men who, because of remaining nationals of the former colonial power, have now become aliens in the country in which they serve. We are inclined to think that, when things are stripped of their veils and reduced to their essentials, these new states run the risk of finding themselves in the throes of a subjection graver than that from which they claim to have emancipated themselves. On the other hand . . . we have been witnessing, and I fear we shall be witnessing with growing frequency, a process of retrogression in economic and social life and a return to certain practices which are incompatible with the desired prosperity and progress. . . .

The independence of African nations has, in general, been based on two erroneous premises that will work to those nations' detriment: anti-white racism and the alleged unity of the peoples of that continent. This latter supposition will tend to subordinate the Negro to the Arab; black racism will tend to bring about the rejection of all that the more progressive white men had brought in capital, labor, and culture. It would be wiser to replace clear-cut segregation with the working together which we have considered to be indispensable. For this reason we hold that the economic, social, and political advancement of those territories will only be possible on a multiracial basis in which the responsibilities of leadership in all fields fall to the most qualified, irrespective of their color.

I know we are accused of trying, by taking this stand, to ensure domination by the white race in Africa, the basis for this accusation being the fact that our multiracialism has not yet been implemented widely enough in the distribution of responsibilities throughout the Portuguese provinces in Africa. It is true that we are still far from attaining the point at which we might be fully satisfied with our achievements. However, it cannot be denied that not only is the road we are following the surest, but also the progress of the various Portuguese territories tends to spread to the whole of their population and not merely to the many groups already benefitted. It is impossible to deny this progress, since what has been achieved can, in many instances, be favorably compared with that of other African countries. And if our critics are so convinced that such is not the case, it is difficult to understand why they did not accept the suggestion that a trip for the purpose of studying overseas Portugal be undertaken by prominent foreign personalities, under the auspices of the United Nations. Unfortunately, harangues were preferred to a dispassionate study of the realities under debate—a project to which we gave our support.

A word about Angola. We are being subjected there to attacks which, at first, were presented as an uprising of people anxious not to continue integrated in the Portuguese nation. However, the enthusiasm of the liberators of Africa did not allow them, except for a short time, to hide their intervention in the recruitment, financing and training of the foreign persons who infiltrate into Angola from neighboring states. Today, therefore, it is no longer possible to claim that what is happening in Angola is a revolt of a more or less nationalistic character. In point of fact, a war is being conducted by several states against Portugal in one of Portugal's overseas territories. Under the circumstances, two things must be considered certain. The first is that in such aggression, it is not only the Portuguese who are being attacked: one of the aggressors' aims is to weaken the positions—and not only the strategic positions—of the entire Western world. The second is that those who attack us, those who support the aggressors, and those who assist them by their indifference are acting against the real interest of the tribes in Angola simply by delaying their peaceful self-improvement and by attempting to sow there the seed of racial antagonism, which did not exist among us and which is today, as I specified above, the principal obstacle to progress and well-being in the African continent.

6. Eduardo Mondlane rejects Portuguese apologetics.

Supporters of independence in the Portuguese colonies, such as Eduardo Mondlane in Mozambique, rejected Salazar's defense of colonialism as a fraud. How, he argues, could anyone take seriously the claim that the Portuguese would encourage democratic change and economic development in Africa when the country itself had been a dictatorship for most of the twentieth century (and a monarchy before that), and the poorest country in Europe to boot? Like Mandela and Umkonto We Sizwe, Mondlane argues that with no opportunity given to Africans to express their views publicly without becoming victims of the Portuguese secret police (the dreaded PIDE), the only option open was to use violence to overthrow the colonial regime.[6]

6. Eduardo Mondlane, *The Struggle for Mozambique* (Harmondsworth: Penguin Books, 1969), pp. 123–26.

The need for armed struggle.

Although determined to do everything in our power to try to gain independence by peaceful means, we were already convinced . . . that a war would be necessary. People more familiar with the policies of other colonial powers have accused us of resorting to violence without due cause. This is partly refuted by the fate met by every type of legal, democratic and reformist activity tried over the preceding forty years.

The character of the government in Portugal itself makes a peaceful solution inherently unlikely. Within Portugal the government has promoted neither sound economic growth nor social well-being, and has gained little international respect. The possession of colonies has helped to conceal these failures: the colonies contribute to the economy; they add to Portugal's consequence in the world, particularly the world of finance; they have provided a national myth of empire which helps discourage any grumbling by a fundamentally dissatisfied population. The government knows how ill it can afford to lose the colonies. For similar reasons it cannot afford to liberalize its control of them. The colonies contribute to the metropolitan economy only because labour is exploited and resources are not ploughed back into local development; the colonies ease the discontent of the Portuguese population only because immigration offers to the poor and uneducated a position of special privilege. Not least, since the fascist government has eliminated democracy within Portugal itself, it can scarcely allow a greater measure of freedom to the supposedly more backward people of its colonies.

Despite all this, attempts were made to use persuasion, encouraged by the acceptance elsewhere of the principle of self-determination. But such efforts were never rewarded with any kind of "dialogue." The only reaction to them was prison, censorship, and the strengthening of the PIDE, the secret police. The character of the PIDE is itself an important factor. For it has a strong tradition of violence—its officers were trained by the Gestapo—and it enjoys a considerable measure of autonomy, allowing it to act outside the control of the official law.

This is why political activity in Mozambique has called for the techniques of the "underground," for secrecy and exile. On the only recent occasion when an open approach was made, what happened is instructive. It was the incident . . . at Mueda in 1960, when some 500 Africans were killed. It had been planned as a peaceful demonstration and to some extent owed its origin to police provocation: the authorities knew that there was political agitation in the region, much of it clandestine, and they had given out that the governor would attend a public meeting on 16 June where he would grant independence to the Makonde people. The police thus brought the disaffection into the open and immediately killed or arrested as many as they could of those involved. They had hoped to remove the leaders, intimidate the population and set an example to other regions. But despite its ferocity, the action was only partially and temporarily successful. It eliminated some of the leaders, but others remained; while, far from being intimidated, the population became more determined than ever to resist.

Some of the exiles and those involved in clandestine opposition hoped at first that, even if Portugal was impervious to peaceful demands from the people of her colonies, she might listen to international organizations and the great nations of the world, if these would intervene on our behalf. Stemming from the Goan issue, some international pressure was brought to bear on Portugal during the fifties. But Portugal's only response was the legislation of the early sixties, which supposedly introduced reforms but made no concession to the principle of self-determination. Since then Portugal has ignored or rejected all appeals from other states or international bodies made on behalf of the people in her colonies. Besides this, not all the major states support us. Since 1961 most Western powers, including the United States, have not cooperated with United Nations resolutions urging Portugal to give the right of self-determination to the people of her non-self-governing territories.

By 1961 two conclusions were obvious. First, Portugal would not admit the principle of self-determination and independence, or allow for any extension of democracy under her own rule, although by then it was clear that her own "Portuguese" solutions to our oppressed condition, such as assimilation by multi-racial *colonatos,* multi-racial schools, local elections etc., had proved a meaningless fraud. Secondly, moderate political action such as strikes, demonstrations and petitions, would result only in the destruction of those who took part in them. We were,

therefore, left with these alternatives: to continue indefinitely living under a repressive imperial rule, or to find a means of using force against Portugal which would be effective enough to hurt Portugal without resulting in our own ruin.

This was why, to FRELIMO [Frente de Libertação de Moçambique] leaders, armed action appeared to be the only method. Indeed, the absence of any opposition to the use of force was one of the factors accounting for the very short period which elapsed between the formation of FRELIMO in 1962 and the beginning of the armed struggle on 25 September 1964.

7. Is neo-colonialism rationalized imperialism?

Even before Eduardo Mondlane and FRELIMO (Frente de Libertação de Moçambique) *embarked on armed struggle in Mozambique, the proponents of African independence in Portuguese Guinea (present day Guinea and Cape Verde), the Partido Africano da Independência da Guiné e Cabo Verde (PAIGC), had begun to fight a war of liberation that did not end until Portuguese troops themselves, weary of an endless colonial struggle that they did not believe they could win, overthrew the Portuguese dictatorship of Marcelo Caetano in 1974 and gave up the wars being fought throughout Africa (in Guinea, Angola, and Mozambique).*

The founder and leader of the PAIGC, Amílcar Cabral (1921–1973), trained as an agronomist in Portugal and worked in the colonial service in Guinea before voluntarily going into exile so that he could pursue his political goals. Cabral led an insurgency movement in Guinea and was assassinated in the capital city, Conakry, in 1973. Here he speaks at the beginning of the liberation war of the even greater struggles that he foresees ahead once liberation has been achieved. Speaking to European opponents of colonialism gathered for a seminar on revolution and the future at the symbolically named Frantz Fanon center in Milan, Cabral poses a number of questions. Is the national liberation struggle itself an imperialist initiative? Is neo-colonialism really just a form of rationalized imperialism? In a society such as that of Guinea and of most colonies in Africa, in which no middle class equivalent to that of the West existed because colonialism prevented its development, what role should the "stratum" of people who learned to manipulate the "apparatus of the state"— the African petty bourgeoisie (who are also the inheritors of state power in the post-colonial period)—pursue? Should the petty bourgeoisie class "commit suicide"? Is it likely to? And what happens if it does not?[7]

---

7. Richard Handyside, trans. and ed., *Revolution in Guinea: Selected Texts by Amílcar Cabral* (New York: Monthly Review Press, 1969), pp. 69–75. © 1969 by Monthly Review Press. Reprinted with the permission of the Monthly Review Press.

Seminar held at the Frantz Fanon Centre in Treviglio, Milan, May 1964.

Our problem is to see who is capable of taking control of the state apparatus when the colonial power is destroyed. In Guinea the peasants cannot read or write, they have almost no relations with the colonial forces during the colonial period except for paying taxes, which is done indirectly. The working class hardly exists as a defined class, it is just an embryo. There is no *economically viable* bourgeoisie because imperialism prevented it being created. What there is is a stratum of people in the service of imperialism who have learned how to manipulate the apparatus of the state—the African petty bourgeoisie: this is the only stratum capable of controlling or even utilising the instruments which the colonial state used against our people. So we come to the conclusion that in colonial conditions it is the petty bourgeoisie which is the inheritor of state power (though I wish we could be wrong). The moment national liberation comes and the petty bourgeoisie takes power we enter, or rather return to history, and thus the internal contradictions break out again.

When this happens, and particularly as things are now, there will be powerful external contradictions conditioning the internal situation, and not just internal contradictions as before. What attitude can the petty bourgeoisie adopt? Obviously people on the left will call for the revolution; the right will call for the "non-revolution," i.e. a capitalist road or something like that. The petty bourgeoisie can either ally itself with imperialism and the reactionary strata in its own country to try and preserve itself as a petty bourgeoisie or ally itself with the workers and peasants, who must themselves take power or control to make the revolution. We must be very clear exactly what we are asking the petty bourgeoisie to do. Are we asking it to commit suicide? Because if there is a revolution, then the petty bourgeoisie will have to abandon power to the workers and the peasants and cease to exist qua [as] petty bourgeoisie. For a revolution to take place depends on the nature of the party (and its size), the character of the struggle which led up to liberation, whether there was an armed struggle, what the nature of this armed struggle was and how it developed and, of course, on the nature of the state.

Here I would like to say something about the position of our friends on the left; if a petty bourgeoisie comes to power, they obviously demand of it that it carry out a revolution. But the important thing is whether they took the precaution of analysing the position of the petty bourgeoisie during the struggle; did they examine its nature, see how it worked, see what instruments it used and see whether this bourgeoisie committed itself with the left to carrying out a revolution, before the liberation? As you can see, it is the struggle in the underdeveloped countries which endows the petty bourgeoisie with a function; in the capitalist countries the petty bourgeoisie is only a stratum which serves, it does not determine the historical orientation of the country; it merely allies itself with one group or another. So that to hope that the petty bourgeoisie will just carry out a revolution when it comes to power in an underdeveloped country is to hope for a miracle, although it is true that it *could* do this.

This connects with the problem of the true nature of the national liberation struggle. In Guinea, as in other countries, the implantation of imperialism by force and the presence of the colonial system considerably altered the historical conditions and aroused a response—the national liberation struggle—which is generally considered a revolutionary trend; but this is something which I think needs further examination. I should like to formulate this question: is the national liberation movement something which has simply emerged from within our country, is it a result of the internal contradictions created by the presence of colonialism, or are there external factors which have determined it? And here we have some reservations; in fact I would even go so far as to ask whether, given the advance of socialism in the world, the national liberation movement is not an imperialist initiative. Is the judicial institution which serves as a reference for the right of all peoples to struggle to free themselves a product of the peoples who are trying to liberate themselves? Was it created by the socialist countries who are our historical associates? It is signed by the imperialist countries, it is the imperialist countries who have recognised the right of all peoples to national independence, so I ask myself whether we may not be considering as an initiative of our people what is in fact an initiative of the enemy? Even Portugal, which is using napalm bombs against our people in Guinea, signed the declaration of the right of all peoples to independence. One may well ask oneself why they were so mad as to do something which goes against their own interests—and whether or not it was partly forced on them, the real point is that they signed it. This is where we think there is something wrong with the simple interpretation of the national liberation movement as a revolutionary trend. The objective of the imperialist countries was to prevent the enlargement of the socialist camp, to liberate the reactionary forces in our countries which were being stifled by colonialism and to enable these forces to ally themselves with the international bourgeoisie. The fundamental objective was to create a bourgeoisie where one did not exist, in order specifically to strengthen the imperialist and the capitalist camp. This rise of the bourgeoisie in the new countries, far from being at all surprising, should be considered absolutely normal, it is something that has to be faced by all those struggling against imperialism. We are therefore faced with the problem of deciding whether to engage in an out and out struggle against the bourgeoisie right from the start or whether to try and make an alliance with the national bourgeoisie, to try to deepen the absolutely necessary contradiction between the national bourgeoisie and the international bourgeoisie which has promoted the national bourgeoisie to the position it holds.

To return to the question of the nature of the petty bourgeoisie and the role it can play after the liberation, I should like to put a question to you. What would you have thought if Fidel Castro had come to terms with the Americans? Is this possible or not? Is it possible or impossible that the Cuban petty bourgeoisie, which set the Cuban people marching towards revolution, might have come to terms with the Americans? I think this helps to clarify the character of the revolutionary petty bourgeoisie. If I may put it this way, I think one thing that can be said is this: the revolutionary petty bourgeoisie is honest; i.e. in spite of all the hostile conditions, it remains identified with the fundamental interests of the popular masses. To do this it may have to commit suicide, but it will not lose, by sacrificing itself it can reincarnate itself, but in the condition of workers or peasants. In speaking of honesty I am not trying to establish moral criteria for judging the role of the petty bourgeoisie when it is in power; what I mean by honesty, in a political context, is total commitment and total identification with the toiling masses.

Again, the role of the petty bourgeoisie ties up with the possible social and political transformations that can be effected after liberation. We have heard a great deal about the state of national democracy, but although we have made every effort we have thus far been unable to understand what this means; even so, we should like to know what it is all about, as we want to know what we are going to do when we have driven out the Portuguese. Likewise, we have to face the question whether or not socialism can be established immediately after the liberation. This depends on the instruments used to effect the transition to socialism; the essential factor is the nature of the state, bearing in mind that after the liberation there will be people controlling the police, the prisons, the army and so on, and a great deal depends on who they are and what they try to do with these instruments. Thus we return again to the problem of which class is the agent of history and who are the inheritors of the colonial state in our specific conditions. . . .

What really interests us here is neocolonialism. After the Second World War, imperialism entered on a new phase: on the one hand, it worked out the new policy of aid, i.e. granted independence to the occupied countries plus "aid" and, on the other hand, concentrated on preferential investment in the European countries; this was, above all, an attempt at rationalising imperialism. Even if it has not yet provoked reactions of a nationalist kind in the European countries, we are convinced that it will soon do so. As we see it, neocolonialism (which we may call rationalised imperialism) is more a defeat for the international working class than for the colonised peoples. Neocolonialism is at work on two fronts—in Europe as well as in the underdeveloped countries. Its current framework in the underdeveloped countries is the policy of aid, and one of the essential aims of this policy is to create a false bourgeoisie to put a brake on the revolution and to enlarge the possibilities of the petty bourgeoisie as a neutraliser of the revolution; at the same time it invests capital in France, Italy, Belgium, England and so on. In our opinion the aim of this is to stimulate the growth of a workers' aristocracy, to enlarge the field of action of the petty bourgeoisie so as to block the revolution. In our opinion it is under this aspect that neocolonialism and the relations between the international working class movement and our movements must be analysed. If there have ever been any doubts about the close relations between our struggle and the struggle of the international working class movement, neocolonialism has proved that there need not be any. Obviously I don't think it is possible to forge closer relations between the peasantry in Guinea and the working class movement in Europe; what we must do first is try and forge closer links between the peasant movement and the wage-earners' movement in our own country. The example of Latin America gives you a good idea of the limits on closer relations; in Latin America you have an old neocolonial situation and a chance to see clearly the relations between the North American proletariat and the Latin American masses. Other examples could be found nearer home.

There is, however, another aspect I should like to raise and that is that the European left has an intellectual responsibility to study the concrete conditions in our country and help us in this way, as we have very little documentation, very few intellectuals, very little chance to do this kind of work ourselves, and yet it is of key importance; this is a major contribution you can make. Another thing you can do is to support the really revolutionary national liberation movements by all possible means. You must analyse and study these movements and combat in Europe, by all possible means, everything which can be used to further the repression against our peoples. I refer especially to the sale of arms. I should like to say to our Italian friends that we have captured a lot of Italian arms from the Portuguese, not to mention French arms, of course. Moreover, you must unmask courageously all the national liberation movements which are under the thumb of imperialism. People whisper that so-and-so is an American agent, but nobody in the European left has taken a violent and open attitude against these people; it is we ourselves who have to try and denounce these people, who are sometimes even those accepted by the rest of Africa, and this creates a lot of trouble for us.

I think that the left and the international working class movement should confront those states which claim to be socialist with their responsibilities; this does not of course, mean cutting off all their possibilities of action, but it does mean denouncing all those states which are neocolonialists.

To end up with, I should just like to make one last point about solidarity between the international working class movement and our national liberation struggle. There are two alternatives: either we admit that there really is a struggle against imperialism which interests everybody, or we deny it. If, as would seem from all the evidence, imperialism exists and is trying simultaneously to dominate the working class in all the advanced countries and smother the national liberation movements in all the underdeveloped countries, then there is only one enemy against whom we are fighting. If we are fighting together, then I think the main aspect of our solidarity is extremely simple: it is to fight— I don't think there is any need to discuss this very much. We are struggling in Guinea with guns in our hands, you must struggle in your countries as well—I don't say with guns in your hands, I'm not going to tell you how to struggle, that's your business; but you must find the best means and the best forms of fighting against our common enemy: this is the best form of solidarity.

8. A man of the people.

Chinua Achebe, whose novel Things Fall Apart *about the impact of conquest on the Igbo people of southeastern Nigeria has become a literary classic, took up the problems of independent Nigeria in a less well-known, but equally penetrating account,* A Man of the People. *In this account, based on Achebe's reactions to developments in Nigeria in the early 1960s, politics in the ex-colony become an opportunity for the petty bourgeoisie feared by Amílcar Cabral to exercise a self-seeking and corrupting influence on the new state. As these "new men" grasp after economic and political spoils for themselves, they adopt an anti-foreign rhetoric—easily transferred from the anti-colonial struggle—as a means to disguise their own self-interest. M. A. Nanga, Achebe's "man of the people," is clearly a certain type of colonial product, schooled as British officials would have wished in Africa, a longtime member of Baden-Powell's scouting movement, and, despite his pretensions to serving the needs of the community at large, fundamentally corrupt.*[8]

No one can deny that Chief the Honorable M. A. Nanga, M.P., was the most approachable politician in the country. Whether you asked in the city or in his home village, Anata, they would tell you he was a man of the people. I have to admit this from the outset or else the story I'm going to tell will make no sense.

That afternoon he was due to address the staff and students of the Anata Grammar School where I was teaching at the time. But as usual in those highly political times the villagers moved in and virtually took over. The Assembly Hall must have carried well over thrice its capacity. Many villagers sat on the floor, right up to the foot of the dais. I took one look and decided it was just as well we had to stay outside—at least for the moment.

Five or six dancing groups were performing at different points in the compound. The popular "Ego Women's Party" wore a new uniform of expensive accra cloth. In spite of the din you could still hear as clear as a bird the high-powered voice of their soloist, whom they admiringly nicknamed "Grammar-phone." Personally I don't care too much for our women's dancing but you just had to listen whenever Grammar-phone sang. She was now praising Micah's handsomeness, which she likened to the perfect, sculpted beauty of a carved eagle, and his popularity which would be the envy of the proverbial traveller-to-distant-places who must not cultivate enmity on his route. Micah was of course Chief the Honourable M. A. Nanga, M.P.

The arrival of the members of the hunters' guild in full regalia caused a great stir. Even Grammar-phone stopped—at least for a while. These people never came out except at the funeral of one of their number, or during some very special and outstanding event. I could not remember when I last saw them. They wielded their loaded guns as though they were playthings. Now and again two of them would meet in warriors' salute and

---

8. Chinua Achebe, *A Man of the People* (London: Heinemann, 1966), pp. 1–6. Reprinted with the permission of Heinemann Educational Publishers, a division of Reed Educational and Professional Publishing Ltd.

knock the barrel of their guns together from left to right and again from right to left. Mothers grabbed their children and hurriedly dragged them away. Occasionally a hunter would take aim at a distant palm branch and break its mid-rib. The crowd applauded. But there were very few such shots. Most of the hunters reserved their precious powder to greet the Minister's arrival—the price of gunpowder like everything else having doubled again and again in the four years since this government took control.

As I stood in one corner of that vast tumult waiting for the arrival of the Minister I felt intense bitterness welling up in my mouth. Here were silly, ignorant villagers dancing themselves lame and waiting to blow off their gunpowder in honour of one of those who had started the country off down the slopes of inflation. I wished for a miracle, for a voice of thunder, to hush this ridiculous festival and tell the poor contemptible people one or two truths. But of course it would be quite useless. They were not only ignorant but cynical. Tell them that this man had used his position to enrich himself and they would ask you–as my father did–if you thought that a sensible man would spit out the juicy morsel that good fortune placed in his mouth.

I had not always disliked Mr. Nanga. Sixteen years or so ago he had been my teacher in standard three and I something like his favourite pupil. I remember him then as a popular, young and handsome teacher, most impressive in his uniform as scoutmaster. There was on one of the walls of the school a painting of a faultlessly handsome scoutmaster wearing an impeccable uniform. I am not sure that the art teacher who painted the picture had Mr. Nanga in mind. There was no facial resemblance; still we called it the picture of Mr. Nanga. It was enough that they were both handsome and that they were both impressive scoutmasters. This picture stood with arms folded across its chest and its raised right foot resting neatly and lightly on a perfectly cut tree stump. Bright red hibiscus flowers decorated the four corners of the frame, and below were inscribed the memorable

words: *Not what I have but what I do is my kingdom*. That was in 1948.

Nanga must have gone into politics soon afterwards and then won a seat in Parliament. (It was easy in those days—before we knew its cash price.) I used to read about him in the papers some years later and even took something like pride in him. At that time I had just entered the University and was very active in the Students' branch of the People's Organization Party. Then in 1960 something disgraceful happened in the Party and I was completely disillusioned.

At that time Mr. Nanga was an unknown back-bencher in the governing P.O.P. A general election was imminent. The P.O.P. was riding high in the country and there was no fear of its not being returned. Its opponent, the Progressive Alliance Party, was weak and disorganized.

Then came the slump in the international coffee market. Overnight (or so it seemed to us) the Government had a dangerous financial crisis on its hands. Coffee was the prop of our economy just as coffee farmers were the bulwark of the P.O.P.

The Minister of Finance at the time was a first-rate economist with a Ph.D. in public finance. He presented to the Cabinet a complete plan for dealing with the situation.

The Prime Minister said "No" to the plan. He was not going to risk losing the election by cutting down the price paid to coffee planters at that critical moment; the National Bank should be instructed to print fifteen million pounds. Two-thirds of the Cabinet supported the Minister. The next morning the Prime Minister sacked them and in the evening he broadcast to the nation. He said the dismissed ministers were conspirators and traitors who had teamed up with foreign saboteurs to destroy the new nation.

I remember this broadcast very well. Of course no one knew the truth at that time. The newspapers and the radio carried the Prime Minister's version of the story. We were very indignant. Our Students' Union met in emergency session and passed a vote of confidence in the leader and called for a detention law to deal with the miscreants. The whole country was behind the leader. Protest marches and demonstrations were staged up and down the land.

It was at this point that I first noticed a new, dangerous and sinister note in the universal outcry.

The *Daily Chronicle*, an official organ of the P.O.P., had pointed out in an editorial that the Miscreant Gang, as the dismissed ministers were now called, were all university people and highly educated professional men. (I have preserved a cutting of that editorial.)

"Let us now and for all time extract from our body-politic as a dentist extracts a stinking tooth all those decadent stooges versed in text-book economics and aping the white man's mannerisms and way of speaking. We are proud to be Africans. Our true leaders are not those intoxicated with their Oxford, Cambridge or Harvard degrees but those who speak the language of the people. Away with the damnable and expensive university education which only alienates an African from his rich and ancient culture and puts him above his people. . . ."

This cry was taken up on all sides. Other newspapers pointed out that even in Britain where the Miscreant Gang got its "so-called education" a man need not be an economist to be Chancellor of the Exchequer or a doctor to be Minister of Health. What mattered was loyalty to the party.

I was in the public gallery the day the Prime Minister received his overwhelming vote of confidence. And that was the day the truth finally came out; only no one was listening. I remember the grief-stricken figure of the dismissed Minister of Finance as he led his team into the chamber and was loudly booed by members of the public. That week his car had been destroyed by angry mobs and his house stoned. Another dismissed minister had been pulled out of his car, beaten insensible, and dragged along the road for fifty yards, then tied hand and foot, gagged and left by the roadside. He was still in the orthopaedic hospital when the house met.

The Prime Minister spoke for three hours and his every other word was applauded. He was called the Tiger, the Lion, the One and Only, the Sky, the Ocean and many other names of praise. He said that the Miscreant Gang had been caught "red-handed in their nefarious plot to overthrow the Government of the people by the people and for the people with the help of enemies abroad."

"They deserve to be hanged," shouted Mr. Nanga from the back benches. This interruption was so loud and clear that it appeared later under his own name in the *Hansard*. Throughout the session he led the pack of back-bench hounds straining their leash to get at their victims. If any one had cared to sum up Mr. Nanga's interruptions they would have made a good hour's continuous yelp. Perspiration poured down his face as he sprang up to interrupt or sat back to share in the derisive laughter of the hungry hyena.

When the Prime Minister said that he had been stabbed in the back by the very ingrates he had pulled out of oblivion some members were in tears.

"They have bitten the finger with which their mother fed them," said Mr. Nanga. This too was entered in the Hansard, a copy of which I have before me. It is impossible, however, to convey in cold print the electric atmosphere of that day.

I cannot now recall exactly what my feelings were at that point. I suppose I thought the whole performance rather peculiar. You must remember that at that point no one had any reason to think there might be another side to the story. The Prime Minister was still talking. Then he made the now famous (or infamous) solemn declaration, "From today we must watch and guard our hard-won freedom jealously. Never again must we entrust our destiny and the destiny of Africa to the hybrid class of Western-educated and snobbish intellectuals who will not hesitate to sell their mothers for a mess of pottage. . . ."

Mr. Nanga pronounced the death sentence at least twice more but this was not recorded, no doubt because his voice was lost in the general commotion.

I remember the figure of Dr. Makinde the ex-Minister of Finance as he got up to speak—

tall, calm, sorrowful and superior. I strained my ears to catch his words. The entire house, including the Prime Minister, tried to shout him down. It was a most unedifying spectacle. The Speaker broke his mallet ostensibly trying to maintain order but you could see he was enjoying the commotion. The public gallery yelled down its abuses. "Traitor," "Coward," "Doctor of Fork your Mother." This last was contributed from the gallery by the editor of the *Daily Chronicle* who sat close to me. Encouraged, no doubt, by the volume of laughter this piece of witticism had earned him in the gallery he proceeded the next morning to print it in his paper. The spelling is his.

Although Dr. Makinde read his speech, which was clearly prepared, the Hansard later carried a garbled version which made no sense at all. It said not a word about the plan to mint fifteen million pounds—which was perhaps to be expected—but why put into Dr Makinde's mouth words that he could not have spoken? In short the Hansard boys wrote a completely new speech suitable to the boastful villain the ex-minister had become. For instance they made him say he was a brilliant economist whose reputation was universally acclaimed in Europe. When I read this I was in tears—and I don't cry all that easily.

9. Tearing things apart.

The contradictions of post-colonial independence exploded in Africa's first coup on January 15, 1966, when Nigerian military officers, most of them Igbo from the southeast, assassinated Nigeria's prime minister, Abubakar Tafawa Balewa (a Muslim northerner), as well as the leaders of the western and northern regions of the country. (Nnamdi Azikiwe, Nigeria's president, was in Britain seeking medical treatment at the time of the coup.) The coup leaders stated that they had been forced to take action by the endemic corruption that was crippling the country, by the corrupt election that had taken place in October of the previous year, and by Nigeria's need for a strong and efficient central government rather than the federal system that had been put in place by Britain.

Aside from opposition to people like those represented by Chinua Achebe's semi-fictional M. A. Nanga, the Igbo officers were concerned also that the divide and rule policies left in place by the British transfer of power had privileged the north at the expense of the south. This imbalance, the coup leaders felt, had been further reinforced by the 1962 census, a highly suspect head count that had concluded that the north had almost two-thirds of Nigeria's population, an impossibly high proportion, and therefore was entitled to an equivalent share of the parliamentary seats. Northerners, most of them Muslim, for their part viewed the coup as an attempt by mainly Christian Igbo to impose themselves upon the country. The coup leaders were themselves deposed, by army officers led by an Igbo general. But rioting broke out, especially in northern Nigeria where large numbers of Igbo were massacred and thousands fled to their southeastern homeland fearing genocide. As the country became enmeshed in violence, northern officers staged a coup of their own, which in turn increased Igbo fears of pogroms. In the following speech made in 1967, C. Odumegwu Ojukwu, an Igbo military officer who led the Biafran secessionist movement from 1967 until its defeat in 1970 (with between one and three million people dead from hostilities, disease, and starvation), describes why he and his supporters (who included Chinua Achebe) felt it necessary to withdraw from the Nigerian federation. [9]

Proclamation of the Republic of Biafra, May 30, 1967.

It is right and just that we of this generation of Eastern Nigeria should record for the benefit of posterity some of the reasons for the momentous decision we have taken at this crucial time in the history of our people.

The military government of Eastern Nigeria has, in a series of publications, traced the evils and injustices of the Nigerian political association through the decades, stating also the case and standpoint of Eastern Nigeria in the recent crisis.

Throughout the period of Nigeria's precarious existence as a single political entity, Eastern Nigerians have always believed in fundamental human rights and principles as they are accepted and enjoyed in civilized communities. Impelled by their belief in these rights and principles and in their common citizenship with other Nigerians after Amalgamation, Eastern Nigerians employed their ideas and skills, their resourcefulness and dynamism, in the development of areas of Nigeria outside the East. Eastern Nigerians opened up avenues of trade and industry throughout the country; overlooked the neglect of their homeland in the disposition of national institutions, projects, and utilities; made available their own natural resources to the rest of the country; and confidently invested in the general economic and social development of Nigeria. Politically, Eastern Nigerians advocated a strong, united Nigeria: for ONE COUNTRY, ONE CONSTITUTION, ONE DESTINY. Eastern Nigerians were in the vanguard of the struggle for national independence and made sacrifices and concessions for the cause of national unity. They conceded the inauguration of a federal instead of a unitary system of government in Nigeria.

Leaders of Northern Nigeria have told us several times that what our former colonial masters made into "Nigeria" consisted of an agglomeration of people, distinct in every way except in the color of their skins, and organized as a unit for their own commercial interests and administrative convenience. The name "Nigeria" was regarded by many as a mere "geographical expression."

In course of time, the peoples of the other parts of Southern Nigeria found that they possessed many things in common with those of Eastern Nigeria, and while the colonial master made adjustments to accommodate these common ties between the Southern inhabitants, the peoples of the North insisted on maintaining their separateness.

On October 1, 1960, independence was granted to the people of Nigeria in a form of "federation," based on artificially made units. The Nigerian Constitution installed the North in perpetual dominance over Nigeria. The Federation was predicated on the perpetual rule by one unit over the others. The Constitution itself contained provisions which negated the fundamental human freedoms which it purported to guarantee for the citizens. Thus were sown, by design or by default, the seeds of factionalism and hate, of struggle for power at the center, and of the worst types of political chicanery and abuse of power. One of two situations was bound to result from that arrangement: either perpetual domination of the rest of the country by the North, not by consent but by force and fraud, or a dissolution of the federation bond. National independence was followed by successive crises, each leading to near-disintegration of the country. Some of the major events which are directly attributable to the defective and inadequate Constitution may here be mentioned.

---

9. C. Odumegwu Ojukwu, *Biafra: Selected Speeches and Random Thoughts of C. Odumegwu Ojukwu, General of the People's Army, With Diaries of Events* (New York: Harper and Row, 1969), pp. 177–84. Reprinted with the permission of HarperCollins Publishers, Inc.

In 1962, an emergency was imposed on Western Nigeria. Jurists agree that the imposition was unconstitutional; it was a ruse to remove certain elements in Western Nigeria known to have taken a firm stand against the misuse of political power. A puppet of the North was maneuvered into power in Western Nigeria.

Also in 1962, and again in 1963, Nigerians tried for the first time to count themselves. What should ordinarily be a statistical and dull exercise was, because of the nature of the Constitution, turned into a fierce political struggle. The official figures established by these censuses have been discredited.

Federal elections followed in December, 1964—elections which have been described as the most farcical in our history. Candidates were kidnapped, killed, or forced to withdraw from the elections. Results announced were in direct opposition to the actual facts. The Southern parties had boycotted the election, and the deadlock which followed brought the country near to dissolution. The situation was patched up; the conflagration was brought under control, but its embers lay smoldering.

On October 11, 1965, elections were held to the Western House of Assembly. The puppet government of that region existed not by the will of the people of Western Nigeria but because of the combined power of the federal government and the Northern Nigeria government which installed it. The electorate of Western Nigeria was not permitted to declare its will in the elections. Fraud, foul play, and murder were committed with impunity. The smoldering embers of the recent past erupted with unquenchable virulence. The irate electorate showed its resentment in its own way. Complete disorder followed. Yet the federal government dominated by the North fiddled with the issue and even refused to recognize what the whole world had known, namely, that Nigeria was on the brink of disaster.

Only the armed forces remained politically uncommitted and nonpartisan. Some of their officers and men revolted against the injustices which were perpetrated before their very

eyes and attempted to overthrow the federal government and regional governments. In desperation, the ministers of the federal government handed over power to the armed forces under the supreme command of Major General J. T. U. Aguiyi-Ironsi.

The military administration under Major General Aguiyi-Ironsi made the first real attempt to unite the country and its peoples. The Northerners saw in his efforts the possibility of losing their control of the affairs of the country. So while its leaders paid lip service to unity, they laid plans for making sure that it could never be achieved. Major General Aguiyi-Ironsi was, of course, an Easterner, but the majority of the individuals at the head of affairs were not. At no time under the civilian rule did Eastern Nigerians hold a dominating position in the government of the Federation.

On May 24, 1966, the military government issued a decree designed to provide a more unified administration in keeping with the military command. The people of Northern Nigeria protested against the decree, and on May 29, 1966, thousands of Easterners residing in the North were massacred by Northern civilians. They looted their property. The Supreme Military Council set up a tribunal to look into the causes of those unprovoked acts of murder and pillage and determine what compensations might be paid to the victims. The Northern emirs declared their intention to pull Northern Nigeria out of the Federation rather than face the tribunal. But the Supreme Military Council justly decided that the tribunal must do its duty.

Then, on July 29, 1966, two months after the May murders and despoliation, and four days before the tribunal was due to commence its sitting, the real pogrom against Eastern Nigerians residing in the Federation began. Major General Aguiyi-Ironsi and his host, Lieutenant Colonel Francis Fajuyi, were kidnapped at Ibadan and murdered. This time Northern soldiers acted in concert with Northern civilians. Defenseless men, women, and children were shot down or hacked to death; some were burned, and some buried alive. Women and young girls were ravished with unprecedented bestiality; unborn children were torn out of the womb of their mothers.

Again, on September 29, 1966, the pogrom was resumed. Thirty thousand Eastern Nigerians are known to have been killed by Northerners. They were killed in the North, in Western Nigeria, in Lagos; some Eastern soldiers in detention at Benin were forcibly removed from prison by Northern soldiers and murdered.

At the time of the incident, millions of Eastern Nigerians resided outside the East, and persons from other parts of the country lived in this region. While Eastern Nigerians who assembled at Northern airports, railway stations, and motor parks were set upon by Northern soldiers and civilians armed with machine guns, rifles, daggers, and poisoned arrows, the army and police in the East were specifically instructed to shoot at sight any Eastern Nigerian found molesting non-Easterners living in the region. By early October the sight of mutilated refugees, orphaned children, widowed mothers, and decapitated corpses of Eastern Nigerians arriving at our airports and railway stations inflamed passions to such an extent that it was found necessary to ask all non-Easterners to leave the region in their own interest. Since the events of July, 1966, there has been a mass movement of population in this country. Nigerian society has undergone a fundamental change; it is no longer possible for Eastern Nigerians to live outside their region without fear of loss of life or of property.

Two facts emerge from the events described above. The widespread nature of the massacre and its periodicity—May 29, July 29, and September 29—show first, that they were premeditated and planned, and second, that Eastern Nigerians are no longer wanted as equal partners in the Federation of Nigeria. It must be recalled that this was the fourth in a series of massacres of Eastern Nigerians in the last two decades.

At the early stages of the crisis, the world was told that it was a conflict between the North and the East. That pretense collapsed when it became clear that Northern soldiers

moved into Western Nigeria and Lagos as another step in Northern Nigeria's bid to continue her so-called conquest to the sea. Belatedly, it was generally accepted that the fundamental issue was not a struggle between the East and the North, but one involving the very existence of Nigeria as one political entity.

Throughout the Nigerian crises, some of the indigenous judges have been found quite unequal to their calling by reason of their involvement in partisan politics. People soon lost faith in them and would not go to their courts for redress. In some measure, they were responsible for the collapse of the rule of law in certain parts of Nigeria. Providence has spared us in the East from this terrible calamity.

It is now necessary to summarize the attempt of the government and people of Eastern Nigeria to solve the crisis, and the bad faith with which these attempts have been received.

On August 9, 1966, representatives of the military governors meeting in Lagos made decisions for restoring peace and for clearing the way for constitutional talks, notably the decision that troops be all repatriated to their region of origin. These decisions were not fully implemented.

On September 12, the Ad Hoc Constitutional Conference, consisting of delegates representing all the governments of the Federation, met in Lagos and for three weeks sought to discover a form of association best suited to Nigeria, having regard to the prevailing circumstances and their causes, and future possibilities. This conference was unilaterally dismissed by Lieutenant Colonel Gowon, the head of the Lagos government.

It had become then impossible for the Supreme Military Council, the highest governing body in the Federation, to meet on Nigerian soil. As long as Northern troops were in Lagos and the West, no venue could be found acceptable to all the military governors for a meeting of the Supreme Military Council in Nigeria. It met at Aburi in Ghana, January 4–5, 1967, on the basis of an agenda previously determined by the officials of the governments of the country and adopted by the Supreme Military Council. Decisions reached at the meeting were ignored by Lieutenant Colonel Gowon and the North. In the interest of this region and of the whole country, the East stood firmly by those decisions and warned that they would be applied to Eastern Nigeria if steps were not taken by the Lagos government to apply them generally. The East rejected all measures which did not reflect the decisions at Aburi.

The Aburi Accord was not implemented by the Lagos government. All the meetings of military leaders held since Aburi were held without the East. All the decisions taken by Lagos were taken without comment and concurrence from the East.

It became evident that each time Nigerians came close to a realistic solution to the current crisis by moving toward a loose form of association or confederation, Lieutenant Colonel Gowon unilaterally frustrated their efforts. When the representatives of the military governors decided on August 9, 1966, that troops be repatriated to their regions of origin, and it appeared to him that this would lead to confederation, he unilaterally refused to fully implement that decision. When in September, 1967, the Ad Hoc Constitutional Conference appeared near to agreement on a loose federation, he unilaterally dismissed them indefinitely. When in January, 1967, the military leaders agreed at Aburi on what the federal permanent secretaries correctly interpreted as confederation, he unilaterally rejected the agreement to which he had voluntarily subscribed. When in May, 1967, all the Southern military governors and the Leaders of Thought of their regions spoke out in favor of confederation, he dismissed the Supreme Military Council and proclaimed himself the dictator of Nigeria—an act which, to say the least, is treasonable.

Following the pogrom of 1966, some 7,000,000 Eastern Nigerians have returned from other regions, refugees in their own country. Money was needed to care for them—not to give them mere relief but to rehabilitate them and, in time, restore their outraged feelings. The Lagos government was urged to give the Eastern Nigeria government its share of the statutory revenues. Lieutenant Colonel Gowon refused to do so in the hope that the weight of the burden would lead to the economic collapse of Eastern Nigeria.

10. Black consciousness.

With black opposition parties banned in South Africa (the apartheid regime viewed all Africans as aliens who were permitted residence in South Africa only so long as their services were needed as migrant workers) and Umkonto we Sizwe crushed in the mid-1960s by police and military action, young African opponents of the apartheid regime looked back to the Africanist ideas of Anton Lembede (Part 3, document 21), to the arguments of Kwame Nkrumah for "positive action (Part 3, document 29; Part 4, document 2)," and to the developing black power movement in the United States to develop new ways of critiquing racism in South Africa. The founder of the black South African Students' Organization (SASO), Steve Biko (1946–1977), argued that apartheid persisted in part because people allowed themselves to be colonized and that they should break the psychological bonds that bound them into subservience. Moreover, Biko argued, black consciousness should be a way of life, not just a political expedient. Through the development of a new self-awareness and pride, and the adoption of peaceful means of organization, Africans would be able to bring about the end of apartheid. It did not mean hatred of whites. Looked upon favorably at first by the Afrikaner rulers of South Africa, because his ideas seemed to support their aim of complete racial separation, Biko soon was viewed as a serious threat because of the popularity of his ideas among young people. Though Biko did argue for peaceful change, he also envisaged a future South Africa ruled by a black government. Proponents of white supremacy feared such a future and in October 1977, a year after the Soweto uprising, white police officers killed Biko while he was in their custody. The extract below is from a paper that Biko presented to a meeting in Edendale, South Africa, in 1971.[10]

What are we talking about?

Here we are primarily concerned with SASO and its work. We talk glibly of "Black Consciousness" and yet we show that we hardly understand what we are talking about. In this regard it is essential for us to realise a few basic facts about "Black Consciousness."

"Black Consciousness" is essentially a slogan directing us away from the traditional political big talk to a new approach. This is an inward-looking movement calculated to make us look at ourselves and see ourselves, not in terms of what we have been taught through the absolute values of white society, but with new eyes. It is a call upon us to see the innate value in us, in our institutions, in our traditional outlook to life and in our own worth as people. The call of "Black Consciousness" is by no means a slogan driving people to think in a certain way politically. Rather it is a social slogan directed at each member of the black community calling upon him to discard the false mantle that he has been forced to wear for so many years and to think in terms of himself as he should. In this regard therefore Black Consciousness is a way of life that must permeate through the society and be adopted by all. The logic behind it is that if you see yourself as a person in your own right there are certain basic questions that you must ask about the conditions under which you live. To get to this stage there are three basic steps that have to be followed.

(i) We have to understand thoroughly what we are talking about and to impart it in the right context. This becomes especially necessary in a country like ours where such

an approach lends itself easily to misinterpretation. For this reason we have made provision for a historical study of the theory of "black power" in this formation school.

(ii) We have to create channels for the adoption of the same approach by the black community at large. Here, again, one has to be realistic. An approach of this nature, to be successful, has to be adopted by as large a fraction of the population as possible in order to be effective. Whilst the student community may be instrumental in carrying the idea across to the people and remaining the force behind it, the approach will remain ineffective unless it gains grass roots support. This is why it is necessary to create easily acceptable slogans and follow these up with in-depth explanations. Secondary institutions built up from members of the community and operating amongst the community have to be encouraged and these must be run by people who themselves understand what is involved in these institutions and in the approach we are adopting. One can expand and give many examples of such institutions but we expect this to come out of discussions at this formation school. Let it suffice to say that such institutions must cover all fields of activity of the black community—educational, social, economic, religious, etc.

(iii) People have to be taught to see the advantages of group action. Here one wonders whether a second look should not be taken at the government-instituted bodies like Urban Bantu Councils and bantustans. It is a universal fact that you cannot politicise people and hope to limit their natural and

---

10. Hendrik van der Merwe, et al., eds., *African Perspectives on South Africa: A Collection of Speeches, Articles & Documents* (Stanford: Hoover Institution Press, 1978), pp. 101–05. Reprinted with the agreement of the Hoover Institution Press.

legitimate aspirations. If the people demand something and get it because they have an Urban Bantu Council or "territorial authority" to talk for them, then they shall begin to realise the power they wield as a group. Political modernisation of the black people may well find good expression in these institutions which at present are repugnant to us. In contrasting the approach adopted in the United States by the black people and our own approach here, it will be interesting to know what this formation school thinks of the various "territorial authorities" in our various "own areas."

There are some dangers that we have to guard against as we make progress in the direction we are pursuing. The first and foremost is that we must not make the mistake of wishing to get into the white man's boots. Traditional indigenous values tell us of a society where poverty was foreign and extreme richness unknown except for the rulers of our society. Sharing was at the heart of our culture. A system that tends to exploit *many* and favour a few is as foreign to us as hair which is not kinky or a skin which is not dark. Where poverty reigned, it affected the whole community simply because of weather conditions beyond our control. Hence even in our aspirations basic truth will find expression. We must guard against the danger of creating a black middle class whose blackness will only be literally skin-deep. . . .

Secondly we must not be limited in our outlook. There is a mile of difference between preaching Black Consciousness and preaching hatred of whites. Telling people to hate whites is an outward and reactionary type of preaching which, though understandable, is undesirable and self-destructive. It makes one think in negative terms and preoccupies one with peripheral issues. In a society like ours it is a "positive feed-forward" approach that leads one into a vicious circle and ultimately to self-destruction through ill-advised and impetuous action. In fact it is usually an extreme form of inferiority complex where the sufferer has lost hope of "making it" because of conditions imposed upon him. His actual

aspirations are to be like the white man and the hatred arises out of frustration.

On the other hand Black Consciousness is an inward-looking process. It takes cognisance of one's dignity and leads to positive action. It makes you seek to assert yourself and to rise to majestic heights as determined by you. No doubt you resent all forces that seek to thwart your progress but you meet them with strength, resilience and determination because in your heart of hearts you are convinced you will get where you want to get to. In the end you are a much more worthy victor because you do not seek to revenge but to implement the truth for which you have stood all along during your struggle. You were no less angry than the man who hated whites but your anger was channelled to positive action. Because you had a vision detached from the situation you worked hard regardless of immediate setbacks. White hatred leads to precipitate and short-run methods whereas we are involved in an essentially long-term struggle where cool-headedness must take precedence over everything else.

The third point is that we must not make the mistake of trying to categorise whites. Essentially all whites are the same and must be viewed with suspicion. This may apparently sound contradictory to what I have been saying but it is not in actual fact. A study of the history of South Africa shows that at almost all times whites have been involved in black struggles and in almost all instances led to the death or confusion of what they were involved in. This may not have been calculated sometimes but it arises out of genuine differences in approach and commitments. That blacks are deciding to go it alone is not an accident but a result of years of history behind black-white co-operation. Black-white co-operation in this country leads to limitations being imposed on the programme adopted. We must by all means encourage "sympathetic whites" to stand firm in their fight but this must be away from us. In many ways this is dealt with adequately in an article that appears in the August SASO Newsletter, "Black Souls in White Skins." The fact that "sympathetic whites" have in the past made themselves the traditional pace-setters in the black man's struggle has led to the black man's taking a backseat in a struggle essentially his own. Hence excluding whites tends to activate black people and in the ultimate analysis gives proper direction to whatever is being done. This is a fact that overseas observers visiting the country find hard to accept but it remains very true. Racial prejudice in this country has gone beyond all proportions and has subconsciously affected the minds of some of the most well-known liberals.

Where are we today?

SASO stands today at a very important stage of its life. The establishment of the organisation has had a very great impact in three major directions.

Firstly we have created a mood on the black campuses, which has set the stage for a complete revision of thinking. Our "blacks only" attitude has infused a sense of pride and self-reliance on almost all black campuses. Where originally one met with stiff opposition to all exclusive talk, it is now generally accepted that blacks must go it alone. This attitude is welcome to us but has to be guided very carefully and steadily least it falls prey to some of the dangers we have already mentioned. It is hoped that we shall translate all the intellectual talk about "black is beautiful" into some kind of meaningful practical language.

Secondly we have given impetus to meaningful thinking outside the campus. Suddenly black people are beginning to appreciate the value of their own efforts, unpolluted by half-hearted support from the white world.

Though this kind of thinking is still limited to the black "intelligentsia" at present, there are all the signs that it will spread to the rest of the community.

Thirdly we have dealt an almost fatal blow at all black-white movements. One does not know whether to take pride in this or not, but definitely it is obvious that we have wasted a lot of valuable time in the so-called non-racial organisations trying to cheat ourselves into believing we were making progress while in fact by the very nature of these bodies we liquidated ourselves into inactivity. The more radical whites have in fact rejoiced at the emergence of SASO and some of them have even come up with useful support in terms of valuable contacts etc., but radical whites are very rare creatures in this country.

Our strength has been difficult to assess because of the battle we were waging for members. With the latest affiliations by Fort Hare and Ngoye we now stand in a position to get down to practical stuff.

Whither are we going?

At all costs we must make sure that we are marching to the same tune as the rest of the community. At no stage must we view ourselves as a group endowed with special characteristics. While we may be playing the tune, it is the rhythmic beating of the community's boots that spurs us to march on and at no stage should that rhythm be disturbed. As the group grows larger and more boots join the rhythmic march, let us not allow the beating of the boots to drown the pure tones of our tune for the tune is necessary and essential to the rhythm.

11. An emperor and his court.

There was no more famous autocrat in Africa than Haile Selassie ("Might of the Trinity") (1892–1975), born Tafari Makonnen at the end of the nineteenth century. Educated by French missionaries, he was considered representative of a new generation of Ethiopian leaders, determined to strengthen national independence (Ethiopia was the only African country—apart from the two states set up as refuges for freed slaves [Sierra Leone and Liberia]—to resist success-

fully European imperialism) by encouraging economic and political reform. He successfully negotiated Ethiopia's admission to the League of Nations in 1923 and traveled widely in Europe. Over time, however, he became more and more of an autocrat. Crowned emperor in 1930, he gave much of his attention to developing the power of Ethiopia's central government, aiming especially to concentrate power in his own hands. He gained even greater fame leading Ethiopia's unsuccessful resistance against the invasion by Italy in 1935 and returned a hero in 1941 when the British re-established him as emperor. Though viewed in the West as some sort of slightly romanticized and quaint African monarch, in Africa as one of the leading figures of the Organization of African Unity (OAU), and in the Americas as the symbolic head of the Rastafarian movement, Selassie's image was much less glowing in Ethiopia where he brooked no opposition. In particular, people complained of his aloofness, his reliance on a coterie of sycophants, and his refusal to improve the difficult economic and political conditions under which most Ethiopians lived.

Ryszard Kapúscínski, a Polish journalist, here paints a devastating portrait of the emperor, shuffling around his palace while listening constantly to stories brought to him by the spies that he had placed in every part of his domain. In this account, all the emperor cares about is his hold on power, and he will do whatever it takes to maintain that power. Yet autocracy had its limits. Though Haile Selassie ruled Ethiopia for almost half a century, his power waned in the 1970s in the face of famine and starvation. Marxist-inspired army officers mutinied in 1974 and placed him under arrest. He was dead within a year, either from natural causes as publicly reported or strangled by the coup leaders as rumored. The leader of the coup, Haile Mariam Mengistu, buried Selassie's body under his office floor so that his grave did not become a symbol of opposition to the new regime.[11]

The Emperor began his day by listening to informers' reports. The night breeds dangerous conspiracies, and Haile Selassie knew that what happens at night is more important than what happens during the day. During the day he kept his eye on everyone; at night that was impossible. For that reason, he attached great importance to the morning reports. And here I would like to make one thing clear: His Venerable Majesty was no reader. For him, neither the written nor the printed word existed; everything had to be relayed by word of mouth. His Majesty had had no schooling. His sole teacher—and that only during his childhood—was a French Jesuit, Monsignor Jerome, later Bishop of Harar and a friend of the poet Arthur Rimbaud. This cleric had no chance to inculcate the habit of reading in the Emperor, a task made all the more difficult, by the way, because Haile Selassie occupied responsible administrative positions from his boyhood and had no time for regular reading.

But I think there was more to it than a lack of time and habit. The custom of relating things by word of mouth had this advantage: if need be, the Emperor could say that a given dignitary had told him something quite different from what had really been said, and the latter could not defend himself, having no written proof. Thus the Emperor heard from his subordinates not what they told him, but what he thought should be said. His Venerable Highness had his ideas, and he would

---

11. Ryszard Kapúscínski, *The Emperor: Downfall of an Autocrat* (New York: Harcourt Brace Jovanovich, 1983), pp. 7–12. Reprinted with the permission of Harcourt Brace Jovanovich, Publishers.

adjust to them all the signals that came from his surroundings. It was the same with writing, for our monarch not only never used his ability to read, but he also never wrote anything and never signed anything in his own hand. Though he ruled for half a century, not even those closest to him knew what his signature looked like.

During the Emperor's hours of official functions, the Minister of the Pen always stood at hand and took down all the Emperor's orders and instructions. Let me say that during working audiences His Majesty spoke very softly, barely moving his lips. The Minister of the Pen, standing half a step from the throne, had to bend his ear close to the Imperial lips in order to hear and write down the Imperial decisions. Furthermore, the Emperor's words were usually unclear and ambiguous, especially when he did not want to take a definite stand on a matter that required his opinion. One had to admire the Emperor's dexterity. When asked by a dignitary for the Imperial decision, he would not answer straight out, but would rather speak in a voice so quiet that it reached only the Minister of the Pen, who moved his ear as close as a microphone. The minister transcribed his ruler's scant and foggy mutterings. All the rest was interpretation, and that was a matter for the minister, who passed down the decision in writing.

The Minister of the Pen was the Emperor's closest confidant and enjoyed enormous power. From the secret cabala of the monarch's words he could construct any decision that he wished. If a move by the Emperor dazzled everyone with its accuracy and wisdom, it was one more proof that God's Chosen One was infallible. On the other hand, if from some corner the breeze carried rumors of discontent to the monarch's ear, he could blame it all on the minister's stupidity. And so the minister was the most hated personality in the court. Public opinion, convinced of His Venerable Highness's wisdom and goodness, blamed the minister for any thoughtless or malicious decisions, of which there were many. True, the servants whispered about why Haile Selassie didn't replace

the minister, but in the Palace questions were always asked from top to bottom, and never vice versa. When the first question was asked in a direction opposite to the customary one, it was a signal that the revolution had begun.

But I'm getting ahead of myself and must go back to the moment when the Emperor appears on the Palace steps in the morning and sets out for his early walk. He enters the park. This is when Solomon Kedir, the head of the Palace spies, approaches and gives his report. The Emperor walks along the avenue and Kedir stays a step behind him, talking all the while. Who met whom, where, and what they talked about. Against whom they are forming alliances. Whether or not one could call it a conspiracy. Kedir also reports on the work of the military cryptography department. This department, part of Kedir's office, decodes the communications that pass among the divisions; it's good to be sure that no subversive thoughts are hatching there. His Distinguished Highness asks no questions, makes no comments. He walks and listens. Sometimes he stops before the lions' cage to throw them a leg of veal that a servant has handed to him. He watches the lions' rapacity and smiles. Then he approaches the leopards, which are chained, and gives them ribs of beef. His Majesty has to be careful as he approaches the unpredictable beasts of prey. Finally he moves on, with Kedir behind continuing his report. At a certain moment His Highness bows his head, which is a signal for Kedir to move away. He bows and disappears down the avenue, never turning his back on the Emperor.

At this moment the waiting Minister of Industry and Commerce, Makonen Habte-Wald, emerges from behind a tree. He falls in, a step behind the Emperor, and delivers his report. Makonen Habte-Wald keeps his own network of informers, both to satisfy a consuming passion for intrigue and to ingratiate himself with His Venerable Highness. On the basis of his information, he now briefs the Emperor on what happened last night. Again, His Majesty walks on, listening without questions or comments, keeping his hands behind his back. He approaches a flock of flamingos, but the shy birds scatter when he comes near. The Emperor smiles at the sight of creatures that refuse to obey him. At last, still walking, he nods his head; Habte-Wald falls silent and retreats backward, disappearing down the avenue.

Next, as if springing up from the ground, rises the hunched silhouette of the devoted confidant Asha WaldeMikael. This dignitary supervises the government political police. He competes with Solomon Kedir's Palace intelligence service and battles fiercely against private informer networks like the one that Makonen Habte-Wald has at his disposal.

The occupation to which these people devoted themselves was hard and dangerous. They lived in fear of not reporting something in time and falling into disgrace, or of a competitor's reporting it better so that the Emperor would think, "Why did Solomon give me a feast today and Makonen only bring me leftovers? Did he say nothing because he didn't know, or did he hold his tongue because he belongs to the conspiracy?" Hadn't His Distinguished Highness often experienced, at cost to himself, betrayal by his most trusted allies? That's why the Emperor punished silence. On the other hand, incoherent streams of words tired and irritated the Imperial ear, so nervous loquaciousness was also a poor solution. Even the way these people looked told of the threat under which they lived. Tired, looking as if they hadn't slept, they acted under feverish stress, pursuing their victims in the stale air of hatred and fear that surrounded them all: They had no shield but the Emperor, and the Emperor could undo them with one wave of his hand. No, His Benevolent Majesty did not make their lives easy.

As I've mentioned, Haile Selassie never commented on or questioned the reports he received, during his morning walks, about the state of conspiracy in the Empire. But he knew what he was doing, as I shall show you. His Highness wanted to receive the reports in a pure state, because if he asked questions or expressed opinions the informant would obligingly adjust his report to meet the Emperor's expectations. Then the whole system of informing would collapse into subjectivity and fall prey to anyone's willfulness. The monarch would not know what was going on in the country and the Palace.

Finishing his walk, the Emperor listens to what was reported last night by Asha's people. He feeds the dogs and the black panther, and then he admires the anteater that he recently received as a gift from the president of Uganda. He nods his head and Asha walks away, bent over, wondering whether he said more or less than what was reported by his most fervent enemies: Solomon, the enemy of Makonen and Asha; and Makonen, the enemy of Asha and Solomon.

Haile Selassie finishes his walk alone. It grows light in the park; the fog thins out, and reflected sunlight glimmers on the lawns. The Emperor ponders. Now is the time to lay out strategies and tactics, to solve the puzzles of personality, to plan his next move on the chessboard of power. He thinks deeply about what was contained in the informants' reports. Little of importance; they usually report on each other. His Majesty has made mental notes of everything. His mind is a computer that retains every detail; even the smallest datum will be remembered. There was no personnel office in the Palace, no dossiers full of personal information. All this the Emperor carried in his mind, all the most important files about the elite. I see him now as he walks, stops, walks again, lifts his head upward as though absorbed in prayer. O God, save me from those who, crawling on their knees, hide a knife that they would like to sink into my back. But how can God help? All the people surrounding the Emperor are just like that, on their knees, and with knives. It's never comfortable on the summits. An icy wind always blows, and everyone crouches, watchful lest his neighbor hurl him down the precipice.

12. Who will start another fire?

Many of the first-generation leaders of independent African nations did not take criticism very well. They tended to be autocratic, paranoid about any form of criticism, and violently opposed to losing their positions of power. Some declared themselves presidents-for-life, and one named himself an emperor. Freedom of speech was rare in independent Africa, rare especially for writers who pointed out the shortcomings of those who governed the new states. Malawi, where John Chilembwe (Part 3, document 2) had led his revolt against British colonialism and which had been ruled since independence by Hastings Kamuzu Banda, was one of the most restrictive states when it came to such criticism. Banda had spent much of his life as a medical doctor in Britain, but he returned home to become Malawi's first prime minister in 1964. Over time, he became increasingly dictatorial, naming himself President-for-Life, banning opposition parties, and arresting anyone who spoke against his regime. One of Banda's most eloquent critics was Jack Mapanje who sought in verse "a way of preserving sanity" in an otherwise oppressively insane society. In "Before Chilembwe Tree," Mapanje looks to the great martyr figure as a model for resistance to repression and wonders who will take up the call. Because of this poem, and other scathing depictions of corruption and self-seeking in independent Malawi, Banda banned Mapanje's volume of poems and imprisoned the author.[12]

Before Chilembwe Tree

1

Didn't you say we should trace
 your footprints unmindful of
quagmires, thickets and rivers
until we reached your *nsolo* tree?
Now, here I seat my gourd of beer
on my little fire throw my millet
flour and my smoked meat
while I await the second coming.

2

Why does your mind boggle:
Who will offer another gourd
Who will force another step
To hide our shame?

The goat blood on the rocks
The smoke that issued
The drums you danced to
And the rains hoped for-

You've chanted yourselves hoarse
Chilembwe is gone in your dust
Stop lingering then:
Who will start another fire?

13. The fate of political dissidents.

The methods that Africa's new dictators used to silence their critics were often brutal. One of the favored treatments was to "detain" people as political prisoners, though without ever calling them such—for that implied a lack of re-

---

12. Jack Mapanje, *Of Chameleons and Gods* (London: Heinemann, 1981), pp. 18–19. Reprinted with the permission of Heinemann Educational Publishers, a division of Reed Educational & Professional Publishing Ltd.

spect for freedom of speech—and keep them in prison for an indefinite period. What one had to do to earn this punishment was usually arbitrary; one could even be a party supporter and be detained if the leader was concerned about losing his power base. President-for-Life Hastings Kamuzu Banda of Malawi threw numerous people into prison for views that they expressed and, as the case below shows, for those that they did not necessarily espouse. Sam Mpasu, currently a member of parliament, was imprisoned by Banda in 1975. Mpasu was a civil servant at the time, working on a major financial project for the government, when members of the Special Branch escorted him from his work-place to Mikuyu Maximum Security Prison where he remained for two years, even though he was never formally charged or brought to trial. This extract relates the ordeals that Sam Mpasu went through as a political prisoner. It also captures well the precarious nature of existence for members of Africa's post-colonial elite, who could often find themselves either prisoner or warder with-out any apparent action on their own part.[13]

The interrogation of Sam Mpasu.

When the large, metal door of Zomba Central Prison closed with a bang behind me, I came face to face with the prison warders. They seemed too busy to attend to me so I sat down on a form. It seemed to me that good manners were out of place.

"Sit down on the floor!" one of them shouted at me very angrily. "A prisoner does not sit on a chair!" he added.

It did not make sense to me that I should sit down on the floor while there were unoccupied chairs in the office. Nevertheless, although dressed in a suit, I sat down on the floor. I was simmering with rage at my humiliation and helplessness.

At last one of them took out a blank, red folder and started to take down my personal details of name, village, date of birth, next of kin and so forth. Then I was ordered to empty all my pockets, take off my wrist-watch and wedding-ring. I surrendered all to him. Then he demanded my tie, belt, shoes and socks as well. He shoved all of these into a cloth bag which he tossed at the corner of the office. He was through with me.

I was taken out of the administration block into the courtyard. We immediately turned right. The next block served as a clinic on top but underneath were three cells. The prison warder opened the middle cell and pushed me in. He closed the door and bolted it from outside. It was a bare, empty cell. A few minutes later, the door opened again. The guard tossed an old threadbare blanket at me. I caught it with my hands before it could fall on the floor. He looked at me with contempt as if I was not worth speaking to. As far as he was concerned, I was probably less than human or an animal.

He walked away without saying a word. His colleague, who carried a gun, closed the door and then stood guard outside. He used a peep-hole to check on me regularly. I wondered if they would spare the life of that warder if by any chance I escaped. It seemed to me that they, too, were prisoners of a sort. They had to do what they were doing even if they hated it.

The thought of escape was utterly unrealistic. The walls were very thick. The door itself was thick and made of hardwood. There was a tiny window at the top but it was full of thick, steel bars. Besides, the window itself was so high that one would need a ladder to reach it. And it was on the same side where the guard stood. The ceiling was the concrete floor of the upper storey. There was no lighting. Digging the floor was impossible with bare hands. It was concrete.

---

13. Sam Mpasu, *Political Prisoner 3/75* (Harare, Zimbabwe: African Publishing Group, 1995), pp. 30–40.

My threadbare blanket was more than a blanket. It was a bed, a mattress, a bedsheet and a blanket, all rolled into one. It was the only thing between me and the bare concrete floor. I was so bewildered that I could not believe or understand what was happening to me. Luckily, the weather in January was fairly warm, but I dreaded what it was like in June when the temperatures dropped.

I spread the blanket on the bare floor. I lay down. I folded my jacket to use it as a pillow. I blinked wide awake for a good part of the night wondering what was happening to me. I was very worried about my wife and her delicate condition. I had not eaten anything the whole day yet they had locked me up for the night without giving me a glass of water or a morsel of food.

It was a long, long night. Morning broke in the end. I heard the sound of keys in the padlock and then the bolt being pulled back. The door was opened to check if I was still in. For some strange reason they kept the door open this time. Later on they allowed me to step outside if I wanted to, but not much farther than the doorstep. The armed guard was trying to be friendly as soon as he ensured that none of his colleagues was looking at him. I sat on the doorstep.

"Is it possible for me to go to the toilet, wherever it is?" I asked him.

"Let us go. I will escort you," he replied. "But you must not speak with anyone."

With his gun on the shoulder he came behind me. He stood by as I faced the urinal. The thought of walking barefoot in that busy toilet, which was hardly clean, filled me with fear about contracting all sorts of diseases.

On return to my cell we found an old prisoner with a wizened, weather-beaten face and a head which was entirely covered with grey hair, waiting for me. He had brought me an old, badly dented, aluminium plate, half-full of porridge. He looked at me with understanding. He shook his head in dismay.

"Eat!" he said. "Prison food is not anything like home food, but that is the only way to stay alive here."

"Where is the spoon and the sugar?" I asked him in all sincerity.

"Sugar and a spoon, in prison?" he asked me, in total disbelief over my naivety.

He laughed a little. He then demonstrated how I could eat the porridge. Eating on a table while sitting on a chair was a luxury that was not available. I sat on the floor.

I lifted the plate to my lips with both hands. I sucked the porridge into my mouth a little at a time. He watched me excitedly as if he was watching a child who was beginning to walk. He displayed a big smile after I had finished.

"Do not be disheartened, this is what men must sometimes go through in life," he told me encouragingly.

"Why am I not allowed to speak to you or to anyone?" I asked.

"That is nonsense. Do not bother about them," he said nonchalantly. "They are trying to intimidate you."

I was really glad to have someone to talk to. At least someone who was not afraid of the arbitrary rules. Apparently, they had appointed him to look after me as a way of preventing me from meeting the other prisoners. He brought me food from the kitchen every day and took back the plate. They did not want me to move away from my cell.

"What are you in prison for?" I asked him. "Theft," he said quite happily, as if theft was something to be proud of.

"How long have you been here and when are you getting released?" I asked him again.

He laughed a bellyful.

"You see," he said, "they built this prison in 1938 and that was the first time I came in. I built it. I have been here ever since."

This was 1975. I could not believe that the man had been in this horrible place for 37 years.

"Are you here for murder perhaps?" I asked him.

"No, no. The only crime I know is theft," he replied honestly.

"You see, when they first locked me up, I was young. After my sentence I went home but I felt out of place. I had no family and no friends. They all felt ashamed of me. They kept away from me. So I stole again in order to come back. This is my home now. I will die here. Whenever my sentence is over, I reserve my place in the cell. I get back the same day. All I do is pick somebody's pocket at the bus station in full view of a policeman. Sometimes I just snatch a banana from a baby's hand and if it cries then that is it; I run a little to allow the people to catch me. When they take me to the police station, I know I am back in prison. The only regret I have is that such small thefts do not get me many years of imprisonment," he said with a straight face.

I could not believe what this old man was saying. One day in that place was too long for me. Yet he wanted to spend the rest of his life there.

"When they let you out, why don't you get a job?" I asked him.

"And look after myself?" he asked me as an answer. Then he laughed. "I tried that once but got bored with waiting for my pay-day. I stole my employer's wrist-watch in order to come back here."

"Don't you feel like having a wife and children? Having a family you can really be proud of?" I asked him.

"What can I give to a family?" he replied.

I got the impression that life had no real meaning to the man. His permanent stay in prison was all that life meant to him.

He disappeared at two o'clock in the afternoon and brought me a plate of badly cooked *nsima* and a metal mug half-full of badly cooked pigeon peas. That was both my lunch and dinner. The food was very unpalatable, but he encouraged me to eat it in order to preserve my life. At four o'clock in the afternoon I was ordered back into my cell. The door was bolted from outside and locked.

When they opened my cell again in the morning I was surprised to see a white man sitting on the doorsteps of the next cell. He, too, was completely bewildered. I gathered a little bit of courage to defy the orders. I greeted the white man in the presence of the prison guard. We got talking. The guard ignored us. The only thing the white man could not stomach was the terrible food. He refused to touch it. He told them that he was prepared to die from starvation. They buckled down and brought him half a loaf of bread

and a small can of sardines. His problem was how to eat that bounty without the aid of a table knife, a fork or a spoon. But he soon overcame that by using his unwashed fingers.

Apparently his crime was that he had made some remarks about the political situation in the country when one of his employees was picked up by the Special Branch. Without checking out the veracity of the allegation he was pulled out of his car and rushed to Zomba prison in a police car. That was his arrest, trial, conviction and sentence. That morning he was making a great deal of fuss about the need to see his ambassador urgently. He was a South African and a General Manager of a company in Blantyre. In the afternoon his ambassador, accompanied by his wife, arrived to see him. Later in the evening the police came to take him out. I learnt that he was deported out of the country on twenty-four hours' notice.

On Friday morning, I was on my way to the common toilet when a sick man called my name out from the balcony of the upper storey which served as a clinic.

"Hey Sam, it's me, Richard. Richard Sembereka!" The name did not fit the appearance of the man. I was horrified with what I saw. I had known Richard Sembereka for many years. The last time I had seen him he was the Minister of Labour, a plump and well-dressed man. That was several years before but here was a pathetic-looking skeleton of a man, completely disfigured and destroyed by his long imprisonment. My eyes welled up with tears as I desperately tried to take in the entire picture. The unanswered question I asked myself in my mind was, if this cruel and beastly government could do that to its own Cabinet Minister, then how much more would it do to me, a humble civil servant.

According to the story which circulated at the time Mr. Richard Sembereka disappeared, he had been driving in his ministerial black Mercedes Benz car from Zomba to Blantyre, with the pennant flying on the bonnet, when the police stopped the car at a roadblock. Without much ceremony the police pulled him out of the ministerial car and shoved him into a waiting police vehicle. He was then driven straight to Zomba prison for his long, indefinite imprisonment without charge or trial. Five or so years on, he had been reduced to this pathetic skeleton in front of my eyes. I think he saw the distress in my eyes and read my mind.

"Steel yourself up," he said, "it is a very tough world!"

I waved my hand feebly at him, but the prison guard pushed me on. We continued to the public toilet.

On return from the toilet, I was called out to the administration block. Charles Ngwata had come for me. I was led out of the prison to a waiting small van. I was told to go into the back of that van. He closed the door from outside and turned to join the driver in the cab. There were no seats in the van. I sat on the floor.

On arrival at Zomba Police Headquarters, I was led to the Special Branch offices which were in a two-storey block on its own. We climbed stairs to the upper storey where the office of Focus Gwede was. He was not in. I was made to wait in an adjoining office. What I immediately noticed was the atmosphere of fear and trepidation which pervaded the whole place. The policemen could not even mention the name of Focus Gwede but referred to him reverently as "Bwana." He was obviously something of a small god around there. On the grass lawn outside sat small groups of men, women and children, waiting fearfully for this small god to give them permits to visit their relatives in Zomba and Mikuyu prisons.

Focus Gwede was Deputy Head of the Special Branch at the time but he behaved very much as if he owned the place entirely. His close association with Albert Muwalo, who was both the Secretary General and Administrative Secretary of the Malawi Congress Party, ensured that he wielded a lot of power. Mr. Muwalo was virtually Home Affairs Minister, although none of that was reflected in his job title. Pretty soon, the Head of the Special Branch, Mr. Kumpukwe, was appointed into the Diplomatic Service and posted to Britain. Focus Gwede then formally took over as Head of the Special Branch.

A poor messenger was getting out of Gwede's office where he had gone to leave files. He was spotted by none other than Gwede himself. Gwede came up the stairs seething and trembling with rage. He went straight for the poor messenger. Gwede repeatedly and threateningly jabbed his right-hand forefinger on the messenger's chest.

"You do not enter my office when I am not there! Do you understand?" shouted Gwede repeatedly in his rage.

"Yes Sir! No Sir! I am sorry Sir! I will not do it again Sir!" whined the poor messenger subserviently.

He was expecting the whole world to explode in his face any moment.

I watched the whole incident with disgust. I do not know if the incident was stage-managed by Gwede for effect on me and the others. If it was, then it certainly lowered my opinion of Gwede in my mind. I had known Gwede before for some years. I had never known him or even imagined him to be such a mean-spirited terror. If a messenger in full police uniform could not enter Gwede's office, then why on earth was the office left open and why didn't Gwede clean his own office?

Anyway, Gwede cooled down. The poor messenger gratefully walked away, thankful that his explanations and apologies had been accepted. The fact that he had been humiliated in public counted for nothing. I could not understand why he did not stand up for his own human dignity and tell Gwede to piss off. Maybe the job meant much to him or maybe he could have been locked up summarily as well.

It was my turn. Gwede sat me on a chair in his office, opposite his. Between us was his large wooden desk. The desk was totally bare except for an old tape recorder and a horse-whip. Charles Ngwata sat on another chair but on Gwede's side.

"Yes, my friend! Why are you here?" Gwede asked me.

"You called for me," I replied.

He then pulled out the drawer of the desk and laid a sheath of blank paper on the desk. He pulled out another drawer, pulled out a revolver for me to see and then put it back. From his jacket he pulled out a Bic pen and got himself ready to write.

"Who appointed you to go into the Diplomatic Service?" he bellowed at me.

"You should know!" I said to him.

"I am asking you!" he retorted angrily.

"Listen," I said, "I never applied for the job. Nobody applies for that kind of job. I was just told that the President had appointed me to go into the Diplomatic Service. How the hell would I know who had recommended my name?"

Gwede tore up whatever he had been writing and tossed the pieces of paper into a waste-paper basket by his side.

"Alright, let us start again," he said getting another blank sheet of paper ready.

"Who did you meet while you were in the Diplomatic Service?" he asked.

I really thought it was an asinine question.

"You meet and see thousands of people everyday. And you ask me who I met in a period of over two years?" I replied.

"Okay, did you meet any of the rebels?" he asked me.

"Look," I said, "even if I met any of them now, I could not recognize them. I saw both Mr. Kanyama Chiume and Mr. Henry Chipembere, here on Malawi soil, when I was a young boy in secondary school and they were cabinet ministers."

"We know that. If you had met any of them we would have known immediately," replied Gwede boastfully.

"So, why did you ask me?" I said angrily as I stood up.

I leaned on his desk with my left hand and attempted to reach out for his shirt-collar with my right hand. Gun or no gun, I was going to punch his face. He drew back out of my reach.

"Alright, let us start again," he said when he realised that my temper was not as long as he thought it was. "Sit down. Do you want a cup of coffee?" he asked.

"I do not want your coffee!" I replied as I sat down.

He tore up the piece of paper he had been scribbling on and threw the bits into the waste-paper basket again.

"You came back from the Diplomatic Service over a year ago. Why were you still using a diplomatic passport? We found a diplomatic passport in your house!" he started again.

"Every time I go out of the country or come in, I pass through the Immigration. Are you suggesting that the Immigration Officers of Malawi do not recognize a Malawi diplomatic passport?" I asked him.

"Answer the question!" he demanded.

"For your information, I went to the Immigration Office immediately after my return from the Diplomatic Service. I gave them my diplomatic passport and asked for my ordinary passport, but they refused. They said that I should hang on to my diplomatic passport because they are wasting a lot of money. They exchange an ordinary passport for a diplomatic passport and a few months later the same person is appointed into the diplomatic service again. Ask them! Ring them now!" I said to him.

Gwede tore up the sheet he had been writing on and threw the pieces into the waste-paper basket.

"Alright, let us begin again," he said. "You wrote a book about the President. You said that he has no friends."

"Have you read the book?" I asked him.

"Answer me!" he demanded.

"*Nobody's Friend* is the title of the small novel I wrote. It has absolutely nothing to do with Dr. Banda or anyone else. It is a book about ordinary people. It is fiction. You should have read it," I told him.

"But there is a passage about a president being assassinated in that book," he said triumphantly.

"That is rubbish!" I said. "Have you read Hamlet, Macbeth or King Lear, all by William Shakespeare? There are passages in all those books about Kings being assassinated. Have you banned those books because they mention the assassination of Kings? Have you banned the Holy Bible because it mentions that Jesus was killed?"

"Let us begin again," Gwede said as he tore up the sheet of paper he had been writing on. He threw the pieces into the waste-paper basket. This time he did not bother to write again.

"Listen to me, my friend! You are finished, finished, finished! I am the last word on detention in Malawi. No one else is above me. As you sit there I have three options for you. Firstly, I can release you now. Yes, you can go home to your wife and back to your job. Secondly, I can take you to court for trial where you will get many years of imprisonment. Lastly, I can send you to Mikuyu Maximum Security Prison, without trial, where you will count the hair on your head. You will never come out. I have decided to send you to Mikuyu where others like you are rotting," he said chillingly. "As long as I sit on this chair, you will never come out. You will rot there!"

He said all this emphatically as he banged the top of the desk with his right-hand fist. I looked at him very defiantly.

"Gwede," I said, "last year, you were not sitting on that chair. Next year, you do not know if you will still be sitting on that chair.

Only the Almighty God knows. If God has made it for me to live the rest of my life and die in Mikuyu prison, so be it. It is not you who has done it. You are just an instrument used by God. But I assure you that if God has not made it for me to die in Mikuyu, I shall come out alive and well. And much earlier than you think."

What I said unnerved him a bit. He had played his last card. He had failed to reduce me to a cowering, tearful coward, crying for mercy at his feet. The degree of my defiance shook his self-confidence thoroughly.

"You go for lunch. We shall meet again this afternoon," he said to me as he terminated the interrogation.

Charles Ngwata took me outside. Gwede closed the door of his office. A police constable brought me a plate of rice and red beans. What was strange was that they gave me a spoon as well. That was on Friday, 25 January 1975. My interrogation had taken Gwede's entire morning.

14. The rebellion begins, South Africa, June 1976.

A major turning point occurred in South African history on Wednesday, June 16, 1976, when armed police in Soweto fired on a peaceful demonstration of school children. The children were participating in a march to protest the recently decreed Bantu Education amendment requiring African schools to teach much of their curriculum in Afrikaans, viewed by most Africans as the language of their oppressors. They were also protesting the continued implementation of apartheid, then a three-decade old policy and one that had long come to be viewed (other than in the public pronouncements of its proponents) as impossible—in its theoretical goal of total racial separation—to achieve. The police shooting, reminiscent of the killing of protestors at Sharpeville a decade and a half earlier, led to international outrage and alerted the world to the tragedy of racism in South Africa. More importantly, it galvanized another generation of young people in South Africa (much like World War II had influenced Nelson Mandela's generation—see Part 3, documents 19, 20, 21, 22, 23, 25, 26) to resist with physical force the violence of the apartheid state.

Mark Mathabane was born in 1961 and raised in Alexandra township, a teeming ghetto that supplied cheap labor for white industries near Johannesburg. His parents came from different ethnic groups, but his life was quite disconnected from the rural base of either culture. He was very much a product of the township. In this selection from his hugely popular book, Kaffir Boy, *Mathabane describes the events that took place in Alexandra as people heard of the massacre in Soweto. In particular, he captures the process by which mass protest developed in a situation in which all the prominent leaders of African resistance (such as Nelson Mandela, Steve Biko, and others) were either in prison or forced into exile. Revolution did not need to be led; it could take off from the massive discontent of the people.* [14]

No one thought it would happen, yet everyone knew it had to happen. All the hate, bitterness, frustration and anger that had crystallized into a powder keg in the minds of black students, waiting for a single, igniting spark, found that spark when the Department of Bantu Education suddenly decreed that all black schools had to teach courses in Afrikaans instead of English.

The first spontaneous explosion took place in Soweto on the afternoon of Wednesday, June 16, 1976, where about ten thousand students marched through the dirt streets of Soweto protesting the Afrikaans decree. The immense crowd was orderly and peaceful, and included six- and seven-year-olds, chanting along with older students, who waved placards reading: To Hell with Afrikaans, We Don't Want to Learn the Language of Our Oppressors, Stop Feeding Us a Poisonous Education and We Want Equal Education Not Slave Education.

Unknown to the marchers, along one of the streets leading to Phefeni High School, where a protest rally was to be held, hundreds of policemen, armed with tear gas canisters, rifles, shotguns and sjamboks, had formed a barricade across the street. When they reached the barricaded street the marchers stopped, but continued waving placards and chanting:

"AMANDLA! AWETHU! AMANDLA! AWETHU! (POWER IS OURS! POWER IS OURS!)"

While student leaders argued about what to do to diffuse the situation, the police suddenly opened fire. Momentarily the crowd stood dazed, thinking that the bullets were plastic and had been fired into the air. But when several small children began dropping down like swatted flies, their white uniforms soaked in red blood, pandemonium broke out.

The police continued firing into the crowd. Students fled into houses alongside the street; others tripped, fell and were trampled underfoot. Some were so shocked they didn't know what to do except scream and cry. Still others fought bullets with rocks and schoolbags. One youth saw a thirteen-year-old go down, a bullet having shattered his forehead. He picked the dying boy up, and carried him to a yard nearby. The photo of the two—the lifeless boy in the hands of a youth whose face blazed with anger, hate and defiance—made headlines around the world.

In the school bus from Tembisa, reading the gruesome accounts of what took place in Soweto in the late afternoon edition of the *World*, I felt hate and anger well up inside me. I cried. The entire edition of the *World* was devoted to the story. One of the pictures of the carnage showed a hacked white policeman near an overturned, burnt police car, surrounded by groups of students shouting defiant slogans, fists upraised in the black power salute. I gloated, and wished that more white people had been killed.

The bus was packed, yet silent. Heads were buried inside newspapers. Tears flowed freely down the cheeks of youths returning from school, and men and women returning from work. I again looked at the photo of the two boys, and then and there I knew that my life would never, could never, be the same again.

"They opened fire," mumbled David, who was sitting alongside me, shaking his head with disbelief. "They didn't give any warning. They simply opened fire. Just like that. Just like that," he repeated. "And small children, small defenseless children, dropped

---

14. Mark Mathabane, *Kaffir Boy: Growing Out of Apartheid* (London: Pan Books, 1986), pp. 259–68.

down like swatted flies. This is murder, cold-blooded murder."

There was nothing I could say in reply, except stare back. No words could possibly express what I felt. No words could express the hatred I felt for the white race.

"This is the beginning of something too ugly to contemplate," David said. "Our lives can, and should, never be the same after this."

I nodded.

At school assembly the next day, the mood was somber. There was tension in the air. There was a fire, a determination, in students that I had never seen before. The first thing the principal said was, "I guess you've all heard about the tragedy that took place in Soweto yesterday."

"Yes," the crowd of students roared.

"It is indeed a dark moment in our lives," the principal said. "But we here have to go on learning. The government has ordered all other schools to stay open. I'm sure things will settle down and will return to normal soon."

A murmur of disapproval surged through the crowd. One student in the back row shouted, "There can be no school while our brothers and sisters are being murdered in Soweto!"

"Yes, yes, no school, no school!" erupted the rest of the students.

"There will be no demonstrations in this school," the principal said authoritatively. "We've had enough bloodshed in Soweto already."

"The struggle in Soweto is our struggle too," some students clamored. "The Afrikaans decree applies to us as well. We too want an equal education. The bloody Boers should stop force-feeding us slave education. To hell with Afrikaans! To hell with Afrikaans!" The cry infected everybody. Students began organizing into groups to plot strategy for a peaceful rally in solidarity with our brothers and sisters in Soweto. The principal tried to restore order but was ignored. Most teachers helped us with the planning of the rally. "Be peaceful and orderly," one teacher said, "or else you'll have the whole Boer army down your necks in no time."

We painted placards that condemned Bantu Education, Afrikaans and apartheid. We demanded an equal education with whites. We urged the government to stop the killings in Soweto. Student leaders were chosen to lead the march to other schools in the area, where we planned to pick up more students for a rally at a nearby stadium. Within an hour we had filled the street and formed columns. We began marching.

"AMANDLA! AWETHU! AMANDLA! AWETHU!" we chanted and waved placards.

From government buildings nearby white people who headed the Tembisa city councils hurriedly stepped out, jumped into cars and zoomed off under police escort. Our ranks swelled with youths who didn't attend school. Black men and women cheered and exhorted us from yards alongside the streets. "TO HELL WITH A FOURTH-CLASS EDUCATION!" "STOP THE GENOCIDE IN SOWETO!" "AMANDLA! AWETHU! AMANDLA! AWETHU!" The cries reverberated through the air.

We picked up hundreds of students from other schools and then headed for the stadium. As the river of black faces coursed through the street leading to the stadium, a group of police vans and trucks suddenly appeared from nowhere and barricaded the street.

"Don't panic! Don't panic!" the student leaders yelled at the restless crowd. "Let's remain peaceful and orderly. They'll leave us alone if we don't provoke them."

Policemen with riot gear, rifles, tear gas canisters and sjamboks poured out of the trucks and formed a phalanx across the wide street. As in Soweto, most of them were black. From one of the trucks the husky voice of a white man suddenly boomed through a megaphone: "DISPERSE AND RETURN TO YOUR HOMES AND SCHOOLS! OR WE'LL BE FORCED TO USE FORCE!"

A few students started turning back, but the majority stood and waited, chanting defiantly with fists raised in the black power salute. We began singing, *Nkosi Sikelel'i Afrika* ("God Bless Africa"), the ANC's anthem:

God bless Africa
Raise up our descendants
Hear our prayers.
Come, holy spirit,
Come, holy spirit,
Lord bless us,
Us, your children.

The police charged. Several shots rang out. Pandemonium broke out. Students fled for cover. It rained tear gas canisters. David and I managed to flee into one of the nearby yards, jumped its fence and ran all the way to school, where teachers told us to go home immediately, for police were raiding schools. The bus stop was a mile or so away. As we made our way through the matchbox-type Tembisa houses, we saw fires and palls of black smoke in the distance. Some beer halls and vehicles had been gutted.

"I hope there's still a bus out of this place," David panted.

We found what turned out to be one of the last buses out of Tembisa, for the police were quarantining the ghetto, barring all company vehicles and public transportation. On our way to Alexandra there was unusual traffic on the highway leading to the Jan Smuts Airport.

"White folks are fleeing by the droves," I remarked.

"They're afraid this whole thing may turn into a revolution," David replied.

Approaching Alexandra, we saw several armoured cars formed into roadblocks, sealing all the roads leading in and out of Alexandra. All vehicles were being stopped and searched. Our bus was stopped, and several soldiers in camouflage uniforms, carrying automatic weapons, ordered us out and lined us up alongside the body of the bus. I shook like a leaf. In the distance, Alexandra resembled a battlefield. Smoke and fire engulfed the area, and from time to time, the sound of gunfire reverberated through the clouds of smoke.

"You'll have to walk home," one of the white soldiers ordered us. "Buses can't go in there. You bloody Kaffirs are burning down everything."

We immediately headed homeward across the veld. From time to time, people glanced nervously over their shoulders, afraid of being shot in the back. When David and I entered Alexandra, we saw several burning government buildings, beer halls, schools, stores belonging to Indians and Chinamen. A bus had been overturned and set afire. People were looting all around, making off with drums of paraffin, bags of mealie meal, carcasses of beef still dripping blood, Primus stoves, boxes of canned goods, loaves of bread and so on. There were power and energy in men, women and children that I had never seen before.

The rebellion had begun in Alexandra.

15. Torture under apartheid.

Fearful of the challenge to white rule, the apartheid regime embarked on a massive campaign to crush the protest movement that had begun in Soweto on June 16, 1976, and that soon expanded enormously throughout the rest of South Africa. Over the course of the following six to nine months, the police arrested at least 6,000 people, "detained" thousands more under the Terrorism Act (which permitted detention without charge, trial, or even the informing of the next of kin that an individual had been detained), and killed at least 700 individuals, the great majority of them under the age of 25. One of the protestors arrested was Dan Montsisi, then a teenager, who, in testimony that he was finally able to give in public in 1996, describes the torture to which he was subjected by the police two decades earlier. Montsisi and his generation emerged from their ordeals even more committed to the struggle to end apartheid. Many sought refuge overseas and became soldiers in a renewed armed struggle that the African National Congress (ANC) embarked upon in the late 1970s and the 1980s. In 1994, when South Africa elected its first post-apartheid government, Montsisi won a seat in the new parliament as a representative of the ANC. The white electorate for its part also hardened in its attitudes. In the 1977 parliamentary election, the National Party returned to power with its largest number of seats ever, supported by an overwhelming majority of both Afrikaans and English-speaking white voters. The white electorate continued to return the National Party to power throughout the 1980s.[15]

Mr. Montsisi: Ja [yes] I was subjected to torture. I was not the only one. It was quite a number of us and I have spoken to some of the officials about that issue. I mean like I said about the detention we got detained on the 10th in 1977. They started quite early. Probably they were eager; on the 13th June we were taken to Protea Police Station where the torture actually started, and the type of questions they asked obviously they wanted to know if we are working for the ANC, and they wanted Paul Langa. They arrested Paul before me, so what they wanted to do was that I must testify and say that Paul did all these things and so on and so on. At that time I didn't know Paul, I mean that's what I said to them. So they were quite angry. They asked about Winnie Mandela, whether I have been to Winnie Mandela's place. And they asked also about activities in the demonstration, where I participated. I tried to cooperate with them concerning student activities because I was a student and even those demonstrations where I did not go I said I did, those meetings where students were, where I was not even there, I said I did, simply because I did not want them to press me on other issues. I was not a member of the suicide squad. I knew about the suicide squad but I denied it. So well they got fed up with me and they actually began in a sense, so there was this trolley and Van Roy, those who fetched me from John Vorster Square and we drove down to Protea Police Station, and they used the rubber truncheon to beat you all over the head and it was quite difficult because I was blindfolded and I couldn't see the direction from which the truncheon was coming from, so it was quite easy for them. It went on for quite some time. And then you could also be kicked and beaten with fists, stomach and so on. And there was also one other method they used, the rifle. They used the rifle to stamp on your toes. So every time you talk what they do not agree with they use the rifle on your toes. And one method they referred to as an airplane, I didn't know what they were talking about, but I was grabbed and they swung me and they threw me right into the air but when you land, fortunately it was a wooden floor so they did that several times. All along I mean they were like laughing and so on and so on, ridicule you and so on. And they were pulling the muscles on the back to put a strain on you so they come from behind and they pull the muscles with their own hands. And so they also forced me to squat. That time I was quite weak and I didn't have much power left in me. I could have collapsed any time but they still continued, so I had to squat against the wall and a brick was placed on my hands as I squatted against the wall. I don't know what happened because I think the brick fell and it hit me on the head and when I regained consciousness they had poured water all over me. So the first person I saw looking down at me was Visser, Captain Visser from Protea Police Station. So all I said to him when I saw him was that "Baas they are killing me," that is what I said to him. And I never thought I would say "baas" but I did. So they explained to him that—they used very strong language . . . so they were going to continue. That

---

15. The full transcript of Dan Montsisi's testimony to the Truth and Reconciliation Commission is available at <www.truth.org.za/hrvtrans/Soweto/Montsisi.htm>. Accessed June 1, 2000.

time they had removed the blindfold and he left the room, and then as soon as he left I could see the people who were instrumental in the torture. Although there were something like eight policemen inside there were two others Trollip and Van Rooyen, those were the ones who were the leaders and the senior was this Lieutenant van Rooyen. So they blindfolded me again and this time they took off my pants and my underpants and they used what we referred to later as we were talking about it as a USO, an unidentified squeezing object, but probably it was a plier to actually press my testes. They did that twice or thrice and when they do that it becomes very difficult for you to scream because you like choke. When they leave you then you are able to scream. So they did that twice, thrice. I don't know what happened and again they poured water all over me. And I was taken to John Vorster and ja I was dumped there. Later I saw a doctor, a district surgeon Williamson, so he was able to treat me. He wasn't supposed to see me, it was just a mistake on the part of the police, because in the cells in John Vorster Square when they were opening the cells they opened my own cell by mistake. Those who were tortured must not be seen by the doctor because they will be . . . (indistinct), so this policeman opened my door unaware and then I couldn't go on my own so I used the wall to walk towards the part of the cells was a surgery where the doctor saw us, so I crawled and so on and so on. When the security police saw me they wanted to take me back to the cells so I screamed, so fortunately the doctor came out and he saw me, then he said I want to see that man. So our own political activists, the students who were tortured were there to see the doctor but fortunately if he doesn't . . . (indistinct) allow you. My whole body was swollen, there were stripes all over the body and so on. So the doctor was able to see me and he made a profile of a human being to indicate all areas of injury. My medical record was subsequently submitted in court so it's properly recorded. When I recovered this was some time in September they took me again. This time it was on the 10th Floor of John Vorster

Square and there it was De Meyer, Sergeant de Meyer, Captain . . . (tape ends)

. . . they didn't touch the face and Stroewig was just concentrating on the head. He didn't hit anything except the head. So he just focused on the head and so on and so forth. For the whole day he did not hit anything except the head and I think I collapsed and again I was taken to hospital. So this time they took me to the Florence Nightingale Clinic in Hillbrow. It was a White hospital so no Africans can see one of the student activist casualties, unlike if you had to take him to an African clinic, quite a number of people could have seen him. So I was smuggled into an exclusive White clinic. There they did brain scanning and well they checked me and they wanted to do a lumbar puncture. At that time I didn't understand what a lumbar puncture was so they explained that they are going to stick a needle in my spine and extract the liquid. I refused because I wasn't quite sure whether I could trust them to do that to me. I knew the spine to be quite sensitive so I refused. So the security cops came again to try and talk to me to do the lumbar puncture, I refused. They promised that they would take me back to prison and beat me up and bring me . . . (indistinct) and so on and so on, but once I was with the doctor I was able to tell the doctor that he shouldn't, so fortunately the doctor did not do it. I recovered after some time. I was taken back to the cells. Later well we were tried I was sentenced to Robben Island and Mandela wanted a report about June 16 including Mr. Sisulu there and Govan Mbeki. So together with . . . (indistinct) we had liked to write a comprehensive report about the events. They also saw the truth, I mean the Cilliers Commission report [the official government report on the Soweto uprising] and we were able in fact to get a copy of that and actually criticise it.

But having said all this that I have said, I want to say that the students at that time they had a support base and members of the community whom even up to this point in time we hold very, very dear. People for instance like Fanyana Mazibuko, Tom Manthata and Ligau Matabata, those were teachers during that period with whom we worked very, very closely. And there was Dr. Abu Asfad, Dr. Massari and Dr. Motlana, most of the casualties, those that we did not want to take to hospital we took to them and student activists who no longer had parents, who no longer had their homes were just wandering around, whenever they are sick these are the doctors who used to attend to them. There is one other doctor whom I have actually forgotten the name but somewhere in Molapo, those were some of the kind people who used to treat us when we are ill, whether it's flu, cold or that. And you had people like Beyers Naude for instance. From Beyers we could be able to like I said print pamphlets, get vehicles and also get financial resources from him. Beyers was banned that time but he was amongst some of the Whites who were able to come into the township of Soweto in the evening to be with the students. I remember at one stage when we were in town and we had seen him he had to drive all the way from town to actually bring us into the township.

When I started to read the Freedom Charter very early in the 70s and so on, later in the 80s I didn't understand what the ANC meant when they said South Africa belonged to all those who live in it, both Black and White, but immediately I saw practically a White man like Beyers Naude risking his own life to come into the township I knew that there were White South Africans in South Africa who were quite prepared to lend a hand and be part of this lovely country.

16. A task which shook my whole being.

Torture was no more effective in crushing opposition in South Africa than it was in Hastings Banda's Malawi (see documents 12 and 13) or elsewhere in Africa. Indeed, state repression became itself a further instigator of public protest, especially in South Africa where opposition to apartheid grew massively in the late 1970s and throughout the 1980s. The basis of this opposition rested on ordinary people fighting daily against racism. Ellen Kuzwayo, a prominent leader of this opposition, did much to promote awareness of the way in which women were ill-treated under apartheid. She was ready to put her own person at risk in order to speak out for what she thought was right. In the following extract, Kuzwayo describes why she agreed to give evidence at the trial of some youths who she did not even know (they included Dan Montsisi—document 15). At the time Kuzwayo was approached by the defense lawyer, she had just been released from a banning order. Though speaking out in court risked further state sanction, Kuzwayo decided that she could not stand by and allow the courts to act without getting some understanding of what urban family life was like for young Africans growing up in Soweto, Alexandra, and other apartheid ghettos in the 1970s. Like Montsisi, Kuzwayo was elected to parliament in South Africa's first fully democratic election in 1994.[16]

[O]nce in my life I was called upon to do a task which shook my whole being as it involved me mentally, emotionally, physically and, I have no doubt, spiritually too.

It was on my release from detention, when there was very alarming talk that eleven students—ten boys and one girl—who had been arrested under the Terrorism Act were facing very serious charges which could lead to

---

16. The extract reprinted is from *Call Me Woman* by Ellen Kuzwayo published in Great Britain by The Women's Press Ltd., 1985, 34 Great Sutton Street, London EC1V OLQ. *Used by permission of The Women's Press, Ltd.*

long prison sentences, or worse. I had only been out of detention myself about two months when I received a letter from Advocate Ernest Wentzel, a leading Johannesburg lawyer, well-known for dealing with political cases. He wanted me to see him in his office. When I delayed responding, he sent me a second letter expressing the urgency of the matter he wished to talk to me about. This weighed rather heavily on my mind, with the scar of detention still very fresh in my memory. But his letter, which should have clarified the issue and thus eased my mind, was vague as well as pressing and when I arrived in his office, I had numerous unanswered questions on my mind.

Advocate Wentzel started by outlining in detail the case of the eleven students, emphasising the gravity of the charges they faced, and expressing his fears of what the outcome could be. Genuinely puzzled by this story, as I had absolutely no contact with this case, I bluntly put a question to him, "What has all this to do with me, Mr. Wentzel?" It was only at this point that he disclosed to me in his gentle way the need to find a social worker

Photo is from *Call Me Woman* by Ellen Kuzwayo, first published in Great Britain by the Women's Press Ltd., 1985, 34 Great Sutton Street, London EC1V 0LQ; it is used by permission of the Women's Press Ltd.

of repute and an unimpeachable record of service in the black community, to plead in mitigation for those students. It was hoped in this way to reduce the possibility of heavy sentences—then estimated at nothing less than life imprisonment for some, without ruling out capital punishment for one of them.

But, I simply could not come to terms with why this lawyer was sharing this very delicate and challenging subject with me. Looking straight into his face, and very much agitated, I replied, "Why do you tell me all this? It has nothing to do with me." He continued to share with me his fears for the outcome of the case and revealed that after consideration he had concluded that he could not find anyone better qualified than myself to make the plea in mitigation for the students.

I frankly told him that the fact that I had just been released from detention alone disqualified me from carrying out that assignment, as it might have an adverse influence on the court; further that this would place me in jeopardy with the authorities, who already saw me as a troublemaker and might thus find good reason to put me back in prison. I completely turned down the request. No amount of persuasion would change my mind. I was too disoriented by my recent experiences to accept the challenge.

Yet Advocate Wentzel did not give up. He painted a picture of the judge expected to be on the Bench that day. He said he needed someone who would be able to get through to the humanity of the man. He needed in particular a social worker who would be able to describe in court some of the very oppressive conditions experienced by the majority of the young population in Soweto. Everyone had advised him to approach me. But my reaction to this was precise, simple and clear; that there were many of us with my training and experience in our practice in Soweto.

His last words to me were: "I approached you because I have great fears about the outcome of the sentence. I appealed to you in the firm belief that you are the only person who would bring home to the judge the truth about the conditions and circumstances which contribute to some of the seemingly

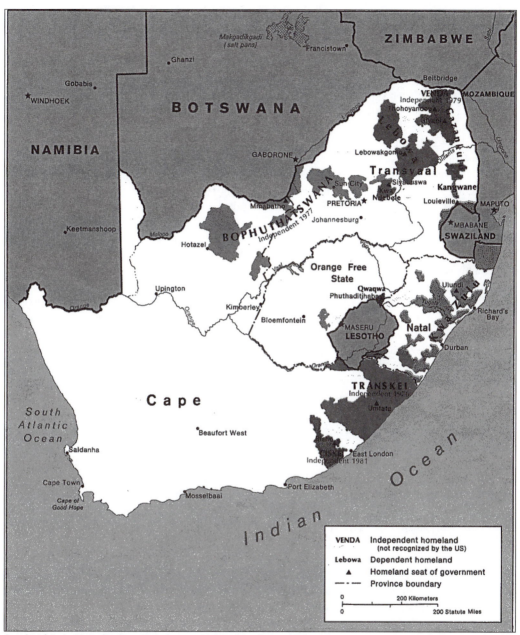

South Africa's Homelands, 1986. *Source:* University of Texas Library Web site, <www.lib.utexas.edu/libs/pcl/ map_collection/africa/southern_african_homelands.gif>, accessed June 26, 2000. Map originally from the Central Intelligence Agency (CIA).

negative behaviour of youth in Soweto. I am not saying your mitigation would have a favourable effect on the sentences of the day; on the other hand, I have a hope it might. If some of them end up with life imprisonment or capital punishment after your mitigation, then we shall say we tried, and our best was not good enough. Now that you say you cannot, when the worst comes to the worst, we shall have nothing to test what could have been our best performance against the sentence they will get."

It was at that point that something sparked a completely new feeling in me. Fear, doubt, hesitation, all three deserted me. I turned to Advocate Wentzel saying, "If I am the last and only person you placed your hopes on for this case, in the name of the black child, I have no choice but to plead in mitigation for their safety and for my conscience. If they get life imprisonment or capital punishment after I refused to assist, I will carry a guilt feeling to my dying day."

I had hardly left his office when I found my mind immersed in the decision I had made. Had I done the right thing? Would this involvement not have repercussions which would see me back in prison? Was there still a chance of backing out of this arrangement? But if I did that, what would happen to the students?

There was still about a month to go before the trial, and I passed a very tedious four weeks, endlessly reviewing the decision I had made. This was often accompanied by sleepless nights spent in an effort to reconcile myself to this very frightening commitment which left me frantic and quite isolated. I did not share my decision with my family and close friends, to avoid severe criticism and possible ridicule from them for making a martyr of myself.

The fateful day and hour finally arrived and found me still full of doubts, regrets, fears and completely withdrawn from any possible source of support, encouragement and understanding. On my arrival at court that morning I felt completely numb and cold. The unfamiliar location of the court and its surroundings in Kempton Park added to my bewilderment. I moved from one end of the corridor to the other in the hope of bumping into the defending counsel or someone I knew. Instead, the interior seemed to be full of black and white uniformed police who all appeared very unfriendly, or so I saw them. Here and there were intimate groups of ordinary people who I assumed were either relatives of the accused or their close friends. I finally collected myself and sat down in one place hoping to see the advocate or his colleague walk in. As I raised my eyes I saw Mathabo Pharase, one of the women I had been detained with. We were both so preoccupied with our own thoughts that we greeted each other very casually, just a "How do you do?", both cool and vacant.

At about eight fifty-five, I could not contain my panic, and at that point approached one of the court officials to find out the whereabouts of the lawyers' offices. I walked in after a distant "Come in," to find the gentlemen on their feet ready to go into court. They didn't dismiss me ungraciously, rather, as they walked out they left me with the impression of how much depended on me. But I still had not received the support I had so much hoped for.

Five minutes dragged by. I was experiencing hot and cold flushes. I was aware of the heavy thump of my heart, and my short intake of breath in between. As people moved into court, I mingled apologetically with them and found myself a protected seat amongst the spectators.

I fixed my eyes on the steps leading from somewhere under the building from where I expected the accused to emerge. I was very keen to see them as I knew nothing about them, yet, when they finally walked up the steps, I felt a cold chill run down my spine. They were so composed and very strong, a condition which strangely unsettled me. I suddenly felt altogether unequal to the task.

I listened with great interest to Mr. Montsisi, the father of Dan Montsisi, the first accused. He pleaded the case of his son with courage, composure and absolute conviction. He encouraged and inspired me. The priest who followed, on the other hand, sounded frightened when he was called to testify about Dan Montsisi as a member of his congregation.

When my name was called to enter the witness box, my mind was in complete turmoil. At that point, I turned to the long-standing, living practice of mine, which has seen me through some of the most awesome experiences in my life. I handed over the challenge which faced me to the "powers" which were fed to me by my mother in my early childhood, as the "foundations of living": "Nothing is too big or difficult for the Creator," and "Always turn to Him when you are in need." Those words came alive at that moment of reckoning.

I remember very clearly standing in the witness box with my hand up, saying, "So help me God" as I faced the judge, still in the grips of fear. When he started questioning me I was completely at a loss as I did not know how to address him. This was my very first experience in the witness box. The quick-thinking, supportive interpreter handed me a piece of paper on which he had scribbled: "Address the judge 'Your Lordship'." You can be sure I still made mistakes, but I managed.

I did fairly well with the advocate. He asked for my name, established my profession and occupation, and asked me to say why, as a social worker, I saw the black children in the country as very deprived. My response to this was to highlight the complete absence of recreational facilities in the form of playgrounds and leisure equipment, to point to the overcrowding in homes where ten to fifteen people living in a three-roomed house was a common condition; to describe how the youth gathered on street corners at night; to explain that parents—mothers in particular—had to leave their young children sometimes as early as four o'clock in the morning and come back long after six or seven o'clock in the evening, in a desperate effort to augment their husbands' appallingly low wages.

It was against this background that I appealed to the judge to see and understand the life of the Soweto child. When I thought that I read doubt on his face, I supported all that I had said by outlining a very nasty and recent experience that the Orlando Home for Children had had. Thugs had walked into the children's Home at night, ignoring the staff on duty there, and had removed the TV set donated to the Home by some well-wishers. The children, all aged less than twelve years, were left shaken with fright, puzzled and robbed of the best, last and only instrument of joy and entertainment they cherished in their lives. This offence the police, perhaps for reasons beyond their control, failed to investigate to the fullest, and it was left to the staff to discover the stolen TV set, which they brought back, reporting their find to the police.

In his amazement the judge wanted to know whether what I had just related was true. I reminded him that I was giving my evidence under oath. That was sufficient. There was no doubt he was puzzled beyond all understanding, but believed my story, which was true in all respects.

Unfamiliar with court procedure, and accepting my first evidence as final, I was taken aback when the prosecutor took over from the defence advocate, displaying an attitude of impatience and superiority. After reminding me that he had heard that I was a social worker of standing in Soweto with long dealings with youth, he wanted to know if I had any knowledge of Black Consciousness, and what my opinion of it was; further, if I believed in it. A very loaded question by any standard. I was rather disturbed by his arrogant manner, but I felt the need to give him an unflinching and convincing reply. "Yes, I know something about 'Black Consciousness'," I said. I went on to tell the court, interrupted by the prosecutor's retorts and unsettling interjections, that I saw it as a very significant period in the history and life of the black people in South Africa; a stage when they had been compelled to pause, stunned by the overwhelming impact of political events, and assess who they were, where they came from and where they were going. The prosecutor's irritating interjections were undoubtedly affecting my speech and disposition at this stage.

Unexpectedly, the judge, seeing my predicament, I suppose, addressed me by name. I raised my head from the gradual droop it was taking and looked up startled. "I am the only person in this court you should address yourself to and be conscious of. Be free to express your convictions and beliefs without any inhibition." I took in the message, resumed my courage and followed his guidance to the letter with confidence. I ended up saying that, to me, Black Consciousness was an institution, a process whereby blacks in South Africa were beginning to take a serious took at themselves against the perilous political plight of a history of close on 350 years, and to find a way of redeeming themselves from that crippling situation. "This is our dilemma," I finished. "I believe in Black Consciousness."

By now I was very tired, having spent two hours in the witness box, and dry from my non-stop presentation, I appealed to the judge saying, "My Lord, am I allowed to drink water in your court?" His subtle support and protection from the haughty prosecutor had fully restored my confidence. With a wry smile, he then ordered that I be given a glass of water and let me drink it at my leisure. I recognised a clear and unspoken expression of justice and felt good.

I had hardly taken my seat with the rest of those who had come to court when suddenly someone took me in his arms and crushed me, almost squeezing the very last breath out of me. As I turned to see who this very brave person was, I saw a man who looked beside himself, as if under some strange influence.

All he said to me was, "You are not an ordinary woman, you pleaded like a man, only a man could speak the way you did." Before I could respond or ask a question, he was kissing me and thanking me. He was one of the parents of the eleven appearing in court that morning. I was just overwhelmed both by the mill I had been through in the witness box and the unexpected response of this parent. I sat huddled in my seat as if nailed to it.

When sentence was passed, four were found guilty including Dan Montsisi, who was sentenced to four years; the other three received shorter sentences. The remaining seven were given a warning and discharged.

17. Another coup in Ghana.

Africa had undergone its second coup in February 1966 when army officers overthrew Kwame Nkrumah while he was out of the country. Discontent was fueled by a disastrous drop in the international price of Ghana's major export—cocoa—coupled with the extravagant cost of Nkrumah's development projects. Nevertheless, the coup leaders justified their action by citing the problems of authoritarian rule and corruption. Their aim, they argued, was to restore democracy in Ghana. Thirteen years and another coup later, junior officers led by Flight Lieutenant Jerry Rawlings attempted a coup in May 1979 against senior officers who, they argued, had become as anti-democratic and as corrupt as the politicians they had overthrown. Rawlings and his co-conspirators were not successful and were imprisoned. A few weeks later, however, other junior officers sympathetic to Rawlings's aims removed the senior generals who had ruled Ghana since the country's second coup in January 1972, and released Rawlings from prison. The generals were later executed. The speech below, in which he seeks to explain the aims of the coup leaders, was broadcast by Rawlings two weeks after he came to power on June 4, 1979. Rawlings has been one of the more charismatic and successful politicians in post-colonial Africa. He returned Ghana to civilian rule in September 1979, but again led a coup—based on the argument that the new government was unable to cope with economic crises (often arising from the falling price of cocoa prices)—in December 1981. Since that time, Rawlings has dominated politics in Ghana, either as military ruler or as popularly elected president, an office in which he currently serves.[17]

17. Barbara E. Okeke, *4 June: A Revolution Betrayed* (Enugu: Ikenga Publishers, 1982), pp. 135–38.

Radio Broadcast: 17 June 1979.

I came to the studio tonight to talk to you about the crucial presidential and parliamentary elections scheduled for tomorrow, Monday, 18 June 1979. In my maiden broadcast to the nation I made it abundantly clear that the elections would go on as planned, and the Armed Forces Revolutionary Council would not do anything that would disrupt the programme for the election. In fulfilment of this promise, the Armed Forces Revolutionary Council has had consultations with the Electoral Commissioner and has been offered all the necessary assistance needed to accomplish it.

The Council has issued directives to all government departments to assist the Electoral Commission. Aircraft have been made available to the Commission to distribute their election material and equipment. A communications network has been set up for the collation and relaying of election results. [Police] officers are going to be deployed and attached to the country's polling booths, and security coverage is to be provided for the security of all its papers and other electorally sensitive material.

Let me at this juncture refer briefly to some of the glaring injustices of the society which made the Armed Forces Revolutionary Council take over the reins of government of this country in the course of this month. These injustices are in the main due to the unfair distribution of the national cake; there are two aspects to this: in the first instance, we have our fellow countrymen and women using their connections to lay their hands on certain portions of [words indistinct] national resources, they then come round and use this position and the factor of [word indistinct] to exploit their fellow countrymen by manipulations of various types. In this category of nation wreckers are the hoarders and profiteers as well as Shylock landlords and transport owners. Another group of thieves are those who refuse to return to the national coffer what they know to be legitimately due from them. The result of this is that the national coffers are absolutely empty. This

group, no less than the first—though by different means—exploits the ordinary Ghanaian and must bear their full share of the blame for the intolerable plight that is the lot of majority. By their action, they have reduced the vital resources which would otherwise be available to improve the lot of the ordinary man, by their rationing these same resources to themselves, their families, and their friends, by illegally keeping for themselves what is not theirs, they deprive others of what should be a fair share of the national resources.

The activities of these groups of Ghanaians—including some non-Ghanaians—who have used the safety from detection and punishment provided them by their connection with those in power, have led to a situation of a widening divergence between productive effort and reward. The nation is full of numerous stories and examples of the non-productive but well-connected individual getting increasingly and openly wealthy, while the hard-working but lowly, get increasingly impoverished.

We intend, in the short period at our disposal, to wage a relentless war against these social injustices. We intend to ensure that whatever resources we have should be used to improve the living conditions of Ghanaians as a whole, and not for any privileged minority. We intend to ensure that only those living within the law and selling at the official prices will remain within the distributive trade. We do not promise the impossible; we recognize that while Ghana is potentially rich, we have problems. We are, at present, a developing country, and hence poor. All we ask is that all those connected with the distribution system to desist forthwith from any act which leads to the unnecessary exploitation of the common man. . . .

The basic task is that together we must try to use all the resources at our disposal to increase the overall supply of goods in the system and ensure that the goods thus produced are fairly distributed.

I wish to avail myself of this opportunity to emphasize once again our resolve not to entrench ourselves in office; we are professional soldiers, and we want to return to the line. It was for the resuscitation and the preservation of the traditions of our profession, and the correction of injustices in the society to which we all belong [that led us] to overthrow the Supreme Military Council. We are in for house-cleaning, and not for the government of this country. In this situation, we would like to assure the nation that we do not favour or support any of the political parties or presidential candidates contesting the election. Let the people choose freely, honestly and wisely for themselves the people they want to rule them. As soldiers, we are prepared to cooperate with, and be loyal to, any democratically and popularly elected government. . . .

Since our assumption of office we have had several proposals on the return of the country to civilian rule. After careful consideration of all the proposals, the Armed Forces Revolutionary Council has decided that Monday, 1st October 1979, should be the target date for the return of the country to civilian rule.

18. The crisis of the state in Africa.

Yoweri Museveni (b. 1944), the president of Uganda, is considered one of a new generation of leaders, coming of age in independent rather than colonial Africa. Museveni studied in Tanzania in the 1960s where he imbibed the socialism of Julius Nyerere and viewed the working out of FRELIMO's (Frente de Libertação de Moçambique) socialist policies in northern Mozambique in the 1970s. An opponent of Idi Amin, the dictatorial ruler of Uganda in the 1970s, Museveni first supported the return to Uganda of Milton Obote who had led the country to independence. But when Obote won election to the presidency in a process marked by widespread fraud, Museveni formed the National Resistance Movement. He succeeded in winning power by armed struggle, forcing Obote to flee Uganda and appointing himself president in 1986. His position as president was confirmed by popular vote in 1996.

Despite his disavowal of earlier ideologues, Museveni echoes the analyses of Frantz Fanon (document 1) that the petty bourgeoisie is trained to serve power, of Chinua Achebe (document 8) that technocrats are necessary to solve Africa's problems, and of Kwame Nkrumah (document 2) that African unity is the path to success. Though Museveni sees the answer to Africa's problems in the free market rather than socialism, he recognizes like his forbears the difficulty of attaining political stability on a continent where the mono-crop export economies inherited from colonialism remain fundamentally unstable.[18]

The crisis of the state in Africa, May 13, 1990.

"The lack of ideological independence in Africa has been a very destabilising factor because it has generated wrong ideas. The regimes which said they were rightist are in a state of crisis; those which said they were leftist are also in a state of crisis. So what is the problem? How can they all be in a crisis?

The main problem was that our leaders were besieged by advice and threats from East and West. If we do not solve this crisis, I think we shall remain in a lot of turmoil for a long time and keep jumping from one mistake to another. We can borrow ideas, but nobody

18. Yoweri Museveni, *What Is Africa's Problem: Speeches and Writings on Africa by Yoweri Kaguta Museveni* (Kampala: NRM Publications, 1992), pp. 185–95. Reprinted with the permission of the Directorate of Information and Public Relations, The Republic of Uganda.

should force us to adopt them if they are not suited to our conditions."

When I received the invitation to come and address this seminar, I tried to put some thoughts down but I shall not read the written speech. I shall summarise what I think are the salient points of this important subject: "The Crisis of the State in Africa."

Soon after the formal departure of colonial rulers at independence, the state in Africa was beset by many problems and I shall concentrate on the most crucial of them. The first problem was that the state was economically dependent on the former colonial powers, especially for technology. We often talk of economic dependence, but this dependence is coupled with and aggravated by an absence of technology: we do not have the technical and managerial skills to enable us to solve our own problems.

After a number of years of independence—more than 30 years in some countries—we have been able to train a few economists and some scientists, professional people like yourselves. If these people could have helped us, we would have got somewhere. But because we have not solved the problem of technological dependence and been able to participate in technological developments, we are not making much headway.

The only way we can participate at present is by someone giving us technology in the form of aid. The donor finances it and then his people come and build a factory in our country. Occasionally, we buy technology with our own money. Right here in this area, there is a salt factory but it is not producing anything because our people bought technology from Germany and found that it was the wrong kind of technology. They are completely dependent on the Germans or some other outsiders to come and put it right. This is a very big handicap indeed.

Since the modern Africa state cannot be independent, it becomes easy prey to manipulation. If our states can be so manipulated, how can they expect to solve the problems of the people except with the permission of the former colonial rulers? A state which does not have capacity to tell the colonial or neo-colonial rulers that it will act independently, in spite of what those rulers think, is completely handicapped. If you need ideas on how to solve problems, why must you borrow from or imitate somebody outside?

Ideological dependence.

The problem of economic and technological dependence was aggravated by ideological dependence. If you want a microphone, like this one I am using now, you must import it because you do not have anyone in your country who can make it, which is bad enough. In addition to that, however, you are also ideologically dependent: you need ideas on how to solve problems and you must borrow from or imitate somebody outside.

In Africa's case, this problem was very serious because our states were born during a time of conflict between the Eastern and Western European countries which had their own arguments about how best to organise themselves. Some said that we should use market forces and others that we should have planned economies. Behind these ideological arguments was European nationalism and chauvinism. There were ideological and nationalist tussles and there was always the old quest for domination, more organised peoples dominating less organised ones.

Africa was thus dragged into European arguments. As soon as any country came to the fore—as soon as any country became independent—the question would come up: "Are you pro-East or pro-West? You must answer that question first before you can do any business with us. What is your ideological colour? You have to take a position." Some of our people did not have the capacity to be able to say: "This is not my argument or my quarrel. Or even if it is my quarrel, it is only partially so." Some countries tried to be pro-capitalist and others tried to be pro-Marxist, even when the conditions were not conducive to being either.

In Uganda for instance, in 1980 and earlier on, we had political groups which had existed since the days of colonial rule. These groups were artificially divided between those called "leftist" and others called "rightist." But when you examined them closely, there was no substance as to why one was called rightist and the other leftist. These were simply opportunistic groupings seeking platforms from which to seek external support. When some people want to get aid from the Russians, they say they are leftist; when they want to get aid from America, they say they are rightist. But when you examine the content of their programmes there is nothing that shows that they are either one thing or the other. They are just small élite groups seeking power, and in order to take political power, they need foreign support. In order to qualify for that support, therefore, they must sing the song of their benefactors.

We, in our [National Resistance] Movement, however, refused to join these opportunists. We refused even to recognise the so called leftist-rightist categorisation. We felt that the opportunistic groups should be got rid of altogether so that we could make a fresh start. We would not join them because they had no genuine platforms. The ideological debate in Africa was thus taken over by opportunists, and opportunism became their ideology: how to qualify for aid from so and so. Even the liberation movements were affected—both the Soviets and the Chinese supported liberation movements which had to declare whether they were pro-Soviet or pro-Chinese and this was very disruptive indeed.

I think the lack of ideological independence has been a very destabilising factor because it has generated wrong ideas most of the time. This is why you see that the state in Africa is now in a crisis, as the theme of your conference states. The regimes which said they were rightist are in a state of crisis; those which said they were leftist are also in a state of crisis. So what is the problem? How can they all be in crisis? That means there is something fundamentally wrong. The main problem is that our leaders did not find time to define the issues confronting them. They borrowed foreign ideas and superimposed them on their countries: this could not, and did not, work.

If you examine the scene in Africa, it is quite difficult to find a model solution. Those who followed the planned economy system got into very serious problems with their economies; those who adopted the so-called market forces approach fared no better either. In very few cases was there real structural economic transformation to generate sustained growth. Those who adopted the planned economy approach over-extended the involvement of the state and went into all sorts of little ventures, which in itself undermined production. The economy was taken over by bureaucrats who had no interest in it and the consequence was that the population was not given a chance to take part in meaningful production. Economies which adopted the market forces approach concentrated on producing raw materials like coffee and tea but these were not integrated with the industrial sector. Therefore, whenever there is a price crisis, it is heavily reflected in the concerned country. Capitalist-oriented regimes were successful only for as long as commodity prices were high.

My personal view, therefore, is that we should have used a mixture of market force and planned economy approaches, depending on convenience and individual countries' circumstances. Above all, we should have aimed at integrating the various economic sectors: the industrial sector interacting with the agricultural sector; agriculture producing raw materials for industry; and industry transforming these into finished products for domestic consumption, leaving the surplus for export. Our industries should have been geared to producing inputs like tools and chemicals for agricultural use.

This, however, was not done and economies which were supposed to follow the capitalist approach were only concerned with producing raw materials and exporting them in an unprocessed, raw form. The prices of these raw materials are, however, very uncertain. The problem was that even where our people could have detected the impending crisis and done something about it, they were besieged by advice and threats from East and West. If we do not solve this crisis, I think we shall remain in a lot of turmoil for a long time and we shall keep jumping from one mistake to another. We must have ideological independence, we can borrow ideas but nobody should force us to adopt them if they are not suited to our conditions.

Africa's "big armies."

Another problem of the state in Africa is the inadequacy of its means to assert its independence. There is a belief, which I personally do not share, that the armies in Africa are too big, for instance. I often hear these opinions expressed on the radio that Africa is not developing because its big armies are consuming all the resources. But where are these big armies? Sudan, for instance, is 2.5 million square miles, without modern communication systems. How do you maintain the unity of such a country without a big army? Therefore, my view, which is contrary to what some people have been saying, is that one of the biggest problems in Africa is the weakness of the state apparatus, i.e. the armies, the police, etc. When the state tries to strengthen these institutions, however, it sometimes acquires equipment which is not suited to its circumstances. Sometimes a state may build up a wrong type of army, for example, a mechanised army instead of an adequately equipped infantry.

If we take the police, I am informed that in Europe the ratio of police to population is one policeman to every 500 people. But here in Uganda, at one time there was one policeman to every 100,000 people. The population was, therefore, left at the mercy of criminals. For instance, the law here says that you are not supposed to beat your wife because she has her citizen's rights like everybody else. But who will enforce this? Who will even detect that you have beaten your wife? Nobody!

Of course, I should be careful here: do not think that I am supporting the strengthening of every type of state. We must first of all define the character of the state. Is this state democratic or not? If it is undemocratic but strong, it will be very dangerous. But even if it is democratic but weak, the people will suffer as much as if it were not democratic.

Low cultural level.

Another problem which beset [the] African state was the low cultural level of the people who took charge of our affairs. You must have heard of people like Idi Amin and [Emperor] Bokassa. If you examine the matter carefully and pose the question: "Who was Idi Amin?" you will find that Idi Amin was a sergeant in the British Army. A sergeant is ordinarily taught to manage 30 people under the supervision of an officer. He is not allowed to manage those 30 people on his own: he must do so under supervision of someone more cultured and better trained than himself.

But here we had a situation where suddenly people who were simply ignorant and hopelessly out of their depth were propelled into positions of very great power. This is a big problem. The endemic corruption in Africa is partly caused by this low level of culture. Culture first generates knowledge, then it generates ethics. How do you define right and wrong? How do you differentiate between what is acceptable and what is not acceptable in society?

In addition to the problems already discussed, the state in Africa also had a problem of the cultural slavery of the small élite groups. I am informed that at independence, Tanganyika only had 13 university graduates. How can you run a country with such a small number of graduates? We had very few educated people, but even the few we had were cultural slaves to foreign ideas. If you did not do things the way they were done in Europe you were not proper and our élites put pressure on governments to make wrong decisions. Even when they were not themselves in government, the élites exerted all kinds of pressure on governments. The ability to improvise and find solutions was thus completely impaired by cultural slavery.

Our élites do not have the capacity to educate our people to use the means which are within their reach: they are always hoping for things which they can never get. As a result, nothing useful is ever done. When you are a slave to certain ideas, you incapacitate yourself because you make yourself incapable of taking another route from that taken by people you regard as superior. Any initiative is stifled because you must do things the way they are done somewhere else.

Interrupted state-formation.

When the imperial powers started penetrating Africa, the process of state formation—the amalgamation of clans into tribes and of tribes into nations—was beginning to crystallise in different places throughout the continent, although it had not yet become consolidated. Some empires had emerged in west, central and east Africa but there was no urgency for the formation of centralised states. When you are living in the tropics with a small population, there is no great urge for one clan to go and conquer another in order to form an empire. The problems we face here are not so numerous. If you live in the Middle East, however, you have a lot of urge to conquer others because you need their resources. Here each clan can stay in its own area: once in a while they all go and raid cattle from another clan, but they will come back home. There is no great need to establish hegemony over other people.

Therefore, the urge to form states was not as strong as in other parts of the world. All the same, there was some linkage at various levels. The clans were linked culturally, although politically they were not centrally organised. Linguistic groupings like the Bantu and the Luo are a manifestation of cultural linkage. A few chiefs tried to unite these clans in order to control resources in their areas and put them under one authority. When colonialism came, however, this process was interrupted and frozen. The territories were channelled to deal with European powers so that horizontal contact between them was discouraged, or stopped altogether in many cases.

Instead, the colonialists encouraged vertical interaction: between the colonised and the colonising people. They also brought new contradictions like factional religious sectors. Religions have played a prominently disruptive role in confusing and dividing our illiter-

ate people and this added to the crisis of the state where you will find people killing one another in the name of religion. However, this sectarianism is sometimes over-stressed in writings on Africa which talk so much about tribes in Africa. People are not aware that the problems were caused by colonial and neo-colonial political organisation and that there is, in fact, a great deal of cultural homogeneity.

Africa is still pre-capitalist.

Another problem confronting the state in Africa is the pre-capitalist nature of African societies today. African societies are still living either at clan or, in some cases, at feudal levels of organisation. Hardly any African state has reached the capitalist stage. The European capitalist class was very useful for integration. If you want pan-Africanists, you should look for capitalists because capitalists would be very good pan-Africanists. Why? Because a capitalist is a producer of wealth: he needs a market for his products and he needs labour in some cases. He cannot, therefore, afford to be parochial: he will work for integration and expansion and he will not support the splitting up of a country because this will split up his market.

It was the capitalist middle class which caused the unification of the German states. Until 1870, the Germans were living more or less as we were living here. People in Bavaria and Prussia spoke the same language but they were not politically united. It was the industrialists and capitalists who wanted a united market, and it was they who pushed Bismarck for German unification.

In Africa, this class does not exist. The middle classes in Africa are not producers of wealth; instead they are salesmen selling other people's products. Fanon said this middle class became senile before they were young. The African middle class is a caricature of the European middle class. Any resemblance between the African middle class and the European middle class is limited merely to the wearing of suits and ties, because in terms of their relationship with the means of production, they could hardly be more different.

In order to have integration, one must use one of the two things. You could use either vested economic interests or ideologically committed people who can work for integration if they are intellectually convinced that it is the right thing to do. The churches offer a good example. Although churches have economic interests, they also have evangelists who preach with conviction. Such people can advance the cause for which they are preaching—although they are often used for other, less laudable, purposes by some interest groups.

If you do not have ideologically committed people and you do not have people with vested interests who can push for integration and, therefore, the stability of the state, then you are in a crisis. You must have one or the other. For instance, the Tanzanians have pushed the process of integration a bit further than some of us, because the leaders who were in charge of state affairs from the very beginning, for instance, used the Swahili language to advance the integration of their country.

Lack of democracy and accountability.

Another problem that has plagued the state in Africa has been the lack of democracy and accountability. When I talk of democracy, I should not be confused with those who are talking about multi-parties. The talk about multi-parties is about form, it is not about substance. Each country's circumstances should dictate what form of democratic expression should be used. There should be control of the top leadership by the population; there must be regular elections; leaders must submit themselves to elections and be thrown out if they are rejected by the electorate. As long as that is happening, I think there will be democracy and accountability, although the exact form this democracy assumes is a different matter. I do not agree with those who are trying to push the idea of multi-parties down everybody's throats.

Having outlined all these crises, is the situation in Africa hopeless? Should we become despondent and give up? I would not myself agree with such a pessimistic view. In fact, the situation in Africa is very bright and it can be turned around very quickly because we have a lot of resources and manpower in many of our countries. There are a few countries, especially those in the Sahel belt, with real problems because they lack water and other resources, but in most cases, we can turn the situation around. I am firmly convinced of this.

What is the solution to the crisis?

How can we correct the present situation? These are some of the steps we need to take:

1. First of all, we must acquire ideological independence. We must stop ourselves being pushed around by exporters of ideas. We should be very adamant about doing what is good for our people. If we do not do this the crisis will continue.

2. Secondly, we must acquire technology. We must take deliberate steps to acquire access to the scientific know-how which can transform our natural products into finished goods. We should pay scientists handsomely, so that the few we have do not keep running to Europe and America. My own view is that these scientists should be bribed. If they are not committed to working for their countries, let us bribe them! They should be given very huge salaries, vehicles, and other incentives to make them stay here so that they can help us solve the problem of our technological dependence. We have tried to put this programme into action here in Uganda but I do not know why there are so many vested interests opposed to it. However, we shall soon sort it out. Ideological conviction is not a very common attribute, so we cannot rely on it. Let us instead rely on the mercenary instinct and bribe our scientists to make them stay here!

Let us also deliberately push the teaching of science in our schools and universities by providing laboratories and other scientific materials. I am sure these two methods will enable us to overcome this problem over the next 10 years or so. We should also open more technical schools and institutions for artisans.

3. Thirdly, we should co-ordinate better among African countries because acting singly is not good enough. We are really not so weak as is generally assumed. For instance, Cuba, a small country, and Angola, were able to break the myth of the power of the South African army and change strategic thinking completely. I had occasion to tell Sir Geoffrey Howe in this very room—he was British Foreign Secretary at the time—that, in my view, the South Africans were making a mistake by thinking that their present superiority over African countries was a perpetual phenomenon. We are disorganised, we are uncoordinated, we are not mobilised, so they seem superior, when actually that is not the case.

My view is that the South Africans should have looked for political solutions while there was still time to do so. The events in Angola were an example of what a sizeable force we can muster if we act together. Not only would better co-ordination make us strong, it would also minimise the conflicts between African states which sap the energy of the continent as a whole.

4. Fourthly, we should institute universal education. We must aim at providing universal education up to the twelfth year of school because we still have millions of people in Africa who are ignorant. Uganda for instance, has a population of 18 million, but of these, perhaps as many as 17 million are still ignorant, illiterate and superstitious. Because of lack of knowledge, these millions are either completely immobilised or only partly mobilised. If we had universal education, however, we would have a big strategic advantage.

5. Fifthly, we must encourage the African languages that can be easily spoken by a wide range of the African population. In East Africa, I would recommend Kiswahili. There are other languages in other regions, such as Lingala in Central Africa and Hausa in West Africa. Language can be a major factor in promoting integration and stability.

6. Finally, we must have democratisation. Without democracy things are bound to go wrong. You cannot manage states properly without democracy. We must have elections and democratic practices which ensure against sectarianism and opportunism. If you campaign on a sectarian platform, you should be automatically disqualified. If the political process is about real issues, they must be submitted to democratic debate and decision by the population.

I think that if we implemented some of these measures, we would resolve the situation on our continent. There are a lot of resources, although they are still untapped, and there is quite a lot of homogeneity on the continent in terms of culture and language. There is an impression that there is so much conflict in Africa that Africans cannot work together: this is not correct. We must stop highlighting our differences and instead highlight the many similarities which can unite and help us develop our continent.

19. The elements of democracy in Africa.

Olesegun Obasanjo, the current president of Nigeria, has long been involved in the politics of the country. In 1970, he led the forces that finally ended the Biafran secessionist movement. In 1976, he succeeded Murtala Muhammad as head of state when Murtala was assassinated in an abortive coup, and he led the country until the return of civilian rule in 1979. Obasanjo became well known internationally during the 1980s, acting as an arbitrator in disputes between certain African countries and taking a prominent role as a critic of apartheid. Though a military officer, he spoke of the importance of democracy and saw intervention by the armed forces in government matters as necessary only in exceptional circumstances and for short periods of time. In the early

1990s, he became especially associated with the Africa Leadership Forum, which he helped form and which aimed at bringing African leaders together to engage in dialogues about how to encourage democracy in Africa. In the following speech to a meeting of the forum, he argued that there was a "phenomenal spread of democracy" in Africa, but that this democracy had to take a distinct African form, echoing Julius Nyerere's analysis (see document 3) from the 1960s. Western practices could not be imported "lock, stock, and barrel" with any real hope of success. While Obasanjo's views were much admired outside Nigeria, he did not find a receptive audience among those who governed the country. In 1995, he was imprisoned on the orders of Sani Abacha, the then dictator of Nigeria, and remained in detention until Abacha's death in 1998. He stood for the presidency in 1999 and won an overwhelming victory. He now has the opportunity at the beginning of a new century to implement his ideas for African democracy.[19]

There is an ongoing and ever spreading wind of change in the air all over the world. Even in spite of its bewildering and sometimes confounding notation, the freshness of its appeal has neither grown stale nor become any less attractive. It is the concept and practice of democracy, which forms the focus of our gathering this weekend.

Democracy is an expression and expansion of man's freedom and has over time become synonymous with man's progress. Democracy is the option which the governed prefers but which is often denied them by the governor under one pretext and pretence or the other. Taken in its totality and at a more ecumenical level, the natural instinct of man as a governed animal is for democracy. I believe that the basic reason for the persistence and recent phenomenal spread of democracy is the ever alluring appeal it has to man's finer instincts and ideas about the process of governance.

As a form of power, it is of course never ideal and it probably might not be ideal but more than any other form of power, it embodies an immanent tendency of man towards freedom and thereby remains the best and the most humane form of power.

Democracy is not a static phenomenon, it has an in-built dynamism which requires that it must be developed and consolidated.

This is made all the more important because democracy releases the total energy of all citizens for development. On the other hand, restraint, curtailment, suppression and oppression, associated with authoritarian regimes, breed resentment, apathy, and withdrawal syndrome which release negative thoughts and tendencies to the development process.

In the Nigerian situation, democracy is the only integrative glue that can bind different sub-national groups together into a nation with a common destiny, equal status and common identity on a permanent basis. The appeal of democracy when firmly established, also lies in its pragmatism and realism as a means of guaranteeing individual rights, interests and social justice. It preserves harmony within communities through consensus and agreement, it thereby integrates societies. It can be made to generate growth and development and distribute wealth more equitably. To admit that democracy is unworkable in a place is to imply that freedom is not cherished in that place.

Agreeably, the variegated nature of the Nigerian polity is an added dimension to the problems of institutionalising democratic process. More often than not, the democratic process has been touted as a destabilizing mechanism in Nigeria. I neither share nor

---

19. Olusegun Obasanjo and Akin Mabogunje, eds., *Elements of Democracy* (Abeokuta: ALF Publications, 1992), pp. 59–62. Reprinted with the permission of the African Leadership Forum.

appreciate this opinion. For me a true and genuine democratic process must make the game of politics a game of inclusion rather than exclusion. It must be a game of service rather than a game of cake sharing.

The important point for us in Nigeria is the need to ensure that both the minority and the majority have adequate access to the institutions of governance. In other words the form and nature of our democratic structure and processes must be aimed at assisting us in allaying our hidden and explicit fears about the system.

Our two attempts at democratic governance have proved that democracy ala West, lock, stock, and barrel cannot resolve our problems. The inability of our structures and processes during these periods has bred and injected a disturbing modicum of cynicism among the citizenry. The important point to think of resolving this weekend is the need to visualize a modality capable of assisting us to expel the choking air of cynicism and its epi-phenomenon of apathy among the populace. Perhaps the first step would be the need to prevent the constant privatisation of the state by our power elites. This must be done in addition to a move to separate the business of governance from the business of economic transactions; it is time to move from the power state of *Ibn Khaldun* to the popular state. It is only in this regard that we can make the democratic process relevant to the daily existence of the people. One of the anchoring bases of this move is the need to embrace, integrate, imbibe and acculturate the spirit of mutual empowerment between the state and the people.

Democratic process must become a way of instituting cultural identity and promoting national unity. It must not be used to disintegrate as was the case in the past. Democratic process in a multi-nationality like ours must be anchored and premised on an order that guarantees justice and equity. We must seek a process that unifies law, morality and justice. It must, as a matter of necessity, be an order that conforms and agrees with our culture, with the will and nature of the humanity of our populace. It must not stultify

or limit ambitions by practice, convention or constitution. It must give hope and inspiration to all.

Our process, as a multi-national society, must move to particularize the will of the varying sections of the society. The aim must be to make our society seek the well-being of its different sections by establishing good relationships among them. As a form of self government it must be self creating, while ebbing away the tendency towards authoritarianism.

It is important that we must not allow our democratic process to be used as a legitimating influence for corruption and tyranny, be it of a group or a person. Genuine democratic process must have embodied in it safeguards against the possibility of its being hi-jacked by any group. Justice and its pursuit are essential ingredients in the democratic process. In addition to all of these let me say that some essential and vital ingredients for the proper institutionalization of a genuine democratic process include among others:

a). Trust creation and confidence building between the leaders and the populace.

b). Periodic election of political leadership through the secret ballot.

c). Creation of an appropriate political machinery.

d). Promotion and defence of human rights.

e). Political communication.

f). Decentralization of political power and authority.

g). Education and political education.

Democracy, as a game of inclusion rather than exclusion, requires and demands popular participation of all adults particularly in the election process. Freedom and choice are two cardinal pillars of democracy and the elections must be free and fair and allow for choice of programmes and personalities.

There must be orderly and periodic succession of leaders at all levels. The society must be open with an independent judiciary. Freedom of the press must include freedom of ownership. Other freedoms enshrined in the United Nations Charter on Human Rights including the OAU [Organization of African Unity] declaration on Human Rights and People's Rights including the Right of the

Child must be promoted and defended. Freedom also connotes obligations and duties which must neither be ignored nor abused. The point must be made, that without fundamental human rights, there can be no democracy. And sustenance of democracy can only be made on democratic culture and democratic spirit both of which have to be engendered and watered.

Democracy need not be too expensive as a form of government. And what is gained in unity, freedom, consensus, stability, commitment and development in a truly democratic society easily outweighs the cost of maintaining and sustaining the structures of democracy. Effective democratic process provides checks and balances which limit the abuses of power, corruption, oppression and dictatorial and authoritarian tendencies.

Democratic principles will only have their full effect if the democratic state operates in such a manner as to guarantee individual liberties through the observance of separation of powers, separation of the state and religious institutions and forces and separation of the state and political party/parties.

The suppression of national interest by tribal interest, favouritism, clientelism and nepotism accentuates social inequalities and undermines the ethics and practice of democracy. Democracy cannot operate successfully within a tribalistic society. Tribalism often stems from perceived or real frustrations assumed or caused by cultural contempt, the refusal to recognise the other in its specificity, the act of basing oneself on one's culture in order to practise discriminations of all sorts. Cultural pluralism is an effort to recognise the specificity of the different cultures or sub-cultures of one nation while avoiding ranking them and yet giving each an equal chance to develop. Without cultural pluralism in a multi-national society, political pluralism will be at risk.

Political authority must be institutionalised and it must not take a patrimonial character. Those who govern must not behave as if authority or power is their personal property and something they can hand down to their heirs. To institutionalize political authority is to compel rulers to conform to pre-established texts and to change them is to suit personal ambitions. They should be made to acknowledge that they are only representatives of the nation and not the owners or proprietors of sovereignty.

20. Negotiating democracy in South Africa.

In the late 1980s, faced by ever-growing mass-based opposition to its apartheid policies, the National Party government of South Africa decided to adopt a policy of "reform." Why the government adopted that policy, and what it hoped to achieve, remain questions of considerable debate among scholars. What is indisputable, however, is that the government did take certain key steps that in themselves set in motion an unstoppable process: it repealed most apartheid legislation during the late 1980s, it unbanned the African National Congress (ANC) and other previously illegal organizations, and it freed Nelson Mandela from prison (where he had been for almost 30 years) in 1990. It also began a process of negotiation to implement a new political structure for South Africa, one that would not recognize racial differences and that would permit all citizens to vote for the first time in the country's history. The negotiations were held under the auspices of the Convention for a Democratic South Africa (CODESA), an umbrella organization (including the ANC, the National Party, and several other political groups) that met for the first time in December 1991 and that continued negotiations—with occasional breaks—until the first na-

tionwide election was held in 1994 (won by Mandela and the ANC). The pamphlet reproduced in full below lists the aims agreed upon by the members of CODESA.[20]

Declaration of intent.

We, the duly authorized representatives of political parties, political organizations, administrations and the South African Government, coming together at this first meeting of the Convention for a Democratic South Africa, mindful of the awesome responsibility that rests on us at this moment in the history of our country, declare our solemn commitment:

1. to bring about an undivided South Africa with one nation sharing a common citizenship, patriotism and loyalty, pursuing amidst our diversity freedom, equality and security for all irrespective of race, colour, sex or creed; a country free from apartheid or any other form of discrimination or domination;

2. to work to heal the divisions of the past, to secure the advancement of all, and to establish a free and open society based on democratic values where the dignity, worth and rights of every South African are protected by law;

3. to strive to improve the quality of life of our people through policies that will promote economic growth and human development and ensure equal opportunities and social justice for all South Africans;

4. to create a climate conducive to peaceful constitutional change by eliminating violence, intimidation and destabilisation and by promoting free political participation, discussion and debate;

5. to set in motion the process of drawing up and establishing a constitution that will ensure, inter alia:

a. that South Africa will be a united, democratic, nonracial and non-sexist state in which sovereign authority is exercised over the whole of its territory;

b. that the Constitution will be the supreme law and that it will be guarded over by an independent, non-racial and impartial judiciary;

c. that there will be a multiparty democracy with the right to form and join political parties and with regular elections on the basis of universal adult suffrage on a common voters' roll; in general the basic electoral system shall be that of proportional representation;

d. that there shall be a separation of powers between the legislature, executive and judiciary with appropriate checks and balances;

e. that the diversity of languages, cultures and religions of the people of South Africa shall be acknowledged;

f. that all shall enjoy universally accepted human rights, freedoms and civil liberties including freedom of religion, speech and assembly protected by an entrenched and justiciable Bill of Rights and a legal system that guarantees equality of all before the law.

We agree:

1. that the present and future participants shall be entitled to put forward freely to the Convention any proposal consistent with democracy.

2. that CODESA will establish a mechanism whose task it will be, in co-operation with administrations and the South African Government, to draft the text of all legislation required go give effect to the agreements reached in CODESA.

[Signatures attached of Mandela, de Klerk, and representatives of seventeen other political parties and/or homeland governments].

Addendum:

For the avoidance of doubt as to the interpretation of the Declaration of Intent, it is declared by its signatories that irrespective of their individual interpretive views thereof, no provisions of the Declaration, interpreted alone or in conjunction with any other provision thereof shall be construed as:

1. favouring or inhibiting or precluding the adoption of any particular constitutional

---

20. CODESA (Convention for a Democratic South Africa), pamphlet entitled "Declaration of Intent," [1991–1993].

model, whether unitary, federal, confederal, or otherwise, consistent with democracy;

2. preventing any participant from advocating the same or the separation, in terms of any constitutional model, of powers between a central government and the regions; during the proceedings of CODESA or any of its committees or Working Groups;

3. and that this Addendum shall be added to and form part of the Declaration.

21. Scrubbing the furious walls of Mikuyu prison.

For his poetry (see document 12), Jack Mapanje of Malawi was imprisoned for three years, seven months, and sixteen days. No charges were ever brought against him. He was released from prison in May 1991 and sent into exile in Britain. Hastings Banda remained President-for-Life of Malawi for another three years, not leaving office until 1994 when the growth of public protest forced him out. (He was then in his early 90s and of debatable mental capacity.) In a volume of poems that he wrote describing his prison ordeal, Mapanje describes in one the evidence that he found in even the harshest of circumstances of the willingness of people to continue to resist their oppressors.[21]

Scrubbing the Furious Walls of Mikuyu

Is this where they dump those rebels,
these haggard cells stinking of bucket
shit and vomit and the acrid urine of
yesteryears? Who would have thought I
would be gazing at these dusty, cobweb
ceilings of Mikuyu Prison, scrubbing
briny walls and riddling out impetuous
scratches of another dung-beetle locked
up before me here? Violent human palms
wounded these blood-bloated mosquitoes
and bugs (to survive), leaving these vicious
red marks. Monstrous flying cockroaches
crashed here. Up there the cobwebs trapped
dead bumblebees. Where did black wasps
get clay to build nests in this corner?

But here, scratches, insolent scratches!
I have marvelled at the rock paintings
of Mphunzi Hills once but these grooves
and notches on the walls of Mikuyu Prison,
how furious, what barbarous squiggles!

How long did this anger languish without
charge without trial without visit here and
what justice committed? This is the moment
we dreaded; when we'd all descend into
the pit, alone; without a wife or a child
without mother; without paper or pencil
without a story (just three Bibles for
ninety men) without charge without trial.
This is the moment I never needed to see.

Shall I scrub these brave squiggles out
of human memory then or should I perhaps
superimpose my own, less caustic; dare I
overwrite this precious scrawl? Who'd
have known I'd find another prey without
charge without trial (without bitterness)
in these otherwise blank walls of Mikuyu
Prison? No, I will throw my water and mop
elsewhere. We have liquidated too many
brave names out of the nation's memory;
I will not rub out another nor inscribe
my own, more ignoble, to consummate this
moment of truth I have always feared!

---

21. Jack Mapanje, *The Chattering Wagtails of Mikuyu Prison* (London: Heinemann, 1993), pp. 53–54. Reprinted with the permission of Heinemann Educational Publishers, a division of Reed Educational & Professional Publishing Ltd.

22. An intimate genocide.

One of the terrible facts of the twentieth century is the periodic campaigns of mass killing by various groups. The Nazis murdered Jews in Europe, the Serb Christians killed Albanian Muslims in Kosovo, and the Hutu massacred thousands of Tutsis in Rwanda. In Europe, military technology and rapid transit helped facilitate the slaughter of millions of people, but in Africa the implementation of genocide has been an intimate affair. Much of the time it was personal and achieved with hand-held weapons, seldom firearms.

Rwanda, primarily home to two ethnic groups, the majority Hutu (89 percent) and the minority Tutsi (10 percent), lost close to a million people between April and July 1994 when supporters of the Hutu-dominated central government sought to exterminate all potential opponents in the country. In their divide and rule policies, the Belgians had long favored the Tutsi at the expense of the Hutu. Upon abandoning their colonial possessions in 1959, however, the Belgians did nothing to protect their former collaborators, and the Hutu massacred tens of thousands of their Tutsi oppressors. Many Tutsi fled as refugees into Uganda from which they began to plan their return to Rwanda. A collapse of world coffee prices in 1989—coffee accounted for 75 percent of Rwanda's export earnings—provided an opportunity for the refugees to invade, and also provided the difficult economic conditions in which Hutu extremists in the Rwandan government began to demonize their opponents. In order to make pointless any military victory for the former refugees, the Hutu extremists planned genocide against the Tutsi still living within Rwanda.

The killing began in the middle of 1994. Precipitated by the mysterious assassination of the presidents of Rwanda and Burundi (when the plane carrying them was shot out of the sky as it was about to land in Rwanda's capital), and carried out by mobs incited by radio broadcasts in which Hutu government officials called on all "loyal" Rwandans to hunt down and kill every Tutsi who could be found, the slaughter extended also to Hutu opponents of the ruling party. In this case, ethnicity served as a useful camouflage for political persecution. Despite calls for international intervention, the West did practically nothing. Minute in numbers, the few Belgian and UN "peacekeepers" stood by and watched as people were macheted to death in front of them. The genocide ended only when a rebel army of Tutsi-led soldiers infiltrated Rwanda from Uganda, defeated the Rwandan national army, and forced the Hutu terrorist gangs (the Interahamwe) to flee into neighboring countries (especially Zaire where they have remained a destabilizing force ever since).

Fergal Keane is an award-winning BBC reporter who traveled to Rwanda just after the genocide to investigate its lingering effects. During that time, he talked to many of the victims of the genocidal campaign, to members of the rebel army, to Hutu officials who had ordered the killings (and who have since sought refugee status themselves outside Rwanda), and to members of relief organizations. He also witnessed scenes of immense carnage, since the perpetrators of the genocide left their victims' bodies to rot where they fell. In this extract, Keane describes what he saw at Nyarubuye parish, site of an awful massacre in which hundreds were killed. His description evokes the intimacy required of the perpetrators to accomplish their goal and of the situation in which each victim was involved prior to his or her death. Near the beginning of his book he impresses upon the reader the following chilling fact: "Before you read this book and while you read it, remember the figures, never ever forget them: in one hundred days up to one million people were hacked, shot, strangled, clubbed and burned to death. Remember, carve this into your consciousness: one million."[22]

[Note: Keane shifts regularly between italic and regular text]

Begin with the river. From where I stand near the bridge it looks like a great soup. It is brown with upland silt and thick with elephant grass. It has come swirling down from the far reaches of the land and is fat with rain. I am arguing with Frank. "Marriage is for old men and idiots," says Frank. "You should try it first, you old cynic," I tell him. Frank believes in loving and leaving, or so he says. I think he had some kind of special feeling for Rose but he won't admit it. I think his talk about having girlfriends everywhere is just a front. Frank is quiet and shy around women. There is an exaggerated politeness about him, even when he is with women soldiers of the RPF [Rwandan Patriotic Front]. "How could I be married anyway doing this job?" he asks. Valence is standing behind us and polishing his rifle. Frank says something to him in Kinyarwanda and he laughs. "What was that?" I ask. "Oh, I just told him you were looking for a wife for me," he replies and we both laugh. The talk goes on like this for several more minutes. It is pleasantly distracting. So much so that at first I do not notice them. And then I turn around and for the first time I see two bodies bobbing along. Then three more. They nudge in and out of the grass and the leaves and are carried towards the falls. One swirls in towards the bank and I notice that it is a woman who has been chopped and hacked. But it is not the gash in her head, the gouges in her back and arms, that frighten and offend. Rather, I am shocked by her nakedness. Like the others she is bloated and her bare body turns and drops and turns

and drops in the current. Near the bridge the current picks up and I watch her tumble down into the white water, disappearing fast. She comes up again, headfirst, and is bounced against the rocks.

"Don't worry man. Don't be surprised," says Frank. "They've been coming through in their hundreds." I look down directly on to the falls and see that there are two bodies wedged tight into the rocks. One is that of a man wearing a pair of shorts. He appears to be white, but this is because the days in the water have changed his colour. Near by there is a baby, but I can only make out the head and an arm. The infant is tossed around by the falling water but is tangled in the weeds that cover the lower part of the rocks. The force of the water is unable to dislodge the baby and so it bounces up and down in the foam. At this I turn and walk away from the bridge and quietly take my place in the back of the car.

The aKagera River flows from the highlands of Rwanda, down through the country until it crosses the border into Tanzania and then Uganda, finally filtering out into the vastness of Lake Victoria. The river therefore became an ideal carriageway for the dispersal of evidence of Rwanda's genocide. People were routinely lined up beside the river for execution and then pushed into the flood. An alternative method of killing was to force people to jump into the fast running water. Most drowned within a few minutes. The Interahamwe gangs noted that this was a particularly efficient way of killing small children, who were more easily carried off in the current. The exhortations of the extremist leaders . . . to send the Tutsis "back to Ethio-

---

22. Fergal Keane, *Season of Blood: A Rwandan Journey* (New York: Viking, 1995), pp. 73–81.

pia" were coming home with a terrible vengeance. Many of the illiterate peasants who were roused to acts of murder believed that the aKagera did actually flow to Ethiopia. But almost every other river and lake in the country also became dumping grounds for the dead. There were so many bodies it seemed the earth could not hold them. When the dead finally reached Lake Victoria, Ugandan fishermen went out in their boats to recover them and give them a decent burial. Moses and Edward had heard of many men going out day after day without being paid, to gather in the corpses. Colleagues had seen the bodies of mothers and children who had been tied together and thrown into the water. There were thousands of corpses.

Driving down to the river, deeper into the heart of the killing grounds, I began to notice the first odours of death. As we drove along the road, the presence of corpses would be announced from a long distance, the rank smells reaching into the interior of our vehicles. I looked back and caught Glenn's eye. He shook his head and then buried his face in a small towel. But we could not see any dead people. They were lying out of view in the plantations and the storm drains, covered now by the thickly spreading vegetation of the summer. In this part of the country close to the border with Tanzania, there was nothing left. There were no people, no cattle, no cats and dogs. The militias had swept through the hills destroying everything before them in a plague of knives and spears.

That morning, as we were leaving Byumba, Frank told us about a massacre that had taken place in the townland of Nyarubuye near the Tanzanian border. An estimated 3,000 Tutsis had taken refuge in and around the parish church. Frank said that a handful of people had survived and were being looked after at a small camp in the offices of the former local administration. "We can get there by this afternoon, if you want to. The tar road is good as far as Rusomo Commune and then we have to leave and go into the bush." The journey passed in quietness and we half slept for several hours, until Frank

directed the Land Rovers off the main road and on to a rough bush track.

This was always going to be the hardest part, this remembrance of what lay ahead in the dusk on that night in early June. My dreams are the fruit of this journey down the dirt road to Nyarubuye. How do I write this, how do I do justice to what awaits at the end of this road? As simply as possible. This is not a subject for fine words. We bounce and jolt along the rutted track on an evening of soft, golden light. The air is sweet with the smell of warm savannah grass. Clouds of midges hover around the cars, dancing through the windows. Although I can sense the nervousness of everybody in the car, we are exhausted and hungry from the long day's travelling, and we are too tired to bother fighting off the insects. Moses shifts down into first gear as we face into a long climb. The wheels begin to lose their grip and they spin in the loose sand of the incline. "Oh, shit," mutters Moses. We climb out and begin to shove and push, but the car rolls back down the hill and we have to jump out of the way. The countryside is vastly different to the deep green hills around Byumba. From the top of the hill we can see a great expanse of yellow savannah grass, dotted here and there with thornbush and acacia. Glenn says it reminds him of home. He is right. This could be the bushveld around Louis Trichardt in the far Northern Transvaal. After about fifteen minutes of manoeuvring Moses eventually gets the car going again and we move off. Frank has become very quiet and he is fingering the stock of his assault rifle. After about another fifteen minutes we come to a straight stretch of track, wider than before and with a line of tall trees on either side. Up ahead is the facade of a church built from red sandstone. "This is Nyarubuye," says Frank. Moses begins to slow the car down and Glenn is preparing his camera to film. As we drive closer the front porch of the church comes into view. There is a white marble statue of Christ above the door with hands outstretched. Below it is a banner proclaiming the celebration of Easter, and below that there is the body of a man lying across the steps, his knees buckled underneath his body and his arms cast behind his head. Moses stops the car but he stays hunched over the wheel and I notice that he is looking down at his feet.

I get out and start to follow Frank across the open ground in front of the church. Weeds and summer grasses have begun to cover the gravel. Immediately in front of us is a set of classrooms and next to that a gateway leading into the garden of the church complex. As I walk towards the gate, I must make a detour to avoid the bodies of several people. There is a child who has been decapitated and there are three other corpses splayed on the ground. Closer to the gate Frank lifts a handkerchief to his nose because there is a smell unlike anything I have ever experienced. I stop for a moment and pull out my own piece of cloth, pressing it to my face. Inside the gate the trail continues. The dead lie on either side of the pathway. A woman on her side, an expression of surprise on her face, her mouth open and a deep gash in her head. She is wearing a red cardigan and a blue dress but the clothes have begun to rot away, revealing the decaying body underneath. I must walk on, stepping over the corpse of a tall man who lies directly across the path, and, feeling the grass brush against my legs, I look down to my left and see a child who has been hacked almost into two pieces. The body is in a state of advanced decay and I cannot tell if it is a girl or a boy. I begin to pray to myself. "Our Father who art in heaven . . ." These are prayers I have not said since my childhood but I need them now. We come to an area of wildly overgrown vegetation where there are many flies in the air. The smell is unbearable here. I feel my stomach heave and my throat is completely dry. And then in front of me I see a group of corpses. They are young and old, men and women, and they are gathered in front of the door of the church offices. How many are there? I think perhaps a hundred, but it is hard to tell. The bodies seem to be melting away. Such terrible faces. Horror, fear, pain, abandonment. I cannot think of prayers now. Here the dead have no dignity. They are twisted and turned into grotesque shapes, and the rains have left pools of stagnant, stinking water all around them. They must have fled

here in a group, crowded in next to the doorway, an easy target for the machetes and the grenades. I look around at my colleagues and there are tears in Tony's eyes. Glenn is filming, but he stops every few seconds to cough. Frank and Valence have wandered away from us into a clump of trees and the older man is explaining something to the boy. I do not know what he is saying, but Valence is looking at him intensely. I stay close to David because at this moment I need his age and strength and wisdom. He is very calm, whispering into Glenn's ear from time to time with suggestions, and moving quietly. The dead are everywhere. We pass a classroom and inside a mother is lying in the corner surrounded by four children. The chalk marks from the last lesson in mathematics are still on the board. But the desks have been upturned by the killers. It looks as if the woman and her children had tried to hide underneath the desks. We pass around the corner and I step over the remains of a small boy. Again he has been decapitated. To my immediate left is a large room filled with bodies. There is blood, rust coloured now with the passing weeks, smeared on the walls. I do not know what else to say about the bodies because I have already seen too much. As we pass back across the open ground in front of the church I notice Moses and Edward standing by the cars and I motion to them to switch on the headlights because it is growing dark. The sound of insects grows louder now filling in the churchyard silence. David and the crew have gone into the church and I follow them inside, passing a pile of bones and rags. There are other bodies between the pews and another pile of bones at the foot of the statue of the Virgin Mary. In a cloister, next to the holy water fountain, a man lies with his arms over his head. He must have died shielding himself from the machete blows. "This is fucking unbelievable," whispers Tony into my ear. We are all whispering, as if somehow we might wake the dead with our voices. "It is just fucking unbelievable. Can you imagine what these poor bastards went through?" he continues. And I answer that no, I cannot imagine it because my powers of visualization cannot possibly encompass the *magnitude of the terror. David and Glenn say nothing at all and Frank has also lapsed into silence. Valence has gone to join the drivers. I do not know the things Valence has seen before this and he will not talk about them. I imagine that the sight of these bodies is bringing back unwelcome memories. Outside the church the night has come down thick and heavy. Tony shines a camera light to guide our way. Even with this and the car lights I nearly trip on the corpse of a woman that is lying in the grass. Moths are dancing around the lights as I reach the sanctuary of the car. While we are waiting for Glenn and Tony to pack the equipment away, we hear a noise coming from one of the rooms of the dead. I turn to Moses and Edward. "What is that? Did you hear that?" I ask. Edward notices the edge of fear in my voice and strains his ear to listen. But there is no more sound. "It is only rats, only rats," says Moses. As we turn to go I took back and in the darkness see the form of the marble Christ gazing down on the dead. The rats scuttle in the classrooms again.*

There was little talk on the way back to the main road. Tony produced one of our whisky bottles and we passed it around. I took several long draughts and lit a cigarette and noticed then that my hands were shaking. Frank watched the road ahead closely and told Moses to drive as quickly as he could. The men who had done the killing, the Interahamwe of Rusomo Commune and Nyarubuye itself, might have fled to Tanzania, but they crossed the border at night to stage guerrilla attacks and to kill any Tutsis who might have escaped the massacres. I

should have felt fear at that moment but I had too much anger inside. After a long silence it was Moses who spoke. "How can they do that to people, to children? Just how can they do it?" he asked. Nobody answered him and he said nothing else. The journey back to the main road seemed to last an eternity. All along the way I could think only of the churchyard and the dead lying there in the dark. Although the sight of the massacre made me feel ill, I was not frightened of the dead. They were not the source of evil that filled the air at Nyarubuye and that now began to undermine my belief in life. Now that we had left, the killing ground would be quiet again. Perhaps the militia men passed there from time to time as they crossed back and forth into Tanzania. Were they still able to pass the scene of their crimes without feeling guilt? Did the rotting dead frighten them? The killers must have moved in close to their victims. Close enough to touch their shaking bodies and smell their fear. Were there faces among the crowd that they recognized? After all, the militia men came from the same neighbourhood. Some of them must have been on speaking terms with the people who pleaded for mercy. I thought of Seamus Heaney's line about "each neighbourly murder" in the backroads of County Fermanagh. Back in the north of Ireland I had reported on numerous cases of people being murdered by men who worked with them or who bought cattle and land from them. In Rwanda that intimate slaughter was multiplied by tens of thousands.

23. Nelson Mandela and a new Africa.

Released from prison in 1990, Nelson Mandela—for years denounced by leaders of the apartheid regime as a communist, a terrorist, a traitor—was elected president in 1994, the first person to hold that office on the basis of universal suffrage. He delivered his inaugural address on May 10, 1994, in Pretoria, the administrative capital of South Africa, before a huge crowd of people. Despite his years of incarceration, he showed no bitterness toward his former captors but counseled reconciliation in the interest of society at large. At the end of the twentieth century and the beginning of the twenty-first, Mandela is the domi-

nant figure in African politics. Though retired now from the presidency, he continues to symbolize the determination of people to struggle against oppression, their readiness to reconcile with their former enemies rather than treat them as they had been treated themselves, and the avoidance of the trappings of post-colonial majesty so favored by the dictators, supporters of one-party states, and other politicians no longer in power in the rest of Africa at the end of the millenium.[23]

Statement of the president of the African National Congress, Nelson Rolihlahla Mandela, at his inauguration as president of the Democratic Republic of South Africa, Union Buildings, May 10, 1994.

Your Majesties, your Highnesses, Distinguished Guests, Comrades and Friends:

Today, all of us do, by our presence here, and by our celebrations in other parts of our country and the world, confer glory and hope to newborn liberty.

Out of the experience of an extraordinary human disaster that lasted too long must be born a society of which all humanity will be proud.

Our daily deeds as ordinary South Africans must produce an actual South African reality that will reinforce humanity's belief in justice, strengthen its confidence in the nobility of the human soul, and sustain all our hopes for a glorious life for all.

All this we owe both to ourselves and to the peoples of the world who are so well represented here today.

To my compatriots, I have no hesitation in saying that each one of us is as intimately attached to the soil of this beautiful country as are the famous jacaranda trees of Pretoria and the mimosa trees of the bushveld.

Each time one of us touches the soil of this land, we feel a sense of personal renewal. The national mood changes as the seasons change.

We are moved by a sense of joy and exhilaration when the grass turns green and the flowers bloom.

That spiritual and physical oneness we all share with this common homeland explains the depth of the pain we all carried in our hearts as we saw our country tear itself apart in terrible conflict, and as we saw it spurned, outlawed, and isolated by the peoples of the world, precisely because it has become the universal base of the pernicious ideology and practice of racism and racial oppression.

We, the people of South Africa, feel fulfilled that humanity has taken us back into its bosom, that we, who were outlaws not so long ago, have today been given the rare privilege to be host to the nations of the world on our own soil. We thank all our distinguished

Nelson Mandela voting in South Africa's first post-apartheid election, 1994. *Source:* ANC Web site, <www.anc.org.za/ancdocs/history/images/sannc.html>, accessed June 26, 2000.

23. ANC Web site, <www.anc.org.za/ancdocs/mandela/1994/inaugpta.html>. Accessed June 1, 2000.

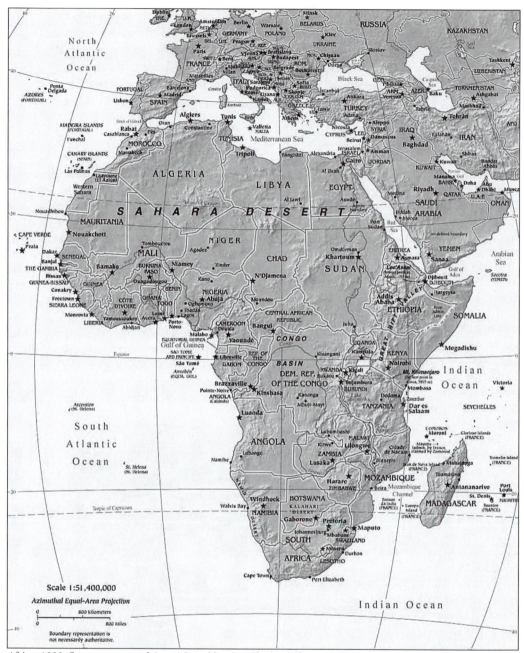

Africa, 1999. Source: <www.odci.gov/cia/publications/factbook/figures/802641.jpg>, accessed June 26, 2000.

international guests for having come to take possession with the people of our country of what is, after all, a common victory for justice, for peace, for human dignity.

We trust that you will continue to stand by us as we tackle the challenges of building peace, prosperity, nonsexism, nonracialism, and democracy.

We deeply appreciate the role that the masses of our people and their democratic, religious, women, youth, business, traditional, and other leaders have played to bring about this conclusion. Not least among them is my Second Deputy President, the Honorable F. W. de Klerk.

We would also like to pay tribute to our security forces, in all their ranks, for the distinguished role they have played in securing our first democratic elections and the transition to democracy, from bloodthirsty forces which still refuse to see the light.

The time for the healing of the wounds has come.

The moment to bridge the chasms that divide us has come.

The time to build is upon us.

We have, at last, achieved our political emancipation. We pledge ourselves to liberate all our people from the continuing bondage of poverty, deprivation, suffering, gender, and other discrimination.

We succeeded to take our last steps to freedom in conditions of relative peace. We commit ourselves to the construction of a complete, just, and lasting peace.

We have triumphed in the effort to implant hope in the breasts of the millions of our people. We enter into a covenant that we shall build the society in which all South Africans, both black and white, will be able to walk tall, without any fear in their hearts, assured of their inalienable right to human dignity—rainbow nation at peace with itself and the world.

As a token of its commitment to the renewal of our country, the new interim government of national unity will, as a matter of urgency, address the issue of amnesty for various categories of our people who are currently serving terms of imprisonment.

We dedicate this day to all the heroes and heroines in this country and the rest of the world who sacrificed in many ways and surrendered their lives so that we could be free.

Their dreams have become reality. Freedom is their reward.

We are both humbled and elevated by the honor and privilege that you, the people of South Africa, have bestowed on us, as the first president of a united, democratic, nonracial, and nonsexist government.

We understand it still that there is no easy road to freedom.

We know it well that none of us acting alone can achieve success.

We must therefore act together as a united people, for national reconciliation, for nation building, for the birth of a new world.

Let there be justice for all.

Let there be peace for all.

Let there be work, bread, water, and salt for all.

Let each know that for each the body, the mind, and the soul have been freed to fulfill themselves.

Never, never, and never again shall it be that this beautiful land will again experience the oppression of one by another and suffer the indignity of being the skunk of the world.

Let freedom reign.

The sun shall never set on so glorious a human achievement!

Let freedom reign.

God bless Africa!

Thank you.

Index

by Janet Perlman

Abacha, Sani, 405
Abacrampah, 170
Abbeokuta, 150, 151
Abolition, 65, 91–92,113, 130–32, 136–39
Abrah, 170
Accra, 170
Achebe, Chinua, 338, 265–69, 398
Adangme, 170
Adjumacon people, 131
Adookoo (king of Fantee), 131
Africa. *See also* Maps
    "civilized man's burden" and, 357–61
    democracy in, 347–51, 404–07
    economy of, 398, 402–03
    expanding trade by taking territory in, 161–63
    historical maps (1891 and 1914), 206
    hunter's map of Africa (1875), 174
    Industrial revolution and, 111–12
    interior wealth of, 194
    post-World War II strikes in, 296–302
    World War II and, 232–33, 286–92, 294
Africa Leadership Forum, 405
African Christian Union, 237–39
African Inland Commercial Company, 150
African Morning Post, article by Azikiwe, 285–86
African National Congress (ANC), 253, 266, 268,
        294, 317
    Defiance Campaign, 309, 310, 311
    policy of violence after 1960, 355–57, 389
    Umkonto We Sizwe, 355–57, 372
    unbanning of, 338, 407
    Web site, 323
    Women's League, 272
    Youth League, 294, 295–96
Aggery (Cape Coast king), 131
Ajayi, 149
aKagera River, 411
Akianvah, 131
Akim, 180
Alexander, Lt. William, 148
Algarve (kingdom), 11
Amabomvanas people, 153
Ambris River, 61
Aminnie (king of Wassaw), 131
Amonoo (king of Annamaboe), 130
Anamaboo, 42
Angola
    post-colonial independence of, 338, 339
    slave trade and, 19, 61
Angonha, 149
Angoulvant, G.L., instructions to civil administra-
        tors, 246–49
Animals, cost of to Western zoos, 173
Apartheid. *See also* South Africa
    explained by Verwoerd, 304–09
    living conditions under, 312
    protest against, 309

reaffirmation of, 328–31, 338, 385
    torture under, 388–91
    women under, 391–96
Aquapim, 170
Araibi River, 215
Armaments, 112, 150, 203
Arthur (ship), log of, 23–27
Arusha, Declaration (Nyerere), 347, 351–54, 357
Asante
    defeat in 1827, 130
    history of, 179
    indigenous slavery by, 141–45
    Karikari, Kofi, 179–80
    king disputes text of a treaty, 118–22
    peace treaty with in 1831, 131–32
    Prempeh I, 202
    runaway slaves, 144
    sack of Kumasi, 181–85
    Sai Tootoo Quamina, 118, 120, 121
    slave trade and, 5, 91
Assin, 131, 170, 180
Assinia, treaty with native chief, 164
Atshashe, 84
Azikiwe, Nnamdi, 275–77, 285, 286, 368
Azurara, Gomes, 5

Baden-Powell, R.S.S., 202, 209–11, 213–14
Baganda people, 265
Bahúkeng people, 159
Bakalai people, 146
Bakari, Bwana Mtoro Mwinyi, 98–103
Bakatla people, 159
Bakwain people, 159
Balewa, Abubakar Tafawa, 368
Bambara people, 165
Bambarra (kingdom), 70
Bamosétla people, 159
Banda, Hastings, 268, 339, 379, 380, 409
Baniserile, 75
Bankole-Bright, H.C., 268
Banks, Sir Joseph, 67
Bann (ship), 91
Bantu Education Bill, 312, 385
Bantu society, 272–75
Barbados, slave trade and, 23, 27, 29, 32, 35, 49
Bargas, 83
Barnard, F.L., 140, 147–148
Barry, Sir J.D., 186
Bartholomew, Joseph, 90
Bassas de India Rocks, 148
Bathurst, 84, 90, 91
Batlókua people, 159
Baukurre, 41
Beaumont Commission, 250
Bechuana people, 159
Bedingfeld, Norman B., 162
Before Chilembwe Tree (Mapanje), 379

Index

Belgian Congo
  independence of, 331–32
  map (1906), 240
  rubber workers, 232, 236, 239–41, 339
Bemba people, slave trade and, 106
Bembezi, 220
Benga, Féral, 277
Bentang, 72
Benue River, 150
Berlin Conference of 1885, 196–97, 200
Bey, Prunner, 170
Biafra, 368–72, 404
Biko, Steve, 339, 372–75
"Black consciousness" movement, 339, 372–75,
  395
Blood River, Battle of, 129, 328
Blyden, Edward, 112, 189
  education and, 249
  inaugural address, 189–94
Boating, 57
Boer War, 219
Boers, 123, 155, 157–59
Boitinnee Quama (king of Dwabin), 121, 122
Bondou, 76
Bonny, King Pepple, 131, 132
Bonny River, slave trade and, 55, 61, 62
Booth, Joseph, 236, 239
Bopape, David, 311
Bornu, 81, 82
Bosman, Willem, Dutch slave trade, 35–37
Bowdich, Thomas, 118, 121
Brackenbury, Henry, 179
Brandaon, Luis, 19
Brass traders, 218, 223–25
Brazil, 3, 19, 35, 139, 140, 147–49
Breaking trade, 54
British Central African Protectorate, 204
British East Africa, 204
British East Africa Company, 200–01, 237
British East Africa Protectorate, 264
British South Africa Company, 199–201
Brookes (ship), 64–65
Broteer, capture into slavery described, 39–42
Bruce Estates, 237
Buccaneers, slave trade and, 17
Bugunese slaves, 53
Bulawayo, 220, 221
Burton, Capt. Richard, 169
Bymba people, slave trade and, 17
Byumba, 412

Cabral, Amílcar, 338, 361–65
Caetano, Marcelo, 361
Caffre people, 157
Caledon, Earl of, 113–15
Canary Islands, 11
Cape Castle, 118
Cape Coast, 119–20, 122
Cape Coast Castle, 21, 29, 34, 116, 122, 131, 179
Cape Colony, 153
Cape of Good Hope, 4, 20, 93, 113, 122–23
Cape Lopez, 145
Cape Three Points, 117
Cape Verde, 11, 18, 361
Caribbean Sea, 3, 16, 21, 35, 37, 62

Casement, Roger, 239–41, 339
Cashan Mountains, 155, 157
Catholic church, slave trade and, 4, 13–16, 19, 27
Cattle killing, 152–55
Censorship, under colonialism, 285–86
Cetshwayo (Zulu king), 186–89, 194, 233
Chamberlain, Joseph, 202, 215–18
Champion, George, conversation with Zulu king,
  125, 127–29
Charles I (king of England), 21
Charles I (king of Spain), 16
Charles II (king of Spain), 27
Charlestown (ship), 76
Chartered companies, 200–01
Chawa people, 105
Chibboo (king of Assin), 131
Chilembwe, John, 232, 236–39, 275, 339, 379
Chipembere, Henry, 384
Chiume, Kanyama, 384
Church Missionary Society (CMS), 91, 167
Cilliers Commission Report, 390
Clarkson, Thomas, 54, 64
Clay, Captain, 30, 31
CMS. *See* Church Missionary Society
Cocoa, Ghana politics and price of, 396
CODESA. *See* Convention for a Democratic South
  Africa
Collingwood, Captain, 42
Colonialism, 231–33. *See also* Great Britain
  African Christian Union, 237–39
  African defiance of, 219, 226–28
  after World War II, 296–302
  in Belgian Congo, rubber worker atrocities, 232,
    236, 239–41, 339
  censorship under, 285–86
  Du Bois on, 257
  in East Africa, 200–06, 208–09, 218–19, 241
  forced labor, 244–46, 280–81
  forms of governance, 231–32
  by France, 246–49
  by Great Britain. *See* Great Britain
  Gold Coast disturbance, 303–04
  hanging of Africans, illustration, 220
  harsh treatment of workers, 234, 236
  higher education under, 285–77
  in Kenya, 232
  Kenyatta, Jomo, 281, 316–19
  kipande system, 264–65, 281–85
  in Malawi, 232, 236–37
  Mandela, Nelson, 294, 309–16, 323–25, 338,
    340, 355, 407, 414–17
  Native Administration Law, 234–36
  police harassment under, 281–85
  post-World War II strikes, 296–302
  repressiveness of, 232
  in Rhodesia, 232
  in South Africa, 231
  taxation under, 131, 244, 278–80
  "traditional" indigenous institutions, 233, 241–
    42
  women and family, impact on, 272–75
  World War II and, 232–33, 286–92
Company of Adventurers of London Trading into
  Parts of Africa, 21
Company of Merchants, 37, 115, 118

Company of Royal Adventurers Trading to Africa, 21
Congo
    as Belgian colony, 232
        Lumumba, Patrice, 233, 332–33
        rubber workers, 232, 236, 239–41, 339
Congo River, map of, 195
Convention for a Democratic South Africa (CODESA), 407–09
Coomassie. See Kumasi
Council of the Indies, 27
Cowrie shells, 33, 36
Crobboe, 170
Crown Lands Ordinance, 317
Crowther, Samuel, 83, 85, 91, 112, 149–52
Cruickshank, Brodie, 139, 140–45
Cuba, slave trade and, 16, 140, 147

Dabou, treaty with native chief, 164
Dadoo, Yusuf, 311
Dahomey, 5, 163, 279
Dakar, 167
De Beers Consolidated Mines, 175
de Gomenot, Lorenzo, 16
de Klerk, F.W., 416
Deed of manumission, 103
Defensivo (ship), 149
Delagoa Bay, 149
Denkera, 170
Denkyera, 180
Dentila, 75
Denyssen, Fiscal D., speech as prosecutor in slave revolt, 95–98
Diamonds, in South Africa, 112, 172, 174–75
Dickie, Alexander, 239
Dingane (Dingaan) (Zulu king), 125, 127–30, 328
Docemo (king of Lagos), 161, 162
Doegood, Robert, 23
"Donko," 142
Dove, F.W., 268
Du Bois, W.E.B., 255, 275
    history of Africans in Africa, 255–59
    League of Nations and, 259–60
    Pan-African movement, 259, 325
    resolutions of Pan African Congress (1919), 260
    Treaty of Versailles and, 259, 266
du Chaillu, Paul, 140, 145–47
Dube, John L., 232, 254
Dukandara, 39
Dupuis, Joseph, 91, 118, 122
Dutch East Indies Company, 20, 65
Dutch slave trade, 35–37

East Africa
    British East Africa Company, 200–01, 237
    imperialism in, 200–06, 208–09
    Lugard, Frederick, 200–06, 208–09, 218–19, 241
    "Native Policy in East Africa," 318
    slave trade and, 3, 20, 113, 139
    Thuku, Harry, 260–66
East Africa Association, 261, 265–66, 317
East-India Merchant (ship), 35
Eastern Akim, 170

Eboe, 58
Education
    Bantu Education Bill, 312, 385
    Blyden, Edward, 249
    by missionaries, 249–50
    colonialism and, 275
    memories of U.S. education, 275–77
    need for universal education, 404
Edward and Ann (ship), 27
Egba dialect, 88
Egerton-Shyngle, J., 268
Eisami, Ali, 81–85
Elmina, 18, 35, 121, 179, 180
Equiano, Olaudah, 39, 42–50
Essacoomah people, 131
Ethiopia, 338, 375–78
Eugenius IV (pope), 13

Faidherbe, Louis, 164–67
Falconbridge, Alexander, experiences as physician on slave ships, 54–64
Falemé River, 75
Fanon, Frantz, 337, 340–44, 361, 398
Fante Confederation, 180
Fantee people, 130–31, 142, 143, 179
Forced labor, under colonialism, 244–46, 280–81
France
    African trade, 163–64
    colonial rule by submission, 246–49
    post-colonial independence, 339
    slave trade, 163
Freetown, 91
FRELIMO, 361, 398
French West Africa, 246, 277
    forced labor in, 280–81
    French instructions to civilian administrators, 246–49
    taxation under colonialism, 278–80
Fulbe people, 81
Fundi Kira (chief), 103, 104
Furkoomah River, 74

Gabon, treaty with native chief, 164
Galant, testimony about revolt, 93–98
Gambia, 75, 112
Gambia River, slave trade and, 22, 67, 71–77, 76, 163
Gandani, 219–20
Gankaran-Kooro, 73
Garvey, Marcus, 325–26, 327
Gatheru, Mugo, 233, 281–85, 292–94
Gee, Joshua, 37
Genocide
    in Rwanda, 339, 410–14
    worldwide, twentieth century, 410
German East Africa, 219, 239, 259
German Southwest Africa, 218
Germany, end of colonialism, 259
Ghana
    coups in, 396–98
    independence of, 325–26, 338, 396–98
    Nkrumah, Kwame, 233, 317, 325–28, 337, 338, 344–47, 357, 372, 398
    Rawlings, Jerry, 340, 396–98
    slave trade and, 21, 35

Index

Gichuru, James, 281
Gikuyu people, 260, 319
God's Bits of Wood (Ousmane), 296–302
Gold Coast, 118, 179
    forts, 115, 117
    Horton, Africanus, 112, 167–70
    post-World War II Gold Coast disturbance,
        303–04
    runaway slaves, 144
    slave trade and, 3, 21, 56, 58
Gold Coast Colony, 204, 214
Gold industry, 198
Goldie, Sir George, 200, 202, 214–15
Gonçalvez, Antam, early slave trading, 6–13
Goree, 76, 115, 116, 164
Gorer, Geoffrey, 277–81
Goterres, Affonso, 6, 8
Grand Bassam, treaty with native chief, 164
Great Britain
    African defiance of, 219, 226–28
    African explorers, 207
    annexation of Lagos, 161–62
    Boer War, 219
    Chamberlain, Joseph, 202
    chartered companies, 200–01
    forced labor, 244–46
    instructions to Niger Commissioners, 133–36
    King's African Rifles, 287
    labor regulations of 1809 and 1812, 122
    maintaining, 202
    Mau Mau rebellion, 317
    National Congress for British West Africa, 266–
      68
    national movement for West Africa, 266
    Niger basin, 214–15
    Proclamation of 1809, 114–15
    Royal African Company, 21–27, 37
    sack of Kumasi, 181–85
    sea power in the nineteenth century, 112, 133
    slave trade
        abolition by treaty, 130–32, 136–39
        interventionist policy to end, 132–36
        legislation to abolish, 77–79, 180
        permitted, 4, 37–38, 65
        prohibited, 113, 139, 180
        supporting slavery and against monopoly,
          37–38
    Smuth denunciation of Britain, 219, 225–26
    South Africa, 250–53
    theory of indirect rule, 233, 241–46
    trade with Africa, 21, 38, 115–18
    traditional indigenous institutions, 233, 241–42
    treaty for Zimbabwe gold lands, 198–99
    war plans of 1899, Chamberlain-Milner
        correspondence, 215–18
    war with Zulu, 185–86
    West African forts, 115–18
    West African treaties of 1800's, 130–32
    World War II and, 286
"Great Trek," 123, 157
Grenada, slave trade and, 62
Groundnut, 286

Gubr, 83
Guinea, 39, 138, 338, 361–65
Guns, 12, 150
Gwede, Focus, 383

Hannibal (ship), 29–35
Harris, Charles, 76
Hausa people, slave trade and, 83
Hawkins, Sir John, expeditions to Africa, 17
Hayford, Casely, 268, 327
Helena (ship), 149
Herero people, 218
Hispaniola, slave trade and, 16
Horton, James Africanus B., 112, 167
    advice to rising generation, 171–72
    biography of, 167
    Fantee people, 180, 194
    portrait of, 169
    on racism, 167–70
    on self-government, 170–71
Hottentots, 114, 123
Hutton, William, 118
Hutton-Mills, T., 268
Hutu people, Rwandan genocide, 410–11

I Speak of Freedom (Nkrumah), 344–47
Idi Amin, 398
Igbo people, 42, 149, 167, 365, 368
Ijaye, 88
Ijebu, 88
Ikereku-iwre, 88
Ikosi, 89
Ilorin, 215
Imperialism, 231. *See also* Great Britain; Treaties
    African "tribute," 131
    Berlin Conference of 1885, 196–97, 200
    chartered companies, 200–01
    East Africa, 200–06, 208–09
    France, 162–65
    history of, 112–13
    interior wealth, 194
    Lagos annexation treaty, 161–63
    ships and, 112
    South Africa, 112–13, 113–15
    taxation, 131, 244
    trade and, 111–12, 164
    voices of resistance, 218–28
    West Africa, 112, 161–63
Independence. *See* Post-colonial independence
Indigenous slavery, in West Africa, 140–47
Indirect rule, 233, 241–46
Industrial and Commercial Workers' Union (South
    Africa), 172, 232, 268–72
Industrial Revolution, 111–12
Inhamban, 149
Iphigenia (ship), 90
Isandlwana, 185, 233
Iseyin, 87
Isles of Herons, 11
Itoko, 88
Itote, Waruhui, 233, 287–92, 296
Ivory trade, 103–05
Ivory Coast, 163

Jabbo, 88
Jallacotta, 75
Jamaica, slave trade and, 16, 63
James I (king of England), 21
Jindey, 76
Johnson, Wallace, 285
Jonas, Simon, 150
Jones, Henry M., 268
Jowett, Rev. William, 86
Julia (ship), 148

Kaarta (kingdom), 70
Kadalie, Clements, 172, 232, 268–69
Kaffir Boy (Mathabane), 385–88
Kajaaga, 75
Kamalia, 71–77
Kapúscínski, Ryszard, portrait of Heile Selassie, 376–78
Karfa Taura, 68
Karikari, Kofi (king of Asante), 179–80
Kataba Treaty, 136, 138–39
Katanga, 334
Katsina, 83
KAU. *See* Kenya African Union
Kaye, 76
Keane, Fergal, account of Rwandan genocide, 410–14
Kentucky (ship), 149
Kenya
    colonialism in, 232
    Gatheru, Mugo, 233, 281–85, 292–94
    Gichuru, James, 281
    Itote, Waruhui, 287–92, 296
    Kenyatta, Jomo, 281, 316–19
    Thuku, Harry, 261–66
Kenya African Union (KAU), 317–19
Kenyatta, Jomo, 281, 316–19
Khoisan people, 114, 123
Kigonsera, 228
Kikuyu Central Association, 317, 318
Kimberley, 172, 269
Kimberley, Earl of, 180
King's African Rifles, 287
Kingston (Jamaica), slave trade and, 63
Kingston, George, 27
Kinjikitile, 219, 226
Kinytakooro, 72
Kipande system, 264–65, 281–85
Kirwani, 75
Knox, Dr. Robert, 169
Koba, 74
Koelle, S.W., 81
Kofi Karikari (king of Asante), 179–80
Koinange (chief), 264
Kolobeng, 159
Kopper, Simon, 222
Kosoko (king of Lagos), 161
Kotane, Moses, 311
Kumalo, Ndansi (Ndebele chief), 218
Kumasi, 91, 119
    sack of, 181–85
    second British torching of, 202
    sketch map of march to (1895-1896), 212
Kuzwayo, Ellen, 391–96

Labor. *See also* Slave trade; Slavery; Slaves
    Belgian Congo rubber workers, 232, 236, 239–41, 339
    forced labor under colonialism, 244–46
    Industrial and Commercial Workers' Union (South Africa), 172, 232, 268–72
    post-World War II Gold Coast disturbance, 303–04
    post-World War II strikes, 296–302
Lagos, 11–13, 85, 161–63
Lagos River, slave trade and, 90
Lake Albert, 207
Lake Albert Edward, 207
Lake Nyasa, 207
Lake Tanganyika, 207
Lake Victoria, 207
Language, independence and, 404
League of Nations, Du Bois involvement with, 259–60
Leeke, Captain H.J., 90
Lembede, Anton, 233, 294–96, 323, 372
Leopold (king of Belgium), Belgian Congo, 232, 239, 339
Leutwein, Theodor, Witbooi letter to, 222–23
Liberia, 4, 189
Lingicotta, 75
Livingstone, David, 149, 155–59, 196, 207
Lobengula (king of Zimbabwe), 198, 218, 219–22
Luabo, 148
luBemba, 106
Lucy Penniman (ship), 149
Lugard, Frederick
    imperialism in East Africa, 200–06, 208–09, 218–19, 241
    theory of indirect rule, 241–46
Lumumba, Patrice, 233, 332–33
Luthuli, Albert, 355

Macaulay, Zachary, 115
MacCarthy, Sir Charles, 118–19, 130
Maccartney, Lord, 65
McCoskry, William, 162
MacDonald, Major, 223–24
Mackinnon, George, 237
Mackinnon, Sir William, 200, 202
Mackrons, 36
Maclean, George, 130–31
Madagascar, slave trade and, 20, 53, 113
Magaliesberg, 155
Magasco, 41
Magriari Tapsoua, 81
Maguire, Rochfort, 199
Maji maji movement, 219, 226–28
Majojo people, 149
Makonnen, Tafari, 375
Malabar, 53
Malaria, 112, 150
Malawi
    Banda, Hastings and, 268, 339, 379, 380, 409
    Chilembwe, John and, 232, 236–37, 275, 339, 379
    history of, 237
    Mapanje, Jack and, 339, 379, 409
    Mpasu, Sam and, 380–85
    post-colonial independence of, 338, 379

Malinka, Morrison, 239
A Man of the People (Achebe), 365–68
Mandela, Nelson, 294, 309, 340
    emancipation of, 338, 407, 414
    Freedom Charter, 323–25
    inaugural speech, 414–17
    "No Easy Walk to Freedom," 309–16
    presidency of, 340, 414–17
    Umkonto We Sizwe, 355–57, 372
Mandingoes, slave trade and, 72, 75
Mansong (king of Bambarra), 70
Manumission, 103
Mapanje, Jack, 339
    Before Chilembwe Tree, 379
    imprisonment of, 409
    Scrubbing the Furious Walls of Mikuyu, 409
Maps
    Belgian Congo (1906), 240
    British South Africa Company, territory owned
      by, 199
    Central Africa (sixteenth and seventeenth
      centuries), 38
    Congo River, 195
    current map of Africa (1999), 416
    Gold Coast Colony, 204
    historical map of independence of nations, 327
    historical maps (1891 and 1914), 206
    hunter's map of Africa (1875), 174
    Livingstone's travels, 156
    march to Kumasi (1895-1896), 212
    Natal (circa 1850), 126
    Nigeria (1912), 243
    Portuguese maritime exploration (fifteenth and
      sixteenth centuries), 7
    South Africa's homelands, 393
Maraboo, 72
Mariangombe, 149
Marks, J.B., 311
Mashona people, 198, 220
Matabele people, 198, 204
Mathabane, Mark, 385–88
Matoppos, 221
Mau Mau, 316–22
Mauritania, slave trade and, 5–13
Mauritius, slave trade and, 20
Maxeke, Charlotte, 272–75
Maxim gun, 12, 203
Mbeki, Govan, 390
Melo, 74
Mends, Capt. Sir Robert, 90
Mengistu, Haile Mariam, 376
Milner, Sir Alfred, 202, 215–18
Mines and Works Act of 1911 (South Africa), 250
Missionaries, 111, 112
    cattle killing and, 152–55
    conversation with Zulu king, 125, 127–29
    Crowther, Samuel, 83, 85–91, 112, 149–52
    educational role of, 166–67
    Goliath, William (Mhlakaza), 152–55
    Tyamzashe, Gwayi, 172
Mobutu Sese Seko, 332, 339
Mombasa, 205
Mondlane, Eduardo, 338, 359–61
Montsisi, Dan, 388–91, 396

Mosilikátze (Caffre chief), 157
Mount Kenya, 316
Mozambique
    Mondlane, Eduardo and, 338, 359–61
    post-colonial independence of, 338, 339, 359–
      61
    slave trade in, 53, 147–49
Mpambalyoto, 228
Mpande (Zulu king), 129
Mpasu, Sam, 380–85
Msimanimoto, 228
Mugabe, Robert, 338
Muhammad, Murtala, 404
Mumford, Robertson, 42
Museveni, Yoweri, 340, 398–404
Muslims, slavery and, 98–103
Mutine (ship), 149
Muwalo, Albert, 383
Mwanga (king of Uganda), 201, 207
Myrmidon (ship), 90

Naicker, Dr. G.M., 311
Nama people, 218
Namibia, 218, 219, 339
Nana-rivier, 51
Natal, 126, 233–36
National African Company, 194, 196, 200
National Congress for British West Africa, 266–68
National Party (South Africa), 389, 407
Nationalism, 292
Native Administration Law, 234–36
Native Policy in East Africa, 318
Natives Land Act (South Africa), 250–53
Naude, Beyers, 391
Ndansi Kumalo (Ndebele chief), 218
Ndebele people, 198, 204, 218
The Negro (Du Bois), 255–59
Neo-colonialism, 338, 340, 342, 361–65
Netherlands, slave trade by, 20, 35–37
New Calabar, 23, 24, 55, 56, 61
Ngesm, 83
Ngololo, 83
Ngwale, Kinjikitile, 219
Ngwata, Charles, 383
Ngwevela, Johnson, 311
Nicholas V (pope), papal bull of 1455, 13–16
Niger, imperialism in, 112, 214–15
Niger Commissioners, Lord John Russell's
    instructions to, 133
Niger Company, 218, 223–25
Niger Delta, 131, 218, 223–25
Niger River, 131, 150, 163
Nigeria, 149, 150
    Abacha, Sani, 405
    Achebe, Chinua, 338, 365–68, 369, 398
    Azikiwe, Nnamdi, 275–77, 285–86
    Biafra secessionist movement, 368–72, 404
    coup of 1966, 368–72
    democracy, 404–07
    Igbo people, 149, 167, 365, 368
    imperialism in, 112, 214–15
    map (1912), 243
    Muhammad, Murtala, 404
    Obasanjo, Olesegun, 340, 404–05

post-colonial independence of, 338, 339–40, 365–68, 404–07
slave trade and, 81, 85
theory of indirect rule, 241–46
Njonjo, Josiah, 263
Nkrumah, Kwame, 233, 317, 337, 338, 357, 372, 398
life of, 325–26
pan-Africanism, 344–47
speech at independence ceremony, 326–28
"No Easy Walk to Freedom" (Mandela), 309–16
Nongqawuse (Nonquase), cattle killing, 153–55
Northey, General, 264
Nyarubuye, 412
Nyasaland, 172, 232, 237, 268–69
Nyerere, Julius, 337, 357, 398, 405
Arusha Declaration, 347, 351–54
life of, 347
on socialism, 347–55

OAU. See Organization of African Unity
Obasanjo, Olesegun, 340, 404–07
Obote, Milton, 398
OFS. See Orange Free State
Ojukwu, C. Odumegwu, and Biafran secessionist movement, 368–72
Old Calabar, 55, 61
Old Oyo, 85
Oluwa (king of Lagos), 268
Orange Free State (OFS), 159–60
Organization of African Unity (OAU), 376
Osei Bonsu, 91–92, 118
Osugun, 86
Otieno, Wambui, women as Mau Mau fighters, 318–22
Ouilinda, 147–48
Ousmane, Sembene, post-World War II strike, 296–302
Owen, Francis, account of Dingane's killing of first settlers, 129–30
Oyo, 85, 86
Oyon River, 215

PAIGC. See Partido Africano da Independencia de Guiné e Cabo Verde
Palm oil, 131, 163
Pan-African movement, 189, 232
Du Bois on, 259, 325
Nkrumah on, 344, 347
resolutions of Pan Africanist Congress (1919), 260
Pan-Africanist Congress, 295, 317, 355
Papal Bull (1455), 13–16
Park, Mungo, 67–71, 111, 150
Partido Africano da Independencia de Guiné e Cabo Verde (PAIGC), 361
"Pawning," 139, 143–44
Peirson, Joseph, 29, 35
Pemba, slave trade and, 98, 140
Pepple (king of Bonny), 131, 132
Peramiho, 228
Phillips, Thomas, 27
Phillips, Capt. Charles, 91
PIDE. See Portuguese secret police

Pisania, 76
Pixley, S., 253
Plantations, slave trade and, 3, 21, 35, 37, 38, 98, 139–40
Pleiad (steamship), 150
Police harassment, under colonialism, 281–85
Political prisoners, 379–85
Popo country, 88, 89
Port Maria (Jamaica), 63
Portugal
early exploration of Africa, 3, 5, 7
slave trade by, 3, 5–13, 16, 19, 22, 23
Portuguese colonialism, 338, 357–61
Portuguese Guinea, 361
Portuguese secret police (PIDE), 359, 360
Post-colonial independence, 337–40
Achebe, Chinua, 338, 365–68, 369, 398
of Angola, 338, 339
autocracy in, 379
of Belgian Congo, 331–32
"black consciousness" movement, 339, 372–75, 395
Chilembwe, John, 232, 236–37, 275, 339, 379
democracy, 347–51, 404–07
economies, 398
Fanon on African independence, 337, 340–44, 361, 398
Freedom Charter (South Africa), 323–25
of Ghana, 325–26, 338, 396–98
of Guinea, 361–65, 368–72
Kenyatta, Jomo, 281, 316–19
Lumumba, Patrice, 233, 332–33
Mandela, Nelson, 294, 309–16, 323–25, 338, 340, 355, 407, 414–17
of Mozambique, 338, 339, 359–61
of Namibia, 339
neo-colonialism, 338, 340, 342, 361–65
of Nigeria, 338, 339–40, 365–68, 404–07
Nkrumah, Kwame, 233, 317, 325–28, 337, 338, 344–47, 357, 372, 398
Nyerere, Julius, 337, 347–54, 357, 398, 405
political dissidents in, fate of, 379–85
political prisoners, 379–85
Rawlings, Jerry, 396–98
repression in, 379–85, 391, 409
of South Africa, 323–25, 338, 385–88
torture, 388–96
of Uganda, 398–404
of Zambia, 339
of Zimbabwe, 339
Potgeiter, Hendrick, 157
Prempeh I (Asante king), 202, 209–11, 213–14
Prester John, 3, 5
Principe, 3
Puerto Rico, slave trade and, 16

Quagua, 131
Quillimane, 147–48, 149
Quinine, 150

Racism, Africanus Horton, 168–70
Ramaquaban River, 199
Rastafarian movement, 376
Rawlings, Jerry, 340, 396–98

Index

Repression, 379–85, 391, 409
Retief, Piet, 123–25, 129, 328
Rhodes, Cecil
  biography of, 172, 175
  British South Africa Company, 200
  confession of faith, 176–78
  De Beers Consolidated Mines, 175
  diamond industry, 175
  gold industry, 189, 200
  Lobengula and the Zulu, 218
  scholarship, 175, 178–79
  treaty for Zimbabwe gold lands, 198–99
Rhodes scholarship, 175, 178–79
Rhodesia, 175, 232, 338
Rio Volta, 117
Roderigue, Paulo, 149
Roode Vos (ship), 20
Royal African Company, 21–27
Royal Niger Company, 194, 200
Rubber workers, Belgian Congo, 232, 236, 239–41
Rudd, C.D., 199
Russell, Lord John, 133–36, 161
Rwanda, genocide in, 339, 410–14

Sai, 83
Sai Tootoo Quamina (king of Asante), 118, 120, 121
Saint-Louis, 164
Salazar, António de Oliveira, 357–59
Sandoval, Father, 19
Sangaya, 83
SANNC. *See* South African Native National Congress
Sao Tomé, 3
Sappho (ship), 149
SAR. *See* South African Republic
SASO. *See* South African Students' Organization
Schoeman, Ben, 312
Scott, Sir Francis, 210
Scramble, 62
Selassie, Haile, 375–78
Seme, Pixley, life of, 253
Senegal, 112, 164, 165, 296
Senegal River, 163
Serawoolli, 75
Settlement of Sierra Leone, 116
Shagou, 83
Shaka, 125, 234
Shangani, 220
Shekiani people, 146
Shepstone, Theophilus, 233–34
Ships
  British, nineteenth century, 112, 133, 150
  steam-powered, 112, 133, 150
Shoas people, 82
Sichyajunga, Chisi Ndjurisiye, first-hand account of slavery, 105–08
Sierra Leone, 115, 116
  post-colonial independence of, 339
  slave trade and, 4, 18, 54, 81, 90, 91
  trade with, 115
Sierra Leone Company, 115
Sisulu, W.M., 311
Slabber-sauce, 58

Slave ships
  accounts of physician on, 54–64
  Arthur, 23–27
  Bann, 91
  Brookes, 64–65
  Charlestown, 76
  condition of, 34–35, 48–49, 57–61, 77, 84, 89, 148
  Defensivo, 149
  East-India Merchant, 35
  Edward and Ann, 27
  Hannibal, 29–35
  Julia, 148
  loss of to mutiny, 37
  plan of, 60, 64-65
  Roode Vos, 20
Slave trade. *See also* Abolition; Slave ships; Slavery; Slaves
  banned in United States and Great Britain, 4
  boating, 57
  breaking trade, 54
  canoes for, 33, 146
  Catholic church and, 4, 13–16, 19, 27
  choosing slaves, 31, 36, 54–57
  conditions on ship, 34–35, 48–49, 57–61, 74, 77, 89, 148
  destinations, 3
  during colonial era, 105–08
  Dutch, 20, 35–37
  East Africa, 3, 20, 113, 139
  English monopoly of, 21
  first-hand accounts of
    capture and freedom, 81–85, 85–91
    capture and transport, 39–42, 42–50
    indigenous slavery, 140–47
    procuring slaves, 54–57, 71–77
    sale of slaves, 39, 62–64, 146
    slave revolt in South Africa, 93–98
    slavery in colonial era, 105–08
    treatment of slaves, 57–62
  France and, 163
  Great Britain and, 4, 21–22, 65
  history, 3, 105
  "illegal slaving," 139–49
  impact on Africa, 5
  importation of slaves into Cape of Good Hope, 4, 20, 93
  justification of slavery to Council of the Indies, 27–29
  managing, 4, 37
  in mid-1800s, 139, 140
  plantations and, 3, 21, 35, 37, 38, 98, 139–40
  Portugal and, 3, 5–13, 16, 19, 22, 23
  regulated by king of Spain, 16–17
  rights of masters, 53
  Royal African Company, 21–27, 37
  scramble, 62
  shipboard uprisings, 4
  slave raiding, 4–5
  slave revolts, 4, 34, 37
  South Africa and, 4, 20, 50–54, 65–67
  Spain and, 16–17
  treatment of slaves, 57–62
  United States and, 4
  voyage of *Hannibal* to Barbados, 29–35

Slavery. *See also* Abolition; Slave ships; Slave trade; Slaves
    "indigenous slavery," 139, 140–45
    "pawning," 139, 143–44
    under colonialism, 244–46
Slaves. *See also* Slave ships; Slave trade; Slavery
    Boers and, 155, 157–59
    capture and transport in Africa, 4, 23–24, 39–42, 42–50, 54–62, 68, 70–71
    choosing, 31, 36
    choosing slaves, 31, 36, 54–56
    conditions on ship, 34–35, 48–49, 57–61, 77, 84, 89, 148
    death of, 23, 25–26, 59–60, 76–77, 148
    emancipation of, 180
    escape attempts, 32
    first view of Western culture, 50, 85
    first-hand accounts
        Alexander Falconbridge (ship's physician), 54–62
        Ali Eisemi, 81–85
        Chisi Ndjurisiye Sichyajunga, 105–08
        Galant, 93–98
        Olaudah Equiano (Gustavus Vassa), 42–50
        Samuel Crowther, 85–91
        Venture Smith (Broteer), 39–42
    illness of, 25–26, 59–62, 76
    manumission, 103
    marriage of, 101–02
    Muslims and, 98–103
    mutiny by, 4, 34, 37
    price of, 32–33, 36, 142
    provisions and feeding, 27, 35, 37, 58
    punishment of, 52, 89, 142
    revolt by, 4, 93–98
    rights of masters, 53
    runaway slaves, 144
    sale of, 39, 62–64, 146
    sexual contact with, 59
    slave raiding, 4–5
    songs of, 100
    trans-Atlantic transport, 4, 23–27, 47–49, 76
    treatment of, 34–35, 47–49, 57–62, 84
Small, E.F., 268
Smith, John Hope, Asante king disputes text of treaty, 118, 120
Smith, Venture, capture into slavery, 39–42
Smuts, Jan, 219, 225–26
Sobukwe, Robert, 355
Socialism, Nyerere on, 347–55
The Souls of Black Folk (Du Bois), 255
South Africa, 232, 250. See also Apartheid; Mandela, Nelson
    abolitionists and labor legislation, 122–23
    African National Congress (ANC). *See* African National Congress
    Bantu Education Bill, 312, 385
    Beaumont Commission, 250
    Biko, Steve, 339, 372–75
    "black consciousness" movement, 339, 372–75, 395
    Boer slaving, 155, 157–59
    Boer War, 219
    Cilliers Commission Report, 390
    Convention for a Democratic South Africa (CODESA), 407–09
    democracy in, 407–09
    diamond trade, 112, 172, 174–75
    Dutch settlers, 112, 123–24, 157
    "Great Trek," 123, 157
    Industrial and Commercial Workers' Union, 172, 232, 268–72
    Lembede, Anton, 233, 294–95, 323, 372
    Mandela, Nelson. *See* Mandela, Nelson
    Manifesto of Emigrant Farmers, 124–25
    map of homelands, 393
    Mathabane, Mark, 385–88
    Mines and Works Act of 1911, 250
    Montsisi, Dan, 388–91, 396
    National Party, 389, 407
    Native Labour Bill, 312
    Natives Land Act, 250–53
    Orange Free State (OFS), 159–60
    organizing laborers, 268–72
    plan for war in 1899, Chamberlain-Milner correspondence, 215–18
    post-colonial independence of, 338, 385–88
    SANNC, 250–56
    slavery in, 4, 20, 50–54, 65–67, 93, 111, 155, 157–59, 180
    South African Republic (SAR), 159–60
    Soweto, 294, 385–87, 391, 395
    subordination of labor in, 114–15
    Suppression of Communism Act, 309
    Terrorism Act, 388
    Transvaal Republic, 159–60
    Union of South Africa, 250
    urbanization of, 294
    Verwoerd, Hendrik, 233, 304–09, 328–31
    World War II and, 294
South African Company, 204
South African Native National Congress (SANNC), 250, 253
    constitution of, 254–55
    delegation, photo, 251
    objections to Natives Land Act, 253–56
South African Republic (SAR), 159–61
South African Students' Organization (SASO), 372
Soweto, 294, 385–87, 391, 395
Spain, 16–17, 27–29
    justification of slavery to Council of the Indies, 27–29
Sparrman, Anders, treatment of slaves in South Africa, 50–54
Spice plantations, need for slaves, 139–40
Stanley, Henry Morton, 196, 207
Steamships, 112, 133, 150
Strikes, after World War II, 296–302
Suppression of Communism Act, South Africa, 309
Swedish East India Company, 50

Tabora, 103, 104
Tanganyika, 286, 347
Tangier, slave trade and, 11
Tanzania, 219, 412
    groundnut scheme, 286
    Nyerere, Julius, 337, 347–54, 357, 398, 405
    slave trade and, 98

Index

Tati Concession, 199
Taxation, under colonialism, 131, 244, 278–80
Tenda Wilderness, 75
Terrorism Act, South Africa, 388
Things Fall Apart (Achebe), 365
Thompson, F.R., 199
Thuku, Harry, 260–61, 265–66
Thurloe, Thomas, 22
Timbuktu, slave trade and, 67
Tinkingtang, 75
Tinmah, 46
Tippu Tip, 103–05
Torture, post-colonial independence movement, 388–96
Trade
    cost of animals to Western zoos, 173
    between England and Africa, 38
    expanding by taking territory, 161–63
    palm oil, 131, 163
Transvaal, gold industry, 198
Transvaal Republic, 159–60
Treaties, 112, 118, 201
    1880s and 1890s, 194
    abolition by, 130–32, 136–39
    Asante king disputes text of a treaty, 118–22
    Berlin Conference of 1885, 196–97, 200
    British-West African treaties of 1800s, 130–32
    chartered companies, 200–01
    with French, 164
    Kataba Treaty, 136, 138–39
    Lagos annexation treaty, 161–63
    templates for, 194–96
    Treaty of Fomena (1874), 180
    Treaty of Paris (1814), 164
    Treaty of Versailles, Du Bois influence on, 259, 266
    for Zimbabwe gold lands, 198–99
Treaty of Fomena (1874), 180
Treaty of Paris (1814), 164
Treaty of Versailles, Du Bois influence on, 259, 266
Tristam, Nuno, 8
Tshombe, Moise, 331, 332
Tutsi people, Rwandan genocide, 410–11
Tyamzashe, Gwayi, 172
Tyamzashe, Henry Daniel, 172

Uganda, 201, 207, 340, 398–404
Ugangi, 103
Ujiji, 104
Umkonto We Sizwe (ANC), 355–57, 372
Union of South Africa, 250–53

United States, 4, 79–80, 113, 139
Urua, 104
uSafwa, 107

van der Meerwe, Willem, 93
Van Hien, H., 268
van Ryneveld, W.S., 65
Vassa, Gustavus, capture and transport of, 42–50
Velten, Carl, 98
Versailles, Treaty of, Du Bois influence on, 259, 266
Verwoerd, Hendrik, 233, 304–09, 328–31
Vogt, Carl, 170
von Bismarck, Chancellor Otto, 196

Wentzel, Ernest, 392, 393
West Africa. *See also* Slave trade; Slavery
    Blyden, Edward, 189
    forts, 115–18
    Horton, James Africanus B., 112, 167–72
    imperialism in, 112, 163–67
    mid-1860s, 179
    national movement for, 266–68
Western Akim, 170
Whidaw, 29, 35, 36
Windward Coast, 56, 61, 67
Winnebah, 170
Witbooi, Hendrik, 218, 222–23
Wolseley, Sir Garnet, 179, 180, 182, 185, 234
Women
    colonialism, impact on, 272–75
    as Mau Mau fighters, 318–22
Wonda River, 72
Woradoo, 75
World War II
    colonialism and, 232–33
    impact on Africa, 286–87, 294
    Itote's experiences in, 287–92
    King's African Rifles, 287, 290–92
    South Africa and, 294

Xhosa people, 152–55, 159, 172

Yauri, 83
Yoruba people, slave trade and, 83, 85

Zaire, independence of, 332
Zambi (chief), 107
Zambia, post-colonial independence of, 339
Zanzibar, slave trade and, 98, 103, 104, 140
Zimbabwe, 198, 339
Zulu kingdom, 125, 127–30, 185–89, 194, 204, 233

William H. Worger is a professor of history at UCLA. Trained in African history at the University of Auckland (New Zealand) and at Yale University, he is the author of *South Africa's City of Diamonds*. He is currently at work on a study of colonialism in nineteenth-century southern Africa, *Cosmologies of Power*. Professor Worger has also taught at the University of Michigan, Ann Arbor, and at Stanford University.

Nancy L. Clark is a professor of history at Cal Poly, San Luis Obispo, where she also directs the university's Honors Program. She studied African history at UCLA and at Yale University and is the author of *Manufacturing Capital: State Corporations in South Africa*. Currently she is at work on a history of South Africa during World War II, focusing especially on the impact of the war on African and female workers.

Edward A. Alpers is a professor of history at UCLA. His research and writing focuses on the political economy of international trade in eastern Africa through the nineteenth century. Throughout his career he has been involved in African liberation support and action groups. Dr. Alpers previously served as dean of honors and undergraduate programs at UCLA, during which time he was also elected president of the African Studies Association, the largest international scholarly organization devoted to the study of Africa.